Complete Works of Geoffrey Chaucer

in Seven Volumes

Volume I
Romaunt of the Rose, Minor Poems

GEOFFREY CHAUCER
EDITED BY W.W. SKEAT

COSIMO CLASSICS

NEW YORK

Complete Works of Geoffrey Chaucer, Vol. I
Cover Copyright © 2008 by Cosimo, Inc.

Complete Works of Geoffrey Chaucer, Vol. I
was originally published in 1894.

For information, address:
P.O. Box 416, Old Chelsea Station
New York, NY 10011

or visit our website at:
www.cosimobooks.com

Ordering Information:
Cosimo publications are available at online bookstores. They may also be purchased for educational, business or promotional use:
- *Bulk orders:* special discounts are available on bulk orders for reading groups, organizations, businesses, and others. For details contact Cosimo Special Sales at the address above or at info@cosimobooks.com.
- *Custom-label orders:* we can prepare selected books with your cover or logo of choice. For more information, please contact Cosimo at info@cosimobooks.com.

Cover Design by www.popshopstudio.com

ISBN: 978-1-60520-517-5

The briddes, that han left hir song,
Whyl they han suffred cold so strong,
In wedres grille, and derk to sighte,
Ben in May, for the sonne brighte,
So glade, that they shewe in singing,
That in her herte is swichh lyking,
That they mote singen and be light
Than doth the nightingale hir might
To make noyse, and singen blythe.

—from "The Romaunt of the Rose"

Lo here the fourme of hir mageste
And lo hir two trwe floure and fructifie

Al thogh his lyfe be queynt the resemblaunce
Of him hath in me so fressh lyflynesse
Yat to putte other men in remembraunce
Of his persone I haue heere his liknesse
Do make to this ende in sothfastnesse
Yat thei that haue of him lest thought & mynde
By this peynture may ageyn him fynde

The ymages that in the chirches been
Maken folk thynke on god & on his seyntes
Whan the ymages thei beholden & seen
Were oft vnsyte of hem causith restreyntes

GEOFFREY CHAUCER: FROM MS. HARL. 4866

CONTENTS.

*** The Portrait of Chaucer in the frontispiece is noticed at p. lix.

	PAGE
GENERAL INTRODUCTION	vii
LIFE OF CHAUCER	ix
LIST OF CHAUCER'S WORKS	lxii
ERRATA AND ADDENDA	lxiv

INTRODUCTION TO THE ROMAUNT OF THE ROSE.—§ 1. Why (the chief part of) the Romaunt of the Rose is not Chaucer's. § 2. The English Version of the Romaunt. § 3. Internal evidence. § 4. Dr. Lidner's opinion. § 5. Dr. Kaluza's opinion. The three Fragments. § 6. Discussion of Fragment B. Test. I.—Proportion of English to French. § 7. Test II.—Dialect. § 8. Test III.—The Riming of *-y* with *-yĕ*. § 9. Test IV.—Assonant Rimes. § 10. Result: Fragment B is not by Chaucer. § 11. Discussion of Fragment C. § 12. Rime-tests. § 13. Further considerations. § 14. Result: Fragment C is not by the author of Fragment B, and perhaps not by Chaucer. § 15. Discussion of Fragment A. (1) Rimes in *-y*. (2) Rimes in *-yĕ*. § 16. No false rimes. § 17. The three Fragments seem to be all distinct. § 18. Fragment A is probably Chaucer's. § 19. Summary. § 20. Probability of the results. § 21. The external evidence. § 22. The Glasgow MS. § 23. Th.—Thynne's Edition; 1532 § 24. Reprints. § 25. The Present Edition. § 26. Some corrections. § 27. The French Text. §§ 28, 29. Brief Analysis of the French Poem: G. de Lorris. § 30. Jean de Meun; to the end of Fragment B. § 31. Gap in the Translation. § 32. Fragment C. § 33. Chaucer's use of 'Le Roman.' § 34. Méon's French text 1

INTRODUCTION TO THE MINOR POEMS.—§ 1. Principles of selection. § 2. Testimony of Chaucer regarding his Works. § 3. Lydgate's List. § 4. Testimony of Shirley. § 5. Testimony of Scribes. § 6. Testimony of Caxton. § 7. Early Editions of Chaucer. § 8. Contents of Stowe's Edition (1561): Part I.—Reprinted Matter. § 9. Part II.—Additions by Stowe. § 10. Part I. discussed. § 11. Part II. discussed. § 12. Poems added by Speght.

CONTENTS.

§ 13. Poems added by Morris. § 14. Description of the MSS. List of the MSS. § 15. Remarks on the MSS. at Oxford. § 16. MSS. at Cambridge. § 17. London MSS. § 18. I.—A. B. C. § 19. II.—The Compleynt unto Pitè. § 20. III.—The Book of the Duchesse. § 21. IV.—The Compleynt of Mars. § 22. V.—The Parlement of Foules. § 23. VI.—A Compleint to his Lady. § 24. VII.—Anelida and Arcite. § 25. VIII. Chaucers Wordes unto Adam. § 26. IX.—The Former Age. § 27. X.—Fortune. § 28. XI.—Merciless Beauty. § 29. XII.—To Rosemounde. § 30. XIII.—Truth. § 31. XIV.—Gentilesse. § 32. XV.—Lak of Stedfastnesse. § 33. XVI—Lenvoy to Scogan. § 34. XVII.—Lenvoy to Bukton. § 35. XVIII.—Compleynt of Venus. § 36. XIX.—The Compleint to his Purse. § 37. XX.—Proverbs. § 38. XXI.—Against Women Unconstaunt. § 39. XXII.—An Amorous Complaint. § 40. XXIII.—Balade of Compleynt. § 41. Concluding Remarks 20

THE ROMAUNT OF THE ROSE.
   FRAGMENT A. (with the French Text). 93
   FRAGMENT B. (containing Northern forms) 164
   FRAGMENT C. 229

THE MINOR POEMS.
    I. An A. B. C. (with the French original) 261
    II. The Compleynte unto Pitè 272
    III. The Book of the Duchesse 277
    IV. The Compleynt of Mars 323
    V. The Parlement of Foules 335
    VI. A Compleint to his Lady 360
    VII. Anelida and Arcite 365
    VIII. Chaucers Wordes unto Adam 379
    IX. The Former Age 380
    X. Fortune 383
    XI. Merciles Beautè 387
    XII. Balade to Rosemounde 389
    XIII. Truth 390
    XIV. Gentilesse 392
    XV. Lak of Stedfastnesse 394
    XVI. Lenvoy to Scogan 396
    XVII. Lenvoy to Bukton 398
    XVIII. The Compleynt of Venus (with the French original) . 400
    XIX. The Compleint of Chaucer to his empty Purse . . 405
    XX. Proverbs of Chaucer 407
    XXI. APPENDIX: Against Women Unconstaunt . . . 409
    XXII. An Amorous Complaint 411
    XXIII. A Balade of Compleynt 415

NOTES TO THE ROMAUNT OF THE ROSE 417

NOTES TO THE MINOR POEMS 452

GENERAL INTRODUCTION.

THE present edition of Chaucer contains an entirely new Text, founded solely on the manuscripts and on the earliest accessible printed editions. For correct copies of the manuscripts, I am indebted, except in a few rare instances, to the admirable texts published by the Chaucer Society.

In each case, the best copy has been selected as the basis of the text, and has only been departed from where other copies afforded a better reading. All such variations, as regards the wording of the text, are invariably recorded in the footnotes at the bottom of each page; or, in the case of the Treatise on the Astrolabe, in Critical Notes immediately following the text. Variations in the spelling are also recorded, wherever they can be said to be of consequence. But I have purposely abstained from recording variations of reading that are certainly inferior to the reading given in the text.

The requirements of metre and grammar have been carefully considered throughout. Beside these, the phonology and spelling of every word have received particular attention. With the exception of reasonable and intelligible variations, the spelling is uniform throughout, and consistent with the highly phonetic system employed by the scribe of the very valuable Ellesmere MS. of the Canterbury Tales. The old reproach, that Chaucer's works are chiefly remarkable for bad spelling, can no longer be fairly made; since the spelling here given is a fair guide to the old pronunciation of nearly every word. For further particulars, see the Introduction to vol. iv. and the remarks on Chaucer's language in vol. v.

The present edition comprises the whole of Chaucer's Works, whether in verse or prose, together with a commentary (contained in the Notes) upon every passage which seems to present any difficulty or to require illustration. It is arranged in six volumes, as follows.

Vol. I. commences with a Life of Chaucer, containing all the known facts and incidents that have been recorded, with authorities for the same, and dates. It also contains the Romaunt of the Rose and the Minor Poems, with a special Introduction and illustrative Notes. The Introduction discusses the genuineness of the poems here given, and explains why certain poems, formerly ascribed to Chaucer with more rashness than knowledge, are here omitted.

The attempt to construct a reasonably good text of the Romaunt has involved great labour; all previous texts abound with corruptions, many of which have now for the first time been amended, partly by help of diligent collation of the two authorities, and partly by help of the French original.

Vol. II. contains Boethius and Troilus, each with a special Introduction. The text of Boethius is much more correct than in any previous edition, and appears for the first time with modern punctuation. The Notes are nearly all new, at any rate as regards the English version.

The text of Troilus is also a new one. The valuable 'Corpus MS.' has been collated for the first time; and several curious words, which have been hitherto suppressed because they were not understood, have been restored to the text, as explained in the Introduction. Most of the explanatory Notes are new; others have appeared in Bell's edition.

Vol. III. contains The House of Fame, the Legend of Good Women, and the Treatise on the Astrolabe; with special Introductions. All these have been previously edited by myself, with Notes. Both the text and the Notes have been carefully revised, and contain several corrections and additions. The latter part of the volume contains a discussion of the Sources of the Canterbury Tales.

Vol. IV. contains the Canterbury Tales, with the Tale of Gamelyn appended. The MSS. of the Canterbury Tales, and the mode of printing them, are discussed in the Introduction.

Vol. V. contains a full Commentary on the Canterbury Tales, in the form of Notes. Such as have appeared before have been carefully revised; whilst many of them appear for the first time. The volume further includes all necessary helps for the study of Chaucer, such as remarks on the pronunciation, grammar, and scansion.

Vol. VI. contains a Glossarial Index and an Index of Names.

LIFE OF GEOFFREY CHAUCER.

※ Many of the documents referred to in the foot-notes are printed *at length* in Godwin's Life of Chaucer, 2nd ed. 1804 (vol. iv), or in the Life by Sir H. Nicolas. The former set are marked (G.); the latter set are denoted by a reference to 'Note A,' or 'Note B'; &c.

§ 1. The name CHAUCER, like many others in England in olden times, was originally significant of an occupation. The Old French *chaucier* (for which see Godefroy's Old French Dictionary) signified rather 'a hosier' than 'a shoemaker,' though it was also sometimes used in the latter sense. The modern French *chausse* represents a Low Latin *calcia*, fem. sb., a kind of hose, closely allied to the Latin *calceus*, a shoe. See *Chausses, Chaussure*, in the New English Dictionary.

It is probable that the Chaucer family came originally from East Anglia. Henry le Chaucier is mentioned as a citizen of Norfolk in 1275; and Walter le Chaucer as the same, in 1292[1]. But Gerard le Chaucer, in 1296, and Bartholomew le Chaucer, in 1312-3, seem to have lived near Colchester[2].

In several early instances, the name occurs in connexion with Cordwainer Street, or with the small Ward of the City of London bearing the same name. Thus, Baldwin le Chaucer dwelt in 'Cordewanerstrete' in 1307; Elyas le Chaucer in the same, in 1318-9; Nicholas Chaucer in the same, in 1356; and Henry Chaucer was a man-at-arms provided for the king's service by Cordwanerstrete Ward[3]. This is worthy of remark, because, as

---

[1] See Rot. Claus. 3 Edw. I., and Kirkpatrick's History of Religious Orders in Norwich, pp. 109, 113. (The Athenæum, Nov. 25, 1876; p. 688.)

[2] Rolls of Parliament, i. 234, 448.

[3] For authorities, see Riley's Memorials of London, pp. xxxiii, xxxiv.

we shall see presently, both Chaucer's father and his grandmother once resided in the same street, the northern end of which is now called Bow Lane, the southern end extending to Garlick Hithe. (See the article on Cordwainer Street Ward in Stowe's Survey of London.)

§ 2. ROBERT LE CHAUCER. The earliest relative with whom we can certainly connect the poet is his grandfather Robert, who is first mentioned, together with Mary his wife, in 1307, when they sold ten acres of land in Edmonton to Ralph le Clerk, for 100s.[4] On Aug. 2, 1310, Robert le Chaucer was appointed 'one of the collectors in the port of London of the new customs upon wines granted by the merchants of Aquitaine[5].' It is also recorded that he was possessed of one messuage, with its appurtenances, in Ipswich[6]; and it was alleged, in the course of some law-proceedings (of which I have more to say below), that the said estate was only worth 20 shillings a year. He is probably the Robert Chaucer who is mentioned under the date 1310, in the Early Letter-books of the City of London[7].

Robert Chaucer was married, in or before 1307 (see above), to a widow named Maria or Mary Heyroun[8], whose maiden name was probably Stace[9]; and the only child of whom we find any mention was his son and heir, named John, who was the poet's father. At the same time, it is necessary to observe that Maria had a son still living, named Thomas Heyroun, who died in 1349[10].

---

[4] See The Athenæum, Nov. 19, 1892, p. 704.

[5] Life-Records of Chaucer (Chaucer Soc.), p. 128; The Athenæum, Jan. 29, 1881, p. 165. From membrane 17 of the Fine Roll, 4 Edw. II.; Parliamentary Writs, vol. ii. pt. 2. p. 30.

[6] The same, p. 126; from mem. 13 of the Coram Rege Roll of Hilary, 19 Edw. II. (1326).

[7] Riley, Mem. London, p. xxxiii.

[8] From Richard Chaucer's will (below); see p. xiv.

[9] Inferred from law-proceedings (below); and cf. note 5, above. Thomas Stace was appointed collector of customs on wine at Ipswich in 1310; Parl. Writs, vol. ii. pt. 2.

[10] Thomas Heyroun, by his will dated April 7, 1349. and proved in the Hustings Court of the City of London, appointed his brother [i.e. his half-brother], John Chaucer, as his executor. In July of the same year, John Chaucer, by the description of 'citizen and vintner, executor of the will of my brother Thomas Heyroun,' executed a deed relating to some lands. See Morris's Chaucer, i. 03, or Nicolas, Life of Chaucer, Note A; from the Records of the Hustings Court, 23 Edw. III.

John Chaucer was born, as will be shewn, in 1312; and his father Robert died before 1316 (Close Rolls, 9 Edw. II., p. 318).

§ 3. RICHARD LE CHAUCER. Some years after Robert's death, namely in 1323[11], his widow married for the third time. Her third husband was probably a relative (perhaps a cousin) of her second, his name being Richard le Chaucer, a vintner residing in the Ward of Cordwainer Street; respecting whom several particulars are known.

Richard le Chaucer was 'one of the vintners sworn at St. Martin's, Vintry, in 1320, to make proper scrutiny of wines[12]'; so that he was necessarily brought into business relations with Robert, whose widow he married in 1323, as already stated.

A plea held at Norwich in 1326, and entered on mem. 13 of the Coram Rege Roll of Hilary 19 Edw. II.[13], is, for the present purpose, so important that I here quote Mr. Rye's translation of the more material portions of it from the Life-Records of Chaucer (Chaucer Soc.), p. 125:—

'London.—Agnes, the widow of Walter de Westhale, Thomas Stace, Geoffrey Stace, and Laurence 'Geffreyesman Stace[14],' were attached to answer *Richard le Chaucer of London and Mary his wife* on a plea that whereas the custody of the heir and land of *Robert le Chaucer*, until the same heir became of full age, belonged to the said Robert and Mary (because the said Robert held his land in socage, and *the said Mary is nearer in relationship to the heir of the said Robert*, and whereas the said Richard and Mary long remained in full and peaceful seizin of such wardship, the said Agnes, Thomas, Geoffrey, and Laurence by force and arms took away *John, the son and heir of the said Robert*, who was *under age* and in the custody of the said Richard and Mary, and married him[15] against the will of the said R. and M. and of the said heir, and also did other unlawful acts against the said R. and M., to the grave injury of the said R. and M., and against the peace.

'And therefore the said R. and M. complain that, whereas the custody of the land and heir of the said Robert, viz. of *one messuage with its appurtenances in Ipswich*, until the full age of, &c., belonged, &c., . . because the said Robert held the said messuage in socage, and the said Mary *is nearer in relationship to the said Robert*, viz. *mother of the said heir, and formerly*

---

[11] In December, 1324, Richard and Mary Chaucer declared that they had 'remained in full and peaceful possession of the said wardship [of John Chaucer] for a long while, namely, *for one year*.' See Life-Records (as in note 5), p. 126.

[12] Riley, Mem. London, p. xxxiii.

[13] Placitorum Abbreviatio, temp. Ric. I.—Edw. II., 1811; p. 354, col. 2; The Athenæum, Jan. 29, 1881, p. 165.

[14] I.e. Laurence, the man of Geoffrey Stace.

[15] They did not really succeed in this; it was disproved.

the wife of the said Robert, and (whereas) the said R. and M. remained in full and peaceful seizin of *the said wardship* for a long while, viz. *for one year*; they, the said Agnes, T., G., and L., on the *Monday* [Dec. 3] *before the feast of St. Nicholas, in the eighteenth year of the present king* [1324], .. stole and took away by force and arms .. the said John, *son and heir of the said Robert*, who was under age, viz. *under the age of fourteen years*, and then in the wardship of the said R. and M. *at London*, viz. *in the Ward of Cordwanerstrete*, and married him to one *Joan, the daughter of Walter de Esthale* [error for *Westhale*], and committed other unlawful acts, &c.

'Wherefore they say they are injured, and have suffered damage to the extent of 300*l*.'

The defence put in was—

'That, *according to the customs of the borough of Ipswich* .. any heir under age when his heirship shall descend to him shall remain in the charge of the nearest of his blood, but that his inheritance shall not descend to him *till he has completed the age of twelve years* .. and they say that the said heir of the said Robert *completed the age of twelve years* before the suing out of the said writ ⁶.'

And it was further alleged that the said Agnes, T., G., and L. *did not cause the said heir to be married.*

'Most of the rest of the membrane,' adds Mr. Rye, 'is taken up with a long technical dispute as to jurisdiction, of which the mayor and citizens of London apparently got the best; for the trial came on before R. Baynard and Hamo de Chikewell [Chigwell] and Nicholas de Farndon (the two latter sitting on behalf of the City) at St. Martin's the Great (le Grand), London, on the Sunday [Sept. 7, 1326] next before the Nativity of the B. V. M. [Sept. 8]; when, the defendants making default, a verdict was entered for the plaintiffs for 250*l*. damages.'

Further information as to this affair is given in the Liber Albus, ed. Riley, 1859, vol. i. pp. 437-444. A translation of this passage is given at pp. 376-381 of the English edition of the same work, published by the same editor in 1861. We hence learn that the Staces, being much dissatisfied with the heavy damages which they were thus called upon to pay, attainted Richard le Chaucer and his wife, in November, 1328, of committing perjury in the above-mentioned trial. But it was decided that attaint does not lie as to the verdict of a jury in London; a decision so important that the full particulars of the trial and of this appeal were carefully preserved among the city records.

---

[16] As they were trying to make out a case, it is clear that John Chaucer was still *just under twelve* on Dec. 3, 1324, when they abducted him.

Mr. Rye goes on to give some information as to a third document relating to the same affair. It appears that Geoffrey Stace next 'presented a petition to parliament (2 Edw. III., 1328, no. 6), praying for relief against the damages of 250*l.*, which he alleged were excessive, on the ground that the heir's estate was only worth 20*s.* a year[17]. This petition sets out all the proceedings, referring to John as "fuiz [fiz] et heire Robert le Chaucier," but puts the finding of the jury thus: "et trove fu qu'ils avoient ravi le dit heire, *mes ne mie mariee*," and alleges that "le dit heire est al large et ove [*with*] les avantditz Richard et Marie demourant et *unkore dismarie*."' The result of this petition is unknown.

From the above particulars I draw the following inferences.

The fact that Mary le Chaucer claimed to be *nearer in relationship* to the heir (being, in fact, his mother) than the Staces, clearly shews that they also were very near relations. We can hardly doubt that the maiden name of Mary le Chaucer was Stace, and that she was sister to Thomas and Geoffrey Stace.

In Dec. 1324, John le Chaucer was, according to his mother's statement, 'under age'; i.e. less than fourteen years old. According to the Staces, he had 'completed the age of twelve before the suing out, &c.' We may safely infer that John was still under twelve when the Staces carried him off, on Dec. 3, 1324. Hence he was born in 1312, and we have seen that his father Robert married the widow Maria Heyroun not later than 1307 (§ 2). She was married to Richard in 1323 (*one year before* 1324), and she died before 1349, as Richard was then a widower.

The attempt to marry John to Joan de Westhale (probably his cousin) was unsuccessful. He was still unmarried in Nov. 1328, and still only sixteen years old. This disposes at once of an old tradition, for which no authority has ever been discovered, that the poet was born in 1328. The *earliest* date that can fairly be postulated for the birth of Geoffrey is 1330; and even then his father was only eighteen years old.

We further learn from Riley's Memorials of London (Pref. p. xxxiii), that Richard Chaucer was a man of some wealth. He was assessed, in 1340, to lend 10*l.* towards the expenses of the French war; and again, in 1346, for 6*l.* and 1 mark towards

---

[17] Rolls of Parliament, ii. 14. Mr. Rye prints 'nulson' in place of 'unkore.'

xiv   LIFE OF GEOFFREY CHAUCER.

the 3,000*l.* given to the king. In 1345, he was witness to a conveyance of a shop situated next his own tenement and tavern in La Reole or Royal Street, near Upper Thames Street.

The last extant document relative to Richard Chaucer is his will. Sir H. Nicolas (Life of Chaucer, Note A) says that the will of Richard Chaucer, vintner, of London, dated on Easter-day (Apr. 12), 1349, was proved in the Hustings Court of the City of London by Simon Chamberlain and Richard Litlebury, on the feast of St. Margaret (July 20), in the same year. He bequeathed his tenement and tavern, &c., in the street called La Reole, to the Church of St. Aldermary in Bow Lane, where he was buried; and left other property to pious uses. The will mentions only his deceased wife Mary and her son Thomas Heyroun; and appointed Henry at Strete and Richard Mallyns his executors[18]. From this we may infer that his stepson John was, by this time, a prosperous citizen, and already provided for.

The will of Thomas Heyroun (see the same Note A) was dated just five days earlier, April 7, 1349, and was also proved in the Hustings Court. He appointed his half-brother, John Chaucer, his executor; and on Monday after the Feast of St. Thomas the Martyr[19] in the same year, John Chaucer, by the description of 'citizen and vintner, executor of the will of my brother Thomas Heyroun,' executed a deed relating to some lands. (Records of the Hustings Court, 23 Edw. III.)

It thus appears that Richard Chaucer and Thomas Heyroun both died in 1349, the year of the first and the most fatal pestilence.

§ 4. JOHN CHAUCER. Of John Chaucer, the poet's father, not many particulars are known. He was born, as we have seen, about 1312, and was not married till 1329, or somewhat later. His wife's name was Agnes, described in 1369 as the kinswoman (consanguinea) and heiress of the city moneyer, Hamo de Copton, who is known to have owned property in Aldgate[20]. He was

---

[18] See the Calendar of Wills in the Hustings Court, by R. R. Sharpe, vol. i. p. 591.

[19] Here Sir H. Nicolas inserts '13th of July,' which I do not understand. His own Chronology of History correctly tells us that the day of St. Thomas the Martyr is Dec. 29, which in 1349 fell on Tuesday. The Monday after it was Jan. 4, 1350; the 23rd year of Edw. III. ended Jan. 24, 1350.

[20] Hustings Roll, Guildhall; see The Athenæum, Dec. 13, 1873, p. 772;

a citizen and vintner of London, and owned a house in Thames Street[21], close to Walbrook, a stream now flowing underground beneath Walbrook Street[22]; so that it must have been near the spot where the arrival platform of the South-Eastern railway (at Cannon Street) now crosses Thames Street. In this house, in all probability, Chaucer was born; at any rate, it became his own property, as he parted with it in 1380. It is further known that John and Agnes Chaucer were possessed of a certain annual quit-rent of 40d. sterling, arising out of a tenement in the parish of St. Botolph-without-Aldgate[23].

In 1338 (on June 12), John Chaucer obtained letters of protection, being then on an expedition to Flanders, in attendance on the king[24]. Ten years later, in the months of February and November, 1348, he is referred to as being deputy to the king's butler in the port of Southampton[25]. In 1349, as we have seen, he was executor to the will of his half-brother, Thomas Heyroun. There is a mention of him in 1352[26]. His name appears, together with that of his wife Agnes, in a conveyance of property dated Jan. 16, 1366[27]; but he died shortly afterwards, aged about fifty-four. His widow married again in the course of a few months; for she is described in a deed dated May 6, 1367, as being then the wife of Bartholomew atte Chapel, citizen and vintner of London, and lately wife of John Chaucer, citizen and vintner[28]. The date of her death is not known.

§ 5. CHAUCER'S EARLY YEARS. The exact date of Geoffrey's birth is not known, and will probably always remain a subject of dispute. It cannot, as we have seen, have been earlier than

---

The Academy, Oct. 13, 1877, p. 364. The joint names of John and Agnes Chaucer occur in 1354, and later, in 1363 and 1366.

[21] See below, under the date 1381; and The Athenæum, Nov. 29, 1873, p. 698; Dec. 13, 1873, p. 772.

[22] Timbs, Curiosities of London, p. 815.

[23] See a document printed in full in The Academy, Oct. 13, 1877, p. 364.

[24] Rymer's Fœdera, vol. ii. pt. iv. p. 23.

[25] Original Writs of Privy Seal in the Rolls House (Nicolas).

[26] Riley; Memorials of London, p. xxxiii.

[27] See The Athenæum, Dec. 13, 1873, p. 772; Nov. 19, 1892, p. 704; and The Academy, Oct. 13, 1877, p. 364. Perhaps his father's death enabled Chaucer to marry; he was married in 1366, or earlier.

[28] 'Bartholomeus atte chapel, ciuis et vinitarius Londinie, et Agnes, uxor eius, ac uxor quondam Johannis Chaucer, nuper ciuis et vinitarii dicte ciuitatis.'—Communicated to The Academy (as in note 27) by W. D. Selby.

1330; and it can hardly have been later than 1340. That it was nearer to 1340 than 1330, is the solution which best suits all the circumstances of the case. Those who argue for an early date do so solely because the poet sometimes refers to his 'old age'; as for example in the Envoy to Scogan, 35-42, written probably in 1393; and still earlier, probably in 1385, Gower speaks, in the epilogue to the former edition of his Confessio Amantis, of the 'later age' of Chaucer, and of his 'dayes olde'; whereas, if Chaucer was born in 1340, he was, at that time, only forty-five years old. But it is essential to observe that Gower is speaking comparatively; he contrasts Chaucer's 'later age' with 'the floures of his youth,' when he 'fulfild the land,' in sundry wise, 'of ditees and of songes glade.' And, in spite of all the needless stress that has been laid upon such references as the above, we must, if we really wish to ascertain the truth without prejudice, try to bear in mind the fact that, in the fourteenth century, men were deemed old at an age which we should now esteem as almost young. Chaucer's pupil, Hoccleve, describes himself as worn out with old age, and ready to die, at the age of *fifty-three*; all that he can look forward to is making a translation of a treatise on 'learning to die.'

'Of age am I fifty winter and thre;
Ripeness of dethe fast vpon me hasteth.'
Hoccleve's Poems, ed. Furnivall, p. 119[29].

And further, if, in order to make out that Chaucer died at the age of nearly 70, we place his birth near the year 1330, we are at once confronted with the extraordinary difficulty, that the poet was already nearly 39 when he wrote 'The Book of the Duchesse,' certainly one of the earliest of his poems that have been preserved, and hardly to be esteemed as a highly satisfactory performance. But as the exact date still remains uncertain, I can only say that we must place it between 1330 and 1340. The reader can incline to whichever end of the decade best pleases him. I merely record my opinion, for what it is worth, that 'shortly before 1340' fits in best with *all* the facts.

---

[29] It is needless to multiply instances. Dante speaks of 35 years as being 'the middle of life's journey'; and Jean de Meun (Le Testament, ed. Méon, iv. 9) says that a man flourishes till he is 30 or 40 years old; after which he does nothing but languish (ne fait que langorir).

CHAUCER'S EARLY YEARS.

The earliest notice of Geoffrey Chaucer, on which we can rely, refers to the year 1357. This discovery is due to Mr. (now Dr.) E. A. Bond, who, in 1851, found some fragments of an old household account which had been used to line the covers of a MS. containing Lydgate's Storie of Thebes and Hoccleve's De Regimine Principum, and now known as MS. Addit. 18,632 in the British Museum. They proved to form a part of the Household Accounts of Elizabeth, Countess of Ulster, wife of Lionel, Duke of Clarence, the third son of King Edward III., for the years 1356-9 [30]. These Accounts shew that, in April, 1357, when the Countess was in London, an entire suit of clothes, consisting of a paltock or short cloak, a pair of red and black breeches, and shoes, was provided for Geoffrey Chaucer at a cost of 7s., equal to about 5l. of our present money. On the 20th of May another article of dress was purchased for him in London. In December of the same year (1357), when the Countess was at Hatfield (near Doncaster) in Yorkshire, her principal place of residence, we find a note of a donation of 2s. 6d. to Geoffrey Chaucer for necessaries at Christmas. It further appears that John of Gaunt, the Countess's brother-in-law, was a visitor at Hatfield at the same period; which indicates the probable origin of the interest in the poet's fortunes which that illustrious prince so frequently manifested, during a long period of years.

It is further worthy of remark that, on several occasions, a female attendant on the Countess is designated as Philippa Pan', which is supposed to be the contracted form of Panetaria, i. e. mistress of the pantry. 'Speculations suggest themselves,' says Dr. Bond, 'that the Countess's attendant Philippa may have been Chaucer's future wife . . The Countess died in 1363, . . and nothing would be more likely than that the principal lady of her household should have found shelter after her death in the family of her husband's mother,' i. e. Queen Philippa. It is quite possible; it is even probable.

Perhaps it was at Hatfield that Chaucer picked up some knowledge of the Northern dialect, as employed by him in the Reves Tale. The fact that the non-Chaucerian Fragment B of the Romaunt of the Rose exhibits traces of a Northern dialect is

---

[30] Life-Records of Chaucer, p. 97 (Chaucer Soc.); Fortnightly Review, Aug. 15, 1866.

quite a different matter; for Fragment A, which is certainly Chaucer's, shews no trace of anything of the kind. What was Chaucer's exact position in the Countess of Ulster's household, we are not informed. If he was born about 1340, we may suppose that he was a page; if several years earlier, he would, in 1357, have been too old for such service. We only know that he was attached to the service of Lionel, duke of Clarence, and of the Countess of Ulster his wife, as early as the beginning of 1357, and was at that time at Hatfield, in Yorkshire. 'He was present,' says Dr. Bond, 'at the celebration of the feast of St. George, at Edward III's court, in attendance on the Countess, in April of that year; he followed the court to Woodstock; and he was again at Hatfield, probably from September, 1357, to the end of March, 1358, and would have witnessed there the reception of John of Ghent, then Earl of Richmond.' We may well believe that he accompanied the Countess when she attended the funeral of Queen Isabella (king Edward's mother), which took place at the Church of the Friars Minors, in Newgate Street, on Nov. 27, 1358.

§ 6. CHAUCER'S FIRST EXPEDITION. 1359-60. A year later, in November, 1359, Chaucer joined the great expedition of Edward III. to France. 'There was not knight, squire, or man of honour, from the age of twenty to sixty years, that did not go [31].' The king of England was 'attended by the prince of Wales and three other sons,' including 'Lionel, earl of Ulster [32]'; and we may be sure that Chaucer accompanied his master prince Lionel. The march of the troops lay through Artois, past Arras to Bapaume; then through Picardy, past Peronne and St. Quentin, to Rheims, which Edward, with his whole army, ineffectually besieged for seven weeks. It is interesting to note that the army must, on this occasion, have crossed the Oise, somewhere near Chauny and La-Fère, which easily accounts for the mention of that river in the House of Fame (l. 1928); and shews the uselessness of Warton's suggestion, that Chaucer learnt the name of that river by studying Provençal poetry ! In one of the numerous skirmishes that took place, Chaucer had the misfortune to be taken prisoner. This appears from his own evidence, in the 'Scrope and Grosvenor' trial, referred to below under the date

---

[31] Johnes, tr. of Froissart, bk. i. c. 206.   [32] The same, c. 207.

HIS FIRST EXPEDITION.

of 1386; he then testified that he had seen Sir Richard Scrope wearing arms described as 'azure, a bend or,' before the town of 'Retters,' an obvious error for Rethel [33], not far from Rheims; and he added that he 'had seen him so armed during the whole expedition, until he (the said Geoffrey) was taken.' See the evidence as quoted at length at p. xxxvi. But he was soon ransomed, viz. on March 1, 1360; and the King himself contributed to his ransom the sum of 16*l*. [34] According to Froissart, Edward was at this time in the neighbourhood of Auxerre [35].

After a short and ineffectual siege of Paris, the English army suffered severely from thunder-storms during a retreat towards Chartres, and Edward was glad to make peace; articles of peace were accordingly concluded, on May 8, 1360, at Bretigny, near Chartres. King John of France was set at liberty, leaving Eltham on Wednesday, July 1; and after stopping for three nights on the road, viz. at Dartford, Rochester, and Ospringe, he arrived at Canterbury on the Saturday [36]. On the Monday he came to Dover, and thence proceeded to Calais. And surely Chaucer must have been present during the fifteen days of October which the two kings spent at Calais in each other's company; the Prince of Wales and his two brothers, *Lionel* and Edmund, being also present [37]. On leaving Calais, King John and the English princes 'went on foot to the church of our Lady of Boulogne, where they made their offerings most devoutly, and afterward returned to the abbey at Boulogne, which had been prepared for the reception of the King of France and the princes of England [38].'

---

[33] Certainly not Retiers, near Rennes, in Brittany, more than 200 miles on the other side of Paris, as suggested by Sir H. Nicolas. Froissart mentions 'Rhetel' expressly. 'Detachments from the [English] army scoured the country... Some of them went over the whole country of Rhetel;' bk. i. c. 208.

[34] The Athenæum, Nov. 22, 1873; p. 663. From the Wardrobe Book, 63/9, in the Record Office.

[35] He was lodging at Guillon, in Burgundy, from Ash-Wednesday (Feb. 18) until Mid-lent (March 12); Fr. bk. i. c. 210.

[36] This is well worth notice; it shews that it took several days to travel to Canterbury, even for a king who was anxious to return to his own land. In Froissart, bk. iv. c. 118, is an account of two knights who stopped at the same places. See Temp. Preface to the Cant. Tales, by F. J. Furnivall, p. 129.

[37] Johnes, tr. of Froissart, bk. i. c. 213.

[38] Johnes, tr. of Froissart, bk. i. c. 213. The Wyf of Bathe (see Cant. Tales, Prol. 465) once went on a pilgrimage to Boulogne. Chaucer probably did the same, viz. in the last week of October, 1360.

On July 1, 1361, prince Lionel was appointed lieutenant of Ireland, probably because he already bore the title of Earl of Ulster. It does not appear that Chaucer remained in his service much longer; for he must have been attached to the royal household not long after the return of the English army from France. In the Schedule of names of those employed in the Royal Household, for whom robes for Christmas were to be provided, Chaucer's name occurs as seventeenth in the list of thirty-seven esquires. The list is not dated, but is marked by the Record Office '? 40 Edw. III,' i. e. 1366[39]. However, Mr. Selby thinks the right date of this document is 1368.

§ 7. CHAUCER'S MARRIAGE: PHILIPPA CHAUCER. In 1366, we find Chaucer already married. On Sept. 12, in that year, Philippa Chaucer received from the queen, after whom she was doubtless named, a pension of ten marks (or 6*l.* 13*s.* 4*d.*) annually for life, perhaps on the occasion of her marriage; and we find her described as 'una domicellarum camerae Philippae Reginae Angliae[40].' The first known payment on behalf of this pension is dated Feb. 19, 1368[41]. Nicolas tells us that her pension 'was confirmed by Richard the Second; and she apparently received it (except between 1370[42] and 1373, in 1378, and in 1385, the reason of which omissions does not appear) from 1366 until June 18, 1387. The money was usually paid to her through her husband; but in November, 1374, by the hands of John de Hermesthorpe, and in June, 1377 (the Poet being then on his mission in France), by Sir Roger de Trumpington, whose wife, Lady Blanche de Trumpington, was [then], like herself[43], in the service of the Duchess of Lancaster.' As no payment appears after June, 1387, we may conclude that she died towards the end of that year[44].

---

[39] Exchequer, Q. R. Wardrobe Accounts, 39/10; Life-Records, p. xvii.

[40] Rot. Pat. 40 Edw. III. p. 2, membrane 30. The title 'domicella camerae' implies that she was married; N. and Q., 8 S., iii. 355.

[41] Issue Rolls of the Exchequer, Mich., 42 Edw. III.; Nicolas, Note DD.

[42] This exception is incorrect. In the Issue Roll of Thomas de Brantingham, (for 1370), p. 359, it is noted that Philippa Chaucer received 10 marks (i. e. for the whole year), on Nov. 7, 1370.

[43] Here Nicolas inserts 'like herself'; this assumes her identity with 'Philippe Chausy,' which seems to be right; see p. xxi.

[44] Issue Rolls of the Exchequer; Roll for Easter, 10 Ric. II.; Issue Roll, Mich., 44 Edw. III.; ed. Devon, 1835; p. 359.

PHILIPPA CHAUCER.

Philippa's maiden name is not known. She cannot be identified with Philippa Picard, because both names, viz. Philippa Chaucer and Philippa Picard, occur in the same document [45]. Another supposition identifies her with Philippa Roet, on the assumption that Thomas Chaucer, on whose tomb appear the arms of Roet, was her son. This, as will be shewn hereafter, is highly probable, though not quite certain.

It is possible that she was the same person as Philippa, the 'lady of the pantry,' who has been already mentioned as belonging to the household of the Countess of Ulster. If so, she doubtless entered the royal household on the Countess's death in 1363, and was married in 1366, or earlier. After the death of the queen in 1369 (Aug. 15), we find that (on Sept. 1) the king gave Chaucer, as being one of his squires of lesser degree, three ells of cloth for mourning; and, at the same time, six ells of cloth, for the same, to Philippa Chaucer [46].

In 1372, John of Gaunt married (as his second wife) Constance, elder daughter of Pedro, king of Castile; and in the same year (Aug. 30), he granted Philippa Chaucer a pension of 10*l.* per annum, in consideration of her past and future services to his dearest wife, the queen of Castile [47]. Under the name of Philippa Chaucy (as the name is also written in this volume), the duke presented her with a 'botoner,' apparently a button-hook, and six silver-gilt buttons as a New Year's gift for the year 1373 [48]. In 1374, on June 13, he granted 10*l.* per annum to his well-loved Geoffrey Chaucer and his well-beloved Philippa, for their service to Queen Philippa and to his wife the queen [i. e. of Castile], to be received at the duke's manor of the Savoy [49]. In 1377, on May 31, payments were made to Geoffrey Chaucer, varlet, of an annuity of 20 marks that day granted, and of 10 marks to Philippa Chaucer (granted to her for life) as being one of the damsels of the chamber to the late queen, by the hands of

---

[45] Writ of Privy Seal, dated March 10, 43 Edw. III., 1369. It mentions Philippa Chaucer, 'damoiselle,' and Philippa Pykart, 'veilleresse.' See Nicolas, life of Chaucer, Note EE.

[46] The Athenæum, Nov. 22, 1873; p. 663.

[47] Register of John of Gaunt, vol. i. fol. 159*b*; Notes and Queries, 7 Ser., v. 289; Trial-Forewords, p. 129.

[48] The same, vol. i. fol. 195*b*; N. and Q., 7 S., v. 289.

[49] The same, fol. 90; N. and Q. (as above).

Geoffrey Chaucer, her husband[50]. In 1380, the duke gave Philippa a silver hanap (or cup) with its cover, as his New Year's gift; and a similar gift in 1381 and 1382[51]. A payment of 5*l*. to Geoffrey 'Chaucy' is recorded soon after the first of these gifts. In 1384, the sum of 13*l*. 6*s*. 8*d*. (20 marks) is transmitted to Philippa Chaucer by John Hinesthorp, chamberlain[52]. The last recorded payment of a pension to Philippa Chaucer is on June 18, 1387; and it is probable, as said above, that she died very shortly afterwards.

Sir H. Nicolas mentions that, in 1380-2, Philippa Chaucer was one of the three ladies in attendance on the Duchess of Lancaster, the two others being Lady Senche Blount and Lady Blanche de Trompington; and that in June, 1377, as mentioned above, her pension was paid to Sir Roger de Trumpington, who was Lady Blanche's husband. This is worth a passing notice; for it clearly shews that the poet was familiar with the name of Trumpington, and must have known of its situation near Cambridge. And this may account for his laying the scene of the Reves Tale in that village, without necessitating the inference that he must have visited Cambridge himself. For indeed, it is not easy to see why the two 'clerks' should have been benighted there; the distance from Cambridge is so slight that, even in those days of bad roads, they could soon have returned home after dark without any insuperable difficulty.

§ 8. **1367.** To return to Chaucer. In 1367, we find him 'a valet of the king's household'; and by the title of 'dilectus valettus noster,' the king, in consideration of his *former* and his future services, granted him, on June 20, an annual salary of 20 marks (13*l*. 6*s*. 8*d*.) for life, or until he should be otherwise provided for[53]. Memoranda are found of the payment of this pension, in half-yearly instalments, on November 6, 1367, and May 25, 1368[54]; but not in November, 1368, or May, 1369. The next entry as to its payment is dated October, 1369[55]. As to the

---

[50] Issue Roll, Easter, 50 Edw. III.; N. and Q. (as in note 48).
[51] Register of John of Gaunt, vol. ii. foll. 33*b*, 49, 61; Nicolas, Note DD.
[52] Issue Roll, Mich., 8 Ric II., Sept. 20.
[53] Rymer's Fœdera, new ed.; vol. iii. p. 829. (G.)
[54] Issue Rolls of the Exchequer; Michaelmas, 42 Edw. III. (1367); Easter, 42 Edw. III. (1368); see Nicolas, Notes B and C. On Nov. 6, 1367, it is expressly noted that he received his pension himself (per manus propriis).
[55] Issue Rolls; Michaelmas, 43 Edw. III. (Nicolas.)

duties of a valet in the royal household, see Life-Records of Chaucer, part ii. p. xi. Amongst other things, he was expected to make beds, hold torches, set boards (i.e. lay the tables for dinner), and perform various menial offices.

§ 9. **1368.** The note that he received his pension, in 1368, on May 25, is of some importance. It renders improbable a suggestion of Speght, that he accompanied his former master, Lionel, Duke of Clarence, to Italy in this year. Lionel set off with an unusually large retinue, about the 10th of May [56], and passed through France on his way to Italy, where he was shortly afterwards married, for the second time, to Violante, daughter of Galeazzo Visconti. But his married life was of short duration; he died on Oct. 17 of the same year, not without suspicion of poison. His will, dated Oct. 3, 1368, is given in Testamenta Vetusta, ed. Nicolas, p. 70. It does not appear that Chaucer went to Italy before 1372-3; but it is interesting to observe that, on his second journey there in 1378, he was sent to treat with Barnabo Visconti, Galeazzo's brother, as noted at p. xxxii.

§ 10. **1369.** In this year, Chaucer was again campaigning in France. An advance of 10*l.* is recorded as having been made to him by Henry de Wakefeld, the Keeper of the King's Wardrobe; and he is described as 'equitanti de guerre (*sic*) in partibus Francie [57].' In the same year, there is a note that Chaucer was to have 20*s.* for summer clothes [58].

This year is memorable for the last of the three great pestilences which afflicted England, as well as other countries, in the fourteenth century. Queen Philippa died at Windsor on Aug. 15; and we find an entry, dated Sept. 1, that Geoffrey Chaucer, a squire of less estate, and his wife Philippa, were to have an allowance for mourning [59], as stated above. Less than a month later, the Duchess Blaunche died, on Sept. 12; and her death was com-

---

[56] Rymer's Fœdera; vol. iii. p. 845. The names of many of those who accompanied the Duke are printed in the same volume, pp. 842-4; but the name of Chaucer is not among them.

[57] The Athenæum, Nov. 29, 1873; p. 698. Exch. L. T. R. Wardrobe, 43 Edw. III. Box A. no. 8. (Ch. Soc., Trial-Forewords, p. 129).

[58] Exch. Q. R. Wardrobe, 64/3; leaf 16, back. See The Athenæum, Nov. 22. 1873, p. 663. A similar entry occurs in 1372; and again in 1373.

[59] Exch. Q. R. Wardrobe, 40/9. (Ch. Soc., Trial-Forewords, p. 129).

memorated by the poet in one of the earliest of his extant poems, the Book of the Duchesse (see p. 277).

§ 11. 1370-1372. In the course of the next ten years (1370-80), the poet was attached to the court, and employed in no less than seven diplomatic services. The first of these occasions was during the summer of 1370, when he obtained the usual letters of protection, dated June 10, to remain in force till the ensuing Michaelmas[60]. That he returned immediately afterwards, appears from the fact that he received his half-yearly pension in person on Tuesday, the 8th of October[61]; though on the preceding occasion (Thursday, April 25), it was paid to Walter Walssh instead of to himself[62].

In 1371 and 1372, he received his pension himself[63]. In 1372 and 1373 he received 2*l.* for his clothes each year. This was probably a customary annual allowance to squires[64]. A like payment is again recorded in 1377.

Towards the end of the latter year, on Nov. 12, 1372, Chaucer, being then 'scutifer,' or one of the king's esquires, was joined in a commission with James Provan and John de Mari, the latter of whom is described as a citizen of Genoa, to treat with the duke, citizens, and merchants of Genoa, for the purpose of choosing an English port where the Genoese might form a commercial establishment[65]. On Dec. 1, he received an advance of 66*l.* 13*s.* 4*d.* towards his expenses[66]; and probably left England before the close of the year

§ 12. 1373. CHAUCER'S FIRST VISIT TO ITALY. All that is known of this mission is that he visited Florence as well as Genoa, and that he returned before Nov. 22, 1373, on which day he received his pension in person[67]. It further appears that his

---

[60] Rot. Pat. 44 Edw. III. p. 2. m. 20. (G.)

[61] Issue Rolls of Thomas de Brantingham, 44 Edw. III., ed. F. Devon, 1835; p. 289.

[62] The same; p. 19.

[63] Issue Rolls, 45-47 Edw. III.

[64] The Athenæum, Nov. 22, 1873; p. 663

[65] Rot. Franc. 46 Edw. III. m. 8. (G.) See Rymer's Fœdera, new edition, vol. iii. p. 964.

[66] Issue Roll, Michaelmas, 47 Edw. III., 1373. See Nicolas, Note D. In this document Chaucer is called 'armiger.'

[67] Issue Roll, Michaelmas. 48 Edw. III., 1374. See Nicolas, Note E. The Foreign Accounts, 47 Edw. III. roll 3, include Chaucer's accounts for this journey from Dec. 1, 1372, to May 23, 1373.

expenses finally exceeded the money advanced to him; for on Feb. 4, 1374, a further sum was paid to him, on this account, of 25*l.* 6*s.* 8*d.*[68] It was probably on this occasion that Chaucer met Petrarch at Padua, and learnt from him the story of Griselda, reproduced in the Clerkes Tale. Some critics prefer to think that Chaucer's assertions on this point are to be taken as imaginative, and that it was the Clerk, and not himself, who went to Padua; but it is clear that in writing the Clerkes Tale, Chaucer actually had a copy of Petrarch's Latin version before him; and it is difficult to see how he came by it unless he obtained it from Petrarch himself or by Petrarch's assistance. For further discussion of this point, see remarks on the Sources of the Clerkes Tale, in vol. iii., and the notes in vol. v.[69] We must, in any case, bear in mind the important influence which this mission to Italy, and a later one in 1378-9 to the same country, produced upon the development of his poetical writings.

It may be convenient to note here that Petrarch resided chiefly at Arquà, within easy reach of Padua, in 1370-4. His death took place there on July 18, 1374, soon after Chaucer had returned home.

§ 13. **1374.** We may fairly infer that Chaucer's execution of this important mission was satisfactorily performed; for we find that on the 23rd of April, 1374, on the celebration at Windsor of the festival of St. George, the king made him a grant of a pitcher of wine daily, to be received in the port of London from the king's butler[70]. This was, doubtless, found to be rather a troublesome gift; accordingly, it was commuted, in 1378 (April 18), for the annual sum of 20 marks (13*l.* 6*s.* 8*d.*)[71]. The original grant was made 'dilecto Armigero nostro, Galfrido Chaucer.'

---

[68] The same.

[69] Much of Sir H. Nicolas's argument against this reasonable supposition is founded on the assertion that Chaucer was 'not acquainted with Italian'; which is now known to be the reverse of the truth. He even urges that not a single Italian word occurs in Chaucer's writings, whereas it would have been absurd for him to use words which his readers could not understand. Nevertheless, we find mention of a '*ducat* in Venyse'; Ho. Fame, 1348.

[70] Rot. Pat., 48 Edw. III., p. i. m. 20. (G.) See Rymer's Fœdera, new ed. vol. iii. p. 1001.

[71] Writ of Privy Seal (in French); 18 Apr. 1 Ric. II. (1378); see Nicolas, Note K.

On May 10, in the same year, the corporation of London granted Chaucer a lease for his life of the dwelling-house situate above the city-gate of Aldgate, on condition that he kept the same in good repair; he seems to have made this his usual residence till 1385, and we know that he retained possession of it till October, 1386 [72].

Four weeks later, on June 8, 1374, he was appointed Comptroller of the Customs and Subsidy of wools, skins, and tanned hides in the Port of London, with the usual fees. Like his predecessors, he was to write the rolls of his office with his own hand, to be continually present, and to perform his duties personally (except, of course, when employed on the King's service elsewhere); and the other part of the seal called the 'coket' (quod dicitur *coket*) was to remain in his custody [73]. The warrant by which, on June 13, 1374, the Duke of Lancaster granted him 10*l*. for life, in consideration of the services of himself and his wife, has been mentioned at p. xxi. In the same year, he received his half-yearly pension of 10 marks as usual; and again in 1375.

§ 14. **1375.** On Nov. 8, 1375, his income was, for a time, considerably increased. He received from the crown a grant of the custody of the lands and person of Edmond, son and heir of Edmond Staplegate of Kent [74], who had died in 1372 [75]; this he retained for three years, during which he received in all, for his wardship and on Edmond's marriage, the sum of 104*l*. This is ascertained from the petition presented by Edmond de Staplegate to Richard II. at his coronation, in which he laid claim to be permitted to exercise the office of chief butler to the king [76]. And further, on Dec. 28, 1375, he received a grant from the king of the custody of five 'solidates' of rent for land at Soles, in Kent, during the minority of William de Solys, then an infant aged 1 year, son and heir of John Solys, deceased; together with a fee due on the marriage of the said heir [77]. But the value of this grant cannot have been large.

---

[72] Memorials of London, ed. Riley, p. 377. See § 26 below, p. xxxviii.

[73] Rot. Pat., 48 Edw. III., p. 1. m. 7, in Turri Londinensi; see Fœdera, new ed. vol. iii. p. 1004. (G.)

[74] Rot. Pat., 49 Edw. III., p. 2. m. 8.

[75] Calendarium Inquisitionum post Mortem, 46 Edw. III. no. 58.

[76] Rot. Claus., 1 Ric. II., m. 45. (G.) The petition, in French, is printed in full in Liber Custumarum, ed. Riley, ii. 466.

[77] Rot. Pat. 49 Edw. III., p. 2. m. 4. (G.) Calend. Inquis. post Mortem,

THE MISSION TO FLANDERS.

§ 15. **1376.** In 1376, on May 31, he received at the exchequer his own half-yearly pension of ten marks and his wife's of five marks, or 10*l.* in all (see Notes and Queries, 3rd Ser. viii. 63); and in October he received an advance from the exchequer of 50*s.* on account of his pension[78]. He also duly received his annuity of 10*l.* from the duke of Lancaster (Oct. 18, 1376, and June 12, 1377)[79].

In the same year, we also meet with the only known record connected with Chaucer's exercise of the Office of Comptroller of the Customs. On July 12, 1376, the King granted him the sum of 71*l.* 4*s.* 6*d.*, being the value of a fine paid by John Kent, of London, for shipping wool to Dordrecht without having paid the duty thereon[80].

Towards the end of this year, Sir John Burley and Geoffrey Chaucer were employed together on some secret service (in secretis negociis domini Regis), the nature of which is unknown; for on Dec. 23, 1376, Sir John 'de Burlee' received 13*l.* 6*s.* 8*d.*, and Chaucer half that sum, for the business upon which they had been employed[81].

§ 16. **1377.** On Feb. 12, 1377, Chaucer was associated with Sir Thomas Percy (afterwards Earl of Worcester) in a secret mission to Flanders, the nature of which remains unknown; and on this occasion Chaucer received letters of protection during his mission, to be in force till Michaelmas in the same year[82]. Five days later, on Feb. 17, the sum of 33*l.* 6*s.* 8*d.* was advanced to Sir Thomas, and 10*l.* to Chaucer, for their expenses[83]. They started immediately, and the business was transacted by March 25; and on April 11 Chaucer himself received at the exchequer the sum of 20*l.* as a reward from the king for the various journeys which he had made abroad upon the king's

---

49 Edw. III., part 2, no. 40. A solidate of land is supposed to be a quantity of land (Blount suggests 12 acres) yielding 1*s.* of yearly rent. *Sole* means 'a pond'; see Pegge's Kenticisms. Soles is the name of a manor in Bonnington, not far from Chillenden, about half-way between Canterbury and Deal.

[78] Issue Roll, Mich., 50 Edw. III.

[79] Receiver's Accounts in the Office of the Duchy of Lancaster, from Mich. 1376 to Mich. 1377; see Nicolas, Note F.

[80] Rot. Pat., 50 Edw. III., p. i. m. 5. (G.)

[81] Issue Roll, Mich., 51 Edw. III.; see Nicolas, Note G.

[82] Rot. Franc., 51 Edw. III., m. 7. (G.)

[83] Issue Roll, Mich., 51 Edw. III.; see Nicolas, Note H.

service (pro regardo suo causâ diuersorum viagiorum per ipsum Galfridum factorum, eundo ad diuersas partes transmarinas ex precepto domini Regis in obsequio ipsius domini Regis)[84].

While Sir Thomas Percy and Chaucer were absent in Flanders, viz. on Feb. 20, 1377, the Bishop of Hereford, Lord Cobham, Sir John Montacu (i.e. Montague), and Dr. Shepeye were empowered to treat for peace with the French King[85]. Their endeavours must have been ineffectual; for soon after Chaucer's return, viz. on April 26, 1377, Sir Guichard d'Angle and several others were also appointed to negotiate a peace with France[86]. Though Chaucer's name does not expressly appear in this commission, he was clearly in some way associated with it; for only six days previously (Apr. 20), letters of protection were issued to him, to continue till Aug. 1, whilst he was on the king's service abroad[87]; and on April 30, he was paid the sum of 26*l*. 13*s*. 4*d*. for his wages on this occasion[88]. We further find, from an entry in the Issue Roll for March 6, 1381 (noticed again at p. xxix), that he was sent to Moustrell (Montreuil) and Paris, and that he was instructed to treat for peace.

This is clearly the occasion to which Froissart refers in the following passage. 'About Shrovetide[89], a secret treaty was formed between the two kings for their ambassadors to meet at Montreuil-sur-Mer; and the king of England sent to Calais sir Guiscard d'Angle, Sir Richard Sturey, and sir Geoffrey Chaucer. On the part of the French were the lords de Coucy and de la Rivieres, sir Nicholas Bragues and Nicholas Bracier. They for a long time discussed the subject of the above marriage [the marriage of the French princess with Richard, prince of Wales]; and the French, *as I was informed*, made some offers, but the others demanded different terms, or refused treating. These lords returned therefore, with their treaties, to their sovereigns; and

---

[84] Issue Roll, Easter, 51 Edw. III.; Nicolas, Note I; Trial-Forewords, p. 131.

[85] Rymer's Fœdera, new ed., vol. iii. p. 1073 (in French).

[86] The same, p. 1076 (in French).

[87] Rot. Franc., 51 Edw III., m. 5. (G.)

[88] Issue Roll, Easter, 51 Edw. III. 'Galfrido Chaucer armigero regis misso in nuncium in secretis negociis domini Regis versus partes Francie.' See Nicolas, Note I.

[89] In 1377, Easter fell on March 29, Ash Wednesday on Feb. 11, and Shrove Tuesday on Feb. 10.

the truces were prolonged to the first of May.'—Johnes, tr. of Froissart, bk. i. c. 326.

I think Sir H. Nicolas has not given Froissart's meaning correctly. According to him, 'Froissart states that, in Feb. 1377, Chaucer was joined with Sir Guichard d'Angle, &c., to negociate a secret treaty for the marriage of Richard, prince of Wales, with Mary, daughter of the king of France,' &c.; and that the truce was prolonged till the first of May. And he concludes that Froissart has confused two occasions, because there really was an attempt at a treaty about this marriage in 1378 (see below). It does not appear that Froissart is wrong. He merely gives the date of about Shrovetide (Feb. 10) as the time when 'a secret treaty was formed'; and this must refer to the ineffectual commission of Feb. 20, 1377. After this 'the king of England' really sent 'Sir Guiscard d'Angle' in April; and Chaucer either went with the rest or joined them at Montreuil. Neither does it appear that discussion of the subject of the marriage arose on the English side; it was the French who proposed it, but the English who declined it, for the reason that they had received no instructions to that effect. On the other hand, the English ambassadors, having been instructed to treat for peace, procured, at any rate, a short truce. This explanation seems to me sufficient, especially as Froissart merely wrote what he had been informed; he was not present himself. The very fact that the marriage was proposed by the French on this occasion explains how the English came to consider this proposal seriously in the following year.

Fortunately, the matter is entirely cleared up by the express language employed in the Issue Roll of 4 Ric. II., under the date Mar. 6, as printed in Nicolas, Note R; where the object of the deliberations at Montreuil is definitely restricted to a treaty for peace, whilst the proposal of marriage (from the *English* side) is definitely dated as having been made in the reign of Richard, not of Edward III. The words are: 'tam tempore regis Edwardi . . . in nuncium eiusdem . . . versus Moustrell' et Parys . . . causa tractatus pacis . . . quam tempore domini regis nunc, causa locutionis habite de maritagio inter ipsum dominum regem nunc et filiam eiusdem aduersarii sui Francie.'

The princess Marie, fifth daughter of Charles V., was born in 1370 (N. and Q., 3 S. vii. 470), and was therefore only seven years old in 1377; and died in the same year. It is remarkable that Richard married Isabella, daughter of Charles VI., in 1396, when she was only eight.

It is worth notice that Stowe, in his Annales, p. 437, alludes to the same mission. He mentions, as being among the ambassadors, 'the Earle of Salisbury and Sir Richard Anglisison a Poyton [can this be Sir Guiscard D'Angle?], the Bishop of Saint Dauids, the Bishop of Hereford, [and] Geffrey Chaucer, the famous Poet of England.' See Life-Records of Chaucer, p. 133, note 3.

The payments made to Chaucer by John of Gaunt on May 31 of this year have been noticed above in § 7, at p. xxi.

The long reign of Edward III. terminated on June 21, 1377, during which Chaucer had received many favours from the king and the Duke of Lancaster, and some, doubtless, from Lionel, Duke of Clarence. At the same time, his wife was in favour with the queen, till her death in August, 1369; and afterwards, with the second duchess of Lancaster. The poet was evidently, at this time, in easy circumstances; and it is not unlikely that he was somewhat lavish in his expenditure. The accession of Richard, at the early age of eleven, made no difference to his position for some nine years; but in 1386, the adverse supremacy of Thomas, Duke of Gloucester, caused him much pecuniary loss and embarrassment for some time, and he frequently suffered from distress during the later period of his life.

§ 17. CHAUCER'S EARLIER POEMS: TILL THE DEATH OF EDWARD III. It is probable that not much of Chaucer's extant poetry can be referred to the reign of Edward III. At the same time, it is likely that he wrote many short pieces, in the form of ballads, complaints, virelayes, and roundels, which have not been preserved; perhaps some of them were occasional pieces, and chiefly of interest at the time of writing them. Amongst the lost works we may certainly include his translation of 'Origenes upon the Maudelayne,' 'The Book of the Lion,' all but a few stanzas (preserved in the Man of Lawes Tale) of his translation of Pope Innocent's 'Wrecched Engendring of Mankinde,' and all but the first 1705 lines of his translation of Le Roman de la Rose. His early work entitled 'Ceyx and Alcioun' is partly preserved in the Book of the Duchesse, written in 1369-70. His A B.C is, perhaps, his earliest extant complete poem.

It seems reasonable to date the poems which shew a strong

DEATH OF EDWARD III.

Italian influence after Chaucer's visit to Italy in 1373. The Compleint to his Lady is, perhaps, one of the earliest of these; and the Amorous Complaint bears so strong a resemblance to it that it may have been composed nearly at the same time. The Complaint to Pity seems to belong to the same period, rather than, as assumed in the text, to a time preceding the Book of the Duchesse. The original form of the Life of St. Cecily (afterwards the Second Nonnes Tale) is also somewhat early, as well as the original Palamon and Arcite, and Anelida. I should also include, amongst the earlier works, the original form of the Man of Lawes Tale (from Anglo-French), of the Clerkes Tale (from Petrarch's Latin), and some parts of the Monkes Tale. But the great bulk of his poetry almost certainly belongs to the reign of Richard II. See the List of Works at p. lxii.

§ 18. **1377. (CONTINUED).** In the commencement of the new reign, Chaucer was twice paid 40s. by the keeper of the king's Wardrobe, for his half-yearly allowance for robes as one of the (late) king's esquires[90]. He also received 7l. 2s. 6½d. on account of his daily allowance of a pitcher of wine, calculated from October 27, 1376, to June 21, 1377, the day of king Edward's death[91].

§ 19. **1378.** In 1378, on Jan. 16, Chaucer was again associated with Sir Guichard d'Angle (created Earl of Huntingdon at the coronation of the new king), with Sir Hugh Segrave, and Dr. Skirlawe, in a mission to France to negotiate for the king's marriage with a daughter of the king of France[92]; this is in accordance with a suggestion which, as noted at p. xxix., originated with the French. The negotiations came, however, to no result.

On Mar. 9, 1378, Geoffrey Chaucer and John Beauchamp are mentioned as sureties for William de Beauchamp, Knight, in a business having respect to Pembroke Castle[93].

On Mar. 23, 1378, Chaucer's previous annuity of 20 marks was confirmed to him by letters patent[94]; on April 18, his previous grant of a pitcher of wine was commuted for an annual sum of

---

[90] Wardrobe Accounts of 50 and 51 Edw. III. (Nicolas).
[91] The same.
[92] Rymer's Fœdera, vol. vii. p. 184.
[93] Fine Roll, 1 Ric. II., pt. 2. m. 11; Athenæum, May 26, 1888, p. 661.
[94] This appears from the Patent of May 1, 1388, by which Chaucer's pensions were assigned to John Scalby; see Rot. Pat., 11 Ric. II., pt. 2. m. 1.

twenty marks[95]; and, on May 14, he received 20*l.* for the arrears of his pension, and 26*s.* 8*d.* in advance, for the current half-year[96].

CHAUCER'S SECOND VISIT TO ITALY: BARNABO VISCONTI. On May 10, 1378, he received letters of protection, till Christmas[97]; on May 21, he procured letters of general attorney, allowing John Gower (the poet) and Richard Forrester to act for him during his absence from England[98]; and on May 28, he received 66*l.* 13*s.* 4*d.* for his wages and the expenses of his journey, which lasted till the 19th of September[99]. All these entries refer to the same matter, viz. his second visit to Italy. On this occasion, he was sent to Lombardy with Sir Edward Berkeley, to treat with Barnabo Visconti, lord of Milan, and the famous free-lance Sir John Hawkwood, on certain matters touching the king's expedition of war (pro certis negociis expeditionem guerre regis tangentibus); a phrase of uncertain import. This is the Barnabo Visconti, whose death, in 1385, is commemorated by a stanza in the Monkes Tale, B 3589-3596. Of Sir John Hawkwood, a soldier of fortune, and the most skilful general of his age, a memoir is given in the Bibliotheca Topographica Britannica, vol. vi. pp. 1-35. The appointment of Gower as Chaucer's attorney during his absence is of interest, and shews the amicable relations between the two poets at this time. For a discussion of their subsequent relations, see Sources of the Canterbury Tales, vol. iii. § 38, p. 413.

§ 20. **1379-80.** In 1379 and 1380, the notices of Chaucer refer chiefly to the payment of his pensions. In 1379, he received 12*l.* 13*s.* 4*d. with his own hands* on Feb. 3[100]; on May 24, he received the sums of 26*s.* 4*d.* and 13*l.* 6*s.* 4*d.* (the latter on account of the original grant of a pitcher of wine), both *by assignment*[101], which indicates his absence from London at the time;

---

[95] Rot. Pat., 11 Ric. II., pt. 2. m. 1 (as in the last note); Writ of Privy Seal (in French), Apr. 18, 1 Ric. II. (see Nicolas, Note K); Issue Roll, Easter, 1 Ric. II. (May 14; see Nicolas, Note L).
[96] Issue Roll, Easter, 1 Ric. II., (as above).
[97] Rot. Franc., 1 Ric. II., pt. 2. m. 6.
[98] The same; see Nicolas, Note M.
[99] Issue Roll, Easter, 1 Ric. II.; Trial-Forewords, p. 131; Nicolas, Note L.
[100] Issue Roll, Mich., 2 Ric. II.; see Nicolas, Note N.
[101] Issue Roll, Easter, 2 Ric. II.; see Nicolas, Note O.

CECILIA CHAUMPAIGNE.

and on Dec. 9 he received, *with his own hands*, two sums of 6*l*. 13*s*. 4*d*. each on account of his two pensions [102]. In 1380, on July 3, he received the same *by assignment* [103]; and on Nov. 28, he received the same *with his own hands* [104], together with a sum of 14*l*. for wages and expenses in connexion with his mission to Lombardy in 1378 [104], in addition to the 66*l*. 13*s*. 4*d*. paid to him on May 28 of that year. He also received 5*l*. from the Duke of Lancaster on May 11 (N. and Q., 7 S. v. 290).

By a deed dated May 1, 1380, a certain Cecilia Chaumpaigne, daughter of the late William Chaumpaigne and Agnes his wife, released to Chaucer all her rights of action against him 'de raptu meo [105].' We have no means of ascertaining either the meaning of the phrase, or the circumstances referred to. It may mean that Chaucer was accessory to her abduction, much as Geoffrey Stace and others were concerned in the abduction of the poet's father; or it may be connected with the fact that his 'little son Lowis' was ten years old in 1391, as we learn from the Prologue to the Treatise on the Astrolabe.

§ 21. **1381.** On March 6, Chaucer received 22*l*. for his services in going to Montreuil and Paris in the time of the late king, i. e. in 1377, in order to treat for peace; as well as for his journey to France in 1378 to treat for a marriage between king Richard and the daughter of his adversary (adversarii sui) [106]. The Treasury must, at this time, have been slack in paying its just debts. On May 24, he and his wife received their usual half-yearly pensions [107].

By a deed dated June 19, 1380, but preserved in the Hustings Roll, no. 110, at the Guildhall, and there dated 5 Ric. II. (1381-2), Chaucer released his interest in his father's house to Henry Herbury, vintner, in whose occupation it then was; and it is here that he describes himself as 'me Galfridum Chaucer,

---

[102] Issue Roll, Mich. 3 Ric. II.; see Nicolas, Note P.

[103] The same; Easter, 3 Ric. II.; see the same, Note Q.

[104] The same; 4 Ric. II.; see the same, Note R.

[105] The Athenæum, Nov. 29, 1873, p. 698. From the Close Roll of 3 Ric. II. And see the whole matter discussed at length in Trial-Forewords, pp. 136-144 (Ch. Soc.).

[106] Issue Roll, 4 Ric. II.; see Nicolas, Note R; Devon's Issues of the Exchequer, 1837, p. 315.

[107] Godwin's Life of Chaucer, iv. 284.

filium Johannis Chaucer, Vinetarii Londonie [108].' This is the best authority for ascertaining his father's name, occupation, and abode. Towards the close of the year we find the following payments to him; viz. on Nov. 16, sums of 6*l.* 13*s.* 4*d.* and 6*s.* 8*d.*; on Nov. 28, the large sum of 46*l.* 13*s.* 4*d.*, paid to Nicholas Brembre and John Philipot, Collectors of Customs, and to Geoffrey Chaucer, Comptroller of the Customs; and on Dec. 31, certain sums to himself and his wife [109].

§ 22. **1382.** We have seen that, in 1378, an ineffectual attempt was made to bring about a marriage between the king and a French princess. In 1382, the matter was settled by his marriage with Anne of Bohemia, who exerted herself to calm the animosities which were continually arising in the court, and thus earned the title of the 'good queen Anne.' It was to her that Chaucer was doubtless indebted for some relaxation of his official duties in February, 1385, as noted below.

On May 8, 1382, Chaucer's income was further increased. Whilst retaining his office of Comptroller of the Customs of Wools, the duties of which he discharged personally, he was further appointed Comptroller of the Petty Customs in the Port of London, and was allowed to discharge the duties of the office by a sufficient deputy [110]. The usual payments of his own and his wife's pensions were made, in this year, on July 22 and Nov. 11. On Dec. 10, a payment to him is recorded, in respect of his office as Comptroller of the Customs [111].

§ 23. **1383.** In 1383, the recorded payments are: on Feb. 27, 6*s.* 8*d.*; on May 5, his own and his wife's pensions; and on Oct. 24, 6*l.* 13*s.* 4*d.* for his own pension [112]. Besides these, is the following entry for Nov. 23: 'To Nicholas Brembre and John Philipot, Collectors of Customs, and Geoffrey Chaucer, Comptroller; money delivered to them this day in regard of the assiduity, labour, and diligence brought to bear by them on the duties of their office, for the year late elapsed, 46*l.* 13*s.* 4*d.*';

---

[108] Thynne's Animadversions, &c., ed. F. J. Furnivall, p. 12, note 2; cf. The Athenæum, Nov. 29, 1873, p. 698.

[109] Issue Roll, Mich., 5 Ric. II.; see Notes and Queries, 3rd Ser. viii. 367.

[110] Rot. Pat., 5 Ric. II., pt. 2. m. 15. (G.)

[111] For these payments, see Issue Roll, Easter, 5 Ric. II.; in Notes and Queries, 3rd Ser. viii. 367.

[112] Issue Rolls, Easter, 5 and 6 Ric. II.; see N. and Q. (as above).

being the same amount as in 1381[113]. It is possible that the date Dec. 10, on which he tells us that he began his House of Fame, refers to this year.

§ 24. **1384.** In 1384, on Apr. 30, he received his own and his wife's pensions[114]. On Nov. 25, he was allowed to absent himself from his duties for one month, on account of his own urgent affairs; and the Collectors of the Customs were commanded to swear in his deputy[115]. On Dec. 9, one *Philip* Chaucer is referred to as Comptroller of the Customs, but Philip is here an error for Geoffrey, as shewn by Mr. Selby[116].

§ 25. **1385.** In 1385, a stroke of good fortune befell him, which evidently gave him much relief and pleasure. It appears that Chaucer had asked the king to allow him to have a sufficient deputy in his office as Comptroller at the Wool Quay (in French, *Wolkee*) of London[117]. And on Feb. 17, he was released from the somewhat severe pressure of his official duties (of which he complains feelingly in the House of Fame, 652–660) by being allowed to appoint a permanent deputy[118]. He seems to have revelled in his newly-found leisure; and we may fairly infer from the Prologue to the Legend of Good Women, which seems to have been begun shortly afterwards, that he was chiefly indebted for this favour to the good queen Anne. (See the Introduction to vol. iii. p. xix.) On April 24, he received his own pensions as usual, in two sums of 6*l*. 13*s*. 4*d*. each; and, on account of his wife's pension, 3*l*. 6*s*. 8*d*.[119]

§ 26. **1386.** In 1386, as shewn by the Issue Rolls, he received his pensions as usual. In other respects, the year was eventful. Chaucer was elected a knight of the shire[120] for the county of Kent, with which he would therefore seem to have had some connexion, perhaps by the circumstance of residing at

---

[113] Issue Roll, Mich., 7 Ric. II.; *ib*. It was usual to make up accounts at Michaelmas; which may explain 'the year late elapsed.'

[114] Issue Roll, Easter, 7 Ric. II.; *ib*.

[115] Rot. Claus., 8 Ric. II., m. 30. G.

[116] Notes and Queries, 3 S. viii. 368; The Athenæum, Apr. 14, 1888; p. 468.

[117] The Athenæum, Jan. 28, 1888; p. 116.

[118] Rot. Pat., 8 Ric. II., p. 2. m. 31. (G.)

[119] Issue Roll, Easter, 8 Ric. II.; see Notes and Queries, 3rd Ser. viii. 368.

[120] 'Ful ofte tyme he was knight of the shire'; Cant. Ta., A 356. It was usual, but not necessary, for such knights to reside within their county (Nicolas, Note S).

Greenwich (see § 32). He sat accordingly in the parliament which met at Westminster on Oct. 1, and continued its sittings till Nov. 1. He and his colleague, William Betenham, were allowed 24*l.* 8*s.* for their expenses in coming to and returning from the parliament, and for attendance at the same; at the rate of 8*s.* a day for 61 days [121]. The poet was thus an unwilling contributor to his own misfortunes; for the proceedings of this parliament were chiefly directed against the party of the duke of Lancaster, his patron, and on Nov. 19 the king was obliged to grant a patent by which he was practically deprived of all power. A council of regency of eleven persons was formed, with the duke of Gloucester at their head; and the partisans of John of Gaunt found themselves in an unenviable position. Among the very few persons who still adhered to the king was Sir Nicholas Brembre [122], Chaucer's associate in the Customs (see note above, Nov. 23, 1383); and we may feel confident that Chaucer's sympathies were on the same side. We shall presently see that, when the king regained his power in 1389, Chaucer almost immediately received a valuable appointment.

It was during the sitting of this parliament, viz. on Oct. 15, that Chaucer was examined at Westminster in the case of Richard, lord Scrope, against the claim of Sir Robert Grosvenor, as to the right of bearing the coat of arms described as 'azure, a bend or.' The account of Chaucer's evidence is given in French [123]; the following is a translation of it, chiefly in the words of Sir H. Nicolas:—

'Geoffrey Chaucer, Esquire, of the age of 40 years and upwards, armed for 27 years, produced on behalf of Sir Richard Scrope, sworn and examined.

'Asked, whether the arms, "azure, a bend or," belonged or ought to belong to the said Sir Richard of right and heritage? Said—Yes, for he had seen them armed in France before the town of Retters [124], and Sir Henry Scrope armed in the same arms with a white label, and with a banner, and the said Sir Richard armed in the entire arms, Azure, a bend Or, and he had so seen them armed during the whole expedition, till the said Geoffrey was taken.

'Asked, how he knew that the said arms appertained to the said Sir Richard?

---

[121] Rot. Claus., 10 Ric. II., m. 16 d.

[122] See Annals of England, Oxford, 1876; p. 206. Sir Nicholas Brembre had been Lord Mayor of London for the three preceding years, 1383-5.

[123] Printed in Godwin's Life of Chaucer; in The Scrope and Grosvenor Roll, ed. Nicolas, i. 178; and in Moxon's Chaucer, p. xiii.

[124] An error for Rethel, near Rheims; see above, footnote 33.

Said—by hearsay from old knights and squires, and that they had always continued their possession of the said arms; and that they had always been reputed to be their arms, as the common fame and the public voice testifies and had testified; and he also said, that when he had seen the said arms in banners, glass, paintings, and vestments, they were commonly called the arms of Scrope.

'Asked, if he had ever heard say who was the first ancestor of the said Sir Richard who first bore the said arms? Said—No; nor had he ever heard otherwise than that they were come of old ancestry and of old gentry, and that they had used the said arms.

'Asked, if he had ever heard say how long a time the ancestors of the said Sir Richard had used the said arms? Said—No; but he had heard say that it passed the memory of man.

'Asked, if he had ever heard of any interruption or claim made by Sir Robert Grosvenor or by his ancestors or by any one in his name, against the said Sir Richard or any of his ancestors? Said—No; but said, that he was once in Friday Street, London, and, as he was walking in the street, he saw a new sign, made of the said arms, hanging out; and he asked what inn it was that had hung out these arms of Scrope? And one answered him and said— No, sir; they are not hung out as the arms of Scrope, nor painted for those arms; but they are painted and put there by a knight of the county of Chester, whom men call Sir Robert Grosvenor; and that was the first time that he had ever heard speak of Sir Robert Grosvenor, or of his ancestors, or of any one bearing the name of Grosvenor.'

The statement that Chaucer was, at this time, of the age of 'forty and upwards' (xl. ans et plus) ought to be of assistance in determining the date of his birth; but it has been frequently discredited on the ground that similar statements made, in the same account, respecting other persons, can easily be shewn to be incorrect. It can hardly be regarded as more than a mere phrase, expressing that the witness was old enough to give material evidence. But the testimony that the witness had borne arms for twenty-seven years (xxvii. ans) is more explicit, and happens to tally exactly with the evidence actually given concerning the campaign of 1359; a campaign which we may at once admit, on his own shewing, to have been his first. Taken in connexion with his service in the household of the Countess of Ulster, where his position was probably that of page, we should expect that, in 1359, he was somewhere near 20 years of age, and born not long before 1340. It is needless to discuss the point further, as nothing will convince those who are determined to make much of Chaucer's allusions to his 'old age' (which is, after all, a personal affair), and who cannot understand why Hoccleve should speak of himself as 'ripe for death' when he was only fifty-three.

It was during the session of this same parliament (Oct. 1386) that Chaucer gave up the house in Aldgate which he had occupied since May, 1374; and the premises were granted by the corporation to one Richard Forster, possibly the same person as the Richard Forrester who had been his proxy in 1378 [125]. In this house he must have composed several of his poems; and, in particular, The Parlement of Foules, The House of Fame, and Troilus, besides making his translation of Boethius. The remarks about 'my house' in the Prologue to the Legend of Good Women, 282, are inconsistent with the position of a house above a city-gate. If, as is probable, they have reference to facts, we may suppose that he had already practically resigned his house to his friend in 1385, when he was no longer expected to perform his official duties personally.

Meanwhile, the duke of Gloucester was daily gaining ascendancy; and Chaucer was soon to feel the resentment of his party. On Dec. 4, 1386, he was deprived of his more important office, that of Comptroller of the Customs of Wool, and Adam Yerdeley was appointed in his stead. Only ten days later, on Dec. 14, he lost his other office likewise, and Henry Gisors became Comptroller of the Petty Customs [126]. This must have been a heavy loss to one who had previously been in good circumstances, and who seems to have spent his money rather freely [127]. He was suffered, however, to retain his own and his wife's pensions, as there was no pretence for depriving him of them.

§ 27. **1387.** In 1387, the payment of his wife's pension, on June 18, appears for the last time [128]. It cannot be doubted that she died during the latter part of this year. In the same year,

---

[125] Letter-book in the Guildhall, discovered by Prof. Hales; see The Academy, Dec. 6, 1879, p. 410, and Hales, Folia Litteraria, p. 87. In Riley's Memorials of London, p. 469, is recorded a resolution by the corporation to let no more houses situated over a city-gate.

[126] Rot. Pat., 10 Ric. II., p. 1. m. 5 and m. 9. Perhaps this new Controller was a descendant of the Henry Gisors who was Sheriff of London in 1328.

[127] It was once a fashion to ascribe his misfortunes to the part he was supposed to have taken with respect to a quarrel in 1384 between the court party and the citizens of London regarding John of Northampton, who had been Mayor in 1382. There is no evidence whatever to shew that Chaucer had anything to do with it, beyond an unauthorised and perhaps false interpretation of certain obscure passages in a piece called *The Testament of Love*, which (as is now known) he certainly did not write!

[128] Issue Roll, Easter, 10 Ric. II.

and in the spring of 1388, he received his own pensions, as usual [129]; but his wife's pension ceased at her death, at a time when his own income was seriously reduced.

§ 28. **1388.** In 1388, on May 1, the grants of his two annual pensions, of 20 marks each, were cancelled at his own request, and assigned, in his stead, to John Scalby [130]. The only probable interpretation of this act is that he was then hard pressed for money, and adopted this ready but rather rash method for obtaining a considerable sum at once. He retained, however, the pension of 10*l.* per annum, granted him by the duke of Lancaster in 1374. Chaucer was evidently a hard worker and a practical man. We have every reason for believing that he performed his duties assiduously, as he himself asserts; and the loss of his offices in Dec. 1386 must have occasioned a good deal of enforced leisure. This explains at once why the years 1387 and 1388 were, as appears from other considerations, the most active time of his poetical career; he was then hard at work on his Canterbury Tales. And though the loss of his wife, at the close of 1387, must have caused a sad interruption in his congenial task, we can hardly wonder if, after a reasonable interval, he resumed it; it was perhaps the best thing that he could do.

§ 29. **1389.** This period of almost complete leisure came to an end in July, 1389; owing, probably, to the fact that the king, on May 3 in that year, suddenly took the government into his own hands. The influence of the duke of Gloucester was on the wane; the duke of Lancaster returned to England; and the cloud that had lain over Chaucer's fortunes was once more dispersed. His public work required some attention, though he was allowed to have a deputy, and the time devoted to the Canterbury Tales was diminished. It is doubtful whether, with the exception of a few occasional pieces, Chaucer wrote much new poetry during the last ten years of his life.

On July 12, Chaucer received the valuable appointment of Clerk of the King's Works at the palace of Westminster, the

---

[129] Issue Rolls, Easter, 10 Ric. II.; Mich. and Easter, 11 Ric. II.

[130] Rot. Pat., 11 Ric. II., p. 2. m. 1. (G.) Nicolas remarks that a John Scalby, of Scarborough in Yorkshire, was one of the persons of that town who were excepted from the king's pardon for insurrection in October, 1382; Rot. Parl. vol. iii. p. 136. (Scalby is the name of a village near Scarborough.)

LIFE OF GEOFFREY CHAUCER.

Tower of London, the Mews at Charing Cross, and other places. Among them are mentioned the Castle of Berkhemsted (Berkhamstead, Herts.), the King's manors of Kennington (now in London), Eltham (Kent), Clarendon (near Salisbury), Sheen (now Richmond, Surrey)[131], Byfleet (Surrey), Childern Langley (i.e. King's Langley, Hertfordshire), and Feckenham (Worcestershire); also the Royal lodge of Hatherbergh in the New Forest, and the lodges in the parks of Clarendon, Childern Langley, and Feckenham. He was permitted to execute his duties by deputy, and his salary was 2s. per day, or 36l. 10s. annually, a considerable sum[132]. A payment to Chaucer, as Clerk of the Works, is recorded only ten days later (July 22); and we find that, about this time, he issued a commission to one Hugh Swayn to provide materials for the king's works at Westminster, Sheen, and elsewhere[133].

§ 30. **1390.** In 1390, on March 13, Chaucer was appointed on a commission, with five others, to repair the banks of the Thames between Woolwich and Greenwich (at that time, probably, his place of residence); but was superseded in 1391[134].

In the same year, Chaucer was entrusted with the task of putting up scaffolds in Smithfield for the king and queen to see the jousts which took place there in the month of May; this notice is particularly interesting in connexion with the Knightes Tale (A 1881-92). The cost of doing this, amounting to 8l. 12s. 6d., was allowed him in a writ dated July 1, 1390; and he received further payment at the rate of 2s. a day[135].

About this time, in the 14th year of king Richard (June 22, 1390-June 21, 1391), he was appointed joint forester, with Richard Brittle, of North Petherton Park, in Somersetshire, by the earl of March, the grandson of his first patron, Prince Lionel. Perhaps in consequence of the death of Richard Brittle, he was made sole forester in 21 Ric. II. (1397-8) by the countess of March; and he probably held the appointment till his death in 1400. No appointment, however, is known to have been then

---

[131] Cf. 'at Eltham or at Shene'; Leg. Good Women, 497; but this passage is of an earlier date.
[132] Rot. Pat., 13 Ric. II., p. 1. m. 30. (G.)
[133] The Athenæum, Jan. 28, 1888; p. 116; Trial-Forewords, p. 133.
[134] Originalia, 13 Ric. II., m. 30; Trial-Forewords, p. 133.
[135] The Athenæum, Feb. 7, 1874; p. 196.

made, and we find that the next forester, appointed in 4 Hen. V. (1416-17), was no other than Thomas Chaucer, who may have been his son[136]. It is perhaps worthy of remark that some of the land in North Petherton, as shewn by Collinson, descended to Emma, third daughter of William de Placetis, which William had the same office of 'forester of North Petherton' till his death in 1274; and this Emma married John Heyron, who died in 1326-7, seised of lands at Enfield, Middlesex, and at Newton, Exton, and North Petherton, in the county of Somerset (Calend. Inquis. post Mortem, 1806, vol. i. p. 333; col. 1). If this John Heyron was related to the Maria Heyron who was Chaucer's grandmother, there was perhaps a special reason for appointing Chaucer to this particular office.

On July 12, 1390, he was ordered to procure workmen and materials for the repair of St. George's Chapel, Windsor, then in a ruinous condition; this furnishes a very interesting association[137].

On Sept. 6, 1390, a curious misfortune befell the poet. He was robbed twice on the same day, by the same gang of robbers; once of 10*l.* of the king's money, at Westminster, and again of 9*l.* 3*s.* 2*d.*, of his horse, and of other property, near the 'foul oak' (*foule ok*) at Hatcham, Surrey (now a part of London, approached by the Old Kent Road, and not far from Deptford and Greenwich). One of the gang confessed the robberies; and Chaucer was forgiven the repayment of the money[138].

§ 31. **1391.** In 1391, on Jan. 22, Chaucer appointed John Elmhurst as his deputy, for superintending repairs at the palace of Westminster and the tower of London; this appointment was confirmed by the king[139]. It was in this year that he wrote his Treatise on the Astrolabe, for the use of his son Lowis. By this time, the Canterbury Tales had ceased to make much progress. For some unknown reason, Chaucer lost his appointment in the

---

[136] Collinson, Hist. of Somersetshire, iii. 54-74; The Athenæum, Nov. 20, 1886, p. 672; Life-Records (Chaucer Soc.), p. 117.

[137] Rot. Pat., 14 Ric. II., m. 33; Issue Roll, Easter, 13 Ric. II. (G.); Trial-Forewords, p. 133.

[138] The Athenæum, Feb. 7 and 14, 1874, pp. 196, 227; Life-Records (Ch. Soc.), p. 5.

[139] Rot. Pat., 14 Ric. II., p. 2. m. 24: 'quem dilectus serviens noster Galfridus Chaucer clericus operationum nostrarum sub se deputavit'; &c. 'Clericus' is here literal; 'clerk' of the works.

summer; for on June 17, a writ was issued, commanding him to give up to John Gedney [140] all his rolls, &c. connected with his office [141]; and on Sept. 16, we find, accordingly, that the office was held by John Gedney [142]; nevertheless, payments to Chaucer as 'late Clerk of the Works' occur on Dec. 16, 1391, Mar. 4 and July 13, 1392, and even as late as in 1393 [143].

§ 32. **1392-3.** Chaucer was now once more without public employment. No doubt the Canterbury Tales received some attention, and perhaps we may assign to this period various alterations in the original plan of the poem. The author must by this time have seen the necessity of limiting each of his characters to the telling of *one* Tale only. The Envoy to Scogan and the Complaint of Venus were probably written in 1393. According to a note written opposite l. 45 of the former poem, Chaucer was then residing at Greenwich, a most convenient position for frequent observation of pilgrims on the road to Canterbury. See §§ 26 and 30.

§ 33. **1394.** Chaucer was once more a poor man, although, as a widower, his expenses may have been less. Probably he endeavoured to draw attention to his reduced circumstances, or Henry Scogan may have done so for him, in accordance with the poet's suggestion in l. 48 of the Envoy just mentioned. In 1394, on Feb. 28, he obtained from the king a grant of 20*l.* per annum for life, payable half-yearly at Easter and Michaelmas, being 6*l.* 13*s.* 8*d.* less than the pensions which he had disposed of in 1388 [144]; but the first payment was not made till Dec. 20, when he received 10*l.* for the half-year from Easter to Michaelmas, and the proportional sum of 1*l.* 16*s.* 7*d.* for the month of March [145].

§ 34. **1395.** The difficulties which Chaucer experienced at this time, as to money matters, are clearly illustrated during the year 1395. In this year he applied for a loan from the exchequer, in advance of his pension, no less than four times. In this way he borrowed 10*l.* on April 1; 10*l.* on June 25; 1*l.* 6*s.* 8*d.* on

---

[140] Afterwards Sheriff of London, viz. in 1417-8 (Fabyan).
[141] Archæologia, vol. xxxiv. 45.
[142] Rot. Pat., 15 Ric. II., p. 1. m. 27; see Godwin, Life of Chaucer, iv. 67.
[143] Issue Rolls, Mich. and Easter, 15 Ric. II.; and Easter, 16 Ric. II.
[144] Rot. Pat., 17 Ric. II., pt. 2. m. 35; printed in full in Godwin's Life of Chaucer, and again in Furnivall's Trial-Forewords to the Minor Poems, p. 26.
[145] Issue Roll, Mich., 18 Ric. II.; see Nicolas, Note U.

Sept. 9; and 8*l*. 6*s*. 8*d*. on Nov. 27. He repaid the first of these loans on May 28; and the second was covered by his allowance at Michaelmas. He must also have repaid the small third loan, as the account was squared by his receipt of the balance of 1*l*. 13*s*. 4*d*. (instead of 10*l*.) on March 1, 1396 [146]. All the sums were paid into his own hands, so that he was not far from home in 1395. The fact that he borrowed so small a sum as 1*l*. 6*s*. 8*d*. is significant and saddening.

In 19 Ric. II. (June, 1395–June, 1396), Chaucer was one of the attorneys of Gregory Ballard, to receive seizin of the manor of Spitalcombe, and of other lands in Kent [147].

§ 35. **1396.** In 1396, as noted above, he received the balance of his first half-year's pension on March 1. The second half-year's pension was not paid till Dec. 25 [148]. The Balades of Truth, Gentilesse, and Lak of Stedfastnesse possibly belong to this period, but some critics would place the last of these somewhat earlier.

§ 36. **1397.** In 1397, the payment of the pension was again behindhand; there seems to have been some difficulty in obtaining it, due, probably, to the lavish extravagance of the king. Instead of receiving his half-yearly pension at Easter, Chaucer received it much later, and in two instalments; viz. 5*l*. on July 2, and 5*l*. on Aug. 9. But after this, things mended; for his Michaelmas pension was paid in full, viz. 10*l*., on Oct. 26 [149]. It was received for him by John Walden, and it is probable that at this time he was in infirm health.

§ 37. **1398.** We may certainly infer that, at this time, Chaucer was once more in great distress for money, and considerably in debt. It is also probable that he was becoming infirm; for indeed, his death was now approaching. In the Easter term of 1398 (Apr. 24–May 20), one Isabella Buckholt sued him for the sum of 14*l*. 1*s*. 11*d*. He did not, however, put in an appearance; for the sheriff's return, in the Michaelmas term (Oct. 9–Nov. 28), was—'non est inventus'; and a similar return was again made in the Trinity term of 1399 (June 4–25) [150].

---

[146] Issue Rolls, Mich. and Easter, 18 Ric. II., and Mich., 19 Ric. II.; see Nicolas, Notes U, V, and W.
[147] Rot. Claus., 19 Ric. II. m. 8 d.
[148] Issue Roll, Mich., 21 Ric. II. See Nicolas, Note X.
[149] Issue Roll, Mich., 21 Ric. II. See Nicolas, Note X
[150] The Athenæum, Sept. 13, 1879; p. 338.

We are tempted to suspect that the sheriff was not particularly diligent in his search after the debtor. That Chaucer was well aware of the awkwardness of his position, is shewn by the fact that on May 4, 1398, just at the very time when the suit was brought, he applied for, and obtained, letters of protection from the king against his enemies, forbidding any one to sue or arrest him on any plea, except it were connected with land, for the term of two years[151]. This furnishes an additional reason why the sheriff did not 'find' him. When the two years terminated, in May, 1400, he had not half a year to live.

On June 3, 1398, Chaucer was again unable to receive his pension himself, but it was conveyed to him by William Waxcombe[152]. At the close of the next month, he was reduced to such pitiable straits that we find him applying *personally* to the exchequer, for such a trifling advance as 6s. 8d., on July 24; and for the same sum only a week later, on July 31[152].

On Aug. 23, he personally received a further advance of 5l. 6s. 8d.[152]

In his distress, he determined to send in a petition to the king. A copy of this, in French, is still preserved. On Oct. 13, 1398, he prayed to be allowed a hogshead of wine (tonel de vin), to be given him by the king's butler[153]; he even asked this favour 'for God's sake and as a work of charity' (pur Dieu et en œure de charitee). It is satisfactory to find that his request met with a prompt response; for only two days afterwards, on Oct. 15, the king made him a grant of a tun of wine annually for life, from the king's butler or his deputy; Sir H. Nicolas computes the value of this grant at about 5l. a year. Moreover, the grant was made to date as from Dec. 1, 1397; so that he necessarily received from it some immediate benefit[154]. He also received from the exchequer, with his own hands, the sum of 10l. on Oct. 28[155].

§ 38. **1399.** In 1399, the great change in political affairs practically brought his distress to an end; and it is pleasant to think that, as far as money matters were concerned, he ended his

---

[151] Rot. Pat., 21 Ric. II., p. 3. m. 26. (G.)
[152] Issue Roll, Easter, 21 Ric. II. See Nicolas, Note Y.
[153] The Athenæum, Jan. 28, 1888; p. 116.
[154] Rot. Pat., 22 Ric. I., p. 1. m. 8. (G.)
[155] Issue Roll, Mich., 22 Ric. II.; see Nicolas, Note Z.

days in comparative ease. Henry of Lancaster was declared king on Sept. 30; and Chaucer lost no time in laying his case before him. This he did by sending in a copy of his 'Compleint to his Empty Purse,' a poem which seems to have been originally written on some other occasion. He added to it, however, an Envoy of five lines, which, like a postscript to some letters, contained the pith of the matter:—

> 'O conquerour of Brutes Albioun,
> Which that by lyne and free eleccioun
> Ben verray king, this song to you I sende;
> And ye, that mowen al our harm amende,
> Have mind upon my supplicacioun!'

The king was prompt to reply; it must have given him real satisfaction to be able to assist the old poet, with whom he must have been on familiar terms. On Oct. 3, only the fourth day after the king's accession, the answer came. He was to receive 40 marks yearly (26*l*. 13*s*. 4*d*.), in addition to the annuity of 20*l*. which king Richard had granted him; so that his income was more than doubled. Even then, he met with a slight misfortune, in losing his letters patent; but, having made oath in Chancery, that the letters patent of Feb. 28, 1394 (referring to king Richard's grant of 20*l*.), and the new letters patent of Oct. 3, 1399, had been accidentally lost, he procured, on Oct. 13, exemplifications of these records [156]. These grants were finally confirmed by the king on Oct. 21 [157].

On Christmas eve, 1399, he covenanted for a lease of 53 years (a long term for one at his age to contemplate) of a house situate in the garden of the Chapel of St. Mary, Westminster, near Westminster Abbey, at the annual rent of 2*l*. 13*s*. 4*d*. This lease, from the Custos Capellae Beatae Mariae to Geoffrey Chaucer, dated Dec. 24, 1399, is in the Muniment Room of Westminster Abbey. The house stood on or near the spot now occupied by Henry the Seventh's Chapel [158]. We find, however, that he had only a life-interest in the lease, as the premises were to revert to the Custos Capellae if the tenant died within the term.

---

[156] Rot. Pat., 1 Hen. IV., p. 1. m. 18; and p. 5. m. 12. (G.)
[157] See Issue Roll, Easter, 1 Hen. IV.; in Nicolas, Note BB.
[158] Godwin, Life of Chaucer, iv. 365, where the document is printed; Hist. MSS. Commission, i. 95.

§ 39. **1400.** In 1400, payments to him are recorded on Feb. 21, of the pension of 20*l*. granted by king Richard[159], in respect of the half-year ending at Michaelmas, 1399; and on June 5, the sum of 5*l*., being part of a sum of 8*l*. 13*s*. 5*d*. due for a portion of the next half-year, calculated as commencing on Oct. 21, 1399, and terminating on the last day of March, 1400, was sent him by the hands of Henry Somere[160].

We should notice that this Henry Somere was, at the time, the Clerk of the Receipt of the Exchequer; he was afterwards Under Treasurer, at which time Hoccleve addressed to him a Balade, printed in Furnivall's edition of Hoccleve's Works, at p. 59, followed by a Roundel containing a pun upon his name; as well as a second Balade, addressed to him after he had been made a Baron, and promoted to be Chancellor (see the same, p. 64). Perhaps he was related to John Somere, the Frere, mentioned in the Treatise on the Astrolabe (Prol. 62).

Chaucer died on Oct. 25, 1400, and was buried in Westminster Abbey. The date of his death is only known from an inscription on the tomb of gray marble erected near his grave, in 1556, by Nicholas Brigham, a man of letters, and an admirer of the poet's writings; but it is probably correct, and may have rested on tradition[161]. We have no note of him after June 5, and no record of a payment of the pension in October. According to Stowe, Chaucer's grave is in the cloister, where also lies the body of 'Henrie Scogan, a learned poet,' i. e. the Scogan who was Chaucer's friend.

§ 40. CHAUCER'S ARMS AND TOMB. 'In front of the tomb,' says Sir. H. Nicolas, 'are three panelled divisions of starred quarterfoils (*sic*), containing shields with the Arms of Chaucer, viz. Per pale argent and gules, a bend counterchanged; and the same Arms also occur in an oblong compartment at the back of the recess, where the following inscription was placed, but which is now almost obliterated, from the partial decomposition and crumbling state of the marble. A small whole-length portrait of Chaucer was delineated *in plano* on the north side of the inscription, but

---

[159] Issue Roll, Mich., 1 Hen IV.; see Nicolas, Note AA.
[160] Issue Roll, Easter, 1 Hen. IV.; see Nicolas, Note BB.
[161] Stowe's Survey of London, ed. Thoms, p. 171; Nicolas, Life of Chaucer.

CAXTON'S TRIBUTE TO CHAUCER.

not a vestige of it is left; and the whole of the recess and canopy has recently been coloured black.

M.S.
Qui fuit Anglorum Vates ter maximus olim,
Galfridus Chaucer conditur hoc tumulo :
Annum si quaeras domini, si tempora vitae,
Ecce notae subsunt, quae tibi cuncta notant.
25 Octobris 1400.
Ærumnarum requies mors.
N. Brigham hos fecit musarum nomine sumptus
1556.

On the ledge of the tomb the following verses were engraved :—

'Si rogites quis eram, forsan te fama docebit :
Quod si fama negat, mundi quia gloria transit,
Haec monumenta lege.'

We learn from an interesting note at the end of Caxton's edition of Boethius, that the good printer was not satisfied with printing some of Chaucer's works, but further endeavoured to perpetuate the poet's memory by raising a pillar near his tomb, to support a tablet containing an epitaph consisting of 34 Latin verses. This epitaph was composed by Stephanus Surigonus of Milan, licentiate in decrees, and is reprinted in Stowe's edition of Chaucer's Works (1561), at fol. 355, back. The last four lines refer to Caxton's pious care :—

'Post obitum Caxton voluit te viuere cura
Willelmi, Chaucer, clare poeta, tui.
Nam tua non solum compressit opuscula formis,
Has quoque sed laudes iussit hic esse tuas.'

A description, by Dean Stanley, of the Chaucer window in Westminster Abbey, completed in 1868, is given in Furnivall's Temporary Preface (Ch. Soc.), p. 133. Some of the subjects in the window are taken from the poem entitled 'The Flower and the Leaf,' which he did not write.

It will be observed that Sir H. Nicolas speaks, just above, of 'the arms of Chaucer,' which he describes. But it should be remembered that this is, practically, an assumption, which at once launches us into an uncertain and debateable position. These arms certainly belonged to *Thomas* Chaucer, for they occur on a seal of his of which a drawing is given in MS. Julius C 7, fol. 153; an accurate copy of which is given by Sir H. Nicolas. It is therefore quite possible that the same arms were assigned to the poet in 1556, only because it was then assumed that Thomas was Geoffrey's son; the fact being that the relationship of Thomas to Geoffrey is open to doubt, and the case requires to be stated with great care.

§ 41. THOMAS CHAUCER. Few things are more remarkable than the utter absence of unequivocal early evidence as to the above-mentioned point. That Geoffrey Chaucer was a famous man, even in his own day, cannot be doubted; and it is equally certain that Thomas Chaucer was a man of great wealth and of some consequence. Sir H. Nicolas has collected the principal facts relating to him, the most important being the following. On Oct. 26, 1399, Henry IV. granted him the offices of Constable of Wallingford Castle and Steward of the Honours of Wallingford and St. Valery and of the Chiltern Hundreds for life, receiving therefrom 40*l.* a year, with 10*l.* additional for his deputy [162]. On Nov. 5, 1402, he was appointed Chief Butler for life to King Henry IV.[163]; and there is a note that he had previously been Chief Butler to Richard II.[164], but the date of that appointment has not been ascertained. He was also Chief Butler to Henry V. until March, 1418, when he was superseded [165]; but was again appointed Chief Butler to Henry VI. after his accession. He represented Oxfordshire in Parliament in 1402, 1408, 1409, 1412, 1414, 1423, 1427, and 1429; and was Speaker of the House of Commons in 1414 [166], and in other years. 'He was employed on many occasions of trust and importance during the reigns of Henry IV., Henry V., and Henry VI.;' to which Sir H. Nicolas adds, that he 'never attained a higher rank than that of esquire.'

His wealth, at his death in 1434, was unusually great, as shewn by the long list of his landed possessions in the Inquisitiones post Mortem. This wealth he doubtless acquired by his marriage

---

[162] Rot. Pat., 1 Hen. IV., p. 1. m. 10.
[163] Rot. Pat., 4 Hen. IV., m. 19; Rot. Parl. iv. 178 b.
[164] Rot. Pat., 12 Hen. IV., m. 34.
[165] Rot. Norman., 5 Hen. V., m. 7; ed. 1835, p. 284.
[166] Rot. Parl. vol. iv. p. 35.

with an heiress, viz. Matilda, second daughter and co-heiress of Sir John Burghersh, who died Sept. 21, 1391, when Matilda was 12 years old. Unfortunately, the date of this marriage is uncertain, though Sir H. Nicolas shews that it was probably earlier than 1403. The exact date would be very useful; for if it took place before 1399, it becomes difficult to understand why the poet was left so poor, whilst his son had vast possessions.

It should be noticed that there is but little to connect even Thomas Chaucer (still less Geoffrey) with Woodstock, until 1411; when the Queen (Joan of Navarre) granted Thomas the farm of the manors of Woodstock, Hanburgh, Wotton, and Stonfield, which, by the king's assignment, he enjoyed for life[167]. That the poet visited Woodstock in 1357, when in the service of Prince Lionel, is almost certain; but beyond this, we have no sure information on the matter. It is true that 'Wodestok' is mentioned in the last line of the Cuckow and the Nightingale, but this supposed connecting link is at once broken, when we find that the said poem was certainly not of his writing[168]. The suggested reference to Woodstock in the Parliament of Foules, l. 122, is discussed below, at p. 510.

The only child of Thomas and Matilda Chaucer was Alice, whose third husband was no less a person than William de la Pole, then Earl and afterwards Duke of Suffolk, who was beheaded in 1450. Their eldest son was John de la Pole, Duke of Suffolk, who married Elizabeth, sister of King Edward IV. Their eldest son bore the same name, and was not only created Earl of Lincoln, but was actually declared heir-apparent to the throne by Richard III; so that there was, at one time, a probability that Thomas Chaucer's great-grandson would succeed to the throne. But the battle of Bosworth, in 1485, set this arrangement aside; and the Earl of Lincoln was himself killed two years later, in the battle of Stoke.

§ 42. THE RELATIONSHIP OF THOMAS TO GEOFFREY CHAUCER. Considering the great eminence of these two men, the almost

---

[167] Rot. Pat., 12 Hen. IV., m. 7.

[168] It actually begins by quoting two lines from the Knightes Tale, A 1785-6; so it is later than 1386. There is at least one non-Chaucerian rime, viz. at l. 61, where *gren-e* (dissyllabic in Chaucer) rimes with the pp. *been*. See p. 30 below.

LIFE OF GEOFFREY CHAUCER.

total silence of early evidence, establishing a connexion between them, is in a high degree remarkable.

The earliest connecting link is the fact that a deed by Thomas Chaucer still exists, written (in English) at Ewelme, and dated May 20, 1409, to which a seal is appended. This seal exhibits the arms which were certainly borne by Thomas Chaucer (viz. party per pale, argent and gules, a bend counterchanged); but the legend, though somewhat indistinct, can only be read as: 'S' Ghofrai Chaucier[169]'; where S' signifies 'Sigillum.'

The spelling 'Ghofrai' is hardly satisfactory; but if Geoffrey be really meant, we gain a piece of evidence of high importance. It proves that Geoffrey bore the same arms as Thomas, and *not* the same arms as his father John; whose seal displays a shield ermine, on a chief, three birds' heads issuant (The Academy, Oct. 13, 1877, p. 364). Moreover, the use of Geoffrey's seal by Thomas goes far to establish that the latter was the son of the former.

The next link is that Geoffrey Chaucer was succeeded by Thomas Chaucer in the office of forester of North Petherton in Somersetshire; but even here there is a gap in the succession, as Thomas was not appointed till 1416-7, the fourth year of Henry V.[170]

It is not till the reign of Henry VI. that we at last obtain an unequivocal statement. Thomas Gascoigne, who died in 1458, wrote a Theological Dictionary, which still exists, in MS., in the Library of Lincoln College, Oxford. He tells us that Chaucer, in his last hours, frequently lamented the wickedness of his writings, though it is transparent that he here merely repeats, in a varied form, the general tenour of the well-known final paragraph of the Persones Tale. But he adds this important sentence: 'Fuit idem Chawserus pater Thomae Chawserus, armigeri, qui Thomas sepelitur in Nuhelm iuxta Oxoniam[171].' The statement is the more important because Gascoigne ought to have known the

---

[169] The seal has lately been re-examined by experts, after application to the Record Office by Dr. Furnivall. See Archæologia, xxxiv. 42, where an engraving of the seal is (inexactly) given, and the deed is printed at length.

[170] Collinson, Hist. of Somersetshire, iii. 54-74; Life-Records, p. 117.

[171] MS. in Lincoln College, p. 377, quoted in Chalmers' English Poets, vol. i. p. x; Letter by Prof. Hales to the Athenæum, Mar. 31, 1888; Hales, Folia Litteraria, p. 109; Lounsbury, Studies, i. 108.

exact truth. He was Chancellor of Oxford, and Thomas Chaucer held the manor of Ewelme, at no great distance, at the same date. As he mentions Thomas's sepulture, he wrote later than 1434, yet before 1458. Even in the case of this decisive statement, it were to be wished that he had shewn greater accuracy in the context; surely he gives a quite unfair turn to the poet's own words.

On the whole, I can only admit at present, that there is a high probability that Thomas was really Geoffrey's son. Perhaps we shall some day know the certainty of the matter.

§ 43. THOMAS'S MOTHER. The chief reason why it is so desirable to know the exact truth as to the relationship of Thomas to Geoffrey, is that a good deal depends upon it. If such was the case, it follows that Philippa Chaucer was Thomas's mother; in which case, we may feel tolerably confident that her maiden name was Roet or Rouet. This has been inferred from the fact that the arms (apparently) of Roet 'occur repeatedly on Thomas Chaucer's tomb, as his paternal coat, instead of the arms usually attributed to him and to the poet.' These arms bore 'three wheels, evidently in allusion to the name [172].' Having thus assigned to Philippa Chaucer the name of Roet, the next step (usually accepted, yet not absolutely proved) is to assume that she was the sister of the Katherine de Roet of Hainault [173], who married Sir Hugh Swynford, and afterwards became the mistress, and, in 1396, the third wife of John of Gaunt. Her father is supposed to have been Sir Payne Roet, of Hainault, upon the evidence of his epitaph, which (in Weever's Funeral Monuments, p. 413) is thus given:—' Hic jacet Paganus Roet, Miles, Guyenne Rex Armorum, Pater Catherine Ducisse Lancastriae [174].' It is obvious that, if all the inferences are correct, they clearly establish an important and close connexion between the poet and John of Gaunt. Further arguments, whether in favour of or against this connexion, need hardly be repeated here. They may be found

---

[172] So says Nicolas; 'evidently' means that such is the most likely explanation. The O. F. *roe* (Lat. *rota*) means 'a wheel'; and *roet* is its diminutive.

[173] She is described as 'the most renowned Lady Katherine de Roelt [error for Roet or Roett] deceased, late Duchess of Lancaster,' and as having had 'divers inheritances in the county of Hainault,' in Rot. Pat., 13 Hen. IV., p. 1. m. 35; see Rymer's Fœdera, viii. 704, and the Account of the Swynford family in the Excerpta Historica, p. 158. Nicolas, Note CC.

[174] This seems to be the sole trace of Sir Payne Roet's existence.

LIFE OF GEOFFREY CHAUCER.

in Nicolas's Life of Chaucer, and in Lounsbury's Studies in Chaucer, vol. i.

Thynne has the following remark in his Animadversions, &c. (ed. Furnivall, p. 22): 'Althoughe I fynde a recorde of the *pellis exitus*, in the tyme of Edwarde the thirde, of a yerely stypende to Elizabethe Chawcer, *Domicelle regine Philippe*, whiche *Domicella* dothe signyfye one of her weytinge gentlewomen: yet I cannott... thinke this was his wyfe, but rather his sister or kinneswoman, who, after the deathe of her mystresse Quene Philippe, did forsake the worlde and became a nonne at Seinte Heleins in London.' And we find, accordingly (as Nicolas shews), that 'on July 27, 1377, the King exercised his right to nominate a Nun in the Priory of St. Helen's, London, after the coronation, in favour of Elizabeth Chausier.' Another Elizabeth Chaucy (who may have been the poet's daughter) is also noticed by Nicolas, for whose noviciate, in the Abbey of Berking in Essex, John of Gaunt paid 51*l*. 8*s*. 2*d*., on May 12, 1381. But these are mere matters for conjecture.

§ 44. The preceding sections include all the most material facts that have been ascertained with respect to Geoffrey Chaucer, and it is fortunate that, owing to his connexion with public business, they are so numerous and so authentic. At the same time, it will doubtless be considered that such dry details, however useful, tell us very little about the man himself; though they clearly shew the versatility of his talents, and exhibit him as a page, a soldier, a valet and esquire of the royal household, an envoy, a comptroller of customs, a clerk of works, and a member of Parliament. In the truest sense, his own works best exhibit his thoughts and character; though we must not always accept all his expressions as if they were all his own. We have to deal with a writer in whom the dramatic faculty was highly developed, and I prefer to leave the reader to draw his own inferences, even from those passages which are most relied upon to support the theory that his domestic life may have been unhappy, and others of the like kind. We can hardly doubt, for example, that he refers to his wife as 'oon that I coude nevene,' i. e. one that I could name, in the Hous of Fame, 562; and he plainly says that the eagle spoke something to him in a kindly tone, such as he never heard from his wife. But when we notice that the something said was the word 'awake,' in order that he should 'the bet abrayde,' i. e. the sooner recover from his dazed state, it is possible that a sentence which at first seems decidedly spiteful is no more than a mild and gentle jest.

§ 45. PERSONAL ALLUSIONS IN CHAUCER'S WORKS. Instead of drawing my own inferences, which may easily be wrong, from various passages in Chaucer's Works, I prefer the humbler task of giving the more important references, from which the reader may perform the task for himself, to his greater satisfaction. I will only say that when a poet complains of hopeless love, or expresses his despair, or tells us (on the other hand) that he has no idea as to what love means, we are surely free to believe, in each case, just as little or as much as we please. It is a very sandy foundation on which to build up a serious autobiographical structure.

The only remark which I feel justified in making is, that I believe his wife's death to have been a serious loss to him in one respect at least. Most of his early works are reasonably free from coarseness; whereas such Tales as those of the Miller, the Reeve, the Shipman, the Merchant, and the Prologue to the Wife's Tale, can hardly be defended. All these may confidently be dated after the year 1387.

I have also to add one caution. We must not draw inferences as to Chaucer's life from poems or works with which he had nothing to do. Even Sir H. Nicolas, with all his carefulness, has not avoided this. He quotes the 'Cuckoo and Nightingale' as mentioning Woodstock; and he only distrusts the 'Testament of Love' because it is 'an allegorical composition[175].' As to the numerous fables that have been imported into the early Lives of Chaucer, see the excellent chapter in Lounsbury's Studies in Chaucer, entitled 'The Chaucer Legend.'

§ 46. REFERENCES. I here use the following abbreviations.

---

[175] The Testament of Love was greatly relied upon by Godwin and others. They thence inferred that Chaucer was mixed up with the dispute as to the appointment of John of Northampton to the mayoralty of London in 1382; that he was imprisoned; that he fled to Zealand; that he was in exile for two years; that, on his return, he was sent to the Tower for three years, and not released till 1389; with more rubbish of the same sort. However, it so happens that Chaucer did not write this piece (see p. 35, note 4). More than this, I have lately discovered that the initial letters of the chapters form an acrostic, which reads thus: MARGARET OF VIRTW, HAVE MERCI ON TSKNVI. The last word may be an anagram for KITSVN, i. e. Kitson; it is certainly not an anagram for Chaucer. See my letter in The Academy, Mar. 11, 1893, p. 222.

LIFE OF GEOFFREY CHAUCER.

Ast. (Treatise on the Astrolabe); B. D. (Book of the Duchesse); C. T. (Canterbury Tales); H. F. (Hous of Fame); L. G. W. (Legend of Good Women); T. (Troilus and Criseyde).

1. PERSONAL ALLUSIONS. The poet's name is Geffrey, H. F. 729; and his surname, Chaucer, C. T., B 47. He describes himself, C. T., B 1886; Envoy to Scogan, 31. His poverty, H. F. 1349; Envoy to Scogan, 45; Compl. to his Purse. Refers to the sale of wine (his father being a vintner), C. T., C 564. Is despondent in love, Compl. unto Pity; B. D. 1-43; T. i. 15-18. His Complaints, viz. unto Pity; to his Lady; and an Amorous Complaint. Has long served Cupid and Venus; H.F. 616. Is no longer a lover, P. F. 158-166; H. F. 639; T. ii. 19-21; L. G. W. 490. Is love's clerk, T. iii. 41. Is love's foe, L. G. W. 323. His misery, H. F. 2012-8. His religious feeling, A.B.C., Second Nun's Tale, Prioress's Tale, &c. Refers to his work when Comptroller of the Customs, H. F. 652. Is unambitious of fame, H. F. 1870-900; and has but little in his head, ib. 621. Is sometimes a mere compiler, Ast. prol. 43. Addresses his little son Lowis, Ast. prol. 1-45[176]. Expresses his gratitude to the queen, L. G. W. 84-96, 445-461, 496. His old age, L. G. W., A 262, A 315; Envoy to Scogan, 31-42; Compl. of Venus, 76[177]. He will not marry a second time, Envoy to Bukton, 8. He exhibits his knowledge of the Northern dialect in the Reeve's Tale. The whole of the Prologue to the Legend of Good Women deserves particular attention.

Chaucer mentions several friends, viz. Gower the poet, T. v. 1856; Strode, T. v. 1857 (cf. the colophon to Ast. pt. ii. § 40); and a lady named Rosemounde, in the Balade addressed to her. He also addresses Envoys to Henry Scogan and to Bukton. The Envoy to the Compleint to his Purse is addressed to king Henry IV.

He is fond of books and of reading, P. F. 15; H. F. 657; L. G. W. 17-35; and even reads in bed, B. D. 50, 274, 1326.

---

[176] Sir H. Nicolas says that some have inferred that Chaucer was living near Oxford in 1391, and refers to Ast. prol. 7, which mentions 'oure orizonte.' We are not justified in drawing such an inference.

[177] Prof. Lounsbury includes H. F. 995, where the poet declines to be taught astronomy (under the most uncomfortable circumstances) because he is 'too old.' Any man of thirty (or less) might have said the same; the passage tells us nothing at all.

PERSONAL ALLUSIONS.

For a full account of the books which he quotes, see vol. vi. I may just notice here the lists in C. T., B 2088; L. G. W., A 272-307; and his references to his own works in L. G. W. 329, 332, 417-28; C. T., B 57-76; C. T., I 1086[178]. His love of nature appears in several excellent descriptions; we may particularly notice his lines upon the sunrise, C. T., A 1491, F 385; on the golden-tressed Phoebus, T. v. 8; on the daisy, L. G. W. 41; his description of the birds, P. F. 330; of a blooming garden, P. F. 182; of the golden age, The Former Age; of fine weather for hunting, B. D. 336, and of the chase itself, B. D. 360, L. G. W. 1188. He frequently mentions the fair month of May, L. G. W. 36, 45, 108, 176, T. ii. 50, C. T. A 1500, 1510; and St. Valentine's day, Compl. of Mars, 13; P. F. 309, 322, 386, 683; Amorous Compleint, 85.

He was our first great metrist, and has frequent references to his poetical art. He never slept on Parnassus, C. T., F 721; and the Host (in the C. T.) even accused him of writing 'dogerel,' B 2115. He cannot write alliterative verse, C. T., I 43. He admits that his rime is 'light and lewed,' and that some lines fail in a syllable, H. F., 1096-8. Yet he hopes that none will 'mismetre' him, T. v. 1796. He writes books, songs, and ditties in rime or 'cadence,' H. F. 622; also hymns, balades, roundels, and virelays, L. G. W. 422; and complaints, such as the Complaint to Pity, to his Lady, to his Purse, the Complaints of Mars, Anelida, and Venus, and the Complaint D'amours (or Amorous Complaint). Specimens of his graphic and dramatic power, of his skill in story and metre, of his tenderness and his humour, need not be here specified. He is fond of astronomy, as shewn by his Treatise on the Astrolabe; and, though he has but little faith in astrology (Ast. ii. 4. 37), he frequently refers to it as well as to astronomy; see B. D. 1206; Compl. Mars, 29, 54, 69, 79, 86, 113, 120, 129, 139, 145; P. F., 56, 59, 67, 117; Envoy to Scogan, 3, 9; H. F. 932, 936, 965, 993-1017; T. ii. 50, iii. 2, 618, 625, 716, iv. 1592, v. 1809; L. G. W. 113, 2223, 2585-99; C. T., A 7, 1087, 1328, 1463, 1537, 1566, 1850, 2021, 2035, 2059, 2217, 2271, 2367, 2454-69, 3192, 3209, 3516; B 1-14, 191, 295-

---

[178] Sir H. Nicolas says that, in L. G. W. 189, he alludes to his poem called The Flower and the Leaf. But that poem is not his, though its title was doubtless suggested by the expressions which Chaucer there uses

308, 312, 4045-8, 4378-89; D 613, 704; E 1795, 1969, 2132, 2222; F 47-51, 263-5, 386, 906, 1032-5, 1045-59, 1130, 1245-9, 1261-6, 1273-96; I 2-12. Even his alchemy has some reference to astrology; C. T., G 826-9; cf. H. F. 1430-1512.

He refers to optics, C. T., F 228-235; to Boethius on music, C. T., B 4484, H. F. 788-818; and to magical arts, H. F. 1259-81, C. T., F 115, 132, 146, 156, 219, 250, 1142-51, 1157-62, 1189-1208.

2. HISTORICAL ALLUSIONS. The references to contemporary history are but few. The death of the Lady Blaunche is commemorated in the Book of the Duchesse. He refers to good queen Anne, L. G. W. 255, 275, 496; to the archbishop of Canterbury, C. T., B 4635; to 'this pestilence,' C 679; to Tyler's rebellion, A 2459; and Jack Straw, B 4584. Perhaps the Complaints of Mars and Venus refer to real personages; see the Notes to those poems. He mentions Dante, H. F. 450, L. G. W. 360, C. T. B 3651, D 1126; Petrarch, C. T., E 31, 1147; Pedro the Cruel, king of Spain, C. T., B 3565, Bertrand du Gueschlin, 3573, and Sir Oliver Mauny, 3576; Peter, king of Cyprus, 3581; Bernabo Visconti, duke of Milan, 3589, and the 'tyrants' of Lombardy, L. G. W. 374; Ugolino of Pisa and the archbishop Ruggieri, C. T., B 3597, 3606. There are several allusions to recent events in the Prologue, A 51-66, 86, 276, 399; and perhaps in C. T., E 995-1001.

His literary allusions are too numerous to be here recited. The reader can consult the Index in vol. vi.

§ 47. ALLUSIONS TO CHAUCER. One of the earliest allusions to Chaucer as a poet occurs in the works of Eustache Deschamps, a contemporary poet of France. It is remarkable that he chiefly praises him as being 'a great translator.' Perhaps this was before his longest poems were written; there is express reference to his translation of Le Roman de la Rose, and, possibly, to Boethius. The poem tells us that Deschamps had sent Chaucer a copy of some of his poems by a friend named Clifford, and he hopes to receive something of Chaucer's in return. The poem is here quoted entire, from the edition of Deschamps by le Marquis de Queux de Saint-Hilaire, published for the Société des Anciens Textes Français, t. ii. p. 138:—

'O Socrates plains de philosophie,
 Seneque en meurs et Anglux en pratique,

EUSTACHE DESCHAMPS.

Ovides grans en ta poeterie,
Bries en parler, saiges en rethorique,
Aigles treshaulz, qui par ta theorique
Enlumines le regne d'Eneas,
L'Isle aux Geans, ceuls de Bruth, et qui as
Semé les fleurs et planté le rosier,
Aux ignorans de la langue pandras,
Grant translateur, noble Geffroy Chaucier.

Tu es d'amours mondains Dieux en Albie:
Et de la Rose, en la terre Angelique,
Qui d'Angela saxonne, est puis flourie
Angleterre, d'elle ce nom s'applique
Le derrenier en l'ethimologique;
En bon anglès le livre translatas;
Et un vergier ou du plant demandas
De ceuls qui font pour eulx autorisier,
A ja longtemps que tu edifias,
Grant translateur, noble Geffroy Chaucier.

A toy pour ce de la fontaine Helye
Requier avoir un buvraige autentique,
Dont la doys est du tout en ta baillie,
Pour rafrener d'elle ma soif ethique,
Qui en Gaule seray paralitique
Jusques a ce que tu m'abuveras.
Eustaces sui, qui de mon plant aras:
Mais pran en gré les euvres d'escolier
Que par Clifford de moy avoir pourras,
Grant translateur, noble Geffroy Chaucier.

LENVOY.

Poete hault, loenge destruye,
En ton jardin ne seroye qu'ortie:
Consideré ce que j'ay dit premier
Ton noble plant, ta douce mélodie,
Mais pour sçavoir, de rescripre te prie,
Grant translateur, noble Geffroy Chaucier.'

Gower alludes to Chaucer in the first edition of the Confessio Amantis; see the passage discussed in vol. iii. p. 414.

Henry Scogan wrote 'a moral balade' in twenty-one 8-line stanzas, in which he not only refers to Chaucer's poetical skill, but quotes the whole of his Balade on Gentilesse; see vol. i. p. 83.

Hoccleve frequently refers to Chaucer as his 'maister,' i. e. his teacher, with great affection; and, if he learnt but little more, he certainly learnt the true method of scansion of his master's lines,

LIFE OF GEOFFREY CHAUCER.

and imitates his metres and rimes with great exactness. The passages relating to Chaucer are as follows [179].

(1) From the Governail of Princes, or De Regimine Principum (ed. Wright, p. 67, st. 267):—

> 'Thou were acqueynted with Chaucer, pardee—
> God save his soule—best of any wight.'

(2) From the same, p. 75, stanzas 280, 281-283, 297-299, 301:—

> 'But weylawey! so is myn herte wo
> That the honour of English tonge is deed,
> Of which I wont was han conseil and reed.
>
> O maister dere and fader reverent,
> My maister Chaucer, flour of eloquence,
> Mirour of fructuous entendement,
> O universel fader in science,
> Allas! that thou thyn excellent prudence
> In thy bed mortel mightest not bequethe!
> What eyled Deeth? Allas! why wolde he slee thee?
>
> O Deeth! thou didest not harm singuler
> In slaghtre of him, but al this land it smerteth!
> But nathelees, yit hast thou no power
> His name slee; his hy vertu asterteth
> Unslayn fro thee, which ay us lyfly herteth
> With bokes of his ornat endyting,
> That is to al this land enlumining. . . .
>
> My dere maister—God his soule quyte—
> And fader, Chaucer, fayn wolde han me taught;
> But I was dul, and lernede right naught [180].
>
> Allas! my worthy maister honorable,
> This landes verray tresor and richesse!
> Deeth, by thy deeth, hath harm irreparable
> Unto us doon; hir vengeable duresse
> Despoiled hath this land of the swetnesse
> Of rethoryk; for unto [181] Tullius
> Was never man so lyk amonges us.

---

[179] Mr. Wright printed his text from MS. Reg. D. vi. Dr. Furnivall gives these passages from MS. Harl. 4866, in his edition of Hoccleve's Minor Poems, p. xxxi. I give a corrected text, due to a collation of these copies, with very slight alterations.

[180] *Or*, and lerned lyte or naught (MS. Harl. 4866).

[181] *So* Harl.; Reg. Of rethoryk fro vs; to Tullius.

HOCCLEVE'S TESTIMONY.

> Also who was heyr[182] in philosophye
> To Aristotle, in our tonge, but thou?
> The steppes of Virgyle in poesye
> Thou folwedest eek, men wot wel y-now.
> That combre-world, that thee (my maister) slow—
> Wolde I slayn werë—Deeth, was to hastyf
> To renne on thee, and reve thee thy lyf. . . .
>
> She mighte han taried hir vengeance a whyle
> Til that som man had egal to thee be;
> Nay, lat be that! she knew wel that this yle
> May never man forth bringe lyk to thee,
> And hir offyce nedes do mot she:
> God bad hir so, I truste as for the beste;
> O maister, maister, God thy soule reste!

(3) From the same, p. 179, stanzas 712–4:—

> The firste finder of our fair langage
> Hath seyd in caas semblable, and othere mo,
> So hyly wel, that it is my dotage
> For to expresse or touche any of tho.
> Allas! my fader fro the worlde is go,
> My worthy maister Chaucer, him I mene:
> Be thou advóket for him, hevenes quene!
>
> As thou wel knowest, O blessèd virgyne,
> With loving herte and hy devocioun
> In thyn honour he wroot ful many a lyne.
> O, now thy help and thy promocioun!
> To God, thy Sonë, mak a mocioun
> How he thy servaunt was, mayden Marië,
> And lat his lovë floure and fructifyë.
>
> Al-thogh his lyf be queynt, the résemblaunce
> Of him hath in me so fresh lyflinesse
> That, to putte othere men in rémembraunce
> Of his persone, I have heer his lyknesse
> Do makë, to this ende, in sothfastnesse,
> That they, that have of him lest thought and minde,
> By this peynturë may ageyn him finde.'

Here is given, in the margin of the MS., the famous portrait of Chaucer which is believed to be the best, and probably the only one that can be accepted as authentic. A copy of it is prefixed to the present volume, and to Furnivall's Trial-Forewords, Chaucer Soc., 1871; and an enlarged copy accompanies the Life-Records of Chaucer, part 2. It is thus described by Sir H. Nicolas:—
'The figure, which is half-length, has a back-ground of green

---

[182] *Both* MSS. *have* hyer (= higher); *an obvious error for* heyr (= heir).

tapestry. He is represented with grey hair and beard, which is biforked; he wears a dark-coloured dress and hood; his right hand is extended, and in his left he holds a string of beads. From his vest a black case is suspended, which appears to contain a knife, or possibly a 'penner,' or pen-case [183]. The expression of the countenance is intelligent; but the fire of the eye seems quenched, and evident marks of advanced age appear on the countenance.' Hoccleve did not paint this portrait himself, as is often erroneously said; he 'leet do make it,' i.e. had it made. It thus became the business of the scribe, and the portraits in different copies of Hoccleve's works vary accordingly. There is a full-length portrait in MS. Reg. 17 D. vi, marked as 'Chaucers ymage'; and another in a MS. copy once in the possession of Mr. Tyson, which was engraved in the Gentleman's Magazine for 1792, vol. lxii. p. 614; perhaps the latter is the copy which is now MS. Phillipps 1099. A representation of Chaucer on horseback, as one of the pilgrims, occurs in the Ellesmere MS.; an engraving of it appears as a frontispiece to Todd's Illustrations of Chaucer. A small full-length picture of Chaucer occurs in the initial letter of the Canterbury Tales, in MS. Lansdowne 851. Other portraits, such as that in MS. Addit. (or Sloane) 5141, the painting upon wood in the Bodleian Library, and the like, are of much later date, and cannot pretend to any authenticity.

Lydgate has frequent references to his 'maister Chaucer.' The most important is that in the Prologue to his Fall of Princes, which begins thus:—

> 'My maister Chaucer, with his fresh comédies,
> Is deed, allas! cheef poete of Bretayne,
> That somtym made ful pitous tragédies;
> The "fall of princes" he dide also compleyne,
> As he that was of making soverayne,
> Whom al this land of right[e] ought preferre,
> Sith of our langage he was the loodsterre.'

The 'fall of princes' refers to the Monkes Tale, as explained in vol. iii. p. 431. He next refers to 'Troilus' as being a translation of a book 'which called is Trophe' (see vol. ii. p. liv.); and to the Translation of Boethius and the Treatise of the Astrolabe.

---

[183] I think not; it is too short. I take it to be a small pen-knife in a sheath; useful for making erasures. So Todd, Illustrations of Chaucer, s. v. *Anelace*; Fairholt, on Costume in England, s. v. *Knives*.

LYDGATE'S TESTIMONY.

He then mentions many of the Minor Poems (in the stanzas quoted below, p. 23), the Legend of Good Women (see vol. iii. p. xx.), and the Canterbury Tales; and concludes thus:—

> 'This sayd poete, my maister, in his dayes
> Made and composed ful many a fresh dites,
> Complaintes, balades, roundels, virelayes,
> Ful delectable to heren and to see;
> For which men shulde, of right and equitee,
> Sith he of English in making was the beste,
> Praye unto God to yeve his soule reste.'

So also, in his Siege of Troye, fol. K 2 :—

> 'Noble Galfryde, chefe Poete of Brytayne,
> Among our English that caused first to rayne
> The golden droppes of Rethorike so fyne,
> Our rudë language onely t'enlumine,' &c.

And again, in the same, fol. R 2, back :—

> 'For he our English gilt[e] with his layes,
> Rude and boystous first, by oldë dayes,
> That was ful fer from al perfeccioun
> And but of lytel reputacioun,
> Til that he cam, and with his poetrye
> Gan our tungë first to magnifye,
> And adourne it with his eloquence'; &c.

And yet again, at fol. Ee 2 :—

> 'And, if I shal shortly him discryve,
> Was never noon [un]to this day alyve,
> To reken all[e], bothe of yonge and olde,
> That worthy was his inkhorn for to holde.'

Similar passages occur in some of his other works, and shew that he regarded Chaucer with affectionate reverence.

Allusions in later authors have only a literary value, and need not be cited in a Life of Chaucer.

I subjoin (on p. lxii.) a List of Chaucer's genuine works, arranged, as nearly as I can conjecture, in their chronological order. Of his poetical excellence it is superfluous to speak; Lowell's essay on 'Chaucer' in My Study Windows gives a just estimate of his powers.

LIST OF CHAUCER'S WORKS.

THE following list is arranged, *conjecturally*, in chronological order. It will be understood that much of the arrangement and some of the dates are due to guesswork; on a few points scholars are agreed. See further in pp. 20-91 below, &c. Of the Poems marked (a'), there seem to have been *two* editions, (a) being the earlier. The letters and numbers appended at the end denote the *metres*, according to the following scheme.

A = octosyllabic metre; **B** = ballad metre, in Sir Thopas; **C** = 4-line stanza, in the Proverbes; **P** = Prose.

The following sixteen metres are original (i. e. in *English*); viz. **1** = 8-line stanza, *ababbcbc*; **1** *b* = the same, thrice, with refrain. **2** = 7-line stanza, *ababbcc*; **2** *b* = the same, thrice, with refrain; **2** *c* = 7-line stanza, *ababbab*. **3** = terza rima. **4** = 10-line stanza, *aabaabcddc*. **5** = 9-line stanza, *aabaabbab*; **5** *b* = the same, with internal rimes. **6** = virelai of 16 lines. **7** = 9-line stanza, *aabaabbcc*. **8** = roundel. **9** = heroic couplet. **10** = 6-line stanza, *ababcb*, repeated six times. **11** = 10-line stanza, *aabaabbaab*. **12** = 5-line stanza, *aabba*.

*** C. T. = Canterbury Tales; L. G. W. = Legend of Good Women; M. P. = Minor Poems.

       Origenes upon the Maudeleyne (*See* L. G. W., A 418; *lost.*)
       Book of the Leoun (C. T., I. 1087; *lost*).
       (*a*) Ceys and Alcion (C. T., B. 57; Bk. Duch. 62-214).—**A**.
       Romaunt of the Rose, ll. 1-1705; *rest lost*.—**A**.
       A. B. C.; *in* M. P. I.—**1**.
1369. Book of the Duchesse; M. P. III.—**A**.
       (*a*) Lyf of Seynt Cecyle (L. G. W., B 426; C. T., G. 1-553).—**2**[1].
       (*a*) Monkes Tale (parts of); *except* B. 3565-3652.—**1**.

---

[1] I see no reason for placing this after 1372; surely ll. 36-56 (from Dante) are a later insertion. Observe 'us wrecches' in G. 32, and 'Me wrecche' in G. 58. These parallel lines must (I think) have once been in closer proximity.

LIST OF CHAUCER'S WORKS.   lxiii

ab. 1372-3. (*a*) Clerkes Tale; except E. 995-1008, and the Envoy.—**2**.
    (*a*) Palamon and Arcite (*scraps preserved*).—**2**.
    Compleint to his Lady; M. P. VI.—**2. 3. 4**.
    An Amorous Compleint, made at Windsor; M. P. XXII.—**2**.
    Compleint unto Pitè; M. P. II.—**2**.
    Anelida and Arcite (10 stt. *from* Palamon); M. P. VII.—**2.**
       5. 6. 5 *b*.
    (*a*) The Tale of Melibeus.—**P**.
    (*a*) The Persones Tale.—**P**.
    (*a*) Of the Wreched Engendring of Mankinde (L. G. W., A. 414; cf. C. T., B. 99-121, &c.)—**2**.
    (*a*) Man of Lawes Tale; *amplified in* C. T.—**2**.
1377-81. Translation of Boethius.—**P**.
1379? Compleint of Mars; M. P. IV.—**2. 7**.
1379-83. Troilus and Criseyde (3 stt. *from* Palamon).—**2**.
    Wordes to Adam (*concerning* Boece *and* Troilus); M. P. VIII.—**2**.
    The Former Age (*from* Boece); M. P. IX.—**1**.
    Fortune (*hints from* Boece); M. P. X.—**1** *b*. **2** *c*.
1382. Parlement of Foules (16 stt. *from* Palamon); M. P. V.—**2. 8**.
1383-4. House of Fame.—**A**.
1385-6. Legend of Good Women.—**9**.
1386. Canterbury Tales begun.
1387-8. Central period of the Canterbury Tales.
1389, &c. The Tales continued.—**B. 1. 2. 9. 10. P**.
1391. Treatise on the Astrolabe.—**P**.
1393? Compleint of Venus; M. P. XVIII.—**1** *b*. **11**.
1393. Lenvoy to Scogan; M. P. XVI.—**2**.
1396. Lenvoy to Bukton; M. P. XVII.—**1**.
1399. *Envoy to* Compleint to his Purse; M. P. XIX.—**12**.

The following occasional triple roundel and balades *may* have been composed between 1380 and 1396:—

Merciless Beautè; M. P. XI.—**8**.   Balade to Rosamounde; M. P. XII.—**1** *b*.   Against Women Unconstaunt; M. P. XXI.—**2** *b*. (*a*) Compleint to his Purse; M. P. XIX.—**2** *b*.   Lak of Stedfastnesse; M. P. XV.—**2** *b*.   Gentilesse; M. P. XIV.—**2** *b*. Truth; M. P. XIII.—**2** *b*.   Proverbes of Chaucer; M. P. XX.—**C**.

ERRATA AND ADDENDA

P. 95 : l. 47. Insert a comma after 'oughte'
P. 98 : l. 114. Omit the comma at the end of the line.
P. 123 : l. 705. It would be better to read 'Withoute.' The scansion then is:
Without | e fabl ' | I wol | descryve.
P. 126 : l. 793. Delete the comma at the end of the line.
P. 127 : l. 806. Delete the comma at the end of the line.
P. 135 : l. 997. *For* shall *read* shal
P. 136 : ll. 1015–6. Improve the punctuation thus:—
As whyt as lilie or rose in rys
Hir face, gentil and tretys.
P. 136 : l. 1021. Delete the comma after 'yelowe'
P. 141 : l. 1154. Delete the comma after 'seide'
P. 168 : l. 1962. *For* Bu -if *read* But-if
P. 176 : l. 2456. *For* joy *read* Ioy
P. 201 : l. 4035. For the comma substitute a semicolon.
P. 249 : l. 7087. *For* echerye *read* trecherye
P. 253 : l. 7324. *For* weary *read* wery
P. 255 : l. 7437. Supply a comma at the end of the line.
P. 258 : l. 7665. Insert a comma after 'helle'
P. 269 : l. 145. The stop at the end should be a comma.
P. 278 : l. 49. *For* aud *read* and
P. 282 : l. 145. *For* Aud *read* And
P. 301 : l. 716. The comma should perhaps be a semicolon or a full stop.
P. 313 : l. 1069. For 'Antilegius,' a better form would be 'Antilogus,' a French form of Antilochus.
P. 326 : l. 74. Perhaps 'let' should be 'lete'
P. 330 : l. 206. *For* folke *read* folk
P. 338 : l. 91. *For* Aud *read* And
P. 340 : l. 133. *For* the *read* thee
P. 362 : l. 76. The final stop should be a comma.
P. 374 : ll. 243, 248. *For* desteny *and* ful *better forms are* destinee *and* fulle
P. 377 : l. 328. *For* furlong wey *read* furlong-wey

INTRODUCTION.

THE ROMAUNT OF THE ROSE.

§ 1. In the Third Edition of my volume of Chaucer Selections, containing the Prioress's Tale, &c., published by the Clarendon Press in 1880, I included an essay to shew 'why the Romaunt of the Rose is not Chaucer's,' meaning thereby the particular English version of Le Roman de la Rose which happens to be preserved. I have since seen reason to modify this opinion as regards a comparatively short portion of it at the beginning (here printed in large type), but the arguments then put forward remain as valid as ever as regards the main part of it (here printed in smaller type, and in double columns). Some of these arguments had been previously put forward by me in a letter to the Academy, Aug. 10, 1878, p. 143. I ought to add that the chief of them are not original, but borrowed from Mr. Henry Bradshaw, whose profound knowledge of all matters relating to Chaucer has been acknowledged by all students.

§ 2. That Chaucer translated the French poem called Le Roman de la Rose, or at least some part of it[1], no one doubts; for he tells us so himself in the Prologue of his Legend of Good Women (A 255, B 329), and the very frequent references to it, in many of his poems, shew that many parts of it were familiarly known to him. Nevertheless, it does not follow that the particular version of it which happens to be preserved, is the very one which he made; for it was a poem familiar to many others besides him, and it is

---

[1] It is not very likely that he ever *finished* his translation, when we consider his frequent habit of leaving his works incomplete, and the enormous length of the French text (22074 lines in Méon's edition).

extremely probable that Middle English versions of it were numerous. In fact, it will presently appear that the English version printed in this volume actually consists of *three* separate fragments, *all by different hands*.

The English version, which I shall here, for brevity, call 'the translation,' has far less claim to be considered as Chaucer's than unthinking people imagine. Modern readers find it included in many editions of his Works, and fancy that such a fact is conclusive; but it is the merest prudence to enquire how it came there. The answer is, that it first appeared in Thynne's edition of 1532, a collection of Chaucer's (supposed) works made more than *a hundred and thirty years* after his death. Such an attribution is obviously valueless; we must examine the matter for ourselves, and on independent grounds.

§ 3. A critical examination of the internal evidence at once shews that by far the larger part of 'the translation' cannot possibly be Chaucer's; for the language of it contradicts most of his habits, and presents peculiarities such as we never find in his genuine poems. I shewed this in my 'Essay' by the use of several unfailing tests, the nature of which I shall explain presently. The only weak point in my argument was, that I then considered 'the translation' as being the production of *one* author, and thought it sufficient to draw my examples (as I unconsciously, for the most part, did) from the central portion of the whole.

§ 4. The next step in this investigation was made by Dr. Lindner. In a painstaking article printed in *Englische Studien*, xi. 163, he made it appear highly probable that at least *two* fragments of 'the translation' are *by different hands*. That there are two fragments, *at least*, is easily discerned; for after l. 5810 there is a great gap, equivalent to an omission of more than 5000 lines.

§ 5. Still more recently, Dr. Max Kaluza has pointed out that there is another distinct break in the poem near l. 1700. The style of translation, not to speak of its accuracy, is much better in the first 1700 lines than in the subsequent portions. We may notice, in particular, that the French word *boutons* is translated by *knoppes* in ll. 1675, 1683, 1685, 1691, 1702, whilst, in l. 1721 and subsequent passages, the same word is merely Englished by *botoun* or *botouns*. A closer study of the passage extending from l. 1702 to l. 1721 shews that there is a very marked break at the end of l. 1705. Here the French text has (ed. Méon, l. 1676):—

THE THREE FRAGMENTS.

> 'L'odor de lui entor s'espent;
> La soatime qui en ist
> Toute la place replenist.'

The English version has :—

> 'The swote smelle sprong so wyde
> That it dide al the place aboute'—

followed by :—

> 'Whan I had smelled the savour swote,
> No wille hadde I fro thens yit go'; &c.

It will be observed that the sentence in the two former lines is incomplete; *dide* is a mere auxiliary verb, and the real verb of the sentence is lost; whilst the two latter lines lead off with a new sentence altogether. It is still more interesting to observe that, at this very point, we come upon a false rime. The word *aboute* was then pronounced (abuu·tə), where (uu) denotes the sound of *ou* in *soup*, and (ə) denotes an obscure vowel, like the *a* in *China*. But the vowel *o* in *swote* was then pronounced like the German *o* in G. *so* (nearly E. *o* in *so*), so that it was quite unlike the M.E. *ou*; and the rime is no better than if we were to rime the mod. E. *boot* with the mod. E. *goat*. It is clear that there has been a *join* here, and a rather clumsy one. The supply of 'copy' of the first translation ran short, perhaps because the rest of it had been torn away and lost, and the missing matter was supplied from some other source. We thus obtain, as the result to be tested, the following arrangement :—

Fragment A.—Lines 1–1705. French text, 1–1678.
Fragment B.—Lines 1706–5810. French text, 1679–5169.
Fragment C.—Lines 5811–7698. French text, 10716–12564.

It should be noted, further, that l. 7698 by no means reaches to the *end*. It merely corresponds to l. 12564 of the French text, leaving 9510 lines untouched towards the end, besides the gap of 5547 lines between Fragments B and C. In fact, the three fragments, conjointly, only represent 7018 lines of the original, leaving 15056 lines (more than double that number) wholly untranslated.

§ 6. Discussion of Fragment B.

TEST I.—PROPORTION OF ENGLISH TO FRENCH.—As regards these fragments, one thing strikes us at once, viz. the much greater *diffuseness* of the translation in fragment B, as may be seen from the following table :—

4 THE ROMAUNT OF THE ROSE.

A.—English, 1705 lines; French, 1678; as 101·6 to 100.
B.—English, 4105 lines; French, 3491; as 117·5 to 100.
C.—English, 1888 lines; French, 1849; as 102·1 to 100.

Thus, in A and C, the translation runs nearly line for line; but in B, the translator employs, on an average, 11 lines and three-quarters for every 10 of the original.

§ 7. TEST II.—DIALECT.—But the striking characteristic of Fragment B is the use in it of a Northern dialect. That this is due to the author, and not merely to the scribe, is obvious from the employment of Northern forms in rimes, where any change would destroy the rime altogether. This may be called the Dialect-test. Examples abound, and I only mention some of the most striking.

1. Use of the Northern pres. part. in -*and*. In l. 2263, we have *wel sittand* (for *wel sitting*), riming with *hand*. In l. 2708, we have *wel doand* (for *wel doing*), riming with *fand*. Even *fand* is a Northern form. Chaucer uses *fond*, riming with *hond* (Cant. Ta. A 4116, 4221, &c.), *lond* (A 702, &c.); cf. the subj. form *fond-e*, riming with *hond-e*, *lond-e*, *bond-e* (B 3521).

2. In l. 1853, we have the rimes *thar*, *mar* (though miswritten *thore*, *more* in MS. G.), where the Chaucerian forms *there*, *more*, would not rime at all. These are well-known Northern forms, as in Barbour's Bruce. So again, in l. 2215, we find *mar*, *ar* (though *mar* is written as *more* in MS. G.). In l. 2397, we find *stat*, *hat*; where *hat* is the Northern form of Chaucer's *hoot*, adj., 'hot.' So also, in 5399, we have North. *wat* instead of Ch. *wot* or *woot*, riming with *estat*. In l. 5542, we find the Northern *certis* (in place of Chaucer's *certes*), riming with *is*.

3. Chaucer (or his scribes) admit the use of the Northern *til*, in place of the Southern *to*, very sparingly; it occurs, e.g. in Cant. Ta. A 1478, before a vowel. But it never occurs after its case, nor at the end of a line. Yet, in fragment B, we twice find *him til* used finally, 4594, 4852.

4. The use of *ado* (for *at do*), in the sense of 'to do,' is also Northern; see the New E. Dict. It occurs in l. 5080, riming with *go*.

5. The dropping of the inflexional *e*, in the infin. mood or gerund, is also Northern. In fragment B, this is very common; as examples, take the rimes *lyf*, *dryf*, 1873; *feet*, *lete* (= *leet*), 1981; *sit*, *flit*, 2371; *may*, *convay*, 2427; *may*, *assay*, 453; *set*, *get*, 2615; *spring*, *thing*, 2627; *ly*, *by*, 2629; *ly*, *erly*, 2645; &c. The Chaucerian

forms are *dryv-e, let-e, flit-te, convey-e, assay-e, get-e, spring-e, ly-e.* That the Northern forms are not due to the scribe, is obvious; for he usually avoids them where he can. Thus in l. 2309, he writes *sitting* instead of *sittand*; but in l. 2263, he could not avoid the form *sittand*, because of the rime.

§ 8. TEST III.—THE RIMING OF -y WITH -y-ë.—With two intentional exceptions (both in the ballad metre of Sir Thopas, see note to Cant. Ta. B 2092), Chaucer *never* allows such a word as *trewely* (which etymologically ends in *-y*) to rime with French substantives in *-y-ë*, such as *fol-y-ë, Ielos-y-ë* (Ital. *follia, gelosia*). But in fragment B, examples abound; e. g. *I, malady(e)*[1], 1849; *hastily, company(e),* 1861; *generally, vilany(e),* 2179; *worthy, curtesy(e),* 2209; *foly(e), by,* 2493, 2521; *curtesy(e), gladly,* 2985; *foly(e), utterly,* 3171; *foly(e), hastily,* 3241; and many more.

This famous test, first proposed by Mr. Bradshaw, is a very simple but effective one; it separates the spurious from the genuine works of Chaucer with ease and certainty in all but a few cases, viz. cases wherein a spurious poem happens to satisfy the test; and these are rare indeed.

§ 9. TEST IV.—ASSONANT RIMES. Those who know nothing about the pronunciation of Middle English, and require an easy test, appreciable by any child who has a good ear, may observe this. Chaucer does not employ mere assonances, i. e. rimes in which only the vowel-sounds correspond. He does not rime *take* with *shape*, nor *fame* with *lane*. But the author of fragment B had no ear for this. He actually has such rimes as these: *kepe, eke,* 2125; *shape, make,* 2259; *escape, make,* 2753; *take, scape,* 3165; *storm, corn,* 4343; *doun, tourn,* 5469.

OTHER STRANGE RIMES.—Other rimes which occur here, but not in Chaucer, are these and others like them: *aboute, swote,* 1705 (already noticed); *desyre, nere,* 1785, 2441; *thar* (Ch. *there*), *to-shar,* 1857; *Ioynt, queynt*[2], 2037; *soon* (Ch. *son-e*), *doon,* 2377; *abrede, forweried,* 2563; *anney* (Ch. *annoy*), *awey,* 2675; *desyre, manere,* 2779; *Ioye, convoye* (Ch. *conveye*), 2915, &c. It is needless to multiply instances.

---

[1] By the spelling *malady(e)*, I mean that the word must be pronounced *malady* in the text, whereas the Chaucerian form is *malady-ë* in four syllables. And so in other cases.

[2] Doubtless the author meant to employ the form *quoynt* or *coint*; but Chaucer as *queynt*, Cant. Ta. A 2333, G 752.

THE ROMAUNT OF THE ROSE.

§ 10. It would be easy to employ further tests; we might, for example, make a minute critical examination of the method in which the final -*e* is grammatically employed. But the results are always the same. We shall always find irrefragable proof that fragment B exhibits usages far different from those which occur in the undoubted works of Chaucer, and cannot possibly have proceeded from his pen. Repeated investigations, made by me during the past thirteen years, have always come round to this result, and it is not possible for future criticism to alter it.

Hence our first result is this. Fragment B, consisting of ll. 1706–5810 (4105 lines), containing more than fragments A and C together, and therefore more than half of 'the translation,' *is not Chaucer's, but was composed by an author who, to say the least, frequently employed Northern English forms and phrases. Moreover, his translation is too diffuse; and, though spirited, it is not always accurate.*

§ 11. Discussion of Fragment C.

I shall now speak of fragment C. The first noticeable point about it is, that it does *not* exhibit many of the peculiarities of B. There is nothing to indicate, with any certainty, a Northern origin, nor to connect it with B. In fact, we may readily conclude that B and C are by different authors. The sole question that remains, as far as we are now concerned, is this. Can we attribute it to Chaucer?

The answer, in this case, is not quite so easily given, because the differences between it and Chaucer's genuine works are less glaring and obvious than in the case above. Nevertheless, we at once find some good reasons for refraining to attribute it to our author.

§ 12. Rime-tests.—If, for instance, we apply the simple but effective test of the rimes of words ending in -*y* with those ending in -*y-e*, we at once find that this fragment fails to satisfy the text.

Examples: *covertly, Ipocrisy*(*e*), 6112; *company*(*e*), *outerly*, 6301; *loteby, company*(*e*), 6339; *why, tregetry*(*e*), 6373; *company'e*), *I*, 6875; *mekely, trechery*(*e*), 7319. These six instances, in less than 1900 lines, ought to make us hesitate.

If we look a little more closely, we find other indications which should make us hesitate still more. At l. 5919, we find *hors* (horse) riming with *wors* (worse); but Chaucer rimes *wors* with *curs* (Cant. Ta.

A 4349), and with *pervers* (Book Duch. 813). At l. 6045, we find *fare, are*; but Chaucer never uses *are* at the end of a line; he always uses *been*. At l. 6105, we find *atte last, agast*; but Chaucer only has *atte last-e* (which is never monosyllabic). At l. 6429, we find *paci-ence, venge-aunce*, a false rime which it would be libellous to attribute to Chaucer; and, at l. 6469, we find *force, croce*, which is still worse, and makes it doubtful whether it is worth while to go on. However, if we go a little further, we find the pl. form *wrought* riming with *nought*, 6565; but Chaucer usually has *wrought-e*, which would destroy the rime. This, however, is not decisive, since Chaucer has *bisought* for *bisoughte*, Cant. Ta. A. 4117, and *brought* for *broughte*, id. F. 1273. But when, at l. 6679, we find *preched* riming with *teched*, we feel at once that this is nothing in which Chaucer had a hand, for he certainly uses the form *taughte* (Prologue, 497), and as certainly does *not* invent such a form as *praughte* to rime with it. Another unpleasant feature is the use of the form *Abstinaunce* in l. 7483, to gain a rime to *penaunce*, whilst in l. 7505, only 22 lines lower down, we find *Abstinence*, to rime with *sentence*; but the original has similar variations.

§ 13. I will just mention, in conclusion, one more peculiarity to be found in fragment C. In the Cant. Tales, B 480 (and elsewhere), Chaucer uses such rimes as *clerkes, derk is*, and the like; but not very frequently. The author of fragment C was evidently much taken with this peculiarity, and gives us plenty of examples of it. Such are: *requestis, honést is*, 6039; *places, place is*, 6119; *nede is, dedis*, 6659; *apert is, certis*, 6799; *chaieris, dere is*, 6915; *enquestes, honést is*, 6977; *prophetis, prophete is*, 7093; *ypocritis, spite is*, 7253. Here are eight instances in less than 1900 lines. However, there are five examples (at ll. 19, 75, 387, 621, 1349) in the Hous of Fame, which contains 2158 lines in the same metre as our 'translation'; and there are 19 instances in the Cant. Tales.

We should also notice that the character called *Bialacoil* throughout Fragment B is invariably called *Fair-Welcoming* in C.

We should also remark how Dr. Lindner (*Engl. Studien*, xi. 172) came to the conclusion that Chaucer certainly never wrote fragment C. As to the rest he doubted, and with some reason; for he had not before him the idea of splitting lines 1–5810 into two fragments.

§ 14. A consideration of the above-mentioned facts, and of others similar to them, leads us to our second result, which is this. Fragment C, containing 1888 lines, and corresponding to ll. 10716–

12564 of the French original, is *neither by the author of fragment B, nor by Chaucer, but is not so glaringly unlike Chaucer's work as in the case of fragment B.*

§ 15. DISCUSSION OF FRAGMENT A.

It remains to consider fragment A. The first test to apply is that of rimes in *-y* and *-y-e*; and, when we remember how indiscriminately these are used in fragments B and C, it is at least instructive to observe the perfect regularity with which they are employed in fragment A. The student who is unacquainted with the subtle distinctions which this test introduces, and who probably is, on that account, predisposed to ignore it, may learn something new by the mere perusal of the examples here given.

1. Words that should, etymologically, end in *-y* (and not in *-y-e*) are here found riming together, and never rime with a word of the other class.

Examples: *covertly, openly*, 19; *redily, erly*, 93; *by, I*, 111; *bisily, redily*, 143; *by, I*, 163; *I, by*, 207; *povrely, courtepy*[1], 219; *beggarly, by*, 223; *enemy, hardily*, 269; *awry*[2], *baggingly*, 291; *certeinly, tenderly*, 331; *prively, sikerly*, 371; *redily, by*, 379; *Pope-holy, prively*, 415; *I, openly*, 501; *queyntely, fetisly*, 569; *fetisly, richely*, 577; *only, uncouthly*, 583; *I, namely*, 595; *sikerly, erthely*, 647; *lustily, semely*, 747; *parfitly, sotilly*, 771; *queyntely, prively*, 783; *fetisly, richely*, 837; *sotilly, I*, 1119; *enemy*[3], *tristely*, 1165; *sotilly, therby*, 1183; *newely, by*, 1205; *fetisly, trewely*, 1235; *I, by*, 1273; *trewely, comunly*, 1307; *lustily, sikerly*, 1319; *merily, hastely*, 1329; *I, sikerly*, 1549; *I, craftely*, 1567; *openly, therby*, 1585; *diversely, verily*, 1629; *openly, by*, 1637. Thirty-eight examples.

We here notice how frequently words in *-ly* rime together; but this peculiarity is Chaucerian; cf. *semely, fetisly,* C. T. prol. A 123, &c.

2. Words that, etymologically, should end in *-y-e*, rime together. These are of two sorts: (*a*) French substantives; and (*b*) words in *-y*, with an inflexional *-e* added.

Examples: (*a*) *felony-e, vilany-e*, 165; *envy-e, masonry-e*, 301;

---

[1] *Courtepy* rimes with *sobrely*; Cant. Ta. prol. 289.
[2] As to *awry* (or *awry-e*?), we have little evidence beyond the present passage.
[3] *Enemy* rimes with *I*, Cant. Ta. A 1643, *royally*, id. 1793; &c.

company-e, curtesy-e, 639; *melody-e, reverdy-e*, 719; *curtesy-e, company-e*, 957; *vilany-e, felony-e*, 977; *envy-e, company-e*, 1069; *chivalry-e, maistry-e*, 1207; *villany-e, sukkeny-e*, 1231; *envye*, Pavie, 1653.

(*b*) *dy-e*, infin. mood, *dry-e*, dissyllabic adj. (A. S. *drȳge*), 1565.

(*a*) and (*b*) mixed: *melody-e*, F. sb., *dy-e*, infin. mood, 675; *espy-e*, gerund, *curtesy-e*, F. sb., 795; *hy-e*, dat. adj., *maistry-e*, 841; *dy-e*, gerund, *flatery-e*, F. sb., 1063; *curtesy-e*, F. sb., *hy-e*, dat. case, pl. adj., 1251; *dy-e*, infin. mood, *remedy-e*, F. sb., 1479. Seventeen examples. (In all, fifty-five examples.)

Thus, in more than fifty cases, the Chaucerian habit is maintained, and there is *no* instance to the contrary. Even the least trained reader may now fairly begin to believe that there is some value in this proposed test, and may see one reason for supposing that fragment A may be genuine.

§ 16. A still closer examination of other rimes tends to confirm this. There are no Northern forms (as in B), no merely assonant rimes (as in B), nor any false or bad or un-Chaucerian rimes (as in both B and C), except such as can be accounted for. The last remark refers to the fact that the scribe or the printer of Thynne's edition frequently misspells words so as to obscure the rime, whereas they rime perfectly when properly spelt; a fact which tells remarkably in favour of the possible genuineness of the fragment. Thus, at l. 29, Thynne prints *befal*, and at l. 30, *al*. Both forms are wrong; read *befalle, alle*. Here Thynne has, however, preserved the rime by making a *double* mistake; as in several other places. A more important instance is at l. 249, where the Glasgow MS. has *farede, herede*, a bad rime; but Thynne correctly has *ferde, herde*, as in Chaucer, Cant. Ta. A 1371. So again, at ll. 499, 673, where the Glasgow MS. is right (except in putting *herd* for *herde* in l. 673).

At l. 505, there is a false rime; but it is clearly due to a misreading, as explained in the notes. A similar difficulty, at l. 1341, is explicable in the same way.

§ 17. So far, there is no reason why fragment A may not be Chaucer's; and the more closely we examine it, the more probable does this supposition become. Dr. Kaluza has noticed, for instance, that the style of translation in fragment A is distinctly better, clearer, and more accurate than in fragment B. I find also another significant fact, viz. that in my essay written to shew that 'the translation' is not Chaucer's (written at a time when I unfortunately regarded the whole translation as being the work of *one* writer, a position which is no longer tenable), nearly all my arguments were drawn from certain peculiarities contained in fragments B and C, especially the former. I have therefore nothing, of any consequence, to retract; nor do I even now find that I made any serious mistake.

§ 18. The third result may, accordingly, be arrived at thus. Seeing that Chaucer really translated the 'Roman de la Rose,' and that three fragments of English translations have come down to us, of which two cannot be his, whilst the third may be, *we may provisionally accept fragment A as genuine; and we find that, the more closely we examine it, the more probable does its genuineness become.*

§ 19. SUMMARY.—Having now discussed the three fragments A, B, C, successively and separately (though in a different order), we may conveniently sum up the three results as follows.

1. Fragment A appears to be a real portion of Chaucer's own translation. Its occurrence, at the *beginning*, is, after all, just what we should expect. The scribe or editor would naturally follow it as far as it was extant; and when it failed, would as naturally piece it out with any other translation or translations to which he could gain access. This fragment ceases suddenly, at the end of l. 1705, in the middle of an incomplete sentence. The junction with the succeeding portion is clumsily managed, for it falsely assumes that the previous sentence is complete, and leads off with a false rime.

2. Fragment B is obviously from some other source, and is at once dissociated from both the other fragments by the facts (*a*) that it was *originally* written in a Northumbrian dialect, though this is somewhat concealed by the manipulation of the spelling by a later scribe; (*b*) that it was written in a more *diffuse* style, the matter being expanded to the extent, on an average, of nearly twelve lines to ten; (*c*) that many licences appear in the rimes, which sometimes degenerate into mere assonances; and (*d*) that it is less exact and less correct in its method of rendering the original.

3. After fragment B, there is a large gap in the story, more than 5000 lines of the original being missing. Hence Fragment C is from yet a third source, not much of which seems to have been accessible. It neither joins on to Fragment B, nor carries the story much further; and it comes to an end somewhat suddenly, at a point more than 9000 lines from the end of the original. It is,

however, both more correct than Fragment B, and more in Chaucer's style; though, at the same time, I cannot accept it as his.

§ 20. There is little that is surprising in this result. That translations of this then famous and popular French poem should have been attempted by many hands, is just what we should expect. At the same time, the enormous length of the original may very well have deterred even the most persevering of the translators from ever arriving at the far end of it. Chaucer's translation was evidently the work of his younger years, and the frequent use which he made of the French poem in his later works may have made him careless of his own version, if indeed he ever finished it, which may be doubted. All this, however, is mere speculation, and all that concerns us now is the net result. It is clear, that, in the 1705 lines here printed in the larger type, we have recovered all of Chaucer's work that we can ever hope to recover. With this we must needs rest satisfied, and it is a great gain to have even so much of it; the more so, when we remember how much reason there was to fear that the whole of Chaucer's work was lost. It was not until Dr. Kaluza happily hit upon the resolution of lines 1–5810 into two fragments, that Chaucer's portion was at last discovered.

§ 21. THE EXTERNAL EVIDENCE.

In what has preceded, we have drawn our conclusions from the most helpful form of evidence—the internal evidence. It remains to look at the external form of the poem, and to enquire how it has come down to us.

The apparent sources are *two*, viz. Thynne's edition of 1532 (reprinted in 1542, 1550, 1561, and at later dates), and a MS. in the Hunterian collection at Glasgow. But a very slight examination shews that these are nearly duplicate copies, both borrowed from one and the same original, which is now no longer extant. I shall denote these sources, for convenience, by the symbols Th., G., and O., meaning, respectively, Thynne, Glasgow MS., and the (lost) Original.

The resemblance of Th. and G. is very close; however, each sometimes corrects *small* faults in the other, and the collation of them is, on this account, frequently helpful. Both are remarkable for an extraordinary misarrangement of the material, in which respect they closely agree; and we are enabled, from this circumstance, to say, definitely, that the C-portion of O. (i. e. their common original) was written (doubtless on vellum) in quires containing 8 leaves (or 16 pages) each, there being, on an average, 24 lines upon every page. Of these quires, the fourth had its leaves transposed, by mistake, when the MS. was bound, in such a manner that the *middle* pair of leaves of this quire was displaced, so as to come next the two *outer* pair of leaves; and this displacement was never suspected till of late years, nor ever (so far as I am aware[1]) fully appreciated and explained till now[2]. This displacement of the material was first noticed in Bell's edition, where the editor found it out by the simple process of comparing the English 'translation' with the French 'Roman'; but he gives no account of how it came about. But a closer investigation is useful as showing how exactly 'Th.' and 'G.' agree in following an original displacement in 'O.', or rather in the still older MS. from which the C-portion of O. was copied.

In the fourth sheet (as said above), the pair of middle leaves, containing its 7th, 8th, 9th, and 10th pages (G, H, I, K, with the contents recorded in note 2 below) was subtracted from the middle of the quire, and placed so that the 7th page (G) followed the 2nd (B), whilst at the same time, the 10th page (K) came to precede the 15th page (P). The resulting order of pages was, necessarily, A, B, G, H, C, D, E, F, L, M, N, O, I, K, P, Q; as is easily seen by help of a small paper model. And the resulting order of the lines was, accordingly, 6965-6988, 6989-7012, 7109-7133, 7134-7158, 7013-7036, 7037-60, 7061-84, 7085-7108, 7209-7232, 7233-7256, 7257-7280, 7281-7304, 7159-7183, 7184-7208, 7305-7328, 7329-7352; or, collecting the successive numbers, . . . -7012, 7109-7158, 7013-7108, 7209-7304, 7159-7208, 7305, &c. And this is precisely the order found, both in Th. and G.

---

[1] As it is the natural instinct of many critics to claim for themselves even small discoveries, I note that this paragraph was written in July, 1891, and that the curious, but not very important fact above announced, was first noticed by me some three months previously.

[2] The calculation is as follows. A quire of 16 pages, at 24 lines a page, contains 384 lines. Three such quires contain about 1152 lines, which, added to 5810 (in A and B), bring us to l. 6962 (say, 6964). In the fourth quire, if A, B, C, &c., be successive pages, these pages contained the lines following. A, 6965-6988; B, 6989-7012; C, 7013-36; D, 7037-60; E, 7061-84; F, 7085-7108; G (25 lines), 7109-33; H (25 lines), 7134-7158; I (25 lines), 7159-7183; K (25 lines), 7184-7208; L, 7209-32; M, 7233-56; N, 7257-80; O, 7281-7304; P, 7305-28; Q, 7329-52.

We see further that the fourth and last quire of this C-portion of O. consisted of 7 leaves only, the rest being torn away. For 7 leaves containing 48 lines apiece give a total of 336 lines, which, added to 7352, make up 7688 lines; and, as 10 of the pages seem to have had 25 lines, we thus obtain 7698 lines as the number found in O.

The A-portion of O. was probably copied from a MS. containing usually 25 lines on a page, and occasionally 26. Four quires at 50 lines to the leaf give 32 × 50, or 1600 lines; and 2 leaves more give 100 lines, or 1700 lines in all. If 5 of the pages had 26 lines, we should thus make up the number, viz. 1705. Of the B-portion we can tell nothing, as we do not know how it was made to join on.

As O. was necessarily older than G., and G. is judged by experts [1] to be hardly later than 1440, it is probable that O. was written out not much later than 1430; we cannot say how much earlier, if earlier it was.

§ 22. G. (the Glasgow MS.) is a well-written MS., on vellum; the size of each page being about 11 inches by 7½, with wide margins, especially at the bottom. Each page contains about 24 lines, and each quire contains 8 leaves. The first quire is imperfect, the 1st leaf (ll. 1–44) and the 8th (ll. 333–380) being lost. Nine other leaves are also lost, containing ll. 1387–1482, 2395–2442, 3595–3690, and 7385–7576; for the contents of which (as of the former two) Th. remains the sole authority. The date of the MS. is about 1440; and its class-mark is V. 3. 7.

It begins at l. 45—'So mochel pris,' &c. At the top of the first extant leaf is the name of Thomas Griggs, a former owner. On a slip of parchment at the beginning is a note by A. Askew (from whom Hunter bought the MS.) to this effect:—'Tho. Martin*us*. Ex dono dom' Iacobi Sturgeon de Bury sci Edmundi in agro Suffolc: Artis Chirurgicæ Periti. Nov. 9, 1720.' It ends very abruptly in the following manner:—

>'Ne half so lettred as am I
>I am licenced boldely
>To Reden in diuinite
>And longe haue red
>Explicit.'

---

[1] I have been greatly assisted in this matter by D. Donaldson, Esq., who gave me some beautifully executed photographic copies of three pages of the MS., which I have shewn to many friends, including Mr. Bond and Mr Thompson at the British Museum.

14   THE ROMAUNT OF THE ROSE.

The third of these lines is incorrect, and the fourth is corrupt and imperfect; moreover, Thynne's copy gives four more lines after them. It would thus appear that G. was copied from O. at a later period than the MS. used by Thynne and now lost, viz. at a period when O. was somewhat damaged or torn at the end of its last page. A careful and exact copy of this MS. is now (in 1891) being printed for the Chaucer Society, edited by Dr. Kaluza.

§ 23. TH.—The version printed in Thynne's edition, 1532, and reprinted in 1542, 1550, 1561, &c. The first four editions, at least, are very much alike. The particular edition at first used by me for constructing the present text is that which I call the edition of 1550. (It is really undated, but that is about the date of it.) Its variations from the earlier editions are trifling, and I afterwards reduced all the readings to the standard of the *first* edition (1532). The MS. used by Thynne was obviously a copy of 'O.', as explained above; and it shews indications of being copied at an earlier date than 'G.', i.e. before 1440. On the whole, 'Th.' appears to me more correct than 'G.', and I have found it very serviceable. We learn from it, for example, that the scribe of 'G.' frequently dropped the prefix *y-* in past participles, giving l. 890 in the form 'For nought *clad* in silk was he,' instead of *y-clad*. Cf. ll. 892, 897, 900, &c.; see the foot-notes.

'Th.' supplies the deficiencies in G., viz. ll. 1-44, 333-380, &c., as well as four lines at the end; and suggests numerous corrections.

§ 24. The various later reprints of the 'Romaunt,' as in Speght (1598) and other editions, are merely less correct copies of 'Th.', and are not worth consulting. The only exceptions are the editions by Bell and Morris. Bell's text was the first for which 'G.' was consulted, and he follows the MS. as his general guide, filling up the deficiencies from Speght's edition, which he describes as 'corrupt and half-modernised.' Why he chose Speght in preference to Thynne, he does not tell us. In consequence, he has left lines incomplete in a large number of instances, owing to putting too much faith in the MS., and neglecting the better printed sources. Thus, in l. 890, he gives us 'clad' instead of '*y*-clad'; where any of the printed texts would have set him right.

Morris's edition is 'printed from the unique MS. in the Hunterian Museum, Glasgow'; but contains numerous corrections, apparently from Thynne. Thus, in l. 890, he reads '*y*-clad'; the *y-* being printed in italics to shew that it is not in the MS.

THE PRESENT EDITION.

§ 25. THE PRESENT EDITION.

The present edition principally follows 'G.', but it has been collated with 'Th.' throughout. Besides this, a large number of spellings in Fragment A. have been slightly amended on definite principles, the rejected spellings being given in the footnotes, whenever they are of the slightest interest or importance. Silent alterations are changes such as *i* for *y* in *king* for *kyng* (l. 10), and *whylom* for *whilom* (in the same line), to distinguish vowel-length; the use of *v* for consonantal *u* in *avisioun* for *auisioun* (l. 9); the use of *ee* for (long) *e* in *Iolitee* for *Iolite* (l. 52) for the sake of clearness; and a few other alterations of the like kind, which make the text easier to read without at all affecting its accuracy. I have also altered the suffix *-is* into *-es* in such words as *hertes* for *hertis* (l. 76); and changed the suffixes *-id* and *-ith* into the more usual *-ed* and *-eth*, both of which are common in the MS., usually giving notice; and in other similar minute ways have made the text more like the usual texts of Chaucer in appearance. But in Fragments B and C such changes have been made more sparingly.

I have also corrected numerous absolute blunders, especially in the use of the final *e*. For example, in l. 125, I have no hesitation in printing *wissh* for *wysshe*, because the use of final *e* at the end of a strong past tense, in the first person singular, is obviously absurd. Owing to the care with which the two authorities, 'G.' and Th.', have been collated, and my constant reference to the French original, I have no hesitation in saying that the present edition, if fairly judged, will be found to be more correct than its predecessors. For Dr. Kaluza's help I am most grateful.

§ 26. For example, in l. 1188, all the editions have *sarlynysh*, there being no such word. It is an obvious error for *Sarsinesshe* (riming with *fresshe*); for the F. text has *Sarrazinesche*, i.e. Saracenic.

In l. 1201, the authorities and Bell have *gousfaucoun*, which Morris alters to *gounfaucoun* in his text, and to *gownfaucoun* in his glossary. But all of these are 'ghost-words,' i.e. non-existent. Seeing that the original has *gonfanon*, it is clear that Chaucer wrote *gonfanoun*, riming with *renoun*.

In l. 1379, late editions have *lorey*; in l. 1313, Bell has *loreryes*, which Morris alters to *loreyes*. There is no such word as *lorey*. Thynne has *laurer*, *laurelles*. Considering that *loreres* rimes with *oliveres*, it is obvious that the right forms are *lorer* and *loreres* (French, *loriers*); see *laurer* in Stratmann.

In l. 1420, where the authorities have *veluet*, the modern editions have *velvet*. But the *u* (also written *ou*) was at that time a vowel, and *velu-et* (or *velou-et*) was trisyllabic, as the rhythm shews. The modern *velvet* seems to have arisen from a mistake.

Several other restorations of the text are pointed out in the notes, and I need not say more about them here.

N.B. After l. 4658, the lines in Morris's edition are misnumbered. His l. 4670 is really l. 4667; and so on. Also, 5700 is printed in the wrong place; and so is 6010; but without throwing out the numbering. Also, 6210 is only *nine* lines after 6200, throwing out the subsequent numbering, so that his l. 6220 is really 6216. At his l. 6232, 6231 is printed, and so counted; thus, his 6240 is really 6237. His 6380 is *eleven* lines after 6370, and is really 6378. After l. 7172, I insert two lines by translation, to fill up a slight gap. This makes his l. 7180 agree with my l. 7180, and brings his numbering right again.

For a few of the Notes, I am indebted to Bell's edition; but most of the work in them is my own.

§ 27. THE FRENCH TEXT.

For some account of the famous French poem entitled 'Le Roman de la Rose,' see Morley's English Writers, 1889, iv. 1. It was commenced by Guillaume de Lorris, born at Lorris, in the valley of the Loire, who wrote it at the age of five-and-twenty, probably between the years 1200 and 1230[1]. He must have died young, as he left the poem incomplete, though it then extended to 4070 lines. It was continued, a little more than 40 years after Guillaume's death, by Jean de Meun (or Meung), born (as he tells us) at Meung-sur-Loire, and surnamed *le Clopinel* (i. e. the hobbler, the lame). See, for these facts, the French text, ll. 10601, 10603, 10626. He added 18004 lines, so that the whole poem finally extended to the enormous length of 22074 lines.

Jean de Meun was a man of a very different temperament from his predecessor. Guillaume de Lorris merely planned a fanciful allegorical love-poem, in which the loved one was represented as a Rose in a beautiful garden, and the lover as one who desired

---

[1] The allusion to prince Edward, 'son of the lord of Windsor' (see note to l. 1250), is not in all the copies; so it may have been added afterwards. Edward I. was not born till 1239.

THE FRENCH ORIGINAL.

to pluck it, but was hindered by various allegorical personages, such as Danger, Shame, Jealousy, and Fear, though assisted by others, such as *Bel Accueil* (Fair Reception), Frankness, Pity, and the like. But Jean de Meun took up the subject in a keener and more earnest spirit, inserting some powerful pieces of satire against the degraded state of many women of the day and against various corruptions of the church. This infused a newer life into the poem, and made it extremely popular and successful. We may look upon the former part, down to l. 4432 of the translation, as a pretty and courtly description of a fanciful dream, whilst the remaining portion intersperses with the general description many forcible remarks, of a satirical nature, on the manners of the time, and affords numerous specimens of the author's erudition. Jean de Meun was the author of several other pieces, including a poem which he called his 'Testament.' He probably lived into the beginning of the fourteenth century, and died about 1318.

§ 28. Professor Morley gives a brief analysis of the whole poem, which will be found to be a useful guide through the labyrinth of this rambling poem. The chief points in it are the following.

The poet's dream begins, after a brief introduction, with a description of allegorical personages, as seen painted on the outside of the walls of a garden, viz. Hate and Felony, Covetousness, &c.; ll. 147–474 of the translation.

We may next note a description of Idleness, the young girl who opens the door of the garden (531–599); of Sir Mirth (600–644); of the garden itself (645–732); again, of Sir Mirth, the lady Gladness, Cupid, or the God of Love, with his two bows and ten arrows, and his bachelor, named Sweet-looking (733–998). Next comes a company of dancers, such as Beauty, Riches, Largesse (Bounty), Frankness, Courtesy, and Idleness again (999–1308). The poet next describes the trees in the garden (1349–1408), and the wells in the same (1409–1454); especially the well of Narcissus, whose story is duly told (1455–1648). THE ROSE-TREE (1649–1690). THE ROSE-BUD (1691–1714).

At l. 1705, Fragment A ends.

§ 29. Just at this point, the descriptions cease for a while, and the action, so to speak, begins. The God of Love seeks to wound the poet, or lover, with his arrows, and succeeds in doing so; after which he calls upon the lover to yield himself up as a prisoner, which he does (1715–2086). Love locks up the lover's heart, and gives him full instructions for his behaviour (2087–2950); after which Love vanishes (2951–2966). The Rose-tree is defended by a hedge; the lover seeks the assistance of Bialacoil or Belacoil (i. e. Fair-Reception), but is warned off by Danger, Wicked-Tongue, and Shame (2967–3166); and at last, Fair-Reception flees away (3167–3188). At this juncture, Reason comes to the lover, and gives him good advice; but he rejects it, and she leaves him to himself (3189–3334).

He now seeks the help of a Friend, and Danger allows him to come a little nearer, but tells him he must not pass within the hedge (3335–3498). Frankness and Pity now assist him, and he enters the garden, rejoined by Fair-Reception (3499–3626). THE ROSE appears more beautiful than ever, and the lover, aided by Venus, kisses it (3627–3772). This leads to trouble; Wicked-tongue and Jealousy raise opposition, Danger is reproved, and becomes more watchful than before (3773–4144). Jealousy builds a strong tower of stone, to guard the Rose-tree; the gates of the tower are guarded by Danger, Shame, Dread, and Wicked-tongue (4145–4276); and Fair-Reception is imprisoned within it (4277–4314). The lover mourns, and is inclined to despair (4315–4432).

§ 30. At this point, the work of G. de Lorris ceases, and Jean de Meun begins by echoing the word 'despair,' and declaring that he will have none of it. The lover reconsiders his position (4433–4614). Reason (in somewhat of a new character) revisits the lover, and again instructs him, declaring how love is made up of contrarieties, and discussing the folly of youth and the self-restraint of old-age (4615–5134). The lover again rejects Reason's advice, who continues her argument, gives a definition of Friendship, and discusses the variability of Fortune (5135–5560), the value of Poverty (5561–5696), and the vanity of Covetousness (5697–5810).

§ 31. Here ends Fragment B, and a large gap occurs in the translation. The omitted portion of the French text continues the discourse of Reason, with examples from the stories of Virginia, Nero, and Crœsus, and references to the fall of Manfred (conquered by Charles of Anjou) and the fate of Conradin. But all this is wasted on the lover, whom Reason quits once more. The lover applies a second time to his Friend, who recommends bounty or bribery. Here Jean de Meun discourses on prodigality, on women who take presents, on the Age of Gold, and on jealous husbands, with much satire interspersed, and many allusions, as for example, to Penelope, Lucretia, Abelard, Hercules, and others.

THE FRENCH ORIGINAL.

At last Love pities the lover, and descends to help him ; and, with the further assistance of Bounty, Honour, and other barons of Love's court, proceeds to lay siege to the castle in which Jealousy has imprisoned Fair-Reception.

§ 32. Here begins Fragment C ; in which the ranks of the besiegers are joined by other assistants of a doubtful and treacherous character, viz. False-Semblant and Constrained-Abstinence (5811–5876). Love discusses buying and selling, and the use of bounty and riches (5877-6016). Love's Barons ask Love to take False-Semblant and Constrained-Abstinence into his service (6017–6057). Love consents, but bids False-Semblant confess his true character (6058–6081). False-Semblant replies by truly exposing his own hypocrisy, with keen attacks upon religious hypocrites (6082–7334). Love now begins the assault upon the castle of Jealousy (7335–7352). A digression follows, regarding the outward appearance of False-Semblant and Constrained-Abstinence (7353–7420). The assailants advance to the gate guarded by Wicked-Tongue, who is harangued by Constrained-Abstinence (7421–7605), and by False-Semblant (7606–7696). And here the English version ends.

The above sketch gives a sufficient notion of the general contents of the poem. Of course the lover is ultimately successful, and carries off the Rose in triumph.

§ 33. It deserves to be noted, in conclusion, that, as the three Fragments of the English version, all taken together, represent less than a third of the French poem, we must not be surprised to find, as we do, that Chaucer's numerous allusions to, and citations from, the French poem, usually lie outside that part of it that happens to be translated. Still more often, they lie outside the part of it translated in Fragment A. Hence it seldom happens that we can compare his quotations with his own translation. In the chief instances where we can do so, we find that he has not repeated his own version *verbatim*, but has somewhat varied his expressions. I refer, in particular, to the Book of the Duchess, 284-6, as compared with Rom. Rose, 7–10 ; the same, 340-1, beside R.R., 130-1 ; the same, 410-2, beside R.R., 61-2 ; and the same, 419-426, 429-432, beside R.R., 1391-1403.

§ 34. In the present edition I have supplied the original French text, in the lower part of each page, as far as the end of Fragment A, where Chaucer's work ends. This text is exactly copied from the edition by M. Méon, published at Paris in four volumes in

1813[1]. I omit, however, the occasional versified headings, which appear as summaries and are of no consequence. Throughout the notes I refer to the lines as numbered in this edition. The later edition by M. Michel is practically useless for the purpose of reference, as the numbering of the lines in it is strangely incorrect. For example, line 3408 is called 4008, and the whole number of lines is made out to be 22817, which is largely in excess of the truth.

Fragments B and C are printed in smaller type, to mark their distinction from Fragment A; and the corresponding French text is omitted, to save space.

THE MINOR POEMS.

§ 1. It has been usual, in editions of Chaucer's Works, to mingle with those which he is known to have written, a heterogeneous jumble of poems by Gower, Lydgate, Hoccleve, Henrysoun, and various anonymous writers (some of quite late date), and then to accept a quotation from any one of them as being a quotation 'from Chaucer.' Some principle of selection is obviously desirable; and the first question that arises is, naturally, this: which of the Minor Poems are genuine? The list here given partly coincides with that adopted by Dr. Furnivall in the publications of the Chaucer Society. I have, however, added six, here numbered VI, XI, XII, XXI, XXII, and XXIII; my reasons for doing so are given below, where each poem is discussed separately. At the same time, I have omitted the poem entitled 'The Mother of God,' which is known to have been written by Hoccleve. The only known copy of it is in a MS. now in the library of the late Sir Thomas Phillipps, which contains sixteen poems, all of which are by the same hand, viz. that of Hoccleve. After all, it is only a translation; still, it is well and carefully written, and the imitation of Chaucer's style is good. In determining which poems have the best right to be reckoned as Chaucer's, we have to consider both the external and the internal evidence.

We will therefore consider, in the first place, the external evidence generally.

---

[1] Some copies are dated 1814; but I can detect no difference in them, except that the later copies have an additional frontispiece.

§ 2. Testimony of Chaucer regarding his works.

The most important evidence is that afforded by the poet himself. In an Introduction prefixed to the Man of Law's Prologue (Cant. Tales, B 57), he says—

'In youth he made of *Ceys and Alcion*'—

a story which is preserved at the beginning of the Book of the Duchesse.

In the Prologue to the Legend of Good Women (see vol. iii.), he refers to his translation of the Romaunce of the Rose, and to his Troilus; and, according to MS. Fairfax 16, ll. 417-423, he says—

'He made the book that hight the *Hous of Fame*,
And eke the Deeth of *Blaunche the Duchesse*,
And the *Parlement of Foules*, as I gesse,
And al the love of Palamon and Arcite
Of Thebes, thogh the story ys knowen lyte,
And many an ympne for your halydayes
That highten Balades, Roundels, Virelayes,' &c.

The rest of the passage does not immediately concern us, excepting ll. 427, 428, where we find—

'He made also, goon ys a grete while,
Origenes vpon the Maudeleyne.'

In the copy of the same Prologue, as extant in MS. Gg. 4. 27, in the Cambridge University Library, there are two additional lines, doubtless genuine, to this effect—

'And of the *wrechede engendrynge of mankynde*,
As man may in pope Innocent I-fynde.'

There is also a remarkable passage at the end of his Persones Tale, the genuineness of which has been doubted by some, but it appears in the MSS., and I do not know of any sound reason for rejecting it. According to the Ellesmere MS., he here mentions—'the book of Troilus, the book also of Fame, the book of the xxv. Ladies[1], the book of the Duchesse, the book of seint Valentynes day of the parlement of briddes . . . the book of the Leoun . . . and many a song,' &c.

Besides this, in the House of Fame, l. 729, he mentions his own name, viz. 'Geffrey.' We thus may be quite certain as to the genuineness of this poem, the longest and most important of all the Minor Poems[2], and we may at once add to the list the Book of

---

[1] The Legend of Good Women is here meant: and 'xxv.' is certainly an error for 'xix.'

[2] Printed *separately* in the present edition, in vol. iii.

22   THE MINOR POEMS.

the Duchesse, the next in order of length, and the Parliament of Foules, which is the third in the same order.

We also learn that he composed some poems which have not come down to us, concerning which a few words may be useful.

1. 'Origines vpon the Maudeleyne' must have been a translation from a piece attributed to Origen. In consequence, probably, of this remark of the poet, the old editions insert a piece called the 'Lamentacion of Marie Magdaleine,' which has no pretence to be considered Chaucer's, and may be summarily dismissed. It is sufficient to notice that it contains a considerable number of rimes such as are never found in his genuine works, as, for example, the dissyllabic *dy-e*[1] riming with *why* (st. 13); the plural adjective *ken-e* riming with *y-ën*, i. e. eyes, which would, with this Chaucerian pronunciation, be no rime at all (st. 19); and thirdly, *disgised* riming with *rived*, which is a mere assonance, and saves us from the trouble of further investigation (st. 25). See below, p. 37.

2. 'The wrechede engendrynge of mankynde' is obviously meant to describe a translation or imitation of the treatise by Pope Innocent III, entitled *De Miseria Conditionis Humanae*. The same treatise is referred to by Richard Rolle de Hampole, in his Pricke of Conscience, l. 498. It should be noted, however, that a few stanzas of this work have been preserved, by being incorporated (as quotations) in the Canterbury Tales, viz. in B 99-121, 421-7, 771-7, 925-31, 1135-8; cf. C 537-40, 551-2. See notes to these passages.

3. 'The book of the Leoun,' i. e. of the lion, was probably a translation of the poem called *Le Dit du Lion* by Machault; see the note to l. 1024 of the Book of the Duchesse in the present volume.

§ 3. Lydgate's List of Chaucer's Poems.

The next piece of evidence is that given in what is known as 'Lydgate's list.' This is contained in a long passage in the prologue to his poem known as the 'Fall of Princes,' translated from the French version (by Laurens de Premierfait) of the Latin book by Boccaccio, entitled 'De Casibus Virorum Illustrium[2].' In this

---

[1] Of course I mean that *dy-e* is the Chaucerian form; the author of the Lamentation pronounced it differently, viz. as *dy*.

[2] See the excellent treatise by Dr. E. Köppel entitled 'Laurents de Premierfait und John Lydgates Bearbeitungen von Boccaccios De Casibus Virorum Illustrium'; München, 1885.

Lydgate commends his 'maister Chaucer,' and mentions many of his works, as, e. g. Troilus and Creseide, the translation of Boethius' *De Consolatione Philosophiae*, the treatise on the Astrolabe addressed to his 'sonne that called was Lowys,' the Legend of Good Women, and the Canterbury Tales. The whole passage is given in Morris's edition of Chaucer, vol. i. pp. 79-81 ; but I shall only cite so much of it as refers to the Minor Poems, and I take the opportunity of doing so directly, from an undated black-letter edition published by John Wayland.

> ' He wrote also full many a day agone
> *Dant in English*, him-selfe doth so expresse,
> The piteous story of *Ceix and Alcion* :
> And the death also of *Blaunche the duches* :
> And notably [he] did his businesse
> By great auise his wittes to dispose,
> To translate the *Romaynt of the Rose.*
>
> ' Thus in vertue he set all his entent,
> Idelnes and vyces for to fle :
> Of *fowles* also he wrote *the parliament*,
> Therein remembring of royall Eagles thre,
> Howe in their choyse they felt aduersitye,
> To-fore nature profered the battayle,
> Eche for his partye, if it woulde auayle.
>
> ' He did also his diligence and payne
> In our vulgare to translate and endite
> *Orygene vpon the Maudelayn* :
> And of *the Lyon a boke* he did write.
> Of *Annelida and of false Arcite*
> He made *a complaynt* dolefull and piteous;
> And of *the broche which that Uulcanus*
>
> ' *At Thebes* wrought, ful diuers of nature.
> Ouide[1] writeth : who-so thereof had a syght,
> For high desire, he shoulde not endure
> But he it had, neuer be glad ne light :
> And if he had it once in his myght,
> Like as my master sayth & writeth in dede,
> It to conscrue he shoulde euer liue in dred.'

It is clear to me that Lydgate is, *at first*, simply repeating the information which we have already had upon Chaucer's own authority ; he begins by merely following Chaucer's own language in the extracts above cited. Possibly he knew no more than we do of 'Orygene vpon the Maudelayn,' and of the 'boke of the Lyon.' At any rate,

---

[1] Not Ovid, but Statius ; Lydgate makes a slip here ; see note to IV. 245.

he tells us no more about them. Naturally, in speaking of the Minor Poems, we should expect to find him following, as regards the three chief poems, the order of length ; that is, we should expect to find here a notice of (1) the House of Fame ; (2) the Book of the Duchesse ; and (3) the Parliament of Foules. We are naturally disposed to exclaim with Ten Brink (*Studien*, p. 152)—'Why did he leave out the House of Fame?' But we need not say with him, that 'to this question I know of no answer.' For it is perfectly clear to me, though I cannot find that any one else seems to have thought of it, that 'Dant in English' and 'The House of Fame' are one and the same poem, described in the same position and connexion. If anything about the House of Fame is clear at all, it is that (as Ten Brink so clearly points out, in his *Studien*, p. 89) the influence of Dante is more obvious in this poem than in any other. I would even go further and say that it is the *only* poem which owes its chief inspiration to Dante in the whole of English literature during, at least, the Middle-English period. There is absolutely nothing else to which such a name as 'Dante in English' can with any fitness be applied. The phrase 'himselfe doth so expresse' is rather dubious ; but I take it to mean : '(I give it that name, for) he, i. e. Chaucer, expresses himself like Dante (therein).' In any case, I refuse to take any other view until some competent critic will undertake to tell me, what poem of Chaucer's, other than the House of Fame, can possibly be intended.

To which argument I have to add a second, viz. that Lydgate mentions the House of Fame in yet another way ; for he refers to it at least three times, in clear terms, in other passages of the same poem, i. e. of the Fall of Princes.

'Fame in her palice hath trumpes mo than one,
Some of golde, that geueth a freshe soun'; &c.—Book I. cap. 14.

'Within my house called the house of Fame
The golden trumpet with blastes of good name
Enhaunceth on to ful hie parties,
Wher Iupiter sytteth among the heuenly skies.

'Another trumpet of sownes ful vengeable
Which bloweth vp at feastes funerall,
Nothinge bright, but of colour sable'; &c.—Prol. to Book VI.

'The golden trumpe of the house of Fame [1]
Through the world blew abrode his name.'—Book VI. cap. 15.

---

[1] In Lydgate's Lyfe of St. Albon, ed. Hortsmann, l. 15, this line appears in the more melodious form—'The golden trumpet of the House of Fame.'

Lydgate describes the Parliament of Foules in terms which clearly shew that he had read it. He also enables us to add to our list the Complaint of Anelida and the Complaint of Mars; for it is the latter poem which contains the story of the *broche* of Thebes. We have, accordingly, complete authority for the genuineness of the House of Fame and the four longest of the Minor Poems, which, as arranged in order of length, are these: The House of Fame (2158 lines); Book of the Duchesse (1334 lines); Parliament of Foules (699 lines); Anelida and Arcite (357 lines); and Complaint of Mars (298 lines). This gives us a total of 4846 lines, furnishing a very fair standard of comparison whereby to consider the claims to genuineness of other poems. Lydgate further tells us that Chaucer

> 'Made and compiled many a freshe dittie,
> Complaynts, ballades, rou*n*dels, vyrelaies.'

§ 4. Testimony of John Shirley.

The next best evidence is that afforded by notes in the existing MSS.; and here, in particular, we should first consider the remarks by Chaucer's great admirer, John Shirley, who took considerable pains to copy out and preserve his poems, and is said by Stowe to have died Oct. 21, 1456, at the great age of ninety, so that he was born more than 30 years before Chaucer died. On his authority, we may attribute to Chaucer the A. B. C.; the Complaint to Pity; the Complaint of Mars (according to a heading in MS. T.); the Complaint of Anelida (according to a heading in MS. Addit. 16165); the Lines to Adam, called in MS. T. 'Chauciers Wordes a. Geffrey vn-to Adam his owen scryveyne'; Fortune; Truth; Gentilesse; Lak of Stedfastnesse; the Compleint of Venus; and the Compleint to his Empty Purse. The MSS. due to Shirley are the Sion College MS., Trin. Coll. Cam. R. 3. 20, Addit. 16165, Ashmole 59, Harl. 78, Harl. 2251, and Harl. 7333. See also § 23, p. 75.

§ 5. Testimony of Scribes of the MSS.

The Fairfax MS. 16, a very fair MS. of the fifteenth century, contains several of the Minor Poems; and in this the name of Chaucer is written at the end of the poem on Truth and of the Compleint to his Purse; it also appears in the title of Lenvoy de *Chaucer* a Scogan; in that of Lenvoy de *Chaucer* a Bukton; in that of the Compleint of *Chaucer* to his empty Purse, and in that of 'Proverbe of *Chaucer*.'

THE MINOR POEMS.

Again, the Pepys MS. no. 2006 attributes to Chaucer the A. B. C., the title there given being 'Pryer a nostre Dame, per Chaucer'; as well as the Compleint to his Purse, the title being 'La Compleint de Chaucer a sa Bourse Voide.' It also has the title 'Lenvoy de Chaucer a Scogan.' See also p. 80, note 2.

The 'Former Age' is entitled 'Chawcer vp-on this fyfte metur of the second book' in the Cambridge MS. Ii. 3. 21; and at the end of the same poem is written 'Finit etas prima. Chaucers' in the Cambridge MS. Hh. 4. 12. The poem on Fortune is also marked 'Causer' in the former of these MSS.; indeed, these two poems practically belong to Chaucer's translation of Boethius, though probably written at a somewhat later period. After all, the most striking testimony to their authenticity is the fact that, in MS. Ii. 3. 21, these two poems are inserted in the very midst of the prose text of 'Boethius,' between the fifth metre and the sixth prose of Book II.

The Cambridge MS. Gg. 4. 27, which contains an excellent copy of the Canterbury Tales, attributes to Chaucer the Parliament of Foules; and gives us the title 'Litera directa de Scogon per G. C.' Of course 'G. C.' is Geoffrey Chaucer.

From Furnivall's *Trial Forewords*, p. 13, we learn that there is a verse translation of De Deguileville's *Pèlerinage do la Vie Humaine*, attributed to Lydgate, in MS. Cotton, Vitellius C. XIII. (leaf 256), in which the 'A. B. C.' is distinctly attributed to Chaucer[1].

The Balade 'To Rosamounde' is assigned to Chaucer in the unique copy of it in the Rawlinson MS. 'A Compleint to his Lady' is assigned to Chaucer in the only *complete* copy of it.

We ought also to assign *some* value to the manner in which the poems appear in the MS. copies. This can only be appreciated by inspection of the MSS. themselves. Any one who will *look for himself* at the copies of Gentilesse, Lak of Stedfastnesse, Truth, and Against Women Inconstaunt in MS. Cotton, Cleop. D. 7, will see that the scribe clearly regarded the last of these as genuine, as well as the rest. And the same may be said of some other poems which are not absolutely marked with Chaucer's name. This im-

---

[1] Hoccleve's poem entitled 'Moder of God' is erroneously attributed to Chaucer in two Scottish copies (Arch. Seld. B 24, and Edinb. 18. 2. 8). But it occurs among 16 poems, *all* by Hoccleve, in a MS. in the collection of the late Sir Thos. Phillipps, as already noted in § 1 above. A few of these poems (*not* including the 'Moder of God') were printed from this MS. in the edition of some of 'Occleve's Poems' by G. Mason, in 1796.

portant argument is easily derided by those who cannot read MSS., but it remains valuable all the same.

§ 6. Testimony of Caxton.

At p. 116 of the same *Trial Forewords* is a description by Mr. Bradshaw of a very rare edition by Caxton of some of Chaucer's Minor Poems. It contains: (1) Parliament of Foules; (2) a treatise by Scogan, in which Chaucer's 'Gentilesse' is introduced; (3) a single stanza of 7 lines, beginning—'Wyth empty honde men may no hawkes lure'; (4) Chaucer's 'Truth,' entitled—'The good counceyl of Chawcer'; (5) the poem on 'Fortune'; and (6) part of Lenvoy to Scogan, viz. the first three stanzas. The volume is imperfect at the end. As to the article No. 3, it was probably included because the first line of it is quoted from l. 415 of the Wyf of Bathes Prologue (Cant. Ta. 5997, vol. iv. p. 332).

At p. 118 of the same is another description, also by Mr. Bradshaw, of a small quarto volume printed by Caxton, consisting of only ten leaves. It contains, according to him: (1) Anelida and Arcite, ll. 1–210; (2) The Compleint of Anelida, being the continuation of the former, ll. 211–350, where the poem ends; (3) The Compleint of Chaucer vnto his empty purse, with an Envoy headed—'Thenuoye of Chaucer vnto the kynge'; (4) Three[1] couplets, beginning—'Whan feyth failleth in prestes sawes,' and ending—'Be brought to grete confusioun'; (5) Two couplets, beginning—'Hit falleth for euery gentilman,' and ending—'And the soth in his presence'; (6) Two couplets, beginning—'Hit cometh by kynde of gentil blode,' and ending—'The werk of wisedom berith witnes'; followed by—'Et sic est finis.' The last three articles only make fourteen lines in all, and are of little importance[2].

§ 7. Early Editions of Chaucer's Works.

The first collected edition of Chaucer's Works is that edited by W. Thynne in 1532, but there were earlier editions of his separate poems. The best account of these is that which I here copy from a note on p. 70 of Furnivall's edition of F. Thynne's 'Animaduersions vpon the Annotacions and Corrections of some imperfections of im-

---

[1] Printed 'Six couplets'; clearly a slip of the pen.
[2] They are printed in full below, on p. 46.

pressiones of Chaucer's Workes'; published for the Chaucer Society in 1875.

Only one edition of Chaucer's *Works* had been published before the date of Thynne's, 1532, and that was Pynson's in 1526, without a general title, but containing three parts, with separate signatures, and seemingly intended to sell separately; 1. the boke of Caunterbury tales; 2. the boke of Fame ... with dyuers other of his workes [i. e. Assemble of Foules[1], La Belle Dame[2], Morall Prouerbes]; 3. the boke of Troylus and Cryseyde. But of separate works of Chaucer before 1532, the following had been published:—

Canterbury Tales. **1.** Caxton, about 1477-8, from a poor MS.; **2.** Caxton, ab. 1483, from a better MS.; **3.** Pynson, ab. 1493; **4.** Wynkyn de Worde, 1498; **5.** Pynson, 1526.

Book of Fame. **1.** Caxton, ab. 1483; **2.** Pynson, 1526.

Troylus. **1.** Caxton, ab. 1483; **2.** Wynkyn de Worde, 1517; **3.** Pynson, 1526.

Parliament of Foules[3]. **1.** Caxton, ab. 1477-8; **2.** Pynson, 1526, **3.** Wynkyn de Worde, 1530.

Gentilnesse[3] (in Scogan's poem). **1.** Caxton, ab. 1477-8.

Truth[3]. (The good counceyl of chawcer.) **1.** Caxton, ab. 1477-8.

Fortune[3]. (Balade of the vilage (*sic*) without peyntyng.) **1.** Caxton, ab. 1477-8.

Envoy to Skogan[3]. **1.** Caxton, ab. 1477-8 (all lost, after the third stanza).

Anelida and Arcyte[4]. **1.** Caxton, ab. 1477-8.

Purse[4]. (The compleynt of Chaucer vnto his empty purse.) **1.** Caxton, ab. 1477-8.

Mars; Venus; Marriage (Lenvoy to Bukton). **1.** Julian Notary, 1499-1502.

After Thynne's first edition of the *Works* in 1532 (printed by Thomas Godfray), came his second in 1542 (for John Reynes and Wyllyam Bonham), to which he added 'The Plowman's Tale' *after* the Parson's Tale, i. e. at the end.

---

[1] i. e. the Parliament of Foules.

[2] La Belle Dame sans Merci, a poem translated from the French originally written by 'Maister Aleyn,' chief secretary to the King of France. Certainly not by Chaucer; for Alain Chartier, the author of the original French poem, was only about *four* years old when Chaucer died. Moreover, it is now known that the author of the English poem was Sir Richard Ros. See p. 35, note 2.

[3] All in Caxton's edition of the Minor Poems, described above, p. 27.

[4] Both in the small quarto volume described above, p. 27.

Then came a reprint for the booksellers (Wm. Bonham, R. Kele, T. Petit, Robert Toye), about 1550, which put the Plowman's Tale *before* the Parson's. This was followed by an edition in 1561 for the booksellers (Ihon Kyngston, Henry Bradsha, citizen and grocer of London, &c.), to which, when more than half printed, Stowe contributed some fresh pieces, the spurious *Court of Love*, Lydgate's *S'ge of Thebes*, and other poems. Next came Speght's edition of 1598—on which William Thynne comments in his *Animadversions*—which added the spurious 'Dreme,' and 'Flower and Leaf.' This was followed by Speght's second edition, in 1602, in which Francis Thynne helped him, and to which were added Chaucer's 'A. B. C.', and the spurious 'Jack Upland [1].' Jack Upland had been before printed, with Chaucer's name on the title-page, about 1536-40 (London, J. Gough, no date, 8vo.).

In an Appendix to the Preface to Tyrwhitt's edition of the Canterbury Tales, there is a similar account of the early editions of Chaucer, to which the reader may refer. He quotes the whole of Caxton's preface to his second edition of the Canterbury Tales, shewing how Caxton reprinted the book because he had meanwhile come upon a more correct MS. than that which he had first followed.

If we now briefly consider all the earlier editions, we find that they may be thus tabulated.

SEPARATE WORKS. Various editions before 1532; see the list above, on p. 28.

COLLECTED WORKS. Pynson's edition of 1526, containing only a portion, as above; *La Belle Dame* being spurious. Also the following:—

1. Ed. by Wm. Thynne; London, 1532. Folio. Pr. by Godfray.
2. Reprinted, with additional matter; London, 1542. Folio.

The chief addition is the spurious Plowman's Tale.

3. Reprinted, with the matter rearranged; London, no date, about 1550. Folio. (Of this edition I possess a copy.)

Here the Plowman's Tale is put before the Parson's. Moreover, the three pieces numbered 66-68 below (p. 45), are inserted at the end of the Table of Contents.

4. Reprinted, with large additions by John Stowe. London, 1561. Folio. (See further below, p. 31). I possess a copy.

---

[1] Speght added *three more* pieces, but they are also found in ed. 1550 and ed. 1542, at the end of the Table of Contents; see below, p. 45, nos. 66-8.

5. Reprinted, with additions and alterations by Thomas Speght; London, 1598. Folio.

Here, for the first time, appear 'Chaucer's Dream' and 'The Flower and the Leaf'; both are spurious.

6. Reprinted, with further additions and alterations by Thomas Speght; London, 1602. Folio.

Here, for the first time, appear the spurious Jack Upland[1] and the genuine A. B. C.

7. Reprinted, with slight additions; London, 1687. Folio.

8. Reprinted, with additions and great alterations in spelling, by John Urry; London, 1721. Folio.

This edition is the worst that has appeared. It is not necessary for our purpose to enumerate the numerous later editions. An entirely new edition of the Canterbury Tales was produced by Thomas Tyrwhitt in 1775–8, in 5 vols., 8vo.; to which all later editions have been much indebted [2].

The manner in which these editions were copied one from the other renders it no very difficult task to describe the whole contents of them accurately. The only important addition in the editions of 1542 and 1550 is the spurious Plowman's Tale, which in no way concerns us. Again, the only important additional poems after 1561 are the spurious *Chaucer's Dream, The Flower and the Leaf*, and the genuine *A. B. C.* The two representative editions are really those of 1532 and 1561. Now the edition of 1561 consists of two parts; the former consists of a reprint from former editions, and so differs but little from the edition of 1532; whilst the latter part consists of additional matter furnished by John Stowe. Hence a careful examination of the edition of 1561 is, practically, nearly sufficient to give us all the information which we need. I shall therefore give a complete table of the contents of this edition.

---

[1] Jack Upland is *in prose*, and in the form of a succession of questions directed against the friars.

[2] I have often made use of a handy edition with the following titlepage: 'The Poetical Works of Geoffrey Chaucer, with an Essay on his Language and Versification and an Introductory Discourse, together with Notes and a Glossary. By Thomas Tyrwhitt. London, Edward Moxon, Dover Street, 1855.' I cannot but think that this title-page may have misled others, as it for a long time misled myself. As a fact, Tyrwhitt never edited anything beyond the Canterbury Tales, though he has left us some useful notes upon the Minor Poems, and his Glossary covers the whole ground. The Minor Poems in this edition are merely *reprinted* from the black-letter editions.

§ 8. Table of Contents of Stowe's Edition (1561)[1].

Part I. Reprinted Matter.

1. Caunterburie Tales. (The Prologue begins on a page with the signature A 2, the first quire of six leaves not being numbered; the Knightes Tale begins on a page with the signature B ii, and marked Fol. i. The spurious Plowman's Tale precedes the Parson's Tale.)
2. *The Romaunt of the Rose*[2]. Fol. cxvi.
3. Troilus and Creseide. Fol. cli., back.
4. *The testament of Creseide*. [By Robert Henryson.] Fol. cxciiii. Followed by its continuation, called *The Complaint of Creseide*; by the same.
5. The Legende of Good Women. Fol. cxcvij.
6. *A goodlie balade of Chaucer*; beginning—'Mother of norture, best beloued of all.' Fol. ccx.
7. Boecius de Consolatione Philosophie. Fol. ccx., back.
8. The dreame of Chaucer. [The Book of the Duchesse.] Fol. ccxliiij.
9. Begins—'My master. &c. When of Christ our kyng.' [Lenvoy to Buckton.] Fol. ccxliiii[3].
10. The assemble of Foules. [Parlement of Foules.] Fol. ccxliiii., back.
11. *The Floure of Curtesie, made by Ihon lidgate*. Fol. ccxlviij. Followed by a Balade, which forms part of it.
12. How pyte is deed, etc. [Complaint unto Pite.] Fol. ccxlix., back.
13. *La belle Dame sans Mercy*. [By Sir R. Ros.] Fol. ccl.
14. Of Quene Annelida and false Arcite. Fol. cclv.
15. *The assemble of ladies*. Fol. ccxlvij.
16. The conclucions of the Astrolabie. Fol. cclxi.

---

[1] Probably copies slightly differ. The book described by me is a copy in my own possession, somewhat torn at the beginning, and imperfect at the end. But the three missing leaves only refer to Lydgate's *Storie of Thebes*.

[2] I print *in italics* the names of the pieces which I reject as spurious. In the case of *The Romaunt of the Rose*, the first 1705 lines are genuine; but the rest, which is spurious, is more than three-fourths of the whole. See p. 1 above.

[3] I. e. the folios are misnumbered. Piece 8 begins with fol. ccxliiii, which is followed by ccxlvj (*sic*), ccxli (*sic*), ccxli (*repeated*), ccxlii, and ccxliii; which brings us to 'ccxliiii' over again.

THE MINOR POEMS.

17. *The complaint of the blacke Knight.* [By Lydgate; see p. 35, note 3.] Fol. cclxx.

18. *A praise of Women.* Begins—'Al tho the lyste of women euill to speke.' Fol. cclxxiii.[1], back.

19. The House of Fame. Fol. cclxxiiij., back.

20. *The Testament of Loue* (in prose). Fol. cclxxxiiij., back.

21. *The lamentacion of Marie Magdaleine.* Fol. cccxviij.

22. *The remedie of Loue.* Fol. cccxxj., back.

23, 24. The complaint of Mars and Venus. Fol. cccxxiiij., back. (Printed as *one* poem; but there is a new title—The complaint of Venus—at the beginning of the latter.)

25. *The letter of Cupide.* [By Hoccleve; *dated* 1402.] Fol. cccxxvj., back.

26. *A Ballade in commendacion of our Ladie.* Fol. cccxxix. [By Lydgate; see p. 38.]

27. *Ihon Gower vnto the noble King Henry the .iiij.* Fol. cccxxx., back. [By Gower.]

28. *A saiyng of dan Ihon.* [By Lydgate.] Fol. cccxxxii., back [2].

29. *Yet of the same.* [By Lydgate.] On the same page.

30. *Balade de bon consail.* Begins—If it be fall that God the list visite. (Only 7 lines.) On the same page.

31. *Of the Cuckowe and the Nightingale.* Fol. cccxxxiij. [By Hoccleve?]

32. *Balade with Envoy* (no title). Begins—'O leude booke w*ith* thy foule rudenesse.' Fol. cccxxxiiij., back.

33. *Scogan, vnto the Lordes and Gentilmen of the Kinges house.* (This poem, by H. Scogan, quotes Chaucer's 'Gentilesse' in full.) Fol. cccxxxiiij., back.

34. Begins—'Somtyme the worlde so stedfast was and stable.' [Lak of Stedfastnesse.] Fol. cccxxxv., back.

35. Good counsail of Chaucer. [Truth.] Same page.

36. Balade of the village (*sic*) without paintyng. [Fortune.] Fol. cccxxxvj.

37. Begins—'Tobroken been the statutes hie in heauen'; headed *Lenuoye.* [Lenvoy to Scogan.] Fol. cccxxxvj., back.

38. *Poem in two stanzas of seven lines each.* Begins—'Go foorthe kyng, rule thee by Sapience.' Same page.

39. Chaucer to his emptie purse. Same page.

---

[1] Marked Fol. cclxxvj by mistake.
[2] Nos. 28–30 are in no previous edition.

40. *A balade of good counseile translated out of Latin verses in-to Englishe, by Dan Ihon lidgat cleped the monke of Buri.* Begins— 'COnsyder well euery circumstaunce.' Fol. cccxxxvij.

41. *A balade in the Praise and commendacion of master Geffray Chauser for his golden eloquence.* (Only 7 lines.) Same leaf, back. [See p. 56.]

§ 9. Part II. Additions by John Stowe.

At the top of fol. cccxl. is the following remark:—

¶ Here foloweth certaine woorkes of Geffray Chauser, whiche hath not heretofore been printed, and are gathered and added to this booke by Ihon Stowe.

42. A balade made by Chaucer, teching what is gentilnes[1]. [Gentilesse.] Fol. cccxl.

43. A Prouerbe [*read* Prouerbs] agaynst couitise and negligence. [Proverbs.] Same page.

44. A balade which Chaucer made agaynst women vnconstaunt. Same page. [Certainly genuine, in my opinion; but here relegated to an Appendix, to appease such as cannot readily apprehend my reasons. Cf. p. 26.]

45. *A balade which Chaucer made in the praise or rather dispraise, of women for their doublenes.* [By Lydgate.] Begins—'This world is full of variaunce.' Same page.

46. *This werke folowinge was compiled by Chaucer, and is caled the craft of louers.* Fol. cccxli. [Written in 1448.]

47. A Balade. Begins—'Of their nature they greatly the*m* delite.' Fol. cccxli., back. [Quotes from no. 56.]

48. *The .x. Commaundementes of Loue.* Fol. cccxlij.

49. *The .ix. Ladies worthie.* Fol. cccxlij., back.

50. [*Virelai; no title.*] Begins—'Alone walkyng.' Fol. cccxliij.

51. A Ballade. Begins—'In the season of Feuerere when it was full colde.' Same page.

52. A Ballade. Begins—'O Mercifull and o merciable.' Fol. cccxliij., back. [Made up of scraps from late poems; see p. 57.]

53. *Here foloweth how Mercurie with Pallas, Venus and Minarua, appeared to Paris of Troie, he slepyng by a fountain.* Fol. cccxliiij.

54. *A balade pleasaunte.* Begins—'I haue a Ladie where so she

---

[1] Stowe did not observe that this had occurred already, in the midst of poem no. 33.

bee.' Same page. At the end—'Explicit the discriuyng of a faire Ladie.'

55. *An other Balade.* Begins—'O Mossie Quince, hangyng by your stalke.' Fol. cccxliiij., back.

56. *A balade, warnyng men to beware of deceitptfnll women* (*sic*). Begins—'LOke well aboute ye that louers bee.' Same page. [By Lydgate.]

57. These verses next folowing were compiled by Geffray Chauser, and in the writen copies foloweth at the ende of the complainte of petee. Begins—'THe long nyghtes when euery [c]reature.' [This is the 'Compleint to his Lady,' as I venture to call it.] Fol. cccxlv[1].

58. *A balade declaring that wemens chastite Doeth moche excel all treasure worldly.* Begins—'IN womanhede as auctours al write.' Back of same leaf.

59. *The Court of Loue.* Begins—'WIth temerous herte, and trembling hand of drede.' Fol. cccxlviij.

60. Chaucers woordes vnto his owne Scriuener[2]. Fol. ccclv., back. *At the end*—Thus endeth the workes of Geffray Chaucer. (This is followed by 34 Latin verses, entitled *Epitaphium Galfridi Chaucer,* &c.)

61. *The Storie of Thebes.* [By Lydgate.] Fol. ccclvj.

§ 10. DISCUSSION OF THE POEMS IN PART I. OF ED. 1561.

Of the 41 pieces in Part I. of the above, we must of course accept as Chaucer's the four poems entitled Canterbury Tales, Troilus, Legend of Good Women, and House of Fame; also the prose translation of Boethius, and the prose treatise on the Astrolabie. The remaining number of Minor Poems (excluding the Romaunt of the Rose) is 34; out of which number I accept the 13 numbered above with the numbers 8, 9, 10, 12, 14, 23, 24, 33 (so far as it quotes Chaucer), 34, 35, 36, 37, and 39. Every one of these has already been shewn to be genuine on sufficient external evidence, and it is not likely that their genuineness will be doubted. In the present volume they

---

[1] Miscalled Fol. cccxxxix. Also, the next folio is called cccxlviij., after which follows cccxlix., and so on.

[2] In the Preface to Morris's Chaucer, p. x, we are told that the editor took his copy of this poem from Thynne's edition of 1532. This is an oversight; for it does not occur there; Stowe's edition is meant.

appear, respectively, as nos. III, XVII, V, II, VII, IV, XVIII, XIV, XV, XIII, X, XVI, XIX. Of the remaining 21, several may be dismissed in a few words. No. 4 is well known to have been written by Robert Henryson. Nos. 11, 28, 29, and 40 are distinctly claimed for Lydgate in all the editions; and no. 27 is similarly claimed for Gower. No. 25 was written by Hoccleve[1]; and the last line gives the date—'A thousande, foure hundred and seconde,' i.e. 1402, or two years after Chaucer's death. No. 13 is translated from Alain Chartier, who was only four years old when Chaucer died; see p. 28, note 2. Tyrwhitt remarks that, in MS. Harl. 372, this poem is expressly attributed to a Sir Richard Ros[2]. No one can suppose that no. 41 is by Chaucer, seeing that the first line is — 'Maister Geffray Chauser, that now lithe in graue.' Mr. Bradshaw once assured me that no. 17 is ascribed, on MS. authority, to Lydgate; and no one who reads it with care can doubt that this is correct[3]. It is, in a measure, an imitation of the Book of the Duchesse; and it contains some interesting references to Chaucer, as in the lines— 'Of Arcite, or of him Palemoun,' and 'Of Thebes eke the false Arcite.' No. 20, i.e. the Testament of Love, is *in prose*, and does not here concern us; still it is worth pointing out that it contains a passage (near the end) such as we cannot suppose that Chaucer would have written concerning himself[4].

After thus removing from consideration nos. 4, 11, 13, 17, 20, 25, 27, 28, 29, 40, and 41, half of the remaining 21 pieces have been considered. The only ones left over for consideration are nos. 6, 15, 18, 21, 22, 26, 30, 31, 32, 38. As to no. 6, there is some

---

[1] 'Thomas Occleve mentions it himself, as one of his own compositions, in a *Dialogue* which follows his *Complaint*, MS. Bodley 1504.'—Tyrwhitt.

[2] See Political, Religious, and Love Poems, ed. Furnivall, p. 52. Cf. *Englische Studien*, x. 206.

[3] I have found the reference. It is Shirley who says so, in a poetical 'introduction'; see MS. Addit. 16165, fol. 3.

[4] It runs thus:—'Quod loue, I shall tel thee, this lesson to learne, myne owne true seruaunte, the noble Philosophicall Poete in Englishe, which euermore hym busieth & trauaileth right sore, my name to encrease, wherefore all that willen me good, owe to doe him worship and reuerence both; truly his better ne his pere, in schole of my rules, coud I neuer finde: He, quod she, in a treatise that he made of my seruaunt Troilus, hath this matter touched, & at the full this question [*of predestination*] assoiled. Certainly his noble saiyngs can I not amend; in goodness of gentil manlich spech, without any maner of nicitie of starieres (*sic*) imaginacion, in wit and in good reason of sentence, he passeth al other makers'; ed. 1561. (Read *storieres*, story-writer's.)

external evidence in its favour, which will be duly considered; but as to the rest, there is absolutely nothing to connect them with Chaucer beyond their almost accidental appearance in an edition by Wm. Thynne, published in 1532, i. e. *one hundred and thirty-two years after Chaucer's death*; and it has just been demonstrated that Thynne is obviously wrong in at least *eleven* instances, and that he wittingly and purposely chose to throw into his edition poems which he *knew* to have been written by Lydgate or by Gower! It is ridiculous to attach much importance to such testimony as this. And now let me discuss, as briefly as I can, the above-named poems separately.

6. *A goodlie balade of Chaucer*; begins —' Mother of norture, best beloued of all'; printed in Morris's edition, vi. 275; and in Bell's edition, iii. 413. I have little to say against this poem; yet the rime of *supposeth* with *riseth* (st. 8) is somewhat startling. It is clearly addressed to a lady named *Margaret*[1], as appears from her being likened to the daisy, and called the sun's daughter. I suspect it was merely attributed to Chaucer by association with the opening lines of the Legend of Good Women. The suggestion, in Bell's Chaucer, that it possibly refers to the Countess of Pembroke, is one of those bad guesses which are discreditable. Tyrwhitt shews, in note *n* to his 'Appendix to the Preface,' that she must have died not later than 1370, whereas this Balade must be much later than that date; and I agree with him in supposing that *le Dit de la fleur de lis et de la Marguerite*, by Guillaume de Machault (printed in Tarbé's edition, 1849, p. 123), and the *Dittié de la flour de la Margherite*, by Froissart, may furnish us with the true key to those mystical compliments which Chaucer and others were accustomed to pay to the daisy.

I wish to add that I am convinced that one stanza, probably the sixth is missing. It ought to form a triple Balade, i. e. three Balades of 21 lines each, each with its own refrain; but the second is imperfect. There seems to be some affectation about the letters beginning the stanzas which I cannot solve; these are *M, M, M* (probably for Margaret) in the first Balade; *D, D* in the second; and *J, C, Q* in the third. The poet goes out of his way to bring in these letters. The result looks like *Margaret de Jacques*; but this guess does not help us.

---

[1] Hoccleve appeals to St. Margaret, in his Letter of Cupid, st. 6 from the end. Lydgate wrote 'the Lyfe of St. Margarete.' I have a strong feeling that the poem is one of Lydgate's. Lines 24-26 seem to be imitated from Chaucer's Legend of Good Women, ll. 197-9.

The poem is rather artificial, especially in such inversions as *It receyve, Cauteles whoso useth,* and *Quaketh my penne;* these things are not in Chaucer's manner. In the second stanza there is a faulty rime; for we there find *shal, smal,* answering to the dissyllabic rimes *alle, calle, appalle, befalle,* in stanzas 1 and 3. Lydgate has: 'My pen quake,' &c.; Troy Book, ch. x., fol. F2, back.

15. *The assemble of Ladies.* This poem Tyrwhitt decisively rejects. There is absolutely *nothing* to connect it with Chaucer. It purports to have been written by 'a gentlewoman'; and perhaps it was. It ends with the rime of *done,* pp., with *sone* (soon); which in Chaucer are spelt *doon* and *son-e* respectively, and never rime. Most of the later editions omit this poem. It is conveniently printed in Chalmers' English Poets, vol. i. p. 526; and consists of 108 7-line stanzas. For further remarks, see notes on *The Flower and the Leaf* (p. 44).

At p. 203 of the Ryme-Index to Chaucer's Minor Poems (Chaucer Society), I have printed a Ryme-Index to this poem, shewing that the number of non-Chaucerian rimes in it is about 60.

18. *A praise of Women.* In no way connected with Chaucer. Rejected by Tyrwhitt. Printed in Bell's edition, iv. 416, and in Chalmers' English Poets, vol. i. p. 344; also in Morris's Aldine edition, vol. vi. p. 278. In twenty-five 7-line stanzas. The rime of *lie* (to tell a lie) with *sie* (I saw), in st. 20, is suspicious; Chaucer has *ly-e, sy.* The rime of *queen-e* (usually dissyllabic in Chaucer) with *beene* (miswritten for *been,* they be, st. 23) is also suspicious. It contains the adjective *sere,* i.e. various (st. 11), which Chaucer never uses.

21. *The lamentacion of Marie Magdaleine.* Printed in Bell's Chaucer, iv. 395; and in Chalmers, i. 532. Tyrwhitt's remarks are admirable. He says, in his Glossary, s. v. *Origenes:*—'In the list of Chaucer's Works, in Legend of Good Women, l. 427, he says of himself:—

"He made also, gon is a grete while,
Origenes upon the Maudeleine"—

meaning, I suppose, a translation, into prose or verse, of the Homily *de Maria Magdalena,* which has been commonly, though falsely, attributed to Origen; v. Opp. Origenis, T. ii. p. 291, ed. Paris, 1604. I cannot believe that the poem entitled *The Lamentation of Marie Magdaleine,* which is in all the [older] editions of Chaucer, is really that work of his. It can hardly be considered as a translation, or even as an imitation, of the Homily; and the composition, in every respect, is infinitely meaner than the worst of his genuine pieces. To those who are interested in Chaucer's rimes I will merely point out the following: *die, why* (Ch. *dy-e, why*); *kene, iyen* (Ch. *ken-e, y-ĕn*); *disguised, to-rived*, a mere assonance; *crie, incessauntly* (Ch. *cry-ē, incessauntly*); *slaine, paine* (Ch. *slein, pein-e*); *y-fet, let* (Ch. *y-fet, let-te*); *accept, bewept* (Ch. *accept-e, bewept*); *die, mihi* (Ch. *dy-e, mihi*). To those interested in Chaucer's language, let me point out 'dogges rabiate'—'embesile his presence'—'my woful herte is inflamed so huge'—'my soveraine and very gentilman.' See st. 34, 39, 54, 99.

22. *The remedie of Loue.* Printed in Chalmers' British Poets, i. 539. In sixty-two 7-line stanzas. Rejected by Tyrwhitt. The language is extremely late; it seems to have been written in the 16th century. It contains such words as *incongruitie, deduction, allective, can't* (for *cannot*), *scribable* (fit for writing on), *olibane, pant, babé* (baby), *cokold* (which Chaucer spells *cokewold*), *ortographie, ethimologie, ethimologise* (verb). The provincial word *lait*, to search for, is well known to belong to the Northern dialect. Dr. Murray, s. v. *allective*, dates this piece about A.D. 1560; but it must be somewhat earlier than this, as it was printed in 1532. I should date it about 1530.

26. *A Ballade in commendacion of our Ladie.* Tyrwhitt remarks that 'a poem with the same beginning is ascribed to Lydgate, under the title of *Invocation to our Lady;* see Tanner, s. v. Lydgate.' The poem consists of thirty-five 7-line stanzas. It has all the marks of Lydgate's style, and imitates Chaucer's language. Thus the line—'I have none English conuenient and digne' is an echo of the Man of Law's Tale, l. 778—'O Donegild, I ne haue noon English digne.' Some of the lines imitate Chaucer's A. B. C. But the most remarkable thing is his quotation of the first line of Chaucer's Merciless Beauty, which he applies to the Virgin Mary! See note to that poem, l. 1.

A poem called an 'Invocation to our Lady' is ascribed to Lydgate in MS. Ashmole 59, fol. 39, back. It agrees with the present Ballade; which settles the question.

30. *Balade de bon consail.* Not in previous editions. Printed in Chalmers, i. 552. Only 7 lines, and here they are, duly edited:—

'If it befall that God thee list visite
With any tourment or adversitee,
Thank first the Lord, and [fond] thy-self to quite;
Upon suffraunce and humilitee
Found thou thy quarel, what ever that it be;
Mak thy defence, and thou shalt have no losse,
The remembraunce of Christ and of his crosse.'

In l. 1, ed. 1561 has *the;* 2. *aduersite;* 3. *Thanke; lorde;* I supply *fond*, i.e. endeavour; *thy-selfe;* 4. (scans ill); 5. *Founde;* 6. *Make.*

31. *Of the Cuckowe and the Nightingale.* Printed in Bell's Chaucer, iv. 334; and in Morris's Chaucer, iv. 75. Not uncommon in MSS.; there is a copy in MS. Ff. 1.6 in the Cambridge University Library; another in MS. Fairfax 16; another in MS. Bodley 638; another in MS. Tanner 346; and a fifth (imperfect) in MS. Arch. Selden B. 24, in the Bodleian Library. A sixth is in MS. Harl. 7333, in the British Museum. From some of these, Morris's better text was constructed; see his edition, pref. p. ix.

It is worth a note, by the way, that it is *not* the same poem as one entitled *The Nightingale*, extant in MS. no. 203 in Corpus Christi College, Oxford, and in MS. Cotton, Calig. A. ii., fol. 59, and attributed to Lydgate.

That the first two lines are by Chaucer, we cannot doubt, for they are quoted from the Knightes Tale, ll. 927, 928. Chaucer often quotes his own lines, but it is not likely that he would take them as the subject of a new poem. On the other hand, this is just what we should expect one of his imitators to do. The present poem is a very fair imitation of Chaucer's style, and follows his peculiarities of metre far more closely than is usually the case with Lydgate. The notion, near the end, of holding a parliament of birds, with the Eagle for lord, is evidently borrowed from Chaucer's Parliament of Foules. Whilst admitting that the present poem is more worthy of Chaucer than most of the others with which it has been proposed to burden his reputation, I can see no sufficient reason for connecting him with it; and the external evidence connects it, in fact, with Hoccleve. For the copy in MS. Bodley 638 calls it 'The boke of Cupide god of loue,' at fol. 11, back; whilst Hoccleve's *Letter of Cupid* is called 'The lettre of Cupide god of loue' in the same, fol. 38, back. The copy in the Fairfax MS. ends with the colophon—*Explicit liber Cupidinis.* The rimes are mostly Chaucerian; but the rime of *day* with the gerund *to assay-e* in st. 11 is suspicious; so also is that of *now* with the gerund *to rescow-e* in st. 46. In st. 13, *grene* rimes with *been*, whereas *gren-e*, in Chaucer, is always dissyllabic. Chaucer's biographers have been anxious to father this poem upon him, merely because it mentions Woodstock in l. 285.

One point about this poem is its very peculiar metre; the 5-line stanza, riming *aabba*, is certainly rare. If the question arises, whence is it copied, the answer is clear, viz. from Chaucer's Envoy to his Compleint to his Purse. This is a further reason for dating it later than 1399.

32. *Balade with envoy;* 'O leude book,' &c. Printed in Bell's Chaucer, iv. 347, and in Morris's Chaucer, iv. 85, as if it were part of The Cuckoo and the Nightingale; but obviously unconnected with it. A Balade in the usual form, viz. three 7-line stanzas, with a refrain; the refrain is—' For of all good she is the best living.' The envoy consists of only six lines, instead of seven, rimed *a b a b c c*, and that for a sufficient reason, which has not been hitherto observed. The initial letters of the lines form, in fact, an anagram on the name ALISON; which is therefore the name of the lady to whom the Balade is addressed. There is a copy of this poem in MS. Fairfax 16, and another in MS. Tanner 346. It is therefore as old as the 15th century. But to attribute to Chaucer the fourth line of the Envoy seems hazardous. It runs thus—' Suspiries whiche I effunde in silence.' Perhaps it is Hoccleve's.

38. *Poem in two 7-line stanzas.* There is nothing to connect this with Chaucer; and it is utterly unworthy of him. I now quote the whole poem, just as it stands in the edition of 1561 :—

'Go foorthe king, rule thee by Sapience,
Bishoppe, be able to minister doctrine,
Lorde, to true counsale yeue audience,
Womanhode, to chastitie euer encline;
Knight, let thy deedes worship determine;
Be righteous, Iudge, in sauyng thy name;
Rich, do almose, lest thou lese blisse w*ith* shame.

'People, obeie your kyng and the lawe;
Age, be ruled by good religion;
True seruaunt, be dredfull & kepe the vnder awe;
And, thou poore, fie on presumpcion;
Inobedience to youth is vtter destruccion;
Remembre you, how God hath set you, lo!
And doe your parte, as ye be ordained to.'

In l. 7, ed. 1532 has *almesse* instead of *almose*. Surely it must be Lydgate's. Many of his poems exhibit similar catalogues, if I may so term them.

I have now gone through all the poems published in 1532 and copied into the later editions (with the exception of nos. 66–68, for which see p. 45); and I see no way of augmenting the list of Chaucer's Minor Poems any further from this source.

§ 11. DISCUSSION OF THE POEMS IN PART II. OF ED. 1561.

It is hardly worth while to discuss at length all the poems which it pleased John Stowe to fling together into the edition of 1561. But a few remarks may be useful.

Nos. 42, 43, and 60 are admittedly genuine; and are printed below, nos. XIV., XX., and VIII. I believe nos. 44 and 57 to be so also[1]; they are discussed below, and are printed as nos. XXI. and VI. No. 61 is, of course, Lydgate's. Besides this, no. 45 is correctly ascribed to Lydgate in the MSS.; there are copies of it in MS. Fairfax 16 and in MS. Ashmole 59. No. 56 is also Lydgate's, and is so marked in MS. Harl. 2251. As to no. 46, called the Craft of Lovers, it is dated by help of two lines in the last stanza, which are thus printed by Stowe:—

'In the yere of our lorde a .M. by rekeninge
CCCXL. .&. UIII. yere folowing.'

This *seems* to give the date as 1348; whereas the language is palpably that of the fifteenth century. Whether Stowe or his printer thought fit to alter the date intentionally, I cannot say. Still, the fact is, that in the MS. marked R. 3. 19 in Trinity College Library, at fol. 156, the reading is 'CCCCXL & VIII yere,' so that the true date is rather 1448, or nearly half a century after Chaucer's death[2]. The same MS., which I suppose belonged to Stowe, contains several other of these pieces, viz. nos. 48, 49, 50, 51, 53, 54, 55, 56, and perhaps others. The language and, in some cases, the ruggedness of the metre, forbid us to suppose that Chaucer can have had anything to do with them, and some are palpably of a much later date; one or more of these considerations at once exclude all the rest of Stowe's additions. It may, however, be noted that no. 47 quotes the line 'Beware alwaye, the blind eats many a fly,' which occurs as a refrain in no. 56, and it is therefore later than the time of Lydgate. The author of no. 48 says he is 'a man vnknowne. Many lines in no. 49 are of abnormal length; it begins with—
'Profulgent in preciousnes, O Sinope the queen.' The same is true of no. 51, which is addressed to a Margaret, and begins with—'In the season of Feuerere when it was full colde.' Of no. 52,

---

[1] I leave this sentence as I wrote it in 1888; shortly afterwards, the attribution of no. 57 to Chaucer received confirmation from a note in the Phillipps MS. See p. 75.

[2] There is another copy of The Craft of Lovers in MS. Harl. 2251. It is there dated 1459.

Tyrwhitt says that the four first stanzas are found in different parts of an imperfect poem upon the *Fall of Man*, in MS. Harl. 2251; whilst the 11th stanza makes part of an *Envoy*, which in the same MS. is annexed to the poem entitled the *Craft of Lovers*. No. 53 is a poor affair. No. 54, called a *Balade Pleasaunte*, is very unpleasant and scurrilous, and alludes to the wedding of 'queene Iane[1]' as a circumstance that happened many years ago. No. 55 is scurrilous, odious, and stupid. I doubt if no. 58 is good enough for Lydgate. No. 59 belongs to the sixteenth century.

All the poems here rejected were rejected by Tyrwhitt, with two strange exceptions, viz. nos 50 and 59, the Virelai and the Court of Love. Of both of these, the language is quite late. The *Virelai* is interesting from a metrical point of view, because such poems are scarce; the only similar poem that I can call to mind is the *Balet* (or rather *Virelai*) composed by Lord Rivers during his imprisonment in 1483, and printed by Percy in his Reliques of Ancient English Poetry. Percy says that Lord Rivers copies the *Virelai* mentioned above, which he assumes to be Chaucer's; but it is quite as likely that the copying was in the other direction, and that Lord Rivers copied some genuine *Virelai* (either Chaucer's or in French) that is now lost[4]. The final rime of *end* with *find* is bad enough; but the supposition that the language is of the 14th century is ridiculous. Still the *Virelai* is good in its way, though it can hardly be older than 1500, and may be still later.

Of all poems that have been falsely ascribed to Chaucer, I know of none more amazing than *The Court of Love*. The language is palpably that of the 16th century, and there are absolutely *no* examples of the occurrence in it of a final *-e* that is fully pronounced, and forms a syllable! Yet there are critics who lose their heads over it, and will not give it up. Tyrwhitt says—'I am induced by the internal evidence (!) to consider it as one of Chaucer's genuine productions.' As if the 'internal evidence' of a poem containing no sonant final *-e* is not enough to condemn it at once. The original MS. copy exists in MS. R. 3. 19 in Trinity College, and the writing is later than 1500. The poem itself has all the smoothness of the Tudor period[3]; it excels the style of Hawes, and would do credit

---

[1] *I.e.* Joan of Navarre, who was married to Henry IV in 1403.
[2] A good French *Virelai* is one by Eustace Deschamps, ed. Tarbé, 1849; i. 25.
[3] See remarks on this poem in *The New English*, by T. L. Kington Oliphant, i. 402.

to Sackville. One reference is too interesting to be passed over. In the second stanza, the poet regrets that he has neither the eloquence of Tully, the power of Virgil, nor the 'craft of *Galfride*.' Tyrwhitt explains *Galfride* as 'Geoffrey of Monmouth,' though it is difficult to understand on what ground he could have been here thought of. Bell's 'Chaucer' explains *Galfride* as 'Geoffrey of Vinsauf,' which is still more curious; for Geoffrey of Vinsauf is the very *Gaufride* whom Chaucer holds up to eternal ridicule in the Nonne Prestes Tale (l. 526).

I have no doubt at all that the *Galfrid* here referred to is no other than Geoffrey Chaucer, who was called, indifferently, *Galfrid* or *Geoffrey*. This appears from the testimony of Lydgate, who speaks, in his 'Troy-book,' of 'Noble Galfryde, chefe Poete of Brytayne,' and again, of 'My mayster Galfride'; see Lydgate's Siege of Troye, bk. ii. ch. 15, and bk. iii. ch. 25; ed. 1557, fol. K 2, col. 1, and fol. R 2, back, col. 2. Hence we are not surprised to find that the author makes frequent reference to Chaucer's Works, viz. to Anelida (l. 235), the Death of Pity (701), Troilus (872), the Legend of Good Women (104, 873), and the Parl. of Foules (near the end). The two allusions to the Legend of Good Women at once make the poem later than 1385; and in fact, it must be quite a century later than that date. There are more than 70 rimes that differ from those employed by Chaucer. The Poet introduces to our notice personages named *Philogenet, Philobone*, and *Rosial*. Of these, at least the two former savour of the time of the Renaissance; for, although Chaucer uses the name Philostrate in the Knightes Tale (A 1428, 1558, 1728), he merely *copies* this name from Boccaccio; and it is amusing to find that Boccaccio himself did not understand it[1].

§ 12. POEMS ADDED IN SPEGHT'S EDITIONS OF 1598 AND 1602.

We have now to consider the additions made by Speght in 1598. These were only two, viz. *Chaucer's Dream* and *The Flower and the Leaf*.

---

[1] It is much to be regretted that Prof. Morley, in his new edition of his English Writers, still clings to the notion of 'the Court of Love' being Chaucer's. It is sufficient to say that, after 1385, Chaucer's poems are of a far higher order, especially as regards correctness of idiom and rhythm. Our knowledge of the history of the English language has made some advance of late years, and it is no longer possible to ignore all the results of linguistic criticism.

62. *Chaucer's Dream.* A long poem of 2206 short lines, in metre similar to that of The House of Fame; accepted by Tyrwhitt, and in all the editions. But there is no early trace of it; and we are not bound to accept as Chaucer's a poem first ascribed to him in 1598, and of which the MS. (at Longleat) was written about 1550. The language is of late date, and the sonant final *-e* is decidedly scarce. The poem is badly named, and may have been so named by Speght; the proper title is 'The Isle of Ladies.' We find such rimes as *be, companie* (Ch. *be, company-e*); *know, low,* i.e. law (Ch. *know-e, law-e*); *grene, yene,* i.e. eyes (Ch. *gren-e, y-ën*); *plesaunce, fesaunce* (Ch. *plesaunc-e, fesaunts*); *ywis, kisse* (Ch. *ywis, kis-se*); and when we come to *destroied* riming with *conclude,* it is time to stop. The tediousness of this poem is appalling [1].

63. *The Flower and the Leaf.* This is rather a pretty poem, in 7-line stanzas. The language is that of the fifteenth century. It professes to be written by a gentlewoman, like the Assemble of Ladies; and perhaps it was [2]. Very likely, the same 'gentlewoman' wrote both these poems. If so, the Flower and the Leaf is the better finished, and probably the later of the two. It contains the word *henchman,* for which the earliest dated quotation which I have yet found is 1415 (Royal Wills, ed. Nichols, p. 220). An interesting reference is given in the lines—

> Eke there be knightes old of the garter
> That in hir time did right worthily.'

The order of the Garter was established in 1349; and we should expect that more than half a century would elapse before it would be natural to refer to the Knights as *old* knights, who did worthily *in their time.* Of course the poem cannot be Chaucer's, and it is hardly necessary to look for rimes such as he never uses; yet such may easily be found, such as *grew,* pt. t. sing., riming with the dissyllabic *hew-e, new-e; sid-e* with *espide,* pp. (Ch. *espy-ed*); *eie,* eye

---

[1] A great peculiarity of this poem is the astonishing length of the sentences. Many of them run to fifty lines or more. As to the MS., see Thynne's *Animadversions,* ed. Furnivall, 1875, p. 30. A second MS. is now in the British Museum (Addit. 10303), also written about 1550.

[2] The authoress had an eye for colour, and some knowledge, one would think, of heraldry. There is a tinsel-like glitter about this poem which gives it a flashy attractiveness, in striking contrast to the easy grace of Chaucer's workmanship. In the same way, the authoress of 'The Assembly of Ladies' describes the colours of the dresses of the characters, and, like the authoress of 'The Flower and the Leaf,' quotes occasional scraps of French.

(Ch. *y-ë*) with *sie*, saw (Ch. *sy*); and *plesure*[1] with *desire;* after which we may stop.

In 1602, Speght issued another edition, in which, according to Bohn's edition of Lowndes' *Bibliographer's Manual*, two more pieces were added, viz. the prose treatise against Friars called *Jack Upland*, and the genuine poem entitled 'A. B. C.' But this is not all; for I find, in a still later edition, that of 1687, which is said to be a 'reimpression of Speght's edition of 1602,' that, at the very end of all the prefatory matter, on what was probably a spare blank leaf, three more poems appear, which might as well have been consigned to oblivion. But the editors of Chaucer evidently thought that a thing once added must be added for ever, and so these three productions are retained in Bell's Chaucer, and must therefore be noticed with the rest. I find, however, that they had been printed previously, viz. at the end of the Table of Contents in ed. 1542 and ed. 1550, where they are introduced quite casually, without a word of explanation. Moreover, they are copied from MS. Trin. Coll. Cam. R. 3. 15, a MS. which also contains the Canterbury Tales; and no doubt, this fact suggested their insertion. See Todd's Illustrations of Chaucer, p. 120.

64. *Jack Upland*. An invective against friars, in prose, worth printing, but obviously not Chaucer's.

65. Chaucer's A. B. C. Genuine; here printed as poem no. I.

66. *Eight goodly questions with their answers;* printed in Bell's Chaucer, vol. iv. p. 421; nine 7-line stanzas. In st. 3, *tree* rimes with *profer;* but *tree* is an obvious misprint for *cofer!* In st. 5, the gerund *to lie* (Ch. *ly-e*) rimes with *honestie* (Ch. *honestee*). This is quite enough to condemn it. But it may be Lydgate's.

67. *To the Kings most noble Grace, and to the Lords and Knights of the Garter;* pr. as above, p. 424; eight 8-line stanzas. In MS. Phillipps 8151, and written by Hoccleve; it much resembles his poem printed in *Anglia*, v. 23. The date may be 1416. The 'King' is Henry V.

68. *Sayings.* Really three separate pieces. They are all found on the fly-leaf of the small quarto edition of Caxton, described above, p. 27. When Caxton printed Chaucer's *Anelida* and *Purse* on a quire of ten leaves, it so happened that he only filled up nine of them. But, after adding *explicit* at the bottom of the ninth leaf, to shew that he had come to the end of his Chaucer, he thought it a

---

[1] *Plesir* may be meant, but Chaucer does not use it; he says *plesaunce*.

pity to waste space, and so added three popular sayings on the front of leaf 10, leaving the back of it still blank. Here is what he printed:—

'Whan feyth failleth in prestes sawes
And lordes hestes ar holden for lawes
And robbery is holden purchas
And lechery is holden solas
Than shal the lond of albyon
Be brought to grete confus'oun.

Hit falleth for euery gentilman
To saye the best that he can
In mannes absence
And the soth in his presence.

'Hit cometh by kynde of gentil blode
To cast away al heuynes
And gadre to-gidre wordes good
The werk of wisedom berith witnes
Et sic est finis ***.'

The first of these sayings was probably a bit of popular rime, of the character quoted in Shakespeare's *King Lear*, iii. 2. 81. Shakespeare calls his lines *Merlin's* prophecy; and it has pleased the editors of Chaucer to call the first six lines *Chaucer's* Prophecy[1]. They appear in Bell's Chaucer, vol. iii. p. 427, in an 'improved' form, not worth discussing; and the last eight lines are also printed in the same, vol. iv. p. 426. Why they are separated, is mysterious. Those who think them genuine may thank me for giving them Caxton's spelling instead of Speght's.

§ 13. PIECES ADDED IN MORRIS'S EDITION, 1866.

In Morris's edition are some pieces which either do not appear in previous editions, or were first printed later than 1700.

69. Roundel; pr. in vol. vi. p. 304. The same as Merciless Beaute; here printed as no. XI. It first appeared, however, in Percy's Reliques of English Poetry. See p. 80 below.

70. The Former Age; pr. in vol. vi. p. 300, for the first time. Here printed as no IX. See p. 78.

71. *Prosperity*; pr. in vol. vi. p. 296, for the first time. This is taken from MS. Arch. Selden B. 24, fol. 119, where it follows

---

[1] It is so termed in a table of contents in MS. Trin. Coll. Cam. R. 3. 15, which (as noted on p. 45) contains *all three* of the pieces here numbered 66, 67, and 68.

Chaucer's Poem on 'Truth.' It has but one stanza of eight lines, and I here give it precisely as it stands in this Scottish MS. :—

> 'Richt as pou*ert* caus*i*th so*b*irnes,
> And febilnes enforcith contenence,
> Ry*ch*t so prosperitee and grete riches
> The moder is of vice and negligence;
> And powere also causith Insolence;
> And hono*ur* oftsiss changith gude thewis;
> Thare is no more p*er*ilouss pestilence
> Than hie estate geven v*n*to schrewis.
>   Q*uo*d Chaucere.'

I have no belief in the genuineness of this piece, though it is not ill written. In general, the ascription of a piece to Chaucer in a MS. is valuable. But the scribe of this particular MS. was reckless. It is he who made the mistake of marking Hoccleve's 'Mother of God' with the misleading remark—'Explicit or*aci*o Galfridi Chaucere.' At fol. 119, back, he gives us a poem beginning 'Deuise prowes and eke humylitee' in seven 7-line stanzas, and here again at the end is the absurd remark—'Q*uo*d Chaucer quhen he was ry*ch*t auisit.' But he was himself quite 'wrongly advised'; for it is plainly not Chaucer's at all. His next feat is to mark Lydgate's Complaynt of the Black Knight by saying—'Here endith the Maying and disporte of Chaucere'; which shews how the editors were misled as to this poem. Nor is this all; for he gives us, at fol. 137, back, another poem in six 8-line stanzas, beginning 'O hie Emperice and quene celestial'; and here again at the end is his stupid—'Q*uo*d Chaucere.' The date of this MS. appears to be 1472; so it is of no high authority; and, unless we make some verbal alteration, we shall have to explain how Chaucer came to write *oftsiss* in two syllables instead of *ofte sythe* in four; see his Can. Yem. Tale, Group G, l. 1031.

72. *Leaulte vault Richesse;* pr. in vol. vi. p. 302, for the first time. This is from the same MS., fol. 138, and is as follows :—

> 'This warldly Ioy is onely fantasy,
> Of quhich non erdly wicht ca*n* be co*n*tent;
> Quho most has wit, leste suld In It affy,
> Quho taist*is* It most, most sall him repent;
> Quhat valis all this richess and this rent,
> Sen no ma*n* wate quho sall his tresour haue?
> P*re*sume no*ch*t gevin *that* god has done but lent,
> Within schort tyme the quhiche he think*is* to craue.
>   *Leaulte vault richess.*'

On this poem, I have three remarks to make. The first is that not even the reckless Scottish scribe attributes it to Chaucer. The second is that Chaucer's forms are *content* and *lent* without a final *e*, and *repent-e* and *rent-e* with a final *-e*, so that the poem cannot be his; although *content, repent, rent*, and *lent* rime well enough in the Northern dialect. The third is that if I could be sure that the above lines were by a well-known author, I should at once ascribe them to King James I., who might very well have written these and the lines called *Prosperity* above. It is somewhat of a coincidence that the very MS. here discussed is that in which the unique copy of the *Kingis Quair* is preserved.

73. *Proverbs of Chaucer;* printed in vol. vi. p. 303. The first eight lines are genuine; here printed as no. XX. But two 7-line stanzas are added, which are spurious. In MS. Addit. 16165, Shirley tells us that they were 'made by Halsham Esquyer'; but they seem to be Lydgate's, unless he *added* to them. See Lydgate's Minor Poems (Percy Soc. 1840), pp. 193 and 74. And see pp. 52, 57.

It thus appears that, of the 73 pieces formerly attributed to Chaucer, not more than 26, and a part of a 27th, can be genuine. These are: *Canterbury Tales, Troilus, Legend of Good Women, House of Fame*, about a quarter of *The Romaunt of the Rose*, the *Minor Poems* printed in the present volume and numbered I-XI, XIII-XXI, and two pieces in prose.

§ 14. Description of the MSS.

After the preceding somewhat tedious, but necessary discussion of the contents of the black-letter and other editions (in many of which poems were as recklessly attributed to Chaucer as medieval proverbs used to be to King Solomon), it is some relief to turn to the manuscripts, which usually afford much better texts, and are altogether more trustworthy.

The following is a list of the MSS. which have been followed. I must here acknowledge my great debt to Dr. Furnivall, whose excellent, careful, and exact reproduction in print of the various MSS. leaves nothing to be desired, and is a great boon to all Chaucer scholars. They are nearly all[1] printed among the Chaucer

---

[1] The copy of no. XXI. in MS. Fairfax 16 has not been printed. I made a transcript of it myself. There is another unprinted copy in MS. Harl. 7578. I also copied out nos. XII., XXII., XXIII.

LIST OF THE MSS.

Society's publications. At the same time, I desire to say that I have myself consulted most of the MSS., and have thus gleaned a few hints which could hardly have been otherwise acquired; it was by this process that I became acquainted with the poems numbered XXII. and XXIII., which are probably genuine, and with the poem numbered XII., which is certainly so. An editor should always look at the MSS. for himself, if he can possibly contrive to do so.

LIST OF THE MSS.; WITH ABBREVIATIONS.

N.B. The roman numbers following the name of each MS. denote the numbers of the poems in the present edition.

A.—Ashmole 59, Bodleian Library (Shirley's).—X. XIV. XVIII.

Ad.—Addit. 16165, British Museum.—VII. XX. XXIII.

Add.—Addit. 22139, British Museum.—XIII. XIV. XV. XIX.

Ar.—Arch. Selden B. 24, Bodleian Library.—IV. V. XIII. XVIII.

Arch.—Arch. Selden B. 10, Bodleian Library.—X. XIII.

At.—Addit. 10340, British Museum.—XIII.

B.—Bodley 638 (Oxford).—I. II. III. V. VII. X. XXII.

Bannatyne MS. 1568, Hunterian Museum, Glasgow.—XV.

Bedford MS. (Bedford Library).—I.

C.—Cambridge Univ. Library, Ff. 5. 30.—I.

Corpus.—Corpus Chr. Coll., Oxford, 203.—XIII.

Ct.—Cotton, Cleopatra D. 7; Brit. Mus.—XIII. XIV. XV. XXI.

Cx.—Caxton's editions; see above (p. 27).—V. VII. X. XIII. XIV. XVI. (part); XIX.

D.—Digby 181, Bodleian Library.—V. VII.

E.—Ellesmere MS. (also has the Cant. Tales).—XIII.

ed. 1561.—Stowe's edition, 1561.—VI. VIII. XX. XXI., &c.

F.—Fairfax 16, Bodleian Library.—I. II. III. IV. V. VII. X. XIII. (two copies); XV. XVI. XVII. XVIII. XIX. XX. XXI. XXII.

Ff.—Cambridge Univ. Library, Ff. 1. 6.—II. V. VII. (part); XVIII. XIX.

Gg.[1]—Cambridge Univ. Library, Gg. 4. 27.—I. V. XIII. XVI.

Gl.—Glasgow, Hunterian Museum, Q. 2. 25.—I.

H.—Harleian 2251, Brit. Mus.—I. X. XIV. XIX.

---

[1] Called 'Cm.' in the footnotes to vol. iv.

Ha.—Harleian 7578, Brit. Mus.—I. II. XIV. XV. XX. XXI.
Harl.—Harleian 7333, Brit. Mus.—IV. V. VII. XIII. XIV. XV. XIX. XXII.
Harleian 78, Brit. Mus. (Shirley's). *See* Sh. *below.*
Harleian 372, Brit. Mus.—VII.
Hat.—Hatton 73, Bodleian Library.—XIII. XV.
Hh.—Cambridge Univ. Library, Hh. 4. 12.—V (part); IX.
I.—Cambridge Univ. Library, Ii. 3. 21.—IX. X.
Jo.—St. John's College, Cambridge, G. 21.—I.
Ju.—Julian Notary's edition (see p. 28).—IV. XVII. XVIII.
Kk.—Cambridge Univ. Library, Kk. 1. 5.—XIII.
L.—Laud 740, Bodleian Library.—I.
Lansdowne 699, Brit. Mus.—X. XIII.
Laud.—Laud 416, Bodleian Library.—V (part).
Lt.—Longleat MS. 258 (Marquis of Bath).—II. IV. V. VII.
O.—St. John's College, Oxford (no. lvii.); fol. 22, bk.—V.
P.—Pepys 2006, Magd. Coll., Cambridge.—I. (two copies); IV V. VII (part); X. XI. XIII. XVI. XVIII. (two copies); XIX.
Ph.—Phillipps 9053 (Cheltenham).—II. VI. VII. (part); XIX.
Phil.—Phillipps 8299 (Cheltenham).—XIII.
R.—Rawlinson Poet. 163, Bodleian Library.—XII.
Sh.—Shirley's MS. Harl. 78, Brit. Mus.—II. VI.
Sion College MS. (Shirley's).—I.
T.—Trinity College, Cambridge, R. 3. 20.—IV. VII (part); VIII. X. XIII. (two copies); XIV. XV. XVIII.
Th.—W. Thynne's edition, 1532.—III. XV. XVII., &c.
Tn.—Tanner 346, Bodleian Library.—II. III. IV. V. VII. XVIII.
Trin.—Trinity College, Cambridge, R. 3. 19.—II. V.
Trinity College, Cambridge, R. 14. 51.—XIV. XV.

Conversely, I here give a list of the Poems in the present volume, shewing from which MSS. each one is derived. I mention first the MSS. of most importance. I also note the number of lines in each piece.

I. *A. B. C.* (184 lines).—C. Jo. Gl. L. Gg. F.; *other copies in* H. P.[1] Bedford. Ha. Sion. B.[2]

II. *Pite* (119).—Tn. F. B. Sh. Ff. Trin.; *also* Ha. Lt. Ph.

III. *Duchess* (1334).—F. Tn. B. Th.

IV. *Mars* (298).—F. Tn. Ju. Harl. T. Ar.; also P.[1] Lt.

---

[1] There are *two* copies in MS. P.; they may be called P 1 and P 2.

[2] I make but little use of the copies in the second group.

V. *Parl. Foules* (699).—F. Gg. Trin. Cx. Harl. O. Ff. Tn. D.; *also* Ar. B. Lt. P.; Hh. (365 lines); Laud (142 lines).

VI. *Compleint to his Lady* (133).—Ph. Sh.; ed. 1561.

VII. *Anelida* (357).—Harl. F. Tn. D. Cx.; *also* B. Lt. Ad.; Harl. 372; *partly in* T. Ff. P. Ph.

VIII. *Lines to Adam* (7).—T.; ed. 1561.

IX. *Former Age* (64).—I. Hh.

X. *Fortune* (79).—I. A. T. F. B. H.; *also* P. Cx.; Arch.; Lansd. 699.

XI. *Merciless Beaute* (39).—P.

XII. *To Rosemounde* (24).—R.

XIII. *Truth* (28).—At. Gg. E. Ct. T.[1]; *also* Arch. Harl. Hat. P. F.[2] Add. Cx.; Ar. Kk. Corpus; Lansd. 699; Phil.

XIV. *Gentilesse* (21).—A. T. Harl. Ct. Ha. Add. Cx; *also* H. *and* Trinity.

XV. *Lak of Stedfastnesse* (28).—Harl. T. Ct. F. Add.; *also* Th. Ha.; Hat., Trinity, *and* Bannatyne.

XVI. *To Scogan* (49).—Gg. F. P.; *also* Cx. (21 lines).

XVII. *To Bukton* (32).—F. Th.; *also* Ju.

XVIII. *Venus* (82).—T. A. Tn. F. Ff.; *also* Ar. Ju. P.[3]

XIX. *Purse* (26).—F. Harl. Ff. P. Add.; *also* H. Cx. Ph.

XX. *Proverbs* (8).—F. Ha. Ad.; ed. 1561.

XXI. *Against Women Unconstaunt* (21).—Ct. F. Ha.; ed. 1561.

XXII. *An Amorous Complaint* (91).—Harl. F. B.

XXIII. *Balade of Complaint* (21).—Ad.

§ 15. Remarks on some of the MSS.

Some of these MSS. deserve a few special remarks.

Shirley's MSS. are—A. Ad. H. Harl. Sh. Sion, *and* T.

MSS. in Scottish spelling are—Ar. Bannatyne. Kk.; L. shews Northern tendencies.

MSS. AT OXFORD.

F. (Fairfax 16) is a valuable MS.; not only does it contain as many as sixteen of these Minor Poems, but it is a fairly written MS. of the fifteenth century. The spelling does not very materially

---

[1] Two copies; may be called T 1 and T 2.
[2] Two copies; F 1 and F 2. The copy in P. is unprinted.
[3] Two copies; P 1 and P 2.

differ from that of such an excellent MS. as the Ellesmere MS. of the Canterbury Tales, excepting in the fact that a great number of final *e*'s are added in wrong places, and are dropped where they are required. This is a matter that can be to a large extent rectified, and I have endeavoured to do so, taking it in many instances as the standard text. Next to this misuse of final *e*'s, which is merely due to the fact that it was written out at a time when the true use of them was already lost, its most remarkable characteristic is the scribe's excessive love of the letter *y* in place of *i*; he writes *hyt ys* instead of *hit is*, and the like. In a great number of instances I have restored *i*, where the vowel is short. When the text of the Fairfax MS. is thus restored, it is by no means a bad one. It also contains fair copies of many poems by Hoccleve and Lydgate, such as the former's *Letter of Cupide*[1], and the latter's *Complaint of the Black Knight, Temple of Glass*, and *Balade against Women's Doubleness*, being the very piece which is introduced into Stowe's edition, and is numbered 45 above (see p. 33). We are also enabled, by comparing this MS. with MS. Harl. 7578, to solve another riddle, viz. why it is that Chaucer's Proverbs, as printed in Morris's and Bell's editions, are followed by two 7-line stanzas which have nothing whatever to do with them. In MS. Harl. 7578 these two stanzas immediately *follow*, and MS. F. immediately *precede* Chaucer's Proverbs, and therefore were near enough to them to give an excuse for throwing them in together. However, both these stanzas are by Lydgate, and are mere fragments[2]. The former of them, beginning 'The worlde so wide, thaire so remuable,' really belongs to a poem of 18 stanzas, printed in Halliwell's edition of Lydgate's Minor Poems (Percy Soc.), p. 193. The latter of them, beginning 'The more I goo, the ferther I am behinde,' belongs to a poem of 11 stanzas, printed in the same, p. 74. Perhaps this will serve as a hint to future editors of Chaucer, from whose works it is high time to exclude poems *known* to be by some other hand.

In this MS. there is also a curious and rather long poem upon the game of chess; the board is called the *cheker*, and the pieces are the *kyng*, the *quene or the fers* (described on fol. 294), the *rokys* (*duo*

---

[1] Also a Balade, beginning 'Victorious kyng,' printed in G. Mason's edition of Occleve, 1796; as well as *The Book of Cupid*, which is another name for the *Cuckoo and Nightingale*.

[2] Unless they were composed, as Shirley says, by one Halsham, and adopted by Lydgate as *subjects* for new poems; see pp. 48, 57.

Roci), the *knyghtys*, the *Awfyns* (*duo alfini*), and the *povnys* (*pedini*). This is interesting in connection with the *Book of the Duchess*; see note to l. 654 of that poem. The author tells us how 'he plaid at the chesse,' and 'was mated of a Ferse.'

B. (Bodley 638) is very closely related to MS. F.; in the case of some of the poems, both must have been drawn from a common source. MS. B. is not a mere copy of F., for it sometimes has the correct reading where F. is wrong; as, e.g. in the case of the reading *Bret* in the *House of Fame*, l. 1208. It contains seven of these Minor Poems, as well as *The boke of Cupide god of loue* (*Cuckoo and Nightingale*), Hoccleve's *Lettre of Cupide god of loue*, Lydgate's *Temple of Glass* (oddly called *Temple of Bras* (!), a mistake which occurs in MS. F. also), his *Ordre of Folys*, printed in Halliwell's Minor Poems of Lydgate, p. 164, and his *Complaint of the Black Knight*, imperfect at the beginning.

A. (Shirley's MS. Ashmole 59) is remarkable for containing a large number of pieces by Lydgate, most of which are marked as his. It corroborates the statement in MS. F. that he wrote the *Balade against Women's Doubleness*. It contains the whole of Scogan's poem in which Chaucer's *Gentilesse* is quoted: see the complete print of it, from this MS., in the Chaucer Society's publications.

Another poem in this MS. requires a few words. At the back of leaf 38 is a poem entitled 'The Cronycle made by Chaucier,' with a second title to this effect:—' Here nowe folowe the names of the nyene worshipfullest Ladyes that in alle cronycles and storyal bokes haue beo founden of trouthe of constaunce and vertuous or reproched (*sic*) womanhode by Chaucier.' The poem consists of nine stanzas of eight lines (in the ordinary heroic metre), and is printed in Furnivall's Odd Text of Chaucer's Minor Poems, Part I. It would be a gross libel to ascribe this poem to Chaucer, as it is very poor, and contains execrable rimes (such as *prysoun*, *bycome*; *apply-e*, *pyte*; *thee*, *dy-e*). But we may easily see that the title is likely to give rise to a misconception. It does not really mean that the *poem itself* is by Chaucer, but that it gives a brief epitome of the 'Cronicle made by Chaucier' of 'the nyene worshipfullest Ladyes.' And, in fact, it does this. Each stanza briefly describes one of the nine women celebrated in Chaucer's Legend of Good Women. It is sufficient to add that the author makes a ludicrous mistake, which is quite enough to acquit Chaucer of having had any hand in this wholly valueless production; for he actually addresses 'quene Alceste' as sorrowing for 'Seyse her husbande.' *Seyse* is Chaucer's *Ceyx*, and *Alceste* is the author's comic substitution for *Alcyone*; see Book of the Duchess, l. 220. This is not a fault of the scribe; for *Alceste* rimes with *byheste*, whereas *Alcione* does not. I much suspect that Shirley wrote this poem *himself.* His verses, in MS. Addit. 16165, are very poor.

Tn. (Tanner 346) is a fair MS. of the 15th century, and contains, besides six of the Minor Poems, the *Legend of Good Women*, Hoccleve's *Letter of Cupid* (called *litera Cupidinis dei Amoris directa subditis suis Amatoribus*), the *Cuckoo and Nightingale* (called tne *god of loue*), Lydgate's *Temple of Glas* and *Black Knight*, &c. One of them is the Ballad no. 32 discussed above (p. 40). At fol. 73 is a poem in thirteen 8-line stanzas, beginning 'As ofte as syghes ben in herte trewe.' One stanza begins with these lines:—

'As ofte tymes as Penelapye
Renewed her werk in the *raduore*,' &c.

I quote this for the sake of the extremely rare Chaucerian word spelt *radevore* in the Legend of Good Women. The same line occurs in another copy of the same poem in MS. Ff., fol. 12, back.

Ar. (Arch. Seld. B. 24) is a Scottish MS., apparently written in 1472, and contains, amongst other things, the unique copy of the *Kingis Quair*, by James I. of Scotland. This is the MS. wherein the scribe attributes pieces to Chaucer quite recklessly: see p. 47. It is also the authority for the pieces called *Prosperity* and *Leaulte vault Richesse*. Here, once more, we find the *Letter of Cupid* and the *Cuckoo and Nightingale*; it is remarkable how often these poems occur in the same MS. It also contains *Troilus* and the *Legend of Good Women*.

D. (Digby 181) contains, besides two of the Minor Poems, an imperfect copy of Troilus; also the *Letter of Cupid* and *Complaint of the Black Knight*. At fol. 52 is a piece entitled 'Here Bochas repreuyth hem that yeue hasti credence to euery reporte or tale'; and it begins—'All-though so be in euery maner age'; in nineteen 7-line stanzas. This is doubtless a part of chapter 13 of Book I. of Lydgate's *Fall of Princes*.

R. (Rawlinson, Poet. 163) contains a copy of Chaucer's *Troilus*, followed by the *Balade to Rosemounde*. Both pieces are marked 'Tregentyll' or 'Tregentil' to the left hand, and 'Chaucer' to the right.

§ 16. Cambridge MSS.

Ff. (Ff. 1. 6) contains, besides five of the Minor Poems, many other pieces. One is a copy of *Pyramus and Thisbe*, being part of the Legend of Good Women. There are four extracts from various parts of Gower's *Confessio Amantis*; the *Cuckoo and Nightingale* and *Letter of Cupid*; the Romance of *Sir Degrevaunt*; *La Belle Dame sans Merci*. Some pieces from this MS. are printed in Reliquiae Antiquae, i. 23, 169, 202; and two more, called *The Parliament of Love* and *The Seven Deadly Sins*, are printed in Political, Religious, and Love Poems, ed. Furnivall (E. E. T. S.), pp. 48, 215. We also find here a copy of Lydgate's *Ballad of Good Counsail*, printed in the old editions of Chaucer (piece no. 40; see above, p. 33).

Gg. (Gg. 4. 27) is the MS. which contains so excellent a copy of the Canterbury Tales, printed as the 'Cambridge MS.' in the Chaucer Society's publications. Four leaves are lost at the beginning. On leaf 5 is Chaucer's *A. B. C.*; on leaf 7, back, the *Envoy to Scogan*; and on leaf 8, back, Chaucer's *Truth*, entitled *Balade de bone conseyl*. This is followed by a rather pretty poem, in 15 8-line stanzas, which is interesting as quoting from Chaucer's *Parliament of Foules*. Examples are: '*Qui bien ayme tard oublye*' (l. 32; cf. P. F. 679): 'The fesaunt, scornere of the cok Be nihter-tyme in frostis colde' (ll. 49, 50; cf. P. F. 357); 'Than spak the frosty feldefare' (l. 89; cf. P. F. 364). Line 41 runs—'Robert redbrest and the wrenne'; which throws some light on the etymology of *robin*. This valuable MS. also contains *Troilus* and the *Legend of Good Women*, with the unique earlier form of the Prologue; *The Parlement of Foules*; and Lydgate's *Temple of Glas*. At fol. 467 is a *Supplicacio amantis*, a long piece of no great value, but the first four lines give pretty clear evidence that the author was well acquainted with Chaucer's Anelida, and aspired to imitate it.

> 'Redresse of sorweful, O Cytherea,
> That with the stremys of thy plesaunt hete
> Gladist the cuntreis of al Cirrea,
> Wher thou hast chosyn thy paleys and thy sete.'

It seems to be a continuation of the *Temple of Glas*, and is probably Lydgate's own.

Hh. (Camb. Univ. Lib. Hh. 4. 12) contains much of Lydgate, and is fully described in the Catalogue.

P. (Pepys 2006) consists of 391 pages, and contains Lydgate's

Complaint of the Black Knight, and *Temple of Glass*, part of the *Legend of Good Women*, the *A. B. C.*, *House of Fame*, *Mars and Venus* (two copies), *Fortune*, *Parlement of Foules*, *The Legend of the Three Kings of Cologne*, *The War between Caesar and Pompey*, a Translation of parts of *Cato*, the *Tale of Melibeus* and *Parson's Tale*, *Anelida*, *Envoy to Scogan*, *A. B. C.* (again), *Purse*, *Truth*, and *Merciless Beauty*.

Trin. (Trin. Coll. Camb. R. 3. 19) not only contains two of the Minor Poems, but a large number of other pieces, including the *Legend of Good Women* and many of Lydgate's Poems. In particular, it is the source of most of Stowe's additions to Chaucer: I may mention *The Craft of Lovers*, dated 1448 in the MS. (fol. 156), but 1348 in Stowe; the *Ten Commandments of Love*, *Nine Ladies worthy*, *Virelai* (fol. 160), *Balade* beginning *In the seson of Feuerer* (fol. 160), *Goddesse and Paris* (fol. 161, back), *A balade plesaunte* (fol. 205), *O Mossie Quince* (fol. 205), *Balade* beginning *Loke well aboute* (fol. 207); and *The Court of Love*; see the pieces numbered 46, 48, 49, 50, 51, 53, 54, 55, 56, 59 (p. 33). The piece numbered 41 also occurs here, at the end of the *Parliament of Foules*, and is headed 'Verba translatoris.' One poem, by G. Ashby, is dated 1463, and I suppose most of the pieces are in a handwriting of a later date, not far from 1500. It is clear that Stowe had no better reason for inserting pieces in his edition of Chaucer than their occurrence in this MS. to which he had access. If he had had access to any other MS. of the same character, the additions in his book would have been different, and *The Court of Love* would never have been 'Chaucer's.' Yet this is the sort of evidence which some accept as being quite sufficient to prove that Chaucer learnt the language of a century after his own date, in order to qualify himself for writing that poem.

§ 17. London MSS.

Ad. (MS. Addit. 16165). One of Shirley's MSS., marked with his name in large letters. It contains a copy of Chaucer's *Boethius*; Trevisa's translation of the gospel of *Nichodemus*; the *Maistre of the game* (on hunting); the *Compleint of the Black Knight* and the *Dreme of a Lover*, both by Lydgate. The latter is the same poem, I suppose, as *The Temple of Glas*. It is here we learn from Shirley that the *Complaint of the Black Knight* is Lydgate's. Not only is it headed, on some pages, as 'The complaynte of a knight made by

Lidegate,' but on fol. 3 he refers to the same poem, speaking of it as being a complaint—

> 'al in balade[1],
> That daun Iohan of Bury made,
> Lydgate the Munk clothed in blakke.'

Here also we find two separate fragments of *Anelida*[2]; the two stanzas mentioned above (p. 52, l. 20), called by Shirley 'two verses made in wyse of balade by Halsham, Esquyer'; Chaucer's *Proverbs*; the poem no. 45 above (p. 33), attributed in this MS. to Lydgate; &c. At fol. 256, back, is the *Balade of compleynte* printed in this volume as poem no. XXIII.

Add. (MS. Addit. 22139). This is a fine folio MS., containing Gower's *Confessio Amantis*. At fol. 138 are Chaucer's *Purse, Gentilesse, Lak of Stedfastnesse*, and *Truth*.

At. (MS. Addit. 10340). Contains Chaucer's *Boethius* (foll. 1–40); also *Truth*, with the unique *envoy*, and the description of the 'Persone,' from the Canterbury Tales, on fol. 41, recto[3].

Ct. (MS. Cotton, Cleopatra, D. 7). The Chaucer poems are all on leaves 188, 189. They are all ballads, viz. *Gentilesse, Lak of Stedfastness, Truth*, and *Against Women Unconstaunt*. All four are in the same hand; and we may remark that the last of the four is thus, in a manner, linked with the rest; see p. 58, l. 5, p. 26, l. 29.

H. (MS. Harl. 2251). Shirley's MS. contains a large number of pieces, chiefly by Lydgate. Also Chaucer's *Prioresses Tale, Fortune* (fol. 46), *Gentilesse* (fol. 48, back), *A. B. C.* (fol. 49), and *Purse* (fol. 271). The *Craft of Lovers* also occurs, and is dated 1459 in this copy. Poem no. 56 (p. 34) also occurs here, and is marked as Lydgate's. We also see from this MS. that the first four stanzas of no. 52 (p. 33) form part of a poem on the *Fall of Man*, in which *Truth, Mercy, Righteousness*, and *Peace* are introduced as allegorical personages. The four stanzas form part of Mercy's plea, and this is why the word *mercy* occurs ten times. At fol. 153, back (formerly 158, back), we actually find a copy of Henry Scogan's poem in which Chaucer's *Gentilesse* is *not* quoted, the requisite stanzas being entirely omitted. At fol. 249, back, Lydgate quotes the line 'this world is a thurghfare ful of woo,' and

---

[1] i. e. in the ballad-measure, or 7-line stanzas.
[2] One page of this, in Shirley's writing, has been reproduced in facsimile for the Chaucer Society.
[3] This page has been reproduced, in facsimile, for the Chaucer Society.

says it is from Chaucer's 'tragedyes.' It is from the Knightes Tale, l. 1989 (A 2847).

Ha. (Harl. 7578). Contains Lydgate's *Proverbs*; Chaucer's *Pite* (fol. 13, back), *Gentilesse* and *Lak of Stedfastnesse* (fol. 17), immediately followed by the *Balade against Women unconstaunt*, precisely in the place where we should expect to find it; also Chaucer's *Proverbs*, immediately followed by the wholly unconnected stanzas discussed above; p. 52, l. 20. At fol. 20, back, are six stanzas of Chaucer's *A. B. C.*

Harl. (MS. Harl. 7333). This is a fine folio MS., and contains numerous pieces. At fol. 37, recto, begins a copy of the Canterbury Tales, with a short prose Proem by Shirley; this page has been reproduced in facsimile for the Chaucer Society. At fol. 129, back, begins the *Parliament of Foules*, at the end of which is the stanza which appears as poem no. 41 in Stowe's edition (see p. 33). Then follow the *Broche of Thebes*, i. e. the *Complaint of Mars*, and *Anelida*. It also contains some of the *Gesta Romanorum* and of Hoccleve's *De Regimine Principum*. But the most remarkable thing in this MS. is the occurrence, at fol. 136, of a poem hitherto (as I believe) unprinted, yet obviously (in my opinion) written by Chaucer; see no. XXII. in the present volume. Other copies occur in F. and B.

Sh. (MS. Harl. 78; one of Shirley's MSS.). At fol. 80 begins the *Complaint to Pity*; on fol. 82 the last stanza of this poem is immediately followed by the poem here printed as no. VI; the only mark of separation is a star-like mark placed upon the line which is drawn to separate one stanza from another. At the end of fol. 83, back, l. 123 of the poem occurs at the bottom of the page, and fol. 84 is gone; so that the last stanza of 10 lines and the ascription to Chaucer in the colophon do not appear in this MS.

MS. Harl. 372. This MS. contains many poems by Lydgate. Also a copy of *Anelida*; followed by *La Belle Dame sans mercy*, 'translatid out of Frenche by Sir Richard Ros,' &c.

MS. Lansdowne 699. This MS. contains numerous poems by Lydgate, such as *Guy of Warwick*, the *Dance of Macabre*, the *Horse, Sheep, and Goose*, &c.; and copies of Chaucer's *Fortune* and *Truth*.

§ 18. I. A. B. C.

This piece was first printed in Speght's edition of 1602, with this title: 'Chaucer's A. B. C. called *La Priere de Nostre Dame*: made, as some say, at the Request of Blanch, Duchesse of Lancaster, as a praier for her priuat vse, being a woman in her religion very deuout.' This is probably a mere guess, founded on the fact that Chaucer wrote the Book of the Duchess. It cannot be literally true, because it is not strictly 'made,' or composed, but only translated. Still, it is just possible that it was *translated* for her pleasure (rather than use); and if so, must have been written between 1359 and 1369. A probable date is about 1366. In any case, it may well stand first in chronological order, being a translation just of that unambitious character which requires no great experience. Indeed, the translation shews one mark of want of skill; each stanza begins by following the original for a line or two, after which the stanza is completed rather according to the requirements of rime than with an endeavour to render the original at all closely. There are no less than thirteen MS. copies of it; and its genuineness is attested both by Lydgate and Shirley[1]. The latter marks it with Chaucer's name in the Sion College MS. Lydgate's testimony is curious, and requires a few words of explanation.

Guillaume De Deguilleville, a Cistercian monk in the royal abbey of Chalis[2], in the year 1330 or 1331[3], wrote a poem entitled *Pèlerinage de la Vie humaine*. Of this there are two extant English translations, one in prose and one in verse, the latter being attributed to Lydgate. Of the prose translation[4] four copies exist, viz. in the MSS. which I call C., Gl., Jo., and L. In all of these, Chaucer's A. B. C. is inserted, in order to give a verse rendering of a similar prayer in verse in the original. Of Lydgate's verse translation there is a copy in MS. Cotton, Vitell. C. xiii. (see foll. 255, 256); and when he comes to the place where the verse prayer occurs in his original, he says that, instead of translating the prayer himself, he will quote Chaucer's translation, observing:—

'My mayster Chaucer, in hys tyme,
Afftcr the Frenchs he dyde yt ryme.'

Curiously enough, he does not do so; a blank space was left in the MS.

---

[1] It is also twice attributed to Chaucer in MS. P.
[2] I follow the account in Morley's *English Writers*, 1867, ii. 204; the name is there given as de Guilevile; but M. Paul Meyer writes De Deguilleville.
[3] Morley says 1330; a note in the Camb. MS. Ff. 6. 30 says 1331.
[4] Edited by Mr. W. Aldis Wright for the Roxburghe Club in 1869; see p. 164 of that edition. And see a note in Warton's Hist. Eng. Poetry, ed. Hazlitt, 1871, vol. iii. p. 67.

60   THE MINOR POEMS.

for the scribe to copy it out, but it was never filled in[1]. However, it places the genuineness of the poem beyond doubt; and the internal evidence confirms it; though it was probably, as was said, quite an early work.

In order to illustrate the poem fully, I print beneath it the French original, which I copy from the print of it in Furnivall's *One-text Print of Chaucer's Minor Poems*, Part I. p. 84.

It is taken from Guillaume De Deguilleville's *Pèlerinage de l'Ame*, Part I, *Le Pèlerinage de la Vie humaine*. Edited from the MS. 1645, Fonds Français, in the National Library, Paris (A), and collated with the MSS. 1649 (B), 376 (C), and 377 (D), in the same collection, by Paul Meyer. I omit, however, the collations; the reader only wants a good text.

Chaucer did not translate the last two stanzas. I therefore give them *here*.

'Ethiques[2] s'avoie leü,
Tout recordé et tout sceü,
Et après riens n'en ouvrasse
Du tout seroie deceü.   280
Aussi con cil qui est cheü,
En sa rois et en sa nasse.
Vierge, m'ame je claim lasse,
Quar en toy priant se lasse
Et si ne fait point son deü.
Pou vault chose que je amasse;
Ma priere n'est que quasse
S'a bien je ne sui esmeü.

'Contre[3] moy doubt que ne prie
Ou que en vain merci ne crie.   290
Je te promet amandement;
Et pour ce que je ne nie
Ma promesse, je t'en lie
L'ame de moy en gaigement;
Puis si te pri finablement
Que quant sera mon finement
Tu ne me defailles mie:
Pour moy soies au jugement
Afin que hereditablement
J'aie pardurable vie. AMEN.'   300

MS. C. affords, on the whole, the best text, and is therefore followed, all variations from it being duly noted in the footnotes,

---

[1] See Furnivall's Trial Forewords, pp. 13-15, and p. 100, for further information.

[2] The initial *E* stands for *et*. See next note.

[3] The initial *C* stands for *cetera*. It was usual to place *&c.* (= *et cetera*) at the end of the alphabet.

except (occasionally) when *i* is put for *y*, or *y* for *i*. The scribes are very capricious in the use of these letters, using them indifferently; but it is best to use *i* when the vowel is short (as a general rule), and *y* when it is long. Thus, *it is* is better than *yt ys*, and *wyse* than *wise*, in order to shew that the vowel is long in the latter case. I also use *y* at the end of a word, as usual; as in *lady, my*. When the spelling of the MS. is thus slightly amended, it gives a fair text, which can easily be read with the old and true pronunciation.

We may roughly divide the better MSS. into two sets, thus : (*a*) C. Gl. L. Jo.; (*b*) F. B. Gg. The rest I have not collated. See Koch, in Anglia, iv. b. 100.

The metre of this poem is worthy of notice. Chaucer uses it again, in the *Former Age* (IX), *Lenvoy to Bukton* (XVII), and in the *Monkes Tale*. More complex examples of it, with repeated rimes, are seen in the *Balade to Rosemounde* (XII), *Fortune* (X), and *Venus* (XVIII). See also the two stanzas on p. 47.

§ 19. II. THE COMPLEYNT UNTO PITE.

The word *compleynt* answers to the O. F. *complaint*, sb. masc., as distinguished from O. F. *complainte*, sb. fem., and was the technical name, as it were, for a love-poem of a mournful tone, usually addressed to the unpitying loved one. See Godefroy's Old French Dictionary[1]. Dr. Furnivall's account of this poem begins as follows: 'In seventeen 7-line stanzas: 1 of Proem, 7 of Story, and 9 of Complaint, arranged in three Terns [sets of three] of stanzas; first printed by Thynne in 1532 ... The poem looks not easy to construe; but it is clearly a Complaint *to* Pity, as 5 MSS. read, and not *of* Pity, as Shirley reads in MS. Harl. 78. This Pity once lived in the heart of the loved-one of the poet ... But in his mistress's heart dwells also Pity's rival, Cruelty; and when the poet, after waiting many years[2], seeks to declare his love, even before he can do so, he finds that Pity for him is dead in his mistress's heart, Cruelty has prevailed, and deprived him of her.' His theory is, that this poem is Chaucer's earliest original work, and relates to his own feelings of hopeless love; also, that Chaucer was not married till 1374, when he married his namesake Philippa Chaucer[3]. If

---

[1] Chaucer speaks of writing *compleintes*; Cant. Ta. 11260 (F. 948).

[2] Cf. 'this eight yere'; *Book of the Duchesse*, 37.

[3] 'Philippa Chaucer was a lady of the bedchamber, and therefore married, in 1366'; N. and Q. 7 S. v. 289.

this be so, a probable conjectural date for this poem is about 1367. I have remarked, in the note to l. 14, that the allegory of the poem is somewhat confused; and this implies a certain want of skill and clearness, which makes the supposition of its being an early work the more probable [1]. It is extremely difficult to determine to what extent the sentiments are artificial. If a French poem of a similar character should one day be found, it would not be very surprising. Meanwhile, it is worth observing that the notion of personifying *Pity* is taken from Chaucer's favourite author Statius; see the *Thebaid*, bk. xi. 458-496, and compare the context, ll. 1-457. It is this which enables us to explain the word *Herenus* in l. 92, which is an error for *Herines*, the form used by Chaucer to denote the *Erinnyes* or Furies [2]. The *Erinnyes* are mentioned in Statius, *Theb.* xi. 345 (cf. ll. 58, 60, 383); and Statius leads up to the point of the story where it is an even chance whether there will be peace or war. The Furies urge on the combatants to war; and at this crisis, the only power who can overrule them is *Pietas*, personified by Statius for this express purpose (ll. 458, 465, 466). The struggle between Pity and Cruelty in Chaucer's poem is parallel to the struggle between Pietas and the fury Tisiphone as told in Statius. Pity is called *Herines quene*, or queen of the Furies, because she alone is supposed to be able to control them. See my notes to ll. 57, 64, and 92.

The poem is extant in nine MSS. It is attributed to Chaucer by Shirley in MS. 'Sh.,' and the internal evidence confirms this. There is a fairly good copy in MS. F., on which my edition of it is based. There is, further, an excellent *critical edition* of this poem by Prof. Ten Brink, in *Essays on Chaucer*, Part II, p. 170 (Chaucer Soc.); this I carefully consulted after making my own copy, and I found that the differences were very slight. The least valuable MSS. seem to be Ff., Ph., and Lt. Omitting these, the MSS. may be divided into three sets, viz. A, Ba, and Bb, the two last going back to a common source B. These are: (A.)—Sh. Ha.; (Ba.)—F. B.; (Bb.)—Tn. Trin. See Koch, in Anglia, iv. b. 96.

In this poem we have the earliest example, in English, of the famous 7-line stanza.

---

[1] But Ten Brink (*Sprache und Verskunst*, p. 174) dates it about 1370-1372.

[2] 'O ye *Herines*, nightes doughtren three'; *Troilus*, last stanza of the invocation in bk. iv.

§ 20. III. THE BOOK OF THE DUCHESSE.

Here we are on firm ground. The genuineness of this poem has never been doubted. It is agreed that the word *Whyte* in l. 948, which is given as the name of the lady lately dead, is a translation of *Blanche*, and that the reference is to the wife of the Duke of Lancaster (John of Gaunt), who died Sept. 12, 1369, at the age of twenty-nine, her husband being then of the same age. As the poem would naturally be written soon after this event, the date must be near the end of 1369. In fact, John of Gaunt married again in 1372, whereas he is represented in the poem as being inconsolable. Chaucer's own testimony, in the Legend of Good Women, l. 418, is that he made 'the deeth of Blaunche the Duchesse'; and again, in the Introduction to the Man of Law's Prologue, l. 57, that 'In youthe he made of Ceys and Alcion.' In 1369, Chaucer was already twenty-nine years of age (taking the year of his birth to be 1340, not 1328), which is rather past the period of youth; and the fact that he thus mentions 'Ceys and Alcion' as if it were the name of an independent poem, renders it almost certain that such was once the case. He clearly thought it too good to be lost, and so took the opportunity of inserting it in a more ambitious effort. The original 'Ceys and Alcion' evidently ended at l. 220; where it began, we cannot say, for the poem was doubtless revised and somewhat altered. Ll. 215, 216 hint that a part of it was suppressed. The two subjects were easily connected, the sorrow of Alcyone for the sudden and unexpected loss of her husband being the counterpart of the sorrow of the duke for the loss of his wife. The poem of 'Ceys and Alcion' shews Chaucer under the influence of Ovid, just as part of his Complaint to Pity was suggested by Statius; but in the later part of the poem of the Book of the Duchesse we see him strongly influenced by French authors, chiefly Guillaume de Machault and the authors of Le Roman de la Rose. His familiarity with the latter poem (as pointed out in the notes) is such as to prove that he had already been previously employed in making his translation of that extremely lengthy work, and possibly quotes lines from his own translation [1].

---

[1] Most of the passages which he quotes are not extant in the English version of the Romaunt. Where we can institute a comparison between that version and the Book of the Duchess, the passages are differently worded. Cf. B. Duch. 420, with R. Rose, 1393.

64   THE MINOR POEMS.

The relationship between the MSS. and Thynne's edition has been investigated by Koch, in *Anglia*, vol. iv. Anzeiger, p. 95, and by Max Lange, in his excellent dissertation entitled *Untersuchungen über Chaucer's Boke of the Duchesse*, Halle, 1883. They both agree in representing the scheme of relationship so as to give the following result:

$$a - \begin{cases} \beta - \text{Thynne.} \\ \gamma - \begin{cases} \text{Tanner MS.} \\ \delta - \begin{cases} \text{Fairfax MS.} \\ \text{Bodley MS.} \end{cases} \end{cases} \end{cases}$$

Here a represents a lost original MS., and β and γ are lost MSS. derived from it. Thynne follows β; whilst γ is followed by the Tanner MS. and a lost MS. δ. The Fairfax and Bodley MSS., which are much alike, are copies of δ. The MS. γ had lost a leaf, containing ll. 31-96; hence the same omission occurs in the three MSS. derived from it. However, a much later hand has filled in the gap in MS. F, though it remains blank in the other two MSS. On the whole, the authorities for this poem are almost unusually poor; I have, in general, followed MS. F, but have carefully amended it where the other copies seemed to give a better result. Lange gives a useful set of 'Konjecturen,' many of which I have adopted. I have also adopted, thankfully, some suggestions made by Koch and Ten Brink; others I decline, with thanks.

This poem is written in the common metre of four accents, which was already in use before Chaucer's time, as in the poem of Havelok the Dane, Robert of Brunne's Handling Synne, Hampole's Pricke of Conscience, &c. Chaucer only used it once afterwards, viz. in his House of Fame. It is the metre employed also in his translation (as far as we have it) of the French *Roman de la Rose*.

§ 21.   IV. THE COMPLEYNT OF MARS.

Lydgate tells us that this poem is Chaucer's, referring to it as containing the story of 'the broche which that Vulcanus At Thebes wrought,' &c. Internal evidence clearly shews that it was written by the author of the *Treatise on the Astrolabie*. In MS. Harl. 7333, Shirley gives it the title 'The broche of Thebes, as of the love of Mars and Venus.' Bale oddly refers to this poem as *De Vulcani veru*, but *broche* is here an ornament, not a spit. With the exception of two lines and a half (ll. 13-15), the whole poem is supposed to be sung by a bird, and upon St. Valentine's day. Such a contrivance shews a certain lack of skill, and is an indication of a comparatively early date. The poem begins in the ordinary 7-line stanza, rimed *ababbcc*; but the Complaint itself is in 9-line stanzas, rimed *aabaabbcc*, and exhibits a considerable advance in rhythmical skill. This stanza, unique in Chaucer, was copied by Douglas (*Palace of Honour*, part 3), and by Sir D. Lyndesay (*Prol. to Testament of Papyngo*).

At the end of the copy of this poem in MS. T., Shirley appends the following note:—'Thus eondethe here this complaint, whiche some men sayne was made by [i.e. with respect to] my lady of York, doughter to the kyng of Spaygne, and my lord huntingdon, some tyme Duc of Excestre.' This tradition may be correct, but the intrigue between them was discreditable enough, and would have been better passed over in silence than celebrated in a poem, in which Mars and Venus fitly represent them. In the heading to the poem in the same MS., Shirley tells us further, that it was written to please John of Gaunt. The heading is:—'Loo, yee louers, gladethe and comfortethe you of thallyance etrayted[1] bytwene the hardy and furyous Mars the god of armes and Venus the double [i.e. fickle] goddesse of loue; made by Geffrey Chaucier, at the comandement of the renommed and excellent Prynce my lord the Duc Iohn of Lancastre.' The lady was John of Gaunt's sister-in-law. John of Gaunt married, as his second wife, in 1372, Constance, elder daughter of Pedro, king of Castile; whilst his brother Edmund, afterwards duke of York, married Isabel, her sister. In Dugdale's Baronage, ii. 154, we read that this Isabel, 'having been somewhat wanton in her younger years, at length became a hearty penitent; and departing this life in 1394, was buried in the Friers Preachers at Langele,' i.e. King's Langley in Hertfordshire; cf. Chauncy's *Hertfordshire*, p. 455; Camden's *Anglica*, p. 350. It is possible that Chaucer addressed his Envoy to the Complaint of Venus to the same lady, as he calls her 'Princess.'

Mars is, accordingly, intended to represent John Holande, half-brother to Richard II, Earl of Huntingdon, and afterwards Duke of Exeter. He actually married John of Gaunt's daughter, Elizabeth, whose mother was the Blaunche celebrated in the Book of the Duchess.

If this tradition be true, the date of the poem must be not very many years after 1372, when the Princess Isabel came to England.

---

[1] i.e. *y-treted*, treated.

We may date it, conjecturally, about 1374. See further in Furnivall's *Trial Forewords*, pp. 78-90. I may add that an attempt has been made to solve the problem of the date of this poem by astronomy (see *Anglia*, ix. 582). It is said that Mars and Venus were in conjunction on April 14, 1379. This is not wholly satisfactory; for Chaucer seems to refer to the 12th of April as the time of conjunction. If we accept this result, then the year was 1379. The date 1373-9 is near enough.

The poem is remarkable for its astronomical allusions, which are fully explained in the notes. The story of Mars and Venus was doubtless taken from Ovid, *Metam.* iv. 170-189. The story of the brooch of Thebes is from Statius, ii. 265, &c.; see note to l. 245.

I shall here add a guess of mine which possibly throws some light on Chaucer's reason for referring to the brooch of Thebes. It is somewhat curious that the Princess Isabel, in a will made twelve years before her death, and dated Dec. 6, 1382, left, amongst other legacies, 'to the Duke of Lancaster, a *Tablet of Jasper which the King of Armonie gave her*'; see Furnivall's *Trial Forewords*, p. 82. Here *Armonie* means, of course, Armenia; but it is also suggestive of *Harmonia*, the name of the first owner of the brooch of Thebes. It seems just possible that the brooch of Thebes was intended to refer to this tablet of jasper, which was doubtless of considerable value and may have been talked about as being a curiosity.

MSS. F. Tn. and Lt. are much alike; the rest vary. I follow F. mainly, in constructing the text.

§ 22. V. THE PARLEMENT OF FOULES.

This poem is undoubtedly genuine; both Chaucer and Lydgate mention it. It is remarkable as being the first of the Minor Poems which exhibits the influence upon Chaucer of Italian literature, and was therefore probably written somewhat later than the Complaint of Mars. It is also the first of the Minor Poems in which touches of true humour occur; see ll. 498-500, 508, 514-6, 563-575, 589-616. Dr. Furnivall (*Trial Forewords*, p. 53) notes that the MSS. fall into two principal groups; in the first he places Gg., Trin., Cx., Harl., O., the former part of Ff., (part of) Ar., and the fragments in Hh. and Laud 416; in the second he places F., Tn., D., and the latter part of Ff. Lt. also belongs to the second group. See further

V. THE PARLEMENT OF FOULES.

in *Anglia*, vol. iv. Anzeiger, p. 97. The whole poem, except the Roundel in ll. 680-692, is in Chaucer's favourite 7-line stanza, often called the ballad-stanza, or simply *balade* in the MSS.

The poem itself may be roughly divided into four parts. The first part, ll. 1-84, is mainly occupied with an epitome of the general contents of Cicero's Somnium Scipionis. The second part, ll. 85-175, shews several instances of the influence of Dante, though the stanza containing ll. 99-105 is translated from Claudian. The third part, ll. 176-294, is almost wholly translated or imitated from Boccaccio's Teseide. And the fourth part, ll. 295 to the end, is occupied with the real subject of the poem, the main idea being taken, as Chaucer himself tells us, from Alanus de Insulis. The passages relating to the *Somnium Scipionis* are duly pointed out in the notes; and so are the references to Dante and Claudian. The history of the third and fourth parts requires further explanation.

We have already seen that Chaucer himself tells us, in the Prol. to the Legend, 420, that he made—'al the love of Palamon and Arcyte Of Thebes, thogh the story is knowen lyte.' (N.B. This does not mean that *Chaucer's* version of the story was 'little known,' but that *Boccaccio* speaks of the story as being little known—'che Latino autor non par ne dica'; see note to Anelida, l. 8.) Now, in the first note on *Anelida and Arcite*, it is explained how this story of Palamon and Arcite was necessarily translated, more or less closely, from Boccaccio's Teseide, and was doubtless written in the 7-line stanza; also that fragments of it are preserved to us (1) in sixteen stanzas of the Parliament of Foules, (2) in the first ten stanzas of Anelida, and (3) in three stanzas of Troilus. At a later period, the whole poem was re-written in a different metre, and now forms the Knightes Tale. The sixteen stanzas here referred to begin at l. 183 (the previous stanza being also imitated from a different part of the *Teseide*, bk. xi. st. 24), and end at l. 294. Chaucer has somewhat altered the order; see note to l. 183. I here quote, from Furnivall's *Trial Forewords*, pp. 60-66, a translation by Mr. W. M. Rossetti, of Boccaccio's *Teseide*, bk. vii. stanzas 51-66; and I give, beneath it, the Italian text, from an edition published at Milan in 1819. This passage can be compared with Chaucer's imitation of it at the reader's leisure.

I note, beforehand, that, in the first line of this translation, the word *whom* refers to *Vaghezza*, i.e. Grace, Allurement; whilst *she* is the prayer of Palemo, personified.

68   THE MINOR POEMS.

Tes. vii. stanzas 51–60; cf. *Parl. Foules*, ll. 183–259.

'With whom going forward, she saw that [i. e. Mount Cithaeron]
In every view suave and charming;
In guise of a garden bosky and beautiful,
And greenest, full of plants,
Of fresh grass, and every new flower;
And therein rose fountains living and clear;
And, among the other plants it abounded in,
Myrtle seemed to her more than other.

'Here she heard amid the branches sweetly   P. F. 190.
Birds singing of almost all kinds:
Upon which [branches] also in like wise
She saw them with delight making their nests.
Next among the fresh shadows quickly
She saw rabbits go hither and thither,
And timid deer and fawns,
And many other dearest little beasts.

'In like wise here every instrument   P. F. 197.
She seemed to hear, and delightful chaunt:
Wherefore passing with pace not slow,
And looking about, somewhat within herself suspended
At the lofty place and beautiful adornment
She saw it replete in almost every corner

Colla quale oltre andando vide quello
Per ogni vista soave ed ameno,
A guisa d'un giardin fronzuto e bello
E di piante verdissimo ripieno,
D'erbetta fresca e d'ogni fior novello;
E fonti vive e chiare vi surgieno,
E in fra l'altre piante, onde abbondava,
Mortine più che altro le sembrava.

Quivi sentì pe' rami dolcemente
Quasi d'ogni maniera ucce' cantare,
Sopra de' quali ancor similemente
Gli vide con diletto i nidi a fare:
Poscia fra l'ombre fresche prestamente
Vidi conigli in qua e in là andare,
E timidenti cervi e cavrioli,
E molti altri carissimi bestiuoli.

Similemente quivi ogni stromento
Le parve udire e dilettoso canto;
Onde passando con passo non lento,
E rimirando, in sè sospesa alquanto
Dell' alto loco e del bell' ornamento;
Ripieno il vide quasi in ogni canto

V. THE PARLEMENT OF FOULES.

With spiritlings which, flying here and there,
Went to their bourne. Which she looking at,

'Among the bushes beside a fountain   P. F. 211.
Saw Cupid forging arrows—
He having the bow set down by his feet;
Which [arrows when] selected his daughter Voluptas
Tempered in the waves. And settled down
With them was Ease [*Ozio*, Otium]; whom she saw
That he, with Memory, steeled his darts
With the steel that she [Voluptas] first tempered.

'And then she saw in that pass Grace [*Leggiadria*],   P. F. 218.
With Adorning [*Adornezza*] and Affability,
And the wholly estrayed Courtesy;
And she saw the Arts that have power
To make others perforce do folly,
In their aspect much disfigured.
The Vain Delight of our form
She saw standing alone with Gentilesse.

'Then she saw Beauty pass her by,   P. F. 225.
Without any ornament, gazing on herself;
And with her she saw Attraction [*Piacevolezza*] go,—
She [the prayer] commending to herself both one and other.
With them she saw standing Youth,
Lively and adorned, making great feast:

Di spirite', che qua e là volando
Gieno a lor posta; a' quali essa guardando,

Tra gli albuscelli ad una fonta allato
Vide Cupido a fabbricar saette,
Avendo egli a' suoi piè l'arco posato,
Le qua' sua figlia Voluttade elette
Nell' onde temperava, ed assettato
Con lor s'era Ozio, il quale ella vedette,
Che con Memoria l'aste sue ferrava
De' ferri ch' ella prima temperava.

E poi vide in quel passo Leggiadria
Con Adornezza ed Affabilitate,
E la ismarrita in tutto Cortesia,
E vide l'Arti ch' hanno potestate
Di fare altrui a forza far follia,
Nel loro aspetto molto isfigurate:
Della immagine nostra il van Diletto
Con Gentilezza vide star soletto.

Poi vide appresso a sè passar Bellezza
Sanz' ornamento alcun sè riguardando,
E vide gir con lei Piacevolezza,
E l'una e l'altra seco commendando,
Vide con loro starsi Giovinezza
Destra ed adorna, molto festeggiando:

And on the other side she saw madcap Audacity
Going along with Glozings and Pimps.

'In mid the place, on lofty columns,   P. F. 232.
She saw a temple of copper; round which
She saw youths dancing and women—
This one of them beautiful, and that one in fine raiment,
Ungirdled, barefoot, only in their hair and gowns,
Who spent the day in this alone.
Then over the temple she saw doves hover
And settle and coo.

'And near to the entry of the temple   P. F. 239.
She saw that there sat quietly
My lady Peace, who a curtain
Moved lightly before the door.
Next her, very subdued in aspect,
Sat Patience discreetly,
Pallid in look; and on all sides
Around her she saw artful Promises.

'Then entering the temple, of Sighs   P. F. 246.
She felt there an earthquake, which whirled
All fiery with hot desires.
This lit up all the altars

E d'altra parte vide il folle Ardire
Con Lusinghe e Ruffiani insieme gire.

In mezzo il loco, sur alte colonne
Di rame vide un tempio, al qual d'intorno
Danzanti giovinetti vide e donne,
Qual d'esse bella, e qual d'abito adorno,
Iscinte, iscalze, in capei soli e'n gonne,
Che in questo solo disponeano il giorno:
Poi sopra il tempio vide volitare
E posarsi colombe e mormorare.

E all'entrata del tempio vicina
Vide che si sedava pianamente
Monna Pace, la quale una cortina
Movea innanzi alla porta lievemente;
Appresso a lei in vista assai tapina
Pacienza sedea discretamente;
Pallida nell' aspetto, e d'ogni parte
Intorno a lei vide Promesse ad arte.

Poi dentro al tempio entrata, di sospiri
Vi sentì un terremoto, che girava
Focoso tutto di caldi disiri:
Questi gli altari tutti alluminava

V. THE PARLEMENT OF FOULES.

With new flames born of pangs;
Each of which dripped with tears
Produced by a woman cruel and fell
Whom she there saw, called Jealousy

'And in that [temple] she saw Priapus hold P. F. 253.
The highest place—in habit just such as
Whoever would at night see him
Could [do] when, braying, the animal
Dullest of all awoke Vesta, who to his mind
Was not a little—towards whom he in like guise
Went: and likewise throughout the great temple
She saw many garlands of diverse flowers.'

Tes. vii. 61, 62 ; cf. *P. F.* 281-294.

'Here many bows of the Chorus of Diana P. F. 281.
She saw hung up and broken; among which was
That of Callisto, become the Arctic
Bear. The apples were there of haughty
Atalanta, who was sovereign in racing;
And also the arms of that other proud one
Who brought forth Parthenopaeus,
Grandson to the Calydonian King Oeneus.

Di nuove fiamme nate di martiri,
De' qua' ciascun di lagrime grondava,
Mosse da una donna cruda e ria,
Che vide lì, chiamata Gelosia:

Ed in quel vide Priapo tenere
Più sommo loco, in abito tal quale
Chiunque il volle la notte vedere
Potè, quando ragghiando l'animale
Più pigro destò Vesta, che in calere
Non poco gli era, in vêr di cui cotale
Andava; e simil per lo tempio grande
Di fior diversi assai vide grillande.

Quivi molti archi a' Cori di Diana
Vide appiccati e rotti, in tra quali era,
Quel di Callisto fatta tramontana
Orsa; le pome v'eran della fiera
Atalanta che 'n correr fu sovrana;
Ed ancor l'armi di quell' altra altiera
Che partorì il bel Partenopeo
Nipote al calidonio Re Eneo.

'She saw there histories painted all about;   P. F. 288.
Among which with finer work
Of the spouse of Ninus she there
Saw all the doings distinguished; and at foot of the mulberry-tree
Pyramus and Thisbe, and the mulberries already distained;
And she saw among these the great Hercules
In the lap of Iole, and woeful Biblis
Going piteous, soliciting Caunus.'

Tes. vii. 63–66; cf. *P. F.* 260–280.

'But, as she saw not Venus, it was told her   P. F. 260.
(Nor knew she by whom)—"In secreter
Part of the temple stays she delighting.
If thou wantest her, through that door quietly
Enter." Wherefore she, without further demur,
Meek of manner as she was,
Approached thither to enter within,
And do the embassy to her committed.

'But there she, at her first coming,   P. F. 261.
Found Riches guarding the portal—
Who seemed to her much to be reverenced:
And, being by her allowed to enter there,
The place was dark to her at first going.
But afterwards, by staying, a little light

Videvi storie per tutto dipinte,
In tra le qua' con più alto lavoro
Della sposa di Nino ivi distinte
L'opere tutte vide; e a piè del moro
Piramo e Tisbe, e già le gelse tinte:
E'l grand' Ercole vide tra costoro
In grembo a Jole, e Bibli dolorosa
Andar pregando Cauno pietosa.

Ma non vedendo Vener, le fu detto,
Nè conobbe da cui: 'In più sagreta
Parte del tempio stassi ella a diletto:
Se tu la vuoi, per quella porta, cheta
Te n'entra': ond' essa, sanza altro rispetto,
In abito qual era mansueta,
Là si appressò per entrar dentro ad essa,
E l'ambasciata fare a lei commessa.

Ma essa lì nel primo suo venire
Trovò Richezza la porta guardare;
La qual le parve assai da riverire;
E lasciata da lei quiv'entro entrare,
Oscuro le fu il loco al primo gire;
Ma poca luce poscia nello stare

V. THE PARLEMENT OF FOULES. 73

She gained there; and saw her lying naked
On a great bed very fair to see.

'But she had hair of gold, and shining   P. F. 267.
Round her head without any tress.
Her face was such that most people
Have in comparison no beauty at all.
The arms, breast, and outstanding apples,
Were all seen; and every other part with a
Texture so thin was covered
That it shewed forth almost as [if] naked.

'The neck was fragrant with full a thousand odours.   P. F. 274.
At one of her sides Bacchus was seated,
At the other Ceres with her savours.
And she in her hands held the apple,
Delighting herself, which, to her sisters
Preferred, she won in the Idean vale.
And, having seen all this, she [the prayer] made her request,
Which was conceded without denial.'

Lì prese, e vide lei nuda giacere
Sopra un gran letto assai bella a vedere.

Ma avie d'oro i crini e rilucenti
Intorno al capo sanza treccia alcuna:
Il suo viso era tal che le più genti
Hanno a rispetto bellezza nissuna:
Le braccia, il petto e le poma eminenti
Si vedien tutte, e ogni altra parte d'una
Testa tanto sottil si ricopria,
Che quasimente nuda comparia.

Olíva il collo ben di mille odori:
Dall' un de' lati Bacco le sedea,
Dall' altro Ceres cogli suoi savori:
Ed essa il pomo per le man tenea,
Sè dilettando, il quale alle sorori
Prelata vinse nella valle Idea:
E tutto ciò veduto posse il prego,
Il qual fu conceduto senza niego.

At l. 298 we are introduced to a queen, who in l. 303 is said to be the noble goddess Nature. The general idea is taken from Aleyn's *Pleynt of Kynde* (l. 316), i.e. from the *Planctus Naturae* of Alanus de Insulis; see note to l. 298 of the poem. I here quote the most essential passage from the Anglo-Latin Satirical Poets, ed. T. Wright, ii. 437. It describes the garment worn by the goddess Nature, on which various birds were represented. The phrase *animalium*

74   THE MINOR POEMS.

concilium may have suggested the name given by Chaucer to our poem. But see the remark on p. 75, l. 21.

'Haec autem [vestis] nimis subtilizata, subterfugiens oculorum indaginem, ad tantam materiae tenuitatem advenerat, ut ejus aerisque eandem crederes esse naturam, in qua, prout oculis pictura imaginabatur, *animalium* celebratur *concilium*. Illic *aquila*, primo juvenem, secundo senem, induens, tertio iterum reciprocata priorem, in Adonidem revertebatur a Nestore. Illic *ancipiter* (*sic*), civitatis praefectus aeriae, violenta tyrannide a subditis redditus exposcebat. Illic *milvus*, venatoris induens personam, venatione furtiva larvam gerebat ancipitris. Illic *falco* in *ardeam* bellum excitabat civile, non tamen aequali lance divisum. Non enim illud pugnae debet appellatione censeri, ubi tu pulsas, ego vapulo tantum. Illic *struthio*, vita seculari postposita, vitam solitariam agens, quasi heremita factus, desertarum solitudines incolebat. Illic *olor*, sui funeris praeco, mellitae citherizationis organo vitae prophetabat apocopam. Illic in *pavone* tantum pulcritudinis compluit Natura thesaurum, ut eam postea crederes mendicasse. Illic *phoenix*, in se mortuus, redivivus in alio, quodam Naturae miraculo, se sua morte a mortuis suscitabat. Illic *avis concordiae* (*ciconia*) prolem decimando Naturae persolvebat tributum. Illic *passeres* in atomum pygmeae humilitatis relegati degebant, *grus* ex opposito in giganteae quantitatis evadebat excessum.

' Illic *phasianus*, natalis insulae perpessus angustias, principum futurus deliciae, nostros evolabat in orbes. Illic *gallus*, tanquam vulgaris astrologus, suae vocis horologio horarum loquebatur discrimina. Illic *gallus silvestris*, privatioris galli deridens desidiam, peregre proficiscens, nemorales peragrabat provincias. Illic *bubo*, propheta miseriae, psalmodias funereae lamentationis praecinebat. Illic *noctua* tantae deformitatis sterquilinio sordescebat, ut in ejus formatione Naturam crederes fuisse somnolentam. Illic *cornix*, ventura prognosticans, nugatorio concitabatur garritu. Illic *pica*, dubio picturata colore, curam logices perennebat insomnem. Illic *monedula*, latrocinio laudabili reculas thesaurizans, innatae avaritiae argumenta monstrabat. Illic *columba*, dulci malo inebriata Diones, laborabat Cypridis in palaestra. Illic *corvus*, zelotypiae abhorrens dedecus, suos foetus non sua esse pignora fatebatur, usque dum comperto nigri argumento coloris, hoc quasi secum disputans comprobat. Illic *perdix* nunc aeriae potestatis insultus, nunc venatorum sophismata, nunc canum latratus propheticos abhorrebat. Illic *anas* cum *ansere*, sub eodem jure vivendi, hiemabat in patria fluviali. Illic *turtur*, suo viduata consorte, amorem epilogare dedignans, in altero bigamiae refutabat solatia. Illic *psittacus* cum sui gutturis incude vocis monetam fabricabat humanae. Illic *coturnicem*, figurae draconis ignorantem fallaciam, imaginariae vocis decipiebant sophismata. Illic *picus*, propriae architectus domunculae, sui rostri dolabro clausulam fabricabat in ilice. Illic *curruca*, novercam exuens, materno pietatis ubere alienam cuculi prolem adoptabat in filium ; quae tamen capitali praemiata stipendio, privignum agnoscens, filium ignorabat. Illic *hirundo*, a sua peregrinatione reversa, sub trabe nidi lutabat hospitium. Illic *philomena*, deflorationis querelam reintegrans, harmoniaca tympanizans dulcedine, puritatis dedecus excusabat. Illic *alauda*, quasi nobilis citharista, non studii artificio, sed Naturae magisterio, musicae praedocta scientiam, citharam praesentabat in ore . . . . Haec animalia, quamvis illic quasi allegorice viverent, ibi tamen esse videbantur ad litteram.'

As to the date of this poem, Ten Brink (*Studien*, p. 127) shews that it must have been written later than 1373; and further, that it

VI. A COMPLEINT TO HIS LADY.

was probably written earlier than Troilus, which seems to have been finished in 1383. It may therefore have been written in 1382, in which case it may very well refer to the betrothal (in 1381) of King Richard II to Queen Anne of Bohemia. See, on this subject, Dr. Koch's discussion of the question in Essays on Chaucer, p. 407, published by the Chaucer Society. Prof. Ward (who follows Koch) in his Life of Chaucer, p. 86, says:—'Anne of Bohemia, daughter of the great Emperor Charles IV., and sister of King Wenceslas, had been successively betrothed to a Bavarian prince and to a Margrave of Meissen, before—after negotiations which, according to Froissart, lasted a year[1]—her hand was given to young King Richard II. of England. This sufficiently explains the general scope of the *Assembly of Fowls*, an allegorical poem written on or about St. Valentine's Day, 1381[2]—eleven months or nearly a year after which date the marriage took place[3].'

I here note that Lydgate's *Flour of Curtesie* is a palpable imitation of the *Parliament of Foules*; so also is the earlier part of his *Complaint of the Black Knight*.

On the other hand, it is interesting to find, in the Poésies de Marie de France, ed. Roquefort, Paris, 1820, that Fable 22 (vol. i. p. 130) is entitled :—' Li parlemens des Oiseax por faire Roi.' In this fable, the Birds reject the Cuckoo, and choose the Eagle as king.

§ 23. VI. A COMPLEINT TO HIS LADY.

We may fairly say that this poem is attributed to Chaucer by Shirley, since in MS. Harl. 78 it is copied out by him as if it were a continuation of the Complaint to Pity, and the pages are, throughout, headed with the words—'The Balade of Pytee. By Chauciers.' Stowe implies that he had seen more than one MS. copy of this poem, and says that 'these verses were compiled by Geffray Chauser,' for which he may have found authority in the MSS.[4] Moreover, the

---

[1] See l. 647. The royal tercel eagle is, then, Richard II; and the formel eagle is Queen Anne; the other two tercel eagles were her other two suitors. See Froissart, bk. ii. c. 86.

[2] Rather, 1382. Ch. could not have *foretold* a year's delay.

[3] It is quite impossible that the poem can refer, as some say, to the marriage of John of Gaunt in 1359, or even to that of de Coucy in 1364; see Furnivall's Trial Forewords, p. 70. It is plainly much later than the Book of the Duchess, as the internal evidence incontestably shews.

[4] I leave the remarks upon this poem as I first wrote them in 1888. Very soon

internal evidence settles the matter. It is evident that we have here a succession of metrical experiments, the last of which exhibits a ten-line stanza resembling the nine-line stanza of his Anelida; in fact, we here have that Complaint in a crude form, which was afterwards elaborated; see the references, in the Notes, to the corresponding passages in that poem. But a very great and unique interest is attached to lines 16 to 43. For here we have the *sole* example, in English literature of that period, of the use of *terza rima*, obviously copied from Dante; and Chaucer was the only writer who then had a real acquaintance with that author. I know of no other example of the use of this metre before the time of Lord Surrey and Sir Thomas Wiat, when Englishmen once more sought acquaintance with Italian poetry. Consequently, we have here the pleasure of seeing how Chaucer handled Dante's metre; and the two fragments here preserved shew that he might have handled it quite successfully if he had persevered in doing so.

It is to be regretted that Shirley's spelling is so indifferent; he was rather an amateur than a professional scribe. Some of his peculiarities may be noticed, as they occur not only here, but also in the two last pieces, nos. XXII. and XXIII. He constantly adds a final *e* in the wrong place, producing such forms as *fallethe, howe, frome*, and the like, and drops it where it is necessary, as in *hert* (for *herte*). He is fond of *eo* for *ee* or long *e*, as in *beo, neodethe*. He writes *ellas* for *allas*; also *e* in place of the prefix *y-*, as in *eknytte* for *y-knit*. This last peculiarity is extremely uncommon. I have removed the odd effect which these vagaries produce, and I adopt the ordinary spelling of MSS. that resemble in type the Ellesmere MS. of the Canterbury Tales.

This piece exhibits three distinct metres, viz. the 7-line stanza, terza rima, and the 10-line stanza. Of the last, which is extremely rare, we have here the earliest example. Lines 56 and 59 are lost, and some others are imperfect.

§ 24. VII. ANELIDA AND ARCITE.

The genuineness of this poem is obvious enough, and is vouched for both by Lydgate and Shirley, as shewn above. It is further

---

afterwards, Dr. Furnivall actually *found* the ascription of the poem to Chaucer in MS. Phillipps 9053. I think this proves that I know how to estimate internal evidence aright. MS. Phillips 9053 also completes the poem, by contributing an additional stanza, which, in MS. Harl. 78, has been torn away.

VII. ANELIDA AND ARCITE.

discussed in the Notes. I may add that Lydgate incidentally refers to it in his *Complaint of the Black Knight*, l. 379 :—'Of Thebes eke the false Arcite.' Much later allusions are the following :—

> 'There was also Annelida the queene,
> Upon Arcite how sore she did complaine';
> *Assembly of Ladies*, l. 465.
>
> ...... 'and the weimenting
> Of her Annelida, true as turtle-dove
> To Arcite fals.'
> *Court of Love*, l. 233.

The first three stanzas are from Boccaccio's *Teseide*, as shewn in the Notes; so also are stanzas 8, 9, and 10. Stanzas 4-7 are partly from Statius. The origin of ll. 71-210 is at present unknown. It is difficult to date this poem, but it must be placed after 1373, because of its quotations from the *Teseide*, or rather from Chaucer's own *Palamon and Arcite*. The mention of 'the quene of Ermony' in l. 72 suggests that Chaucer's thoughts may have been turned towards Armenia by the curious fact that, in 1384, the King of Armenia came to England about Christmas time, stayed two months, and was hospitably entertained by King Richard at Eltham; see Fabyan's *Chronicles*, ed. Ellis, p. 532. At an earlier time, viz. in 1362, Walsingham says that some knights of Armenia appeared at a tournament in Smithfield. In the Transactions of the Cambridge Philological Society, May 13, 1886, there is a short paper by Prof. Cowell, from which we learn that Mr. Bradshaw believed the name of *Anelida* to be identical ' with Anáhita ('Αναΐτις), the ancient goddess of Persia and Armenia. . . He supposed that Chaucer got the name *Anelida* from a misreading of the name *Anaetidem* or *Anaetida* in some Latin MS., the *t* being mistaken for *l*.' We must remember that *Creseide* represents a Greek *accusative* form Χρυσηΐδα, of which the gen. Χρυσηΐδος occurs in Homer, *Il.* i. 111; and perhaps the form *Dalida* (for Dalilah) in the Septuagint is also due to association with Greek accusatives in -ιδα. The genitive *Anaetidos* occurs in Pliny, xxxiii. 4; in Holland's translation of Pliny, ii. 470, she appears as 'the goddesse *Diana* syrnamed *Anaitis*.' It may be as well to explain to those who are unaccustomed to MSS. of the fourteenth century, that it was then usual to write *e* in place of *ae* or *æ*, so that the name would usually be written, in the accusative case, *Anetida*. This suggests that *Anelida* should be spelt with but one *n*; and such is the practice of all the better MSS.

It remains to be added that one source of the part of the poem called the *Complaint* (ll. 211-350) is the piece printed in this volume as no. VI. That piece is, in fact, a kind of exercise in metrical experiments, and exhibits specimens of a 10-line stanza, resembling the nine-line stanza of this Complaint. Chaucer seems to have elaborated this into a longer Complaint, with additional varieties in the metre; and then to have written the preceding story by way of introduction. One line (vi. 50) is repeated without alteration (vii. 237); another (vi. 35) is only altered in the first and last words (vii. 222). Other resemblances are pointed out in the Notes.

It is also worth while to notice how the character of the speaking falcon in the second part of the Squire's Tale is precisely that of Anelida. The parallel lines are pointed out in the Notes. The principal MSS. may be thus grouped: A*a*.—F.B. A*b*.—Tn. D. Lt. B.—Harl. Cx. Here A and B are two groups, of which the former is subdivided into A*a* and A*b*. See Koch, in *Anglia*, iv. b. 102.

§ 25. VIII. Chaucer's Wordes unto Adam.

This is evidently a genuine poem, written by the author of the translation of Boethius and of the story of Troilus.

§ 26. IX. The Former Age.

First printed in 1866, in Morris's Chaucer, from a transcript made by Mr. Bradshaw, who pointed out its genuineness. It is ascribed to Chaucer in both MSS., and belongs, in fact, to his translation of Boethius, though probably written at a later date. In MS. I. the poem is headed:—'Chaw*cer* vp-on this fyfte met*ur* of the second book.' In MS. Hh., the colophon is: 'Finit Etas prima: Chaucers.' Dr. Koch thinks that the five poems here numbered IX. X. XIII–XV. 'form a cyclus, as it were, being free transcriptions of different passages in Boethius' *Consolatio Philosophiae*.' There is, in fact, a probability that these were all written at about the same period, and that rather a late one, some years after the prose translation of Boethius had been completed; and a probable date for this completion is somewhere about 1380.

Both MS. copies are from the same source, as both of them omit the same line, viz. l. 56; which I have had to supply by conjecture. Neither of the MSS. are well spelt, nor are they very satisfactory. The mistake in riming l. 47 with l. 43 instead of l. 45 may very well have been due to an oversight on the part of the poet himself. But the poem is a beautiful one, and admirably expressed; and its inclusion among the Minor Poems is a considerable gain.

Dr. Furnivall has printed the Latin text of Boethius, lib. ii. met. 5, from MS. I., as well as Chaucer's prose version of the same, for the sake of comparison with the text of the poem. The likeness hardly extends beyond the first four stanzas. I here transcribe that part of the prose version which is parallel to the poem, omitting a few sentences which do not appear there at all; for the complete text, see vol. ii.

'Blisful was the first age of men. They helden hem apayed with the metes that the trewe feldes broughten furthe. They ne distroyede nor deceivede not hem-self with outrage. They weren wont lightly to slaken hir hunger at even with acornes of okes. [*Stanza* 2.] They ne coude nat medly[1] the yifte of Bachus to the clere hony; that is to seyn, they coude make no piment nor clarree. [*Stanza* 3.] .. they coude nat deyen whyte fleeses[2] of Serien contree with the blode of a maner shelfisshe that men finden in Tyrie, with whiche blode men deyen purpur. [*Stanza* 6.] They slepen hoolsum slepes upon the gras, and dronken of the renninge wateres [*cf*. l. 8]; and layen under the shadwes of the heye pyn-trees. [*Stanza* 3, *continued*.] Ne no gest ne no straungere ne carf yit the heye see with ores or with shippes; ne they ne hadde seyn yit none newe strondes, to leden marchaundyse in-to dyverse contrees. Tho weren the cruel clariouns ful hust[3] and ful stille... [*Stanza* 4.] For wherto or whiche woodnesse of enemys wolde first moeven armes, whan they seyen cruel woundes, ne none medes[4] be of blood y-shad[5]?.. Allas! what was he that first dalf[6] up the gobetes[7] or the weightes of gold covered under erthe, and the precious stones that wolden han ben hid? He dalf up precious perils; ... for the preciousnesse of swiche thinge, hath many man ben in peril.'

The metre is the same as that of the ABC.

§ 27. X. FORTUNE.

Attributed to Chaucer by Shirley in MSS. A. and T.; also marked as Chaucer's in MSS. F. and I. In MS. I., this poem and

---

[1] mix. [2] fleeces. [3] hushed, silent.
[4] rewards. [5] shed. [6] dug. [7] lumps.

THE MINOR POEMS.

the preceding are actually introduced into Chaucer's translation of Boethius, between the fifth metre and the sixth prose of the second book, as has been already said. The metre is the same as that of the ABC and The Former Age, but the same rimes run through three stanzas. The Envoy forms a 7-line stanza, but has only two rimes; the formula is *ababbab*. For further remarks, see the Notes.

§ 28. XI. MERCILES BEAUTE.

The unique copy of this poem is in MS. P[1]. It is the last poem in the MS., and is in excellent company, as it immediately follows several other of Chaucer's genuine poems[2]. This is probably why Bp. Percy attributed it to Chaucer, who himself tells us that he wrote 'balades, *roundels*, virelayes.' It is significant that Mätzner, in his *Altenglische Sprachproben*, i. 347, chose this poem alone as a specimen of the Minor Poems. It is, in fact, most happily expressed, and the internal evidence places its authenticity beyond question. The three roundels express three 'movements,' in the poet's usual manner; and his mastery of metre is shewn in the use of the same rime in *-en-e* in the first and third roundels, requiring no less than *ten* different words for the purpose; whilst in the second roundel the corresponding lines end in *-eyn-e*, producing much the same effect, if (as is probable) the old sounds of *e* and *ey* were not very different. We at once recognise the Chaucerian phrases *I do no fors* (see Cant. Ta. D 1234, 1512), and *I counte him not a bene* (see Troil. v. 363).

Very characteristic is the use of the dissyllabic word *sen-e* (l. 10), which is an adjective, and means 'manifest,' from the A.S. *geséne*, (*gesýne*), and not the past participle, which is *y-seen*. Chaucer rimes it with *clen-e* (Prol. to C. T. 134), and with *gren-e* (Kn. Tale, A 2298). The phrase *though he sterve for the peyne* (l. 23) reminds us of *for to dyen in the peyne* (Kn. Ta. A 1133).

But the most curious thing about this poem is the incidental testimony of Lydgate, in his Ballade in Commendacion of our Ladie;

---

[1] See Todd, Illustrations of Chaucer, p. 116; and see above, pp. 55, 56.

[2] The critics who brush aside such a statement as this should learn to look at MSS. for themselves. The make-up of this MS. shews that it is essentially a Chaucer-Lydgate MS.; and Merciless Beautee is not Lydgate's. To weigh the evidence of a MS., it must be personally inspected by such as have had some experience.

see poem no. 26 above, discussed at p. 38. I here quote st. 22 in full, from ed. 1561, fol. 330 :

> 'Where might I loue euer better beset
> Then in this Lilie, likyng to beholde?
> That lace of loue, the bonde so well thou knit,
> That I maie see thee, or myne harte colde,
> And or I passe out of my daies olde,
> Tofore [thee] syngyng euermore vtterly—
> *Your iyen twoo woll slea me sodainly.*'

I ought to add that this poem is the only one which I have admitted into the set of Minor Poems (nos. I–XX) with incomplete external evidence. If it is not Chaucer's, it is by some one who contrived to surpass him in his own style. And this is sufficient excuse for its appearance here.

Moreover, Lydgate's testimony *is* external evidence, in a high degree. Even the allusion in l. 27 to the Roman de la Rose points in the same direction; and so does Chaucer's statement that he wrote roundels. Excepting that in the Parl. of Foules, ll. 680-692, and the three here given, no roundels of his have ever been found[1].

§ 29. XII. TO ROSEMOUNDE.

This poem was discovered by me in the Bodleian Library on the 2nd of April, 1891. It is written on a fly-leaf at the end of MS. Rawlinson Poet. 163, which also contains a copy of Chaucer's Troilus. At the end of the 'Troilus' is the colophon: 'Here endith the book of Troylus and of Cresseyde.' This colophon is preceded by 'Tregentyll,' and followed by 'Chaucer.' On the next leaf (no. 114) is the Balade, without any title, at the foot of which is 'Tregentil'——'Chaucer,' the two names being written at a considerable distance apart. I believe 'Tregentil' to represent the name of the scribe[2]. In any case, 'Chaucer' represents the name of the author. It is a happy specimen of his humour.

---

[1] Middle-English roundels are very scarce. I know of one by Hoccleve, printed by Mason in 1796, and reprinted in Todd's *Illustrations*, p. 372; and there is a poor one by Lydgate, in Halliwell's edition of his Minor Poems, p. 10. Two more (one being by Lydgate) are given in Ritson, *Anc. Songs*, i. 128, 129.

[2] I do *not* think, as some have guessed, that 'Tregentil Chaucer' means 'Tres gentil Chaucer.' Those who think so had better look at the MS. I see no sense in it; nor do I know why *tres* should be spelt *tre*.

§ 30. XIII. TRUTH.

This famous poem is attributed to Chaucer in MS. F., also (thrice) by Shirley, who in one of the copies in MS. T. (in which it occurs *twice*) calls it a 'Balade that Chaucier made on his deeth-bedde'; which is probably a mere bad guess[1]. The MSS. may be divided into two groups; the four best are in the first group, viz. At., E., Gg., Ct., and the rest (mostly) in the second group. Those of the first group have the readings *Tempest* (8), *Know thy contree* (19), and *Hold the hye wey* (20); whilst the rest have, in the same places, *Peyne* (8), *Look up on hy* (19), and *Weyve thy lust* (20). It is remarkable that the Envoy occurs in MS. At. *only*. It may have been suppressed owing to a misunderstanding of the word *vache* (cow), the true sense of which is a little obscure. The reference is to Boethius, bk. v. met. 5, where it is explained that quadrupeds *look down* upon the earth, whilst man alone *looks up* towards heaven; cf. *lok up* in l. 19 of the poem. The sense is therefore, that we should cease to look down, and learn to look up like true men; 'only the linage of man,' says Chaucer, in his translation of Boethius, 'heveth heyeste his heye heved[2].. this figure amonesteth[3] thee, that axest the hevene with thy righte visage, and hast areysed thy fore-heved to beren up a-heigh thy corage, so that thy thoght ne be nat y-hevied[4] ne put lowe under fote.'

§ 31. XIV. GENTILESSE.

It is curious that this Balade not only occurs as an independent poem, as in MSS. T., Harl., Ct., and others, but is also quoted bodily in a poem by Henry Scogan in MS. A. It is attributed to Chaucer by Shirley in MSS. T. and Harl.; and still more satisfactory is the account given of it by Scogan. The title of Scogan's poem is:—'A moral balade made by Henry Scogan squyer. Here folowethe nexst a moral balade to my lorde the Prince, to my lord of Clarence, to my lord of Bedford, and to my lorde of Gloucestre; by Henry Scogan, at a souper of feorthe merchande (*sic*) in the vyntre in London, at the hous of Lowys Iohan.' It is printed in all the

---

[1] A similar note was made in MS. Cotton, Otho. A. xviii., now destroyed. Todd printed the poem from this MS. in his Illustrations of Chaucer, p. 131; it belongs to the 'first group.'

[2] high head.   [3] admonishes.   [4] weighed down.

XIV. GENTILESSE.

old editions of Chaucer; see poem no. 33, p. 32. Scogan tells us that he was 'fader,' i.e. tutor, to the four sons of Henry IV. above-mentioned[1]. His ballad is in twenty-one 8-line stanzas, and he inserts Chaucer's *Gentilesse*, distinguished by being in 7-line stanzas, between the 13th and 14th stanzas of his own work. He refers to Chaucer in the 9th stanza thus (in MS. A.):—

> 'My maistre Chaucier, God his soule have,
> That in his langage was so curyous,
> He saide that the fader, nowe dede and grave,
> Beqwathe no-thing his vertue with his hous
> Un-to his sone.'

This is a reference to ll. 16, 17 of Chaucer's poem. Again, in his 13th stanza, he says:—

> 'By auncetrye thus may yee no-thing clayme,
> As that my maistre Chaucier dothe expresse,
> But temporell thing, that man may hurte and mayme;
> Thane is gode stocke of vertuous noblesse;
> And, sithe that he is lord of blessednesse
> That made us alle, and for mankynde that dyed,
> Folowe his vertue with full besynesse;
> And of this thinge herke howe my maistre seyde.'

He here refers to lines 15–17, and lines 1–4 of Chaucer's poem; and then proceeds to quote it in full. Having done so, he adds:—

> 'Loo, here this noble poete of Brettayne
> Howe hyely he, in vertuouse sentence,
> The losse [MS. lesse] in youthe of vertue can compleyne.'

Scogan's advice is all good; and, though he accuses himself of having misspent his youth, this may very well mean no more than such an expression means in the mouth of a good man. He is doubtless the very person to whom Chaucer's 'Lenvoy a Scogan' was addressed, and Chaucer (l. 21) there gives him an excellent character for wisdom of speech. Accordingly, he is not to be confused with the Thomas Scogan or Scogin to whom is attributed an idle book called 'Scoggins Iests,' which were said to have been 'gathered' by Andrew Boord or Borde, author of the Introduction of Knowledge[2]. When

---

[1] The poem must have been written not many years before 1413, the date of the accession of Henry V. In 1405, the ages of the princes were 17, 16, 15, and 14 respectively. Shirley's title to the poem was evidently written after 1415, as John was not created Duke of Bedford until that year.

[2] See Furnivall's edition of Borde's Introduction of Knowledge, E. E. T. S.,

Shakespeare, in *2 Hen. IV.* iii. 2. 33, says that Sir John Falstaff broke Scogan's head, he was no doubt thinking of the supposed author of the jest-book, and may have been led, by observation of the name in a black-letter edition of Chaucer, to suppose that he lived in the time of Henry IV. This was quite enough for his purpose, though it is probable that the jester lived in the time of Edward IV.; see Tyrwhitt's note on the Envoy to Scogan. On the other hand, we find Ben Jonson taking his ideas about Scogan solely from Henry Scogan's poem and Chaucer's Envoy, without any reference to the jester. See his Masque of the Fortunate Isles, in which Scogan is first described and afterwards introduced. The description tells us nothing more than we know already.

As for Lewis John (p. 82), Tyrwhitt says he was a Welshman, 'who was naturalised by Act of Parliament, 2 Hen. V., and who was concerned with Thomas Chaucer in the execution of the office of chief butler; *Rot. Parl.* 2 Hen. V. n. 18.'

Caxton's printed edition of this poem seems to follow a better source than any of the MSS.

§ 32. XV. LAK OF STEDFASTNESSE.

Attributed to Chaucer by Shirley in MSS. Harl. and T., and sent to King Richard at Windsor, according to the same authority. The general idea of it is from Boethius; see the Notes. Shirley refers it to the last years of Richard II., say 1397-9. We find something very like it in Piers Plowman, C. iv. 203-210, where Richard is told that bribery and wicked connivance at extortion have almost brought it about—

'That no lond loveth the, and yut leest thyn owene.'

In any case, the date can hardly vary between wider limits than between 1393 and 1399. Richard held a tournament at Windsor in 1399[1], which was but thinly attended; 'the greater part of the knights and squires of England were disgusted with the king.'

Of this poem, MS. Ct. seems to give the best text.

1870. At p. 31 of the Forewords, the editor says there is no evidence for attributing 'Scoggins Iests' to Borde.

[1] Froissart, bk. iv. c. 105 (Johnes' translation).

§ 33. XVI. LENVOY A SCOGAN.

This piece is attributed to Chaucer in all three MSS., viz. F., P., and Gg.; and is obviously genuine. The probable date of it is towards the end of 1393; see the Notes.

For some account of Scogan, see above (p. 83).

§ 34. XVII. LENVOY A BUKTON.

This piece is certainly genuine. In MS. F., the title is—'Lenvoy de Chaucer a Bukton.' In Julian Notary's edition it is—'Here foloweth the counceyll of Chaucer touching Maryag, &c. whiche was sente te (*sic*) Buckcton, &c.' In all the other early printed editions it is inserted *without any title* immediately after the Book of the Duchess.

The poem is one of Chaucer's latest productions, and may safely be dated about the end of the year 1396. This appears from the reference, in l. 23, to the great misfortune it would be to any Englishmen 'to be take in Fryse,' i. e. to be taken prisoner in Friesland. There is but one occasion on which this reference could have had any point, viz. during or just after the expedition of William of Hainault to Friesland, as narrated by Froissart in his Chronicles, bk. iv. capp. 78, 79. He tells that William of Hainault applied to Richard II. for assistance, who sent him 'some men-at-arms and two hundred archers, under the command of three English lords[1].' The expedition set out in August, 1396, and stayed in Friesland about five weeks, till the beginning of October, when 'the weather began to be very cold and to rain almost daily.' The great danger of being taken prisoner in Friesland was because the Frieslanders fought so desperately that they were seldom taken prisoners themselves. Then 'the Frieslanders offered their prisoners in exchange, man for man; but, when their enemies had none to give in return, they put them to death.' Besides this, the prisoners had to endure all the miseries of a bad and cold season, in an inclement climate. Hence the propriety of Chaucer's allusion fully appears. From l. 8, we learn that Chaucer was now a widower; for the word *eft* means 'again.' His wife is presumed to have died in the latter part of 1387. We should also observe the allusion to the Wife of Bath's Tale in l. 29.

---

[1] See Johnes' translation of Froissart, 1839; ii. 612-7.

§ 35. XVIII. THE COMPLEYNT OF VENUS.

This poem is usually printed as if it formed part of the Complaint of Mars; but it is really distinct. It is attributed to Chaucer by Shirley both in MS. T. and in MS. A. It is not original, but translated from the French, as appears from l. 82. Shirley tells us that the author of the French poem was Sir Otes de Graunson, a worthy knight of Savoy. He is mentioned as receiving from King Richard the grant of an annuity of 126*l.* 13*s.* 4*d.* on 17 Nov. 1393; see Furnivall's *Trial Forewords*, p. 123. The association of this poem with the Complaint of Mars renders it probable that the Venus of this poem is the same as the Venus of the other, i. e. the Princess Isabel of Spain, and Duchess of York. This fits well with the word *Princess* at the beginning of the Envoy; and as she died in 1394, whilst Chaucer, on the other hand, complains of his advancing years, we must date the poem about 1393, i. e. just about the time when Graunson received his annuity. Chaucer, if born about 1340, was not really more than 53, but we must remember that, in those days, men often aged quickly. John of Gaunt, who is represented by Shakespeare as a very old man, only lived to the age of 59; and the Black Prince died quite worn out, at the age of 46. Compare the notes to ll. 73, 76, 79, and 82.

Much new light has lately been thrown upon this poem by Dr. A. Piaget, who contributed an article to *Romania*, tome xix., on 'Oton de Granson et ses Poésies,' in 1890. The author succeeded in discovering a large number of Granson's poems, including, to our great gain, the three Balades of which Chaucer's 'Compleynt of Venus' is a translation. I am thus enabled to give the original French beneath the English version, for the sake of comparison.

He has also given us an interesting account of Granson himself, for which I must refer my readers to his article. It appears that Froissart mentions Granson at least four times (twice in bk. i. c. 303, A. D. 1372, once in c. 305, and once in c. 331, A. D. 1379), as fighting on the side of the English; see Johnes' translation. He was in Savoy from 1389 to 1391; but, in the latter year, was accused of being concerned in the death of Amadeus VII., count of Savoy, in consequence of which he returned to England, and in 1393 his estates in Savoy were confiscated. It was on this occasion that Richard II. assigned to him the pension above mentioned. With the hope of clearing himself from the serious charge laid against him,

XIX. THE COMPLEINT TO HIS PURSE.

Granson fought a judicial duel, at Bourg-en-Bresse, on Aug. 7, 1397, in which, however, he was slain.

Now that we have the original before us, we can see clearly, as Dr. Piaget says, that Chaucer has certainly not translated the original Balades 'word for word' throughout. He does so sometimes, as in ll. 27, 28, 30, 31, in which the closeness of the translation is marvellous; but, usually, he paraphrases the original to a considerable extent. In the first Balade, he has even altered the general motive; in the original, Granson sings the praises of his lady; in Chaucer, it is a lady who praises the worthiness of her lover.

It also becomes probable that the title 'The Compleynt of Venus,' which seems to have been suggested by Shirley, is by no means a fitting one. It is not suitable for Venus, unless the 'Venus' be a mortal; neither is it a continuous 'Compleynt,' being simply a linking together of three separate and distinct Balades.

It is clear to me that, when Chaucer added his Envoy, he made the difficulties of following the original 'word by word' and of preserving the original metre his excuse; and that what really troubled him was the difficulty of adapting the French, especially Balade I., so as to be acceptable to the 'Princess' who enjoined him to translate these Balades. In particular, he evidently aimed at giving them a sort of connection, so that one should follow the other naturally; which accounts for the changes in the first of them. It is significant, perhaps, that the allusion to 'youth' (F. *jeunesce*) in l. 70 is entirely dropped.

On the whole, I think we may still accept the theory that this poem was written at the request (practically, the command) of Isabel, duchess of York, the probable 'Venus' of the 'Compleynt of Mars.' Chaucer seems to have thrown the three Balades together, linking them so as to express a lady's constancy in love, and choosing such language as he deemed would be most acceptable to the princess. He then ingeniously, and not without some humour, protests that any apparent alterations are due to his own dulness and the difficulties of translating 'word for word,' and of preserving the rimes.

In l. 31, the F. text shews us that we must read *Pleyne*, not *Pleye* (as in the MSS.). This was pointed out by Mr. Paget Toynbee.

§ 36. XIX. THE COMPLEINT TO HIS PURSE.

Attributed to Chaucer by Shirley, in MS. Harl. 7333; by Caxton; by the scribes of MSS. F., P., and Ff.; and by early editors. I do not know on what grounds Speght removed Chaucer's name, and substituted that of T. Occleve; there seems to be no authority for this change. I think it highly probable that the poem itself is older than the Envoy; see note to l. 17. In any case, the Envoy is almost certainly Chaucer's latest extant composition.

§ 37. XX. Proverbs.

Attributed to Chaucer in MSS. F. and Ha.; see further in the Notes. From the nature of the case, we cannot assign any probable date to this composition. Yet it was, perhaps, written after, rather than before, the Tale of Melibeus.

§ 38. XXI. Against Women Unconstaunt.

For the genuineness of this Balade, we have chiefly the internal evidence to trust to; but this seems to me to be sufficiently strong. The Balade is perfect in construction, having but three rimes (*-esse, -ace, -ene*), and a refrain. The 'mood' of it strongly resembles that of Lak of Stedfastnesse; the lines run with perfect smoothness, and the rimes are all Chaucerian. It is difficult to suppose that Lydgate, or even Hoccleve, who was a better metrician, could have produced so good an imitation of Chaucer's style. But we are not without strong external evidence; for the general idea of the poem, and what is more important, the whole of the refrain, are taken from Chaucer's favourite author Machault (ed. Tarbé, p. 56); whose refrain is—'En lieu de bleu, Damë, vous vestez vert.' Again, the poem is only found in company with other poems by Chaucer. Such collocation frequently means nothing, but those who actually consult[1] MSS. Ct. and Ha. will see how close is its association with the Chaucerian poems in those MSS. I have said that it occurs in MSS. F., Ct., and Ha. Now in MS. Ct. we find, on the back of fol. 188 and on fol. 189, just four poems in the same hand. These are (1) Gentilesse; (2) Lak of Stedfastnesse; (3) Truth; and (4) Against Women Unconstaunt. As three of these are admittedly genuine, there is evidence that the fourth is the same. We may also notice that, in this MS., the poems on Lak of Stedfastnesse and Against Women Unconstaunt are not far apart. On searching

---

[1] It would be decent, on the part of such critics as do *not* examine the MSS., to speak of my opinions in a less contemptuous tone.

MS. Ha. (Harl. 7578), I again found three of these poems in company, viz. (1) Gentilesse; (2) Lak of Stedfastnesse; and (3) Against Women Unconstaunt; the last being, in my view, precisely in its right place. (This copy of the poem was unknown to me in 1887.)

§ 39. XXII. An Amorous Complaint.

Whilst searching through the various MSS. containing Minor Poems by Chaucer in the British Museum, my attention was arrested by this piece, which, as far as I know, has never before been printed. It is in Shirley's handwriting, but he does not claim it for Chaucer. However, the internal evidence seems to me irresistible; the melody is Chaucer's, and his peculiar touches appear in it over and over again. There is, moreover, in the last stanza, a direct reference to the Parliament of Foules [1].

I cannot explain the oracular notice of time in the heading; even if we alter *May* to *day*, it contradicts l. 85, which mentions 'seint Valentines day.' The heading is—'And next folowyng begynnith an amerowse compleynte made at wyndesore in the laste May tofore Nouembre' (*sic*). The date is inexplicable [2]; but the mention of locality is interesting. Chaucer became a 'valet of the king's chamber' in 1367, and must frequently have been at Windsor, where the institution of the Order of the Garter was annually celebrated on St. George's Day (April 23). Some of the parallelisms in expression between the present poem and other passages in Chaucer's Works are pointed out in the Notes.

This Complaint should be compared with the complaint uttered by Dorigen in the Cant. Tales, F. 1311-1325, which is little else than the same thing in a compressed form. There is also much resemblance to the 'complaints' in Troilus; see the references in the Notes.

Since first printing the text in 1888, I found that it is precisely the same poem as one extant in MSS. F. and B., with the title 'Complaynt Damours.' I had noticed the latter some time previously, and had made a note that it ought to be closely examined; but unfortunately I forgot to do so, or I should have seen at once

---

[1] Unless, which is more probable, the *Parliament of Foules* reproduces, nearly, two lines from the present poem.

[2] Perhaps 'tofore' means 'for use in,' or 'to be presented in'; and 'November' was some special occasion.

that it had strong claims to being considered genuine. These claims are considerably strengthened by the fact of the appearance of the poem in these two Chaucerian MSS., the former of which contains no less than *sixteen*, and the latter *seven* of the Minor Poems, besides the Legend and the Hous of Fame.

In reprinting the text in the present volume, I take occasion to give all the more important results of a collation of the text with these MSS. In most places, their readings are inferior to those in the text; but in other places they suggest corrections.

In MS. F. the fourth stanza is mutilated; the latter half of lines 24-28 is missing.

In B., below the word *Explicit*, another and later hand has scrawled 'be me Humfrey Flemyng.' 'Be me' merely means—'this signature is mine.' It is a mere scribble, and does not necessarily relate to the poem at all.

The readings of F. and B. do not help us much; for the text in Harl., on the whole, is better.

It is not at all improbable that a better copy of this poem may yet be found.

§ 40. XXIII. BALADE OF COMPLEYNT.

This poem, which has not been printed before, as far as I am aware, occurs in Shirley's MS. Addit. 16165, at fol. 256, back. It is merely headed 'Balade of compleynte,' without any note of its being Chaucer's. But I had not read more than four lines of it before I at once recognised the well-known melodious flow which Chaucer's imitators (except sometimes Hoccleve) so seldom succeed in reproducing. And when I had only finished reading the first stanza, I decided at once to copy it out, not doubting that it would fulfil all the usual tests of metre, rime, and language; which it certainly does. It is far more correct in wording than the preceding poem, and does not require that we should either omit or supply a single word. But in l. 20 the last word should surely be *dere* rather than *here*; and the last word in l. 11 is indistinct. I read it as *reewe* afterwards altered to *newe*; and *newe* makes very good sense. I may notice that Shirley's *n*'s are very peculiar: the first upstroke is very long, commencing below the line; and this peculiarity renders the reading tolerably certain. Some lines resemble lines in no. VI., as is pointed out in the Notes. Altogether, it is a beautiful poem, and its recovery is a clear gain.

§ 41. Concluding Remarks.

I regret that this Introduction has run to so great a length; but it was incumbent on me to shew reasons for the rejection or acceptance of the very large number of pieces which have hitherto been included in editions of Chaucer's Works. I have now only to add that I have, of course, been greatly indebted to the works of others; so much so indeed that I can hardly particularise them. I must, however, mention very gratefully the names of Dr. Furnivall, Professor Ten Brink, Dr. Koch, Dr. Willert, Max Lange, Rambeau, and various contributors to the publications of the Chaucer Society; and though I have consulted for myself such books as Le Roman de la Rose, the Teseide, the Thebaid of Statius, the poems of Machault, and a great many more, and have inserted in the Notes a large number of references which I discovered, or re-discovered, for myself, I beg leave distinctly to disclaim any merit, not doubting that most of what I have said may very likely have been said by others, and said better. Want of leisure renders it impossible for me to give to others their due meed of recognition in many instances; for I have often found it less troublesome to consult original authorities for myself than to hunt up what others have said relative to the passage under consideration.

I have relegated Poems no. XXI., XXII., and XXIII. to an Appendix, because they are not expressly attributed to Chaucer in the MSS. Such evidence has its value, but it is possible to make too much of it; and I agree with Dr. Koch, that, despite the MSS., the genuineness of no XX. is doubtful; for the rime of *compas* with *embrace* is suspicious. It is constantly the case that poems, well known to be Chaucer's, are not marked as his in the MS. copies; and we must really depend upon a prolonged and intelligent study of the internal evidence. This is why I admit poems nos. XXI–XXIII into the collection; and I hope it will be conceded that I am free from recklessness in this matter. Certainly my methods differ from those of John Stowe, and I believe them to be more worthy of respect.

THE ROMAUNT OF THE ROSE.

FRAGMENT A.

MANY men seyn that in sweveninges
Ther nis but fables and lesinges;
But men may somme swevenes seen,
Which hardely ne false been,
But afterward ben apparaunte.   5
This may I drawe to waraunte
An authour, that hight Macrobes,
That halt not dremes false ne lees,
But undoth us the avisioun
That whylom mette king Cipioun.   10
    And who so sayth, or weneth it be
A Iape, or elles [a] nycetee
To wene that dremes after falle,
Let who-so liste a fool me calle.

LE ROMAN DE LA ROSE.

Maintes gens dient que en songes
N'a se fables non et mençonges;
Mais l'en puet tiex songes songier
Qui ne sunt mie mençongier;
Ains sunt après bien apparant.
Si en puis bien trere à garant
Ung acteur qui ot non Macrobes,
Qui ne tint pas songes à lobes;
Ainçois escrist la vision
Qui avint au roi Cipion.   10
Quiconques cuide ne qui die
Que soit folor ou musardie
De croire que songes aviengne,
Qui ce voldra, pour fol m'en tiengne;

G. = Glasgow MS.; Th. = Thynne's ed. (1532).
1-44. *Lost in G.; from* Th.   3. Th. some sweuen; *but the pl. is required.*
4. Th. that false ne bene.   5. Th. apparaunt.   6. Th. warraunt.   12. Th. els; *om.* a.   13, 14. Th. fal, cal; fole.

THE ROMAUNT OF THE ROSE.

For this trowe I, and say for me, 15
That dremes signifiaunce be
Of good and harme to many wightes,
That dremen in her slepe a-nightes
Ful many thinges covertly,
That fallen after al openly. 20
   Within my twenty yere of age, *The Dream.*
Whan that Love taketh his corage
Of yonge folk, I wente sone
To bedde, as I was wont to done,
And fast I sleep; and in sleping, 25
Me mette swiche a swevening,
That lykede me wonders wel;
But in that sweven is never a del
That it nis afterward befalle,
Right as this dreem wol telle us alle. 30
Now this dreem wol I ryme aright,
To make your hertes gaye and light;
For Love it prayeth, and also
Commaundeth me that it be so
And if ther any aske me, 35
Whether that it be he or she,
How [that] this book [the] which is here
Shal hote, that I rede you here;

Car endroit moi ai-je fiance
Que songe soit senefiance
Des biens as gens et des anuiz,
Car li plusors songent de nuitz
Maintes choses couvertement
Que l'en voit puis apertement. 20
   Où vintiesme an de mon aage,
Où point qu'Amors prend le paage
Des jones gens, couchiez estoie
Une nuit, si cum je souloie,
Et me dormoie moult forment,

Si vi ung songe en mon dormant,
Qui moult fut biax, et moult me plot,
Mès onques riens où songe n'ot
Qui avenu trestout ne soit,
Si cum li songes recontoit. 30
Or veil cel songe rimaier,
Por vos cuers plus fere esgaier,
Qu' Amors le me prie et commande :
Et se nus ne nule demande
Comment ge voil que cilz Romman
Soit apelez, que ge commanz :

---

23. Th. folke; went.   25. Th. slepte.   26. Th. suche.   27. Th. lyked;
wele.   28. Th. dele.   29. Th. afterwarde befal.   30. Th. dreme; tel; al.
31. Th. Nowe; dreme.   35. Th. there.   37. Th. Howe; *om.* that *and* the.
38. Th. hatte; *read* hote.

THE ROMAUNT OF THE ROSE. 95

It is the Romance of the Rose,
In which al the art of love I close. 40
   The mater fair is of to make;
God graunte in gree that she it take
For whom that it begonnen is!
And that is she that hath, y-wis,
So mochel prys; and ther-to she 45
So worthy is biloved be,
That she wel oughte of prys and right,
Be cleped Rose of every wight.
   That it was May me thoughte tho,
It is fyve yere or more ago; 50
That it was May, thus dremed me,
In tyme of love and Iolitee,
That al thing ginneth waxen gay,
For ther is neither busk nor hay
In May, that it nil shrouded been, 55
And it with newe leves wreen.
These wodes eek recoveren grene,
That drye in winter been to sene;
And the erthe wexeth proud withalle,
For swote dewes that on it falle, 60
And [al] the pore estat forget
In which that winter hadde it set,

Ce est li Rommanz de la Rose,
Où l'art d'Amors est tote enclose.
La matire en est bone et noeve:
Or doint Diez qu'en gré le reçoeve
Cele por qui ge l'ai empris. 41
C'est cele qui tant a de pris,
Et tant est digne d'estre amée,
Qu'el doit estre Rose clamée.
   Avis m'iere qu'il estoit mains,
Il a jà bien cincq ans, au mains,
En Mai estoie, ce songoie,

El tems amoreus plain de joie,
El tens où tote riens s'esgaie,
Que l'en ne voit boisson ne haie 50
Qui en Mai parer ne se voille,
Et covrir de novele foille;
Li bois recovrent lor verdure,
Qui sunt sec tant cum yver dure,
La terre méisme s'orgoille
Por la rousée qui la moille,
Et oblie la poverté
Où ele a tot l'yver esté.

---

39. Ed. 1550, Romaunte.   40. Th. arte.   42. Th. graunt me in; *omit* me.
45. *Here begins* G.   46. Th. to be; G. *torn*.   47. Th. G. ought.   49. G.
Th. thought.   55. G. Th. bene.   56. G. Th. wrene.   59. G. erth.
G. Th. proude.   61. G. Th. forgette.   62. G. Th. had; sette.

And than bicometh the ground so proud
That it wol have a newe shroud,
And maketh so queynt his robe and fayr   65
That it hath hewes an hundred payr
Of gras and floures, inde and pers,
And many hewes ful dyvers:
That is the robe I mene, y-wis,
Through which the ground to preisen is.   70
   The briddes, that han left hir song,
Whyl they han suffred cold so strong
In wedres grille, and derk to sighte,
Ben in May, for the sonne brighte,
So glade, that they shewe in singing,   75
That in hir herte is swich lyking,
That they mote singen and be light.
Than doth the nightingale hir might
To make noyse, and singen blythe.
Than is blisful, many a sythe,   80
The chelaundre and the papingay.
Than yonge folk entenden ay
For to ben gay and amorous,
The tyme is than so savorous.
Hard is his herte that loveth nought   85
In May, whan al this mirth is wrought;

Lors devient la terre si gobe,
Qu'ele volt avoir novele robe;   60
Si scet si cointe robe faire,
Que de colors i a cent paire,
D'erbes, de flors indes et perses,
Et de maintes colors diverses.
C'est la robe que ge devise,
Por quoi la terre miex se prise.
   Li oisel, qui se sunt téu
Tant cum il ont le froit éu,
Et le tens divers et frarin,
Sunt en Mai, por le tens serin,   70

Si lié qu'il monstrent en chantant
Qu'en lor cuer a de joie tant,
Qu'il lor estuet chanter par force.
Li rossignos lores s'efforce
De chanter et de faire noise;
Lors s'esvertue, et lors s'envoise
Li papegaus et la kalandre :
Lors estuet jones gens entendre
A estre gais et amoreus
Por le tens bel et doucereus.   80
Moult a dur cuer qui en Mai n'aime,

---

66. G. Th. had.   69-72. *Imperfect in* G.   72. G. so; Th. ful.   73. Th. grylle; G. gryl.   73, 74. G. Th. sight, bright.   76. Th. herte; G. hertis. G. sich.   80. G. *om.* a.   81. G. *om.* the.   82. Th. yonge; G. yong 84. Th. sauorous; G. sauerous.   85. Th. his herte; G. the hert.

THE ROMAUNT OF THE ROSE. 97

Whan he may on these braunches here
The smale briddes singen clere
Hir blisful swete song pitous;
And in this sesoun delytous, 90
Whan love affrayeth alle thing,
Me thoughte a-night, in my sleping,
Right in my bed, ful redily,
That it was by the morowe erly,
And up I roos, and gan me clothe; 95
Anoon I wissh myn hondes bothe;
A sylvre nedle forth I drogh
Out of an aguiler queynt y-nogh,
And gan this nedle threde anon;
For out of toun me list to gon 100
The sowne of briddes for to here,
That on thise busshes singen clere.
And in the swete sesoun that leef is,
With a threde basting my slevis,
Aloon I wente in my playing, 105
The smale foules song harkning;
That peyned hem ful many a payre
To singe on bowes blosmed fayre.
Iolif and gay, ful of gladnesse,

Quant il ot chanter sus la raime
As oisiaus les dous chans piteus.
En iceli tens déliteus,
Que tote riens d'amer s'effroie,
Sonjai une nuit que j'estoie,
Ce m'iert avis en mon dormant,
Qu'il estoit matin durement;
De mon lit tantost me levai,
Chauçai moi et mes mains lavai. 90
Lors trais une aguille d'argent
D'un aguiller mignot et gent,

Si pris l'aguille à enfiler.
Hors de vile oi talent d'aler,
Por oïr des oisiaus les sons
Qui chantoient par ces boissons.
En icele saison novele,
Cousant mes manches à videle,
M'en alai tot seus esbatant,
Et les oiselés escoutant, 100
Qui de chanter moult s'engoissoient
Par ces vergiers qui florissoient.
Jolis, gais et plains de léesce,

---

89. G. blesful; Th. blysful.   91. G. affraieth; Th. affirmeth.   G. Th. al.
96. G. wisshe; hondis.   97. Th. nedyl. G. droughe; Th. drowe.   98. Th.
aguyler; G. Aguler. G. ynoughe; Th. ynowe.   101. Th. sowne; G. song.
102. Th. on; G. in. *Both* buskes.   103. G. *om.* the. G. swete; Th. lefe.
107. Th. That; G. They. G. *om.* a.   109. Th. Iolyfe; G. Ioly.

H

98 THE ROMAUNT OF THE ROSE.

Toward a river I gan me dresse, 110
That I herde renne faste by;
For fairer playing non saugh I
Than playen me by that riveer,
For from an hille that stood ther neer,
Cam doun the streem ful stif and bold. 115
Cleer was the water, and as cold
As any welle is, sooth to seyne;
And somdel lasse it was than Seine,
But it was straighter wel away.
And never saugh I, er that day, 120
The water that so wel lyked me;
And wonder glad was I to see
That lusty place, and that riveer;
And with that water that ran so cleer
My face I wissh. Tho saugh I wel 125
The botme paved everydel
With gravel, ful of stones shene.
The medewe softe, swote, and grene,
Beet right on the water-syde.
Ful cleer was than the morow-tyde, 130
And ful attempre, out of drede.
Tho gan I walke through the mede,
Dounward ay in my pleying,

Vers une riviere m'adresce.
Que j'oi près d'ilecques bruire;
Car ne me soi aillors déduire
Plus bel que sus cele riviere.
D'ung tertre qui près d'iluec iere
Descendoit l'iaue grant et roide,
Clere, bruiant, et aussi froide 110
Comme puiz, ou comme fontaine,
Et estoit poi mendre de Saine,
Mès qu'ele iere plus espanduë.
Onques mès n'avoie véuë
Cele iaue qui si bien coroit:

Moult m'abelissoit et séoit
A regarder le leu plaisant.
De l'iaue clere et reluisant
Mon vis rafreschi et lavé.
Si vi tot covert et pavé 120
Le fons de l'iaue de gravele;
La praérie grant et bele
Très au pié de l'iaue batoit.
Clere et serie et bele estoit
La matinée et atrempeé;
Lors m'en alai parmi la prée
Contre val l'iaue esbanoiant,

---

110. *Both* gan I.   111. G. herd; fast.   113. *Both* ryuere.   114. *Both* nere.   117–120. *Imperfect in* G.   121. *Perhaps om.* that.   123, 4. G. Th. ryuere, clere.   126. Th. botome ypaued.   132. G. walk thorough.

The river-syde costeying.
And whan I had a whyle goon, 135
I saugh a GARDIN right anoon, *The Garden.*
Ful long and brood, and everydel
Enclos it was, and walled wel,
With hye walles enbatailled,
Portrayed without, and wel entailled 140
With many riche portraitures;
And bothe images and peyntures
Gan I biholde bisily.
And I wol telle you, redily,
Of thilke images the semblaunce, 145
As fer as I have remembraunce.

A-midde saugh I HATE stonde, *Hate.*
That for hir wrathe, ire, and onde,
Semed to been a moveresse,
An angry wight, a chideresse; 150
And ful of gyle, and fel corage,
By semblaunt was that ilke image.
And she was no-thing wel arrayed,
But lyk a wood womman afrayed;
Y-frounced foule was hir visage, 155
And grenning for dispitous rage;
Hir nose snorted up for tene.

Tot le rivage costoiant.
 Quant j'oi ung poi avant alé,
Si vi ung vergier grant et lé, 130
Tot clos d'ung haut mur bataillié,
Portrait defors et entaillié
A maintes riches escritures.
Les ymages et les paintures
Ai moult volentiers remiré :
Si vous conteré et diré
De ces ymages la semblance,
Si cum moi vient à remembrance.

Haïne.
Ens où milieu je vi HAÏNE
Qui de corrous et d'ataïne 140
Sembloit bien estre moverresse,
Et correceuse et tencerresse,
Et plaine de grant cuvertage
Estoit par semblant cele ymage.
Si n'estoit pas bien atornée,
Ains sembloit estre forcenée,
Rechignie avoit et froncié
Le vis, et le nés secorcié.

---

138. G. Th. Enclosed was; *see* l. 1652.   139. Th. hye; G. high.   142. G. the ymages and the peyntures; Th. the ymages and peyntures.   146. G. haue in; Th. *om.* in.   147. Th. Amydde; G. Amyd.   149. *Both* mynoresse; *French,* moverresse.   154. *Both* wode.   155. G. *om.* Y-.

H 2

Ful hidous was she for to sene,
Ful foul and rusty was she, this.
Hir heed y-writhen was, y-wis, 160
Ful grimly with a greet towayle.
    An image of another entayle,   *Felonye.*
A lift half, was hir faste by;
Hir name above hir heed saugh I,
And she was called FELONYE. 165
    Another image, that VILANYE   *Vilanye.*
Y-cleped was, saugh I and fond
Upon the walle on hir right hond.
Vilanye was lyk somdel
That other image; and, trusteth wel, 170
She semed a wikked creature.
By countenaunce, in portrayture,
She semed be ful despitous,
And eek ful proud and outrageous.
Wel coude he peynte, I undertake, 175
That swiche image coude make.
Ful foul and cherlish semed she,
And eek vilaynous for to be,
And litel coude of norture,
To worshipe any creature. 180

Par grant hideur fu soutilliée,
Et si estoit entortillée   150
Hideusement d'une toaille.
    Felonnie.
Une autre ymage d'autel taille
A senestre vi delez lui ;
Son non desus sa teste lui ;
Apellée estoit FELONNIE.
    Vilennie.
Une ymage qui VILONIE
Avoit non, revi devers destre,

Qui estoit auques d'autel estre
Cum ces deus et d'autel féture ;
Bien sembloit male créature,   160
Et despiteuse et orgueilleuse,
Et mesdisant et ramponeuse.
Moult sot bien paindre et bien portraire
Cil qui tiex ymages sot faire :
Car bien sembloit chose vilaine,
De dolor et de despit plaine ;
Et fame qui petit séust
D'honorer ceus qu'ele déust.

---

160. Th. ywrithen ; G. writhen.   163. G. *om.* faste.   165, 6. *Both* Felony, Vil(l)any.   167. Th. Ycleped ; G. Clepid. *Both* fonde.   168. G. wal ; Th. wall. *Both* honde.   174. *Both* outragious.   176. Th. suche an ymage.

And next was peynted COVEITYSE,   Coveityse.
That eggeth folk, in many gyse,
To take and yeve right nought ageyn,
And grete tresours up to leyn.
And that is she that for usure   185
Leneth to many a creature
The lasse for the more winning,
So coveitous is her brenning.
And that is she, for penyes fele,
That techeth for to robbe and stele   190
These theves, and these smale harlotes;
And that is routhe, for by hir throtes
Ful many oon hangeth at the laste.
She maketh folk compasse and caste
To taken other folkes thing,   195
Through robberie, or miscounting.
And that is she that maketh trechoures;
And she [that] maketh false pledoures,
That with hir termes and hir domes
Doon maydens, children, and eek gromes   200
Hir heritage to forgo.
Ful croked were hir hondes two;
For Coveityse is ever wood

Couvoitise.
Après fu painte COVEITISE:
C'est cele qui les gens atise   170
De prendre et de noient donner,
Et les grans avoirs aüner.
C'est cele qui fait à usure
Prester mains por la grant ardure
D'avoir conquerre et assembler.
C'est cele qui semont d'embler
Les larrons et les ribaudiaus;
Si est grans pechiés et grans diaus
Qu'en la fin en estuet mains pendre.

C'est cele qui fait l'autrui prendre,
Rober, tolir et bareter,   181
Et bescochier et mesconter;
C'est cele qui les tricheórs
Fait tous et les faus pledéors,
Qui maintes fois par lor faveles
Ont as valés et as puceles
Lor droites herites toluës.
Recorbillies et croçües
Avoit les mains icele ymage;
Ce fu drois: car toz jors esrage   190
Coveitise de l'autrui prendre.

---

184. G. gret tresouris; Th. gret treasours. G. leyne; Th. layne.   185. G. *om*. she.   188. Th. couetous; G. coueitise.   189. G. *om*. she. Th. for; G. that.   196. *Both* myscoueiting.   198. *Both om*. that.   203. *Both* wode.

102   THE ROMAUNT OF THE ROSE.

  To grypen other folkes good.
  Coveityse, for hir winning,   205
  Ful leef hath other mennes thing.
   Another image set saugh I   Avarice.
  Next Coveityse faste by,
  And she was cleped AVARICE.
  Ful foul in peynting was that vice; 210
  Ful sad and caytif was she eek,
  And al-so grene as any leek.
  So yvel hewed was hir colour,
  Hir semed have lived in langour.
  She was lyk thing for hungre deed, 215
  That ladde hir lyf only by breed
  Kneden with eisel strong and egre;
  And therto she was lene and megre.
  And she was clad ful povrely,
  Al in an old torn courtepy,   220
  As she were al with dogges torn;
  And bothe bihinde and eek biforn
  Clouted was she beggarly.
  A mantel heng hir faste by,
  Upon a perche, weyke and smalle; 225
  A burnet cote heng therwithalle,
  Furred with no menivere,

Coveitise ne set entendre
A riens qu'à l'autrui acrochier;
Coveitise à l'autrui trop chier.

   Avarice.

Une autre ymage y ot assise
Coste à coste de Coveitise,
AVARICE estoit apelée :
Lede estoit et sale et foulée
Cele ymage, et megre et chetive,
Et aussi vert cum une cive. 200
Tant par estoit descolorée
Qu'el sembloit estre enlangorée ;

Chose sembloit morte de fain,
Qui ne vesquit fors que de pain
Petri à lessu fort et aigre ;
Et avec ce qu'ele iere maigre,
Iert-ele povrement vestuë,
Cote avoit viés et desrumpuë,
Comme s'el fust as chiens remese ;
Povre iert moult la cote et esrese, 210
Et plaine de viés palestiaus.
Delez li pendoit ung mantiaus
A une perche moult greslete,
Et une cote de brunete ;
Où mantiau n'ot pas penne vaire,

 204. *Both* gode. 208. *Both* fast. 212. Th. any; G. ony. 214. *Both* semed to haue. 219. G. porely; Th. poorely. 220. *Both* courtpy
224. Th. mantel; G. mantyl. *Both* fast.

THE ROMAUNT OF THE ROSE.

But with a furre rough of here,
Of lambe-skinnes hevy and blake;
It was ful old, I undertake. 230
For Avarice to clothe hir wel
Ne hasteth hir, never a del;
For certeynly it were hir loth
To weren ofte that ilke cloth;
And if it were forwered, she 235
Wolde have ful greet necessitee
Of clothing, er she boughte hir newe,
Al were it bad of wolle and hewe.
This Avarice held in hir hande
A purs, that heng [doun] by a bande; 240
And that she hidde and bond so stronge,
Men must abyde wonder longe
Out of that purs er ther come ought,
For that ne cometh not in hir thought;
It was not, certein, hir entente 245
That fro that purs a peny wente.

    And by that image, nygh y-nough, *Envye.*
Was peynt ENVYE, that never lough,
Nor never wel in herte ferde
But-if she outher saugh or herde 250

Mes moult viés et de povre afaire,
D'agniaus noirs velus et pesans.
Bien avoit la robe vingt ans;
Mès Avarice du vestir
Se sot moult à tart aatir : 220
Car sachiés que moult li pesast
Se cele robe point usast;
Car s'el fust usée et mauvese,
Avarice éust grant mesese
De noeve robe et grant disete,
Avant qu'ele éust autre fete.
Avarice en sa main tenoit
Une borse qu'el reponnoit,
Et la nooit si durement,
Que demorast moult longuement 230
Ainçois qu'el en péust riens traire,
Mès el n'avoit de ce que faire.
El n'aloit pas à ce béant
Que de la borse ostat néant.

Envie.

Après refu portrete ENVIE,
Qui ne rist oncques en sa vie,
N'oncques de riens ne s'esjoï,
S'ele ne vit, ou s'el n'oï

---

234. Th. ilke; G. ilk. 239. Th. helde; G. hilde. 240. *Both om.* doun.
241, 2. Th. stronge, longe; G. strong, long. 245, 6. *Both* entent, went.
248. *Both* peynted. 249, 250. *Both* in hir herte. G. farede, herede; Th. ferde, herde.

Som greet mischaunce, or greet disese.
No-thing may so moch hir plese
As mischef and misaventure;
Or whan she seeth discomfiture
Upon any worthy man falle,   255
Than lyketh hir [ful] wel withalle.
She is ful glad in hir corage,
If she see any greet linage
Be brought to nought in shamful wyse.
And if a man in honour ryse,   260
Or by his witte, or by prowesse,
Of that hath she gret hevinesse;
For, trusteth wel, she goth nigh wood
Whan any chaunce happeth good.
Envye is of swich crueltee,   265
That feith ne trouthe holdeth she
To freend ne felawe, bad or good.
Ne she hath kin noon of hir blood,
That she nis ful hir enemy;
She nolde, I dar seyn hardely,   270
Hir owne fader ferde wel.
And sore abyeth she everydel
Hir malice, and hir maltalent:

Aucun grant domage retrere.
Nule riens ne li puet tant plere 240
Cum mefet et mesaventure;
Quant el voit grant desconfiture
Sor aucun prodomme chéoir,
Ice li plest moult à véoir.
Ele est trop lie en son corage
Quant el voit aucun grant lignage
Decheoir et aler à honte;
Et quant aucuns à honor monte
Par son sens ou par sa proéce,
C'est la chose qui plus la bléce. 250

Car sachiés que moult la convient
Estre irée quant biens avient.
Envie est de tel cruauté,
Qu'ele ne porte léauté
A compaignon, ne à compaigne;
N'ele n'a parent, tant li tiengne,
A cui el ne soit anemie:
Car certes el ne vorroit mie
Que biens venist, neis à son pere.
Mès bien sachiés qu'ele com-
 pere   260
Sa malice trop ledement:

---

255. *Perhaps read* On . . . to falle.   256. *Both om.* ful.   259. Th. shamful;
G. shynful.   261. *Both* or by his prowesse.   264. Th. chaunce; G. chaunge.
266. G. trouth.   271. G. farede; Th. fared.   273. *Both* male talent; *see* 330.

THE ROMAUNT OF THE ROSE.

For she is in so greet turment
And hath such [wo], whan folk doth good, 275
That nigh she melteth for pure wood;
Hir herte kerveth and to-breketh
That god the peple wel awreketh.
Envye, y-wis, shal never lette
Som blame upon the folk to sette. 280
I trowe that if Envye, y-wis,
Knewe the beste man that is
On this syde or biyond the see,
Yit somwhat lakken him wolde she.
And if he were so hende and wys, 285
That she ne mighte al abate his prys,
Yit wolde she blame his worthinesse,
Or by hir wordes make it lesse.
I saugh Envye, in that peynting,
Hadde a wonderful loking; 290
For she ne loked but awry,
Or overthwart, al baggingly.
And she hadde [eek] a foul usage;
She mighte loke in no visage
Of man or womman forth-right pleyn, 295
But shette oon yë for disdeyn;

Car ele est en si grant torment,
Et a tel duel quant gens bien font,
Par ung petit qu'ele ne font.
Ses felons cuers l'art et detrenche,
Qui de li Diex et la gent venche.
Envie ne fine nule hore
D'aucun blasme as gens metre sore;
Je cuit que s'ele cognoissoit
Tot le plus prodome qui soit 270
Ne deçà mer, ne delà mer,
Si le vorroit-ele blasmer;
Et s'il iere si bien apris

Qu'el ne péust de tot son pris
Rien abatre ne deprisier,
Si vorroit-ele apetisier
Sa proéce au mains, et s'onor
Par parole faire menor.
Lors vi qu'Envie en la painture
Avoit trop lede esgardéure; 280
Ele ne regardast noient
Fors de travers en borgnoiant;
Ele avoit ung mauvès usage,
Qu'ele ne pooit où visage
Regarder reins de plain en plaing,
Ains clooit ung oel par desdaing,

---

275. G. hath; Th. hate. *I supply* wo.   276. *Read* melt' th *or* melt.
277. *Both* so (*for* to-).   278. Th. people; G. puple.   282. *Both* best.
291. G. Th. awrie.   292. G. -thart; Th. -twharte, *misprint for* -thwart.
293. *I supply* eek. G. *om.* a foul.   296. G. hir eien; Th. her one eye.

106   THE ROMAUNT OF THE ROSE.

So for envye brenned she
Whan she mighte any man [y]-see,
That fair, or worthy were, or wys,
Or elles stood in folkes prys.   300
    SOROWE was peynted next Envye   Sorowe.
Upon that walle of masonrye.
But wel was seen in hir colour
That she hadde lived in langour;
Hir semed have the Iaunyce.   305
Nought half so pale was Avaryce,
Nor no-thing lyk, [as] of lenesse;
For sorowe, thought, and greet distresse,
That she hadde suffred day and night
Made hir ful yelwe, and no-thing bright,   310
Ful fade, pale, and megre also.
Was never wight yit half so wo
As that hir semed for to be,
Nor so fulfilled of ire as she.
I trowe that no wight mighte hir plese,   315
Nor do that thing that mighte hir ese;
Nor she ne wolde hir sorowe slake,
Nor comfort noon unto hir take;

Qu'ele fondoit d'ire et ardoit,
Quant aucuns qu'ele regardoit,
Estoit ou preus, ou biaus, ou gens,
Ou amés, ou loés de gens.   290

    Tristesse.

Delez Envie auques près iere
TRISTECE painte en la maisiere;
Mès bien paroit à sa color
Qu'ele avoit au cuer grant dolor,
Et sembloit avoir la jaunice.
Si n'i feïst riens Avarice
Ne de paleur, ne de mégrece,
Car li soucis et la destrece,

Et la pesance et les ennuis
Qu'el soffroit de jors et de nuis,   300
L'avoient moult fete jaunir,
Et megre et pale devenir.
Oncques mès nus en tel martire
Ne fu, ne n'ot ausinc grant ire
Cum il sembloit que ele éust :
Je cuit que nus ne li séust
Faire riens qui li péust plaire :
N'el ne se vosist pas retraire,
Ne réconforter à nul fuer
Du duel qu'ele avoit à son cuer.   310

---

298. *Both* se.   299. *So* Th.; G. fairer or worthier.   303. G. seyn;
Th. sene.   305. *Both* to haue; *read* hav-ë. Th. iaundice.   307. *I supply* as.
310. Th. yelowe; G. yolare.

So depe was hir wo bigonnen,
And eek hir herte in angre ronnen,   320
A sorowful thing wel semed she.
Nor she hadde no-thing slowe be
For to forcracchen al hir face,
And for to rende in many place
Hir clothes, and for to tere hir swire,   325
As she that was fulfilled of ire;
And al to-torn lay eek hir here
Aboute hir shuldres, here and there,
As she that hadde it al to-rent
For angre and for maltalent.   330
And eek I telle you certeynly
How that she weep ful tenderly.
In world nis wight so hard of herte
That hadde seen hir sorowes smerte,
That nolde have had of hir pitee,   335
So wo-bigoon a thing was she.
She al to-dasshte hir-self for wo,
And smoot togider her handes two.
To sorwe was she ful ententyf,
That woful recchelees caityf;   340
Hir roughte litel of pleying,
Or of clipping or [of] kissing;
For who-so sorweful is in herte

Trop avoit son cuer correcié,	De maltalent et de corrous.
Et son duel parfont commencié.	Et sachiés bien veritelment
Moult sembloit bien qu'el fust dolente,	Qu'ele ploroit profondément:
	Nus, tant fust durs, ne la véist,
Qu'ele n'avoit mie esté lente	A cui grant pitié n'en préist,
D'esgratiner tote sa chiere;	Qu'el se desrompoit et batoit,
N'ele n'avoit pas sa robe chiere,	Et ses poins ensemble hurtoit.
Ains l'ot en mains leus descirée	Moult iert à duel fere ententive
Cum cele qui moult iert irée.	La dolereuse, la chetive; 330
Si cheveul tuit destrecié furent,	Il ne li tenoit d'envoisier,
Et espandu par son col jurent, 320	Ne d'acoler, ne de baisier:
Que les avoit trestous desrous	Car cil qui a le cuer dolent,

---

324. *Both* rent.   333-380. *Lost in* G; *from* Th.   334. Th. had sene.
340. Th. rechelesse.   341. Th. rought.   342. *I supply* of.

Him liste not to pleye ne sterte,
Nor for to daunsen, ne to singe, 345
Ne may his herte in temper bringe
To make Ioye on even or morowe;
For Ioye is contraire unto sorowe.
 ELDE was peynted after this, *Elde.*
That shorter was a foot, ywis, 350
Than she was wont in her yonghede.
Unnethe hir-self she mighte fede;
So feble and eek so old was she
That faded was al hir beautee.
Ful salowe was waxen hir colour, 355
Hir heed for-hoor was, whyt as flour.
Y-wis, gret qualm ne were it noon,
Ne sinne, although hir lyf were gon.
Al woxen was hir body unwelde,
And drye, and dwyned al for elde. 360
A foul forwelked thing was she
That whylom round and softe had be.
Hir eres shoken fast withalle,
As from her heed they wolde falle.
Hir face frounced and forpyned, 365
And bothe hir hondes lorn, fordwyned.

Sachiés de voir, il n'a talent
De dancier, ne de karoler,
Ne nus ne se porroit moller
Qui duel éust, à joie faire,
Car duel et joie sont contraire.
  Vieillesse.
Après fu VIELLECE portraite,
Qui estoit bien ung pié retraite 340
De tele cum el soloit estre;
A paine se pooit-el pestre,
Tant estoit vielle et radotée.
Bien estoit si biauté gastée,
Et moult ert lede devenuë.

Toute sa teste estoit chenuë,
Et blanche cum s'el fust florie.
Ce ne fut mie grant morie
S'ele morust, ne grans pechiés,
Car tous ses cors estoit sechiés 350
De viellece et anoiantis :
Moult estoit jà ses vis fletris,
Qui jadis fut soef et plains;
Mès or est tous de fronces plains,
Les oreilles avoit mossues,
Et trestotes les dens perdues,
Si qu'ele n'en avoit neis une.
Tant par estoit de grant viellune,

---

344. Th. luste; play. 349. Th. contrarie. 352. Th. might. 356. Th for hore.

THE ROMAUNT OF THE ROSE. 109

So old she was that she ne wente
A foot, but it were by potente.
   The TYME, that passeth night and day,   **Time.**
And restelees travayleth ay,   370
And steleth from us so prively,
That to us seemeth sikerly
That it in oon point dwelleth ever,
And certes, it ne resteth never,
But goth so faste, and passeth ay,   375
That ther nis man that thinke may
What tyme that now present is:
Asketh at these clerkes this;
For [er] men thinke it redily,
Three tymes been y-passed by.   380
The tyme, that may not soiourne,
But goth, and never may retourne,
As water that doun renneth ay,
But never drope retourne may;
Ther may no-thing as tyme endure,   385
Metal, nor erthely creature;
For alle thing it fret and shal:
The tyme eek, that chaungeth al,
And al doth waxe and fostred be,
And alle thing distroyeth he: 390

Qu'el n'alast mie la montance
De quatre toises sans potance. 360
  Li tens qui s'en va nuit et jor,
Sans repos prendre et sans sejor,
Et qui de nous se part et emble
Si celéement, qu'il nous semble
Qu'il s'arreste adés en ung point,
Et il ne s'i arreste point,
Ains ne fine de trepasser,
Que nus ne puet néis penser
Quex tens ce est qui est présens;
Sel' demandés as clers lisans, 370

Ainçois que l'en l'éust pensé,
Seroit-il jà trois tens passé.
Li tens qui ne puet sejourner,
Ains vait tous jors sans retorner,
Cum l'iaue qui s'avale toute,
N'il n'en retorne arriere goute:
Li tens vers qui noient ne dure,
Ne fer ne chose tant soit dure,
Car il gaste tout et menjue;
Li tens qui tote chose mue,   380
Qui tout fait croistre et tout norist,
Et qui tout use et tout porrist;

367, 368. Th. went, potent.   370. Th. restlesse.   379. *Supply* er (Kaluza).   381. G. *begins again.*   382. *Both* may neuer.   387. *Both* frette. Th. shal; G. shall*e*.   388. Th. al; G. all*e*.   389. Th. al; G. all*e*.   390. *Both* al.

THE ROMAUNT OF THE ROSE.

The tyme, that eldeth our auncessours
And eldeth kinges and emperours,
And that us alle shal overcomen
Er that deeth us shal have nomen:
The tyme, that hath al in welde   395
To elden folk, had maad hir elde
So inly, that, to my witing,
She mighte helpe hir-self no-thing,
But turned ageyn unto childhede;
She had no-thing hir-self to lede,   400
Ne wit ne pith in[with] hir holde
More than a child of two yeer olde.
But natheles, I trowe that she
Was fair sumtyme, and fresh to see,
Whan she was in hir rightful age: 405
But she was past al that passage
And was a doted thing bicomen.
A furred cope on had she nomen;
Wel had she clad hir-self and warm,
For cold mighte elles doon hir harm.   410
These olde folk have alwey colde,
Hir kinde is swiche, whan they ben olde.
    Another thing was doon ther write,   **Pope-holy.**
That semede lyk an ipocrite,

Li tens qui enviellist nos peres,
Et viellist roys et emperieres,
Et qui tous nous enviellira,
Ou mort nous desavancera;
Li tens qui toute a la baillie
Des gens viellir, l'avoit viellie
Si durement, qu'au mien cuidier
El ne se pooit mès aidier,   390
Ains retornoit jà en enfance,
Car certes el n'avoit poissance,
Ce cuit-je, ne force, ne sens
Ne plus c'un enfés de deus ans.
Ne porquant, au mien escient,
Ele avoit esté sage et gent,

Quant cle iert en son droit aage;
Mais ge cuit qu'el n'iere mès sage,
Ains iert trestote rassotée.
Si ot d'une chape forrée   400
Moult bien, si cum je me recors,
Abrié et vestu son corps:
Bien fu vestue et chaudement,
Car el éust froit autrement.
Les vielles gens ont tost froidure;
Bien savés que c'est lor nature.

    Papelardie.

Une ymage ot emprès escrite,
Qui sembloit bien estre ypocrite;

---

398. *Both* myght.   401. *Both* witte; pithe; in.   404. *Both* faire.   408. Th. cappe.

THE ROMAUNT OF THE ROSE.

And it was cleped POPE-HOLY. 415
That ilke is she that prively
Ne spareth never a wikked dede,
Whan men of hir taken non hede;
And maketh hir outward precious,
With pale visage and pitous, 420
And semeth a simple creature;
But ther nis no misaventure
That she ne thenketh in hir corage.
Ful lyk to hir was that image,
That maked was lyk hir semblaunce. 425
She was ful simple of countenaunce,
And she was clothed and eek shod,
As she were, for the love of god,
Yolden to religioun,
Swich semed hir devocioun. 430
A sauter held she faste in honde,
And bisily she gan to fonde
To make many a feynt prayere
To god, and to his seyntes dere.
Ne she was gay, fresh, ne Iolyf, 435
But semed be ful ententyf
To gode werkes, and to faire,
And therto she had on an haire.
Ne certes, she was fat no-thing,

PAPELARDIE ert apelée.	Qu'el fu de simple contenance; 420
C'est cele qui en recelée, 410	Et si fu chaucie et vestue
Quant nus ne s'en puet prendre garde,	Tout ainsinc cum fame rendue.
De nul mal faire ne se tarde.	En sa main ung sautier tenoit,
El fait dehors le marmiteus,	Et sachiés que moult se penoit
Si a le vis simple et piteus,	De faire à Dieu prieres faintes,
Et semble sainte créature;	Et d'appeler et sains et saintes.
Mais sous ciel n'a male aventure	El ne fu gaie, ne jolive,
Qu'ele ne pense en son corage.	Ains fu par semblant ententive
Moult la ressembloit bien l'ymage	Du tout à bonnes ovres faire;
Qui faite fu à sa semblance,	Et si avoit vestu la haire. 430
	Et sachiés que n'iere pas grasse,

---

421. Th. symple; G. semely.   435. G. ne fresh; Th. *om*. ne.   436. *Both* to be.

But semed wery for fasting; 440
Of colour pale and deed was she.
From hir the gate [shal] werned be
Of paradys, that blisful place;
For swich folk maketh lene hir face,
As Crist seith in his evangyle, 445
To gete hem prys in toun a whyle;
And for a litel glorie veine
They lesen god and eek his reine.

    And alderlast of everichoon,   **Povert.**
Was peynted POVERT al aloon, 450
That not a peny hadde in wolde,
Al-though [that] she hir clothes solde,
And though she shulde anhonged be;
For naked as a worm was she.
And if the weder stormy were, 455
For colde she shulde have deyed there.
She nadde on but a streit old sak,
And many a clout on it ther stak;
This was hir cote and hir mantel,
No more was there, never a del, 460
To clothe her with; I undertake,
Gret leyser hadde she to quake.

De jeuner sembloit estre lasse,
S'avoit la color pale et morte.
A li et as siens ert la porte
Dévéée de Paradis;
Car icel gent si font lor vis
Amegrir, ce dit l'Evangile,
Por avoir loz parmi la ville,
Et por un poi de gloire vaine
Qui lor toldra Dieu et son raine. 440

    Povreté.
Portraite fu au darrenier

POVRETÉ, qui ung seul denier
N'éust pas, s'el se déust pendre,
Tant séust bien sa robe vendre;
Qu'ele iere nuë comme vers:
Se li tens fust ung poi divers,
Je cuit qu'ele acorast de froit,
Qu'el n'avoit c'ung vié sac estroit
Tout plain de mavès palestiaus;
Ce iert sa robe et ses mantiaus. 450
El n'avoit plus que afubler,
Grant loisir avoit de trembler.

---

442. *Both* ay (*giving no sense*); *read* shal.   444. *Both* grace (*for* face).
446. G. *om.* hem.   448. G. *om.* eek.   452. *I supply* that.   455. G. wedir; Th. wether.   456. G. deyd; Th. dyed.   462. *Both* had.

THE ROMAUNT OF THE ROSE. 113

And she was put, that I of talke,
Fer fro these other, up in an halke;
There lurked and there coured she, 465
For povre thing, wher-so it be,
Is shamfast, and despysed ay.
Acursed may wel be that day,
That povre man conceyved is;
For god wot, al to selde, y-wis, 470
Is any povre man wel fed,
Or wel arayed or y-cled,
Or wel biloved, in swich wyse
In honour that he may aryse.
 Alle these thinges, wel avysed, 475
As I have you er this devysed,
With gold and asure over alle
Depeynted were upon the walle.
Squar was the wal, and high somdel;
Enclosed, and y-barred wel, 480
In stede of hegge, was that gardin;
Com never shepherde therin.
Into that gardyn, wel [y-]wrought,
Who-so that me coude have brought,
By laddre, or elles by degree, 485
It wolde wel have lyked me.

Des autres fu un poi loignet;
Cum chien honteus en ung coignet
Se cropoit et s'atapissoit,
Car povre chose, où qu'ele soit,
Est adès boutée et despite.
L'eure soit ore la maudite,
Que povres homs fu concéus!
Qu'il ne sera jà bien péus, 460
Ne bien vestus, ne bien chauciés,
Néis amés, ne essauciés.
 Ces ymages bien avisé,

Qui, si comme j'ai devisé,
Furent à or et à asur
De toutes pars paintes où mur.
Haut fu li mur et tous quarrés,
Si en fu bien clos et barrés,
En leu de haies, uns vergiers,
Où onc n'avoit entré bergiers. 470
Cis vergiers en trop bel leu sist:
Qui dedens mener me vousist
Ou par échiele ou par degré,
Je l'en séusse moult bon gré;

---

466. G. pouer. 467. G. shamefast; dispised. 471. G. ony pouere;
fedde. Th. yfedde. 472. G. cledde; Th. ycledde. 478. Th. were:
G. newe. 479. *Both* Square. 480. Th. ybarred; G. barred. 483. *Both*
wrought. 485. G. laddris; Th. ladders; *read* laddre; *see* 523.

114 THE ROMAUNT OF THE ROSE.

For swich solace, swich Ioye, and play,
I trowe that never man ne say,
As in that place delitous.
The gardin was not daungerous 490
To herberwe briddes many oon.
So riche a yerd was never noon
Of briddes songe, and braunches grene.
Therin were briddes mo, I wene,
Than been in alle the rewme of Fraunce. 495
Ful blisful was the accordaunce
Of swete and pitous songe they made,
For al this world it oughte glade.
And I my-self so mery ferde,
Whan I hir blisful songes herde, 500
That for an hundred pound nolde I,—
If that the passage openly
Hadde been unto me free—
That I nolde entren for to see
Thassemblee, god [it kepe and were!]— 505
Of briddes, whiche therinne were,
That songen, through hir mery throtes,
Daunces of love, and mery notes.
  Whan I thus herde foules singe,
I fel faste in a weymentinge, 510

Car tel joie ne tel déduit
Ne vit nus hons, si cum ge cuit,
Cum il avoit en ce vergier :
Car li leus d'oisiaus herbergier
N'estoit ne dangereux ne chiches.
Onc mès ne fu nus leus si riches 480
D'arbres, ne d'oisillons chantans :
Qu'il i avoit d'oisiaus trois tans
Qu'en tout le remanant de France.
Moult estoit bele l'acordance
De lor piteus chant à oïr :
Tous li mons s'en dust esjoïr.

Je endroit moi m'en esjoï
Si durement, quant les oï,
Que n'en préisse pas cent livres,
Se li passages fust delivres, 490
Que ge n'entrasse ens et véisse
L'assemblée (que Diex garisse !)
Des oisiaus qui léens estoient,
Qui envoisiement chantoient
Les dances d'amors et les notes
Plesans, cortoises et mignotes.
  Quant j'oï les oisiaus chanter,
Forment me pris à dementer

---

489. *Both* As was in.   492. G. yeer ; Th. yere ; *read* yerd ; *see* 656.   494. Th. Therin ; G. Therynne.   498. *Both* ought.   501. Th. hundred ; G. hundreth. *Both* wolde (*by confusion*).   503. *Both* be.   505. *Both* kepe it fro care ; *a false rime*.   506. *Both* ware ; *a false spelling*.   510. *Both* weymentyng.

THE ROMAUNT OF THE ROSE.

By which art, or by what engyn
I mighte come in that gardyn;
But way I couthe finde noon
Into that gardin for to goon.
Ne nought wiste I if that ther were   515
Eyther hole or place [o]-where,
By which I mighte have entree;
Ne ther was noon to teche me;
For I was al aloon, y-wis,
Ful wo and anguissous of this.   520
Til atte laste bithoughte I me,
That by no weye ne mighte it be;
That ther nas laddre or wey to passe,
Or hole, into so fair a place.
　Tho gan I go a ful gret pas   525
Envyroning even in compas
The closing of the square wal,
Til that I fond a wiket smal
So shet, that I ne mighte in goon,
And other entree was ther noon.   530
　Upon this dore I gan to smyte,   The Door.
That was [so] fetys and so lyte;
For other wey coude I not seke.
Ful long I shoof, and knokked eke,

Par quel art ne par quel engin
Je porroie entrer où jardin ;   500
Mès ge ne poi onques trouver
Leu par où g'i péusse entrer.
Et sachiés que ge ne savoie
S'il i avoït partuis ne voie,
Ne leu par où l'en i entrast,
Ne hons nés qui le me monstrast
N'iert illec, que g'iere tot seus,
Moult destroit et moult angoisseus ;
Tant qu'au darrenier me sovint
C'oncques à nul jor ce n'avint   510

Qu'en si biau vergier n'éust huis,
Ou eschiele ou aucun partuis.
　Lors m'en alai grant aléure
Açaignant la compasséure
Et la cloison du mur quarré,
Tant que ung guichet bien barré
Trovai petitet et estroit ;
Par autre leu l'en n'i entroit.
A l'uis commençai à ferir,
Autre entrée n'i soi querir.   520
　Assez i feri et boutai,
Et par maintes fois escoutai

---

512. *Both* into.　　516. *Both* where; *read* o-where.　　517. *Both* myght.
520. *Both* For; *read* Ful. G. angwishis; *see* F. text.　　532. *I supply* 1st so.

116   THE ROMAUNT OF THE ROSE.

  And stood ful long and of[t] herkning 535
  If that I herde a wight coming;
  Til that the dore of thilke entree
  A mayden curteys opened me. *Ydelnesse.*
  Hir heer was as yelowe of hewe
  As any basin scoured newe. 540
  Hir flesh [as] tendre as is a chike,
  With bente browes, smothe and slike;
  And by mesure large were
  The opening of hir yën clere.
  Hir nose of good proporcioun, 545
  Hir yën greye as a faucoun,
  With swete breeth and wel savoured.
  Hir face whyt and wel coloured,
  With litel mouth, and round to see;
  A clove chin eek hadde she. 550
  Hir nekke was of good fasoun
  In lengthe and gretnesse, by resoun,
  Withoute bleyne, scabbe, or royne.
  Fro Ierusalem unto Burgoyne
  Ther nis a fairer nekke, y-wis, 555
  To fele how smothe and softe it is.
  Hir throte, al-so whyt of hewe
  As snow on braunche snowed newe.

Se j'orroie venir nulle arme.
Le guichet, qui estoit de charme,
M'ovrit une noble pucele
Qui moult estoit et gente et bele.
Cheveus ot blons cum uns bacins,
La char plus tendre qu'uns pocins,
Front reluisant, sorcis votis.
Son entr'oil ne fu pas petis, 530
Ains iert assez grans par mesure;
Le nés ot bien fait à droiture,
Les yex ot plus vairs c'uns faucons,
Por faire envie à ces bricons.

Douce alene ot et savorée,
La face blanche et colorée,
La bouche petite et grocete,
S'ot où menton une fossete.
Le col fu de bonne moison,
Gros assez et lons par raison, 540
Si n'i ot bube ne malen.
N'avoit jusqu'en Jherusalen
Fame qui plus biau col portast,
Polis iert et soef au tast.
La gorgete ot autresi blanche
Cum est la noif desus la branche

---

535. G. and of herknyng; Th. al herkenyng. 536. G. ony; Th. any; *read* a.
537. G. *om.* the. 540. G. ony; Th. any. 541. *I supply 1st* as. 542. *Both*
bent. 546. *Both* as is a; *omit* is *or* a. 558. G. snawe; Th. snowe. G.
snawed; Th. snowed.

THE ROMAUNT OF THE ROSE. 117

Of body ful wel wrought was she
Men neded not, in no cuntree, 560
A fairer body for to seke.
And of fyn orfrays had she eke
A chapelet: so semly oon
Ne wered never mayde upon; ....
And faire above that chapelet 565
A rose gerland had she set.
She hadde [in honde] a gay mirour,
And with a riche gold tressour
Hir heed was tressed queyntely;
Hir sleves sewed fetisly. 570
And for to kepe hir hondes faire
Of gloves whyte she hadde a paire.
And she hadde on a cote of grene
Of cloth of Gaunt; withouten wene,
Wel semed by hir apparayle 575
She was not wont to greet travayle.
For whan she kempt was fetisly,
And wel arayed and richely,
Thanne had she doon al hir Iournee;
For mery and wel bigoon was she. 580

Quant il a freschement negié.
Le cors ot bien fait et dougié,
L'en ne séust en nule terre
Nul plus bel cors de fame querre. 550
D'orfrois ot un chapel mignot;
Onques nule pucele n'ot
Plus cointe ne plus desguisié,
Ne l'aroie adroit devisié
En trestous les jors de ma vie.
Robe avoit moult bien entaillie ;
Ung chapel de roses tout frais
Ot dessus le chapel d'orfrais :
En sa main tint ung miroër,

Si ot d'ung riche treçoër 560
Son chief trecié moult richement,
Bien et bel et estroitement
Ot ambdeus cousues ses manches;
Et por garder que ses mains blanches
Ne halaissent, ot uns blans gans.
Cote ot d'ung riche vert de gans,
Cousue à lignel tout entour.
Il paroit bien à son atour
Qu'ele iere poi embesoignie.
Quant ele s'iere bien pignie, 570
Et bien parée et atornée,
Ele avoit faite sa jornée.

---

560. G. neded; Th. neden. 564. *Some lines lost?* 567. *I supply* in honde. 568. Th. tressour; G. tresour; (*cf.* Gawain, 1739). 569. *Both* queyntly; *see* l. 783. 570. *Both* fetously; *see* l. 577.

She ladde a lusty lyf in May,
She hadde no thought, by night ne day,
Of no-thing, but it were oonly
To graythe hir wel and uncouthly.
  Whan that this dore hadde opened me   585
This mayden, semely for to see,
I thanked hir as I best mighte,
And axede hir how that she highte,
And what she was, I axede eke.
And she to me was nought unmeke,   590
Ne of hir answer daungerous,
But faire answerde, and seide thus:—
'Lo, sir, my name is YDELNESSE;
So clepe men me, more and lesse.
Ful mighty and ful riche am I,   595
And that of oon thing, namely;
For I entende to no-thing
But to my Ioye, and my pleying,
And for to kembe and tresse me.
Aqueynted am I, and privee   600
With Mirthe, lord of this gardyn,
That fro the lande of Alexandryn
Made the trees be hider fet,
That in this gardin been y-set.

Moult avoit bon tems et bon May,
Qu'el n'avoit soussi ne esmay
De nule riens, fors solement
De soi atorner noblement.
  Quant ainsinc m'ot l'uis deffermé
La pucele au cors acesmé,
Je l'en merciai doucement,
Et si li demandai comment   580
Ele avoit non, et qui ele iere.
Ele ne fu pas envers moi fiere,
Ne de respondre desdaigneuse :
' Je me fais apeler Oiseuse,'
Dist-ele, ' à tous mes congnoissans ;

Si sui riche fame et poissans.
S'ai d'une chose moult bon tens,
Car à nule riens je ne pens
Qu'à moi joer et solacier,
Et mon chief pignier et trecier :   590
Quant sui pignée et atornée,
Adonc est fete ma jornée.
Privée sui moult et acointe
De Déduit le mignot, le cointe ;
C'est cil cui est cest biax jardins,
Qui de la terre as Sarradins
Fist çà ces arbres aporter,
Qu'il fist par ce vergier planter.

---

583. *Both* but if; *om.* if.   586. *Both* may; *see* l. 538.   587, 588. *Both* myght, hyght.   592. G. answeride ; Th. answerde.   603. G. hidre be ; Th. hyther be. *Both* fette.   604. G. sette ; Th. ysette.

THE ROMAUNT OF THE ROSE. 119

And whan the trees were woxen on highte, 605
This wal, that stant here in thy sighte,
Dide Mirthe enclosen al aboute;
And these images, al withoute,
He dide hem bothe entaile and peynte,
That neither ben Iolyf ne queynte, 610
But they ben ful of sorowe and wo,
As thou hast seen a whyle ago.
　'And ofte tyme, him to solace,
Sir Mirthe cometh into this place,
And eek with him cometh his meynee, 615
That liven in lust and Iolitee.
And now is Mirthe therin, to here
The briddes, how they singen clere,
The mavis and the nightingale,
And other Ioly briddes smale. 620
And thus he walketh to solace
Him and his folk ; for swetter place
To pleyen in he may not finde,
Although he soughte oon in-til Inde.
The alther-fairest folk to see 625
That in this world may founde be
Hath Mirthe with him in his route,
That folowen him alwayes aboute.'

Quant li arbres furent créu,
Le mur que vous avez véu, 600
Fist lors Deduit tout entor faire,
Et si fist au dehors portraire
Les ymages qui i sunt paintes,
Que ne sunt mignotes ne cointes ;
Ains sunt dolereuses et tristes,
Si cum vous orendroit véistes.
　Maintes fois por esbanoier
Se vient en cest leu umbroier
Déduit et les gens qui le sivent,
Qui en joie et en solas vivent. 610

Encores est léens, sans doute,
Déduit orendroit qui escoute
A chanter gais rossignolés,
Mauvis et autres oiselés.
Il s'esbat iluec et solace
O ses gens, car plus bele place
Ne plus biau leu por soi joer
Ne porroit-il mie trover ;
Les plus beles gens, ce sachiés,
Que vous jamès nulleu truissiés, 620
Si sunt li compaignon Déduit
Qu'il maine avec li et conduit.'

---

605. *Both* hight. 　 606. *Both* sight. 　 617. Th. therin ; G. therynne.
623. Th. playen in ; G. pleyn ynne.

When Ydelnesse had told al this,
And I hadde herkned wel, y-wis,   630
Than seide I to dame Ydelnesse,
'Now al-so wisly god me blesse,
Sith Mirthe, that is so fair and free,
Is in this yerde with his meynee,
Fro thilke assemblee, if I may,   635
Shal no man werne me to-day,
That I this night ne mote it see.
For, wel wene I, ther with him be
A fair and Ioly companye
Fulfilled of alle curtesye.'   640
And forth, withoute wordes mo,
In at the wiket wente I tho,
That Ydelnesse hadde opened me,
Into that gardin fair to see.

And whan I was [ther]in, y-wis,   645
Myn herte was ful glad of this.   **The Garden.**
For wel wende I ful sikerly
Have been in paradys erth[e]ly;
So fair it was, that, trusteth wel,
It semed a place espirituel.   650
For certes, as at my devys,
Ther is no place in paradys
So good in for to dwelle or be
As in that GARDIN, thoughte me;

Quant Oiseuse m'ot ce conté,
Et j'oi moult bien tout escouté,
Je li dis lores : 'Dame Oiseuse,
Jà de ce ne soyés douteuse,
Puis que Déduit li biaus, li gens
Est orendroit avec ses gens
En cest vergier, ceste assemblée
Ne m'iert pas, se je puis, emblée, 630
Que ne la voie encore ennuit ;
Véoir la m'estuet, car ge cuit
Que bele est cele compaignie,
Et cortoise et bien enseignie.'

Lors m'en entrai, ne dis puis mot,
Par l'uis que Oiseuse overt m'ot,
Où vergier ; et quant je fui ens
Je fui liés et baus et joiens.
Et sachiés que je cuidai estre
Por voir en Paradis terrestre,   640
Tant estoit li leu delitables,
Qu'il sembloit estre esperitables :
Car si cum il m'iert lors avis,
Ne féist en nul Paradis
Si bon estre, cum il faisoit
Où vergier qui tant me plaisoit.

---

631. Th. Than; G. Thanne.   645, 653. Th. in ; G. Inne.   654. *Both* thought.

THE ROMAUNT OF THE ROSE.

For there was many a brid singing, 655
Throughout the yerde al thringing.
In many places were nightingales,
Alpes, finches, and wodewales,
That in her swete song delyten
In thilke place as they habyten. 660
Ther mighte men see many flokkes
Of turtles and [of] laverokkes.
Chalaundres fele saw I there,
That wery, nigh forsongen were.
And thrustles, terins, and mavys, 665
That songen for to winne hem prys,
And eek to sormounte in hir song
These other briddes hem among.
By note made fair servyse
These briddes, that I you devyse; 670
They songe hir song as faire and wel
As angels doon espirituel.
And, trusteth wel, whan I hem herde,
Full lustily and wel I ferde;
For never yit swich melodye 675
Was herd of man that mighte dye.

D'oisiaus chantans avoit assés
Par tout le vergier amassés ;
En ung leu avoit rossigniaus,
En l'autre gais et estorniaus ; 650
Si r'avoit aillors grans escoles
De roietiaus et torteroles,
De chardonnereaus, d'arondeles,
D'aloes et de lardereles ;
Calendres i ot amassées
En ung autre leu, qui lassées
De chanter furent à envis :
Melles y avoit et mauvis
Qui baoient à sormonter

Ces autres oisiaus par chanter. 660
Il r'avoit aillors papegaus,
Et mains oisiaus qui par ces gaus
Et par ces bois où il habitent,
En lor biau chanter se délitent.
Trop parfesoient bel servise
Cil oisel que je vous devise ;
Il chantoient ung chant itel
Cum s'il fussent esperitel.
De voir sachiés, quant les oï,
Moult durement m'en esjoï : 670
Que mès si douce mélodie
Ne fu d'omme mortel oïe.

---

655. Th. byrde; G. bridde; *read* brid.   660. *Both* places (*badly*).   661. *Both* might.   668. *Both* That (*for* These).   673. Th. whan; G. that. Th. herde; G. herd.   676. *Both* myght.

Swich swete song was hem among,
That me thoughte it no briddes song,
But it was wonder lyk to be
Song of mermaydens of the see; 680
That, for her singing is so clere,
Though we mermaydens clepe hem here
In English, as in our usaunce,
Men clepen hem sereyns in Fraunce.
 Ententif weren for to singe 685
These briddes, that nought unkunninge
Were of hir craft, and apprentys,
But of [hir] song sotyl and wys.
And certes, whan I herde hir song,
And saw the grene place among, 690
In herte I wex so wonder gay,
That I was never erst, er that day,
So Iolyf, nor so wel bigo,
Ne mery in herte, as I was tho.
And than wiste I, and saw ful wel, 695
That Ydelnesse me served wel,
That me putte in swich Iolitee.
Hir freend wel oughte I for to be,
Sith she the dore of that gardyn
Hadde opened, and me leten in. 700

Tant estoit cil chans dous et biaus,
Qu'il ne sombloit pas chans d'oi- siaus,
Ains le péust l'en aesmer
A chant de seraines de mer,
Qui par lor vois, qu'eles ont saines
Et series, ont non seraines.
 A chanter furent ententis
Li oisillon qui aprenti 680
Ne furent pas ne non sachant;
Et sachiés quant j'oï lor chant,
Et je vi le leu verdaier,
Je me pris moult à esgaier;
Que n'avoie encor esté onques
Si jolif cum je fui adonques;
Por la grant délitableté
Fui plains de grant jolieté.
Et lores soi-je bien et vi
Que Oiseuse m'ot bien servi, 690
Qui m'avoit en tel déduit mis:
Bien déusse estre ses amis,
Quant ele m'avoit deffermé
Le guichet du vergier ramé.

---

684. *Both* clepe.
gardyn; G. gardyne.
688. Th. But; G. For. *Both om.* hir.
700. G. inne; Th. in.
699. Th

THE ROMAUNT OF THE ROSE. 123

From hennesforth how that I wroughte,
I shal you tellen, as me thoughte.
First, whereof Mirthe served there,
And eek what folk ther with him were,
Withoute fable I wol descryve. 705
And of that gardin eek as blyve
I wol you tellen after this.
The faire fasoun al, y-wis,
That wel [y-]wrought was for the nones,
I may not telle you al at ones: 710
But as I may and can, I shal
By ordre tellen you it al.
Ful fair servyse and eek ful swete
These briddes maden as they sete.
Layes of love, ful wel sowning 715
They songen in hir Iargoning;
Summe highe and summe eek lowe songe
Upon the braunches grene y-spronge.
The sweetnesse of hir melodye
Made al myn herte in reverdye. 720
And whan that I hadde herd, I trowe,
These briddes singing on a rowe,
Than mighte I not withholde me
That I ne wente in for to see

Dès ore si cum je sauré,
Vous conterai comment j'ovré.
Primes de quoi Déduit servoit,
Et quel compaignie il avoit
Sans longue fable vous veil dire,
Et du vergier tretout à tire 700
La façon vous redirai puis.
Tout ensemble dire ne puis,
Mès tout vous conteré par ordre,
Que l'en n'i sache que remordre.
  Grant servise et dous et plaisant

Aloient cil oisel faisant;
Lais d'amors et sonnés cortois
Chantoit chascun en son patois,
Li uns en haut, li autre en bas;
De lor chant n'estoit mie gas. 710
La douçor et la mélodie
Me mist où cuer grant reverdie;
Mès quant j'oi escouté ung poi
Les oisiaus, tenir ne me poi
Que dant Déduit véoir n'alasse;
Car à savoir moult desirasse

---

701. G. hens-; wrought. 702. *Both* thought. 709. *Both* wrought. 716. Th. her; G. their. Th. iargonyng; G. yarkonyng. 718. Th. ispronge; G. spronge. 720. Th. reuelrye; G. reuerye; *see* French. 724. Th. in; G. inne.

124   THE ROMAUNT OF THE ROSE.

  Sir Mirthe; for my desiring   725
Was him to seen, over alle thing,
His countenaunce and his manere:
That sighte was to me ful dere.
  Tho wente I forth on my right hond
Doun by a litel path I fond   730
Of mentes ful, and fenel grene;
And faste by, withoute wene,
SIR MIRTHE I fond; and right anoon Sir Mirthe.
Unto sir Mirthe gan I goon,
Ther-as he was, him to solace.   735
And with him, in that lusty place,
So fair folk and so fresh hadde he,
That whan I saw, I wondred me
Fro whennes swich folk mighte come,
So faire they weren, alle and some;   740
For they were lyk, as to my sighte,
To angels, that ben fethered brighte.
  This folk, of which I telle you so,
Upon a carole wenten tho.
A lady caroled hem, that highte   745
GLADNES, [the] blisful and the lighte; Gladnesse.
Wel coude she singe and lustily,
Non half so wel and semely,
And make in song swich refreininge,
It sat hir wonder wel to singe.   750

Son contenement et son estre.
 Lors m'en alai tout droit à destre,
Par une petitete sente
Plaine de fenoil et de mente;   720
Mès auques près trové Déduit,
Car maintenant en ung réduit
M'en entré où Déduit estoit.
Déduit ilueques s'esbatoit;
S'avoit si bele gent o soi,
Que quant je les vi, je ne soi
Dont si tres beles gens pooient

Estre venu; car il sembloient
Tout por voir anges empennés,
Si beles gens ne vit homs nés.   730
 Ceste gent dont je vous parole,
S'estoient pris à la carole,
Et une dame lor chantoit,
Qui Léesce apelée estoit :
Bien sot chanter et plesamment,
Ne nule plus avenaument,
Ne plus bel ses refrains ne fist,
A chanter merveilles li sist;

---

728. *Both* sight (*wrongly*).   732. Th. faste; G. fast. *Both* without.   739.
Th. whence; G. whenne. *Both* might.   741, 2. *Both* sight, bright.   743.
Th. These; G. This.   745. *Both* hyght.   746. *Both* blisfull. Th. and
lyght; G. and the light; *see* 797.   749. *Both add* couthe *before* make.

THE ROMAUNT OF THE ROSE.

Hir vois ful cleer was and ful swete.
She was nought rude ne unmete,
But couthe y-now of swich doing
As longeth unto caroling:
For she was wont in every place 755
To singen first, folk to solace;
For singing most she gaf hir to;
No craft had she so leef to do.
 Tho mightest thou caroles seen,
And folk [ther] daunce and mery been, 760
And make many a fair tourning
Upon the grene gras springing.
Ther mightest thou see these floutours,
Minstrales, and eek Iogelours,
That wel to singe dide hir peyne. 765
Somme songe songes of Loreyne;
For in Loreyne hir notes be
Ful swetter than in this contree.
Ther was many a timbestere,
And saylours, that I dar wel swere 770
Couthe hir craft ful parfitly.
The timbres up ful sotilly
They caste, and henten [hem] ful ofte
Upon a finger faire and softe,

Qu'ele avoit la vois clere et saine;
Et si n'estoit mie vilaine; 740
Ains se savoit bien desbrisier,
Ferir du pié et renvoisier.
Ele estoit adès coustumiere
De chanter en tous leus premiere:
Car chanter estoit li mestiers
Qu'ele faisoit plus volentiers.
 Lors véissiés carole aler,
Et gens mignotement baler,
Et faire mainte bele tresche,
Et maint biau tor sor l'erbe fresche. 750

Là véissiés fléutéors,
Menesterez et jougléors;
Si chantent li uns rotruenges,
Li autres notes Loherenges,
Por ce qu'en set en Loheregne
Plus cointes notes qu'en nul regne.
Assez i ot tableterresses
Ilec entor, et tymberresses
Qui moult savoient bien joer,
Et ne finoient de ruer 760
Le tymbre en haut, si recuilloient
Sor ung doi, c'onques n'i failloient.

---

760. *I supply* ther.   761. *Both* made (*for* make).   770. Th. saylours;
G. saillouris.   773. *Both* hente; *I supply* hem.

THE ROMAUNT OF THE ROSE.

That they [ne] fayled never-mo.　　　775
Ful fetis damiselles two,
Right yonge, and fulle of semlihede,
In kirtles, and non other wede,
And faire tressed every tresse,
Hadde Mirthe doon, for his noblesse,　　780
Amidde the carole for to daunce;
But her-of lyth no remembraunce,
How that they daunced queyntely.
That oon wolde come al prively
Agayn that other: and whan they were　　785
Togidre almost, they threwe y-fere
Hir mouthes so, that through hir play
It semed as they kiste alway;
To dauncen wel coude they the gyse;
What shulde I more to you devyse?　　790
Ne bede I never thennes go,
Whyles that I saw hem daunce so.
　Upon the carole wonder faste,
I gan biholde; til atte laste
A lady gan me for to espye,　　795
And she was cleped CURTESYE,　　　*Curtesye.*
The worshipful, the debonaire;
I pray god ever falle hir faire!

Deus damoiseles moult mignotes, | Bien se savoient desbrisier.
Qui estoient en pures cotes, | Ne vous en sai que devisier;
Et trecies à une tresce, | Mès à nul jor ne me quéisse
Faisoient Déduit par noblesce | Remuer, tant que ge véisse
Enmi la karole baler; | Ceste gent ainsine efforcier
Mès de ce ne fait à parler | De caroler et de dancier.　　780
Comme el baloient cointement. | 　La karole tout en estant
L'une venoit tout belement　　770 | Regardai iluec jusqu'à tant
Contre l'autre; et quant el estoient | C'une dame bien enseignie
Près à près, si s'entregetoient | Me tresvit: ce fu Cortoisie
Les bouches, qu'il vous fust avis | La vaillant et la debonnaire,
Que s'entrebaisassent où vis: | Que Diex deffende de contraire.

---

776. G. damysels; Th. damosels.　　782. *Both* lieth.　　783. *Both* queyntly;
see l. 569.　　791. *Both* bode; *read* bede; *see* note.　　798. *Both* pray to God.

THE ROMAUNT OF THE ROSE.

Ful curteisly she called me,
'What do ye there, beau sire?' quod she, 800
'Come [neer], and if it lyke yow
To daunccen, daunceth with us now.'
And I, withoute tarying,
Wente into the caroling.
I was abasshed never a del, 805
But it me lykede right wel,
That Curtesye me cleped so,
And bad me on the daunce go.
For if I hadde durst, certeyn
I wolde have caroled right fayn, 810
As man that was to daunce blythe.
Than gan I loken ofte sythe
The shap, the bodies, and the cheres,
The countenaunce and the maneres
Of alle the folk that daunced there, 815
And I shal telle what they were.
  Ful fair was Mirthe, ful long and high; **Mirthe.**
A fairer man I never sigh.
As round as appel was his face,
Ful rody and whyt in every place. 820
Fetys he was and wel beseye,
With metely mouth and yën greye;

Cortoisie lors m'apela :
'Biaus amis, que faites-vous là?'
Fait Cortoisie, 'çà venez,
Et avecque nous vous prenez 790
A la karole, s'il vous plest.'
Sans demorance et sans arrest
A la karole me sui pris,
Si n'en fui pas trop entrepris,
Et sachiés que moult m'agréa
Quant Cortoisie m'en pria,
Et me dist que je karolasse ;
Car de karoler, se j'osasse,
Estoie envieus et sorpris.

A regarder lores me pris 800
Les cors, les façons et les chieres,
Les semblances et les manieres
Des gens qui ilec karoloient :
Si vous dirai quex il estoient.
  Déduit fu biaus et lons et drois,
Jamés en terre ne venrois
Où vous truissiés nul plus bel homme :
La face avoit cum une pomme,
Vermoille et blanche tout entour,
Cointes fu et de bel atour. 810

---

801. *I supply* neer. 806. *Both* it to me liked. 811. *Both* right blythe; *om.* right. 812. Th. Than ; G. Thanne. 819. Th. appel; G. appille.

His nose by mesure wrought ful right;
Crisp was his heer, and eek ful bright.
His shuldres of a large brede, 825
And smalish in the girdilstede.
He semed lyk a portreiture,
So noble he was of his stature,
So fair, so Ioly, and so fetys,
With limes wrought at poynt devys, 830
Deliver, smert, and of gret might;
Ne sawe thou never man so light.
Of berde unnethe hadde he no-thing,
For it was in the firste spring.
Ful yong he was, and mery of thought, 835
And in samyt, with briddes wrought,
And with gold beten fetisly,
His body was clad ful richely.
Wrought was his robe in straunge gyse,
And al to-slitered for queyntyse 840
In many a place, lowe and hye.
And shod he was with greet maistrye,
With shoon decoped, and with laas.
By druerye, and by solas,
His leef a rosen chapelet 845
Had maad, and on his heed it set.

Les yex ot vairs, la bouche gente,
Et le nez fait par grant entente;
Cheveus ot blons, recercelés,
Par espaules fu auques lés,
Et gresles parmi la ceinture :
Il resembloit une painture,
Tant ere biaus et acesmés,
Et de tous membres bien formés.
Remuans fu, et preus, et vistes,
Plus legier homme ne véistes; 820
Si n'avoit barbe, ne grenon,
Se petiz peus folages non,

Car il ert jones damoisiaus.
D'un samit portret à oysiaus,
Qui ere tout à or batus,
Fu ses cors richement vestus.
Moult iert sa robe desguisée,
Et fu moult riche et encisée,
Et décopée par cointise ;
Chauciés refu par grant mes-
trise 830
D'uns solers décopés à las ;
Par druerie et par solas
Li ot s'amie fet chapel
De roses qui moult li sist bel.

---

834. *Both* first.   836. *Both* samette.   837. *Both* beten ful; *om.* ful.
844. *Both* drury.   845. Th. rosen; G. rosyn.

And wite ye who was his leef?
Dame GLADNES ther was him so leef,   Gladnesse.
That singeth so wel with glad corage,
That from she was twelve yeer of age,   850
She of hir love graunt him made.
Sir Mirthe hir by the finger hadde
[In] daunsing, and she him also;
Gret love was atwixe hem two.
Bothe were they faire and brighte of hewe;   855
She semede lyk a rose newe
Of colour, and hir flesh so tendre,
That with a brere smale and slendre
Men mighte it cleve, I dar wel sayn.
Hir forheed, frounceles al playn.   860
Bente were hir browes two,
Hir yën greye, and gladde also,
That laughede ay in hir semblaunt,
First or the mouth, by covenaunt.
I not what of hir nose descryve;   865
So fair hath no womman alyve. . . .
Hir heer was yelowe, and cleer shyning,
I wot no lady so lyking.

Savés-vous qui estoit s'amie?
Léesce qui nel' haoit mie,
L'envoisie, la bien chantans,
Qui dès lors qu'el n'ot que sept ans
De s'amor li donna l'otroi;
Déduit la tint parmi le doi   840
A la karole, et ele lui,
Bien s'entr'amoient ambedui:
Car il iert biaus, et ele bele,
Bien resembloit rose novele
De sa color. S'ot la char tendre,
Qu'en la li péust toute fendre
A une petitete ronce.
Le front ot blanc, poli, sans fronce,

Les sorcis bruns et enarchiés,
Les yex gros et si envoisiés,   850
Qu'il rioient tousjors avant
Que la bouchete par convant.
Je ne vous sai du nés que dire,
L'en nel' féist pas miex de cire.
Ele ot la bouche petitete,
Et por baisier son ami, preste;
Le chief ot blons et reluisant.
Que vous iroie-je disant?
Bele fu et bien atornée;
D'ung fil d'or ere galonnée,   860
S'ot ung chapel d'orfrois tout nuef;
Je qu'en oi véu vint et nuef,

---

848. *Both* gladnesse.   859. G. seye; Th. sey (*for* sayn).   860. G. pleye; Th. pley (*for* pleyn).   861. *Both* Bent.   863. *Both* laugheden.   865. *Both* I wot not what of hir nose I shal descryve (*eleven syllables*).   866. *Two lines lost.*

130   THE ROMAUNT OF THE ROSE.

Of orfrays fresh was hir gerland;
I, whiche seen have a thousand,   870
Saugh never, y-wis, no gerlond yit,
So wel [y]-wrought of silk as it.
And in an over-gilt samyt
Clad she was, by gret delyt,
Of which hir leef a robe werde,   875
The myrier she in herte ferde.
   And next hir wente, on hir other syde, **Cupide.**
The god of Love, that can devyde
Love, as him lyketh it [to] be.
But he can cherles daunten, he,   880
And maken folkes pryde fallen.
And he can wel these lordes thrallen,
And ladies putte at lowe degree,
Whan he may hem to proude see.
   This God of Love of his fasoun   885
Was lyk no knave, ne quistroun;
His beautee gretly was to pryse.
But of his robe to devyse
I drede encombred for to be.
For nought y-clad in silk was he,   890
But al in floures and flourettes,
Y-painted al with amorettes;

A nul jor mès véu n'avoie
Chapel si bien ouvré de soie.
D'un samit qui ert tous dorés
Fu ses cors richement parés,
De quoi son ami avoit robe,
Si en estoit assés plus gobe.
  A li se tint de l'autre part
Li Diex d'Amors, cil qui départ 870
Amoretes à sa devise.
C'est cil qui les amans justise,
Et qui abat l'orguel des gens,

Et si fait des seignors sergens,
Et des dames refait bajesses,
Quant il les trove trop engresses.
  Li Diex d'Amors, de la façon,
Ne resembloit mie garçon:
De beaulté fist moult à prisier,
Mes de sa robe devisier   880
Criens durement qu'encombré soie.
Il n'avoit pas robe de soie,
Ains avoit robe de floretes,
Fete par fines amoretes

---

869. Th. orfrayes.   870. Th. whiche; G. which. Th. sene; G. seyen.
873. Th. samyte; G. samet.   875, 6. Th. werde, ferde; G. werede, ferede.
Both ins. hir *bef.* herte.   877. Th. on; G. in.   879. *Both* Love, and as hym
likith it be.   887. Th. prise; G. preyse.   890. Th. ycladde; G. clad.
891. G. and in; Th. *om.* in.   892. *From* Th.; G. *om.*

THE ROMAUNT OF THE ROSE.

And with losenges and scochouns,
With briddes, libardes, and lyouns,
And other beestes wrought ful wel. 895
His garnement was everydel
Y-portreyd and y-wrought with floures,
By dyvers medling of coloures.
Floures ther were of many gyse
Y-set by compas in assyse; 900
Ther lakked no flour, to my dome,
Ne nought so muche as flour of brome,
Ne violete, ne eek pervenke,
Ne flour non, that man can on thenke,
And many a rose-leef ful long 905
Was entermedled ther-among:
And also on his heed was set
Of roses rede a chapelet.
But nightingales, a ful gret route,
That flyen over his heed aboute, 910
The leves felden as they flyen;
And he was al with briddes wryen,
With popiniay, with nightingale,
With chalaundre, and with wodewale,
With finch, with lark, and with archaungel. 915
He semede as he were an aungel

A losenges, à escuciaus,
A oiselés, à lionciaus,
Et à bestes et à liépars;
Fu la robe de toutes pars
Portraite, et ovrée de flors
Par diverseté de colors. 890
Flors i avoit de maintes guises
Qui furent par grant sens assises;
Nulle flor en esté ne nest
Qui n'i soit, neis flor de genest,
Ne violete, ne parvanche,
Ne fleur inde, jaune ne blanche;
Si ot par leus entremeslées
Foilles de roses grans et lées.
Il ot où chief ung chapelet
De roses; mès rossignolet 900
Qui entor son chief voletoient,
Les foilles jus en abatoient:
Car il iert tout covers d'oisiaus,
De papegaus, de rossignaus,
De calandres et de mesanges;
Il sembloit que ce fust uns anges

---

893. Th. losenges; G. losynges. 897. Th. Ypurtrayed; G. Portreied.
Th. ywrought; G. wrought. 900. Th. Yset; G. Sett. 902. Th.
moche; G. mych. 903, 4. *Both* peruynke, thynke. 906. G. -melled;
Th. -medled; *see* l. 898.

That doun were comen fro hevene clere.
  Love hadde with him a bachelere,
That he made alweyes with him be;
SWETE-LOKING cleped was he. 920
This bachelere stood biholding   Swete-Loking.
The daunce, and in his honde holding
Turke bowes two hadde he.
That oon of hem was of a tree
That bereth a fruyt of savour wikke; 925
Ful croked was that foule stikke,
And knotty here and there also,
And blak as bery, or any slo.
That other bowe was of a plante
Withoute wem, I dar warante, 930
Ful even, and by proporcioun
Tretys and long, of good fasoun.
And it was peynted wel and thwiten,
And over-al diapred and writen
With ladies and with bacheleres, 935
Ful lightsom and [ful] glad of cheres.
These bowes two held Swete-Loking,
That semed lyk no gadeling.
And ten brode arowes held he there,
Of which five in his right hond were. 940

Qui fust tantost venus du ciau.
  Amors avoit ung jovenciau
Qu'il faisoit estre iluec delés ;
Douz-Regard estoit apelés. 910
Ici bachelers regardoit
Les caroles, et si gardoit
Au Dieu d'Amors deux ars turquois.
Li uns des ars si fu d'un bois
Dont li fruit iert mal savorés ;
Tous plains de nouz et bocerés
Fu li ars dessous et dessore,

Et si estoit plus noirs que mores.
Li autres ars fu d'un plançon
Longuet et de gente façon ; 920
Si fu bien fait et bien dolés,
Et si fu moult bien pipelés.
Dames i ot de tous sens pointes,
Et valés envoisiés et cointes.
Ices deux ars tint Dous-Regars
Qui ne sembloit mie estre gars,
Avec dix des floiches son mestre.
Il en tint cinq en sa main destre ;

923. *Both* Turke bowes two, full wel deuysed had he (*too long*). 928. Th. any ; G. ony. 929, 930. Th. plante, warante ; G. plant, warant. *Both* Without. 932. G. Treitys ; Th. Trectes. *Both ins.* ful *after* of. 933. G. twythen ; Th. thwitten (*printed* twhitten). 936. *I supply* ful. 939. Th. helde ; G. hilde

THE ROMAUNT OF THE ROSE. 133

But they were shaven wel and dight,
Nokked and fethered a-right;
And al they were with gold bigoon,
And stronge poynted everichoon,
And sharpe for to kerven weel. 945
But iren was ther noon ne steel;
For al was gold, men mighte it see,
Out-take the fetheres and the tree.
   The swiftest of these arowes fyve
Out of a bowe for to dryve, 950
And best [y]-fethered for to flee,
And fairest eek, was cleped BEAUTEE.   **Beautee.**
That other arowe, that hurteth lesse,
Was cleped, as I trowe, SIMPLESSE.   **Simplesse.**
The thridde cleped was FRAUNCHYSE, 955
That fethered was, in noble wyse,   **Fraunchyse.**
With valour and with curtesye.
The fourthe was cleped COMPANYE   **Companye.**
That hevy for to sheten is;
But who-so sheteth right, y-wis, 960
May therwith doon gret harm and wo.
The fifte of these, and laste also,

Mès moult orent ices cinq floiches
Les penons bien fais, et les
   coiches: 930
Si furent toutes à or pointes,
Fors et tranchans orent les pointes,
Et aguës por bien percier,
Et si n'i ot fer ne acier;
Onc n'i ot riens qui d'or ne fust,
Fors que les penons et le fust :
Car el furent encarrelées
De sajetes d'or barbelées.
   La meillore et la plus isnele
De ces floiches, et la plus bele, 940

Et cele où li meillor penon
Furent entés, Biautes ot non.
Une d'eles qui le mains blece,
Ot non, ce m'est avis, Sim-
   plece.
Une autre en i ot apelée
Franchise; cele iert empenée
De Valor et de Cortoisie.
La quarte avoit non Compaignie :
En cele ot moult pesant sajete.
Ele n'iert pas d'aler loing preste; 950
Mès qui de près en vosist traire,
Il en péust assez mal faire.

---

942. Th. aryght; G. right.   944. G. peynted (!).   945. Th. sharpe; G. sharp. Th. wele; G. welle.   946. Th. stele; G. steelle.   948. Th. Out take; G. Outake.   953. G. lasse; Th. lesse.   958. Th. companye; G. compaigny.   959. *Both* shoten; *see* l. 989.   960. *For* right *read* nigh (K.).

FAIR-SEMBLAUNT men that arowe calle, **Fair-**
The leeste grevous of hem alle; **Semblaunt.**
Yit can it make a ful gret wounde, 965
But he may hope his sores sounde,
That hurt is with that arowe, y-wis;
His wo the bet bistowed is.
For he may soner have gladnesse,
His langour oughte be the lesse. 970
 Fyve arowes were of other gyse,
That been ful foule to devyse;
For shaft and ende, sooth to telle,
Were al-so blak as feend in helle.
 The first of hem is called PRYDE; **Pryde.** 975
That other arowe next him bisyde,
It was [y]-cleped VILANYE; **Vilanye.**
That arowe was as with felonye
Envenimed, and with spitous blame.
The thridde of hem was cleped SHAME. **Shame.** 980
The fourthe, WANHOPE cleped is, **Wanhope.**
The fifte, the NEWE-THOUGHT, y-wis. **Newe-**
 These arowes that I speke of here, **Thought.**
Were alle fyve of oon manere,
And alle were they resemblable. 985
To hem was wel sitting and able

La quinte avoit non Biau-Semblant,
Ce fut toute la mains grévant.
Ne porquant el fait moult grant
  plaie ;
Mès cis atent bonne menaie,
Qui de cele floiche est plaiés,
Ses maus en est mielx emplaiés ;
Car il puet tost santé atendre,
S'en doit estre sa dolor mendre. 960
 Cinq floiches i ot d'autre guise,
Qui furent lédes à devise :
Li fust estoient et li fer
Plus noirs que déables d'enfer.

La premiere avoit non Orguex,
L'autre qui ne valoit pas miex,
Fu apelée Vilenie ;
Icele fu de felonie
Toute tainte et envenimée.
La tierce fu Honte clamée, 970
Et la quarte Desesperance :
Novel-Penser fu sans doutance
Apelée la darreniere.
 Ces cinq floiches d'une maniere
Furent, et moult bien resem
  blables ;
Moult par lor estoit convenables

---

964. *Both* leest.   969. Th. soner; G. sonner.   970. Th. Hys; G. Hir.
Th. ought be; G. ought to be.   973. *Both* for to telle.   984. *Both* on;
read of (K.).

THE ROMAUNT OF THE ROSE. 135

The foule croked bowe hidous,
That knotty was, and al roynous.
That bowe semede wel to shete
These arowes fyve, that been unmete, 990
Contrarie to that other fyve.
But though I telle not as blyve
Of hir power, ne of hir might,
Her-after shal I tellen right
The sothe, and eek signifiaunce, 995
As fer as I have remembraunce:
Al shall be seid, I undertake,
Er of this boke an ende I make.
  Now come I to my tale ageyn.
But alderfirst, I wol you seyn 1000
The fasoun and the countenaunces
Of al the folk that on the daunce is.
The God of Love, Iolyf and light,
Ladde on his honde a lady bright,
Of high prys, and of greet degree. 1005
This lady called was BEAUTEE, Beautee.
[As was] an arowe, of which I tolde.
Ful wel [y]-thewed was she holde;
Ne she was derk ne broun, but bright,
And cleer as [is] the mone-light, 1010

Li uns des arcs qui fu hideus,
Et plains de neus, et eschardeus ;
Il devoit bien tiex floiches traire,
Car el erent force et contraire 980
As autres cinq floiches sans doute.
Mès ne diré pas ore toute
Lor forces, ne lor poestés.
Bien vous sera la verités
Contée, et la sénefiance
Nel'metré mie en obliance ;
Ains vous dirai que tout ce monte,
Ainçois que je fine mon conte.

Or revendrai à ma parole :
Des nobles gens de la karole 990
M'estuet dire les contenances,
Et les façons et les semblances.
Li Diex d'Amors se fu bien pris
A une dame de haut pris,
Et delez lui iert ajoustés :
Icele dame ot non Biautés,
Ainsinc cum une des cinq fleches.
En li ot maintes bonnes teches :
El ne fu oscure, ne brune,
Ains fu clere comme la lune, 1000

---

991. *Both* And contrarye.   998. Th. booke ; G. book.   1007. G. Th.
And ; *read* As was ; F. *Ainsinc cum.*   1010. *I supply* is.

Ageyn whom alle the sterres semen
But smale candels, as we demen.
Hir flesh was tendre as dewe of flour,
Hir chere was simple as byrde in bour;
As whyt as lilie or rose in rys, 1015
Hir face gentil and tretys.
Fetys she was, and smal to see;
No windred browes hadde she,
Ne popped hir, for it neded nought
To windre hir, or to peynte hir ought. 1020
Hir tresses yelowe, and longe straughten,
Unto hir heles doun they raughten:
Hir nose, hir mouth, and eye and cheke
Wel wrought, and al the remenaunt eke.
A ful gret savour and a swote 1025
Me thinketh in myn herte rote,
As helpe me god, whan I remembre
Of the fasoun of every membre!
In world is noon so fair a wight;
For yong she was, and hewed bright, 1030
[Wys], plesaunt, and fetys withalle,
Gente, and in hir middel smalle.
    Bisyde Beaute yede RICHESSE,   Richesse.
An high lady of greet noblesse,

Envers qui les autres estoiles
Resemblent petites chandoiles.
Tendre ot la char comme rousée,
Simple fu cum une espousée,
Et blanche comme flor de lis;
Si ot le vis cler et alis,
Et fu greslete et alignie;
Ne fu fardée ne guignie:
Car el n'avoit mie mestier
De soi tifer ne d'afetier. 1010
Les cheveus ot blons et si lons
Qu'il li batoient as talons;
Nez ot bien fait, et yelx et bouche.
Moult grant douçor au cuer me touche,
Si m'aïst Diex, quant il me membre
De la façon de chascun membre
Qu'il n'ot si bele fame où monde.
Briément el fu jonete et blonde,
Sade, plaisant, aperte et cointe,
Grassete et grele, gente et jointe. 1020
Près de Biauté se tint Richece,
Une dame de grant hautece,

1015. *For* As *read* And (K.). 1017. *Both* smale. 1018. *Both* wyntred;
see l. 1020. 1026. *Both* thought; *read* thinketh (K.). 1031. *Both* Sore (!);
read Wys (?). 1034. *Both* And hight (!).

THE ROMAUNT OF THE ROSE. 137

And greet of prys in every place. 1035
But who-so durste to hir trespace,
Or til hir folk, in worde or dede,
He were ful hardy, out of drede;
For bothe she helpe and hindre may:
And that is nought of yisterday 1040
That riche folk have ful gret might
To helpe, and eek to greve a wight.
The beste and grettest of valour
Diden Richesse ful gret honour,
And besy weren hir to serve; 1045
For that they wolde hir love deserve,
They cleped hir 'Lady,' grete and smalle;
This wyde world hir dredeth alle;
This world is al in hir daungere.
Hir court hath many a losengere, 1050
And many a traytour envious,
That been ful besy and curious
For to dispreisen, and to blame
That best deserven love and name.
Bifore the folk, hem to bigylen, 1055
These losengeres hem preyse, and smylen,
And thus the world with word anoynten;
But afterward they [prikke] and poynten

De grant pris et de grant affaire.
Qui à li ne as siens meffaire
Osast riens par fais, ou par dis,
Il fust moult fiers et moult hardis;
Qu'ele puet moult nuire et aidier.
Ce n'est mie ne d'ui ne d'ier
Que riches gens ont grant poissance
De faire ou aïde, ou grévance. 1030
Tuit li greignor et li menor
Portoient à Richece honor:
Tuit baoient à li servir,
Por l'amor de li deservir;

Chascuns sa dame la clamoit,
Car tous li mondes la cremoit;
Tous li mons iert en son dangier.
En sa cort ot maint losengier,
Maint traïtor, maint envieus:
Ce sunt cil qui sunt curieus 1040
De desprisier et de blasmer
Tous ceus qui font miex à amer.
Par devant, por eus losengier,
Loent les gens li losengier;
Tout le monde par parole oignent,
Mès lor losenges les gens poignent

1037. *Both* in werk (!). 1043. G. and the; Th. *om.* the. 1045. Th. weren; G. were. 1058. Th. But; G. And. Th. prill; G. prile; *prob. error for* prike, *or* prikke.

138   THE ROMAUNT OF THE ROSE.

The folk right to the bare boon,
Bihinde her bak whan they ben goon,   1060
And foule abate the folkes prys.
Ful many a worthy man and wys,
An hundred, have [they] don to dye,
These losengeres, through flaterye;
And maketh folk ful straunge be,   1065
Ther-as hem oughte be prive.
Wel yvel mote they thryve and thee,
And yvel aryved mote they be,
These losengeres, ful of envye!
No good man loveth hir companye.   1070
  Richesse a robe of purpre on hadde,
Ne trowe not that I lye or madde;
For in this world is noon it liche,
Ne by a thousand deel so riche,
Ne noon so fair; for it ful wel   1075
With orfrays leyd was everydel,
And portrayed in the ribaninges
Of dukes stories, and of kinges.
And with a bend of gold tasseled,
And knoppes fyne of gold ameled.   1080
Aboute hir nekke of gentil entaile
Was shet the riche chevesaile,

Par derriere dusques as os,
Qu'il abaissent des bons les los,
Et desloent les aloés,
Et si loent les desloés.   1050
Maint prodommes ont encusés,
Et de lor honnor reculés
Li losengier par lor losenges;
Car il font ceus des cors estranges
Qui déussent estre privés :
Mal puissent-il estre arivés
Icil losengier plain d'envie!
Car nus prodons n'aime lor vie.

Richece ot une porpre robe,
Ice ne tenés mie à lobe,   1060
Que je vous di bien et afiche
Qu'il n'ot si bele, ne si riche
Où monde, ne si envoisie.
La porpre fu toute orfroisie ;
Si ot portraites à orfrois
Estoires de dus et de rois.
Si estoit au col bien orlée
D'une bende d'or néélée
Moult richement, sachiés sans faille.
Si i avoit tretout à taille   1070

1062. Th. and wyse; G. ywys.   1063. G. haue do; Th. and ydon.   1065.
Th. And maketh; G. Haue maad.   1066. G. *om.* as. *Both* ought.   1068.
Th. aryued; G. achyued.   1071. G. purpur; Th. purple.   1073. Th. it; G.
hir.   1080. Th. amyled; Speght, ameled; G. enameled.   1082 G. shete;
Th. shette.

THE ROMAUNT OF THE ROSE. 139

In which ther was ful gret plentee
Of stones clere and bright to see.
   Rychesse a girdel hadde upon,   1085
The bokel of it was of a stoon
Of vertu greet, and mochel of might;
For who-so bar the stoon so bright,
Of venim [thurte] him no-thing doute,
While he the stoon hadde him aboute.   1090
That stoon was greetly for to love,
And til a riche mannes bihove
Worth al the gold in Rome and Fryse.
The mourdaunt, wrought in noble wyse,
Was of a stoon ful precious,   1095
That was so fyn and vertuous,
That hool a man it coude make
Of palasye, and of tooth-ake.
And yit the stoon hadde suche a grace,
That he was siker in every place,   1100
Al thilke day, not blind to been,
That fasting mighte that stoon seen.
The barres were of gold ful fyne,
Upon a tissu of satyne,
Ful hevy, greet, and no-thing light,   1105
In everich was a besaunt-wight.
   Upon the tresses of Richesse
Was set a cercle, for noblesse,

De riches pierres grant plenté
Qui moult rendoient grant clarté.
   Richece ot ung moult riche ceint
Par desus cele porpre ceint ;
La boucle d'une pierre fu
Qui ot grant force et grant vertu :
Car cis qui sor soi la portoit,
Nes uns venins ne redotoit :
Nus nel pooit envenimer,
Moult faisoit la pierre à aimer. 1080
Ele vausist à ung prodomme
Miex que trestous li ors de Romme.

D'une pierre fu li mordens,
Qui garissoit du mal des dens ;
Et si avoit ung tel éur,
Que cis pooit estre asséur
Tretous les jors de sa véue,
Qui à géun l'avoit véue.
Li clou furent d'or esmeré,
Qui erent el tissu doré ;   1090
Si estoient gros et pesant,
En chascun ot bien ung besant.
   Richece ot sus ses treces sores
Ung cercle d'or ; onques encores

1089. *Both* durst (!); *read* thurte *or* thurfte.   1092. Th. mannes; G. man.
1098. G. *om*. of. *Both* tothe.   1101. Th. thylke; G. thilk.   1102. *Both* myght.

140   THE ROMAUNT OF THE ROSE.

Of brend gold, that ful lighte shoon;
So fair, trowe I, was never noon.　　　　1110
But he were cunning, for the nones,
That coude devysen alle the stones
That in that cercle shewen clere;
It is a wonder thing to here.
For no man coude preyse or gesse　　　　1115
Of hem the valewe or richesse.
Rubyes there were, saphyres, iagounces,
And emeraudes, more than two ounces.
But al bifore, ful sotilly,
A fyn carboucle set saugh I.　　　　　　 1120
The stoon so cleer was and so bright,
That, al-so sone as it was night,
Men mighte seen to go, for nede,
A myle or two, in lengthe and brede.
Swich light [tho] sprang out of the stoon, 1125
That Richesse wonder brighte shoon,
Bothe hir heed, and al hir face,
And eke aboute hir al the place.
　Dame Richesse on hir hond gan lede
A yong man ful of semelihede,　　　　 1130
That she best loved of any thing;
His lust was muche in housholding.

Ne fu si biaus véus, ce cuit,
Car il fu tout d'or fin recuit;
Mès cis seroit bons devisierres
Qui vous sauroit toutes les pierres,
Qui i estoient, devisier,
Car l'en ne porroit pas prisier 1100
L'avoir que les pierres valoient,
Qui en l'or assises estoient.
Rubis i ot, saphirs, jagonces,
Esmeraudes plus de dix onces.
Mais devant ot, par grant mestrise,
Une escharboucle où cercle assise,

Et la pierre si clere estoit,
Que maintenant qu'il anuitoit,
L'en s'en véist bien au besoing
Conduire d'une liue loing.　　1110
Tel clarté de la pierre yssoit,
Que Richece en resplendissoit
Durement le vis et la face,
Et entor li toute la place.
　Richece tint parmi la main
Ung valet de grant biauté plain,
Qui fu ses amis veritiez.
C'est uns hons qui en biaus ostiez

1109. *Both* light.　　1111. Th. he; G. she.　　1112. *Both* deuyse.
1116. Th. the; G. that.　1117. *Both* ragounces (!).　1125. Morris *supplies*
tho.　1132. G. mych.

In clothing was he ful fetys,
And lovede wel have hors of prys.
He wende to have reproved be   1135
Of thefte or mordre, if that he
Hadde in his stable an hakeney.
And therfore he desyred ay
To been aqueynted with Richesse;
For al his purpos, as I gesse,   1140
Was for to make greet dispense,
Withoute werning or defence.
And Richesse mighte it wel sustene,
And hir dispenses wel mayntene,
And him alwey swich plentee sende   1145
Of gold and silver for to spende
Withoute lakking or daungere,
As it were poured in a garnere.

    And after on the daunce wente   *Largesse.*
LARGESSE, that sette al hir entente   1150
For to be honourable and free;
Of Alexandres kin was she;
Hir moste Ioye was, y-wis,
Whan that she yaf, and seide, 'have this.'
Not Avarice, the foule caytyf,   1155
Was half to grype so ententyf,

Maintenir moult se délitoit.
Cis se chauçoit bien et vestoit, 1120
Si avoit les chevaus de pris ;
Cis cuidast bien estre repris
Ou de murtre, ou de larrecin,
S'en s'estable éust ung roucin.
Por ce amoit-il moult l'acointance
De Richece et la bien-voillance,
Qu'il avoit tous jors en porpens
De demener les grans despens,
Et el les pooit bien soffrir,
Et tous ses despens maintenir ; 1130
El li donnoit autant deniers
Cum s'el les puisast en greniers.
    Après refu Largece assise,
Qui fu bien duite et bien aprise
De faire honor, et de despendre :
El fu du linage Alexandre ;
Si n'avoit-el joie de rien
Cum quant el pooit dire, 'tien.'
Neis Avarice la chétive
N'ert pas si à prendre ententive   1140

1134. Th. loued wel to haue ; G. loued to haue well.   1137. Th. an ; G. ony.
1139. Th. ben ; G. be.   1141. Th. Was ; G. And.   1142. Th. or defence ;
G. of diffense.   1144. Th. dispences ; G. dispence.   1146. Th. for to
spende ; G. for to dispende ; *see* 1157.   1147. Th. lackynge ; G. lakke.
1150. Th. sette ; G. settith.

142   THE ROMAUNT OF THE ROSE.

As Largesse is to yeve and spende.
And god y-nough alwey hir sende,
So that the more she yaf awey,
The more, y-wis, she hadde alwey.   1160
Gret loos hath Largesse, and gret prys;
For bothe wys folk and unwys
Were hoolly to hir baundon brought,
So wel with yiftes hath she wrought.
And if she hadde an enemy,   1165
I trowe, that she coude craftily
Make him ful sone hir freend to be,
So large of yift and free was she;
Therfore she stood in love and grace
Of riche and povre in every place.   1170
A ful gret fool is he, y-wis,
That bothe riche and nigard is.
A lord may have no maner vice
That greveth more than avarice.
For nigard never with strengthe of hond   1175
May winne him greet lordship or lond.
For freendes al to fewe hath he
To doon his wil perfourmed be.
And who-so wol have freendes here,
He may not holde his tresour dere.   1180
For by ensample I telle this,
Right as an adamaunt, y-wis,

Cum Largece ere de donner;
Et Diex li fesoit foisonner
Ses biens si qu'ele ne savoit
Tant donner, cum el plus avoit.
Moult a Largece pris et los;
Ele a les sages et les fos
Outréement à son bandon,
Car ele savoit fere biau don;
S'ainsinc fust qu'aucuns la haïst,
Si cuit-ge que de ceus féist   1150
Ses amis par son biau servise;
Et por ce ot-ele à devise
L'amor des povres et des riches.

Moult est fos haus homs qui est
  chiches!
Haus homs ne puet avoir nul vice,
Qui tant li griet cum avarice :
Car hons avers ne puet con-
  querre
Ne seignorie ne grant terre;
Car il n'a pas d'amis plenté,
Dont il face sa volenté.   1160
Mès qui amis vodra avoir
Si n'ait mie chier son avoir,
Ains par biaus dons amis acquiere:
Car tout en autretel maniere

1162. G. *om.* wys. 1166. Th. craftely; G. tristely. 1172. Th. nygarde; G. nygart.
1176. G. *om.* him. 1178. Th. wyl; G. wille. 1182. Th. adamant; G. adamaund.

THE ROMAUNT OF THE ROSE. 143

Can drawen to him sotilly
The yren, that is leyd therby,
So draweth folkes hertes, y-wis, 1185
Silver and gold that yeven is.
   Largesse hadde on a robe fresshe
Of riche purpur Sarsinesshe.
Wel fourmed was hir face and clere,
And opened had she hir colere; 1190
For she right there hadde in present
Unto a lady maad present
Of a gold broche, ful wel wrought.
And certes, it missat hir nought;
For through hir smokke, wrought with silk, 1195
The flesh was seen, as whyt as milk.
Largesse, that worthy was and wys,
Held by the honde a knight of prys,
Was sib to Arthour of Bretaigne.
And that was he that bar the enseigne 1200
Of worship, and the gonfanoun.
And yit he is of swich renoun,
That men of him seye faire thinges
Bifore barouns, erles, and kinges.
This knight was comen al newely 1205
Fro tourneyinge faste by;

Cum la pierre de l'aïment
Trait à soi le fer soutilment,
Ainsinc atrait les cuers des gens
Li ors qu'en donne et li argens.
   Largece ot robe toute fresche 1170
D'une porpre Sarrazinesche;
S'ot le vis bel et bien formé;
Mès el ot son col deffermé,
Qu'el avoit iluec en présent
A une dame fet présent,
N'avoit gueres, de son fermal,
Et ce ne li séoit pas mal,
Que sa cheveçaille iert overte,
Et sa gorge si descoverte,
Que parmi outre la chemise
Li blanchoioit sa char alise. 1180
Largece la vaillant, la sage,
Tint ung chevalier du linage
Au bon roy Artus de Bretaigne;
Ce fu cil qui porta l'enseigne
De Valor et le gonfanon.
Encor est-il de tel renom,
Que l'en conte de li les contes
Et devant rois et devant contes.
Cil chevalier novelement
Fu venus d'ung tornoiement, 1190

1187. Th. fresshe; G. fresh.   1188. G. sarlynysh; Th. Sarlynyssche.
1199. *Both* sibbe. Th. Arthour; G. Artour. Th. Breteigne; G. Britaigne.
1200. Th. enseigne; G. ensaigne.   1201. *Both* gousfaucoun.   1205.
Both newly.   1206. Th. tourneyeng; G. tournerying.

Ther hadde he doon gret chivalrye
Through his vertu and his maistrye;
And for the love of his lemman
[Had] cast doun many a doughty man.　　　1210
　　And next him daunced dame FRAUNCHYSE,
Arrayed in ful noble gyse.　　　*Fraunchyse.*
She was not broun ne dun of hewe,
But whyt as snowe y-fallen newe.
Hir nose was wrought at poynt devys,　　1215
For it was gentil and tretys;
With eyen gladde, and browes bente;
Hir heer doun to hir heles wente.
And she was simple as dowve on tree,
Ful debonaire of herte was she.　　　1220
She durste never seyn ne do
But that [thing] that hir longed to.
And if a man were in distresse,
And for hir love in hevinesse,
Hir herte wolde have ful greet pitee,　　1225
She was so amiable and free.
For were a man for hir bistad,
She wolde ben right sore adrad
That she dide over greet outrage,
But she him holpe his harm to aswage;　1230

Où il ot faite por s'amie
Mainte jouste et mainte envaïe,
Et percié maint escu bouclé,
Maint hiaume i avoit desserclé,
Et maint chevalier abatu,
Et pris par force et par vertu.
　Après tous ceus se tint Fran-
　　chise,
Qui ne fu ne brune ne bise,
Ains ere blanche comme nois;
Et si n'ot pas nés d'Orlenois,　　1200
Ainçois l'avoit lonc et traitis,
Iex vairs rians, sorcis votis:
S'ot les chevous et blons, et lons,

Et fu simple comme uns coulons.
Le cuer ot dous et debon-
　　naire:
Ele n'osast dire ne faire
A nuli riens qu'el ne déust;
Et s'ele ung homme cognéust
Qui fust destrois por s'amitié,
Tantost éust de li pitié,　　　1210
Qu'ele ot le cuer si pitéable,
Et si dous et si amiable,
Que se nus por li mal traisist,
S'el ne li aidast, el crainsist
Qu'el féïst trop grant vilonnie.
Vestue ot une sorquanie,

1207. Th. There; G. The.　　1210. *Both* He caste.　　1214. Th. yfallen;
G. fall*e*.　　1219. Th. on; G. of.　　1221. *Both* durst.　　1227, 8. *Both*
bisladde, adradde.　　1230. Th. taswage.

Hir thoughte it elles a vilanye.
And she hadde on a sukkenye,
That not of hempen herdes was;
So fair was noon in alle Arras.
Lord, it was rideled fetysly! 1235
Ther nas nat oo poynt, trewely,
That it nas in his right assyse.
Ful wel y-clothed was Fraunchyse;
For ther is no cloth sitteth bet
On damiselle, than doth roket. 1240
A womman wel more fetys is
In roket than in cote, y-wis.
The whyte roket, rideled faire,
Bitokened, that ful debonaire
And swete was she that it bere. 1245
By hir daunced a bachelere;
I can not telle you what he highte,
But fair he was, and of good highte,
Al hadde he be, I sey no more,
The lordes sone of Windesore. 1250
And next that daunced CURTESYE, **Curtesye.**
That preised was of lowe and hye,
For neither proud ne fool was she.
She for to daunce called me,

Qui ne fu mie de borras:
N'ot si bele jusqu'à Arras;
Car el fu si coillie et jointe,
Qu'il n'i ot une seule pointe 1220
Qui à son droit ne fust assise.
Moult fu bien vestue Franchise;
Car nule robe n'est si bele
Que sorquanie à damoisele.
Fame est plus cointe et plus mignote
En sorquanie que en cote :
La sorquanie qui fu blanche,

Senefioit que douce et franche
Estoit cele qui la vestoit.
Uns bachelers jones s'estoit 1230
Pris à Franchise lez à lez,
Ne soi comment ert apelé,
Mès biaus estoit, se il fust ores
Fiex au seignor de Gundesores.
Après se tenoit Courtoisie,
Qui moult estoit de tous prisie,
Si n'ere orguilleuse ne fole.
C'est cele qui à la karole

1233. Th. hempe; G. hempe ne (*for* hempene). 1235. G. ridled; Th. ryddeled. 1236. G. *om.* nat. *Both* a; *read* oo. 1238. Th. yclothed; G. clothed. 1243; *see* 1235. 1244. *Both* Bitokeneth. 1247, 8. *Both* hight.

146   THE ROMAUNT OF THE ROSE.

  (I pray god yeve hir right good grace!) 1255
Whan I com first into the place.
She was not nyce, ne outrageous,
But wys and war, and vertuous,
Of faire speche, and faire answere;
Was never wight misseid of here; 1260
She bar no rancour to no wight.
Cleer broun she was, and therto bright
Of face, of body avenaunt;
I wot no lady so plesaunt.
She were worthy for to bene 1265
An emperesse or crouned quene.
  And by hir wente a knight dauncing
That worthy was and wel speking,
And ful wel coude he doon honour.
The knight was fair and stif in stour, 1270
And in armure a semely man,
And wel biloved of his lemman.
  Fair YDELNESSE than saugh I,   Ydelnesse.
That alwey was me faste by.
Of hir have I, withouten fayle, 1275
Told yow the shap and apparayle
For (as I seide) lo, that was she
That dide me so greet bountee,

La soe merci m'apela
Ainz que nule, quant je vins là. 1240
El ne fu ne nice, n'umbrage,
Mès sages auques sans outrage,
De biaus respons et de biaus dis,
Onc nus ne fu par li laidis,
Ne ne porta nului rancune.
El fu clere comme la lune
Est avers les autres estoiles
Qui ne resemblent que chandoiles.
Faitisse estoit et avenant,
Je ne sai fame plus plaisant. 1250
Ele ere entoutes cors bien digne

D'estre emperieris, ou roïne.
 A li se tint uns chevaliers
Acointables et biaus parliers,
Qui sot bien faire honor as gens.
Li chevaliers fu biaus et gens,
Et as armes bien acesmés,
Et de s'amie bien amés.
 La bele Oiseuse vint après,
Qui se tint de moi assés près. 1260
De cele vous ai dit sans faille
Toute la façon et la taille;
Jà plus ne vous en iert conté,
Car c'est cele qui la bonté

1255. Th. *om.* right. 1259. G. and of; Th. *om.* of. 1261. G. *om. 1st* no.
1263. G. wenaunt (!). 1265. G. *om.* were. 1274. *Both* fast. 1275. *Both* without.

THE ROMAUNT OF THE ROSE.

That she the gate of the gardin
Undide, and leet me passen in.   1280
    And after daunced, as I gesse,   **Youthe.**
[YOUTHE], fulfild of lustinesse,
That nas not yit twelve yeer of age,
With herte wilde, and thought volage;
Nyce she was, but she ne mente   1285
Noon harm ne slight in hir entente,
But only lust and Iolitee.
For yonge folk, wel witen ye,
Have litel thought but on hir play.
Hir lemman was bisyde alway,   1290
In swich a gyse, that he hir kiste
At alle tymes that him liste,
That al the daunce mighte it see;
They make no force of privetee;
For who spak of hem yvel or wel,   1295
They were ashamed never-a-del,
But men mighte seen hem kisse there,
As it two yonge douves were.
For yong was thilke bachelere,
Of beaute wot I noon his pere;   1300
And he was right of swich an age
As Youthe his leef, and swich corage.
    The lusty folk thus daunced there,
And also other that with hem were,

Me fist si grant qu'ele m'ovri
Le guichet del vergier flori.
    Après se tint mien esciant,
Jonesce, au vis cler et luisant,
Qui n'avoit encores passés,
Si cum je cuit, douze ans d'assés.   1270
Nicete fu, si ne pensoit
Nul mal, ne nul engin qui soit;
Mès moult iert envoisie et gaie,
Car jone chose ne s'esmaie
Fors de joer, bien le savés.
Ses amis iert de li privés
En tel guise, qu'il la besoit
Toutes les fois que li plesoit,
Voians tous ceus de la karole :
Car qui d'aus deus tenist parole,   1280
Il n'en fussent jà vergondeus,
Ains les véissiés entre aus deus
Baisier comme deus columbiaus.
Le valés fu jones et biaus,
Si estoit bien d'autel aage
Cum s'amie, et d'autel corage.
    Ainsi karoloient ilecques,
Ceste gens, et autres avecques,

1282. *Both* And she; *read* Youthe; *see* 1302.   1288. Th. yonge; G. yong. Th. wel; G. wole.   1303. *Both* that; *read* thus; *see* 1310.

148 THE ROMAUNT OF THE ROSE.

That weren alle of hir meynee; 1305
Ful hende folk, and wys, and free,
And folk of fair port, trewely,
Ther weren alle comunly.
   Whan I hadde seen the countenaunces
Of hem that ladden thus these daunces, 1310
Than hadde I wil to goon and see
The gardin that so lyked me,
And loken on these faire loreres,
On pyn-trees, cedres, and oliveres.
The daunces than y-ended were; 1315
For many of hem that daunced there
Were with hir loves went awey
Under the trees to have hir pley.
   A, lord! they lived lustily!
A gret fool were he, sikerly, 1320
That nolde, his thankes, swich lyf lede!
For this dar I seyn, out of drede,
That who-so mighte so wel fare,
For better lyf [thurte] him not care;
For ther nis so good paradys 1325
As have a love at his devys.
   Out of that place wente I tho,
And in that gardin gan I go,

Qui estoient de lor mesnies,
Franches gens et bien ensei-
   gnies, 1290
Et gens de bel afetement
Estoient tuit communément.
   Quant j'oi véues les semblances
De ceus qui menoient les dances,
J'oi lors talent que le vergier
Alasse véoir et cerchier,
Et remirer ces biaus moriers,
Ces pins, ces codres, ces lo-
   riers.

Les karoles jà remanoient,
Car tuit li plusors s'en aloient 1300
O lor amies umbroier
Sous ces arbres por dosnoier.
   Diex, cum menoient bonne vie!
Fox est qui n'a de tel envie;
Qui autel vie avoir porroit,
De mieudre bien se sofferroit,
Qu'il n'est nul greignor paradis
Qu'avoir amie à son devis.
   D'iiecques me parti atant,
Si m'en alai seus esbatant 1310

1307. *Both* faire; truly (truely). 1308. *Both* were. 1313. G. loreyes;
Th. Laurelles. 1315. Th. ended; G. eended (=y-ended?). 1323. *Both* myght.
1324. *Both* durst (*for* thurte). 1326. *Both* As to haue.

Pleying along ful merily.
The God of Love ful hastely　　　　1330
Unto him Swete-Loking clepte,
No lenger wolde he that he kepte
His bowe of golde, that shoon so bright.
He [bad] him [bende it] anon-right;
And he ful sone [it] sette on ende,　　1335
And at a braid he gan it bende,
And took him of his arowes fyve,
Ful sharpe and redy for to dryve.
Now god that sit in magestee
Fro deedly woundes kepe me,　　　　1340
If so be that he [wol] me shete ;
For if I with his arowe mete,
It [wol me greven] sore, y-wis !
But I, that no-thing wiste of this,
Wente up and doun ful many a wey,　　1345
And he me folwed faste alwey ;
But no-wher wolde I reste me,
Til I hadde al the [yerde in] be.
　　The gardin was, by mesuring,
Right even and squar in compassing ;　　1350
It was as long as it was large.
Of fruyt hadde every tree his charge,　**The Trees.**

Par le vergier de çà en là ;	Me prist à suivir, l'arc où poing.
Et li Diex d'Amors apela	Or me gart Diex de mortel plaie !
Tretout maintenant Dous-Regart :	Se il fait tant que à moi traie,
N'a or plus cure qu'il li gart	Il me grevera moult forment.
Son arc : donques sans plus atendre	Je qui de ce ne soi noient, Vois par la vergier à délivre,
L'arc li a commandé à tendre,	Et cil pensa bien de moi sivre ;
Et cis gaires n'i atendi,	Mès en nul leu ne m'arresté,
Tout maintenant l'arc li tendi,	Devant que j'oi par tout esté. 1330
Si li bailla et cinq sajetes	Li vergiers par compasséure
Fors et poissans, d'aler loing prestes. 　　　　1320	Si fu de droite quarréure, S'ot de lonc autant cum de large ;
Li Diex d'Amors tantost de loing	Nus arbres qui soit qui fruit charge,

　　1332. *Both* she (*for 2nd* he). 1334. *Both* hadde (*for* bad); bent; *om.* it. 1335. *I supply* it. *Both* an (*for* on). 1339. *Both* sittith. 1340. *Both* he kepe me ; (*om.* he). 1341. G. hadde me shette ; Th. had me shete. 1342. G. mette ; Th. mete. 1343. *Both* had me greued. 1348. *Both* hadde in all the gardyn be.

150   THE ROMAUNT OF THE ROSE.

But it were any hidous tree
Of which ther were two or three.
Ther were, and that wot I ful wel,   1355
Of pomgarnettes a ful gret del;
That is a fruyt ful wel to lyke,
Namely to folk whan they ben syke.
And trees ther were, greet foisoun,
That baren notes in hir sesoun,   1360
Such as men notemigges calle,
That swote of savour been withalle.
And alemandres greet plentee,
Figes, and many a date-tree
Ther weren, if men hadde nede,   1365
Through the gardin in length and brede.
Ther was eek wexing many a spyce,
As clow-gelofre, and licoryce,
Gingere, and greyn de paradys,
Canelle, and setewale of prys,   1370
And many a spyce delitable,
To eten whan men ryse fro table.
And many hoomly trees ther were,
That peches, coynes, and apples bere,
Medlers, ploumes, peres, chesteynes,   1375
Cheryse, of whiche many on fayn is,

Se n'est aucuns arbres hideus,	Maint figuier, et maint biau datier;
Dont il n'i ait ou ung, ou deus	Si trovast qu'en éust mestier,
Où vergier, ou plus, s'il avient.	Où vergier mainte bone espice,
Pomiers i ot, bien m'en sovient,	Cloz de girofle et requelice, 1350
Qui chargoient pomes grenades,	Graine de paradis novele,
C'est uns fruis moult bons à malades; 1340	Citoal, anis, et canele,
	Et mainte espice délitable,
De noiers i ot grant foison,	Que bon mengier fait après table.
Qui chargoient en la saison	Où vergier ot arbres domesches,
Itel fruit cum sunt nois mugades,	Qui chargoient et coins et pesches,
Qui ne sunt ameres, ne fades;	Chataignes, nois, pommes et poires,
Alemandiers y ot planté,	
Et si ot où vergier planté	Nefles, prunes blanches et noires,

1359. G. of gret; Th. *om.* of.   1360. Th. nuttes.   1363. *Both* almandres.
1365. Th. weren; G. wexen.   1366. *Read* Throughout the yerd?   1369. Th.
Gyngere; G. Gyngevre.   *Both* Parys (!).   1375. Th. plommes.   Th.
chesteynis; G. chesteyns.   1376. G. Cherys; Th. Cheryse.   G. which.

THE ROMAUNT OF THE ROSE. 151

Notes, aleys, and bolas,
That for to seen it was solas;
With many high lorer and pyn
Was renged clene al that gardyn; 1380
With cipres, and with oliveres,
Of which that nigh no plente here is.
Ther were elmes grete and stronge,
Maples, asshe, ook, asp, planes longe,
Fyn ew, popler, and lindes faire, 1385
And othere trees ful many a payre.
　What sholde I telle you more of it?
Ther were so many treës yit,
That I sholde al encombred be
Er I had rekened every tree. 1390
　These trees were set, that I devyse,
Oon from another, in assyse,
Five fadome or sixe, I trowe so,
But they were hye and grete also:
And for to kepe out wel the sonne, 1395
The croppes were so thikke y-ronne,
And every braunch in other knet,
And ful of grene leves set,
That sonne mighte noon descende,
Lest [it] the tendre grasses shende. 1400

Cerises fresches vermeilletes,
Cormes, alies et noisetes; 1360
De haus loriers et de haus pins
Refu tous pueplés li jardin,
Et d'oliviers et de ciprés,
Dont il n'a gaires ici prés;
Ormes y ot branchus et gros,
Et avec ce charmes et fos,
Codres droites, trembles et chesnes,
Erables haus, sapins et fresnes.
　Que vous iroie-je notant?
De divers arbres i ot tant, 1370

Que moult en seroie encombrés,
Ains que les éusse nombrés.
　Sachiés por voir, li arbres furent
Si loing à loing cum estre durent.
Li ung fu loing de l'autre assis
Plus de cinq toises, ou de sis:
Mès li rain furent lonc et haut,
Et por le leu garder de chaut,
Furent si espés par deseure,
Que li solaus en nesune eure 1380
Ne pooit à terre descendre,
Ne faire mal à l'erbe tendre.

1379. Th. laurer; G. lorey (!).　　1381. G. olyuers; Th. olyueris.　　1384. *Both* oke.　　1386-1482. *Lost in* G.　　1397, 8. Th. knytte, sytte; *see* Parl. Fo. 628.　　1399. Th. myght there noon.　　1400. *I supply* it.

Ther mighte men does and roes y-see,
And of squirels ful greet plentee,
From bough to bough alwey leping.
Conies ther were also playing,
That comen out of hir claperes   1405
Of sondry colours and maneres,
And maden many a turneying
Upon the fresshe gras springing.
 In places saw I WELLES there,   **The Welles.**
In whiche ther no frogges were,   1410
And fair in shadwe was every welle;
But I ne can the nombre telle
Of stremes smale, that by devys
Mirthe had don come through condys,
Of which the water, in renning,   1415
Gan make a noyse ful lyking.
 About the brinkes of thise welles,
And by the stremes over-al elles
Sprang up the gras, as thikke y-set
And softe as any veluët,   1420
On which men mighte his lemman leye,
As on a fetherbed, to pleye,
For therthe was ful softe and swete.
Through moisture of the welle wete

Où vergier ot daims et che-
 vrions,
Et moult grant plenté d'escoirions,
Qui par ces arbres gravissoient;
Connins i avoit qui issoient
Toute jor hors de lor tesnieres,
Et en plus de trente manieres
Aloient entr'eus tornoiant
Sor l'erbe fresche verdoiant.   1390
 Il ot par leus cleres fontaines,
Sans barbelotes et sans raines,
Cui li arbres fesoient umbre;
Mès n'en sai pas dire le numbre

Par petis tuiaus que Déduis
Y ot fet fere, et par conduis
S'en aloit l'iaue aval, fesant
Une noise douce et plesant.
 Entor les ruissiaus et les rives
Des fontaines cleres et vives,   1400
Poignoit l'erbe freschete et drue;
Ausinc y poïst-l'en sa drue
Couchier comme sur une coite,
Car la terre estoit douce et
 moite
Por la fontaine, et i venoit
Tant d'erbe cum il convenoit.

1403. Th. bowe; Speght, bough (*twice*).   1404. Th. Connes.   1405, 6.
Th. clapers, maners.   1411, 2. Th. wel, tel.   1413, 4. Th. deuyse, condyse
1423. Th. the erthe; *see* 1428.   1424. Th. wel.

THE ROMAUNT OF THE ROSE.

Sprang up the sote grene gras, 1425
As fair, as thikke, as mister was.
But muche amended it the place,
That therthe was of swich a grace
That it of floures had plente,
That both in somer and winter be. 1430
   Ther sprang the violete al newe,
And fresshe pervinke, riche of hewe,
And floures yelowe, whyte, and rede;
Swich plentee grew ther never in mede.
Ful gay was al the ground, and queynt, 1435
And poudred, as men had it peynt,
With many a fresh and sondry flour,
That casten up ful good savour.
   I wol not longe holde you in fable
Of al this gardin delitable. 1440
I moot my tonge stinten nede,
For I ne may, withouten drede,
Naught tellen you the beautee al,
Ne half the bountee therewithal.
   I wente on right honde and on left 1445
Aboute the place; it was not left,
Til I hadde al the [yerde in] been,
In the estres that men mighte seen.

Mès moult embelissoit l'afaire
Li leus qui ere de tel aire,
Qu'il i avoit tous jours plenté
De flors et yver et esté. 1410
   Violete y avoit trop bele,
Et parvenche fresche et novele;
Flors y ot blanches et vermeilles,
De jaunes en i ot merveilles.
Trop par estoit la terre cointe,
Qu'ele ere piolée et pointe
De flors de diverses colors,
Dont moult sunt bonnes les odors.
   Ne vous tenrai jà longue fable
Du leu plesant et délitable; 1420
Orendroit m'en convenra taire,
Que ge ne porroie retraire
Du vergier toute la biauté,
Ne la grant délitableté.
   Tant fui à destre et à senestre,
Que j'oi tout l'afere et tout l'estre
Du vergier cerchié et véu;
Et li Diex d'Amors m'a séu

1425. Th. Spronge; *see* l. 1419.   1428. Th. suche.   1429. Th. hath.
1431. Th. vyolet.   1440. Th. dilectable.   1445, 6. Th. lefte.   1447. Th. garden; *read* yerde in (K.); cf. 1366 (note).   1448. Th. efters (!).

THE ROMAUNT OF THE ROSE.

  And thus whyle I wente in my pley,
The God of Love me folowed ay,   1450
Right as an hunter can abyde
The beste, til he seeth his tyde
To shete, at good mes, to the dere,
Whan that him nedeth go no nere.
  And so befil, I rested me   1455
Besyde a welle, under a tree,
Which tree in Fraunce men calle a pyn.
But, sith the tyme of king Pepyn,
Ne grew ther tree in mannes sighte
So fair, ne so wel woxe in highte;   1460
In al that yerde so high was noon.
And springing in a marble-stoon
Had nature set, the sothe to telle,
Under that pyn-tree a welle.
And on the border, al withoute,   1465
Was writen, in the stone aboute,
Lettres smale, that seyden thus,
'Here starf the faire Narcisus.'
  NARCISUS was a bachelere,   **Narcisus.**
That Love had caught in his daungere,   1470
And in his net gan him so streyne,
And dide him so to wepe and pleyne,
That nede him muste his lyf forgo.
For a fair lady, hight Echo,

Endementiers en agaitant,
Cum li venieres qui atant   1430
Que la beste en bel leu se mete
Por lessier aler la sajete.
 En ung trop biau leu arrivé,
Au darrenier, où je trouvé
Une fontaine sous ung pin;
Mais puis Karles le fils Pepin,
Ne fu ausinc biau pin véus,
Et si estoit si haut créus,
Qu'où vergier n'ot nul si bel arbre.
Dedens une pierre de marbre   1440

Ot nature par grant mestrise
Sous le pin la fontaine assise:
Si ot dedens la pierre escrites
Où bort amont letres petites
Qui disoient: 'ici desus
Se mori li biaus Narcisus.'
 Narcisus fu uns damoisiaus
Que Amors tint en ses roisiaus,
Et tant le sot Amors destraindre,
Et tant le fist plorer et plaindre, 1450
Que li estuet à rendre l'ame:
Car Equo, une haute dame,

1452. Th. beest.   1453. Th. shoten; *read* shete.   1453. Th. goodmesse; *see* 3462.   1456. Th. Besydes.   1474. Th. that hight; (*om.* that).

Him loved over any creature, 1475
And gan for him swich peyne endure,
That on a tyme she him tolde,
That, if he hir loven nolde,
That hir behoved nedes dye,
Ther lay non other remedye. 1480
But natheles, for his beautee,
So fiers and daungerous was he,
That he nolde graunten hir asking,
For weping, ne for fair praying.
And whan she herde him werne hir so, 1485
She hadde in herte so gret wo,
And took it in so gret dispyt,
That she, withoute more respyt,
Was deed anoon. But, er she deyde,
Ful pitously to god she preyde, 1490
That proude-herted Narcisus,
That was in love so daungerous,
Mighte on a day ben hampred so
For love, and been so hoot for wo,
That never he mighte Ioye atteyne; 1495
Than shulde he fele in every veyne
What sorowe trewe lovers maken,
That been so vilaynsly forsaken.

L'avoit amé plus que riens née.
El fu par lui si mal menée
Qu'ele li dist qu'il li donroit
S'amor, ou ele se morroit.
Mès cis fu por sa grant biauté
Plains de desdaing et de fierté,
Si ne la li volt otroier,
Ne por chuer, ne por proier. 1460
Quant ele s'oï escondire,
Si en ot tel duel et tel ire,
Et le tint en si grant despit,

Que morte en fu sans lonc respit;
Mès ainçois qu'ele se morist,
Ele pria Diex et requist
Que Narcisus au cuer ferasche,
Qu'ele ot trové d'amors si flasche,
Fust asproiés encore ung jor,
Et eschaufés d'autel amor 1470
Dont il ne péust joie atendre;
Si porroit savoir et entendre
Quel duel ont li loial amant
Que l'en refuse si vilment.

1482. Th. feirs.   1483. G. *begins again*.   1485. G. *om*. hir.   1486. Th. hert.   1488. Th. without.   1489. Th. deyde; G. dide.   1495. *Both* might to; *I omit* to.   1496. Th. Than; G. And that. Th. shulde he; G. he shulde.   1498. G. velaynesly; Th. vilaynously.

This prayer was but resonable,
Therefor god held it ferme and stable : 1500
For Narcisus, shortly to telle,
By aventure com to that welle
To reste him in that shadowing
A day, whan he com fro hunting.
This Narcisus had suffred paynes 1505
For renning alday in the playnes,
And was for thurst in greet distresse
Of hete, and of his werinesse
That hadde his breeth almost binomen.
Whan he was to that welle y-comen, 1510
That shadwed was with braunches grene,
He thoughte of thilke water shene
To drinke and fresshe him wel withalle ;
And doun on knees he gan to falle,
And forth his heed and nekke out-straughte 1515
To drinken of that welle a draughte.
And in the water anoon was sene
His nose, his mouth, his yën shene,
And he ther-of was al abasshed ;
His owne shadowe had him bitrasshed. 1520
For wel wende he the forme see
Of a child of greet beautee.

Cele proiere fu resnable,
Et por ce la fist Diex estable,
Que Narcisus, par aventure,
A la fontaine clere et pure
Se vint sous le pin umbroier,
Ung jour qu'il venoit d'archoier,
Et avoit soffert grant travail 1481
De corre et amont et aval,
Tant qu'il ot soif por l'aspreté
Du chault, et por la lasseté
Qui li ot tolue l'alaine.
Et quant il vint à la fontaine

Que li pins de ses rains covroit,
Il se pensa que il bevroit :
Sus la fontaine, tout adens
Se mist lors por boivre dedans. 1490
Si vit en l'iaue clere et nete
Son vis, son nés et sa bouchete,
Et cis maintenant s'esbahi ;
Car ses umbres l'ot si trahi,
Que cuida véoir la figure
D'ung enfant bel à desmesure.

1500. Th. ferme ; G. forme.   1503. G. resten ; Th. rest.   G. that ; Th. the.   1508. G. heet ; Th. herte (*for* heete).   1510. *Both* wel.   Th. y-comen ; G. comen.   1515. G. he straught ; Th. out-straught.   1516. *Both* draught.   1517, 8. G. seen, sheen ; Th. sene, shene.   1520. Th. had ; G. was.

THE ROMAUNT OF THE ROSE.

Wel couthe Love him wreke tho
Of daunger and of pryde also,
That Narcisus somtyme him bere.　　　1525
He quitte him wel his guerdon there;
For he so musede in the welle,
That, shortly al the sothe to telle,
He lovede his owne shadowe so,
That atte laste he starf for wo.　　　1530
For whan he saugh that he his wille
Mighte in no maner wey fulfille,
And that he was so faste caught
That he him couthe comfort naught,
He loste his wit right in that place,　　　1535
And deyde within a litel space.
And thus his warisoun he took
For the lady that he forsook.

　　Ladyes, I preye ensample taketh,
Ye that ayeins your love mistaketh:　　　1540
For if hir deeth be yow to wyte,
God can ful wel your whyle quyte.

　　Whan that this lettre, of whiche I telle,
Had taught me that it was the welle
Of Narcisus in his beautee,　　　1545
I gan anoon withdrawe me,

Lors se sot bien Amors vengier
Du grant orguel et du dangier
Que Narcisus li ot mené.
Lors li fu bien guerredoné,　　　1500
Qu'il musa tant à la fontaine,
Qu'il ama son umbre demaine,
Si en fu mors à la parclose.
Ce est la somme de la chose :
Car quant il vit qu'il ne porroit
Acomplir ce qu'il desirroit,
Et qu'il i fu si pris par sort,
Qu'il n'en pooit avoir confort
En nule guise, n'en nul sens,
Il perdi d'ire tout le sens,　　　1510
Et fu mors en poi de termine.
Ainsinc si ot de la meschine
Qu'il avoit d'amors escondite,
Son guerredon et sa merite.

　　Dames, cest exemple aprenés,
Qui vers vos amis mesprenés;
Car se vous les lessiés morir,
Diex le vous sara bien merir.

　　Quant li escris m'ot fait savoir
Que ce estoit tretout por voir　　　1520
La fontaine au biau Narcisus,
Je m'en trais lors ung poi en sus,

1527. *Both* musede so.　　1528. Th. *om.* al.　　1534. *Both* comforte.

THE ROMAUNT OF THE ROSE.

Whan it fel in my remembraunce,
That him bitidde swich mischaunce.
But at the laste than thoughte I,
That scatheles, ful sikerly,   1550
I mighte unto THE WELLE go.   The Welle.
Wherof shulde I abasshen so?
Unto the welle than wente I me,
And doun I louted for to see
The clere water in the stoon,   1555
And eek the gravel, which that shoon
Down in the botme, as silver fyn;
For of the welle, this is the fyn,
In world is noon so cleer of hewe.
The water is ever fresh and newe   1560
That welmeth up with wawes brighte
The mountance of two finger highte.
Abouten it is gras springing,
For moiste so thikke and wel lyking,
That it ne may in winter dye,   1565
No more than may the see be drye.
  Down at the botme set saw I
Two cristal stones craftely
In thilke fresshe and faire welle.
But o thing soothly dar I telle,   1570

Que dedens n'osai regarder,
Ains commençai à coarder,
Quant de Narcisus me sovint,
Cui malement en mesavint ;
Mès ge me pensai qu'asséur,
Sans paor de mavés éur,
A la fontaine aler pooie,
Por folie m'en esmaioie.   1530
De la fontaine m'apressai,
Quant ge fui près, si m'abessai
Por véoir l'iaue qui coroit,
Et la gravele qui paroit
Au fons plus clere qu'argens fins,
De la fontaine c'est la fins.

En tout le monde n'ot si bele,
L'iaue est tousdis fresche et novele,
Qui nuit et jor sourt à grans ondes
Par deux doiz creuses et par-
  fondes.   1540
Tout entour point l'erbe menue,
Qui vient por l'iaue espesse et
  drue,
Et en iver ne puet morir
Ne que l'iaue ne puet tarir.
  Où fons de la fontaine aval
Avoit deux pierres de cristal
Qu'à grande entente remirai,
Et une chose vous dirai,

1550. G. scathles; Th. scathlesse.   1552. Th. abasshen; G. abaisshen.
1553. *From* Th.; *not in* G.   1561, 2. *Both* bright, hight.   1563. *Both*

THE ROMAUNT OF THE ROSE. 159

That ye wol holde a greet mervayle
Whan it is told, withouten fayle.
For whan the sonne, cleer in sighte,
Cast in that welle his bemes brighte,
And that the heet descended is,   1575
Than taketh the cristal stoon, y-wis,
Agayn the sonne an hundred hewes,
Blewe, yelowe, and rede, that fresh and newe is.
Yit hath the merveilous cristal
Swich strengthe, that the place overal,   1580
Bothe fowl and tree, and leves grene,
And al the yerd in it is sene.
And for to doon you understonde,
To make ensample wol I fonde;
Right as a mirour openly   1585
Sheweth al thing that stant therby,
As wel the colour as the figure,
Withouten any coverture;
Right so the cristal stoon, shyning,
Withouten any disceyving,   1590
The estres of the yerde accuseth
To him that in the water museth;
For ever, in which half that he be,
He may wel half the gardin see;

Qu'à merveilles, ce cuit, tenrés
Tout maintenant que vous l'orrés.   1550
Quant li solaus qui tout aguete,
Ses rais en la fontaine giete,
Et la clartés aval descent,
Lors perent colors plus de cent
Où cristal, qui por le soleil
Devient ynde, jaune et vermeil :
Si ot le cristal merveilleus
Itel force que tous li leus,
Arbres et flors et quanqu'aorne
Li vergiers, i pert tout aorne ; 1560
Et por faire la chose entendre,
Un essample vous veil aprendre.
Ainsinc cum li miréors montre
Les choses qui li sunt encontre,
Et y voit-l'en sans coverture
Et lor color, et lor figure ;
Tretout ausinc vous dis por voir,
Que li cristal, sans décevoir,
Tout l'estre du vergier accusent
A ceus qui dedens l'iaue musent :   1570
Car tous jours quelque part qu'il soient,
L'une moitié du vergier voient ;

1573, 4. *Both* sight, bright.   1581. *Both* foule.   1583. *Both* you to;
I omit to.   1585. *Both* mirrour.   1586. G. stondith; Th. stondeth.
1591. *Both* entrees.   1593, 4. *Both* ye (*for* he).

And if he turne, he may right wel 1595
Seen the remenaunt everydel.
For ther is noon so litel thing
So hid, ne closed with shitting,
That it ne is sene, as though it were
Peynted in the cristal there. 1600
This is the mirour perilous,
In which the proude Narcisus
Saw al his face fair and bright,
That made him sith to lye upright.
For who-so loke in that mirour, 1605
Ther may no-thing ben his socour
That he ne shal ther seen som thing
That shal him lede into [loving].
Ful many a worthy man hath it
Y-blent; for folk of grettest wit 1610
Ben sone caught here and awayted;
Withouten respyt been they bayted.
Heer comth to folk of-newe rage,
Heer chaungeth many wight corage;
Heer lyth no reed ne wit therto; 1615
For Venus sone, daun Cupido,
Hath sowen there of love the seed,
That help ne lyth ther noon, ne reed,

Et s'il se tornent maintenant,
Pueent véoir le remenant.
Si n'i a si petite chose,
Tant reposte, ne tant enclose,
Dont démonstrance n'i soit faite,
Cum s'ele iert es cristaus portraite.
C'est li miréoirs périlleus,
Où Narcisus li orguilleus 1580
Mira sa face et ses yex vers,
Dont il jut puis mors tout envers.
Qui en cel miréor se mire,
Ne puet avoir garant de mire,

Que tel chose à ses yex ne voie,
Qui d'amer l'a tost mis en voie.
Maint vaillant homme a mis à glaive
Cis miréors, car li plus saive,
Li plus preus, li miex afetié
I sunt tost pris et aguetié. 1590
Ci sourt as gens novele rage,
Ici se changent li corage;
Ci n'a mestier sens, ne mesure,
Ci est d'amer volenté pure;
Ci ne se set conseiller nus;
Car Cupido, li fils Venus,

1601, 1605. *Both* mirrour. 1604. *So* Th.; G. swithe to ligge. 1605. Th. loke; G. loketh. 1608. *Both* laughyng (!); *read* loving. 1609. G. *om.* a. 1610 Th. Y-blent; G. Blent. 1617. Th. sowen; G. sowne.

THE ROMAUNT OF THE ROSE.

So cercleth it the welle aboute.
His ginnes hath he set withoute   1620
Right for to cacche in his panteres
These damoysels and bacheleres.
Love wil noon other bridde cacche,
Though he sette either net or lacche.
And for the seed that heer was sowen,   1625
This welle is cleped, as wel is knowen,
The Welle of Love, of verray right,
Of which ther hath ful many a wight
Spoke in bokes dyversely.
But they shulle never so verily   1630
Descripcioun of the welle here,
Ne eek the sothe of this matere,
As ye shulle, whan I have undo
The craft that hir bilongeth to.
    Alway me lyked for to dwelle,   1635
To seen the cristal in the welle,
That shewed me ful openly
A thousand thinges faste by.
But I may saye, in sory houre
Stood I to loken or to poure;   1640
For sithen [have] I sore syked,
That mirour hath me now entryked.

Sema ici d'Amors la graine
Qui toute a çainte la fontaine;
Et fist ses las environ tendre,
Et ses engins i mist por prendre   1600
Damoiseles et Damoisiaus;
Qu' Amors ne velt autres oisiaus.
Por la graine qui fu semée,
Fu cele fontaine clamée
La Fontaine d'Amors par droit,
Dont plusors ont en maint endroit
Parlé, en romans et en livre;

Mais jamès n'orrez miex descrivre
La verité de la matere,
Cum ge la vous vodré retrere.   1610
Adès me plot à demorer
A la fontaine, et remirer
Les deus cristaus qui me monstroient
Mil choses qui ilec estoient.
Mès de fort hore m'i miré:
Las! tant en ai puis souspiré!
Cis miréors m'a decéu;
Se j'éusse avant cognéu

1621, 2. *Both* panters, bachelers.   1638. G. fast; Th. faste.   1641. *I*
supply have. *Both* sighed (*for* syked).   1642, 9. *Both* mirrour.

But hadde I first knowen in my wit
The vertue and [the] strengthe of it,
I nolde not have mused there; 1645
Me hadde bet ben elles-where;
For in the snare I fel anoon,
That hath bitraisshed many oon.
  In thilke mirour saw I tho,
Among a thousand thinges mo, 1650
A ROSER charged ful of roses,   The Roser.
That with an hegge aboute enclos is.
Tho had I swich lust and envye,
That, for Parys ne for Pavye,
Nolde I have left to goon and see 1655
Ther grettest hepe of roses be.
Whan I was with this rage hent,
That caught hath many a man and shent,
Toward the roser gan I go.
And whan I was not fer therfro, 1660
The savour of the roses swote
Me smoot right to the herte rote,
As I hadde al embawmed [be.]
And if I ne hadde endouted me
To have ben hated or assailed, 1665
My thankes, wolde I not have failed

Quex sa force ert et sa vertu,
Ne m'i fusse jà embatu : 1620
Car meintenant où las chaï
Qui meint homme ont pris et traï.
  Où miroer entre mil choses,
Choisi rosiers chargiés de roses,
Qui estoient en ung détor
D'une haie clos tout entor :
Adont m'en prist si grant envie,
Que ne laissasse por Pavie,

Ne por Paris, que ge n'alasse
Là où ge vi la greignor masse. 1630
Quant cele rage m'ot si pris,
Dont maint ont esté entrepris,
Vers les rosiers tantost me très ;
Et sachiés que quant g'en fui près,
L'oudor des roses savorées
M'entra ens jusques es corées,
Que por noient fusse embasmés :
Se assailli ou mesamés

1644. Th. vertue; G. vertues. *I supply* the. *Both* strengthes; *read* strengthe. 1646. *Both* had. 1648. G. bitrisshed; Th. bytresshed. 1649. Th. thylke; G. thilk. 1652. Th. enclos; G. enclosid. 1655. G. att (*for* and). 1663. Th. G. me; **read** be (F. *fusse*). 1666. *So* Th.; G. Me thankis. G. wole; Th. wol; *read* wolde.

THE ROMAUNT OF THE ROSE.

To pulle a rose of al that route
To beren in myn honde aboute,
And smellen to it wher I wente;
But ever I dredde me to repente, 1670
And lest it greved or for-thoughte
The lord that thilke gardyn wroughte.
Of roses were ther gret woon,
So faire wexe never in roon.
Of knoppes clos, some saw I there, 1675
And some wel beter woxen were;
And some ther been of other moysoun,
That drowe nigh to hir sesoun,
And spedde hem faste for to sprede;
I love wel swiche roses rede; 1680
For brode roses, and open also,
Ben passed in a day or two;
But knoppes wilen fresshe be
Two dayes atte leest, or three.
The knoppes gretly lyked me, 1685
For fairer may ther no man see.
Who-so mighte haven oon of alle,
It oughte him been ful leef withalle.
Mighte I [a] gerlond of hem geten,
For no richesse I wolde it leten. 1690

Ne cremisse estre, g'en cuillisse,
Au mains une que ge tenisse 1640
En ma main, por l'odor sentir;
Mès paor oi du repentir:
Car il en péust de legier
Peser au seignor du vergier.
Des roses i ot grans monciaus,
Si beles ne vit homs sous ciaus;
Boutons i ot petit et clos,
Et tiex qui sunt ung poi plus gros.
Si en i ot d'autre moison
Qui se traient à lor soison, 1650

Et s'aprestoient d'espanir,
Et cil ne font pas à haïr.
Les roses overtes et lées
Sunt en ung jor toutes alées;
Mès li bouton durent trois frois
A tout le mains deux jors ou trois.
Icil bouton forment me plurent,
Oncques plus bel nul leu ne crurent.
Qui en porroit ung acroichier,
Il le devroit avoir moult chier; 1660
S'ung chapel en péusse avoir,
Je n'en préisse nul avoir.

1668. *Both* bere. 1671, 2. *Both* -thought, wrought. 1673. *Both* ther were; *both* wone. 1674. Th. ware; G. waxe; *both* Rone. 1679. Th. faste; G. fast. 1683. G. will*e*; Th. wyl. Th. fresshe; G. fresh. 1687. *Both* myght haue. 1688. G. lief; Th. lefe. 1689. *I supply* a

164   THE ROMAUNT OF THE ROSE.

>   Among THE KNOPPES I chees oon **The Knoppe**.
> So fair, that of the remenaunt noon
> Ne preyse I half so wel as it,
> Whan I avyse it in my wit.
> For it so wel was enlumyned   1695
> With colour reed, as wel [y]-fyned
> As nature couthe it make faire.
> And it had leves wel foure paire,
> That Kinde had set through his knowing
> Aboute the rede rose springing.   1700
> The stalke was as risshe right,
> And theron stood the knoppe upright,
> That it ne bowed upon no syde.
> The swote smelle sprong so wyde
> That it dide al the place aboute—   1705

Entre ces boutons en eslui
Ung si très-bel, qu'envers celui
Nus des autres riens ne prisié,
Puis que ge l'oi bien avisié :
Car une color l'enlumine,
Qui est si vermeille et si fine,
Com Nature la pot plus faire.
Des foilles i ot quatre paire   1670

Que Nature par grant mestire
I ot assises tire à tire.
La coe ot droite comme jons,
Et par dessus siet li boutons,
Si qu'il ne cline, ne ne pent.
L'odor de lui entor s'espent ;
La soatime qui en ist
Toute la place replenist.   1678

FRAGMENT B.

Whan I had smelled the savour swote,
No wille hadde I fro thens yit go,
But somdel neer it wente I tho,
To take it; but myn hond, for drede,
Ne dorste I to the rose bede,   1710
For thistels sharpe, of many maneres,

Netles, thornes, and hoked breres;
[Ful] muche they distourbled me,
For sore I dradde to harmed be.
  The God of Love, with bowe bent,   1715
That al day set hadde his talent
To pursuen and to spyen me,
Was stonding by a fige-tree.

1694. G. it in; Th. *om.* it.   1695. G. enlomyned.   1698. *Both* hath ; *om.* wel?   1700. *Both* roses.   1701. Th. rysshe ; G. rish.   1705. Th. dyed (*for* dide ; *wrongly*).   1705, 6. *A false rime* ; l. 1705 *is incomplete in sense, as the sentence has no verb. Here the genuine portion ends.* L. 1706 *is by another hand.*   1711. Th. thystels ; G. thesteles.   1713. Ful] *Both* For. Th. moche ; G. mych.

And whan he sawe how that I
Had chosen so ententifly 1720
The botoun, more unto my pay
Than any other that I say,
He took an arowe ful sharply whet,
And in his bowe whan it was set,
He streight up to his ere drough 1725
The stronge bowe, that was so tough,
And shet at me so wonder smerte,
That through myn eye unto myn herte
The takel smoot, and depe it wente.
And ther-with-al such cold me hente, 1730
That, under clothes warme and softe,
Sith that day I have chevered ofte.
  Whan I was hurt thus in [that] stounde,
I fel doun plat unto the grounde.
Myn herte failed and feynted ay, 1735
And long tyme [ther] a-swone I lay.
But whan I com out of swoning,
And hadde wit, and my feling,
I was al maat, and wende ful wel
Of blood have loren a ful gret del. 1740
But certes, the arowe that in me stood
Of me ne drew no drope of blood,
For-why I found my wounde al dreye.
Than took I with myn hondis tweye
The arowe, and ful fast out it plight, 1745
And in the pulling sore I sight.
So at the last the shaft of tree
I drough out, with the fethers three.
But yet the hoked heed, y-wis,
The whiche Beautee callid is, 1750
Gan so depe in myn herte passe,
That I it mighte nought arace ;
But in myn herte stille it stood,
Al bledde I not a drope of blood.
I was bothe anguissous and trouble 1755
For the peril that I saw double ;
I niste what to seye or do,
Ne gete a leche my woundis to ;
For neithir thurgh gras ne rote,
Ne hadde I help of hope ne bote. 1760
But to the botoun ever-mo
Myn herte drew ; for al my wo,
My thought was in non other thing.
For hadde it been in my keping,
It wolde have brought my lyf agayn. 1765
For certeinly, I dar wel seyn,
The sight only, and the savour,
Alegged muche of my langour.
  Than gan I for to drawe me
Toward the botoun fair to see ; 1770
And Love hadde gete him, in [a] throwe,
Another arowe into his bowe,
And for to shete gan him dresse ;
The arowis name was Simplesse.
And whan that Love gan nyghe me nere, 1775
He drow it up, withouten were,

1721. G. botheum; Th. bothum; *read* botoun.   1727. Th. shotte.   1728. G. me nye (!)   1732. *Both* Sithen; Th. chyuered.   1733. *I supply* that.   1736. *I supply* ther; F. *iluec.*   1743. Th. drey; G. drie.   1749. Th. yet; G. atte.   1750. Th. whiche; G. which it.   1757. G. to do; Th. do.   1758. *Both* two (!).   1761. *Both* bothum.   1766. *Both* certis euenly.   1771. a] *Both* his.

And shet at me with al his might,
So that this arowe anon-right
Thourghout [myn] eigh, as it was founde,
Into myn herte hath maad a wounde. 1780
Thanne I anoon dide al my crafte
For to drawen out the shafte,
And ther-with-al I sighed eft.
But in myn herte the heed was left,
Which ay encresid my desyre, 1785
Unto the botoun drawe nere;
And ever, mo that me was wo,
The more desyr hadde I to go
Unto the roser, where that grew
The fresshe botoun so bright of hewe. 1790
Betir me were have leten be;
But it bihoved nedes me
To don right as myn herte bad.
For ever the body must be lad
Aftir the herte; in wele and wo, 1795
Of force togidre they must go.
But never this archer wolde fyne
To shete at me with alle his pyne,
And for to make me to him mete.
  The thridde arowe he gan to shete, 1800
Whan best his tyme he mighte espye,
The which was named Curtesye;
Into myn herte it dide avale.
A-swone I fel, bothe deed and pale;
Long tyme I lay, and stired nought, 1805
Til I abraid out of my thought.
And faste than I avysed me
To drawen out the shafte of tree;

But ever the heed was left bihinde
For ought I couthe pulle or winde. 1810
So sore it stikid whan I was hit,
That by no craft I might it flit;
But anguissous and ful of thought,
I felte such wo, my wounde ay wrought,
That somoned me alway to go 1815
Toward the rose, that plesed me so;
But I ne durste in no manere,
Bicause the archer was so nere.
For evermore gladly, as I rede,
Brent child of fyr hath muche drede. 1820
And, certis yit, for al my peyne,
Though that I sigh yit arwis reyne,
And grounde quarels sharpe of stele,
Ne for no payne that I might fele,
Yit might I not my-silf with-holde 1825
The faire roser to biholde;
For Love me yaf sich hardement
For to fulfille his comaundement.
Upon my feet I roos up than
Feble, as a forwoundid man; 1830
And forth to gon [my] might I sette,
And for the archer nolde I lette.
Toward the roser fast I drow;
But thornes sharpe mo than y-now
Ther were, and also thistels thikke, 1835
And breres, brimme for to prikke,
That I ne mighte gete grace
The rowe thornes for to passe,
To sene the roses fresshe of hewe.
I must abide, though it me rewe, 1840
The hegge aboute so thikke was,
That closid the roses in compas.

1779. *I supply* myn.   1786. *Both* bothom; *so in* 1790.   1791. *Both* were to haue.   1797, 8. Th. fyne, pyne; G. feyne, peyne.   1806. Th. of; G. on.   1808. *Both* drawe.   1811. Th. stycked G. stikith.   1814. felte] *both* lefte (!).

THE ROMAUNT OF THE ROSE.

But o thing lyked me right wele;
I was so nygh, I mighte fele
Of the botoun the swote odour, 1845
And also see the fresshe colour;
And that right gretly lyked me,
That I so neer it mighte see.
Sich Ioye anoon therof hadde I,
That I forgat my malady. 1850
To sene [it] hadde I sich delyt,
Of sorwe and angre I was al quit,
And of my woundes that I had thar;
For no-thing lyken me might mar
Than dwellen by the roser ay, 1855
And thennes never to passe away.
But whan a whyle I had be thar,
The God of Love, which al to-shar
Myn herte with his arwis kene,
Caste him to yeve me woundis grene. 1860
He shet at me ful hastily
An arwe named Company,
The whiche takel is ful able
To make these ladies merciable.
Than I anoon gan chaungen hewe 1865
For grevaunce of my wounde newe,
That I agayn fel in swoning,
And sighed sore in compleyning.
Sore I compleyned that my sore
On me gan greven more and more. 1870
I had non hope of allegeaunce;
So nigh I drow to desperaunce,
I rought of dethe ne of lyf,
Whither that love wolde me dryf.
If me a martir wolde he make, 1875
I might his power nought forsake.
And whyl for anger thus I wook,

The God of Love an arowe took;
Ful sharp it was and [ful] pugnaunt,
And it was callid Fair-Semblaunt, 1880
The which in no wys wol consente,
That any lover him repente
To serve his love with herte and alle,
For any peril that may bifalle.
But though this arwe was kene grounde 1885
As any rasour that is founde,
To cutte and kerve, at the poynt,
The God of Love it hadde anoynt
With a precious oynement,
Somdel to yeve aleggement 1890
Upon the woundes that he had
Through the body in my herte maad,
To helpe hir sores, and to cure,
And that they may the bet endure.
But yit this arwe, withoute more, 1895
Made in myn herte a large sore,
That in ful gret peyne I abood.
But ay the oynement wente abroad;
Throughout my woundes large and wyde
It spredde aboute in every syde; 1900
Through whos vertu and whos might
Myn herte Ioyful was and light.
I had ben deed and al to-shent
But for the precious oynement.
The shaft I drow out of the arwe, 1905
Roking for wo right wondir narwe;

1845. *Both* bothom. 1848. *Both* mighte it. 1851. *Both* sene I hadde. 1853, 4. *Both* thore, more; *see* l. 1857. 1856. G. thens; Th. thence. 1860. G. Castith; Th. Casteth. 1863. G. which. 1873. Th. dethe; G. deth. 1874. G. Whader; Th. Whether. 1879. *I supply* ful. 1892. *So* Th.; G. (*in late hand*) That he hadde the body hole made. 1895. *Both* without.

But the heed, which made me smerte,
Lefte bihinde in myn herte
With other foure, I dar wel say,
That never wol be take away; 1910
But the oynement halp me wele.
And yit sich sorwe dide I fele,
That al-day I chaunged hewe,
Of my woundes fresshe and newe,
As men might see in my visage. 1915
The arwis were so fulle of rage,
So variaunt of diversitee,
That men in everich mighte see
Bothe gret anoy and eek swetnesse,
And Ioye meynt with bittirnesse. 1920
Now were they esy, now were they wood,
In hem I felte bothe harm and good;
Now sore without aleggement,
Now softening with oynement;
It softned here, and prikked there, 1925
Thus ese and anger togider were.
The God of Love deliverly
Com lepand to me hastily,
And seide to me, in gret rape,
'Yeld thee, for thou may not escape! 1930
May no defence availe thee here;
Therfore I rede mak no daungere.
If thou wolt yelde thee hastily,
Thou shalt [the] rather have mercy.
He is a fool in sikernesse, 1935
That with daunger or stoutnesse
Rebellith ther that he shulde plese;
In such folye is litel ese.
Be meek, wher thou must nedis bowe;

To stryve ageyn is nought thy prowe. 1940
Come at ones, and have y-do,
For I wol that it be so.
Than yeld thee here debonairly.'
And I answerid ful humbly,
'Gladly, sir; at your bidding, 1945
I wol me yelde in alle thing.
To your servyse I wol me take;
For god defende that I shulde make
Ageyn your bidding resistence;
I wol not doon so gret offence; 1950
For if I dide, it were no skile.
Ye may do with me what ye wile,
Save or spille, and also sloo;
Fro you in no wyse may I go.
My lyf, my deth, is in your honde, 1955
I may not laste out of your bonde.
Pleyn at your list I yelde me,
Hoping in herte, that sumtyme ye
Comfort and ese shulle me sende;
Or ellis shortly, this is the ende, 1960
Withouten helthe I moot ay dure,
Bu -if ye take me to your cure.
Comfort or helthe how shuld I have,
Sith ye me hurte, but ye me save?
The helthe of lovers moot be founde 1965
Wher-as they token firste hir wounde.
And if ye list of me to make
Your prisoner, I wol it take
Of herte and wil, fully at gree.
Hoolly and pleyn I yelde me, 1970
Withoute feyning or feyntyse,
To be governed by your empryse.
Of you I here so much prys,
I wol ben hool at your devys

Transpose 1913, 4? 1922. Th. hem; G. hym. 1924. *Both* softyng; *see* 1925. 1925. *Both* prikkith. 1929. Th. iape. 1933. Th. hastely; G. hastly. 1934. *I supply* the. 1946. *Both* al. 1965. *Both* loue (!). 1971. *Both* Without.

For to fulfille your lyking 1975
And repente for no-thing,
Hoping to have yit in som tyde
Mercy, of that [that] I abyde.'
And with that covenaunt yeld I me,
Anoon doun kneling upon my knee, 1980
Profering for to kisse his feet;
But for no-thing he wolde me lete,
And seide, 'I love thee bothe and preyse,
Sen that thyn answer doth me ese,
For thou answerid so curteisly. 1985
For now I wot wel uttirly,
That thou art gentil, by thy speche.
For though a man fer wolde seche,
He shulde not finden, in certeyn,
No sich answer of no vileyn; 1990
For sich a word ne mighte nought
Isse out of a vilayns thought.
Thou shalt not lesen of thy speche,
For [to] thy helping wol I eche,
And eek encresen that I may. 1995
But first I wol that thou obay
Fully, for thyn avauntage,
Anon to do me here homage.
And sithen kisse thou shalt my mouth,
Which to no vilayn was never couth 2000
For to aproche it, ne for to touche;
For sauf of cherlis I ne vouche
That they shulle never neigh it nere.
For curteys, and of fair manere,
Wel taught, and ful of gentilnesse 2005
He muste ben, that shal me kisse,
And also of ful high fraunchyse,
That shal atteyne to that empryse.

And first of o thing warne I thee,
That peyne and gret adversitee 2010
He mot endure, and eek travaile,
That shal me serve, withoute faile.
But ther-ageyns, thee to comforte,
And with thy servise to desporte,
Thou mayst ful glad and Ioyful be 2015
So good a maister to have as me,
And lord of so high renoun.
I bere of Love the gonfanoun,
Of Curtesye the banere;
For I am of the silf manere, 2020
Gentil, curteys, meek and free;
That who [so] ever ententif be
Me to honoure, doute, and serve,
And also that he him observe
Fro trespas and fro vilanye, 2025
And him governe in curtesye
With wil and with entencioun;
For whan he first in my prisoun
Is caught, than muste he uttirly,
Fro thennes-forth ful bisily, 2030
Caste him gentil for to be,
If he desyre helpe of me.'
Anoon withouten more delay,
Withouten daunger or affray,
I bicom his man anoon, 2035
And gave him thankes many a oon,
And kneled doun with hondis Ioynt,
And made it in my port ful queynt;
The Ioye wente to myn herte rote.
Whan I had kissed his mouth so swote, 2040
I had sich mirthe and sich lyking,
It cured me of languisshing.
He askid of me than hostages:—
'I have,' he seide, 'taken fele homages

1982. G. *om.* me. 1984. Th. Sens. 1994. *Supply* to; *see* 2126. 1999. Th. sythe; G. sith; *read* sithen. 2002. *For of read* to? 2006. G. must. *Both* kysse. 2012. *Both* without. 2018. *Both* gonfenoun. 2022. *I supply* so. 2030. G. thens; Th. thence. 2033. *Both* without. 2038. *Perhaps* quoynt. 2044. *Perhaps* tan (*for* taken).

Of oon and other, where I have
    been   2045
Disceyved ofte, withouten wene.
These felouns, fulle of falsitee,
Have many sythes bigyled me,
And through falshede hir lust
    acheved,
Wherof I repente and am
    agreved.   2050
And I hem gete in my daungere,
Hir falshed shulle they bye ful dere.
But for I love thee, I seye thee
    pleyn,
I wol of thee be more certeyn ;
For thee so sore I wol now
    binde,   2055
That thou away ne shalt not winde
For to denyen the covenaunt,
Or doon that is not avenaunt.
That thou were fals it were gret
    reuthe,
Sith thou semest so ful of
    treuthe.'   2060
'Sire, if thee list to undirstande,
I merveile thee asking this demande.
For-why or wherfore shulde ye
Ostages or borwis aske of me,
Or any other sikirnesse,   2065
Sith ye wote, in sothfastnesse,
That ye have me surprysed so,
And hool myn herte taken me fro,
That it wol do for me no-thing
But-if it be at your bidding ?   2070
Myn herte is yours, and myn right
    nought,
As it bihoveth, in dede and
    thought,
Redy in alle to worche your wille,
Whether so [it] turne to good or ille.

So sore it lustith you to plese, 2075
No man therof may you disseise.
Ye have theron set sich Iustise,
That it is werreyd in many wise.
And if ye doute it nolde obeye,
Ye may therof do make a
    keye,   2080
And holde it with you for ostage.'
'Now certis, this is noon outrage,'
Quoth Love, 'and fully I accord ;
For of the body he is ful lord
That hath the herte in his tre-
    sor ;   2085
Outrage it were to asken more.'
    Than of his aumener he drough
A litel keye, fetys y-nough,
Which was of gold polisshed clere,
And seide to me, 'With this keye
    here   2090
Thyn herte to me now wol I shette ;
For al my Iowellis loke and knette
I binde under this litel keye,
That no wight may carye aweye ;
This keye is ful of gret poeste.' 2095
With which anoon he touchid me
Undir the syde ful softely,
That he myn herte sodeynly
Without [al] anoy had spered,
That yit right nought it hath me
    dered.   2100
Whan he had doon his wil al-out,
And I had put him out of dout,
'Sire,' I seide, 'I have right gret
    wille
Your lust and plesaunce to fulfille.
Loke ye my servise take at
    gree,   2105
By thilke feith ye owe to me.
I seye nought for recreaundyse,
For I nought doute of your servyse.

2046. *Both* Disteyned (F. *deceus*). 2049. *Both ins.* her *after* through. 2066. G. wole ; Th. wot (F. *savez*). 2067. *Both* susprised. 2068. *Perhaps* tan (*for* taken). 2074. *I supply* it. 2076. G. disese ; Th. desese (F. *dessaisir*). 2085. Th. tresore ; G. tresour. 2099. *I supply* al. 2105. Th. at ; G. atte.

But the servaunt traveileth in
  vayne,
That for to serven doth his
  payne   2110
Unto that lord, which in no wyse
Can him no thank for his servyse.'
  Love seide, 'Dismaye thee
    nought,
Sin thou for sucour hast me
  sought,
In thank thy servise wol I
  take,   2115
And high of degree I wol thee make,
If wikkidnesse ne hindre thee;
But, as I hope, it shal nought be.
To worship no wight by aventure
May come, but-if he peyne en-
  dure.   2120
Abyde and suffre thy distresse;
That hurtith now, it shal be lesse;
I wot my-silf what may thee save,
What medicyne thou woldist have.
And if thy trouthe to me thou
  kepe,   2125
I shal unto thyn helping eke,
To cure thy woundes and make
  hem clene,
Wher-so they be olde or grene;
Thou shalt be holpen, at wordis fewe.
For certeynly thou shalt wel
  shewe   2130
Wher that thou servest with good
  wille,
For to complisshen and fulfille
My comaundementis, day and night,
Whiche I to lovers yeve of right.'
  'Ah, sire, for goddis love,' seide
  I,   2135
' Er ye passe hens, ententifly
Your comaundementis to me ye say,
And I shal kepe hem, if I may;

For hem to kepen is al my thought.
And if so be I wot hem nought, 2140
Than may I [sinne] unwitingly.
Wherfore I pray you enterely,
With al myn herte, me to lere,
That I trespasse in no manere.'
  The god of love than chargid
    me   2145
Anoon, as ye shal here and see,
Word by word, by right empryse,
So as the Romance shal devyse.
  The maister lesith his tyme to
    lere,
Whan the disciple wol not
  here.   2150
It is but veyn on him to swinke,
That on his lerning wol not thinke.
Who-so lust love, let him entende,
For now the Romance ginneth
  amende.
Now is good to here, in fay, 2155
If any be that can it say,
And poynte it as the resoun is
Set; for other-gate, y-wis,
It shal nought wel in alle thing
Be brought to good undirstond-
  ing: 2160
For a reder that poyntith ille
A good sentence may ofte spille.
The book is good at the ending,
Maad of newe and lusty thing;
For who-so wol the ending
  here,   2165
The crafte of love he shal now
  lere,
If that he wol so long abyde,
Til I this Romance may unhyde,
And undo the signifiaunce
Of this dreme into Romaunce. 2170
The sothfastnesse that now is hid,
Without coverture shal be kid,

2109. *Om.* But? 2116. *Read* gree? 2132. G. compleysshen; Th. accom-
plysshen. 2141. *I supply* sinne. 2142. Th. entierly. 2150. G. Whanne
that; Th. Whan. 2154. *Both* bigynneth to amende. 2167. Th. he; G. ye.

Whan I undon have this dreming,
Wherin no word is of lesing.
  'Vilany, at the biginning, 2175
I wol,' sayd Love, ' over alle thing,
Thou leve, if thou wolt [not] be
Fals, and trespasse ageynes me.
I curse and blame generally
Alle hem that loven vilany; 2180
For vilany makith vilayn,
And by his dedis a cherle is seyn.
Thise vilayns arn without pitee,
Frendshipe, love, and al bounte.
I nil receyve to my servyse 2185
Hem that ben vilayns of empryse.
  'But undirstonde in thyn entent,
That this is not myn entendement,
To clepe no wight in no ages
Only gentil for his linages. 2190
But who-so [that] is vertuous,
And in his port nought outrageous,
Whan sich oon thou seest thee biforn,
Though he be not gentil born,
Thou mayst wel seyn, this is a soth, 2195
That he is gentil, bicause he doth
As longeth to a gentilman;
Of hem non other deme I can.
For certeynly, withouten drede,
A cherl is demed by his dede, 2200
Of hye or lowe, as ye may see,
Or of what kinrede that he be.
Ne say nought, for noon yvel wille,
Thing that is to holden stille;
It is no worship to misseye. 2205
Thou mayst ensample take of Keye,
That was somtyme, for misseying,
Hated bothe of olde and ying;
As fer as Gaweyn, the worthy,
Was preysed for his curtesy, 2210
Keye was hated, for he was fel,
Of word dispitous and cruel.
Wherfore be wyse and aqueyntable,
Goodly of word, and resonable
Bothe to lesse and eek to mar. 2215
And whan thou comest ther men ar,
Loke that thou have in custom ay
First to salue hem, if thou may :
And if it falle, that of hem som
Salue thee first, be not dom, 2220
But quyte him curteisly anoon
Without abiding, er they goon.
  'For no-thing eek thy tunge applye
To speke wordis of ribaudye.
To vilayn speche in no degree 2225
Lat never thy lippe unbounden be.
For I nought holde him, in good feith,
Curteys, that foule wordis seith.
And alle wimmen serve and preyse,
And to thy power hir honour reyse. 2230
And if that any missayere
Dispyse wimmen, that thou mayst here,
Blame him, and bidde him holde him stille.
And set thy might and al thy wille
Wimmen and ladies for to plese, 2235
And to do thing that may hem ese,
That they ever speke good of thee,
For so thou mayst best preysed be.
  'Loke fro pryde thou kepe thee wele;
For thou mayst bothe perceyve and fele, 2240

  2176. G. say; Th. saye.   2178. G. ageyns; Th. ayenst.   2183. G. withouten; Th. without.   2185. G. resseyue; Th. receyue. *Both* vnto (*for* to).
2191. *I supply* that.   2195. *Both* in (*for* a).   2208. G. yong; Th. yonge.
2215. G. more; Th. mare.   2218. Th. hem; G. him.   2219, 20. *Both* somme, domme.   2224. Th. rybaudye; G. rebaudrye.   2234. Th. sette; G. *om.*

That pryde is bothe foly and
    sinne;
And he that pryde hath, him with-
    inne,
Ne may his herte, in no wyse,
Meken ne souplen to servyse.
For pryde is founde, in every
    part,   2245
Contrarie unto Loves art.
And he that loveth trewely
Shulde him contene Iolily,
Withouten pryde in sondry wyse,
And him disgysen in queyntyse. 2250
For queynt array, withouten drede,
Is no-thing proud, who takith
    hede;
For fresh array, as men may see,
Withouten pryde may ofte be.
   'Mayntene thy-silf aftir thy
    rent,   2255
Of robe and eek of garnement;
For many sythe fair clothing
A man amendith in mich thing.
And loke alwey that they be shape,
What garnement that thou shalt
    make,   2260
Of him that can [hem] beste do,
With al that perteyneth therto.
Poyntis and sleves be wel sittand,
Right and streight upon the hand.
Of shoon and botes, newe and
    faire,   2265
Loke at the leest thou have a
    paire;
And that they sitte so fetisly,
That these rude may uttirly
Merveyle, sith that they sitte so
    pleyn,
How they come on or of ageyn. 2270

Were streite gloves, with aumenere
Of silk; and alwey with good chere
Thou yeve, if thou have richesse;
And if thou have nought, spend
    the lesse.
Alwey be mery, if thou may, 2275
But waste not thy good alway.
Have hat of floures fresh as May,
Chapelet of roses of Whitsonday;
For sich array ne cost but lyte.
Thyn hondis wasshe, thy teeth
    make whyte,   2280
And let no filthe upon thee be.
Thy nailes blak if thou mayst see,
Voide it awey deliverly,
And kembe thyn heed right Iolily.
[Fard] not thy visage in no
    wyse,   2285
For that of love is not thempryse;
For love doth haten, as I finde,
A beaute that cometh not of kinde.
Alwey in herte I rede thee
Glad and mery for to be, 2290
And be as Ioyful as thou can;
Love hath no Ioye of sorowful man.
That yvel is ful of curtesye
That [lauhwith] in his maladye;
For ever of love the siknesse 2295
Is meynd with swete and bitter-
    nesse.
The sore of love is merveilous;
For now the lover [is] Ioyous,
Now can he pleyne, now can he
    grone,
Now can he singen, now maken
    mone.   2300
To-day he pleyneth for hevinesse,
To-morowe he pleyeth for Ioly-
    nesse.

2247 *Both* trewly.   2249, 2251, 2254. *Both* Without.   2261. *I supply* hem; *both* best.   2264. G. streght. *Both* on (*for* upon).   2268. G. ruyde; Th. rude (F. *cil vilain*).   2271. G. streit. Th. aumere; G. awmere; *see* 2087.   2278. Th. Whit-; G. wis-.   2279. *Both* costneth (F. *couste*).   2285. *Both* Farce.   2294. G. knowith (!); *so* Th.   2302. *Both* pleyneth (!).

The lyf of love is ful contrarie,
Which stoundemele can ofte varie.
But if thou canst [som] mirthis
    make,   2305
That men in gree wole gladly take,
Do it goodly, I comaunde thee;
For men sholde, wher-so-ever they
    be,
Do thing that hem [best] sitting is,
For therof cometh good loos and
    pris.   2310
Wher-of that thou be vertuous,
Ne be not straunge ne daungerous.
For if that thou good rider be,
Prike gladly, that men may se.
In armes also if thou conne,   2315
Pursue, til thou a name hast wonne.
And if thy voice be fair and clere,
Thou shalt maken no gret daun-
    gere
Whan to singe they goodly preye;
It is thy worship for to obeye. 2320
Also to you it longith ay
To harpe and giterne, daunce and
    play;
For if he can wel foote and daunce,
It may him greetly do avaunce.
Among eek, for thy lady
    sake,   2325
Songes and complayntes that thou
    make;
For that wol meve [hem] in hir
    herte,
Whan they reden of thy smerte.
Loke that no man for scarce thee
    holde,
For that may greve thee many-
    folde.   2330
Resoun wol that a lover be
In his yiftes more large and free

Than cherles that been not of
    loving.
For who ther-of can any thing,
He shal be leef ay for to yeve, 2335
In [Loves] lore who so wolde leve;
For he that, through a sodeyn
    sight,
Or for a kissing, anon-right
Yaf hool his herte in wille and
    thought,
And to him-silf kepith right
    nought,   2340
Aftir [swich yift], is good resoun,
He yeve his good in abandoun.
  'Now wol I shortly here re-
    herce,
Of that [that] I have seid in verse,
Al the sentence by and by,   2345
In wordis fewe compendiously,
That thou the bet mayst on hem
    thinke,
Whether-so it be thou wake or
    winke;
For [that] the wordis litel greve
A man to kepe, whanne it is
    breve.   2350
  'Who-so with Love wol goon or
    ryde
He mot be curteys, and void of
    pryde,
Mery and fulle of Iolite,
And of largesse alosed be.
  'First I Ioyne thee, here in
    penaunce,   2355
That ever, withoute repentaunce,
Thou set thy thought in thy loving,
To laste withoute repenting;
And thenke upon thy mirthis swete,
That shal folowe aftir whan ye
    mete.   2360

2305. *I supply* som.   2309. *I supply* best.   2316. Th. tyl; G. to.   2318.
G. *om.* no.   2327. *Both* meuen.   2336. *Both* londes; *read* Loues.   2341.
G. this swiffte (*so* Th.; F. *si riche don*). *Both* it is; *om.* it.   2344, 9. *I supply*
that.   2347. *Both* better.   2355. G. that heere; Th. *om.* that.

'And for thou trewe to love shalt
  be,
I wol, and [eek] comaunde thee,
That in oo place thou sette, al hool,
Thyn herte, withouten halfen dool,
For trecherie, [in] sikernesse ; 2365
For I lovede never doublenesse.
To many his herte that wol depart,
Everiche shal have but litel part.
But of him drede I me right
  nought,
That in oo place settith his
  thought. 2370
Therfore in oo place it sette,
And lat it never thennes flette.
For if thou yevest it in lening,
I holde it but a wrecchid thing :
Therfore yeve it hool and
  quyte, 2375
And thou shalt have the more
  merite.
If it be lent, than aftir soon,
The bountee and the thank is doon ;
But, in love, free yeven thing
Requyrith a gret guerdoning. 2380
Yeve it in yift al quit fully,
And make thy yift debonairly ;
For men that yift [wol] holde more
  dere
That yeven is with gladsome chere.
That yift nought to preisen is 2385
That man yeveth, maugre his.
Whan thou hast yeven thyn herte,
  as I
Have seid thee here [al] openly,
Than aventures shulle thee falle,
Which harde and hevy been with-
  alle. 2390
For ofte whan thou bithenkist thee
Of thy loving, wher-so thou be,

Fro folk thou must depart in hy,
That noon perceyve thy malady,
But hyde thyn harm thou must
  alone, 2395
And go forth sole, and make thy
  mone.
Thou shalt no whyl be in oo stat,
But whylom cold and whylom hat ;
Now reed as rose, now yelowe and
  fade.
Such sorowe, I trowe, thou never
  hade ; 2400
Cotidien, ne [yit] quarteyne,
It is nat so ful of peyne.
For ofte tymes it shal falle
In love, among thy peynes alle,
That thou thy-self, al hoolly, 2405
Foryeten shalt so utterly,
That many tymes thou shalt be
Stille as an image of tree,
Dom as a stoon, without stering
Of foot or hond, without spek-
  ing. 2410
Than, sone after al thy peyne,
To memorie shalt thou come ageyn,
As man abasshed wondre sore,
And after sighen more and more.
For wit thou wel, withouten
  wene, 2415
In swich astat ful oft have been
That have the yvel of love assayd,
Wher-through thou art so dis-
  mayd.
'After, a thought shal take thee so,
That thy love is to fer thee fro : 2420
Thou shalt say, " God, what may
  this be,
That I ne may my lady see ?
Myne herte aloon is to her go,
And I abyde al sole in wo,

2362. *I supply* eek. 2365. *Both* and (*for* in). 2367, 8. *Both* departe. parte.
2371, 2. *So* Th. ; G. sitte, flitte. 2383. *I supply* wol. 2384. G. *om.* is.
2388. *I supply* al. 2395-2442. *Not in* G. ; *from* Th. 2401. *I supply* yit.
2403, 4. Th. fal, al. 2405. Th. holy. 2413. As] Th. A.

Departed fro myn owne thought, 2425
And with myne eyen see right nought.
'"Alas, myn eyen sende I ne may,
My careful herte to convay!
Myn hertes gyde but they be,
I praise no-thing what ever they see. 2430
Shul they abyde thanne? nay;
But goon visyte without delay
That myn herte desyreth so.
For certeynly, but-if they go,
A fool my-self I may wel holde, 2435
Whan I ne see what myn herte wolde.
Wherfore I wol gon her to seen,
Or esed shal I never been,
But I have som tokening."
Then gost thou forth without dwelling; 2440
But ofte thou faylest of thy desyre,
Er thou mayst come hir any nere,
And wastest in vayn thy passage.
Than fallest thou in a newe rage;
For want of sight thou ginnest morne, 2445
And homward pensif dost retorne.
In greet mischeef than shalt thou be,
For than agayn shal come to thee
Sighes and pleyntes, with newe wo,
That no icching prikketh so. 2450
Who wot it nought, he may go lere
Of hem that byen love so dere.
'No-thing thyn herte appesen may,
That oft thou wolt goon and assay,
If thou mayst seen, by aventure, 2455
Thy lyves joy, thyn hertis cure;
So that, by grace if thou might
Atteyne of hir to have a sight,
Than shalt thou doon non other dede
But with that sight thyn eyen fede. 2460
That faire fresh whan thou mayst see,
Thyn herte shal so ravisshed be,
That never thou woldest, thy thankis, lete,
Ne remove, for to see that swete.
The more thou seest in sothfastnesse, 2465
The more thou coveytest of that swetnesse;
The more thyn herte brenneth in fyr,
The more thyn herte is in desyr.
For who considreth every del,
It may be lykned wondir wel, 2470
The peyne of love, unto a fere;
For ever [the] more thou neighest nere
Thought, or who-so that it be,
For verray sothe I telle it thee,
The hatter ever shal thou brenne, 2475
As experience shal thee kenne.
Wher-so [thou] comest in any cost,
Who is next fyr, he brenneth most.
And yit forsothe, for al thyn hete,
Though thou for love swelte and swete, 2480
Ne for no-thing thou felen may,
Thou shalt not willen to passe away.
And though thou go, yet must thee nede
Thenke al-day on hir fairhede,

2427. Th. sene (F. *envoier*). 2432. Th. gone and visyten. 2437, 8. Th. sene, bene. 2443. G. *begins again*. 2446. *Both* thou dost; *om*. thou. 2454. *For* wolt *read* nilt? 2466. *Om*. of? 2472. *I supply* the. 2473. *For* Thought *read* That swete? 2477. *I supply* thou.

Whom thou bihelde with so good
    wille;   2485
And holde thysilf bigyled ille,
That thou ne haddest non harde-
    ment
To shewe hir ought of thyn en'ent.
Thyn herte ful sore thou wolt dis-
    pyse,
And eek repreve of cowardyse, 2490
That thou, so dulle in every thing,
Were dom for drede, without spek-
    ing.
Thou shalt eek thenke thou didest
    foly,
That thou were hir so faste by,
And durst not auntre thee to
    say   2495
Som-thing, er thou cam away;
For thou haddist no more wonne,
To speke of hir whan thou bi-
    gonne:
But yif she wolde, for thy sake,
In armes goodly thee have
    take,   2500
It shulde have be more worth to
    thee
Than of tresour greet plentee.
    'Thus shalt thou morne and eek
    compleyn,
And gete enchesoun to goon ageyn
Unto thy walk, or to thy place, 2505
Where thou biheld hir fleshly
    face.
And never, for fals suspeccioun,
Thou woldest finde occasioun
For to gon unto hir hous.
So art thou thanne desirous   2510
A sight of hir for to have,
If thou thine honour mightest save,
Or any erand mightist make
Thider, for thy loves sake;

Ful fayn thou woldist, but for
    drede   2515
Thou gost not, lest that men take
    hede.
Wherfore I rede, in thy going,
And also in thyn ageyn-coming,
Thou be wel war that men ne wit;
Feyne thee other cause than it 2520
To go that weye, or faste by;
To hele wel is no folye.
And if so be it happe thee
That thou thy love ther mayst see,
In siker wyse thou hir salewe, 2525
Wherwith thy colour wol trans-
    mewe,
And eke thy blood shal al to-quake,
Thyn hewe eek chaungen for hir
    sake.
But word and wit, with chere ful
    pale,
Shul wante for to telle thy tale. 2530
And if thou mayst so fer-forth winne,
That thou [thy] resoun durst bi-
    ginne,
And woldist seyn three thingis or
    mo,
Thou shalt ful scarsly seyn the two.
Though thou bithenke thee never
    so wel,   2535
Thou shalt foryete yit somdel,
But-if thou dele with trecherye.
For fals lovers mowe al folye
Seyn, what hem lust, withouten
    drede,
They be so double in hir fals-
    hede;   2540
For they in herte cunne thenke a
    thing
And seyn another, in hir speking.
And whan thy speche is endid al,
Right thus to thee it shal bifal;

2492. *Both* do*m*me. 2494, 2521. Th. faste; G. fast. 2499. G. yitt; Th. yet (*for* yif). 2532. *I supply* thy; F. *ta raison.* Th. durste; G. derst. 2541. a] Th. o.

If any word than come to minde,   2545
That thou to seye hast left bihinde,
Than thou shalt brenne in greet martyr;
For thou shalt brenne as any fyr.
This is the stryf and eke the affray,
And the batail that lastith ay.   2550
This bargeyn ende may never take,
But-if that she thy pees wil make.
  'And whan the night is comen, anon
A thousand angres shal come upon.
To bedde as fast thou wolt thee dight,   2555
Where thou shalt have but smal delyt;
For whan thou wenest for to slepe,
So ful of peyne shalt thou crepe,
Sterte in thy bedde aboute ful wyde,
And turne ful ofte on every syde;   2560
Now dounward groffe, and now up-right,
And walowe in wo the longe night,
Thyne armis shalt thou sprede a-brede,
As man in werre were forwerreyd.
Than shal thee come a remembraunce   2565
Of hir shape and hir semblaunce,
Wherto non other may be pere.
And wite thou wel, withoute were,
That thee shal [seme], somtyme that night,
That thou hast hir, that is so bright,   2570
Naked bitwene thyn armes there,
Al sothfastnesse as though it were.
Thou shalt make castels than in Spayne,
And dreme of Ioye, al but in vayne,
And thee delyten of right nought,   2575
Whyl thou so slomrest in that thought,
That is so swete and delitable,
The which, in soth, nis but a fable,
For it ne shal no whyle laste.
Than shalt thou sighe and wepe faste,   2580
And say, "Dere god, what thing is this?
My dreme is turned al amis,
Which was ful swete and apparent,
But now I wake, it is al shent!
Now yede this mery thought away!   2585
Twenty tymes upon a day
I wolde this thought wolde come ageyn,
For it alleggith wel my peyn.
It makith me ful of Ioyful thought,
It sleeth me, that it lastith noght.   2590
A, lord! why nil ye me socoure,
The Ioye, I trowe, that I langoure?
The deth I wolde me shulde slo
Whyl I lye in hir armes two.
Myn harm is hard, withouten wene,   2595
My greet unese ful ofte I mene.
But wolde Love do so I might
Have fully Ioye of hir so bright,
My peyne were quit me richely.
Allas, to greet a thing aske I!   2600
It is but foly, and wrong wening,
To aske so outrageous a thing.
And who-so askith folily,
He moot be warned hastily;
And I ne wot what I may say,   2605
I am so fer out of the way;
For I wolde have ful gret lyking
And ful gret Ioye of lasse thing.

2550. Th. batell; G. batelle.   2563, 4. Th. a-brede, forwerede; G. abrode, forweriede; see 3251.   2569. seme] *Both* se.   2576. Th. slombrest.   2578. G. *om.* a.

For wolde she, of hir gentilnesse,
Withouten more, me onis kesse, 2610
It were to me a greet guerdoun,
Relees of al my passioun.
But it is hard to come therto;
Al is but foly that I do,
So high I have myn herte set, 2615
Where I may no comfort get.
I noot wher I sey wel or nought;
But this I wot wel in my thought,
That it were bet of hir aloon,
For to stinte my wo and moon, 2620
A loke on [me] y-cast goodly,
[Than] for to have, al utterly,
Of another al hool the pley.
A! lord! wher I shal byde the day
That ever she shal my lady be? 2625
He is ful cured that may hir see.
A! god! whan shal the dawning spring?
To ly thus is an angry thing;
I have no loye thus here to ly
Whan that my love is not me by. 2630
A man to lyen hath gret disese,
Which may not slepe ne reste in ese.
I wolde it dawed, and were now day,
And that the night were went away;
For were it day, I wolde upryse. 2635
A! slowe sonne, shew thyn enpryse!
Speed thee to sprede thy bemis bright,
And chace the derknesse of the night,
To putte away the stoundes stronge,
Which in me lasten al to longe." 2640
'The night shalt thou contene so,
Withoute rest, in peyne and wo;
If ever thou knewe of love distresse,
Thou shalt mowe lerne in that siknesse.
And thus enduring shalt thou ly,
And ryse on morwe up erly 2646
Out of thy bedde, and harneys thee
Er ever dawning thou mayst see.
Al privily than shalt thou goon,
What [weder] it be, thy-silf aloon, 2650
For reyn, or hayl, for snow, for slete,
Thider she dwellith that is so swete,
The which may falle aslepe be,
And thenkith but litel upon thee.
Than shalt thou goon, ful foule aferd; 2655
Loke if the gate be unsperd,
And waite without in wo and peyn,
Ful yvel a-cold in winde and reyn.
Than shal thou go the dore bifore,
If thou maist fynde any score, 2660
Or hole, or reft, what ever it were;
Than shalt thou stoupe, and lay to ere,
If they within a-slepe be;
I mene, alle save thy lady free.
Whom waking if thou mayst aspye, 2665
Go put thy-silf in Iupartye,
To aske grace, and thee bimene,
That she may wite, withouten wene,
That thou [a]night no rest hast had,
So sore for hir thou were bistad. 2670
Wommen wel ought pite to take
Of hem that sorwen for hir sake.
And loke, for love of that relyke,
That thou thenke non other lyke,

2610. Th. Withouten; G. Without. Th. kesse; G. kysse. 2617. *Both* I wote not; *read* I noot. 2619. *Both* better. 2621. *Both* on hir I caste. 2622. *Both* That (*for* Than). 2628. *Both* liggen. 2649. Th. shalt; G. shalle. 2650. *Both* whider (!). 2655, 6. Th. aferde, vnsperde; G. aferd, unspered. 2660. Th. shore. 2664. Th. thy; G. the. 2668. *Both* without. 2669. *Both om.* a.

For [whom] thou hast so greet
    annoy, 2675
Shal kisse thee er thou go away,
And hold that in ful gret deyntee.
And, for that no man shal thee see
Bifore the hous, ne in the way,
Loke thou be goon ageyn er
    day. 2680
Suche coming, and such going,
Such hevinesse, and such walking,
Makith lovers, withouten wene,
Under hir clothes pale and lene,
For Love leveth colour ne cleer-
    nesse ; 2685
Who loveth trewe hath no fatnesse.
Thou shalt wel by thy-selfe see
That thou must nedis assayed be.
For men that shape hem other wey
Falsly her ladies to bitray, 2690
It is no wonder though they be fat ;
With false othes hir loves they gat ;
For oft I see suche losengeours
Fatter than abbatis or priours.
    'Yet with o thing I thee
    charge, 2695
That is to seye, that thou be large
Unto the mayd that hir doth serve,
So best hir thank thou shalt de-
    serve.
Yeve hir yiftes, and get hir grace,
For so thou may [hir] thank pur-
    chace, 2700
That she thee worthy holde and
    free,
Thy lady, and alle that may thee
    see.
Also hir servauntes worshipe ay,
And plese as muche as thou may;

Gret good through hem may come
    to thee, 2705
Bicause with hir they been prive.
They shal hir telle how they thee
    fand
Curteis and wys, and wel doand,
And she shal preyse [thee] wel the
    mare.
Loke out of londe thou be not
    fare ; 2710
And if such cause thou have, that
    thee
Bihoveth to gon out of contree,
Leve hool thyn herte in hostage,
Til thou ageyn make thy passage.
Thenk long to see the swete
    thing 2715
That hath thyn herte in hir keping.
    'Now have I told thee, in what
    wyse
A lover shal do me servyse.
Do it than, if thou wolt have
The mede that thou aftir crave.' 2720
    Whan Love al this had boden me,
I seide him :—' Sire, how may
    it be
That lovers may in such manere
Endure the peyne ye have seid here ?
I merveyle me wonder faste, 2725
How any man may live or laste
In such peyne, and such brenning,
In sorwe and thought, and such
    sighing,
Ay unrelesed wo to make,
Whether so it be they slepe or
    wake. 2730
In such annoy continuely,
As helpe me god, this merveile I,

2675. Th. whan ; G. whanne ; *read* wham *or* whom ; F. *De qui tu ne pues avoir aise.* 2676. *Corrupt*; F. *Au departir la porte baise.* Th. awey ; G. away. 2683. Th. *ins.* any (G. ony) *bef.* wene. 2687. Th. selfe ; G. silf. 2688. Th. assayed ; G. assaid. 2690. *Both* for to (*for* to). 2693. Th. ofte ; G. of. 2697. Th. dothe ; G. doith. 2700. *I supply* hir. 2709, 2710. *Both* more, fore ; *read* mare, fare. *I supply* thee. 2712. *Perhaps omit* to. 2729. Th. Aye ; G. A-yee.

THE ROMAUNT OF THE ROSE.

How man, but he were maad of stele,
Might live a month, such peynes to fele.'
The God of Love than seide me, 2735
'Freend, by the feith I owe to thee,
May no man have good, but he it by.
A man loveth more tendirly
The thing that he hath bought most dere.
For wite thou wel, withouten were, 2740
In thank that thing is taken more,
For which a man hath suffred sore.
Certis, no wo ne may atteyne
Unto the sore of loves peyne.
Non yvel therto ne may amounte, 2745
No more than a man [may] counte
The dropes that of the water be.
For drye as wel the grete see
Thou mightist, as the harmes telle
Of hem that with Love dwelle 2750
In servyse; for peyne hem sleeth,
And that ech man wolde flee the deeth,
And trowe they shulde never escape,
Nere that hope couthe hem make
Glad as man in prisoun set, 2755
And may not geten for to et
But barly-breed, and watir pure,
And lyeth in vermin and in ordure;
With alle this, yit can he live,
Good hope such comfort hath him yive, 2760
Which maketh wene that he shal be
Delivered and come to liberte;
In fortune is [his] fulle trust.

Though he lye in strawe or dust,
In hope is al his susteyning. 2765
And so for lovers, in hir wening,
Whiche Love hath shit in his prisoun;
Good-Hope is hir salvacioun.
Good-Hope, how sore that they smerte, 2769
Yeveth hem bothe wille and herte
To profre hir body to martyre;
For Hope so sore doth hem desyre
To suffre ech harm that men devyse,
For Ioye that aftir shal aryse.
Hope, in desire [to] cacche victorie; 2775
In Hope, of love is al the glorie,
For Hope is al that love may yive;
Nere Hope, ther shulde no lover live.
Blessid be Hope, which with desyre
Avaunceth lovers in such manere. 2780
Good-Hope is curteis for to plese,
To kepe lovers from al disese.
Hope kepith his lond, and wol abyde,
For any peril that may betyde;
For Hope to lovers, as most cheef, 2785
Doth hem enduren al mischeef;
Hope is her help, whan mister is.
And I shal yeve thee eek, y-wis,
Three other thingis, that greet solas
Doth to hem that be in my las. 2790
'The firste good that may be founde,
To hem that in my lace be bounde,
Is Swete-Thought, for to recorde
Thing wherwith thou canst accorde

2746. *I supply* may.   2748. Th. great; G. greet.   2752. *For* that *read* yet?
2755, 6. Th. sete, ete; G. sett, ete.   2760. *Both* yeue.   2763. *I supply* his.
Th. trust; G. trist.   2774. *Both* aftirward.   2775. *I supply* to.   2777.
Both yeue.   2786. *Both* endure.   2789, 90. Th. solace, lace. G. Doith.   2791.
Both first.

Best in thyn herte, wher she
  be;   2795
Thought in absence is good to
  thee.
Whan any lover doth compleyne,
And liveth in distresse and peyne,
Than Swete-Thought shal come, as
  blyve,
Awey his angre for to dryve. 2800
It makith lovers have remem-
  braunce
Of comfort, and of high plesaunce,
That Hope hath hight him for to
  winne.
For Thought anoon than shal
  biginne,
As fer, god wot, as he can
  finde,   2805
To make a mirrour of his minde;
For to biholde he wol not lette.
Hir person he shal afore him sette,
Hir laughing eyen, persaunt and
  clere,
Hir shape, hir fourme, hir goodly
  chere,   2810
Hir mouth that is so gracious,
So swete, and eek so saverous;
Of alle hir fetures he shal take
  heede,
His eyen with alle hir limes fede.
  'Thus Swete-Thenking shal a-
  swage   2815
The peyne of lovers, and hir rage.
Thy Ioye shal double, withoute
  gesse,
Whan thou thenkist on hir semli-
  nesse,
Or of hir laughing, or of hir chere,
That to thee made thy lady
  dere.   2820

This comfort wol I that thou take;
And if the next thou wolt forsake
Which is not lesse saverous,
Thou shuldist been to daungerous.
  'The secounde shal be Swete-
  Speche,   2825
That hath to many oon be leche,
To bringe hem out of wo and were,
And helpe many a bachilere;
And many a lady sent socoure,
That have loved par-amour, 2830
Through speking, whan they might-
  en here
Of hir lovers, to hem so dere.
To [hem] it voidith al hir smerte,
The which is closed in hir herte.
In herte it makith hem glad and
  light,   2835
Speche, whan they mowe have
  sight.
And therfore now it cometh to
  minde,
In olde dawes, as I finde,
That clerkis writen that hir knewe
Ther was a lady fresh of hewe, 2840
Which of hir love made a song
On him for to remembre among,
In which she seide, "Whan that I
  here
Speken of him that is so dere,
To me it voidith al [my] smerte, 2845
Y-wis, he sit so nere myn herte,
To speke of him, at eve or morwe,
It cureth me of al my sorwe.
To me is noon so high plesaunce
As of his persone daliaunce." 2850
She wist ful wel that Swete-Speking
Comfortith in ful muche thing.
Hir love she had ful wel assayed,
Of him she was ful wel apayed;

2796. G. Thenkyng; Th. Thynkyng; see 2804.   2798. *Both* and in peyne.
2801. *Both ins.* to *bef.* have.   2824. *Both* not ben; F. *tu seroies*. 2831. *Both*
myght.   2833. *Both* me (*for* hem); see 2845.   2845. *I supply* my; see 2833. 2846.
G. sittith; Th. sytteth.   2854. Th. him; G. hem. Th. apayde; G. apaied; see l. 2891.

To speke of him hir Ioye was
   set.   2855
Therfore I rede thee that thou get
A felowe that can wel concele
And kepe thy counsel, and wel hele,
To whom go shewe hoolly thyn
   herte,
Bothe wele and wo, Ioye and
   smerte :   2860
To gete comfort to him thou go,
And privily, bitween yow two,
Ye shal speke of that goodly thing,
That hath thyn herte in hir ke-
   ping ;
Of hir beaute and hir sem-
   blaunce,   2865
And of hir goodly countenaunce.
Of al thy state thou shalt him sey,
And aske him counseil how thou
   may
Do any thing that may hir plese ;
For it to thee shal do gret ese, 2870
That he may wite thou trust him
   so,
Bothe of thy wele and of thy wo.
And if his herte to love be set,
His companye is muche the bet,
For resoun wol, he shewe to
   thee   2875
Al uttirly his privite ;
And what she is he loveth so,
To thee pleynly he shal undo,
Withoute drede of any shame,
Bothe telle hir renoun and hir
   name.   2880
Than shal he forther, ferre and
   nere,
And namely to thy lady dere,
In siker wyse ; ye, every other
Shal helpen as his owne brother,
In trouthe withoute double-
   nesse,   2885

And kepen cloos in sikernesse.
For it is noble thing, in fay,
To have a man thou darst say
Thy prive counsel every del ;
For that wol comfort thee right
   wel,   2890
And thou shalt holde thee wel
   apayed,
Whan such a freend thou hast
   assayed.
 'The thridde good of greet com-
   fort
That yeveth to lovers most dis-
   port,
Comith of sight and biholding, 2895
That clepid is Swete-Loking,
The whiche may noon ese do,
Whan thou art fer thy lady fro ;
Wherfore thou prese alwey to be
In place, where thou mayst hir
   se.   2900
For it is thing most amerous,
Most delitable and saverous,
For to aswage a mannes sorowe,
To sene his lady by the morowe.
For it is a ful noble thing   2905
Whan thyn eyen have meting
With that relyke precious,
Wherof they be so desirous.
But al day after, soth it is,
They have no drede to faren
   amis,   2910
They dreden neither wind ne reyn,
Ne [yit] non other maner peyn.
For whan thyn eyen were thus in
   blis,
Yit of hir curtesye, y-wis,
Aloon they can not have hir
   Ioye,   2915
But to the herte they [it] convoye ;
Part of hir blis to him [they] sende,
Of al this harm to make an ende.

2895. G. and of ; Th. *om.* of.   2897. G. which.   2912. *I supply* yit.
2916. *I supply* it. Th. conuoye G. conueye.   2917. they] *Both* thou.

The eye is a good messangere,
Which can to the herte in such
  manere   2920
Tidyngis sende, that [he] hath seen,
To voide him of his peynes cleen.
Wherof the herte reioyseth so
That a gret party of his wo
Is voided, and put awey to
  flight.   2925
Right as the derknesse of the night
Is chased with clerenesse of the
  mone,
Right so is al his wo ful sone
Devoided clene, whan that the
  sight
Biholden may that fresshe
  wight   2930
That the herte desyreth so,
That al his derknesse is ago;
For than the herte is al at ese,
Whan they seen that [that] may
  hem plese.
  'Now have I thee declared al-
  out,   2935
Of that thou were in drede and
  dout;
For I have told thee feithfully
What thee may curen utterly,
And alle lovers that wole be
Feithful, and ful of stabilite.   2940
Good-Hope alwey kepe by thy
  syde,
And Swete-Thought make eek
  abyde,
Swete-Loking and Swete-Speche;
Of alle thyn harmes they shal be
  leche.
Of every thou shalt have greet
  plesaunce;   2945
If thou canst byde in sufferaunce,
And serve wel without feyntyse,
Thou shalt be quit of thyn em-
  pryse,
With more guerdoun, if that thou
  live;
But al this tyme this I thee
  yive.'   2950
The God of Love whan al the
  day
Had taught me, as ye have herd
  say,
And enfourmed compendiously,
He vanished awey al sodeynly,
And I alone lefte, al sole,   2955
So ful of compleynt and of dole,
For I saw no man ther me by.
My woundes me greved won-
  dirly;
Me for to curen no-thing I knew,
Save the botoun bright of hew, 2960
Wheron was set hoolly my thought;
Of other comfort knew I nought,
But it were through the God of
  Love;
I knew nat elles to my bihove
That might me ese or comfort
  gete,   2965
But-if he wolde him entermete.
  The roser was, withoute doute,
Closed with an hegge withoute,
As ye to-forn have herd me seyn;
And fast I bisied, and wolde
  fayn   2970
Have passed the haye, if I might
Have geten in by any slight
Unto the botoun so fair to see.
But ever I dradde blamed to be,
If men wolde have suspec-
  cioun   2975
That I wolde of entencioun

2921, 2. *Both* sene, clene; *supply* he.   2934. *I supply* that.   2935. *Both* declared thee.   2946. Th. sufferaunce; G. suffraunce.   2950. *Both* yeue.   2954. Th. vanysshed; G. vanyshide.   2960, 2973. *Both* bothom; *read* botoun.   2970. G. bisiede; Th. besyed.   2971. Th. haye; G. hay.

Have stole the roses that ther
    were;
Therfore to entre I was in fere.
But at the last, as I bithought
Whether I sholde passe or
    nought,   2980
I saw come with a gladde chere
To me, a lusty bachelere,
Of good stature, and of good hight,
And Bialacoil forsothe he hight.
Sone he was to Curtesy,   2985
And he me graunted ful gladly
The passage of the outer hay,
And seide :—' Sir, how that ye may
Passe, if [it] your wille be,
The fresshe roser for to see, 2990
And ye the swete savour fele.
Your warrant may [I be] right
    wele;
So thou thee kepe fro folye,
Shal no man do thee vilanye.
If I may helpe you in ought,   2995
I shal not feyne, dredeth nought;
For I am bounde to your servyse,
Fully devoide of feyntyse.'
Than unto Bialacoil saide I,
' I thank you, sir, ful hertely, 3000
And your biheest [I] take at gree,
That ye so goodly profer me ;
To you it cometh of greet fraun-
    chyse,
That ye me profer your servyse.'
Than aftir, ful delivery,   3005
Through the breres anoon wente I,
Wherof encombred was the hay.
I was wel plesed, the soth to say,
To see the botoun fair and swote,

So fresshe spronge out of the
    rote.   3010
And Bialacoil me served wel,
Whan I so nygh me mighte fele
Of the botoun the swete odour,
And so lusty hewed of colour.
But than a cherl (foule him bi-
    tyde !)   3015
Bisyde the roses gan him hyde,
To kepe the roses of that roser,
Of whom the name was Daunger.
This cherl was hid there in the
    greves,
Covered with grasse and with
    leves,   3020
To spye and take whom that he
    fond
Unto that roser putte an hond.
He was not sole, for ther was mo ;
For with him were other two
Of wikkid maners, and yvel
    fame.   3025
That oon was clepid, by his name,
Wikked-Tonge, god yeve him
    sorwe !
For neither at eve, ne at morwe,
He can of no man [no] good speke;
On many a lust man doth he
    wreke.   3030
Ther was a womman eek, that hight
Shame, that, who can reken right,
Trespas was hir fadir name,
Hir moder Resoun ; and thus was
    Shame
[On lyve] brought of these ilk
    two.   3035
And yit had Trespas never ado

2981. Th. gladde ; G. glad.   2984. F. *Bel-Acueil.*   2987. G. outter; Th. vtter.   2990. Th. fresshe ; G. fresh   2992. *Both* warrans; *I supply* I be ; F. *Ge vous i puis bien garantir.*   3000. Th. hertely ; G. hertly.   3001. *I supply* I.   3009, 3013. *Both* bothom ; *read* botoun.   3010. Th. fresshe ; G. fresh. Th. spronge ; G. sprange.   3012. *Both* myght.   3020. Th. grasse ; G. gras.   3029. *I insert* no.   3035. *Both* Brought ; *I supply* On lyve (i. e. to life). Th. ylke ; G. ilk.

With Resoun, ne never ley hir by,
He was so hidous and ugly,
I mene, this that Trespas hight;
But Resoun conceyveth, of a sight, 3040
Shame, of that I spak aforn.
And whan that Shame was thus born,
It was ordeyned, that Chastitee
Shulde of the roser lady be,
Which, of the botouns more and las, 3045
With sondry folk assailed was,
That she ne wiste what to do.
For Venus hir assailith so,
That night and day from hir she stal
Botouns and roses over-al. 3050
To Resoun than prayeth Chastitee,
Whom Venus flemed over the see,
That she hir doughter wolde hir lene,
To kepe the roser fresh and grene.
Anoon Resoun to Chastitee 3055
Is fully assented that it be,
And grauntid hir, at hir request,
That Shame, bicause she is honest,
Shal keper of the roser be.
And thus to kepe it ther were three, 3060
That noon shulde hardy be ne bold
(Were he yong, or were he old)
Ageyn hir wille awey to bere
Botouns ne roses, that ther were.
I had wel sped, had I not been 3065
Awayted with these three, and seen.
For Bialacoil, that was so fair,
So gracious and debonair,
Quitte him to me ful curteisly,
And, me to plese, bad that I 3070
Shuld drawe me to the botoun nere;
Prese in, to touche the rosere
Which bar the roses, he yaf me leve;
This graunt ne might but litel greve.
And for he saw it lyked me, 3075
Right nygh the botoun pullede he
A leef al grene, and yaf me that,
The which ful nygh the botoun sat;
I made [me] of that leef ful queynt.
And whan I felte I was a-queynt 3080
With Bialacoil, and so prive,
I wende al at my wille had be.
Than wex I hardy for to tel
To Bialacoil how me bifel
Of Love, that took and wounded me, 3085
And seide: 'Sir, so mote I thee,
I may no Ioye have in no wyse,
Upon no syde, but it ryse;
For sithe (it I shal not feyne)
In herte I have had so gret peyne, 3090
So gret annoy, and such affray,
That I ne wot what I shal say;
I drede your wrath to disserve.
Lever me were, that knyves kerve
My body shulde in pecis smalle, 3095
Than in any wyse it shulde falle

3038. Th. so vgly; G. so oughlye; *om.* so.   3045. *Both* bothoms; *read* botouns. Th. las; G. lasse.   3046. Th. sondrie; G. sondre.   3047. Th. wyste; G. wist.   3050, 3064. *Both* Bothoms.   3052. *Both* Venus hath flemed.   3058. G. *om.* is.   3071, 6, 8. *Both* bothom.   3079. *I supply* me; F. *me fis.*   3083. G. waxe; Th. wext.

That ye wratthed shulde been with
    me.'
'Sey boldely thy wille,' quod he,
' I nil be wroth, if that I may,
For nought that thou shalt to me
    say.'   3100
  Thanne seide I, 'Sir, not you dis-
    plese
To knowen of my greet unese,
In which only love hath me
    brought;
For peynes greet, disese and
    thought,
Fro day to day he doth me
    drye;   3105
Supposeth not, sir, that I lye.
In me fyve woundes dide he make,
The sore of whiche shal never
    slake
But ye the botoun graunte me,
Which is most passaunt of beau-
    tee,   3110
My lyf, my deth, and my martyre,
And tresour that I most desyre.'
  Than Bialacoil, affrayed all,
Seyde, 'Sir, it may not fall;
That ye desire, it may not
    ryse.   3115
What? wolde ye shende me in this
    wyse?
A mochel foole than I were,
If I suffrid you awey to bere
The fresh botoun, so fair of sight.
For it were neither skile ne
    right   3120
Of the roser ye broke the rind,
Or take the rose aforn his kind;
Ye ar not courteys to aske it.
Lat it stil on the roser sit,
And growe til it amended be,   3125
And parfitly come to beaute.
I nolde not that it pulled wer
Fro the roser that it ber,
To me it is so leef and dere.'
  With that sterte out anoon Daun-
    gere,   3130
Out of the place where he was hid.
His malice in his chere was kid;
Ful greet he was, and blak of hewe,
Sturdy and hidous, who-so him
    knewe;
Like sharp urchouns his here was
    growe,   3135
His eyes rede as the fire-glow;
His nose frounced ful kirked stood,
He com criand as he were wood,
And seide, ' Bialacoil, tel me why
Thou bringest hider so boldly 3140
Him that so nygh [is] the roser?
Thou worchist in a wrong maner;
He thenkith to dishonour thee,
Thou art wel worthy to have mau-
    gree
To late him of the roser wit;   3145
Who serveth a feloun is yvel quit.
Thou woldist have doon greet
    bountee,
And he with shame wolde quyte
    thee.
Flee hennes, felowe! I rede thee
    go!
It wanteth litel I wol thee slo; 3150
For Bialacoil ne knew thee nought,
Whan thee to serve he sette his
    thought;
For thou wolt shame him, if thou
    might,
Bothe ageyn resoun and right.

3109. *Both* bothom.   3115. *Both* arise; *read* ryse.   3125. *Both* And late (lette) it growe.   3127, 8. *Both* were, bere.   3136. G. *om.* Th. His eyes reed sparclyng as the fyre-glowe (*too long*); F. *S'ot les yex rouges comme feus.*   3037. *Both* kirked.   3150. I] G. it; Th. he; F. *ge.*   3154. Th. agayne; G. ageyns.

THE ROMAUNT OF THE ROSE.

I wol no more in thee affye, 3155
That comest so slyghly for tespye;
For it preveth wonder wel,
Thy slight and tresoun every del.'
  I durst no more ther make abode,
For the cherl, he was so wode; 3160
So gan he threten and manace,
And thurgh the haye he did me chace.
For feer of him I tremblid and quook,
So cherlishly his heed he shook;
And seide, if eft he might me take, 3165
I shulde not from his hondis scape.
  Than Bialacoil is fled and mate,
And I al sole, disconsolate,
Was left aloon in peyne and thought;
For shame, to deth I was nygh brought. 3170
Than thought I on myn high foly,
How that my body, utterly,
Was yeve to peyne and to martyre;
And therto nadde I so gret yre,
That I ne durst the hayes passe; 3175
There was non hope, there was no grace.
I trowe never man wiste of peyne,
But he were laced in Loves cheyne;
Ne no man [wot], and sooth it is,
But-if he love, what anger is. 3180
Love holdith his heest to me right wele,
Whan peyne he seide I shulde fele.
Non herte may thenke, ne tunge seyne,
A quarter of my wo and peyne.
I might not with the anger laste; 3185

Myn herte in poynt was for to braste,
Whan I thought on the rose, that so
Was through Daunger cast me froo.
  A long whyl stood I in that state,
Til that me saugh so mad and mate 3190
The lady of the highe ward,
Which from hir tour lokid thiderward.
Resoun men clepe that lady,
Which from hir tour deliverly
Come doun to me withouten more. 3195
But she was neither yong, ne hore,
Ne high ne low, ne fat ne lene,
But best, as it were in a mene.
Hir eyen two were cleer and light
As any candel that brenneth bright; 3200
And on hir heed she hadde a crown.
Hir semede wel an high persoun;
For rounde enviroun, hir crownet
Was ful of riche stonis fret.
Hir goodly semblaunt, by devys, 3205
I trowe were maad in paradys;
Nature had never such a grace,
To forge a werk of such compace.
For certeyn, but the letter lye,
God him-silf, that is so high, 3210
Made hir aftir his image,
And yaf hir sith sich avauntage,
That she hath might and seignorye
To kepe men from al folye;
Who-so wole trowe hir lore, 3215
Ne may offenden nevermore.
  And whyl I stood thus derk and pale,
Resoun bigan to me hir tale;

3164. Th. he; G. it. 3179. *I supply* wot. 3186. Th. brast; G. barste. 3188. G. That was; Th. *m.* That. Th. through; G. thurgh. 3191. Th. highe; G. high. 3195. *Both* without. 3201. on] G. in (!). 3207. *Both* For nature; *I omit* For. 3209. *Both* but if the. 3213. Th. seignorie; G. seignurie.

She seide: 'Al hayl, my swete frend!
Foly and childhood wol thee shend, 3220
Which thee have put in greet affray;
Thou hast bought dere the tyme of May,
That made thyn herte mery to be.
In yvel tyme thou wentist to see
The gardin, wherof Ydilnesse 3225
Bar the keye, and was maistresse
Whan thou yedest in the daunce
With hir, and haddest aqueyntaunce:
Hir aqueyntaunce is perilous,
First softe, and aftir[ward] noyous; 3230
She hath [thee] trasshed, withoute ween;
The God of Love had thee not seen,
Ne hadde Ydilnesse thee conveyed
In the verger where Mirthe him pleyed.
If Foly have supprised thee, 3235
Do so that it recovered be;
And be wel war to take no more
Counsel, that greveth aftir sore;
He is wys that wol himsilf chastyse.
And though a young man in any wyse 3240
Trespace among, and do foly,
Lat him not tarye, but hastily
Lat him amende what so be mis.
And eek I counseile thee, y-wis,
The God of Love hoolly foryet, 3245
That hath thee in sich peyne set,
And thee in herte tormented so.
I can nat seen how thou mayst go
Other weyes to garisoun;
For Daunger, that is so feloun, 3250
Felly purposith thee to werrey,
Which is ful cruel, the soth to sey.
'And yit of Daunger cometh no blame,
In reward of my doughter Shame,
Which hath the roses in hir warde, 3255
As she that may be no musarde.
And Wikked-Tunge is with these two,
That suffrith no man thider go;
For er a thing be do, he shal,
Where that he cometh, over-al, 3260
In fourty places, if it be sought,
Seye thing that never was doon ne wrought;
So moche tresoun is in his male,
Of falsnesse for to [feyne] a tale.
Thou delest with angry folk, y-wis; 3265
Wherfor to thee [it] bettir is
From these folk awey to fare,
For they wol make thee live in care.
This is the yvel that Love they calle,
Wherin ther is but foly alle, 3270
For love is foly everydel;
Who loveth, in no wyse may do wel,
Ne sette his thought on no good werk.
His scole he lesith, if he be clerk;
Of other craft eek if he be, 3275
He shal not thryve therin; for he
In love shal have more passioun
Than monke, hermyte, or chanoun.
The peyne is hard, out of mesure,
The Ioye may eek no whyl endure; 3280

3219. 20. G. freende, sheende; Th. frende, shende. 3221. Th. the; G. ye. 3227. G. didest (!). 3228. Th. had; G. hadde; *read* haddest. 3230. *I supply* ward. 3231, 2. *Both* wene, sene; *I supply* thee. 3248. G. *om.* nat. 3251. Th. werrey; G. werye. 3264. *Both* seyne; feyne *seems better.* 3266. *I supply* it. 3274. *Both* he be a; *I omit* a. 3279. G. *om.* of.

And in the possessioun
Is muche tribulacioun;
The Ioye it is so short-lasting,
And but in happe is the geting;
For I see ther many in tra-
vaille, 3285
That atte laste foule fayle.
I was no-thing thy counseler,
Whan thou were maad the homager
Of God of Love to hastily;
Ther was no wisdom, but foly. 3290
Thyn herte was Ioly, but not sage,
Whan thou were brought in sich a
rage,
To yelde thee so redily,
And to Love, of his gret maistry.
  'I rede thee Love awey to
dryve, 3295
That makith thee recche not of thy
lyve.
The foly more fro day to day
Shal growe, but thou it putte away.
Take with thy teeth the bridel
faste,
To daunte thyn herte; and eek thee
caste, 3300
If that thou mayst, to gete defence
For to redresse thy first offence.
Who-so his herte alwey wol leve,
Shal finde among that shal him
greve.'
  Whan I hir herd thus me chas-
tyse, 3305
I answerd in ful angry wyse.
I prayed hir cessen of hir speche,
Outher to chastyse me or teche,
To bidde me my thought refreyne,
Which Love hath caught in his
demeyne:— 3310
'What? wene ye Love wol consent,

That me assailith with bowe bent,
To draw myn herte out of his honde,
Which is so quikly in his bonde?
That ye counsayle, may never
be; 3315
For whan he first arested me,
He took myn herte so hool him til,
That it is no-thing at my wil;
He [taughte] it so him for to
obey,
That he it sparred with a key. 3320
I pray yow lat me be al stille.
For ye may wel, if that ye wille,
Your wordis waste in idilnesse;
For utterly, withouten gesse,
Al that ye seyn is but in
veyne. 3325
Me were lever dye in the peyne,
Than Love to me-ward shulde
arette
Falsheed, or tresoun on me sette.
I wol me gete prys or blame,
And love trewe, to save my
name; 3330
Who me chastysith, I him hate.'
  With that word Resoun wente hir
gate,
Whan she saugh for no sermoning
She might me fro my foly bring.
Than dismayed, I lefte al sool, 3335
Forwery, forwandred as a fool,
For I ne knew no chevisaunce.
Than fel into my remembraunce,
How Love bade me to purveye
A felowe, to whom I mighte
seye 3340
My counsel and my privete,
For that shulde muche availe me.
With that bithought I me, that I
Hadde a felowe faste by,

3282. Th. moche; G. mych. 3292. G. arrage (!). 3301. *After* gete,
Th. *ins.* the, *and* G. thee. 3315. Th. counsayle; G. counsele. 3320. *Both*
thought; *read* taughte. 3331. *Both* Who that; *I omit* that. 3337. *Both*
cherisaunce; F. *chevissance.* 3340. *Both* myght. 3344. *Both* fast.

Trewe and siker, curteys, and hend, 3345
And he was called by name a Freend;
A trewer felowe was no-wher noon.
In haste to him I wente anoon,
And to him al my wo I tolde,
Fro him right nought I wold withholde. 3350
I tolde him al withoute were,
And made my compleynt on Daungere,
How for to see he was hidous,
And to-me-ward contrarious;
The whiche through his cruelte 3355
Was in poynt to have meygned me;
With Bialacoil whan he me sey
Within the gardyn walke and pley,
Fro me he made him for to go,
And I bilefte aloon in wo; 3360
I durst no lenger with him speke,
For Daunger seide he wolde be wreke,
Whan that he sawe how I wente
The fresshe botoun for to hente,
If I were hardy to come neer 3365
Bitwene the hay and the roser.
  This Freend, whan he wiste of my thought,
He discomforted me right nought,
But seide, 'Felowe, be not so mad,
Ne so abaysshed nor bistad. 3370
My-silf I knowe ful wel Daungere,
And how he is feers of his chere,
At prime temps, Love to manace;
Ful ofte I have ben in his caas.
A feloun first though that he be, 3375
Aftir thou shalt him souple see.
Of long passed I knew him wele;

Ungoodly first though men him fele,
He wol meek aftir, in his bering,
Been, for service and obeysshing. 3380
I shal thee telle what thou shalt do:—
Mekely I rede thou go him to,
Of herte pray him specialy
Of thy trespace to have mercy,
And hote him wel, [him] here to plese, 3385
That thou shalt nevermore him displese.
Who can best serve of flatery,
Shal plese Daunger most uttirly.'
  My Freend hath seid to me so wel,
That he me esid hath somdel, 3390
And eek allegged of my torment;
For through him had I hardement
Agayn to Daunger for to go,
To preve if I might meke him so.
  To Daunger cam I, al ashamed,
The which aforn me hadde blamed,
Desyring for to pese my wo; 3397
But over hegge durst I not go,
For he forbad me the passage.
I fond him cruel in his rage, 3400
And in his hond a gret burdoun.
To him I knelid lowe adoun,
Ful meke of port, and simple of chere,
And seide, 'Sir, I am comen here
Only to aske of you mercy. 3405
That greveth me, [sir], ful gretly
That ever my lyf I wratthed you,
But for to amende I am come now,

3350. *Both* witholde.   3355. Th. whiche; G. which.   3356. G. *om.* have. Th. meymed.   3364. Th. fresshe; G. fresh. *Both* bothom.   3372. Th. fiers. 3379. Th. meke; G. make.   3385. *I supply* him.   3399. Th. forbode; G. fobede; *read* forbad.   3406. *I supply* sir.   3408. *Both* amenden.

With al my might, bothe loude and
    stille,
To doon right at your owne
    wille;   3410
For Love made me for to do
That I have trespassed hidirto;
Fro whom I ne may withdrawe
    myn herte;
Yit shal I never, for Ioy ne smerte,
What so bifalle, good or ille,   3415
Offende more ageyn your wille.
Lever I have endure disese
Than do that shulde you displese.
  'I you require and pray, that ye
Of me have mercy and pitee,   3420
To stinte your yre that greveth so,
That I wol swere for evermo
To be redressid at your lyking,
If I trespasse in any thing;
Save that I pray thee graunte
    me   3425
A thing that may nat warned be,
That I may love, al only;
Non other thing of you aske I.
I shal doon elles wel, y-wis,
If of your grace ye graunte me
    this.   3430
And ye [ne] may not letten me,
For wel wot ye that love is free,
And I shal loven, [sith] that I wil,
Who-ever lyke it wel or il;
And yit ne wold I, for al
    Fraunce,   3435
Do thing to do you displesaunce.'
  Than Daunger fil in his entent
For to foryeve his maltalent;
But al his wratthe yit at laste
He hath relesed, I preyde so
    faste :   3440
Shortly he seide, 'Thy request

Is not to mochel dishonest;
Ne I wol not werne it thee,
For yit no-thing engreveth me.
For though thou love thus ever-
    more,   3445
To me is neither softe ne sore.
Love wher thee list; what recchith
    me,
So [thou] fer fro my roses be?
Trust not on me, for noon assay,
In any tyme to passe the hay.'   3450
Thus hath he graunted my prayere.
  Than wente I forth, withouten
    were,
Unto my Freend, and tolde him al,
Which was right Ioyful of my tale.
He seide, 'Now goth wel thyn
    affaire,   3455
He shal to thee be debonaire.
Though he aforn was dispitous,
He shal heeraftir be gracious.
If he were touchid on som good
    veyne,
He shuld yit rewen on thy
    peyne.   3460
Suffre, I rede, and no boost make,
Til thou at good mes mayst him
    take.
By suffraunce, and [by] wordis softe,
A man may overcomen ofte
Him that aforn he hadde in
    drede,   3465
In bookis sothly as I rede.'
  Thus hath my Freend with gret
    comfort
Avaunced me with high disport,
Which wolde me good as mich
    as I.
And thanne anoon ful so-
    deynly   3470

3414. G. *om*. I. 3418. G. you shulde. 3429. G. doon elles welle; Th. done al wel, F. *Toutes vos autres volentes Ferai*. 3433. Th. suche; G. sichen; F. *puisqu'il me siet*. 3447. *Both* where that the; *I omit* that. 3448. *I supply* thou; F. *tu*. 3454. Th. tale; G. talle. 3455. Th. affayre; G. affere. 3462. *Both* good mes (*sic*); F. *en bon point*; see l. 1453. 3464. *Both* -come. 3468. G. *om*. me.

I took my leve, and streight I went
Unto the hay; for gret talent
I had to seen the fresh botoun,
Wherin lay my salvacioun;
And Daunger took kepe, if
　that I　　　　　　　　　3475
Kepe him covenaunt trewly.
So sore I dradde his manasing,
I durst not breke[n] his bidding;
For, lest that I were of him shent,
I brak not his comaundement, 3480
For to purchase his good wil.
It was [hard] for to come ther-til,
His mercy was to fer bihinde;
I wepte, for I ne might it finde.
I compleyned and sighed sore, 3485
And languisshed evermore,
For I durst not over go
Unto the rose I loved so.
Thurghout my deming outerly,
[Than] had he knowlege cer-
　teinly,　　　　　　　　　3490
[That] Love me ladde in sich a
　wyse,
That in me ther was no feyntyse,
Falsheed, ne no trecherye.
And yit he, ful of vilanye,
Of disdeyne, and cruelte,　　3495
On me ne wolde have pite,
His cruel wil for to refreyne,
Though I wepe alwey, and com-
　pleyne.
　And while I was in this torment,
Were come of grace, by god
　sent,　　　　　　　　　 3500
Fraunchyse, and with hir Pite
Fulfild the botoun of bountee.
They go to Daunger anon-right
To forther me with al hir might,

And helpe in worde and in
　dede,　　　　　　　　　　3505
For wel they saugh that it was
　nede.
First, of hir grace, dame Fraun-
　chyse
Hath taken [word] of this empryse:
She seide, 'Daunger, gret wrong
　ye do
To worche this man so muche
　wo,　　　　　　　　　　　3510
Or pynen him so angerly;
It is to you gret vilany.
I can not see why, ne how,
That he hath trespassed ageyn you,
Save that he loveth; wherfore ye
　shulde　　　　　　　　　 3515
The more in cherete of him holde.
The force of love makith him do
　this;
Who wolde him blame he dide
　amis?
He leseth more than ye may do;
His peyne is hard, ye may see,
　lo!　　　　　　　　　　　3520
And Love in no wyse wolde con-
　sente
That [he] have power to repente;
For though that quik ye wolde him
　sloo,
Fro Love his herte may not go.
Now, swete sir, is it your ese 3525
Him for to angre or disese?
Allas, what may it you avaunce
To doon to him so greet grevaunce?
What worship is it agayn him take,
Or on your man a werre make, 3530
Sith he so lowly every wyse
Is redy, as ye lust devyse?

3473. *Both* bothom.　3482. Morris *supplies* hard.　3490. *Both* That he had.
3491. G. Thanne; Th. Than; *read* That; F. Qu'Amors.　3498. G. Thou; Th.
Tho. *Both* and me (*for* and).　3502. *Both* bothom.　3508. *I supply* word.
3510. Th. moche; G. mych.　3522. *Both* ye (*for* he); F. Que il.　3525. *Both* it is.

If Love hath caught him in his lace,
You for tobeye in every caas,
And been your suget at your wille,   3535
Shulde ye therfore willen him ille?
Ye shulde him spare more, al-out,
Than him that is bothe proud and stout.
Curtesye wol that ye socour
Hem that ben meke undir your cure.   3540
His herte is hard, that wole not meke,
Whan men of mekenesse him biseke.'
'That is certeyn,' seide Pite;
'We see ofte that humilitee
Bothe ire, and also felonye   3545
Venquissheth, and also melancolye;
To stonde forth in such duresse,
This crueltee and wikkednesse.
Wherfore I pray you, sir Daungere,
For to mayntene no lenger here   3550
Such cruel werre agayn your man,
As hoolly youres as ever he can;
Nor that ye worchen no more wo
On this caytif that languisshith so,
Which wol no more to you trespasse,   3555
But put him hoolly in your grace.
His offense ne was but lyte;
The God of Love it was to wyte,
That he your thral so gretly is,
And if ye harm him, ye doon amis;   3560
For he hath had ful hard penaunce,
Sith that ye refte him thaqueyntaunce

Of Bialacoil, his moste Ioye,
Which alle his peynes might acoye.
He was biforn anoyed sore,   3565
But than ye doubled him wel more;
For he of blis hath ben ful bare,
Sith Bialacoil was fro him fare.
Love hath to him do greet distresse,
He hath no nede of more duresse.   3570
Voideth from him your ire, I rede;
Ye may not winnen in this dede.
Makith Bialacoil repeire ageyn,
And haveth pite upon his peyn;
For Fraunchise wol, and I, Pite,   3575
That merciful to him ye be;
And sith that she and I accorde,
Have upon him misericorde;
For I you pray, and eek moneste,
Nought to refusen our requeste;   3580
For he is hard and fel of thought,
That for us two wol do right nought.'
Daunger ne might no more endure,
He meked him unto mesure.
'I wol in no wyse,' seith Daungere,   3585
'Denye that ye have asked here;
It were to greet uncurtesye.
I wol ye have the companye
Of Bialacoil, as ye devyse;
I wol him letten in no wyse.'   3590
To Bialacoil than wente in hy
Fraunchyse, and seide ful curteisly:—
'Ye have to longe be deignous
Unto this lover, and daungerous,

3534. G. to beye; Th. to bey.   3548. *Both* This; F. *C'est*; This = This is.
3552. Th. he; G. ye.   3554. *Both* Vpon (*for* On).   3560. *Read* mis (*for* amis).   3563. Th. moste; G. most.   3590. G. lette; Th. let.   3591. Th. hye; G. high.

THE ROMAUNT OF THE ROSE. 195

Fro him to withdrawe your pre-
   sence, 3595
Which hath do to him grete
   offence,
That ye not wolde upon him see;
Wherfore a sorowful man is he.
Shape ye to paye him, and to
   plese,
Of my love if ye wol have ese. 3600
Fulfil his wil, sith that ye knowe
Daunger is daunted and brought
   lowe
Thurgh help of me and of Pite;
You [thar] no more afered be.'
'I shal do right as ye wil,' 3605
Saith Bialacoil, 'for it is skil,
Sith Daunger wol that it so be.'
Than Fraunchise hath him sent to
   me.
   Bialacoil at the biginning
Salued me in his coming. 3610
No straungenes was in him seen,
No more than he ne had wrathed
   been.
As faire semblaunt than shewed he
   me,
And goodly, as aforn did he;
And by the honde, withouten
   doute, 3615
Within the haye, right al aboute
He ladde me, with right good
   chere,
Al environ the vergere,
That Daunger had me chased fro.
Now have I leve over-al to go; 3620
Now am I raised, at my devys,
Fro helle unto paradys.
Thus Bialacoil, of gentilnesse,
With alle his peyne and besinesse,

Hath shewed me, only of
   grace, 3625
The estres of the swote place.
   I saw the rose, whan I was nigh,
Was gretter woxen, and more high,
Fresh, rody, and fair of hewe,
Of colour ever yliche newe. 3630
And whan I had it longe seen,
I saugh that through the leves
   grene
The rose spredde to spanishing;
To sene it was a goodly thing.
But it ne was so spred on
   brede, 3635
That men within might knowe the
   sede;
For it covert was and [en]close
Bothe with the leves and with the
   rose.
The stalk was even and grene
   upright,
It was theron a goodly sight; 3640
And wel the better, withouten wene,
For the seed was not [y]-sene.
Ful faire it spradde, [god it]
   blesse!
For suche another, as I gesse,
Aforn ne was, ne more ver-
   mayle. 3645
I was abawed for merveyle,
For ever, the fairer that it was,
The more I am bounden in Loves
   laas.
   Longe I abood there, soth to saye,
Til Bialacoil I gan to praye, 3650
Whan that I saw him in no wyse
To me warnen his servyse,
That he me wolde graunte a thing,
Which to remembre is wel sitting;

3595-3690. *Not in* G.; *from* Th.   3599, 3600. Th. please, ease.   3604. Th. dare (*for* thar), *wrongly*. Th. aferde.   3615. Th. without.   3619. Th. hadde.   3620. Th. leaue.   3622. Th. hel.   3626. Th. eftres.   3633. Th. spaunysshinge.   3641. Th. without.   3642. Th. sene.   3643. Th. the god of blesse; F. *Diex la beneie*.   3646. Th. marueyle.

This is to sayne, that of his
   grace   3655
He wolde me yeve leyser and space
To me that was so desirous
To have a kissing precious
Of the goodly freshe rose,
That swetely smelleth in my
   nose;   3660
'For if it you displesed nought,
I wolde gladly, as I have sought,
Have a cos therof freely
Of your yeft; for certainly
I wol non have but by your
   leve,   3665
So loth me were you for to greve.'
   He sayde, 'Frend, so god me
      spede,
Of Chastite I have suche drede,
Thou shuldest not warned be for
   me,
But I dar not, for Chastite. 3670
Agayn hir dar I not misdo,
For alwey biddeth she me so
To yeve no lover leve to kisse;
For who therto may winnen, y-wis,
He of the surplus of the pray 3675
May live in hope to get som day.
For who so kissing may attayne,
Of loves peyne hath, soth to sayne,
The beste and most avenaunt,
And ernest of the remenaunt.' 3680
   Of his answere I syghed sore;
I durst assaye him tho no more,
I had such drede to greve him ay.
A man shulde not to muche assaye
To chafe his frend out of me-
   sure,   3685

Nor put his lyf in aventure;
For no man at the firste stroke
Ne may nat felle doun an oke;
Nor of the reisins have the wyne,
Til grapes rype and wel afyne 3690
Be sore empressid, I you ensure,
And drawen out of the pressure.
But I, forpeyned wonder stronge,
[Thought] that I abood right longe
Aftir the kis, in peyne and wo, 3695
Sith I to kis desyred so:
Til that, [rewing] on my distresse,
Ther [to me] Venus the goddesse,
Which ay werreyeth Chastite,
Came of hir grace, to socoure
   me,   3700
Whos might is knowe fer and wyde,
For she is modir of Cupyde,
The God of Love, blinde as stoon,
That helpith lovers many oon.
This lady brought in hir right
   hond   3705
Of brenning fyr a blasing brond;
Wherof the flawme and hote fyr
Hath many a lady in desyr
Of love brought, and sore het,
And in hir servise hir hertes
   set.   3710
This lady was of good entayle,
Right wondirful of apparayle;
By hir atyre so bright and shene,
Men might perceyve wel, and seen,
She was not of religioun. 3715
Nor I nil make mencioun
Nor of [hir] robe, nor of tresour,
Of broche, [nor] of hir riche
   attour;

3656. Th. leysar.   3660. Th. That so swetely.   3663. Th. cosse.   3667.
Th. sayd.   3670, 1. Th. dare.   3674. Th. ywisse.   3676. Th.
lyfe; *read* live.   3679. Th. best.   3687. Th. first.   3688. Th. fel downe.
3690. Th. grapes be ripe; *om.* be.   3691. G. *begins again.*   3694. *Both*
Though.   3697. *Both* rennyng (*for* rewing).   3698. *Both* come (*absurdly*);
see l. 3700; *read* to me.   3699. Th. werryeth; G. werieth; F. *guerroie.*   3707.
Th. flame.   3709. *Both* hette.   3710. G. heite is; Th. hert is; *read* hertis
= hertes. *Both* sette.   3716. G. nelle; Th. nyl.   3718. *Both* neithir (*for* nor).

THE ROMAUNT OF THE ROSE.

Ne of hir girdil aboute hir syde,
For that I nil not long abyde. 3720
But knowith wel, that certeynly
She was arayed richely.
Devoyd of pryde certeyn she was;
To Bialacoil she wente a pas,
And to him shortly, in a clause, 3725
She seide: 'Sir, what is the cause
Ye been of port so daungerous
Unto this lover, and deynous,
To graunte him no-thing but a kis?
To werne it him ye doon amis; 3730
Sith wel ye wote, how that he
Is Loves servaunt, as ye may see,
And hath beaute, wher-through [he] is
Worthy of love to have the blis.
How he is semely, biholde and see, 3735
How he is fair, how he is free,
How he is swote and debonair,
Of age yong, lusty, and fair.
Ther is no lady so hauteyne,
Duchesse, countesse, ne chastel-eyne, 3740
That I nolde holde hir ungoodly
For to refuse him outerly.
His breeth is also good and swete,
And eke his lippis rody, and mete
Only to pleyen, and to kisse. 3745
Graunte him a kis, of gentilnesse!
His teeth arn also whyte and clene;
Me thinkith wrong, withouten wene,
If ye now werne him, trustith me,
To graunte that a kis have he; 3750
The lasse [to] helpe him that ye haste,
The more tyme shul ye waste.'
Whan the flawme of the verry brond,
That Venus brought in hir right hond,
Had Bialacoil with hete smete, 3755
Anoon he bad, withouten lette,
Graunte to me the rose kisse.
Than of my peyne I gan to lisse,
And to the rose anoon wente I,
And kissid it ful feithfully. 3760
Thar no man aske if I was blythe,
Whan the savour soft and lythe
Strook to myn herte withoute more,
And me alegged of my sore,
So was I ful of Ioye and blisse. 3765
It is fair sich a flour to kisse,
It was so swote and saverous.
I might not be so anguisshous,
That I mote glad and Ioly be,
Whan that I remembre me. 3770
Yit ever among, sothly to seyn,
I suffre noye and moche peyn.
The see may never be so stil,
That with a litel winde it [nil]
Overwhelme and turne also, 3775
As it were wood, in wawis go.
Aftir the calm the trouble sone
Mot folowe, and chaunge as the mone.
Right so farith Love, that selde in oon
Holdith his anker; for right anoon 3780
Whan they in ese wene best to live,
They been with tempest al fordrive.

3723. G. pruyde. 3730. Th. warne; G. worne. 3742. G. outterly; Th. vtterly. 3745. *Both* pleyne (playne). 3746. *Both* -nysse. 3748. G. thenkith. 3749. Th. warne; G. worne. 3751. *Both* ye helpe; *read* to helpe. 3755. Th. with his hete. 3756. *Both* ins. me *after* bad. 3757. G. Grauntede; Th. Graunt. 3761. Thar] Th. There nede. 3763. *Both* Stroke. 3774. G. it wille; Th. at wyl. 3779. Th. selde; G. yelde.

198 THE ROMAUNT OF THE ROSE.

Who serveth Love, can telle of wo;
The stoundemele Ioye mot overgo.
Now he hurteth, and now he
  cureth, 3785
For selde in oo poynt Love
  endureth.
  Now is it right me to procede,
How Shame gan medle and take
  hede,
Thurgh whom felle angres I have
  had;
And how the stronge wal was
  maad, 3790
And the castell of brede and
  lengthe,
That God of Love wan with his
  strengthe.
Al this in romance wil I sette,
And for no-thing ne wil I lette,
So that it lyking to hir be, 3795
That is the flour of beaute;
For she may best my labour quyte,
That I for hir love shal endyte.
  Wikkid-Tunge, that the covyne
Of every lover can devyne 3800
Worst, and addith more somdel,
(For Wikkid-Tunge seith never wel),
To me-ward bar he right gret hate,
Espying me erly and late,
Til he hath seen the grete
  chere 3805
Of Bialacoil and me y-fere.
He mighte not his tunge withstonde
Worse to reporte than he fonde,
He was so ful of cursed rage;
It sat him wel of his linage, 3810
For him an Irish womman bar.
His tunge was fyled sharp, and
  squar,
Poignaunt and right kerving,
And wonder bitter in speking.

For whan that he me gan
  espye, 3815
He swoor, afferming sikirly,
Bitwene Bialacoil and me
Was yvel aquayntaunce and privee.
He spak therof so folily,
That he awakid Ielousy; 3820
Which, al afrayed in his rysing,
Whan that he herde [him] Iangling,
He ran anoon, as he were wood,
To Bialacoil ther that he stood;
Which hadde lever in this caas 3825
Have been at Reynes or Amyas;
For foot-hoot, in his felonye
To him thus seide Ielousye:—
'Why hast thou been so necligent,
To kepen, whan I was absent, 3830
This verger here left in thy ward?
To me thou haddist no reward,
To truste (to thy confusioun)
Him thus, to whom suspeccioun
I have right greet, for it is
  nede; 3835
It is wel shewed by the dede.
Greet faute in thee now have I
  founde;
By god, anoon thou shalt be bounde,
And faste loken in a tour,
Withoute refuyt or socour. 3840
For Shame to long hath be thee fro;
Over sone she was agoo.
Whan thou hast lost bothe drede
  and fere,
It semed wel she was not here.
She was [not] bisy, in no
  wyse, 3845
To kepe thee and [to] chastyse,
And for to helpen Chastitee
To kepe the roser, as thinkith me.
For than this boy-knave so boldely
Ne sholde not have be hardy, 3850

3790. G. strong; Th. stronge. 3803, 3811. *Both* bare. 3805. G. gret; Th. great. 3807. *Both* myght. 3808. G. report. 3812. *Both* square. 3832. Th. regarde. 3834. **Th. thus;** G. this. 3845. *I supply* not. 3846. *I supply* to. 3848. G. thenkith.

THE ROMAUNT OF THE ROSE.

[Ne] in this verger had such game,
Which now me turneth to gret shame.'
Bialacoil nist what to sey;
Ful fayn he wolde have fled awey,
For fere han hid, nere that he 3855
Al sodeynly took him with me.
And whan I saugh he hadde so,
This Ielousye, take us two,
I was astoned, and knew no rede,
But fledde awey for verrey drede. 3860
Than Shame cam forth ful simply;
She wende have trespaced ful gretly;
Humble of hir port, and made it simple,
Wering a vayle in stede of wimple,
As nonnis doon in hir abbey. 3865
Bicause hir herte was in affray,
She gan to speke, within a throwe,
To Ielousye, right wonder lowe.
First of his grace she bisought,
And seide :—'Sire, ne leveth nought 3870
Wikkid-Tunge, that fals espye,
Which is so glad to feyne and lye.
He hath you maad, thurgh flatering,
On Bialacoil a fals lesing.
His falsnesse is not now anew, 3875
It is to long that he him knew.
This is not the firste day;
For Wikkid-Tunge hath custom ay
Yongé folkis to bewreye,
And false lesinges on hem leye. 3880
'Yit nevertheles I see among,
That the loigne it is so longe
Of Bialacoil, hertis to lure,
In Loves servise for to endure,

Drawing suche folk him to, 3885
That he had no-thing with to do;
But in sothnesse I trowe nought,
That Bialacoil hadde ever in thought
To do trespace or vilanye;
But, for his modir Curtesye 3890
Hath taught him ever [for] to be
Good of aqueyntaunce and privee;
For he loveth non hevinesse,
But mirthe and pley, and al gladnesse;
He hateth alle [trecherous], 3895
Soleyn folk and envious;
For [wel] ye witen how that he
Wol ever glad and Ioyful be
Honestly with folk to pley.
I have be negligent, in good fey, 3900
To chastise him; therfore now I
Of herte crye you here mercy,
That I have been so recheles
To tamen him, withouten lees.
Of my foly I me repente; 3905
Now wol I hool sette myn entente
To kepe, bothe [loude] and stille,
Bialacoil to do your wille.'
'Shame, Shame,' seyde Ielousy,
'To be bitrasshed gret drede have I. 3910
Lecherye hath clombe so hye,
That almost blered is myn ye;
No wonder is, if that drede have I.
Over-al regnith Lechery,
Whos might [yit] growith night and day. 3915
Bothe in cloistre and in abbey
Chastite is werreyed over-al.
Therfore I wol with siker wal

3852. *I supply* Ne. *Both* verge; *see* 3234. G. hadde; Th. had.   3862. Th. wende; G. wente.   3864. Th. vayle; G. bayle. Th. stede; G. stide.   3877. *Both* first.   3880. G. fals. *Both* lye.   3885. G. such.   3889. G. vylonye.   3891. M. *supplies* for.   3895. *Both* trechours.   3897. *I supply* wel.   3902. *Both* herte I crye.   3907. *Both* lowe.   3912. G. yhe; Th. eye.   3915. *I supply* yit.   3917. Th. werreyed; G. werried.

Close bothe roses and roser.
I have to longe in this maner 3920
Left hem unclosid wilfully;
Wherfore I am right inwardly
Sorowful and repente me.
But now they shal no lenger be
Unclosid; and yit I drede sore, 3925
I shal repente ferthermore,
For the game goth al amis.
Counsel I [mot take] newe, y-wis.
I have to longe tristed thee,
But now it shal no lenger be; 3930
For he may best, in every cost,
Disceyve, that men tristen most.
I see wel that I am nygh shent,
But-if I sette my ful entent
Remedye to purveye. 3935
Therfore close I shal the weye
Fro hem that wol the rose espye,
And come to wayte me vilanye,
For, in good feith and in trouthe,
I wol not lette, for no slouthe, 3940
To live the more in sikirnesse,
[To] make anoon a forteresse,
[To enclose] the roses of good savour.
In middis shal I make a tour
To putte Bialacoil in prisoun, 3945
For ever I drede me of tresoun.
I trowe I shal him kepe so,
That he shal have no might to go
Aboute to make companye
To hem that thenke of vilanye; 3950
Ne to no such as hath ben here
Aforn, and founde in him good chere,

Which han assailed him to shende,
And with hir trowandyse to blende.
A fool is eyth [for] to bigyle; 3955
But may I lyve a litel while,
He shal forthenke his fair semblaunt.'
And with that word cam Drede avaunt,
Which was abasshed, and in gret fere,
Whan he wiste Ielousye was there. 3960
He was for drede in such affray,
That not a word durste he say,
But quaking stood ful stille aloon,
Til Ielousye his wey was goon,
Save Shame, that him not forsook; 3965
Bothe Drede and she ful sore quook;
[Til] that at laste Drede abreyde,
And to his cosin Shame seyde:
'Shame,' he seide, 'in sothfastnesse,
To me it is gret hevinesse, 3970
That the noyse so fer is go,
And the sclaundre of us two.
But sith that it is [so] bifalle,
We may it not ageyn [do] calle,
Whan onis sprongen is a fame. 3975
For many a yeer withouten blame
We han been, and many a day;
For many an April and many a May
We han [y]-passed, not [a]shamed,
Til Ielousye hath us blamed 3980
Of mistrust and suspecioun
Causeles, withouten enchesoun.
Go we to Daunger hastily,
And late us shewe him openly,

3928. Th. Counsayle. *Both* must; *read* mot, *and supply* take. 3942. *Both* Do; *read* To. *Both* fortresse; F. *forteresce.* 3943. *Both* Thanne (Than) close; F. *Qui les Roses clorra entor.* 3954. Th. blende; G. blynde. 3955. *I supply* for. 3967. *I supply* Til. *Both* last. 3971. *Both* ferre. 3973. *I supply* so. 3974. *I supply* do. 3977. Th. haue. 3979. *Both* shamed. 3982. G. withoute; Th. without.

That he hath not aright [y]-
  wrought,   3985
Whan that he sette nought his
  thought
To kepe better the purpryse;
In his doing he is not wyse.
He hath to us [y]-do gret wrong,
That hath suffred now so long 3990
Bialacoil to have his wille,
Alle his lustes to fulfille.
He must amende it utterly,
Or ellis shal he vilaynsly
Exyled be out of this londe; 3995
For he the werre may not with-
  stonde
Of Ielousye, nor the greef,
Sith Bialacoil is at mischeef.'
  To Daunger, Shame and Drede
    anoon
The righte wey ben [bothe a]-
  goon.   4000
The cherl they founden hem aforn
Ligging undir an hawethorn.
Undir his heed no pilowe was,
But in the stede a trusse of gras.
He slombred, and a nappe he
  took,   4005
Til Shame pitously him shook,
And greet manace on him gan make.
'Why slepist thou whan thou
  shulde wake?'
Quod Shame; 'thou dost us vil-
  anye!
Who tristith thee, he doth
  folye,   4010
To kepe roses or botouns,
Whan they ben faire in hir se-
  souns.
Thou art woxe to familiere
Where thou shulde be straunge of
  chere,

Stout of thy port, redy to greve. 4015
Thou dost gret foly for to leve
Bialacoil here-in, to calle
The yonder man to shenden us
  alle.
Though that thou slepe, we may
  here
Of Ielousie gret noyse here. 4020
Art thou now late? ryse up [in hy],
And stoppe sone and deliverly
Alle the gappis of the hay;
Do no favour, I thee pray.
It fallith no-thing to thy name 4025
Make fair semblaunt, where thou
  maist blame.
  'If Bialacoil be swete and free,
Dogged and fel thou shuldist be;
Froward and outrageous, y-wis;
A cherl chaungeth that curteis
  is.   4030
This have I herd ofte in seying,
That man [ne] may, for no daunting,
Make a sperhauke of a bosarde.
Alle men wole holde thee for mu-
  sarde,
That debonair have founden
  thee,   4035
It sit thee nought curteis to be;
To do men plesaunce or servyse,
In thee it is recreaundyse.
Let thy werkis, fer and nere,
Be lyke thy name, which is Daun-
  gere.'   4040
  Than, al abawid in shewing,
Anoon spak Dreed, right thus
  seying,
And seide, 'Daunger, I drede me
That thou ne wolt [not] bisy be
To kepe that thou hast to kepe; 4045
Whan thou shuldist wake, thou art
  aslepe.

3985, 6. G. *om.* he.   3994. Th. vilanously; G. vilaynesly.   4000. *Both* right.
I supply bothe a-.   4009, 4016. G. doist.   4011. *Both* bothoms.   4015. *Both*
Stoute, porte.   4021. G. an high; Th. an hye; *read* in hy.   4026. *Both* To make.
4036. *Both* sittith (-eth).   4044. *I supply* not.

Thou shalt be greved certeynly,
If thee aspye Ielousy,
Or if he finde thee in blame.
He hath to-day assailed Shame, 4050
And chased awey, with gret manace,
Bialacoil out of this place,
And swereth shortly that he shal
Enclose him in a sturdy wal;
And al is for thy wikkednesse, 4055
For that thee faileth straungenesse.
Thyn herte, I trowe, be failed al;
Thou shalt repente in special,
If Ielousye the sothe knewe;
Thou shalt forthenke, and sore
  rewe.' 4060
With that the cherl his clubbe
  gan shake,
Frouning his eyen gan to make,
And hidous chere; as man in rage,
For ire he brente in his visage.
Whan that he herde him blamed
  so, 4065
He seide, 'Out of my wit I go;
To be discomfit I have gret wrong.
Certis, I have now lived to long,
Sith I may not this closer kepe;
Al quik I wolde be dolven
  depe, 4070
If any man shal more repeire
Into this garden, for foule or faire.
Myn herte for ire goth a-fere,
That I lete any entre here.
I have do foly, now I see, 4075
But now it shal amended bee.
Who settith foot here any more,
Truly, he shal repente it sore;
For no man mo into this place
Of me to entre shal have
  grace. 4080

Lever I hadde, with swerdis tweyne,
Thurgh-out myn herte, in every
  veyne
Perced to be, with many a wounde,
Than slouthe shulde in me be
  founde.
From hennesforth, by night or
  day, 4085
I shal defende it, if I may,
Withouten any excepcioun
Of ech maner condicioun;
And if I any man it graunte,
Holdeth me for recreaunte.' 4090
  Than Daunger on his feet gan
  stonde,
And hente a burdoun in his honde.
Wroth in his ire, ne lefte he nought,
But thurgh the verger he hath
  sought.
If he might finde hole or trace, 4095
Wher-thurgh that men mot forth-
  by pace,
Or any gappe, he dide it close,
That no man mighte touche a rose
Of the roser al aboute;
He shitteth every man with-
  oute. 4100
  Thus day by day Daunger is wers,
More wondirful and more divers,
And feller eek than ever he was;
For him ful oft I singe 'allas!'
For I ne may nought, thurgh his
  ire, 4105
Recover that I most desire.
Myn herte, allas, wol brest a-two,
For Bialacoil I wratthed so.
For certeynly, in every membre
I quake, whan I me remembre 4110
Of the botoun, which [that] I wolde
Fulle ofte a day seen and biholde.

4059. Th. sothe; G. sooth. G. knowe. 4063. as] G. a. 4065. G. *om*. he.
4072. G. gardyne. 4073. *a-fere*, i. e. on fire. 4089. *Both put* it *after* I.
4096. *Both* me (*for* men). 4098. *Both* myght. 4110. Th. quake; G. quoke.
4111. *Both* bothom. *I supply* that.

And whan I thenke upon the kisse,
And how muche Ioye and blisse
I hadde thurgh the savour
 swete,   4115
For wante of it I grone and grete.
Me thenkith I fele yit in my nose
The swete savour of the rose.
And now I woot that I mot go
So fer the fresshe floures fro, 4120
To me ful welcome were the deeth;
Absens therof, allas, me sleeth!
For whylom with this rose, allas,
I touched nose, mouth, and face;
But now the deeth I must
 abyde.   4125
But Love consente, another tyde,
That onis I touche may and kisse,
I trowe my peyne shal never lisse.
Theron is al my coveityse,
Which brent myn herte in many
 wyse.   4130
Now shal repaire agayn sighinge,
Long wacche on nightis, and no
 slepinge;
Thought in wisshing, torment, and
 wo,
With many a turning to and fro,
That half my peyne I can not
 telle.   4135
For I am fallen into helle
From paradys and welthe, the more
My turment greveth; more and
 more
Anoyeth now the bittirnesse,
That I toforn have felt swet-
 nesse.   4140
And Wikkid-Tunge, thurgh his
 falshede,
Causeth al my wo and drede.
On me he leyeth a pitous charge,
Bicause his tunge was to large.

Now it is tyme, shortly that
 I   4145
Telle you som-thing of Ielousy,
That was in gret suspecioun.
Aboute him lefte he no masoun,
That stoon coude leye, ne querrour;
He hired hem to make a tour. 4150
And first, the roses for to kepe,
Aboute hem made he a diche depe,
Right wondir large, and also
 brood;
Upon the whiche also stood
Of squared stoon a sturdy wal, 4155
Which on a cragge was founded al,
And right gret thikkenesse eek it
 bar.
Abouten, it was founded squar,
An hundred fadome on every syde,
It was al liche longe and wyde. 4160
Lest any tyme it were assayled,
Ful wel aboute it was batayled;
And rounde enviroun eek were set
Ful many a riche and fair touret.
At every corner of this wal 4165
Was set a tour ful principal;
And everich hadde, withoute fable,
A porte-colys defensable
To kepe of enemies, and to greve,
That there hir force wolde
 preve.   4170
And eek amidde this purpryse
Was maad a tour of gret maistryse;
A fairer saugh no man with sight,
Large and wyde, and of gret might.
They [ne] dredde noon assaut 4175
Of ginne, gunne, nor skaffaut.
[For] the temprure of the mortere
Was maad of licour wonder dere;
Of quikke lyme persant and egre,
The which was tempred with vin-
 egre.   4180

4114. Th. moche; G. mych. 4120. Th. fresshe; G. fresh. 4158. G. Aboute; Th. About. 4159. G. fademe. 4175. M. *supplies* ne. 4177. *Supply* For (F. *Car*). *Both* temprure.

The stoon was hard [as] ademant,
Wherof they made the foundement.
The tour was rounde, maad in com-
  pas;
In al this world no richer was,
Ne better ordeigned therwith-
  al.   4185
Aboute the tour was maad a wal,
So that, bitwixt that and the tour,
Rosers were set of swete savour,
With many roses that they bere.
And eek within the castel were 4190
Springoldes, gunnes, bows, archers;
And eek above, atte corners,
Men seyn over the walle stonde
Grete engynes, [whiche] were nigh
  honde;   4194
And in the kernels, here and there,
Of arblasters gret plentee were.
Noon armure might hir stroke with-
  stonde,
It were foly to prece to honde.
Without the diche were listes made,
With walles batayled large and
  brade,   4200
For men and hors shulde not
  atteyne
To neigh the diche over the pleyne.
Thus Ielousye hath enviroun
Set aboute his garnisoun
With walles rounde, and diche
  depe,   4205
Only the roser for to kepe.
And Daunger [eek], erly and late
The keyes kepte of the utter gate,
The which openeth toward the eest.
And he hadde with him atte
  leest   4210
Thritty servauntes, echon by name.
  That other gate kepte Shame,
Which openede, as it was couth,
Toward the parte of the south.
Sergeauntes assigned were hir
  to   4215
Ful many, hir wille for to do.
  Than Drede hadde in hir baillye
The keping of the conestablerye,
Toward the north, I undirstonde,
That opened upon the left
  honde,   4220
The which for no-thing may be
  sure,
But-if she do [hir] bisy cure
Erly on morowe and also late,
Strongly to shette and barre the
  gate.
Of every thing that she may
  see   4225
Drede is aferd, wher-so she be;
For with a puff of litel winde
Drede is astonied in hir minde.
Therfore, for stelinge of the rose,
I rede hir nought the yate un-
  close.   4230
A foulis flight wol make hir flee,
And eek a shadowe, if she it see.
  Thanne Wikked-Tunge, ful of
  envye,
With soudiours of Normandye,
As he that causeth al the bate, 4235
Was keper of the fourthe gate,
And also to the tother three
He went ful ofte, for to see.
Whan his lot was to wake a-night,
His instrumentis wolde he
  dight,   4240
For to blowe and make soun,
Ofter than he hath enchesoun;
And walken oft upon the wal,
Corners and wikettis over-al

4181. *Both* of; *read* as.   4188. *Both* Roses; *read* Rosers; F. *rosiers*.   4191. G. and bows; Th. bowes and.   4194. whiche] *Both* who.   4207. *I supply* eek.   4208. G. *om.* kepte.   4220. Th. lefte; G. lyft.   4222. M. *supplies* hir.   4142. Th. Ofter; G. Ofte.

Ful narwe serchen and espye ; 4245
Though he nought fond, yit wolde
    he lye.
Discordaunt ever fro armonye,
And distoned from melodye,
Controve he wolde, and foule fayle,
With hornpypes of Cornewayle.
                                4250
In floytes made he discordaunce,
And in his musik, with mischaunce,
He wolde seyn, with notes newe,
That he [ne] fond no womman
    trewe,
Ne that he saugh never, in his
    lyf,   4255
Unto hir husbonde a trewe wyf ;
Ne noon so ful of honestee,
That she nil laughe and mery be
Whan that she hereth, or may espye,
A man speken of lecherye.   4260
Everich of hem hath somme vyce ;
Oon is dishonest, another is nyce ;
If oon be ful of vilanye,
Another hath a likerous ye ;
If oon be ful of wantonesse, 4265
Another is a chideresse.
    Thus Wikked-Tunge (god yeve
      him shame !)
Can putte hem everichone in blame
Withoute desert and causeles ;
He lyeth, though they been
    giltles.   4270
I have pite to seen the sorwe,
That waketh bothe eve and morwe,
To innocents doth such grevaunce ;
I pray god yeve him evel chaunce,
That he ever so bisy is   4275
Of any womman to seyn amis !
    Eek Ielousye god confounde,

That hath [y]-maad a tour so rounde,
And made aboute a garisoun
To sette Bialacoil in prisoun ; 4280
The which is shet there in the
    tour,
Ful longe to holde there soiour,
There for to liven in penaunce.
And for to do him more grevaunce,
[Ther] hath ordeyned Ielousye 4285
An olde vekke, for to espye
The maner of his governaunce ;
The whiche devel, in hir enfaunce,
Had lerned [muche] of Loves art,
And of his pleyes took hir part ; 4290
She was [expert] in his servyse.
She knew ech wrenche and every
    gyse
Of love, and every [loveres] wyle,
It was [the] harder hir to gyle.
Of Bialacoil she took ay hede, 4295
That ever he liveth in wo and drede.
He kepte him coy and eek privee,
Lest in him she hadde see
Any foly countenaunce,
For she knew al the olde
    daunce.   4300
And aftir this, whan Ielousye
Had Bialacoil in his baillye,
And shette him up that was so free,
For seure of him he wolde be,
He trusteth sore in his castel ; 4305
The stronge werk him lyketh wel.
He dradde nat that no glotouns
Shulde stele his roses or botouns.
The roses weren assured alle,
Defenced with the stronge
    walle.   4310
Now Ielousye ful wel may be
Of drede devoid, in libertee,

4246. G. wole.   4254. M. *supplies* ne.   4264. Th. eye ; G. ighe.   4269.
Th. deserte ; G. disseit.   4272. *Both* walketh (!).   4283. *Both* lyue.
4285. *Both* Which (*for* Ther) ; *giving no sense.*   4288. Th. whiche ; G.
which.   4289. *I supply* muche.   4291. *Both* except.   4293. *I supply*
loveres.   4294. *I supply* the.   4308. *Both* bothoms.

Whether that he slepe or wake;
For of his roses may noon be take.
　But I, allas, now morne shal; 4315
Bicause I was without the wal,
Ful moche dole and mone I made.
Who hadde wist what wo I hadde,
I trowe he wolde have had pitee.
Love to deere had sold to me　4320
The good that of his love hadde I.
I [wende a bought] it al queyntly;
But now, thurgh doubling of my peyn,
I see he wolde it selle ageyn,
And me a newe bargeyn lere, 4325
The which al-out the more is dere,
For the solace that I have lorn,
Than I hadde it never aforn.
Certayn I am ful lyk, indeed,
To him that cast in erthe his seed;　　　　　　　4330
And hath Ioie of the newe spring,
Whan it greneth in the ginning,
And is also fair and fresh of flour,
Lusty to seen, swote of odour;
But er he it in sheves shere,　4335
May falle a weder that shal it dere,
And maken it to fade and falle,
The stalk, the greyn, and floures alle;
That to the tilier is fordone
The hope that he hadde to sone.　　　　　　　4340
I drede, certeyn, that so fare I;
For hope and travaile sikerly
Ben me biraft al with a storm;
The floure nil seden of my corn.
For Love hath so avaunced me,　　　　　　　4345
Whan I bigan my privitee

To Bialacoil al for to telle,
Whom I ne fond froward ne felle,
But took a-gree al hool my play.
But Love is of so hard assay,　4350
That al at onis he reved me,
Whan I wend best aboven have be.
It is of Love, as of Fortune,
That chaungeth ofte, and nil contune;
Which whylom wol on folke smyle,　　　　　　　4355
And gloumbe on hem another whyle;
Now freend, now foo, [thou] shalt hir fele,
For [in] a twinkling tourneth hir wheel.
She can wrythe hir heed awey,
This is the concours of hir pley; 4360
She can areyse that doth morne,
And whirle adown, and overturne
Who sittith hieghst, [al] as hir list;
A fool is he that wol hir trist.
For it [am] I that am com doun 4365
Thurgh change and revolucioun!
Sith Bialacoil mot fro me twinne,
Shet in the prisoun yond withinne,
His absence at myn herte I fele;
For al my Ioye and al myn hele 4370
Was in him and in the rose,
That but yon [wal], which him doth close,
Open, that I may him see,
Love nil not that I cured be
Of the peynes that I endure,　4375
Nor of my cruel aventure.
A, Bialacoil, myn owne dere!
Though thou be now a prisonere,

　　4314. G. *om.* of.　4322. *Both* wente aboute (a = have).　4337. *Both* make.　4339. G. tiliers; Th. tyllers.　4344. Th. nyl; G. nel.　4352. *Both* wente; aboven to haue.　4355. Th. folke; G. folk.　4356. G. glowmbe; Th. glombe.　4357. M. *supplies* thou.　4358. *I supply* in.　Th. tourneth; G. tourne.　4361. Th. areyse; G. arise.　4363. Th. hyest.　*Both* but; *read* al.　*Both* lust.　4364. *Both* trust.　4365. am] *Both* is.　4366. *Both* charge.　4372. wal] G. wole; Th. wol.

Kepe atte leste thyn herte to me,
And suffre not that it daunted
    be;   4380
Ne lat not Ielousye, in his rage,
Putten thyn herte in no servage.
Although he chastice thee with-
    oute,
And make thy body unto him loute,
Have herte as hard as dya-
    maunt,   4385
Stedefast, and nought pliaunt;
In prisoun though thy body be,
At large kepe thyn herte free.
A trewe herte wol not plye
For no manace that it may drye. 4390
If Ielousye doth thee payne,
Quyte him his whyle thus agayne,
To venge thee, atte leest in thought,
If other way thou mayest nought:
And in this wyse sotilly   4395
Worche, and winne the maistry.
But yit I am in gret affray
Lest thou do not as I say;
I drede thou canst me greet maugree,
That **thou** emprisoned art for
    me;   4400
But that [is] not for my trespas,
For **thurgh** me never discovered
    was
Yit thing that oughte be secree.
Wel more anoy [ther] is in me,
Than **is in thee,** of this mis-
    chaunce;   4405
For I endure more hard penaunce
Than any [man] can seyn or thinke,
That for the sorwe almost I sinke.
Whan I remembre me of my wo,
Ful nygh out of my wit I go.   4410
Inward myn herte I fele blede,
For comfortles the deeth I drede.
Ow I not wel to have distresse,

Whan false, thurgh hir wikked-
    nesse,
And traitours, that arn envy-
    ous,   4415
To noyen me be so coragious?
A, Bialacoil! ful wel I see,
That they hem shape to disceyve
    thee,
To make thee buxom to hir lawe,
And with hir corde thee to
    drawe   4420
Wher-so hem lust, right at hir wil;
I drede they have thee brought
    thertil.
Withoute comfort, thought me
    sleeth;
This game wol bringe me to my
    deeth.
For if your gode wille I lese, 4425
I mote be deed; I may not chese.
And if that thou foryete me,
Myn herte shal never in lyking be;
Nor elles-where finde solace,
If I be put out of your grace, 4430
As it shal never been, I hope;
Than shulde I fallen in wanhope.

[*Here, at* l. 4070 *of the* French
text, *ends the work of* G. de
Lorris; *and begins the work
of* Jean de Meun.]

Allas, in wanhope?—nay, par-
    dee!
For I wol never dispeired be.
If Hope me faile, than am I 4435
Ungracious and unworthy;
In Hope I wol comforted be,
For Love, whan he bitaught hir
    me,

4394. *Both* maist.   4401. *I supply* is.   4403. *Both* ought.   4404.
I supply ther.   4407. *I supply* man.   4413. *Both* Owe.   4414. Th
false; G. fals.   4425. *Both* good.   4432. *Both* falle.

Seide, that Hope, wher-so I go,
Shulde ay be relees to my wo. 4440
But what and she my balis bete,
And be to me curteis and swete?
She is in no-thing ful certeyn.
Lovers she put in ful gret peyn,
And makith hem with wo to dele. 4445
Hir fair biheest disceyveth fele,
For she wol bihote, sikirly,
And failen aftir outrely.
A! that is a ful noyous thing!
For many a lover, in loving, 4450
Hangeth upon hir, and trusteth fast,
Whiche lese hir travel at the last.
Of thing to comen she woot right nought;
Therfore, if it be wysly sought,
Hir counseille, foly is to take. 4455
For many tymes, whan she wol make
A ful good silogisme, I drede
That aftirward ther shal in dede
Folwe an evel conclusioun;
This put me in confusioun. 4460
For many tymes I have it seen,
That many have bigyled been,
For trust that they have set in Hope,
Which fel hem aftirward a-slope.
But natheles yit, gladly she wolde, 4465
That he, that wol him with hir holde,
Hadde alle tymes [his] purpos clere,
Withoute deceyte, or any were.
That she desireth sikirly;
Whan I hir blamed, I did foly. 4470
But what avayleth hir good wille,

Whan she ne may staunche my stounde ille?
That helpith litel, that she may do,
Outake biheest unto my wo.
And heeste certeyn, in no wyse, 4475
Withoute yift, is not to pryse.
Whan heest and deed a-sundir varie,
They doon [me have] a gret contrarie.
Thus am I possed up and doun
With dool, thought, and confusioun; 4480
Of my disese ther is no noumbre.
Daunger and Shame me encumbre,
Drede also, and Ielousye,
And Wikked-Tunge, ful of envye,
Of whiche the sharpe and cruel ire 4485
Ful oft me put in gret martire.
They han my Ioye fully let,
Sith Bialacoil they have bishet
Fro me in prisoun wikkidly,
Whom I love so entierly, 4490
That it wol my bane be,
But I the soner may him see.
And yit moreover, wurst of alle,
Ther is set to kepe, foule hir bifalle!
A rimpled vekke, fer ronne in age, 4495
Frowning and yelowe in hir visage,
Which in awayte lyth day and night,
That noon of hem may have a sight.
Now moot my sorwe enforced be;
Ful soth it is, that Love yaf me 4500

4440. G. reles; Th. relees.   4441. G. baalis; Th. bales.   4448. Th. vtterly.   4452. Th. traueyle.   4460. Th. put; G. putte.   4465. Th. nathelesse; G. neuertheles; *after which* G. *has* yit (Th. yet).   4467. *Both* her (*for* his).   4472. G. no; Th. ne.   4476. *Both* preise; *read* pryse.   4477. Th. a-sondre; G. asundry.   4478. *I supply* me have; F. *Avoir me lest tant de contraires.*   4483. G. Dre (!).   4486. G. putte.   4492. G. sonner.   4495. *Both* ferre.

Three wonder yiftes of his grace,
Which I have lorn now in this place,
Sith they ne may, withoute drede
Helpen but litel, who taketh hede.
For here availeth no Swete-Thought,   4505
And Swete-Speche helpith right nought.
The thridde was called Swete-Loking,
That now is lorn, without lesing.
[The] yiftes were fair, but not forthy
They helpe me but simply,   4510
But Bialacoil [may] loosed be,
To gon at large and to be free.
For him my lyf lyth al in dout,
But-if he come the rather out.
Allas! I trowe it wol not been!   4515
For how shuld I evermore him seen?
He may not out, and that is wrong,
Bicause the tour is so strong.
How shulde he out? by whos prowesse,
Out of so strong a forteresse?   4520
By me, certeyn, it nil be do;
God woot, I have no wit therto!
But wel I woot I was in rage,
Whan I to Love dide homage.
Who was in cause, in sothfastnesse,   4525
But hir-silf, dame Idelnesse,
Which me conveyed, thurgh fair prayere,
To entre into that fair vergere?
She was to blame me to leve,
The which now doth me sore greve.   4530

A foolis word is nought to trowe,
Ne worth an appel for to lowe;
Men shulde him snibbe bittirly,
At pryme temps of his foly.
I was a fool, and she me leved,   4535
Thurgh whom I am right nought releved.
She accomplisshed al my wil,
That now me greveth wondir il.
Resoun me seide what shulde falle.
A fool my-silf I may wel calle,   4540
That love asyde I had not leyde,
And trowed that dame Resoun seyde.
Resoun had bothe skile and right,
Whan she me blamed, with al hir might,
To medle of love, that hath me shent;   4545
But certeyn now I wol repent.
'And shulde I repent? Nay, parde!
A fals traitour than shulde I be.
The develles engins wolde me take,
If I my [lorde] wolde forsake,   4550
Or Bialacoil falsly bitraye.
Shulde I at mischeef hate him? nay,
Sith he now, for his curtesye,
Is in prisoun of Ielousye.
Curtesye certeyn dide he me,   4555
So muche, it may not yolden be,
Whan he the hay passen me lete,
To kisse the rose, faire and swete;
Shulde I therfore cunne him maugree?
Nay, certeynly, it shal not be;   4560
For Love shal never, [if god wil],
Here of me, thurgh word or wil,

4509. *I supply* The.   4510. *Both* symply; *read* simpilly?   4511. *I supply* may.   4513, 4. Th. dout, out; G. doute, oute.   4528. G. verger.   4537. G. Sheo.   4541. G. assayde; G. *om.* not.   4549. Th. engyns; G. engynnes. 4550. *Both* Loue; *read* lorde.   4556. Th. moche that it; G. mych that. 4557. *Both* lete = leet.   4561. *Both* yeue good wille; F. *se Diex plaist.*

Offence or complaynt, more or lesse,
Neither of Hope nor Idilnesse;
For certis, it were wrong that I 4565
Hated hem for hir curtesye.
Ther is not ellis, but suffre and thinke,
And waken whan I shulde winke;
Abyde in hope, til Love, thurgh chaunce,
Sende me socour or allegeaunce, 4570
Expectant ay til I may mete
To geten mercy of that swete.

'Whylom I thinke how Love to me
Seyde he wolde taken atte gree
My servise, if unpacience 4575
Caused me to doon offence.
He seyde, " In thank I shal it take,
And high maister eek thee make,
If wikkednesse ne reve it thee;
But sone, I trowe, that shal not be." 4580
These were his wordis by and by;
It semed he loved me trewly.
Now is ther not but serve him wele,
If that I thinke his thank to fele.
My good, myn harm, lyth hool in me; 4585
In Love may no defaute be;
For trewe Love ne failid never man.
Sothly, the faute mot nedis than
(As God forbede!) be founde in me,
And how it cometh, I can not see. 4590
Now lat it goon as it may go;
Whether Love wol socoure me or slo,
He may do hool on me his wil.
I am so sore bounde him til,
From his servyse I may not fleen; 4595
For lyf and deth, withouten wene,
Is in his hand; I may not chese;
He may me do bothe winne and lese.
And sith so sore he doth me greve,
Yit, if my lust he wolde acheve 4600
To Bialacoil goodly to be,
I yeve no force what felle on me.
For though I dye, as I mot nede,
I praye Love, of his goodlihede,
To Bialacoil do gentilnesse, 4605
For whom I live in such distresse,
That I mote deyen for penaunce.
But first, withoute repentaunce,
I wol me confesse in good entent,
And make in haste my testament, 4610
As lovers doon that felen smerte:—
To Bialacoil leve I myn herte
Al hool, withoute departing,
Or doublenesse of repenting.'

Coment Raisoun vient a L'amant.

Thus as I made my passage 4615
In compleynt, and in cruel rage,
And I not wher to finde a leche
That couthe unto myn helping eche,
Sodeynly agayn comen doun
Out of hir tour I saugh Resoun, 4620
Discrete and wys, and ful plesaunt,
And of hir porte ful avenaunt.
The righte wey she took to me,
Which stood in greet perplexite,
That was posshed in every side, 4625
That I nist where I might abyde,
Til she, demurely sad of chere,
Seide to me as she com nere:—

4567, 4573, 4584. G. thenke.   4574. *Both* take. G. att; Th. at.   4587. *Om.* ne?   4614. G. *om.* Or.   4615. Rubric *in both.*   4617. *For* not *read* nist?   4621. G. wijs.   4623. *Both* right.   4628. Th. came; G. come.

'Myn owne freend, art thou yit
    greved?
How is this quarel yit acheved   4630
Of Loves syde? Anoon me telle;
Hast thou not yit of love thy fille?
Art thou not wery of thy servyse
That thee hath [pyned] in sich
    wyse?
What Ioye hast thou in thy
    loving?   4635
Is it swete or bitter thing?
Canst thou yit chese, lat me see,
What best thy socour mighte be?
'Thou servest a ful noble lord,
That maketh thee thral for thy
    reward,   4640
Which ay renewith thy turment,
With foly so he hath thee blent.
Thou felle in mischeef thilke day,
Whan thou didest, the sothe to say,
Obeysaunce and eek homage; 4645
Thou wroughtest no-thing as the
    sage.
Whan thou bicam his liege man,
Thou didist a gret foly than;
Thou wistest not what fel therto,
With what lord thou haddist to
    do.   4650
If thou haddist him wel knowe,
Thou haddist nought be brought so
    lowe;
For if thou wistest what it were,
Thou noldist serve him half a yeer,
Not a weke, nor half a day,   4655
Ne yit an hour withoute delay,
Ne never [han] loved paramours,
His lordship is so ful of shoures.
Knowest him ought?'
    L'Amaunt. 'Ye, dame, parde!'

Raisoun. 'Nay, nay.'
L'Amaunt. 'Yes, I.'
Raisoun. 'Wherof, lat see?' 4660
L'Amaunt. 'Of that he seyde I
    shulde be
Glad to have sich lord as he,
And maister of sich seignory.'
Raisoun. 'Knowist him no more?'
L'Amaunt.   'Nay, certis, I,
Save that he yaf me rewles
    there,   4665
And wente his wey, I niste where,
And I abood bounde in balaunce.'
Raisoun. 'Lo, there a noble
    conisaunce!
But I wil that thou knowe him
    now
Ginning and ende, sith that
    thou   4670
Art so anguisshous and mate,
Disfigured out of astate;
Ther may no wrecche have more
    of wo,
Ne caitif noon enduren so.
It were to every man sitting 4675
Of his lord have knowleching.
For if thou knewe him, out of dout,
Lightly thou shulde escapen out
Of the prisoun that marreth thee.'
L'Amaunt. 'Ye, dame! sith my
    lord is he,   4680
And I his man, maad with myn
    honde,
I wolde right fayn undirstonde
To knowen of what kinde he be,
If any wolde enforme me.'
Raisoun. 'I wolde,' seid Re-
    soun, 'thee lere,   4685
Sith thou to lerne hast sich desire,

4634. *Both* the. *I insert* pyned. Th. suche.   4638. *Both* myght.   4647.
Both liege.   4657. G. I lovede; Th. I loued; *read* han loved.   4659 (*ends
at* parde); *misnumbered* 4660 *in* M.   Th. Ye; G. Yhe.   4660. Th. Yes; G.
Yhis.   4667. *misnumbered* 4670 *in* M.   4672. G. a state.   4680. G.
Yhe.   4683. *Both* knowe.   4684. G. ony.

And shewe thee, withouten fable,
A thing that is not demonstrable.
Thou shalt [here lerne] without science,
And knowe, withoute experience, 4690
The thing that may not knowen be,
Ne wist ne shewid in no degree.
Thou mayst the sothe of it not witen,
Though in thee it were writen.
Thou shalt not knowe therof more 4695
Whyle thou art reuled by his lore;
But unto him that love wol flee,
The knotte may unclosed be,
Which hath to thee, as it is founde,
So long be knet and not unbounde. 4700
Now sette wel thyn entencioun,
To here of love discripcioun.
'Love, it is an hateful pees,
A free acquitaunce, without relees,
[A trouthe], fret full of falshede,
A sikernesse, al set in drede; 4706
In herte is a dispeiring hope,
And fulle of hope, it is wanhope;
Wyse woodnesse, and wood resoun,
A swete peril, in to droune, 4710
An hevy birthen, light to bere,
A wikked wawe awey to were.
It is Caribdis perilous,
Disagreable and gracious.
It is discordaunce that can accorde, 4715
And accordaunce to discorde.

It is cunning withoute science,
Wisdom withoute sapience,
Wit withoute discrecioun,
Havoir, withoute possessioun. 4720
It is sike hele and hool siknesse,
A thrust drowned [in] dronkenesse,
An helthe ful of maladye,
And charitee ful of envye,
An [hunger] ful of habundaunce, 4725
And a gredy suffisaunce;
Delyt right ful of hevinesse,
And drerihed ful of gladnesse;
Bitter swetnesse and swete errour,
Right evel savoured good savour; 4730
Sinne that pardoun hath withinne,
And pardoun spotted without [with] sinne;
A peyne also it is, Ioyous,
And felonye right pitous;
Also pley that selde is stable, 4735
And stedefast [stat], right mevable;
A strengthe, weyked to stonde upright,
And feblenesse, ful of might;
Wit unavysed, sage folye,
And Ioye ful of turmentrye; 4740
A laughter it is, weping ay,
Rest, that traveyleth night and day;
Also a swete helle it is,
And a sorowful Paradys;
A plesaunt gayl and esy prisoun, 4745
And, ful of froste, somer sesoun;

4689. *I supply* here lerne; *both* withouten.   4690. *Both* withouten.   4700. G. knette; Th. knytte.   4705. *Both* And through the; *read* A trouthe.   *Both* frette.   4709. G. vode (*for* wood); Th. voyde.   4710. G. perelle.   4712. Th. weare.   4713. G. karibdous; Th. Carybdes; F. *Caribdis*.   4721. Th. lyke; G. like; *read* sike. Th. sickenesse; G. sekenesse.   4722. G. trust; Th. truste; (thrust = thirst).   *Both* and (*for* in).   4723. *Both* And. G. helth.   4725. *Both* And. G. anger; Th. angre (!).   4728. *Both* dreried.   4731. *Both* Sen.   4732. *Supply* with.   4736. *Supply* stat; F. *Estat trop fers et trop muable.*

Pryme temps, ful of frostes whyte,
And May, devoide of al delyte,
With seer braunches, blossoms ungrene;
And newe fruyt, fillid with winter tene. 4750
It is a slowe, may not forbere
Ragges, ribaned with gold, to were;
For al-so wel wol love be set
Under ragges as riche rochet;
And eek as wel be amourettes 4755
In mourning blak, as bright burnettes.
For noon is of so mochel prys,
Ne no man founden [is] so wys,
Ne noon so high is of parage,
Ne no man founde of wit so sage, 4760
No man so hardy ne so wight,
Ne no man of so mochel might,
Noon so fulfilled of bounte,
[But] he with love may daunted be.
Al the world holdith this way; 4765
Love makith alle to goon miswey,
But it be they of yvel lyf,
Whom Genius cursith, man and wyf,
That wrongly werke ageyn nature.
Noon suche I love, ne have no cure 4770
Of suche as Loves servaunts been,
And wol not by my counsel fleen.
For I ne preyse that loving,
Wher-thurgh man, at the laste ending,
Shal calle hem wrecchis fulle of wo, 4775
Love greveth hem and shendith so.
But if thou wolt wel Love eschewe,
For to escape out of his mewe,
And make al hool thy sorwe to slake,

No bettir counsel mayst thou take, 4780
Than thinke to fleen wel, y-wis;
May nought helpe elles; for wite thou this :—
If thou flee it, it shal flee thee;
Folowe it, and folowen shal it thee.'
L'Amaunt. Whan I hadde herd al Resoun seyn, 4785
Which hadde spilt hir speche in veyn :
'Dame,' seyde I, 'I dar wel sey
Of this avaunt me wel I may
That from your scole so deviaunt
I am, that never the more avaunt 4790
Right nought am I, thurgh your doctryne;
I dulle under your disciplyne;
I wot no more than [I] wist [er],
To me so contrarie and so fer
Is every thing that ye me lere; 4795
And yit I can it al parcuere.
Myn herte foryetith therof right nought,
It is so writen in my thought;
And depe graven it is so tendir
That al by herte I can it rendre, 4800
And rede it over comunely;
But to my-silf lewedist am I.
' But sith ye love discreven so,
And lakke and preise it, bothe two,
Defyneth it into this letter, 4805
That I may thenke on it the better;
For I herde never [diffyne it ere],
And wilfully I wolde it lere.'
Raisoun. 'If love be serched wel and sought,
It is a sykenesse of the thought 4810

4755. *Both* by (*for* be). 4758. M. *supplies* is. 4762. G. mychel; *see* 4757. 4764. *Both* That; *read* But. 4771, 2. *Both* bene, flene. 4793. *I supply* I. *Both* euer; *read* er. 4796. *Both* al by partuere. 4799. *Both* greven. 4802. Th. lewdest. 4804. Th. lacke; G. lak. 4807. *Both* diffyned here.

THE ROMAUNT OF THE ROSE.

Annexed and knet bitwixe tweyne,
[Which] male and female, with oo cheyne,
So frely byndith, that they nil twinne,
Whether so therof they lese or winne.
The roote springith, thurgh hoot brenning, 4815
Into disordinat desiring
For to kissen and enbrace,
And at her lust them to solace.
Of other thing love recchith nought,
But setteth hir herte and al hir thought 4820
More for delectacioun
Than any procreacioun
Of other fruyt by engendring;
Which love to god is not plesing;
For of hir body fruyt to get 4825
They yeve no force, they are so set
Upon delyt, to pley in-fere.
And somme have also this manere,
To feynen hem for love seke;
Sich love I preise not at a leke. 4830
For paramours they do but feyne;
To love truly they disdeyne.
They falsen ladies traitoursly,
And sweren hem othes utterly,
With many a lesing, and many a fable, 4835
And al they finden deceyvable.
And, whan they her lust han geten,
The hoote ernes they al foryeten.
Wimmen, the harm they byen ful sore;
But men this thenken evermore, 4840
That lasse harm is, so mote I thee,

Disceyve them, than disceyved be;
And namely, wher they ne may
Finde non other mene wey.
For I wot wel, in sothfastnesse, 4845
That [who] doth now his bisynesse
With any womman for to dele,
For any lust that he may fele,
But-if it be for engendrure,
He doth trespasse, I you ensure. 4850
For he shulde setten al his wil
To geten a likly thing him til,
And to sustene[n], if he might,
And kepe forth, by kindes right,
His owne lyknesse and semblable, 4855
For bicause al is corumpable,
And faile shulde successioun,
Ne were ther generacioun
Our sectis strene for to save.
Whan fader or moder arn in grave, 4860
Hir children shulde, whan they ben deede,
Ful diligent ben, in hir steede,
To use that werke on such a wyse,
That oon may thurgh another ryse.
Therfore set Kinde therin delyt, 4865
For men therin shulde hem delyte,
And of that dede be not erke,
But ofte sythes haunt that werke.
For noon wolde drawe therof a draught
Ne were delyt, which hath him caught. 4870
This hadde sotil dame Nature;
For noon goth right, I thee ensure,
Ne hath entent hool ne parfyt;
For hir desir is for delyt,

4811. G. kned; Th. knedde. *Both* bitwixt. 4812. *Both* With. 4813. *Both* frely that; *I omit* that. G. nylle. 4823. *Both* engendrure; *see* 6114. 4830. G. *om.* at. 4834. *Both* swerne. 4837. *Both* han her lust. 4839. Th. *om.* they. 4846. who] *Both* what. 4856. G. *omits; from* Th. 4858. *Both* their; *read* ther. 4865. *Both* sette. 4873. G. parfight; T. parfyte.

The which fortened crece and
   eke   4875
The pley of love for-ofte seke,
And thralle hem-silf, they be so
   nyce,
Unto the prince of every vyce.
For of ech sinne it is the rote,
Unlefulle lust, though it be
   sote,   4880
And of al yvel the racyne,
As Tullius can determyne,
Which in his tyme was ful sage,
In a boke he made of Age,
Wher that more he preyseth
   Elde,   4885
Though he be croked and unwelde,
And more of commendacioun,
Than Youthe in his discripcioun.
For Youthe set bothe man and wyf
In al perel of soule and lyf;   4890
And perel is, but men have grace,
The [tyme] of youthe for to pace,
Withoute any deth or distresse,
It is so ful of wildenesse;
So ofte it doth shame or
   damage   4895
To him or to his linage.
It ledith man now up, now doun,
In mochel dissolucioun,
And makith him love yvel company,
And lede his lyf disrewlily,   4900
And halt him payed with noon es-
   tate.
Within him-silf is such debate,
He chaungith purpos and entent,
And yalt [him] into som covent,
To liven aftir her empryse,   4905
And lesith fredom and fraunchyse,
That Nature in him hadde set,

The which ageyn he may not get,
If he there make his mansioun
For to abyde professioun.   4910
Though for a tyme his herte absente,
It may not fayle, he shal repente,
And eke abyde thilke day
To leve his abit, and goon his way,
And lesith his worship and his
   name,   4915
And dar not come ageyn for shame;
But al his lyf he doth so mourne,
Bicause he dar not hoom retourne.
Fredom of kinde so lost hath he
That never may recured be,   4920
But-if that god him graunte grace
That he may, er he hennes pace,
Conteyne undir obedience
Thurgh the vertu of pacience.
For Youthe set man in al folye, 4925
In unthrift and in ribaudye,
In leccherye, and in outrage,
So ofte it chaungith of corage.
Youthe ginneth ofte sich bargeyn,
That may not ende withouten
   peyn.   4930
In gret perel is set youth-hede,
Delyt so doth his bridil lede.
Delyt thus hangith, drede thee
   nought,
Bothe mannis body and his thought,
Only thurgh Youthe, his cham-
   berere,   4935
That to don yvel is customere,
And of nought elles taketh hede
But only folkes for to lede
Into disporte and wildenesse,   4939
So is [she] froward from sadnesse.
'But Elde drawith hem therfro;
Who wot it nought, he may wel go

4875. Th. crease.   4878. Th. vyce; G. wise.   4882. Th. Tullyus; G.
Tulius.   4889. *Both* sette.   4892. G. perell; Th. parel; *read* tyme. Th.
youthe; G. yougth.   4904. *Both* yalte. *I supply* him.   4921. *Both* But that if.
4926. G. *om.* in.   4931. Th. youth-hede; G. youthede.   4933. thus] *Both*
this.   4935. *Both* youthes chambre (chambere); *read* Youthe his chamberere;
F. *Par Ionesce sa chamberiere.*   4936. G. customere.   4940. *Supply* she.

[Demand] of hem that now arn olde,
That whylom Youthe hadde in holde,
Which yit remembre of tendir
  age,   4945
How it hem brought in many a
  rage,
And many a foly therin wrought.
But now that Elde hath hem thurgh-
  sought,
They repente hem of her folye,
That Youthe hem putte in Iu-
  pardye,   4950
In perel and in muche wo,
And made hem ofte amis to do,
And suen yvel companye,
Riot and avouterye.
  'But Elde [can] ageyn re-
    streyne   4955
From suche foly, and refreyne,
And set men, by hir ordinaunce,
In good reule and in governaunce.
But yvel she spendith hir servyse,
For no man wol hir love, ne
  pryse;   4960
She is hated, this wot I wele.
Hir acqueyntaunce wolde no man
  fele,
Ne han of Elde companye,
Men hate to be of hir alye.
For no man wolde bicomen
  olde,   4965
Ne dye, whan he is yong and bolde.
And Elde merveilith right gretly,
Whan they remembre hem inwardly
Of many a perelous empryse,
Whiche that they wrought in son-
  dry wyse,   4970
How ever they might, withoute
  blame,
Escape awey withoute shame,

In youthe, withoute[n] damage
Or repreef of her linage,
Losse of membre, sheding of
  blode,   4975
Perel of deth, or losse of good.
  'Wost thou nought where Youthe
    abit,
That men so preisen in her wit?
With Delyt she halt soiour,
For bothe they dwellen in oo
  tour.   4980
As longe as Youthe is in sesoun,
They dwellen in oon mansioun.
Delyt of Youthe wol have servyse
To do what so he wol devyse;
And Youthe is redy evermore 4985
For to obey, for smerte of sore,
Unto Delyt, and him to yive
Hir servise, whyl that she may live.
  'Where Elde abit, I wol thee
    telle
Shortly, and no whyle dwelle, 4990
For thider bihoveth thee to go.
If Deth in youthe thee not slo,
Of this journey thou maist not
  faile.
With hir Labour and Travaile
Logged been, with Sorwe and
  Wo,   4995
That never out of hir courte go.
Peyne and Distresse, Syknesse and
  Ire,
And Malencoly, that angry sire,
Ben of hir paleys senatours;
Groning and Grucching, hir her-
  bergeours,   5000
The day and night, hir to turment,
With cruel Deth they hir present,
And tellen hir, erliche and late,
That Deth stant armed at hir gate.

4943. *Both* And mo of (!).   4945. *Both* remembreth.   4948. *Both* him;
read hem.   4950. Th. ieopardye.   4951. Th. moche; G. mych.   4954.
G. avoutrie; Th. avoutrye.   4955. can] *Both* gan.   4956. Th. suche; G.
sich.   4960. *Both* neither preise.   4996. Th. courte; G. court.   5000.
Th. herbegeours; G. herbeiours.   5004. Th. stondeth; G. stondith.

THE ROMAUNT OF THE ROSE.

Than bringe they to hir remem-
  braunce   5005
The foly dedis of hir infaunce,
Which causen hir to mourne in wo
That Youthe hath hir bigiled so,
Which sodeynly awey is hasted.
She wepeth the tyme that she hath
  wasted,   5010
Compleyning of the preterit,
And the present, that not abit,
And of hir olde vanitee,
That, but aforn hir she may see
In the future som socour,   5015
To leggen hir of hir dolour,
To graunt hir tyme of repentaunce,
For hir sinnes to do penaunce,
And at the laste so hir governe
To winne the Ioy that is
  eterne,   5020
Fro which go bakward Youthe [hir]
  made,
In vanitee to droune and wade.
For present tyme abidith nought,
It is more swift than any thought ;
So litel whyle it doth endure   5025
That ther nis compte ne mesure.
  ' But how that ever the game go,
Who list [have] Ioye and mirth also
Of love, be it he or she,
High or lowe, who[so] it be,   5030
In fruyt they shulde hem delyte ;
Her part they may not elles quyte,
To save hem-silf in honestee.
And yit ful many oon I see
Of wimmen, sothly for to
  seyne,   5035
That [ay] desire and wolde fayne
The pley of love, they be so wilde,
And not coveite to go with childe.
And if with child they be per-
  chaunce,

They wole it holde a gret mis-
  chaunce ;   5040
But what-som-ever wo they fele,
They wol not pleyne, but concele ;
But-if it be any fool or nyce,
In whom that shame hath no Ius-
  tyce.
For to delyt echon they drawe,   5045
That haunte this werk, bothe high
  and lawe,
Save sich that ar[e]n worth right
  nought,
That for money wol be bought.
Such love I preise in no wyse,
Whan it is given for coveitise. 5050
I preise no womman, though [she]
  be wood,
That yeveth hir-silf for any good.
For litel shulde a man telle
Of hir, that wol hir body selle,
Be she mayde, be she wyf,   5055
That quik wol selle hir, by hir lyf.
How faire chere that ever she
  make,
He is a wrecche, I undirtake,
That loveth such one, for swete or
  sour,
Though she him calle hir para-
  mour,   5060
And laugheth on him, and makith
  him feeste.
For certeynly no suche [a] beeste
To be loved is not worthy,
Or bere the name of druery.
Noon shulde hir please, but he
  were wood,   5065
That wol dispoile him of his good.
Yit nevertheles, I wol not sey
[But] she, for solace and for pley,
May a Iewel or other thing
Take of her loves free yeving ; 5070

5010. *Both* weped.   5021. *Both* he (*for* hir).   5028. *Both* list to loue.
5030. *Supply* so.   5036. *Supply* ay.   5050. *Both* gouen.   5051. *Both*
so ; *read* she (*or* sho).   5059. *Both* loued.   5062. Th. suche ; G. such ; *I
supply* a.   5064. Th. Drury ; G. drurie.   5068. But] *Both* That ; *cf.* 4764.

But that she aske it in no wyse,
For drede of shame of coveityse.
And she of hirs may him, certeyn,
Withoute sclaundre, yeven ageyn,
And ioyne her hertes togidre so   5075
In love, and take and yeve also.
Trowe not that I wolde hem twinne,
Whan in her love ther is no sinne;
I wol that they togedre go,
And doon al that they han ado,   5080
As curteis shulde and debonaire,
And in her love beren hem faire,
Withoute vyce, bothe he and she;
So that alwey, in honestee,   5084
Fro foly love [they] kepe hem clere
That brenneth hertis with his fere;
And that her love, in any wyse,
Be devoid of coveityse.
Good love shulde engendrid be
Of trewe herte, iust, and secree,   5090
And not of such as sette her thought
To have her lust, and ellis nought,
So are they caught in Loves lace,
Truly, for bodily solace.
Fleshly delyt is so present   5095
With thee, that sette al thyn entent,
Withoute more (what shulde I glose?)
For to gete and have the Rose;
Which makith thee so mate and wood
That thou desirest noon other good.   5100
But thou art not an inche the nerre,
But ever abydest in sorwe and werre,
As in thy face it is sene;
It makith thee bothe pale and lene;

Thy might, thy vertu goth away.
A sory gest, in goode fay,   5106
Thou [herberedest than] in thyn inne,
The God of Love whan thou let inne!
Wherfore I rede, thou shette him out,
Or he shal greve thee, out of doute;   5110
For to thy profit it wol turne,
If he nomore with thee soiourne.
In gret mischeef and sorwe sonken
Ben hertis, that of love arn dronken,
As thou peraventure knowen shal,   5115
Whan thou hast lost [thy] tyme al,
And spent [thy youthe] in ydilnesse,
In waste, and woful lustinesse;
If thou maist live the tyme to see
Of love for to delivered be,   5120
Thy tyme thou shalt biwepe sore
The whiche never thou maist restore.
(For tyme lost, as men may see,
For no-thing may recured be).
And if thou scape yit, atte laste,
Fro Love, that hath thee so faste   5126
Knit and bounden in his lace,
Certeyn, I holde it but a grace.
For many oon, as it is seyn,
Have lost, and spent also in veyn,   5130
In his servyse, withoute socour,
Body and soule, good, and tresour,
Wit, and strengthe, and eek richesse,
Of which they hadde never redresse.'

5085. they] *Both* to.   5099. G. *om.* thee.   5107. G. herberest hem; Th. herborest.   5111. G. profi3t.   5116. thy] *Both* the; F. *ton.*   5117. *Both* by thought; F. *ta Ionesce.*   5124. Th. recoucred.

Thus taught and preched hath
  Resoun, 5135
But Love spilte hir sermoun,
That was so imped in my thought,
That hir doctrine I sette at nought.
And yit ne seide she never a dele,
That I ne understode it wele, 5140
Word by word, the mater al.
But unto Love I was so thral,
Which callith over-al his pray,
He chasith so my thought [alway],
And holdith myn herte undir his
  sele, 5145
As trust and trew as any stele ;
So that no devocioun
Ne hadde I in the sermoun
Of dame Resoun, ne of hir rede ;
It toke no soiour in myn hede. 5150
For alle yede out at oon ere
That in that other she dide lere ;
Fully on me she lost hir lore,
Hir speche me greved wondir sore.
  [Than] unto hir for ire I seide,
For anger, as I dide abraide : 5156
'Dame, and is it your wille al-
  gate,
That I not love, but that I hate
Alle men, as ye me teche ?
For if I do aftir your speche, 5160
Sith that ye seyn love is not
  good,
Than must I nedis say with
  mood,
If I it leve, in hatrede ay
Liven, and voide love away
From me, [and been] a sinful
  wrecche, 5165
Hated of all that [love that] tecche.
I may not go noon other gate,
For either must I love or hate.
And if I hate men of-newe

More than love, it wol me
  rewe, 5170
As by your preching semeth me,
For Love no-thing ne preisith thee.
Ye yeve good counseil, sikirly,
That prechith me al-day, that I
Shulde not Loves lore alowe ; 5175
He were a fool, wolde you not
  trowe !
In speche also ye han me taught
Another love, that knowen is
  naught,
Which I have herd you not re-
  preve,
To love ech other ; by your
  leve, 5180
If ye wolde diffyne it me,
I wolde gladly here, to see,
At the leest, if I may lere
Of sondry loves the manere.'
  Raison. 'Certis, freend, a fool
    art thou 5185
Whan that thou no-thing wolt
  allowe
That I [thee] for thy profit say.
Yit wol I sey thee more, in fay ;
For I am redy, at the leste,
To accomplisshe thy requeste, 5190
But I not wher it wol avayle ;
In veyne, perauntre, I shal tra-
  vayle.
Love ther is in sondry wyse,
As I shal thee here devyse.
For som love leful is and good ; 5195
I mene not that which makith thee
  wood,
And bringith thee in many a fit,
And ravisshith fro thee al thy wit,
It is so merveilous and queynt ;
With such love be no more a-
  queynt. 5200

5144. alway] G. ay ; Th. aye.   5155. *Both* That ; F. *Lors.*   5162. (say =
assay?)   5165. *I supply* and been.   5166. *I supply* love that.   5168.
Th. eyther ; G. other.   5187. *I supply* thee

Comment Raisoun diffinist Amistie.

'Love of Frendshipe also ther is,
Which makith no man doon amis,
Of wille knit bitwixe two,
That wol not breke for wele ne wo;
Which long is lykly to contune, 5205
Whan wille and goodis ben in comune;
Grounded by goddis ordinaunce,
Hool, withoute discordaunce;
With hem holding comuntee
Of al her goode in charitee, 5210
That ther be noon excepcioun
Thurgh chaunging of entencioun;
That ech helpe other at hir neede,
And wysly hele bothe word and dede;
Trewe of mening, devoid of slouthe, 5215
For wit is nought withoute trouthe;
So that the ton dar al his thought
Seyn to his freend, and spare nought,
As to him-silf, without dreding
To be discovered by wreying. 5220
For glad is that coniunccioun,
Whan ther is noon suspecioun
[Ne lak in hem], whom they wolde prove
That trew and parfit weren in love.
For no man may be amiable, 5225
But-if he be so ferme and stable,
That fortune chaunge him not, ne blinde,
But that his freend alwey him finde,
Bothe pore and riche, in oon [e]state.

For if his freend, thurgh any gate, 5230
Wol compleyne of his povertee,
He shulde not byde so long, til he
Of his helping him requere;
For good deed, done [but] thurgh prayere,
Is sold, and bought to dere, y-wis, 5235
To hert that of gret valour is.
For hert fulfilled of gentilnesse
Can yvel demene his distresse.
And man that worthy is of name
To asken often hath gret shame.
A good man brenneth in his thought 5241
For shame, whan he axeth ought.
He hath gret thought, and dredith ay
For his disese, whan he shal pray
His freend, lest that he warned be, 5245
Til that he preve his stabiltee.
But whan that he hath founden oon
That trusty is and trew as stone,
And [hath] assayed him at al,
And found him stedefast as a wal, 5250
And of his freendship be certeyne,
He shal him shewe bothe Ioye and peyne,
And al that [he] dar thinke or sey,
Withoute shame, as he wel may.
For how shulde he ashamed be 5255
Of sich oon as I tolde thee?
For whan he woot his secree thought,
The thridde shal knowe ther-of right nought;

RUBRIC. *Both* Aunsete (*for* Amistie). *Both* oo state; *read* oon estate; *see* 5400. 5223. *I supply* Ne . . hem. 5229. 5234, 49, 53. *Supply* but, hath, he.

For tweyn in nombre is bet than three
In every counsel and secree. 5260
Repreve he dredeth never a del,
Who that biset his wordis wel;
For every wys man, out of drede,
Can kepe his tunge til he see nede;
And fooles can not holde hir tunge; 5265
A fooles belle is sone runge.
Yit shal a trewe freend do more
To helpe his felowe of his sore,
And socoure him, whan he hath nede, 5269
In al that he may doon in dede;
And gladder [be] that he him plesith
Than [is] his felowe that he esith.
And if he do not his requeste,
He shal as mochel him moleste
As his felow, for that he 5275
May not fulfille his voluntee
[As] fully as he hath requered.
If bothe the hertis Love hath fered,
Joy and wo they shul depart,
And take evenly ech his part. 5280
Half his anoy he shal have ay,
And comfort [him] what that he may;
And of his blisse parte shal he,
If love wol departed be.
  'And whilom of this [amitee] 5285
Spak Tullius in a ditee;
["A man] shulde maken his request
Unto his freend, that is honest;
And he goodly shulde it fulfille,
But it the more were out of skile, 5290
And otherwise not graunt therto,
Except only in [cases] two:
If men his freend to deth wolde dryve,
Lat him be bisy to save his lyve.
Also if men wolen him assayle, 5295
Of his wurship to make him faile,
And hindren him of his renoun,
Lat him, with ful entencioun,
His dever doon in ech degree
That his freend ne shamed be, 5300
In this two [cases] with his might,
Taking no kepe to skile nor right,
As ferre as love may him excuse;
This oughte no man to refuse."
This love that I have told to thee 5305
Is no-thing contrarie to me;
This wol I that thou folowe wel,
And leve the tother everydel.
This love to vertu al attendith,
The tothir fooles blent and shendith. 5310
  'Another love also there is,
That is contrarie unto this,
Which desyre is so constreyned
That [it] is but wille feyned; 5314
Awey fro trouthe it doth so varie,
That to good love it is contrarie;
For it maymeth, in many wyse,
Syke hertis with coveityse;
Al in winning and in profyt
Sich love settith his delyt. 5320
This love so hangeth in balaunce
That, if it lese his hope, perchaunce,
Of lucre, that he is set upon,
It wol faile, and quenche anon;
For no man may be amorous, 5325
Ne in his living vertuous,
But-[if] he love more, in mood,
Men for hem-silf than for hir good.

5259. Th. in; G. of.   5261. G. dreded.   5271, 72, 82, 5314, 27. *Supply* be, is, him, it, if.   5277, 8. *Supply* As. Th. requyred, fyred.   *Perhaps om.* the.
5283. his] *Both* this.   5285. *Both* vnyte.   5286. Th. Tullius; G. Tulius.
5287. A man] *Both* And.   5292. Th. causes; G. cause; *see* 5301, 5523.
5301. G. caas; Th. case.   5304. *Both* ought.   5325. G. amerous.

For love that profit doth abyde
Is fals, and bit not in no tyde. 5330
[This] love cometh of dame Fortune,
That litel whyle wol contune;
For it shal chaungen wonder sone,
And take eclips right as the mone,
Whan she is from us [y]-let 5335
Thurgh erthe, that bitwixe is set
The sonne and hir, as it may falle,
Be it in party, or in alle;
The shadowe maketh her bemis
  merke, 5339
And hir hornes to shewe derke,
That part where she hath lost hir
  lyght
Of Phebus fully, and the sight;
Til, whan the shadowe is overpast,
She is enlumined ageyn as faste,
Thurgh brightnesse of the sonne
  bemes 5345
That yeveth to hir ageyn hir lemes.
That love is right of sich nature;
Now is [it] fair, and now obscure,
Now bright, now clipsy of manere,
And whylom dim, and whylom
  clere. 5350
As sone as Poverte ginneth take,
With mantel and [with] wedis blake
[It] hidith of Love the light awey,
That into night it turneth day;
It may not see Richesse shyne 5355
Til the blakke shadowes fyne.
For, whan Richesse shyneth bright,
Love recovereth ageyn his light;
And whan it failith, he wol flit,
And as she [groweth, so groweth]
  it. 5360
'Of this love, here what I sey:—
The riche men are loved ay,

And namely tho that sparand
  bene,
That wol not wasshe hir hertes
  clene
Of the filthe, nor of the vyce 5365
Of gredy brenning avaryce.
The riche man ful fond is, y-wis,
That weneth that he loved is.
If that his herte it undirstood,
It is not he, it is his good; 5370
He may wel witen in his thought,
His good is loved, and he right
  nought.
For if he be a nigard eke,
Men wole not sette by him a leke,
But haten him; this is the
  soth. 5375
Lo, what profit his catel doth!
Of every man that may him see,
It geteth him nought but enmitee.
But he amende him of that
  vyce,
And knowe him-silf, he is not
  wys. 5380
'Certis, he shulde ay freendly be,
To gete him love also ben free,
Or ellis he is not wyse ne sage
No more than is a gote ramage.
That he not loveth, his dede
  proveth, 5385
Whan he his richesse so wel loveth,
That he wol hyde it ay and spare,
His pore freendis seen forfare;
To kepe [it ay is] his purpose,
Til for drede his eyen close, 5390
And til a wikked deth him take;
Him hadde lever asondre shake,
And late his limes asondre ryve,
Than leve his richesse in his lyve.

5330. Th. bydeth; G. bit.   5331, 48, 52, 53. *Supply* This, it, with, It.
5335. *Both* he; *read* she; *see* 5337, 5341.   5345. *Both* Thurgh the; *I omit* the.
5356. Th. blacke; G. blak.   5360. *Both* greueth so greueth.   5367. Th.
fonde; G. fonned.   5375. *Both* sothe.   5376. Th. his; G. this.   5379. *Both*
him silf (selfe) of.   5389. *Both* kepen ay his; *see* 5387.   5390. Th. eyne;
G. iyen.   5393. G. alle hise lymes; Th. al his lymmes; *I omit* alle.

THE ROMAUNT OF THE ROSE.

He thenkith parte it with no
   man ;   5395
Certayn, no love is in him than.
How shulde love within him be,
Whan in his herte is no pite?
That he trespasseth, wel I wat,
For ech man knowith his
   estat ;   5400
For wel him oughte be reproved
That loveth nought, ne is not loved.
  'But sith we arn to Fortune
   comen,
And [han] our sermoun of hir nomen,
A wondir wil I telle thee now, 5405
Thou herdist never sich oon, I trow.
I not wher thou me leven shal,
Though sothfastnesse it be [in] al,
As it is writen, and is sooth, 5409
That unto men more profit doth
The froward Fortune and contraire,
Than the swote and debonaire :
And if thee thinke it is doutable,
It is thurgh argument provable.
For the debonaire and softe   5415
Falsith and bigylith ofte ;
For liche a moder she can cherishe
And milken as doth a norys ;
And of hir goode to hem deles,
And yeveth hem part of her
   Ioweles,   5420
With grete richesse and dignitee ;
And hem she hoteth stabilitee
In a state that is not stable,
But chaunging ay and variable ;
And fedith hem with glorie
   veyne,   5425
And worldly blisse noncerteyne.
Whan she hem settith on hir whele,
Than wene they to be right wele,
And in so stable state withalle,

That never they wene for to
   falle.   5430
And whan they set so highe be,
They wene to have in certeintee
Of hertly frendis [so] gret noumbre,
That no-thing mighte her stat en-
   combre ;
They truste hem so on every
   syde,   5435
Wening with hem they wolde abyde
In every perel and mischaunce,
Withoute chaunge or variaunce,
Bothe of catel and of good ;   5439
And also for to spende hir blood
And alle hir membris for to spille,
Only to fulfille hir wille.
They maken it hole in many wyse,
And hoten hem hir ful servyse,
How sore that it do hem
   smerte,   5445
Into hir very naked sherte !
Herte and al, so hole they yeve,
For the tyme that they may live,
So that, with her flaterye,
They maken foolis glorifye   5450
Of hir wordis [greet] speking,
And han [there]-of a reioysing,
And trowe hem as the Evangyle ;
And it is al falsheed and gyle,
As they shal afterwardes see, 5455
Whan they arn falle in povertee,
And been of good and catel bare ;
Than shulde they seen who freendis
   ware.
For of an hundred, certeynly,
Nor of a thousand ful scarsly, 5460
Ne shal they fynde unnethis oon,
Whan povertee is comen upon.
For [this] Fortune that I of telle,
With men whan hir lust to dwelle,

5399. Th. wate; G. wote.   5400, 1. *Both* estate ; ought to be.   5403. Th. sithe ; G. se.   5404. *Both* hath.   5408. in] G. it ; Th. *om.*   5419, 20, 25, 27, 36. *Both* hym (!) ; F. *les.*   5425. G. glorie and veyne.   5431. *Both* high.   5433. so] *Both* to.   5446. G. *om.* very.   5451. *I supply* greet.   5452. Th. chere (*for* there) ; G. cheer (!).   5455. G. aftirward ; Th. afterwarde.   5463. *Both* thus.

Makith hem to lese hir con-
　isaunce,　　　　　　　5465
And nourishith hem in ignoraunce.
'But froward Fortune and per-
　verse,
Whan high estatis she doth reverse,
And maketh hem to tumble doun
Of hir whele, with sodeyn
　tourn,　　　　　　　　5470
And from hir richesse doth hem
　flee,
And plongeth hem in povertee,
As a stepmoder envyous,
And leyeth a plastre dolorous
Unto her hertis, wounded egre, 5475
Which is not tempred with vinegre,
But with poverte and indigence,
For to shewe, by experience,
That she is Fortune verely
In whom no man shulde affy, 5480
Nor in hir yeftis have fiaunce,
She is so ful of variaunce.
Thus can she maken high and lowe,
Whan they from richesse ar[e]n
　throwe,
Fully to knowen, withouten
　were,　　　　　　　　5485
Freend of effect, and freend of
　chere ;
And which in love weren trew and
　stable,
And whiche also weren variable,
After Fortune, hir goddesse,
In poverte, outher in richesse ; 5490
For al [she] yeveth, out of drede,
Unhappe bereveth it in dede ;
For Infortune lat not oon
Of freendis, whan Fortune is goon ;
I mene tho freendis that wol
　flee　　　　　　　　　5495

Anoon as entreth povertee.
And yit they wol not leve hem
　so,
But in ech place where they go
They calle hem "wrecche," scorne
　and blame,
And of hir mishappe hem
　diffame,　　　　　　　5500
And, namely, siche as in richesse
Pretendith most of stablenesse,
Whan that they sawe him set on-
　lofte,
And weren of him socoured ofte,
And most y-holpe in al hir
　nede :　　　　　　　　5505
But now they take no maner hede,
But seyn, in voice of flaterye,
That now apperith hir folye,
Over-al where-so they fare,
And singe, "Go, farewel felde-
　fare."　　　　　　　　5510
Alle suche freendis I beshrewe,
For of [the] trewe ther be to fewe ;
But sothfast freendis, what so
　bityde,
In every fortune wolen abyde ;
They han hir hertis in suche
　noblesse　　　　　　　5515
That they nil love for no richesse ;
Nor, for that Fortune may hem
　sende,
They wolen hem socoure and de-
　fende ;
And chaunge for softe ne for sore,
For who is freend, loveth ever-
　more.　　　　　　　　5520
Though men drawe swerd his freend
　to slo,
He may not hewe hir love a-
　two.

5465. Th. hem ; G. men.　　5470. Th. Of ; G. Or with.　　5478. *Read* She sheweth, by experience.　　5485. *Both* without.　　5486. *Both* affect ; *see* note. 5489. Th. goddesse ; G. goddes.　　5491. *Both* For al that yeueth here out of drede.　　5493. Th. lette ; G. late.　　5503. Th. they ; G. the.　　5505. Th. yholpe ; G. I hope.　　5510. G. feldfare.　　5512. *I supply* the.

But, in [the] case that I shal sey,
For pride and ire lese it he may,
And for reprove by nycetee,   5525
And discovering of privitee,
With tonge wounding, as feloun,
Thurgh venemous detraccioun.
Frend in this case wol gon his way,
For no-thing greve him more ne
    may;   5530
And for nought ellis wol he flee,
If that he love in stabilitee.
And certeyn, he is wel bigoon
Among a thousand that fyndith oon.
For ther may be no richesse,   5535
Ageyns frendship, of worthinesse;
For it ne may so high atteigne
As may the valoure, sooth to seyne,
Of him that loveth trew and wel;
Frendship is more than is ca-
    tel.   5540
For freend in court ay better is
Than peny in [his] purs, certis;
And Fortune, mishapping,
Whan upon men she is [falling],
Thurgh misturning of hir
    chaunce,   5545
And casteth hem oute of balaunce,
She makith, thurgh hir adversitee,
Men ful cleerly for to see
Him that is freend in existence
From him that is by appar-
    ence.   5550
For Infortune makith anoon
To knowe thy freendis fro thy foon,
By experience, right as it is;
The which is more to preyse, y-wis,
Than [is] miche richesse and tre-
    sour;   5555
For more [doth] profit and valour
Poverte, and such adversitee,
Bifore than doth prosperitee;

For the toon yeveth conisaunce,
And the tother ignoraunce.   5560
 'And thus in poverte is in dede
Trouthe declared fro falsehede;
For feynte frendis it wol declare,
And trewe also, what wey they
    fare.
For whan he was in his
    richesse,   5565
These freendis, ful of doublenesse,
Offrid him in many wyse
Hert and body, and servyse.
What wolde he than ha [yeve] to ha
    bought
To knowen openly her thought,   5570
That he now hath so clerly seen?
The lasse bigyled he sholde have
    been
And he hadde than perceyved it,
But richesse nold not late him wit.
Wel more avauntage doth him
    than,   5575
Sith that it makith him a wys man,
The greet mischeef that he [re-
    ceyveth],
Than doth richesse that him de-
    ceyveth.
Richesse riche ne makith nought
Him that on tresour set his
    thought;   5580
For richesse stont in suffisaunce
And no-thing in habundaunce;
For suffisaunce al-only
Makith men to live richely.
For he that hath [but] miches
    tweyne,   5585
Ne [more] value in his demeigne,
Liveth more at ese, and more is
    riche,
Than doth he that is [so] chiche,

5523, 42, 85, 86, 88. *Supply* the, his, but, more, so.   5544. *Both* fablyng;
F. *cheans.*   5546. *Both* caste.   5555. *Both* in; *read* is.   5556. *Both* depe (*for*
doþ).   5569. Th. haue you to haue; G. ha yow to ha.   5577. *Both* perceyueth.

And in his bern hath, soth to seyn,
An hundred [muwis] of whete
  greyn,   5590
Though he be chapman or mar-
  chaunt,
And have of golde many besaunt.
For in the geting he hath such wo,
And in the keping drede also,
And set evermore his bisy-
  nesse   5595
For to encrese, and not to lesse,
For to augment and multiply.
And though on hepis [it] lye him
  by,
Yit never shal make his richesse
Asseth unto his gredinesse.   5600
But the povre that recchith nought,
Save of his lyflode, in his thought,
Which that he getith with his
  travaile,
He dredith nought that it shal faile,
Though he have lytel worldis
  good,   5605
Mete and drinke, and esy food,
Upon his travel and living,
And also suffisaunt clothing.
Or if in syknesse that he falle,
And lothe mete and drink with-
  alle,   5610
Though he have nought, his mete to
  by,
He shal bithinke him hastely,
To putte him out of al daunger,
That he of mete hath no mister;
Or that he may with litel eke 5615
Be founden, whyl that he is seke;
Or that men shul him bere in
  hast,
To live, til his syknesse be past,
To somme maysondewe bisyde;

He cast nought what shal him
  bityde.   5620
He thenkith nought that ever he
  shal
Into any syknesse falle.
  'And though it falle, as it may be,
That al betyme spare shal he
As mochel as shal to him suf-
  fyce,   5625
Whyl he is syke in any wyse,
He doth [it], for that he wol be
Content with his povertee
Withoute nede of any man.
So miche in litel have he can, 5630
He is apayed with his fortune;
And for he nil be importune
Unto no wight, ne onerous,
Nor of hir goodes coveitous;
Therfore he spareth, it may wel
  been,   5635
His pore estat for to sustene.
  'Or if him lust not for to spare,
But suffrith forth, as nought ne
  ware,
Atte last it hapneth, as it may,
Right unto his laste day,   5640
And taketh the world as it wolde
  be;
For ever in herte thenkith he,
The soner that [the] deeth him slo,
To paradys the soner go
He shal, there for to live in
  blisse,   5645
Where that he shal no good misse.
Thider he hopith god shal him
  sende
Aftir his wrecchid lyves ende.
Pictagoras himsilf reherses,
In a book that the Golden
  Verses   5650

5590. G. mavis; Th. mauys.   5597. G. aument.   5598. it] *Both* that.   5611,
38. G. not; Th. nat.   5612. G. hastly.   5617. *Both* berne.   5627, 43. *Supply* it,
the.   5633. Th. wyght; G. witte.   G. honerous.   5640. Th. laste; G. last.
5641. *Both* take.   5649. G. Pictigoras; Th. Pythagoras.

Is clepid, for the nobilitee
Of the honourable ditee :—
"Than, whan thou gost thy body fro,
Free in the eir thou shalt up go,
And leven al humanitee,   5655
And purely live in deitee."—
He is a fool, withouten were,
That trowith have his countre here.
"In erthe is not our countree,"
That may these clerkis seyn and
    see   5660
In Boece of Consolacioun,
Where it is maked mencioun
Of our countree pleyn at the eye,
By teching of philosophye,
Where lewid men might lere
    wit,   5665
Who-so that wolde translaten it.
If he be sich that can wel live
Aftir his rente may him yive,
And not desyreth more to have,
That may fro povertee him
    save :   5670
A wys man seide, as we may seen,
Is no man wrecched, but he it wene,
Be he king, knight, or ribaud.
And many a ribaud is mery and
    baud,
That swinkith, and berith, bothe
    day and night,   5675
Many a burthen of gret might,
The whiche doth him lasse offense,
For he suffrith in pacience.
They laugh and daunce, trippe and
    singe,
And ley not up for her living, 5680
But in the tavern al dispendith
The winning that god hem sendith.
Than goth he, fardels for to bere,
With as good chere as he dide ere ;

To swinke and traveile he not
    feynith,   5685
For for to robben he disdeynith ;
But right anoon, aftir his swinke,
He goth to tavern for to drinke.
Alle these ar riche in abundaunce,
That can thus have suffisaunce 5690
Wel more than can an usurere,
As god wel knowith, withoute
    were.
For an usurer, so god me see,
Shal never for richesse riche bee,
But evermore pore and indi-
    gent,   5695
Scarce, and gredy in his entent.
'For soth it is, whom it displese,
Ther may no marchaunt live at ese,
His herte in sich a were is set,
That it quik brenneth [more] to
    get,   5700
Ne never shal [enough have] geten;
Though he have gold in gerners
    yeten,
For to be nedy he dredith sore.
Wherfore to geten more and more
He set his herte and his
    desire ;   5705
So hote he brennith in the fire
Of coveitise, that makith him wood
To purchase other mennes good.
He undirfongith a gret peyne,
That undirtakith to drinke up
    Seyne ;   5710
For the more he drinkith, ay
The more he leveth, the soth to say.
[This is the] thurst of fals geting,
That last ever in coveiting,
And the anguisshe and dis-
    tresse   5715
With the fire of gredinesse.

5661. G. Boice.   5668. *Both* rent ; yeue.   5675. G. wynkith (!).   5683. G. fardeles.   5685. G. feyntith.   5686. G. disdeyntith.   5699. *Both* where ; F. *guerre*.   5700. *I supply* more ; F. *plus*.   5701. *Both* shal thogh he hath geten (!).   5713. *Both* Thus is thurst.

She fighteth with him ay, and
    stryveth,
That his herte asondre ryveth;
Such gredinesse him assaylith,
That whan he most hath, most he
    faylith.   5720
    Phisiciens and advocates
Gon right by the same yates;
They selle hir science for winning,
And haunte hir crafte for greet
    geting.
Hir winning is of such swet-
    nesse,   5725
That if a man falle in sikenesse,
They are ful glad, for hir encrese;
For by hir wille, withoute lees,
Everiche man shulde be seke,
And though they dye, they set not
    a leke.   5730
After, whan they the gold have take,
Ful litel care for hem they make.
They wolde that fourty were seke
    at onis,
Ye, two hundred, in flesh and bonis,
And yit two thousand, as I
    gesse,   5735
For to encresen her richesse.
They wol not worchen, in no wyse,
But for lucre and coveityse;
For fysyk ginneth first by *fy*,
The fysycien also sothely;   5740
And sithen it goth fro *fy* to *sy*;
To truste on hem, it is foly;
For they nil, in no maner gree,
Do right nought for charitee.
    'Eke in the same secte are
    set   5745
Alle tho that prechen for to get
Worshipes, honour, and richesse.
Her hertis arn in greet distresse,
That folk [ne] live not holily.
But aboven al, specialy,   5750
Sich as prechen [for] veynglorie,
And toward god have no memorie,
But forth as ypocrites trace,
And to her soules deth purchace,
And outward [shewen] holy-
    nesse,   5755
Though they be fulle of cursidnesse.
Not liche to the apostles twelve,
They deceyve other and hem-selve;
Bigyled is the gyler than.
For preching of a cursed man,   5760
Though [it] to other may profyte,
Himsilf availeth not a myte;
For oft good predicacioun
Cometh of evel entencioun.
To him not vailith his prech-
    ing,   5765
Al helpe he other with his teching;
For where they good ensaumple
    take,
There is he with veynglorie shake.
'But lat us leven these prechoures,
And speke of hem that in her
    toures   5770
Hepe up her gold, and faste shette,
And sore theron her herte sette.
They neither love god, ne drede;
They kepe more than it is nede,
And in her bagges sore it
    binde,   5775
Out of the sonne, and of the winde;
They putte up more than nede ware,
Whan they seen pore folk forfare,
For hunger dye, and for cold quake;
God can wel vengeaunce therof
    take.   5780
[Thre] gret mischeves hem assailith,
And thus in gadring ay travaylith;

5727. G. ther; Th. her (=hir). 5734. G. Yhe. 5740. G. phicicien; *read* fysycien. 5741. G. fy; Th. fye (*for* sy); *see* note. 5742. G. *om.* it. 5749, 51. *Supply* ne, for. 5755. *Both* shewing. 5761. *Supply* it, *wh. follows* Himself *in* 5762. 5763. *Both* ofte. 5771. G. fast. 5781. *Both* The; F. *Trois.*

With moche peyne they winne
    richesse;
And drede hem holdith in distresse,
To kepe that they gadre faste; 5785
With sorwe they leve it at the
    laste;
With sorwe they bothe dye and live,
That to richesse her hertis yive,
And in defaute of love it is,
As it shewith ful wel, y-wis. 5790
For if these gredy, the sothe to
    seyn,
Loveden, and were loved ageyn,
And good love regned over-alle,
Such wikkidnesse ne shulde falle;
But he shulde yeve that most good
    had   5795
To hem that weren in nede bistad,
And live withoute fals usure,
For charitee ful clene and pure.
If they hem yeve to goodnesse,
Defending hem from ydel-
    nesse,   5800
In al this world than pore noon
We shulde finde, I trowe, not oon.
But chaunged is this world unstable;
For love is over-al vendable.
We see that no man loveth
    now   5805
But for winning and for prow;
And love is thralled in servage
Whan it is sold for avauntage;
Yit wommen wol hir bodies selle;
Suche soules goth to the devel of
    helle.'   5810

[*Here ends* l. 5170 *of the* F.
text. *A great gap follows.
The next line answers to*
l. 10717 *of the same.*]

FRAGMENT C.

Whan Love had told hem his entente,
The baronage to councel wente;
In many sentences they fille,
And dyversly they seide hir wille:
But aftir discord they accorded,
    5815
And hir accord to Love recorded.
'Sir,' seiden they, 'we been at oon,
By even accord of everichoon,
Out-take Richesse al-only, 5819
That sworen hath ful hauteynly,
That she the castel nil assaile,
Ne smyte a stroke in this bataile,
With dart, ne mace, spere, ne knyf,
For man that speketh or bereth
    the lyf,
And blameth your empryse, y-
    wis,   5825
And from our hoost departed is,
(At leeste wey, as in this plyte,)
So hath she this man in dispyte;
For she seith he ne loved hir never,
And therfor she wol hate him
    ever.   5830
For he wol gadre no tresore,
He hath hir wrath for evermore.
He agilte hir never in other caas,
Lo, here al hoolly his trespas!
She seith wel, that this other
    day   5835
He asked hir leve to goon the way
That is clepid To-moche-Yeving,
And spak ful faire in his praying;
But whan he prayde hir, pore was
    he,
Therfore she warned him the
    entree.   5840
Ne yit is he not thriven so
That he hath geten a peny or two,

5783. G. mych. 5788. *Both* vnto. 5791. Th. these; G. this. 5793. G. goode. 5814. Th. wyl; G. tille. 5820. *Both* sworne. 5821. G. The (*for* That). *Both* nyl not. 5827. Th. leest; G. lest. 5831. G. tresoure. 5836. G. axide.

That quitly is his owne in hold.
Thus hath Richesse us alle told;
And whan Richesse us this re-
    corded, 5845
Withouten hir we been accorded.
    'And we finde in our accordaunce,
That False-Semblant and Abstin-
    aunce,
With alle the folk of hir bataile,
Shulle at the hinder gate as-
    sayle, 5850
That Wikkid-Tunge hath in keping,
With his Normans, fulle of Iang-
    ling.
And with hem Curtesie and Lar-
    gesse,
That shulle shewe hir hardinesse
To the olde wyf that [kepeth] so
    harde 5855
Fair-Welcoming within her warde.
Than shal Delyte and Wel-
    Helinge
Fonde Shame adoun to bringe;
With al hir hoost, erly and late,
They shulle assailen [thilke]
    gate. 5860
Agaynes Drede shal Hardinesse
Assayle, and also Sikernesse,
With al the folk of hir leding,
That never wist what was fleing.
    'Fraunchyse shal fighte, and eek
    Pitee, 5865
With Daunger ful of crueltee.
Thus is your hoost ordeyned wel;
Doun shal the castel every del,
If everiche do his entente,
So that Venus be presente, 5870
Your modir, ful of vassalage,
That can y-nough of such usage;
Withouten hir may no wight spede
This werk, neither for word ne dede.

Therfore is good ye for hir
    sende, 5875
For thurgh hir may this werk
    amende.'
    Amour. 'Lordinges, my modir,
    the goddesse,
That is my lady, and my maistresse,
Nis not [at] al at my willing,
Ne doth not al my desyring. 5880
Yit can she som-tyme doon labour,
Whan that hir lust, in my socour,
[Al my nedis] for to acheve,
But now I thenke hir not to greve.
My modir is she, and of child-
    hede 5885
I bothe worshipe hir, and eek
    drede;
For who that dredith sire ne dame
Shal it abye in body or name.
And, natheles, yit cunne we
Sende aftir hir, if nede be; 5890
And were she nigh, she comen
    wolde,
I trowe that no-thing might hir
    holde.
    'My modir is of greet prowesse;
She hath tan many a forteresse,
That cost hath many a pound er
    this, 5895
Ther I nas not present, y-wis;
And yit men seide it was my
    dede;
But I come never in that stede;
Ne me ne lykith, so mote I thee,
Such toures take withoute me. 5900
For-why me thenketh that, in no
    wyse,
It may ben cleped but marchandise.
    'Go bye a courser, blak or whyte,
And pay therfor; than art thou
    quyte.

5855. *Both* kepte; F. *qui mestrie.*   5859. G. oost.   5860. *Both* that ilke.
5861. G. Agayns; Th. Agaynst.   5869, 70. *Both* entent, present.   5871. *Both*
vesselage.   5879. *Supply* at.   5883. *Both* As my nede is.   5886. *Om.* eek?
5894. G. fortresse.   5900. *Both* That such; *om.* That. *Both* ben take; *om.* ben.

The marchaunt oweth thee right
    nought,   5905
Ne thou him, whan thou [hast] it
    bought.
I wol not selling clepe yeving,
For selling axeth no guerdoning;
Here lyth no thank, ne no meryte,
That oon goth from that other al
    quyte.   5910
But this selling is not semblable;
For, whan his hors is in the stable,
He may it selle ageyn, pardee,
And winne on it, such hap may be;
Al may the man not lese,
    y-wis,   5915
For at the leest the skin is his.
Or elles, if it so bityde
That he wol kepe his hors to ryde,
Yit is he lord ay of his hors.
But thilke chaffare is wel wors,   5920
There Venus entremeteth nought;
For who-so such chaffare hath
    bought,
He shal not worchen so wysly,
That he ne shal lese al outerly
Bothe his money and his chaf-
    fare;   5925
But the seller of the ware
The prys and profit have shal.
Certeyn, the byer shal lese al;
For he ne can so dere it bye
To have lordship and ful mais-
    trye,   5930
Ne have power to make letting
Neither for yift ne for preching,
That of his chaffare, maugre his,
Another shal have as moche, y-wis,
If he wol yeve as moche as he,   5935
Of what contrey so that he be;
Or for right nought, so happe may,
If he can flater hir to hir pay.

Ben than suche marchaunts wyse?
No, but fooles in every wyse,   5940
Whan they bye such thing wilfully,
Ther-as they lese her good [fully].
But natheles, this dar I saye,
My modir is not wont to paye,
For she is neither so fool ne
    nyce,   5945
To entremete hir of sich vyce.
But truste wel, he shal paye al,
That repente of his bargeyn shal,
Whan Poverte put him in distresse,
Al were he scoler to Rich-
    esse,   5950
That is for me in gret yerning,
Whan she assenteth to my willing.
  'But, [by] my modir seint Venus,
And by hir fader Saturnus,
That hir engendrid by his lyf,   5955
But not upon his weddid wyf!
Yit wol I more unto you swere,
To make this thing the seurere;
Now by that feith, and that leautee
I owe to alle my brethren free,   5960
Of which ther nis wight under
    heven
That can her fadris names neven,
So dyvers and so many ther be
That with my modir have be privee!
Yit wolde I swere, for sikir-
    nesse,   5965
The pole of helle to my witnesse,
Now drinke I not this yeer clarree,
If that I lye, or forsworn be!
(For of the goddes the usage is,
That who-so him forswereth
    amis,   5970
Shal that yeer drinke no clarree).
Now have I sworn y-nough, pardee;
If I forswere me, than am I lorn,
But I wol never be forsworn.

5906, 53. *Supply* hast, by.   5920. G. thilk.   5935. G. myche.   5939.
Th. marchauntes; G. marchauntz.   5942. *Both* folyly.   5946. Th. vyce; G. wise.
5947. G. trust; pay.   5958. Th. surere.   5959. *Both* beaute(!).   5960. *Both* That I.

Sith Richesse hath me failed
    here,   5975
She shal abye that trespas dere,
At leeste wey, but [she] hir arme
With swerd, or sparth, or gisarme.
For certes, sith she loveth not me,
Fro thilke tyme that she may
    see   5980
The castel and the tour to-shake,
In sory tyme she shal awake.
If I may grype a riche man,
I shal so pulle him, if I can,
That he shal, in a fewe
    stoundes,   5985
Lese alle his markes and his
    poundes.
I shal him make his pens out-
    slinge,
But-[if] they in his gerner springe;
Our maydens shal eek plukke him
    so,
That him shal neden fetheres
    mo,   5990
And make him selle his lond to
    spende,
But he the bet cunne him defende.
  'Pore men han maad hir lord of
    me ;
Although they not so mighty be,
That they may fede me in
    delyt,   5995
I wol not have hem in despyt.
No good man hateth hem, as I
    gesse,
For chinche and feloun is Richesse,
That so can chase hem and dispyse,
And hem defoule in sondry
    wyse.   6000
They loven ful bet, so god me
    spede,
Than doth the riche, chinchy grede,

And been, in good feith, more
    stable
And trewer, and more serviable ;
And therfore it suffysith me   6005
Hir goode herte, and hir leautee.
They han on me set al hir thought,
And therfore I forgete hem nought.
I wolde hem bringe in greet
    noblesse,
If that I were god of Richesse, 6010
As I am god of Love, sothly,
Such routhe upon hir pleynt have I.
Therfore I must his socour be,
That peyneth him to serven me ;
For if he deyde for love of
    this,   6015
Than semeth in me no love ther
    is.'
  'Sir,' seide they, 'sooth is, every
    del,
That ye reherce, and we wot wel
Thilk oth to holde is resonable ;
For it is good and covenable,   6020
That ye on riche men han sworn.
For, sir, this wot we wel biforn ;
If riche men doon you homage,
That is as fooles doon outrage ;
But ye shul not forsworen be,   6025
Ne let therfore to drinke clarree,
Or piment maked fresh and newe.
Ladyes shulle hem such pepir
    brewe,
If that they falle into hir laas,
That they for wo mowe seyn
    "Allas ! "   6030
Ladyes shuln ever so curteis be,
That they shal quyte your oth al
    free.
Ne seketh never other vicaire,
For they shal speke with hem so
    faire

5976. *Both* ful dere.   5977. *Both* leest; *supply* she.   5980. Th. thylke; G. thilk.   5983. Th. grype; G. grepe.   5988. *I supply* if.   5997, 9. Th. hem; G. hym.   6002. *Read* gnede.   6006. *Both* good; beaute (*as in* 5959).   6009. Th. wol; G. wole.   6025. G. shulle. *Both* forsworne.   6026. G. lette.

That ye shal holde you payed ful
  wel,   6035
Though ye you medle never a del.
Lat ladies worche with hir thinges,
They shal hem telle so fele tyd-
  inges,
And moeve hem eke so many
  requestis
By flatery, that not honest is, 6040
And therto yeve hem such
  thankinges,
What with kissing, and with
  talkinges,
That certes, if they trowed be,
Shal never leve hem lond ne fee
That it nil as the moeble fare, 6045
Of which they first delivered are.
Now may ye telle us al your wille,
And we your hestes shal fulfille.
  'But Fals-Semblant dar not, for
  drede
Of you, sir, medle him of this
  dede,   6050
For he seith that ye been his fo;
He not, if ye wol worche him wo.
Wherfore we pray you alle, beau-
  sire,
That ye forgive him now your ire,
And that he may dwelle, as your
  man,   6055
With Abstinence, his dere lemman;
This our accord and our wil now.'
  'Parfay,' seide Love, 'I graunte it
  yow;
I wol wel holde him for my man;
Now lat him come:' and he forth
  ran.   6060
'Fals-Semblant,' quod Love, 'in
  this wyse
I take thee here to my servyse,
That thou our freendis helpe alway,
And hindre hem neithir night ne
  day,

But do thy might hem to
  releve,   6065
And eek our enemies that thou
  greve.
Thyn be this might, I graunt it
  thee,
My king of harlotes shalt thou be;
We wol that thou have such honour.
Certeyn, thou art a fals trai-
  tour,   6070
And eek a theef; sith thou were
  born,
A thousand tyme thou art forsworn.
But, natheles, in our hering,
To putte our folk out of douting,
I bid thee teche hem, wostow
  how?   6075
By somme general signe now,
In what place thou shalt founden
  be,
If that men had mister of thee;
And how men shal thee best espye,
For thee to knowe is greet
  maistrye;   6080
Tel in what place is thyn haunting.'
  F. Sem. 'Sir, I have fele dyvers
  woning,
That I kepe not rehersed be,
So that ye wolde respyten me.
For if that I telle you the
  sothe,   6085
I may have harm and shame bothe.
If that my felowes wisten it,
My tales shulden me be quit;
For certeyn, they wolde hate me,
If ever I knewe hir cruelte; 6090
For they wolde over-al holde hem
  stille
Of trouthe that is ageyn hir wille;
Suche tales kepen they not here.
I might eftsone bye it ful dere,
If I seide of hem any thing, 6095
That ought displeseth to hir hering.

6037. G. worthe.   6401. G. hym.   6048. G. heestes.   6057. This = This is.
6063. G. away.   6064. *Both* hindreth.   6073. G. netheles; Th. nathelesse.

For what word that hem prikke or byteth,
In that word noon of hem delyteth,
Al were it gospel, the evangyle,
That wolde reprove hem of hir gyle, 6100
For they are cruel and hauteyn.
And this thing wot I wel, certeyn,
If I speke ought to peire hir loos,
Your court shal not so wel be cloos,
That they ne shal wite it atte last. 6105
Of good men am I nought agast,
For they wol taken on hem nothing,
Whan that they knowe al my mening;
But he that wol it on him take,
He wol himself suspecious make, 6110
That he his lyf let covertly,
In Gyle and in Ipocrisy,
That me engendred and yaf fostring.'
'They made a ful good engendring,'
Quod Love, 'for who-so soothly telle, 6115
They engendred the devel of helle!
'But nedely, how-so-ever it be,'
Quod Love, 'I wol and charge thee,
To telle anoon thy woning-places,
Hering ech wight that in this place is; 6120
And what lyf that thou livest also,
Hyde it no lenger now; wherto?
Thou most discover al thy wurching,
How thou servest, and of what thing,
Though that thou shuldest for thy soth-sawe 6125
Ben al to-beten and to-drawe;

And yit art thou not wont, pardee.
But natheles, though thou beten be,
Thou shalt not be the first, that so
Hath for soth-sawe suffred wo.'
F. Sem. 'Sir, sith that it may lyken you, 6131
Though that I shulde be slayn right now,
I shal don your comaundement,
For therto have I gret talent.' 6134
Withouten wordes mo, right than,
Fals-Semblant his sermon bigan,
And seide hem thus in audience:—
'Barouns, tak hede of my sentence!
That wight that list to have knowing 6139
Of Fals-Semblant, ful of flatering,
He must in worldly folk him seke,
And, certes, in the cloistres eke;
I wone no-where but in hem tweye;
But not lyk even, sooth to seye;
Shortly, I wol herberwe me 6145
There I hope best to hulstred be;
And certeynly, sikerest hyding
Is undirneth humblest clothing.
'Religious folk ben ful covert;
Seculer folk ben more appert. 6150
But natheles, I wol not blame
Religious folk, ne hem diffame,
In what habit that ever they go:
Religioun humble, and trewe also,
Wol I not blame, ne dispyse, 6155
But I nil love it, in no wyse.
I mene of fals religious,
That stoute ben, and malicious;
That wolen in an abit go, 6159
And setten not hir herte therto.
'Religious folk ben al pitous;
Thou shalt not seen oon dispitous.
They loven no pryde, ne no stryf,
But humbly they wol lede hir lyf;
With swich folk wol I never be.
And if I dwelle, I feyne me 6166

6143. *Both* twey. 6144. G. sey; Th. say. 6165. *Both* which; F. *tex*.

I may wel in her abit go ;
But me were lever my nekke atwo,
Than lete a purpose that I take,
What covenaunt that ever I
    make.   6170
I dwelle with hem that proude be,
And fulle of wyles and subtelte ;
That worship of this world co-
    veyten,
And grete nedes cunne espleyten ;
And goon and gadren greet
    pitaunces,   6175
And purchace hem the acqueynt-
    aunces
Of men that mighty lyf may leden ;
And feyne hem pore, and hem-self
    feden
With gode morcels delicious,
And drinken good wyn pre-
    cious,   6180
And preche us povert and distresse,
And fisshen hem-self greet rich-
    esse
With wyly nettis that they caste :
It wol come foul out at the laste.
They ben fro clene religioun
    went ;   6185
They make the world an argument
That hath a foul conclusioun.
"I have a robe of religioun,
Than am I al religious : "
This argument is al roignous ; 6190
It is not worth a croked brere ;
Habit ne maketh monk ne frere,
But clene lyf and devocioun
Maketh gode men of religioun.
Nathelesse, ther can noon
    answere,   6195
How high that ever his heed he
    shere

With rasour whetted never so kene,
That Gyle in braunches cut
    thrittene ;
Ther can no wight distincte it so,
That he dar sey a word therto. 6200
'But what herberwe that ever I
    take,
Or what semblant that ever I make,
I mene but gyle, and folowe that ;
For right no mo than Gibbe our
    cat
[Fro myce and rattes went his
    wyle],   6205
Ne entende I [not] but to begyle ;
Ne no wight may, by my clothing,
Wite with what folk is my dwelling ;
Ne by my wordis yet, pardee,
So softe and so plesaunt they
    be.   6210
Bihold the dedis that I do ;
But thou be blind, thou oughtest so ;
For, varie hir wordis fro hir dede,
They thenke on gyle, withouten
    drede,
What maner clothing that they
    were,   6215
Or what estat that ever they bere,
Lered or lewd, lord or lady,
Knight, squier, burgeis, or bayly.'
    Right thus whyl Fals-Semblant
        sermoneth,
Eftsones Love him aresoneth,   6220
And brak his tale in the speking
As though he had him told lesing ;
And seide : 'What, devel, is that I
    here ?
What folk hast thou us nempned
    here ?
May men finde religioun   6225
In worldly habitacioun ?'

6169. *Both* lette. 6172. G. subtilite. 6174. *Both* nede ; F. *besoignes.* 6183, 4.
G. cast, last. 6187. G. *om.* hath. 6192. *Both* neithir monk ; *om.* neithir. 6195.
Th. Na- ; G. Ne-. 6197. Th. rasour ; G. resoun. 6205. *I supply this line.* 6206.
Supply not. Th. begylen ; G. bigilyng. 6214. *Both* without.

F. Sem. 'Ye, sir; it foloweth not
  that they
Shulde lede a wikked lyf, parfey,
Ne not therfore her soules lese,
That hem to worldly clothes
  chese;   6230
For, certis, it were gret pitee.
Men may in seculer clothes see
Florisshen holy religioun.
Ful many a seynt in feeld and toun,
With many a virgin glorious,   6235
Devout, and ful religious,
Had deyed, that comun clothe ay
  beren,
Yit seyntes never-the-les they
  weren.
I coude reken you many a ten;
Ye, wel nigh alle these holy wim-
  men,   6240
That men in chirchis herie and seke,
Bothe maydens, and these wyves
  eke,
That baren many a fair child
  here,
Wered alwey clothis seculere,
And in the same dyden they,   6245
That seyntes weren, and been alwey.
The eleven thousand maydens dere,
That beren in heven hir ciergis
  clere,
Of which men rede in chirche, and
  singe,
Were take in seculer clothing,   6250
Whan they resseyved martirdom,
And wonnen heven unto her hoom.
Good herte makith the gode thought;
The clothing yeveth ne reveth
  nought.
The gode thought and the worch-
  ing,   6255

That maketh religioun flowring,
Ther lyth the good religioun
Aftir the right entencioun.
  'Who-so toke a wethers skin,
And wrapped a gredy wolf
  therin,   6260
For he shulde go with lambis whyte,
Wenest thou not he wolde hem
  byte?
Yis! never-the-las, as he were
  wood,
He wolde hem wery, and drinke the
  blood;
And wel the rather hem dis-
  ceyve,   6265
For, sith they coude not perceyve
His treget and his crueltee,
They wolde him folowe, al wolde he
  flee.
  'If ther be wolves of sich hewe
Amonges these apostlis newe,   6270
Thou, holy chirche, thou mayst be
  wayled!
Sith that thy citee is assayled
Thourgh knightis of thyn owne
  table,   6273
God wot thy lordship is doutable!
If they enforce [hem] it to winne,
That shulde defende it fro withinne,
Who might defence ayens hem
  make?
Withouten stroke it mot be take
Of trepeget or mangonel;
Without displaying of pensel.   6280
And if god nil don it socour,
But lat [hem] renne in this colour,
Thou moost thyn heestis laten be.
Than is ther nought, but yelde thee,
Or yeve hem tribute, doutelees, 6285
And holde it of hem to have pees:

  6227. G. Yhe. 6237. Th. co*m*men; G. comyn; *read* comun. 6240. G. Yhe;
G. *om.* alle. 6243. *Both* ful many; *om.* ful. 6245. G. dieden. 6247. *Both* xi.
6253. G. hert; *both* good. 6255. *Both* good. 6256. *Both* the religioun; *om.*
the. 6259. G. took. 6263. G. Yhis; Th. Yes. 6271. G. biwailed (!). 6275,
82. *Supply* hem. 6278. *Both* Without. 6285. G. doutlees; Th. doutles.

But gretter harm bityde thee,
That they al maister of it be.
Wel conne they scorne thee withal;
By day stuffen they the wal, 6290
And al the night they mynen there.
Nay, thou most planten elleswhere
Thyn impes, if thou wolt fruyt have;
Abyd not there thy-self to save.
  'But now pees! here I turne
    ageyn; 6295
I wol no more of this thing seyn,
If I may passen me herby;
I mighte maken you wery.
But I wol heten you alway
To helpe your freendis what I
    may, 6300
So they wollen my company;
For they be shent al-outerly
But-if so falle, that I be
Oft with hem, and they with me.
And eek my lemman mot they
    serve, 6305
Or they shul not my love deserve.
Forsothe, I am a fals traitour;
God iugged me for a theef trichour;
Forsworn I am, but wel nygh non
Wot of my gyle, til it be don. 6310
  'Thourgh me hath many oon
    deth resseyved,
That my treget never aper-
    ceyved;
And yit resseyveth, and shal
    resseyve,
That my falsnesse never aper-
    ceyve:
But who-so doth, if he wys be, 6315
Him is right good be war of me.
But so sligh is the [deceyving
That to hard is the] aperceyving.
For Protheus, that coude him
    chaunge

In every shap, hoomly and
    straunge, 6320
Coude never sich gyle ne tresoun
As I; for I com never in toun
Ther-as I mighte knowen be,
Though men me bothe might here
    and see.
Ful wel I can my clothis
    chaunge, 6325
Take oon, and make another
    straunge.
Now am I knight, now chasteleyn;
Now prelat, and now chapeleyn;
Now prest, now clerk, and now
    forstere; 6329
Now am I maister, now scolere;
Now monk, now chanoun, now baily;
What-ever mister man am I.
Now am I prince, now am I page,
And can by herte every langage.
Som-tyme am I hoor and old; 6335
Now am I yong, [and] stout, and
    bold;
Now am I Robert, now Robyn;
Now frere Menour, now Iacobyn;
And with me folweth my loteby,
To don me solas and company, 6340
That hight dame Abstinence-
    Streyned,
In many a queynt array [y]-
    feyned.
Right as it cometh to hir lyking,
I fulfille al hir desiring.
Somtyme a wommans cloth take
    I; 6345
Now am I mayde, now lady.
Somtyme I am religious;
Now lyk an anker in an hous.
Somtyme am I prioresse,
And now a nonne, and now ab-
    besse; 6350

6292. *Both* planten most. 6296. *Both* feyne; F. *dire.* 6314. *Both ins.* shal *bef.* never. 6316. G. warre; Th. ware. 6317, 8. *Words supplied by* Kaluza. 6323. *Both* myght. 6336. *I supply* and. 6341. *Both* and reyned (!) *for* streyned; *see* 7366. 6342. *I supply* y-. 6346. *Both* I a; *om.* a.

And go thurgh alle regiouns,
Seking alle religiouns.
But to what ordre that I am sworn,
I take the strawe, and lete the corn;
To [blynde] folk [ther] I en-habite, 6355
I axe no-more but hir abite.
What wol ye more? in every wyse,
Right as me list, I me disgyse.
Wel can I bere me under weed;
Unlyk is my word to my deed. 6360
Thus make I in my trappis falle,
Thurgh my pryvileges, alle
That ben in Cristendom alyve.
I may assoile, and I may shryve,
That no prelat may lette me, 6365
Al folk, wher-ever they founde be:
I noot no prelat may don so,
But it the pope be, and no mo,
That made thilk establisshing.
Now is not this a propre thing? 6370
But, were my sleightis aperceyved,
[Ne shulde I more been re-ceyved]
As I was wont; and wostow why?
For I dide hem a tregetry;
But therof yeve I litel tale, 6375
I have the silver and the male;
So have I preched and eek shriven,
So have I take, so have [me] yiven,
Thurgh hir foly, husbond and wyf,
That I lede right a Ioly lyf, 6380
Thurgh simplesse of the prelacye;
They know not al my tregetrye.

'But for as moche as man and wyf

Shuld shewe hir paroche-prest hir lyf
Ones a yeer, as seith the book, 6385
Er any wight his housel took,
Than have I pryvilegis large,
That may of moche thing dis-charge;
For he may seye right thus, par-dee:—
"Sir Preest, in shrift I telle it thee, 6390
That he, to whom that I am shriven,
Hath me assoiled, and me yiven
Penaunce soothly, for my sinne,
Which that I fond me gilty inne;
Ne I ne have never entencioun 6395
To make double confessioun,
Ne reherce eft my shrift to thee;
O shrift is right y-nough to me.
This oughte thee suffyce wel,
Ne be not rebel never-a-del; 6400
For certis, though thou haddest it sworn,
I wot no prest ne prelat born
That may to shrift eft me con-streyne.
And if they don, I wol me pleyne;
For I wot where to pleyne wel. 6405
Thou shalt not streyne me a del,
Ne enforce me, ne [yit] me trouble,
To make my confessioun double.
Ne I have none affeccioun
To have double absolucioun. 6410
The firste is right y-nough to me;
This latter assoiling quyte I thee.

6354. G. bete; Th. beate (*for* lete). 6355. *Both* Ioly (*for* blynde); *I supply* ther. 6356. Th. habite. 6359. Th. beare; G. were. 6361. G. *om.* Thus *and* I; *both* in to (*for* in). 6372. *Both omit*; *supplied as in* Morris; F. *Si n'en sui mes si receus.* 6375. *Both* I a; *om.* a. 6377. G. shreuen. 6378. *Both* I (*for* me); *both* yeuen. 6386. G. ony. 6388. G. mych. 6392. *Both* yeuen. 6393. G. *ins.* For *bef.* Penaunce. 6399. *Both* ought. 6407. *Both* not; *read* yit.

I am unbounde; what mayst thou
    finde
More of my sinnes me to unbinde?
For he, that might hath in his
    hond,   6415
Of alle my sinnes me unbond.
And if thou wolt me thus con-
    streyne,
That me mot nedis on thee pleyne,
There shal no Iugge imperial,
Ne bisshop, ne official,   6420
Don Iugement on me; for I
Shal gon and pleyne me openly
Unto my shrift-fadir newe,
(That hight not Frere Wolf un-
    trewe!)
And he shal chevise him for
    me,   6425
For I trowe he can hampre thee.
But, lord! he wolde be wrooth
    withalle,
If men him wolde Frere Wolf calle!
For he wolde have no pacience,
But don al cruel vengeaunce! 6430
He wolde his might don at the
    leest,
[Ne] no-thing spare for goddis heest.
And, god so wis be my socour,
But thou yeve me my Saviour
At Ester, whan it lyketh me, 6435
Withoute presing more on thee,
I wol forth, and to him goon,
And he shal housel me anoon,
For I am out of thy grucching;
I kepe not dele with thee no-
    thing."   6440
Thus may he shryve him, that
    forsaketh
His paroche-prest, and to me taketh.
And if the prest wol him refuse,

I am ful redy him to accuse,
And him punisshe and hampre
    so,   6445
That he his chirche shal forgo.
  'But who-so hath in his feling
The consequence of such shryving,
Shal seen that prest may never
    have might
To knowe the conscience a-
    right   6450
Of him that is under his cure.
And this ageyns holy scripture,
That biddeth every herde honeste
Have verry knowing of his beste.
But pore folk that goon by
    strete,   6455
That have no gold, ne sommes
    grete,
Hem wolde I lete to her prelates,
Or lete hir prestis knowe hir states,
For to me right nought yeve they.'
Amour. 'And why is it?'
  F. Sem. 'For they ne
    may.   6460
They ben so bare, I take no keep;
But I wol have the fatte sheep;—
Lat parish prestis have the lene,
I yeve not of hir harm a bene!
And if that prelats grucchen
    it,   6465
That oughten wroth be in hir wit,
To lese her fatte bestes so,
I shal yeve hem a stroke or two,
That they shal lesen with [the]
    force,
Ye, bothe hir mytre and hir
    croce.   6470
Thus Iape I hem, and have do
    longe,
My priveleges been so stronge.'

6425. G. cheueys; Th. chuse; F. *chevir*.   6426. Th. hamper.   6432. *I supply* Ne.   6452. Th. this is ayenst.   6453. G. heerde.   6454. G. beeste.   6460. *Both* it is; F. *Porquoi*.   6462, 7. G. fat.   6465. G. grucche; Th. grutche.   6466. *Both* woth (!).   6469. *I supply* the.   6470. G. Yhe.

Fals-Semblant wolde have stinted here,
But Love ne made him no such chere
That he was wery of his sawe; 6475
But for to make him glad and fawe,
He seide:—'Tel on more specialy,
How that thou servest untrewly.
Tel forth, and shame thee never a del;
For as thyn abit shewith wel, 6480
Thou [semest] an holy heremyte.'
  F. Sem. 'Soth is, but I am an ypocryte.'
  Amour. 'Thou gost and prechest povertee?'
  F. Sem. 'Ye, sir; but richesse hath poustee.'
  Amour. 'Thou prechest abstinence also?' 6485
  F. Sem. 'Sir, I wol fillen, so mote I go,
My paunche of gode mete and wyne,
As shulde a maister of divyne;
For how that I me pover feyne,
Yit alle pore folk I disdeyne. 6490
  'I love bet the acqueyntaunce
Ten tymes, of the king of Fraunce,
Than of pore man of mylde mode,
Though that his soule be also gode.
For whan I see beggers quaking, 6495
Naked on mixens al stinking,
For hungre crye, and eek for care,
I entremete not of hir fare.
They been so pore, and ful of pyne,
They might not ones yeve me dyne, 6500
For they have no-thing but hir lyf;
What shulde he yeve that likketh his knyf?
It is but foly to entremete,
To seke in houndes nest fat mete.
Let bere hem to the spitel anoon, 6505
But, for me, comfort gete they noon.
But a riche sike usurere
Wolde I visyte and drawe nere;
Him wol I comforte and rehete,
For I hope of his gold to gete. 6510
And if that wikked deth him have,
I wol go with him to his grave.
And if ther any reprove me,
Why that I lete the pore be,
Wostow how I [mot] ascape? 6515
I sey, and swerë him ful rape,
That riche men han more tecches
Of sinne, than han pore wrecches,
And han of counseil more mister;
And therfore I wol drawe hem ner. 6520
But as gret hurt, it may so be,
Hath soule in right gret poverte,
As soul in gret richesse, forsothe,
Al-be-it that they hurten bothe.
For richesse and mendicitees 6525
Ben cleped two extremitees;
The mene is cleped suffisaunce,
Ther lyth of vertu the aboundaunce.
For Salamon, ful wel I woot,
In his Parables us wroot, 6530

6481. *Both* seruest; F. *sembles.* 6482. *Both* I am but an. 6484. G. Yhe. 6487. *Both* good. 6491. *Both* bettir; G. that queyntaunce. 6492. Th. tymes; G. tyme. 6493. *Both* of a pore. 6496. G. myxnes; Th. myxins. 6500. *Both* me a dyne. 6513. G. ony. 6515. *Both* not. 6516. *Both* swere. 6522. *Both* Hath a soule.

As it is knowe of many a wight,
In his [thrittethe] chapitre right :
" God, thou me kepe, for thy
  poustee,
Fro richesse and mendicitee ;
For if a riche man him dresse 6535
To thenke to moche on [his] ri-
  chesse,
His herte on that so fer is set,
That he his creatour foryet ;
And him, that [begging] wol ay greve,
How shulde I by his word him
  leve ?   6540
Unnethe that he nis a micher,
Forsworn, or elles [god is] lyer."
Thus seith Salamones sawes ;
Ne we finde writen in no lawes,
And namely in our Cristen
  lay—   6545
(Who seith "ye," I dar sey
  "nay")—
That Crist, ne his apostlis dere,
Whyl that they walkede in erthe
  here,
Were never seen her bred begging,
For they nolde beggen for no-
  thing.   6550
And right thus were men wont to
  teche ;
And in this wyse wolde it preche
The maistres of divinitee
Somtyme in Paris the citee.
  'And if men wolde ther-geyn ap-
    pose   6555
The naked text, and lete the glose,
It mighte sone assoiled be ;
For men may wel the sothe see,
That, parde, they mighte axe a
  thing

Pleynly forth, without begging. 6560
For they weren goddis herdis dere,
And cure of soules hadden here,
They nolde no-thing begge hir fode ;
For aftir Crist was don on rode,
With [hir] propre hondis they
  wrought,   6565
And with travel, and elles nought,
They wonnen al hir sustenaunce,
And liveden forth in hir penaunce,
And the remenaunt [yeve] awey
To other pore folk alwey.   6570
They neither bilden tour ne halle,
But [leye] in houses smale with-
  alle.
A mighty man, that can and may,
Shulde with his honde and body
  alway
Winne him his food in labor-
  ing,   6575
If he ne have rent or sich a thing,
Although he be religious,
And god to serven curious.
Thus mote he don, or do trespas,
But-if it be in certeyn cas, 6580
That I can reherce, if mister be,
Right wel, whan the tyme I see.
' Seke the book of Seynt Austin,
Be it in paper or perchemin,
There-as he writ of these wor-
  chinges,   6585
Thou shalt seen that non excus-
  inges
A parfit man ne shulde seke
By wordis, ne by dedis eke,
Although he be religious,
And god to serven curious, 6590
That he ne shal, so mote I go,
With propre hondis and body also,

6531. Th. of; G. to.   6532. G. thrittene ; Th. thirtene ; *read* thrittethe
6536. G. myche.   6539. *Both* beggith (-eth).   6542. *Both* goddis (-es).   6543.
G. Salamon ; Th. Salomon.   6546. G. yhe.   6550. *Both* nolden.   6551.
G. was.   6557. *Both* myght.   6565. G. ther ; Th. their.   6569. *Both* yaf.
6570. *Both* folkis (-es).   6572. *Both* they ; *read* leye ; F. *Ains gisoient*.   6581.
Perhaps om. That.

Gete his food in laboring,
If he ne have propretee of thing.
Yit shulde he selle al his sub-
    staunce,   6595
And with his swink have sus-
    tenaunce,
If he be parfit in bountee.
Thus han tho bookes tolde me :
For he that wol gon ydilly,
And useth it ay besily   6600
To haunten other mennes table,
He is a trechour, ful of fable ;
Ne he ne may, by gode resoun,
Excuse him by his orisoun.
For men bihoveth, in som gyse, 6605
Som-tyme [leven] goddes servyse
To gon and purchasen her
    nede.
Men mote eten, that is no drede,
And slepe, and eek do other thing ;
So longe may they leve pray-
    ing.   6610
So may they eek hir prayer blinne,
While that they werke, hir mete to
    winne.
Seynt Austin wol therto accorde,
In thilke book that I recorde.
Justinian eek, that made lawes, 6615
Hath thus forboden, by olde dawes,
" No man, up peyne to be deed,
Mighty of body, to begge his
    breed,
If he may swinke, it for to gete ;
Men shulde him rather mayme or
    bete,   6620
Or doon of him apert Iustice,
Than suffren him in such
    malice."
They don not wel, so mote I go,
That taken such almesse so,
But if they have som privelege, 6625

That of the peyne hem wol allege.
But how that is, can I not see,
But-if the prince disseyved be ;
Ne I ne wene not, sikerly,
That they may have it right-
    fully.   6630
But I wol not determyne
Of princes power, ne defyne,
Ne by my word comprende, y-wis,
If it so fer may strecche in this.
I wol not entremete a del ;   6635
But I trowe that the book seith wel,
Who that taketh almesses, that be
Dewe to folk that men may see
Lame, feble, wery, and bare,
Pore, or in such maner care,   6640
(That conne winne hem nevermo,
For they have no power therto),
He eteth his owne dampning,
But-if he lye, that made al thing.
And if ye such a truaunt finde, 6645
Chastise him wel, if ye be kinde.
But they wolde hate you, percas,
And, if ye fillen in hir laas,
They wolde eftsones do you scathe,
If that they mighte, late or
    rathe ;   6650
For they be not ful pacient,
That han the world thus foule
    blent.
And witeth wel, [wher] that god
    bad
The good man selle al that he had,
And folowe him, and to pore it
    yive,   6655
He wolde not therfore that he live
To serven him in mendience,
For it was never his sentence ;
But he bad wirken whan that nede
    is,
And folwe him in goode dedis. 6660

6598. *Both* tolde (*against grammar*). 6600. G. desily (!). 6601. Th.
To ; G. Go.   6606. *Both* Ben somtyme in ; *see* 6610.   6616. G. old ; Th.
olde.   6650. *Both* myght.   6653. *I supply* wher ; F. *la ou*.   6655. *Both* yeue.

Seynt Poule, that loved al holy chirche,
He bade thapostles for to wirche,
And winnen hir lyflode in that wyse,
And hem defended truaundyse,
And seide, "Wirketh with your honden;" 6665
Thus shulde the thing be undirstonden.
He nolde, y-wis, bidde hem begging,
Ne sellen gospel, ne preching,
Lest they berafte, with hir asking,
Folk of hir catel or of hir thing. 6670
For in this world is many a man
That yeveth his good, for he ne can
Werne it for shame, or elles he
Wolde of the asker delivered be;
And, for he him encombreth so, 6675
He yeveth him good to late him go:
But it can him no-thing profyte,
They lese the yift and the meryte.
The goode folk, that Poule to preched,
Profred him ofte, whan he hem teched, 6680
Som of hir good in charite;
But therof right no-thing took he;
But of his hondwerk wolde he gete
Clothes to wryen him, and his mete.'
Amour. 'Tel me than how a man may liven, 6685
That al his good to pore hath yiven,
And wol but only bidde his bedis,
And never with honde laboure his nedis:

May he do so?'
F. Sem. 'Ye, sir.'
Amour. 'And how?'
F. Sem. 'Sir, I wol gladly telle yow:— 6690
Seynt Austin seith, a man may be
In houses that han propretee,
As templers and hospiteler,
And as these chanouns regulers,
Or whyte monkes, or these blake— 6695
(I wole no mo ensamplis make)—
And take therof his sustening,
For therinne lyth no begging;
But other-weyes not, y-wis,
[If] Austin gabbeth not of this. 6700
And yit ful many a monk laboureth,
That god in holy chirche honoureth;
For whan hir swinking is agoon,
They rede and singe in chirche anoon.
'And for ther hath ben greet discord, 6705
As many a wight may bere record,
Upon the estate of mendience,
I wol shortly, in your presence,
Telle how a man may begge at nede,
That hath not wherwith him to fede, 6710
Maugre his felones Iangelinges,
For sothfastnesse wol non hidinges;
And yit, percas, I may abey,
That I to yow sothly thus sey.
'Lo, here the caas especial: 6715
If a man be so bestial
That he of no craft hath science,
And nought desyreth ignorence,
Than may he go a-begging yerne,
Til he som maner craft can lerne, 6720

6667. *Both* haue bidde; (*om.* haue). 6679. *Both* good. 6682. Th. -of; G. -fore. 6684. *Both* wryne. 6688. G. *omits*: Th. hondis. 6699. Th. -wayes; G. -weys. 6700. If] *Both* Yit. 6707. *Both* mendiciens (-ence); *see* 6657.

R 2

Thurgh which, withoute truaunding,
He may in trouthe have his living.
Or if he may don no labour,
For elde, or syknesse, or langour,
Or for his tendre age also,   6725
Than may he yit a-begging go.
  'Or if he have, peraventure,
Thurgh usage of his noriture,
Lived over deliciously,
Than oughten good folk co-
    munly   6730
Han of his mischeef som pitee,
And suffren him also, that he
May gon aboute and begge his
    breed,
That he be not for hungur deed.
Or if he have of craft cunning, 6735
And strengthe also, and desiring
To wirken, as he hadde what,
But he finde neither this ne that,
Than may he begge, til that he
Have geten his necessitee.   6740
  'Or if his winning be so lyte,
That his labour wol not acquyte
Sufficiantly al his living,
Yit may he go his breed begging;
Fro dore to dore he may go
    trace,   6745
Til he the remenaunt may purchace.
Or if a man wolde undirtake
Any empryse for to make,
In the rescous of our lay,
And it defenden as he may,   6750
Be it with armes or lettrure,
Or other covenable cure,
If it be so e pore be,
Than may he begge, til that he
May finde in trouthe for to
    swinke,   6755
And gete him clothes, mete, and
    drinke.

Swinke he with hondis cor-
    porel,
And not with hondis espirituel.
  'In al thise caas, and in sem-
    blables,
If that ther ben mo resonables, 6760
He may begge, as I telle you here,
And elles nought, in no manere;
As William Seynt Amour wolde
    preche,
And ofte wolde dispute and teche
Of this matere alle openly   6765
At Paris ful solempnely.
And al-so god my soule blesse,
As he had, in this stedfastnesse,
The accord of the universitee,
And of the puple, as semeth
    me.   6770
  'No good man oughte it to re-
    fuse,
Ne oughte him therof to excuse,
Be wrooth or blythe who-so be;
For I wol speke, and telle it thee,
Al shulde I dye, and be put
    doun,   6775
As was seynt Poul, in derk prisoun;
Or be exiled in this caas
With wrong, as maister William
    was,
That my moder Ypocrisye
Banisshed for hir greet envye. 6780
  'My moder flemed him, Seynt
    Amour:
This noble dide such labour
To susteyne ever the loyaltee,
That he to moche agilte me.
He made a book, and leet it
    wryte,   6785
Wherin his lyf he dide al wryte,
And wolde ich reneyed begging,
And lived by my traveyling,

6721. *Both* without.   6728. Th. noriture; G. norture.   6737. *Both* had.
6748. G. Ony.   6756. *Both* clothe; *read* clothes; *see* 6684.   6759. *Both* this.
6766. *Both* solemply.   6782. Th. This; G. The.   6784. Th. agylte; G. agilt.
6786. *So* Th.; G. Of thyngis that he beste myghte (*in late hand*).

If I ne had rent ne other good.
What? wened he that I were
    wood?   6790
For labour might me never plese,
I have more wil to been at ese ;
And have wel lever, sooth to
    sey,
Bifore the puple patre and prey,
And wrye me in my foxerye 6795
Under a cope of papelardye.'
  Quod Love, ' What devel is this
    I here ?
What wordis tellest thou me here ? '
  F. Sem. 'What, sir?'
  Amour. 'Falsnesse, that apert is ;
Than dredist thou not god ? '
  F. Sem.   ' No, certis : 6800
For selde in greet thing shal he
    spede
In this world, that god wol drede.
For folk that hem to vertu yiven,
And truly on her owne liven,
And hem in goodnesse ay con-
    tene,   6805
On hem is litel thrift y-sene ;
Such folk drinken gret misese ;
That lyf [ne] may me never plese.
But see what gold han usurers,
And silver eek in [hir] garners, 6810
Taylagiers, and these monyours,
Bailifs, bedels, provost, countours ;
These liven wel nygh by ravyne ;
The smale puple hem mote enclyne,
And they as wolves wol hem
    eten.   6815
Upon the pore folk they geten
Ful moche of that they spende or
    kepe ;
Nis none of hem that he nil strepe,
And wryen him-self wel atte fulle ;

Withoute scalding they hem
    pulle.   6820
The stronge the feble overgoth ;
But I, that were my simple cloth,
Robbe bothe robbed and robbours,
And gyle gyled and gylours.
By my treget, I gadre and
    threste   6825
The greet tresour into my cheste,
That lyth with me so faste bounde
Myn highe paleys do I founde,
And my delytes I fulfille
With wyne at feestes at my
    wille,   6830
And tables fulle of entremees ;
I wol no lyf, but ese and pees,
And winne gold to spende also.
For whan the grete bagge is go,
It cometh right with my Iapes. 6835
Make I not wel tumble myn apes ?
To winne is alwey myn entent ;
My purchas is better than my rent ;
For though I shulde beten be,
Over-al I entremete me ;   6840
Withoute me may no wight dure.
I walke soules for to cure.
Of al the worlde cure have I
In brede and lengthe ; boldely
I wol bothe preche and eek coun-
    ceilen ;   6845
With hondis wille I not traveilen,
For of the pope I have the
    bulle ;
I ne holde not my wittes dulle.
I wol not stinten, in my lyve, 6849
These emperouris for to shryve,
Or kyngis, dukis, and lordis grete ;
But pore folk al quyte I lete.
I love no such shryving, pardee,
But it for other cause be.

6792. G. wille.   6797. *Both* this that ; *om.* that.   6803. *Both* yeuen.   6806.
G. sene.   6808, 10. *Supply* ne, hir.   6819. *Both* wrine. *Both* hem,
at.   6820. *Both* Without.   6823, 4. *Both* robbyng, gilyng.   6827. G. fast.
6828. *Both* high.   6834. C. gret ; Th. great.   6841. *Both* Without
6844. *Both* boldly.   6850. *Both* **e**mperours.   6851. G. *om.* and.

I rekke not of pore men,   6855
Hir astate is not worth an hen.
Where fyndest thou a swinker of
  labour
Have me unto his confessour?
But emperesses, and duchesses,
Thise quenes, and eek [thise]
  countesses,   6860
Thise abbesses, and eek Bigyns,
These grete ladyes palasyns,
These Ioly knightes, and baillyves,
Thise nonnes, and thise burgeis
  wyves,
That riche been, and eek ples-
  ing,   6865
And thise maidens welfaring,
Wher-so they clad or naked be,
Uncounceiled goth ther noon fro me.
And, for her soules savetee,
At lord and lady, and hir
  meynee,   6870
I axe, whan they hem to me shryve,
The propretee of al hir lyve,
And make hem trowe, bothe meest
  and leest,
Hir paroch-prest nis but a beest
Ayens me and my company,   6875
That shrewis been as greet as I;
For whiche I wol not hyde in hold
No privetee that me is told,
That I by word or signe, y-wis,
[Nil] make hem knowe what it
  is,   6880
And they wolen also tellen me;
They hele fro me no privitee.
And for to make yow hem per-
  ceyven,
That usen folk thus to disceyven,
I wol you seyn, withouten
  drede,   6885
What men may in the gospel rede
Of Seynt Mathew, the gospelere,
That seith, as I shal you sey here.
  'Upon the chaire of Moyses—
Thus is it glosed, douteles: 6890
That is the olde testament,
For therby is the chaire ment—
Sitte Scribes and Pharisen;—
That is to seyn, the cursid men
Whiche that we ypocritis
  calle—   6895
Doth that they preche, I rede you
  alle,
But doth not as they don a del,
That been not wery to seye wel,
But to do wel, no wille have they;
And they wolde binde on folk
  alwey,   6900
That ben to [be] begyled able,
Burdens that ben importable;
On folkes shuldres thinges they
  couchen
That they nil with her fingres
  touchen.'
  Amour. 'And why wol they not
  touche it?'
  F. Sem.   'Why?   6905
For hem ne list not, sikirly;
For sadde burdens that men
  taken
Make folkes shuldres aken.
And if they do ought that good be,
That is for folk it shulde see: 6910
Her burdens larger maken they,
And make hir hemmes wyde
  alwey,
And loven setes at the table,
The firste and most honourable;
And for to han the first chaieris 6915
In synagoges, to hem ful dere is;
And willen that folk hem loute and
  grete,
Whan that they passen thurgh the
  strete,

6860, 6901. *Supply* thise, be.   6862. G. gret; Th. great.   6880. Th. Ne wol;
G. Wol; *read* Nil.   6890. *Both* doutles (-lees).   6902, 7, 11. *Both* burdons.

And wolen be cleped "Maister" also.
But they ne shulde not willen
    so;   6920
The gospel is ther-ageyns, I gesse :
That sheweth wel hir wikkidnesse.
    'Another custom use we :—
Of hem that wol ayens us be,
We hate hem deedly everich-
    oon,   6925
And we wol werrey hem, as oon.
Him that oon hatith, hate we alle,
And coniecte how to doon him falle.
And if we seen him winne honour,
Richesse or preys, thurgh his
    valour,   6930
Provende, rent, or dignitee,
Ful fast, y-wis, compassen we
By what ladder he is clomben so ;
And for to maken him doun to go,
With traisoun we wole him de-
    fame,   6935
And doon him lese his gode name.
Thus from his ladder we him take,
And thus his freendis foes we make ;
But word ne wite shal he noon,
Til alle his freendis been his
    foon.   6940
For if we dide it openly,
We might have blame redily ;
For hadde he wist of our malyce,
He hadde him kept, but he were
    nyce.
    'Another is this, that, if so
    falle   6945
That ther be oon among us alle
That doth a good turn, out of drede,
We seyn it is our alder dede.
Ye, sikerly, though he it feyned,
Or that him list, or that him
    deyned   6950
A man thurgh him avaunced be ;
Therof alle parceners be we,

And tellen folk, wher-so we go,
That man thurgh us is sprongen so.
And for to have of men preys-
    ing,   6955
We purchace, thurgh our flatering,
Of riche men, of gret poustee,
Lettres, to witnesse our bountee ;
So that man weneth, that may us see,
That alle vertu in us be.   6960
And alwey pore we us feyne ;
But how so that we begge or pleyne,
We ben the folk, without lesing,
That al thing have without having.
Thus be we dred of the puple,
    y-wis.   6965
And gladly my purpos is this :—
I dele with no wight, but he
Have gold and tresour gret plentee ;
Hir acqueyntaunce wel love I ;
This is moche my desyr,
    shortly.   6970
I entremete me of brocages,
I make pees and mariages,
I am gladly executour,
And many tymes procuratour ;
I am somtyme messager ;   6975
That falleth not to my mister.
And many tymes I make enquestes;
For me that office not honest is ;
To dele with other mennes thing,
That is to me a gret lyking.   6980
And if that ye have ought to do
In place that I repeire to,
I shal it speden thurgh my wit,
As sone as ye have told me it.
So that ye serve me to pay,   6985
My servyse shal be your alway.
But who-so wol chastyse me,
Anoon my love lost hath he ;
For I love no man in no gyse,
That wol me repreve or
    chastyse ;   6990

6925, 6. *Both* him ; *read* hem.   6936. *Both* good.   6939. Th. wete.
6949. G. Yhe.   6952. Th. parceners ; G. perseners.   6974. *Both* tymes a ;
om. a.

But I wolde al folk undirtake,
And of no wight no teching take ;
For I, that other folk chastye,
Wol not be taught fro my folye.
'I love noon hermitage more ; 6995
Alle desertes, and holtes hore,
And grete wodes everichoon,
I lete hem to the Baptist Iohan.
I quethe him quyte, and him relesse
Of Egipt al the wildirnesse ; 7000
To fer were alle my mansiouns
Fro alle citees and goode tounes.
My paleis and myn hous make I
There men may renne in openly,
And sey that I the world forsake. 7005
But al amidde I bilde and make
My hous, and swimme and pley therinne
Bet than a fish doth with his finne.
'Of Antecristes men am I,
Of whiche that Crist seith openly, 7010
They have abit of holinesse,
And liven in such wikkednesse.
Outward, lambren semen we,
Fulle of goodnesse and of pitee,
And inward we, withouten fable, 7015
Ben gredy wolves ravisable.
We enviroune bothe londe and see ;
With al the world werreyen we ;
We wol ordeyne of alle thing,
Of folkes good, and her living. 7020
'If ther be castel or citee
Wherin that any bougerons be,
Although that they of Milayne were,

For ther-of ben they blamed there :
Or if a wight, out of mesure, 7025
Wolde lene his gold, and take usure,
For that he is so coveitous :
Or if he be to leccherous,
Or [thefe, or] haunte simonye ;
Or provost, ful of trecherye, 7030
Or prelat, living Iolily,
Or prest that halt his quene him by ;
Or olde hores hostilers,
Or other bawdes or bordillers,
Or elles blamed of any vyce, 7035
Of whiche men shulden doon Iustyce :
By alle the seyntes that we pray,
But they defende hem with lamprey,
With luce, with elis, with samons,
With tendre gees, and with capons, 7040
With tartes, or with cheses fat,
With deynte flawnes, brode and flat,
With caleweys, or with pullaille,
With coninges, or with fyn vitaille,
That we, undir our clothes wyde, 7045
Maken thurgh our golet glyde :
Or but he wol do come in haste
Roo-venisoun, [y]-bake in paste :
Whether so that he loure or groine,
He shal have of a corde a loigne, 7050
With whiche men shal him binde and lede,
To brenne him for his sinful dede,
That men shulle here him crye and rore
A myle-wey aboute, and more.

6997. G. gret ; Th. great.   7002. Th. al ; G. om.   7012. *After this line, both in* Th. *and* G., *come* ll. 7109-7158.   7018. G. werrien ; Th. werryen. 7019. *Both* al.   7022. Th. bougerons ; G. begger.   7029. *Both* these that ; F. *lerres ou.*   7035. G. ony.   7037. we] G. me.   7038. hem] *Both* them. 7041. G. cheffis ; Th. cheffes ; F. *fromages.*   7047. he] G. we.   7048. *Both* bake.

THE ROMAUNT OF THE ROSE.

Or elles he shal in prisoun dye, 7055
But-if he wol [our] frendship bye,
Or smerten that that he hath do,
More than his gilt amounteth to.
But, and he couthe thurgh his sleight
Do maken up a tour of height, 7060
Nought roughte I whether of stone or tree,
Or erthe, or turves though it be,
Though it were of no vounde stone,
Wrought with squyre and scantilone,
So that the tour were stuffed wel 7065
With alle richesse temporel;
And thanne, that he wolde updresse
Engyns, bothe more and lesse,
To caste at us, by every syde—
To bere his goode name wyde— 7070
Such sleightes [as] I shal yow nevene,
Barelles of wyne, by sixe or sevene,
Or gold in sakkes gret plente,
He shulde sone delivered be.
And if he have noon sich pitaunces, 7075
Late him study in equipolences,
And lete lyes and fallaces,
If that he wolde deserve our graces;
Or we shal bere him such witnesse
Of sinne, and of his wrecchidnesse, 7080
And doon his loos so wyde renne,
That al quik we shulde him brenne,
Or elles yeve him suche penaunce,
That is wel wors than the pitaunce.
'For thou shalt never, for nothing, 7085
Con knowen aright by her clothing
The traitours fulle of trecherye,
But thou her werkis can aspye.
And ne hadde the good keping be
Whylom of the universitee, 7090
That kepeth the key of Cristendome,
[They] had been turmented, alle and some.
Suche been the stinking [fals] prophetis;
Nis non of hem, that good prophete is;
For they, thurgh wikked entencioun, 7095
The yeer of the incarnacioun
A thousand and two hundred yeer,
Fyve and fifty, ferther ne ner,
Broughten a book, with sory grace,
To yeven ensample in comune place, 7100
That seide thus, though it were fable:—
"This is the Gospel Perdurable,
That fro the Holy Goost is sent."
Wel were it worth to ben [y]-brent.
Entitled was in such manere 7105
This book, of which I telle here.
Ther nas no wight in al Parys,
Biforn Our Lady, at parvys,
That [he] ne mighte bye the book,
To copy, if him talent took. 7110
Ther might he see, by greet tresoun,
Ful many fals comparisoun:—

7056. *Both* his; *read* our.   7059. G. sleght; Th. sleight.   7060. G. hight; Th. heyght.   7063. *Both* vounde.   7070. *Both* good.   7071. G. sleghtes. *I supply* as.   7075. G. *om.* he have.   7092. Th. We had ben turmented al and some (*read* They); G. Of al that here axe juste their dome (*in late hand*); F. *Tout eust este tormente.*   7093. *I supply* fals.   7104. *Both* brent.   7109. G. *has here* l. 7110, *followed by a blank line*; Th. *has* That they [*read* he] ne might the booke by; *and then inserts an extra spurious line*—The sentence pleased hem wel trewly.   7110. Th. To the copye, if hem talent toke; *after which,* Of the Euangelystes booke (*spurious*).

"As moche as, thurgh his grete
    might,
Be it of hete, or of light,
The sunne sourmounteth the
    mone,   7115
That troubler is, and chaungeth
    sone,
And the note-kernel the shelle—
(I scorne nat that I yow telle)—
Right so, withouten any gyle,
Sourmounteth this noble Evan-
    gyle   7120
The word of any evangelist."
And to her title they token Christ ;
And many such comparisoun,
Of which I make no mencioun,
Might men in that boke finde, 7125
Who-so coude of hem have minde.
  'The universitee, that tho was
    aslepe,
Gan for to braide, and taken kepe ;
And at the noys the heed up-caste,
Ne never sithen slepte it faste, 7130
But up it sterte, and armes took
Ayens this fals horrible book,
Al redy bateil for to make,
And to the Iuge the book to take.
But they that broughten the book
    there   7135
Hente it anoon awey, for fere ;
They nolde shewe it more a del,
But thenne it kepte, and kepen wil,
Til such a tyme that they may see
That they so stronge woxen be, 7140
That no wight may hem wel with-
    stonde ;
For by that book they durst not
    stonde.

Away they gonne it for to bere,
For they ne du ste not answere
By exposicioun ne glose   7145
To that that clerkis wole appose
Ayens the cursednesse, y-wis,
That in that boke writen is.
Now wot I not, ne I can not see
What maner ende that there shal
    be   7150
Of al this [boke that they hyde ;
But yit algate they shal abyde
Til that they may it bet defende ;
This trowe I best, wol be hir ende.
  'Thus Antecrist abyden we, 7155
For we ben alle of his meynee ;
And what man that wol not be so,
Right sone he shal his lyf forgo.
We wol a puple on him areyse,
And thurgh our gyle doon him
    seise,   7160
And him on sharpe speris ryve,
Or other-weyes bringe him fro
    lyve,
But-if that he wol folowe, y-wis,
That in our boke writen is.
Thus moche wol our book sig-
    nifye,   7165
That whyl [that] Peter hath mais-
    trye,
May never Iohan shewe wel his
    might.
  'Now have I you declared right
The mening of the bark and rinde
That makith the entenciouns
    blinde.   7170
But now at erst I wol biginne
To expowne you the pith with-
    inne :—

7113. G. gret ; Th. great.   7119, 21. G. ony.   7123. G. many a such.
7125. Th. booke ; G. book.   7127. *Perhaps omit* that.   7133, 37, 42. G.
om. for, it, they.   7143. Th. Awaye ; G. Alwey.   7144. G. durst.   7145.
Both no.   7148. Th. booke ; G. book.   7151. *Supply* boke.   7159. *Both*
vpon.   *Before this line* G. *and* Th. *wrongly insert* ll. 7013-7110, 7209-7304.
7164. Th. booke ; G. book.   7165. G. mych.   7166. *I supply* that.

[And first, by Peter, as I wene,
The Pope himself we wolden mene,]
And [eek] the seculers compre-
    hende,   7175
That Cristes lawe wol defende,
And shulde it kepen and mayn-
    tenen
Ayeines hem that al sustenen,
And falsly to the puple techen.
[And] Iohan bitokeneth hem [that]
    prechen,   7180
That ther nis lawe covenable
But thilke Gospel Perdurable,
That fro the Holy Gost was sent
To turne folk that been miswent.
The strengthe of Iohan they undir-
    stonde   7185
The grace in which, they seye, they
    stonde,
That doth the sinful folk converte,
And hem to Iesus Crist reverte.
  ' Ful many another horriblete
May men in that boke see,   7190
That ben comaunded, douteles,
Ayens the lawe of Rome expres ;
And alle with Antecrist they holden,
As men may in the book biholden.
And than comaunden they to
    sleen   7195
Alle tho that with Peter been ;
But they shal nevere have that
    might,
And, god toforn, for stryf to fight,
That they ne shal y-nough [men]
    finde
That Peters lawe shal have in
    minde,   7200
And ever holde, and so mayntene,
That at the last it shal be sene
That they shal alle come therto,
For ought that they can speke or
    do.
And thilke lawe shal not
    stonde,   7205
That they by Iohan have undir-
    stonde ;
But, maugre hem, it shal adoun,
And been brought to confusioun.
But I wol stinte of this matere,
For it is wonder long to here ;   7210
But hadde that ilke book endured,
Of better estate I were ensured ;
And freendis have I yit, pardee,
That han me set in greet degree.
  ' Of all this world is em-
    perour   7215
Gyle my fader, the trechour,
And emperesse my moder is,
Maugre the Holy Gost, y-wis.
Our mighty linage and our route
Regneth in every regne aboute ;   7220
And wel is worth we [maistres] be,
For al this world governe we,
And can the folk so wel disceyve,
That noon our gyle can perceyve ;
And though they doon, they dar
    not saye ;   7225
The sothe dar no wight biwreye.
But he in Cristis wrath him
    ledeth,
That more than Crist my bretheren
    dredeth.
He nis no ful good champioun,
That dredith such similacioun ; 7230
Nor that for peyne wole refusen
Us to correcten and accusen.
He wol not entremete by right,
Ne have god in his eye-sight,

7173, 4. *Supplied by conjecture* ; F. *Par Pierre voil le Pape entendre.*   7175, 99. *I supply* eek, men.   7178. G. Ayens ; Th. Ayenst.   7180. And] *Both* That. that] *Both* to.   7189. G. orribilite ; Th. horriblete.   7190. Th. booke ; G. book.   7196. G. Petre.   7200. G. Petres.   7205. G. thilk.   7209. *See note to* l. 7159.   7217. Th. Empresse ; G. Emperis.   7221. *Both* worthy ; *see* 7104. *Both* mynystres.   7234. G. iye.

And therfore god shal him
  punyce; 7235
But me ne rekketh of no vyce,
Sithen men us loven comunably,
And holden us for so worthy,
That we may folk repreve echoon,
And we nil have repref of noon. 7240
Whom shulden folk worshipen so
But us, that stinten never mo
To patren whyl that folk us see,
Though it not so bihinde hem be?
  'And where is more wood
    folye, 7245
Than to enhaunce chivalrye,
And love noble men and gay,
That Ioly clothis weren alway?
If they be sich folk as they semen,
So clene, as men her clothis
  demen, 7250
And that her wordis folowe her dede,
It is gret pite, out of drede,
For they wol be noon ypocritis!
Of hem, me thinketh [it] gret spite is;
I can not love hem on no syde. 7255
But Beggers with these hodes wyde,
With sleighe and pale faces lene,
And greye clothis not ful clene,
But fretted ful of tatarwagges,
And highe shoes, knopped with
  dagges, 7260
That frouncen lyke a quaile-pype,
Or botes riveling as a gype;
To such folk as I you devyse
Shuld princes and these lordes wyse
Take alle her londes and her
  thinges, 7265
Bothe werre and pees, in govern-
  inges;
To such folk shulde a prince him
  yive,
That wolde his lyf in honour live.

And if they be not as they seme,
That serven thus the world to
  queme, 7270
There wolde I dwelle, to disceyve
The folk, for they shal not perceyve.
  ' But I ne speke in no such wyse,
That men shulde humble abit dis-
  pyse,
So that no pryde ther-under
  be. 7275
No man shulde hate, as thinketh me,
The pore man in sich clothing.
But god ne preiseth him no-thing,
That seith he hath the world forsake,
And hath to worldly glorie him
  take, 7280
And wol of siche delyces use;
Who may that Begger wel
  excuse?
That papelard, that him yeldeth so,
And wol to worldly ese go,
And seith that he the world hath
  left, 7285
And gredily it grypeth eft,
He is the hound, shame is to seyn,
That to his casting goth ageyn.
  ' But unto you dar I not lye:
But mighte I felen or aspye, 7290
That ye perceyved it no-thing,
Ye shulden have a stark lesing
Right in your hond thus, to biginne,
I nolde it lette for no sinne.'
  The god lough at the wonder
    tho, 7295
And every wight gan laughe also,
And seide:—'Lo here a man aright
For to be trusty to every wight!'
  'Fals Semblant,' quod Love, 'sey
    to me,
Sith I thus have avaunced
  thee, 7300

7236. Th. recketh; G. rekke. 7243. *Both* may us (*om.* may). 7244. G. *om.* hem. 7254. Th. hem; G. hym; *supply* it. 7255. Th. hem; G. hym. 7257. G. steight(!). 7258. Th. graye; G. grey. 7260. G. high. 7262. Th. ryuelyng; G. reuelyng. 7263. G. dyuyse. 7272. The] G. To. 7292. *Both* shulde.

That in my court is thy dwelling,
And of ribaudes shalt be my king,
Wolt thou wel holden my for-
    wardis?'
    F. Sem. 'Ye, sir, from hennes
    forewardis;
Hadde never your fader here-
    biforn   7305
Servaunt so trewe, sith he was born.'
    Amour. 'That is ayeines al
    nature.'
    F. Sem. 'Sir, put you in that
    aventure;
For though ye borowes take of me,
The sikerer shal ye never be 7310
For ostages, ne sikirnesse,
Or chartres, for to bere witnesse.
I take your-self to record here,
That men ne may, in no manere,
Teren the wolf out of his hyde, 7315
Til he be [flayn], bak and syde,
Though men him bete and al
    defyle;
What? wene ye that I wole bigyle?
For I am clothed mekely,
Ther-under is al my trechery; 7320
Myn herte chaungeth never the mo
For noon abit, in which I go.
Though I have chere of simplenesse,
I am not weary of shrewednesse.
My lemman, Streyned-Absti-
    nence,   7325
Hath mister of my purveaunce;
She hadde ful longe ago be deed,
Nere my councel and my reed;
Lete hir allone, and you and me.'
    And Love answerde, 'I truste
    thee   7330
Withoute borowe, for I wol noon.'
And Fals-Semblant, the theef,
    anoon,

Right in that ilke same place,
That hadde of tresoun al his face
Right blak withinne, and whyt
    withoute,   7335
Thanketh him, gan on his knees
    loute.
    Than was ther nought, but
    'Every man
Now to assaut, that sailen can,'
Quod Love, 'and that ful hardily.'
Than armed they hem com-
    munly   7340
Of sich armour as to hem fel.
Whan they were armed, fers and fel,
They wente hem forth, alle in a
    route,
And set the castel al aboute;
They wil nought away, for no
    drede,   7345
Til it so be that they ben dede,
Or til they have the castel take.
And foure batels they gan make,
And parted hem in foure anoon,
And toke her way, and forth they
    goon,   7350
The foure gates for to assaile,
Of whiche the kepers wol not
    faile;
For they ben neither syke ne dede,
But hardy folk, and stronge in dede.
    Now wole I seyn the counte-
    naunce   7355
Of Fals-Semblant, and Absti-
    naunce,
That ben to Wikkid-Tonge went.
But first they helde her parlement,
Whether it to done were
To maken hem be knowen
    there,   7360
Or elles walken forth disgysed.
But at the laste they devysed,

7303. G. forwordis.   7304. G. Yhe. Th. hence; G. hens.   7307. Th. ayenst;
G. ayens.   7316. *Both* slayn; *see* note.   7317. G. alto defyle.   7325. G. Myn;
Th. My.   G. streyneth (!).   7331. *Both* Without.   7336. Th. Thankyng.
7355. G. countynaunce.   7358. G. heelde.   7362. Th. laste; G. last.

That they wold goon in tapinage,
As it were in a pilgrimage,
Lyk good and holy folk un-
 feyned. 7365
And Dame Abstinence-Streyned
Took on a robe of camelyne,
And gan hir graithe as a Begyne.
A large coverchief of threde
She wrapped al aboute hir
 hede, 7370
But she forgat not hir sautere ;
A peire of bedis eek she bere
Upon a lace, al of whyt threde,
On which that she hir bedes bede ;
But she ne boughte hem never a
 del, 7375
For they were geven her, I wot wel,
God wot, of a ful holy frere,
That seide he was hir fader dere,
To whom she hadde ofter went
Than any frere of his covent. 7380
And he visyted hir also,
And many a sermoun seide hir to ;
He nolde lette, for man on lyve,
That he ne wolde hir ofte shryve.
And with so gret devocion 7385
They maden her confession,
That they had ofte, for the nones,
Two hedes in one hood at ones.

Of fair shape I devyse her thee,
But pale of face somtyme was
 she ; 7390
That false traitouresse untrewe
Was lyk that salowe hors of hewe,
That in the Apocalips is shewed,
That signifyeth tho folk beshrewed,
That been al ful of trecherye, 7395
And pale, thurgh hypocrisye ;
For on that hors no colour is,
But only deed and pale, y-wis.
Of suche a colour enlangoured
Was Abstinence, y-wis, co-
 loured ; 7400
Of her estat she her repented,
As her visage represented.

She had a burdoun al of Thefte,
That Gyle had yeve her of his yefte ;
And a scrippe of Fainte Dis-
 tresse, 7405
That ful was of elengenesse,
And forth she walked sobrely :
And False-Semblant saynt, *ie vous
 die*,
[Had], as it were for such mistere,
Don on the cope of a frere, 7410
With chere simple, and ful pitous ;
His looking was not disdeinous,
Ne proud, but meke and ful pesible.
About his nekke he bar a bible,
And squierly forth gan he gon ; 7415
And, for to reste his limmes upon,
He had of Treson a potente ;
As he were feble, his way he wente.
But in his sleve he gan to thringe
A rasour sharp, and wel bytinge,
That was forged in a forge, 7421
Which that men clepen Coupe-
 gorge.

So longe forth hir way they nomen,
Til they to Wicked-Tonge comen,
That at his gate was sitting, 7425
And saw folk in the way passing.
The pilgrimes saw he faste by,
That beren hem ful mekely,
And humblely they with him mette.
Dame Abstinence first him
 grette, 7430
And sith him False-Semblant
 salued,
And he hem ; but he not remued,
For he ne dredde hem not a-del.
For when he saw hir faces wel,

7368. G. gracche ; Th. gratche. G. bygynne ; Th. bygyne. 7371. Th. psaltere ; G. sawter. 7380. G. ony. 7385-7576. *From* Th. ; *lost in* G. 7386. Th. made. 7389. Th. shappe ; deuysed. 7394. tho] Th. to. 7409. Had] Th. And. 7429. Th. humbly. 7432. Th. remeued.

Alway in herte him thoughte so, 7435
He shulde knowe hem bothe two;
For wel he knew Dame Abstinaunce
But he ne knew not Constreynaunce.
He knew nat that she was con-
  strayned,
Ne of her theves lyfe feyned, 7440
But wende she com of wil al free;
But she com in another degree;
And if of good wil she began,
That wil was failed her [as] than.
  And Fals-Semblant had he seyn
    als, 7445
But he knew nat that he was fals.
Yet fals was he, but his falsnesse
Ne coude he not espye, nor gesse;
For semblant was so slye wrought,
That falsnesse he ne espyed
  nought. 7450
But haddest thou knowen him
  beforn,
Thou woldest on a boke have
  sworn,
Whan thou him saugh in thilke aray
That he, that whylom was so gay,
And of the daunce Ioly Robin, 7455
Was tho become a Iacobin.
But sothely, what so men him
  calle,
Freres Prechours been good men
  alle;
Hir order wickedly they beren,
Suche minstrelles if [that] they
  weren. 7460
So been Augustins and Cordileres,
And Carmes, and eek Sakked
  Freres,
And alle freres, shodde and bare,
(Though some of hem ben grete
  and square)

Ful holy men, as I hem deme; 7465
Everich of hem wolde good man
  seme.
But shalt thou never of apparence
Seen conclude good consequence
In none argument, y-wis,
If existence al failed is. 7470
For men may finde alway sophyme
The consequence to envenyme,
Who-so that hath the subteltee
The double sentence for to see.
  Whan the pilgrymes commen
    were 7475
To Wicked-Tonge, that dwelled
  there,
Hir harneis nigh hem was algate;
By Wicked-Tonge adoun they sate,
That bad hem ner him for to come,
And of tydinges telle him some, 7480
And sayde hem:—'What cas
  maketh yow
To come into this place now?'
'Sir,' seyde Strained-Abstinaunce,
'We, for to drye our penaunce,
With hertes pitous and devoute, 7485
Are commen, as pilgrimes gon
  aboute;
Wel nigh on fote alway we go;
Ful dusty been our heles two;
And thus bothe we ben sent
Thurghout this world that is mis-
  went, 7490
To yeve ensample, and preche also.
To fisshen sinful men we go,
For other fisshing ne fisshe we.
And, sir, for that charitee,
As we be wont, herberwe we
  crave, 7495
Your lyf to amende; Crist it save!
And, so it shulde you nat displese,
We wolden, if it were your ese,

7435. Th. thought. 7444. *I supply* as. 7458. Th. Frere. 7460. *Supply* that. 7463. Th. al. 7464. Th. greet. 7471, 72. Th. sopheme, enueneme; F. *sophime, envenime*. 7473. Th. hath hadde the. 7488. Th. doughty (!); F. *poudreus*; *read* dusty. 7494. Th. herborowe.

A short sermoun unto you seyn.'
And Wikked-Tonge answerde
   ageyn,   7500
'The hous,' quod he, 'such as ye see,
Shal nat be warned you for me,
Sey what you list, and I wol here.'
'Graunt mercy, swete sire dere!'
Quod alderfirst Dame Absti-
   nence,   7505
And thus began she hir sentence :
Const. Abstinence. 'Sir, the first
   vertue, certeyn,
The gretest, and most sovereyn
That may be founde in any man,
For having, or for wit he can, 7510
That is, his tonge to refreyne ;
Therto ought every wight him peyne.
For it is better stille be
Than for to speken harm, pardee !
And he that herkeneth it
   gladly,   7515
He is no good man, sikerly.
And, sir, aboven al other sinne,
In that art thou most gilty inne.
Thou spake a Iape not long ago,
(And, sir, that was right yvel
   do)   7520
Of a yong man that here repaired,
And never yet this place apaired.
Thou seydest he awaited nothing
But to disceyve Fair-Welcoming.
Ye seyde nothing sooth of that ; 7525
But, sir, ye lye ; I tell you plat ;
He ne cometh no more, ne goth,
   pardee !
I trow ye shal him never see.
Fair-Welcoming in prison is,
That ofte hath pleyed with you, er
   this,   7530
The fairest games that he coude,
Withoute filthe, stille or loude ;

Now dar [he] nat [him]self solace.
Ye han also the man do chace,
That he dar neither come ne
   go.   7535
What meveth you to hate him so
But properly your wikked thought,
That many a fals lesing hath
   thought ?
That meveth your foole eloquence,
That iangleth ever in audience, 7540
And on the folk areyseth blame,
And doth hem dishonour and
   shame,
For thing that may have no preving,
But lyklinesse, and contriving.
For I dar seyn, that Reson
   demeth,   7545
It is not al sooth thing that semeth,
And it is sinne to controve
Thing that is [for] to reprove ;
This wot ye wel ; and, sir, there-
   fore
Ye arn to blame [wel] the more. 7550
And, nathelesse, he rekketh lyte ;
He yeveth nat now thereof a myte ;
For if he thoughte harm, parfay,
He wolde come and gon al day ;
He coude him-selfe nat ab-
   stene.   7555
Now cometh he nat, and that is
   sene,
For he ne taketh of it no cure,
But-if it be through aventure,
And lasse than other folk, algate.
And thou here watchest at the
   gate,   7560
With spere in thyne arest alway ;
There muse, musard, al the day.
Thou wakest night and day for
   thought ;
Y-wis, thy traveyl is for nought.

7504. Th. sir.   7513. Th. styll.   7532. Th. styl.   7533. Th.
she nat herselfe.   7546. Th. sothe.   7548, 50. *I supply* for, wel.   7553. Th.
thought harme.   7560. Th. her.

And Ielousye, withouten faile, 7565
Shal never quyte thee thy travaile.
And scathe is, that Fair-Welcom-
   ing,
Withouten any trespassing,
Shal wrongfully in prison be,
Ther wepeth and languissheth
   he.   7570
And though thou never yet, y-wis,
Agiltest man no more but this,
(Take not a-greef) it were worthy
To putte thee out of this baily,
And afterward in prison lye, 7575
And fettre thee til that thou dye;
For thou shalt for this sinne dwelle
Right in the devils ers of helle,
But-if that thou repente thee.'
   'Ma fay, thou lyest falsly!' quod
      he.   7580
'What? welcome with mischaunce
   now!
Have I therfore herbered you
To seye me shame, and eek reprove?
With sory happe, to your bihove,
Am I to-day your herbergere! 7585
Go, herber you elleswhere than
   here,
That han a lyer called me!
Two tregetours art thou and he,
That in myn hous do me this
   shame,
And for my soth-sawe ye me
   blame.   7590
Is this the sermoun that ye make?
To alle the develles I me take,
Or elles, god, thou me confounde!
But er men diden this castel
   founde,
It passeth not ten dayes or
   twelve,   7595
But it was told right to my-selve,

And as they seide, right so tolde I,
He kiste the Rose privily!
Thus seide I now, and have seid
   yore;
I not wher he dide any more. 7600
Why shulde men sey me such a
   thing,
If it hadde been gabbing?
Right so seide I, and wol seye yit;
I trowe, I lyed not of it;
And with my bemes I wol
   blowe   7605
To alle neighboris a-rowe,
How he hath bothe comen and gon.'
   Tho spak Fals-Semblant right
      anon,
'Al is not gospel, out of doute,
That men seyn in the toune a-
   boute;   7610
Ley no deef ere to my speking;
I swere yow, sir, it is gabbing!
I trowe ye wot wel certeynly,
That no man loveth him tenderly
That seith him harm, if he wot
   it,   7615
Al be he never so pore of wit.
And sooth is also sikerly,
(This knowe ye, sir, as wel as I),
That lovers gladly wol visyten
The places ther hir loves haby-
   ten.   7620
This man you loveth and eek
   honoureth;
This man to serve you laboureth;
And clepeth you his freend so dere,
And this man maketh you good
   chere,
And every-wher that [he] you
   meteth,   7625
He you saleweth, and he you gret-
   eth,

7568. Th. Without.   7577. G. *begins again.*   7582. Th. herbered; G. herberd.   7585. *Both* herbegere.   7590. *Both* sothe. Th. sawe; G. saugh.   7600. *Both* where. G. ony.   7625. *I supply* he.   7626. G. saloweth.

He preseth not so ofte, that ye
Ought of his come encombred be;
Ther presen other folk on yow
Ful ofter than [that] he doth
    now.   7630
And if his herte him streyned so
Unto the Rose for to go,
Ye shulde him seen so ofte nede,
That ye shulde take him with the
    dede.
He coude his coming not for-
    bere,   7635
Though ye him thrilled with a
    spere;
It nere not thanne as it is now.
But trusteth wel, I swere it yow,
That it is clene out of his thought.
Sir, certes, he ne thenketh it
    nought;   7640
No more ne doth Fair-Welcoming,
That sore abyeth al this thing.
And if they were of oon assent,
Ful sone were the Rose hent;
The maugre youres wolde be. 7645
And sir, of o thing herkeneth me:—
Sith ye this man, that loveth
    yow,
Han seid such harm and shame
    now,
Witeth wel, if he gessed it,
Ye may wel demen in your
    wit,   7650
He nolde no-thing love you so,
Ne callen you his freend also,
But night and day he [wolde]
    wake,
The castel to destroye and take,
If it were sooth as ye devyse; 7655
Or som man in som maner wyse
Might it warne him everydel,
Or by him-self perceyven wel;

For sith he might not come and
    gon
As he was whylom wont to
    don,   7660
He might it sone wite and see;
But now al other-wyse [doth] he.
Than have [ye], sir, al-outerly
Deserved helle, and Iolyly
The deth of helle douteles, 7665
That thrallen folk so gilteles.'
    Fals-Semblant proveth so this
    thing
That he can noon answering,
And seeth alwey such apparaunce,
That nygh he fel in repent-
    aunce,   7670
And seide him:—'Sir, it may wel
    be.
Semblant, a good man semen ye;
And, Abstinence, ful wyse ye seme;
Of o talent you bothe I deme.
What counceil wole ye to me
    yeven?'   7675
    F. Sem. 'Right here anoon thou
    shalt be shriven,
And sey thy sinne withoute more;
Of this shalt thou repente sore;
For I am preest, and have poustee
To shryve folk of most dignitee 7680
That been, as wyde as world may
    dure.
Of al this world I have the cure,
And that had never yit persoun,
No vicarie of no maner toun.
And, god wot, I have of thee   7685
A thousand tymes more pitee
Than hath thy preest parochial,
Though he thy freend be special.
I have avauntage, in o wyse,
That your prelates ben not so
    wyse   7690

7628. Th. comynge.   7630. *Supply* that.   7637. G. I ner*er* (!).   7653. G. wole; Th. wol; *read* wolde.   7662. doth] F. *fait*; *both* wot.   7663. Th. we (*for* ye); G. *om.*   7666. *Both* giltles.   7678. *Both* repent.   7686. Th. tymes; G. tyme.

THE ROMAUNT OF THE ROSE.

Ne half so lettred as am I.
I am licenced boldely
In divinitee to rede,
And to confessen, out of drede.
If ye wol you now confesse,   7695

And leve your sinnes more and
  lesse,
Without abood, knele doun anon,
And you shal have absolucion.'   7698

Explicit.

7693. *So* Th. (*but with* for to *for* to); G. To reden in diuinite.   7694. G. And longe haue red (*wrongly*); *here* G. *abruptly ends*.   7694-8. *From* Th.   7697. Th. abode.   COLOPHON. G. Explicit, *following* And longe haue red (*see note to* 7694); Th. Finis. Here endeth the Romaunt of the Rose.

THE MINOR POEMS.

I. AN A. B. C.

Incipit carmen secundum ordinem literarum Alphabeti.

A<small>LMIGHTY</small> and al merciable quene,
To whom that al this world fleeth for socour,
To have relees of sinne, sorwe and tene,
Glorious virgine, of alle floures flour,
To thee I flee, confounded in errour!   5
Help and releve, thou mighty debonaire,
Have mercy on my perilous langour!
Venquisshed me hath my cruel adversaire.

A toy du monde le refui,
Vierge glorieuse, m'en fui
Tout confus, ne puis miex faire;
A toy me tien, a toy m'apuy.
Relieve moy, abatu suy:
Vaincu m'a mon aversaire.

Puis qu'en toy ont tous repaire
Bien me doy vers toy retraire
Avant que j'aie plus d'annuy.
N'est pas luite necessaire   10
A moy, se tu, debonnayre,
Ne me sequeurs comme a autrui.

The MSS. *used to form this text are*: C. = MS. Ff. 5. 30 in the Camb. Univ. Library; Jo. = MS. G. 21, in St. John's College, Cambridge; Gl. = Glasgow MS. Q. 2. 25; L. = MS. Laud 740, in the Bodleian Library; Gg. = MS. Gg. 4. 27 in the Camb. Univ. Library; F. = MS. Fairfax 16, in the Bodleian Library; B = MS. Bodley 638; Sion = Sion Coll. MS. *The text closely follows the first of these; and all variations from it are recorded (except sometimes* i *for* y, *and* y *for* i).

1. C. Almihty; queene.   3. L. B. sorwe; F. Jo. sorowe; *the rest insert* of *before* sorwe.   4. C. Gloriowse.   6. C. iciecue; mihti.   8. Jo. Venquist; Gg. Venquyst. *Read* m'hath. C. cruelle.

262 THE MINOR POEMS.

Bountee so fix hath in thyn herte his tente,
That wel I wot thou wolt my socour be,   10
Thou canst not warne him that, with good entente,
Axeth thyn help. Thyn herte is ay so free,
Thou art largesse of pleyn felicitee,
Haven of refut, of quiete and of reste.
Lo, how that theves seven chasen me!   15
Help, lady bright, er that my ship to-breste!

Comfort is noon, but in yow, lady dere,
For lo, my sinne and my confusioun,
Which oughten not in thy presence appere,
Han take on me a grevous accioun   20
Of verrey right and desperacioun;
And, as by right, they mighten wel sustene
That I were worthy my dampnacioun,
Nere mercy of you, blisful hevene quene.

Doute is ther noon, thou queen of misericorde, 25
That thou nart cause of grace and mercy here;
God vouched sauf thurgh thee with us tacorde.
For certes, Cristes blisful moder dere,

Bien voy que par toy confortés
Sera mes cuers desconfortés,
Quer tu es de salu porte.
Se je me suis mal tresportez
Par .vij. larrons, pechiés mortez,
Et erre par voie torte,
Esperance me conforte
Qui à toy hui me raporte   20
A ce que soie deportez.
Ma povre arme je t'aporte :
Sauve la : ne vaut que morte ;
En li sont tous biens avortez.

Contre moy font une accion
Ma vergoigne et confusion,

Que devant toy ne doy venir
Pour ma très grant transgression.
Rayson et desperacion
Contre moy veulent maintenir ;   30
Mès pour ce que veil plait fenir,
Devant toy les fès convenir
En faisant replicacion.
C'est que je di appartenir
A toy du tout et convenir
Pitié et miseracion.

Dame es de misericorde
Par qui Diex bien se recorde
A sa gent estre racordé.
Par toy vint pes et concorde,   40

---

10. C. bee.   11. F. B. werne.   12. C. helpe.   14. C. Hauene ; refute.
15. C. Loo ; theeves sevene ; mee.   16. C. briht.   17. C. ladi deere.   18.
C. loo.   19. C. ouhten ; thi ; appeere.   20. C. greevous.   21. C. riht.   22.
C. riht þei mihten ; sustene.   23. C. wurthi.   24. C. queene.   25. C. Dowte.
26. C. merci heere.   27. C. Gl. Gg. saf ; Jo. saff ; L. F. saufe ; B. sauf. C. thoruh ;
L. F. þurgh. Gl. F. B. tacorde ; C. L. to accorde.   28. C. crystes ; mooder deere.

I. AN A. B. C.

Were now the bowe bent in swich manere,
As it was first, of Iustice and of yre, 30
The rightful God nolde of no mercy here;
But thurgh thee han we grace, as we desyre.

Ever hath myn hope of refut been in thee,
For heer-biforn ful ofte, in many a wyse,
Hast thou to misericorde receyved me. 35
But mercy, lady, at the grete assyse,
Whan we shul come bifore the hye Iustyse!
So litel fruit shal thanne in me be founde,
That, but thou er that day me wel chastyse,
Of verrey right my werk me wol confounde. 40

Fleeing, I flee for socour to thy tente
Me for to hyde from tempest ful of drede,
Biseching you that ye you not absente,
Though I be wikke. O help yit at this nede!

Et fu pour oster discorde
L'arc de justice descordé;
Et pour ce me sui acordé
Toi mercier et concordé,
Pour ce que ostas la corde;
Quar, ainsi com j'ay recordé,
S'encore fust l'arc encordé
Comparé l'eust ma vie orde.

En toy ay m'esperance eü
Quant a merci m'as receü 50
Autre foys en mainte guise,
Du bien qui ou ciel fu creü
As ravivé et repeü

M'ame qui estoit occise.
Las! mès quant la grant assise
Sera, se n'y es assise
Pour moy mal y seray veü.
De bien n'ay nulle reprise.
Las m'en clain quant bien m'avise,
Souvent en doy dire heü! 60

Fuiant m'en viens a ta tente
Moy mucier pour la tormente
Qui ou monde me tempeste.
Pour mon pechié ne t'absente,
A moy garder met t'entente,
A mon besoing soiez preste.

---

29. C. maneere. 31. C. rihtful; heere. 32. C. thoruh; Jo. L. F. B. thurgh. 33. C. Euere. C. refuit; Gl. refuyt; Gg. refut; *rest* refute. 35. C. resceyued. 36. C. merci ladi. 37. C. shule. 39. wel *is supplied from the* Sion MS.; *nearly all the copies give this line corruptly; see note.* 40. C. riht; wole. 41. C. Fleeinge; thi. 42. C. tempeste; dreede. 43. C. Biseeching yow. 44. C. Thouh; neede.

THE MINOR POEMS.

Al have I been a beste in wille and dede, 45
Yit, lady, thou me clothe with thy grace.
Thyn enemy and myn—lady, tak hede,
Un-to my deth in poynt is me to chace.

Glorious mayde and moder, which that never
Were bitter, neither in erthe nor in see, 50
But ful of swetnesse and of mercy ever,
Help that my fader be not wroth with me!
Spek thou, for I ne dar not him y-see.
So have I doon in erthe, allas ther-whyle!
That certes, but-if thou my socour be, 55
To stink eterne he wol my gost exyle.

He vouched sauf, tel him, as was his wille,
Bicome a man, to have our alliaunce,
And with his precious blood he wroot the bille
Up-on the crois, as general acquitaunce, 60
To every penitent in ful creaunce ;
And therfor, lady bright, thou for us praye.
Than shalt thou bothe stinte al his grevaunce,
And make our foo to failen of his praye.

Se lonc temps j'ay esté beste
A ce, Vierge, je m'arreste
Que de ta grace me sente.
Si te fais aussi requeste 70
Que ta pitié nu me veste,
Car je n'ay nulle autre rente.

Glorieuse vierge mere
Qui a nul onques amere
Ne fus en terre ne en mer,
Ta douceur ores m'apere
Et ne sueffres que mon pere
De devant li me jecte puer.
Se devant li tout vuit j'apper,
Et par moy ne puis eschapper 80
Que ma faute ne compere.

Tu devant li pour moy te per
En li moustrant que, s'a li per
Ne sui, si est il mon frere.

Homme voult par sa plaisance
Devenir, pour aliance
Avoir a humain lignage.
Avec li crut dès enfance
Pitié dont j'ai esperance
Avoir eu en mon usage. 90
Elle fu mise a forage
Quant au cuer lui vint mesage
Du cruel fer de la lance.
Ne puet estre, se sui sage,
Que je n'en aie avantage,
Se tu veus et abondance.

---

45. C. ben. Jo. wille; C. wil. 46. C. thi. 47. C. Thin ; ladi ; heede.
49. C. Gloriows; mooder; neuere. 50. C. eerthe. 51. C. euere. 54.
C. eerthe. 55. C. bee. 56. C. wole. 57. C. saaf; F. B. sauf; L.
saufe; Jo. saffe; Gl. Gg. saf. 58. C. Bicomen; oure. 59. C. wrot. 61. C.
criaunce; Gg. cryaunce; *rest* creaunce. 62. C. ladi briht. 63. C. Thanne.

I. AN A. B. C. 265

I wot it wel, thou wolt ben our socour, 65
Thou art so ful of bountee, in certeyn.
For, whan a soule falleth in errour,
Thy pitee goth and haleth him ayeyn.
Than makest thou his pees with his sovereyn,
And bringest him out of the crooked strete. 70
Who-so thee loveth he shal not love in veyn,
That shal he finde, as he the lyf shal lete.

Kalenderes enlumined ben they
That in this world ben lighted with thy name,
And who-so goth to you the righte wey, 75
Him thar not drede in soule to be lame.
Now, queen of comfort, sith thou art that same
To whom I seche for my medicyne,
Lat not my foo no more my wounde entame,
Myn hele in-to thyn hand al I resigne. 80

Lady, thy sorwe can I not portreye
Under the cros, ne his grevous penaunce.
But, for your bothes peynes, I you preye,
Lat not our alder foo make his bobaunce,

Ie ne truis par nulle voie
Ou mon salut si bien voie
Com, après Dieu, en toy le voy;
Quar quant aucun se desvoie, 100
A ce que tost se ravoie,
De ta pitié li fais convoy.
Tu li fès lessier son desroy
Et li refaiz sa pais au roy,
Et remez en droite voie.
Moult est donc cil en bon arroy,
En bon atour, en bon conroy
Que ta grace si conroie.

Kalendier sont enluminé
Et autre livre enteriné 110
Quant ton non les enlumine.

A tout meschief ont resiné
Ceus qui se sont acheminé
A toy pour leur medicine.
A moy donc, virge, t'encline,
Car a toy je m'achemine
Pour estre bien mediciné;
Ne sueffre que de gaïnne
Isse justice devine
Par quoy je soye exterminé. 120

La douceur de toy pourtraire
Je ne puis, a qui retraire
Doit ton filz de ton sanc estrait;
Pour ce a toy m'ay volu traire
Afin que contre moy traire
Ne le sueuffres nul cruel trait.

64, 65. C. oure. 66. C. bowntee. 69. C. Thanne. 73. C. Kalendeeres enlumyned. 74. C. thi. 75. C. yow; rihte. 77. C. sithe. 78. C. seeche. 79. C. vntame; Sion, vntaame (*wrongly*); *rest* entame. 80. C. resyne; Gl. B. resigne. 81. C. kan. 82. C. greevous. 84. C. oure.

That he hath in his listes of mischaunce 85
Convict that ye bothe have bought so dere.
As I seide erst, thou ground of our substaunce,
Continue on us thy pitous eyen clere!

Moises, that saugh the bush with flaumes rede
Brenninge, of which ther never a stikke brende, 90
Was signe of thyn unwemmed maidenhede.
Thou art the bush on which ther gan descende
The Holy Gost, the which that Moises wende
Had ben a-fyr; and this was in figure.
Now lady, from the fyr thou us defende 95
Which that in helle eternally shal dure.

Noble princesse, that never haddest pere,
Certes, if any comfort in us be,
That cometh of thee, thou Cristes moder dere,
We han non other melodye or glee 100
Us to reioyse in our adversitee,
Ne advocat noon that wol and dar so preye
For us, and that for litel hyre as ye,
That helpen for an Ave-Marie or tweye.

Je recongnois bien mon mesfait
Et qu'au colier j'ai souvent trait
Dont l'en me devroit detraire;
Mez se tu veus tu as l'entrait 130
Par quoy tantost sera retrait
Le mehain qui m'est contraire.

Moyses vit en figure
Que tu, vierge nete et pure,
Jesu le filz Dieu conceüs :
Un bysson contre nature
Vit qui ardoit sans arsure.
C'es tu, n'en suis point deceüs,
Dex est li feus qu'en toy eüs;
Et tu, buisson des recreüz 140
Es, pour tremper leur ardure.

A ce veoir, vierge, veüs
Soie par toy et receüs,
Oste chaussement d'ordure.

Noble princesse du monde
Qui n'as ne per ne seconde
En royaume n'en enpire,
De toy vient, de toy redonde
Tout le bien qui nous abonde,
N'avons autre tirelire. 150
En toy tout povre homme espire
Et de toy son salu tire,
Et en toy seule se fonde.
Ne puet nul penser ne dire,
Nul pourtraire ne escrire
Ta bonté comme est parfonde.

---

85. C. hise lystes.   86. C. bouht.   87. C. oure.   88. C. thi; cleere.   89. C. sauh; F. B. saugh.   C. flawmes.   93. C. holigost.   94. C. a fyir.   95. C. fyir; Gl. fyr.   C. deufende (sic).   96. C. eternalli.   97. C. neuere; peere.   98. C. bee.   99. C. mooder deere.   100. C. noon ooþer.   101. C. oure.   102. C. wole.   103. C. yee.

1. AN A. B. C.

O verrey light of eyen that ben blinde, 105
O verrey lust of labour and distresse,
O tresorere of bountee to mankinde,
Thee whom God chees to moder for humblesse!
From his ancille he made thee maistresse
Of hevene and erthe, our bille up for to bede. 110
This world awaiteth ever on thy goodnesse,
For thou ne failest never wight at nede.

Purpos I have sum tyme for tenquere,
Wherfore and why the Holy Gost thee soughte,
Whan Gabrielles vois cam to thyn ere. 115
He not to werre us swich a wonder wroughte,
But for to save us that he sithen boughte.
Than nedeth us no wepen us for to save,
But only ther we did not, as us oughte,
Do penitence, and mercy axe and have. 120

Queen of comfort, yit whan I me bithinke
That I agilt have bothe, him and thee,
And that my soule is worthy for to sinke,
Allas, I, caitif, whider may I flee?

O Lumiere des non voians
Et vrai repos des recreans
Et de tout bien tresoriere,
A toy sont toutez gens beans 160
Qui en la foy sont bien creans
Et en toy ont foy entiere;
A nul onques ne fus fiere,
Ains toy deïs chamberiere
Quant en toy vint li grans geans.
Or es de Dieu chanceliere
Et de graces aumosniere
Et confort a tous recreans.

Pris m'est volenté d'enquerre
Pour savoir que Diex vint querre 170
Quant en toy se vint enserrer;
En toy devint vers de terre;
Ne cuit pas que fust pour guerre
Ne pour moy jus aterrer.
Vierge, se ne me sens errer,
D'armes ne me faut point ferrer
Fors sans plus de li requerre.
Quant pour moy se vint enterrer,
Se il ne se veut desterrer
Encor puis s'amour acquerre. 180

Quant pourpensé après me sui
Qu'ay offendu et toy et lui,
Et qu'a mal est m'ame duite,
Que, fors pechié, en moi n'estui,
Et que mal hyer et pis m'est hui,
Tost après si me ranvite,

---

107. C. tresoreere. 108. F. chees; C. ches. C. mooder. 109. C. the.
110. C. eerthe; oure; beede. 111. C. euere; thi. 112. C. neuere; neede.
113. Gg. F. B. tenquere; C. to enquere. 114. C. whi; holi; souhte. 115. C.
Sion, vn-to; *rest* to. 116. C. wunder wrouhte. 117. C. bouhte. 118.
C. Thanne needeth; wepene. 119. C. oonly. Jo. F. B. did; C. diden. C. ouhte.
120. C. Doo; merci. 123. C. wurthi.

Who shal un-to thy sone my mene be? 125
Who, but thy-self, that art of pitee welle?
Thou hast more reuthe on our adversitee
Than in this world mighte any tunge telle.

Redresse me, moder, and me chastyse,
For, certeynly, my fadres chastisinge 130
That dar I nought abyden in no wyse:
So hidous is his rightful rekeninge.
Moder, of whom our mercy gan to springe,
Beth ye my Iuge and eek my soules leche;
For ever in you is pitee haboundinge 135
To ech that wol of pitee you bisecche.

Soth is, that God ne graunteth no pitee
With-oute thee; for God, of his goodnesse,
Foryiveth noon, but it lyke un-to thee.
He hath thee maked vicaire and maistresse 140

Vierge douce, se pren fuite,
Se je fui a la poursuite,
Ou fuiray, qu'a mon refui?
S'a nul bien je ne m'affruite 190
Et mas sui avant que luite,
Plus grief encore en est l'anuy.

Reprens moy, mere, et chastie
Quar mon pere n'ose mie
Attendre a mon chastiement.
Son chastoy si fiert a hie;
Rien n'ataint que tout n'esmie
Quant il veut prendre vengement.

Mere, bien doi tel batement
Douter, quar en empirement 200
A tous jours esté ma vie.
A toy dont soit le jugement,
Car de pitié as l'oingnement,
Mès que merci l'en te prie.

Sans toy nul bien ne foysonne
Et sans toy Diex riens ne donne,
Quar de tout t'a fet maistresse.
Quant tu veus trestout pardonne;
Et par toy est mise bonne
A justice la mairesse; 210

---

125. C. thi; bee. 126. C. thi-. 128. C. miht. 129. C. mooder. 130. F. Fadres; B. fadrys; C. faderes; Jo. fader. 131. C. nouht. 132. Gg. F. B. is his; *rest* it is. C. rihful (*sic*). 133. C. Mooder; merci. 135. C. euere. 136. C. eche; wole; bisecche. 137. C. granteth; F. graunteth. 140. C. vicair; Gg. F. vicaire; Gl. B. Sion, vicayre.

I. AN A. B. C.

Of al the world, and eek goverueresse
Of hevene, and he represseth his Iustyse
After thy wille, and therefore in witnesse
He hath thee crouned in so ryal wyse.

Temple devout, ther god hath his woninge. 145
Fro which these misbileved pryved been,
To you my soule penitent I bringe.
Receyve me! I can no ferther fleen!
With thornes venimous, O hevene queen,
For which the erthe acursed was ful yore, 150
I am so wounded, as ye may wel seen,
That I am lost almost;—it smert so sore.

Virgine, that art so noble of apparaile,
And ledest us in-to the hye tour
Of Paradys, thou me wisse and counsaile, 155
How I may have thy grace and thy socour;
Al have I been in filthe and in errour.
Lady, un-to that court thou me aiourne
That cleped is thy bench, O fresshe flour!
Ther-as that mercy ever shal soiourne. 160

N'est royne ne princesse
Pour qui nul ainsi se cesse
Et de droit se dessaisonne.
Du monde es gouverneresse,
Et du ciel ordeneresse ;
Sans reson n'as pas couronne.

Temple saint ou Dieu habite
Dont privé sont li herite
Et a tous jours desherité,
A toy vieng, de toy me herite, 220
Reçoif moy par ta merite
Quar de toy n'ay point hesité.
Et se je me sui herité
Des espines d'iniquité
Pour quoy terre fu maudite,

Las m'en clain en verité,
Car a ce fait m'a excité
L'ame qui n'en est pas quite.

Vierge de noble et haut atour,
Qui au chastel et a la tour 230
De paradis nous atournes,
Atourne moy ens et entour
De tel atour que au retour
De ta grace me retournes,
Se vil sui, si me raournes.
A toy vieng, ne te destournes,
Quer au besoing es mon destour.
Sequeur moy, point ne sejournes,
Ou tu a la court m'ajournes,
Ou ta pitié fait son sejour. 240

---

141. C. gouernowresse; Gl. Gg. gouerneresse. 143. C. thi wil. 144. L. crowned; Gg. crouwnyd; C. Jo. F. corowned. C. rial. 146. C. misbileeued. Jo. L. pryued; *rest* depriued. 148. C. Resceyve; ferþere. 149. C. venymous. 150. C. eerthe. 151. C. (*alone*) om. so. 156. C. thi (*twice*). 157. Gg. Al; B. C. All. C. ben. 158. C. Ladi. 159. Sion MS. fresshe; Gg. frosche (*sic*); *the rest wrongly omit the final* e. 160. C. merci; euere.

270   THE MINOR POEMS.

Xristus, thy sone, that in this world alighte,
Up-on the cros to suffre his passioun,
And eek, that Longius his herte pighte,
And made his herte blood to renne adoun ;
And al was this for my salvacioun ;   165
And I to him am fals and eek unkinde,
And yit he wol not my dampnacioun—
This thanke I you, socour of al mankinde.

Ysaac was figure of his deeth, certeyn,
That so fer-forth his fader wolde obeye   170
That him ne roughte no-thing to be slayn;
Right so thy sone list, as a lamb, to deye.
Now lady, ful of mercy, I you preye,
Sith he his mercy mesured so large,
Be ye not skant ; for alle we singe and seye   175
That ye ben from vengeaunce ay our targe.

Zacharie you clepeth the open welle
To wasshe sinful soule out of his gilt.
Therfore this lessoun oughte I wel to telle
That, nere thy tender herte, we weren spilt.   180

Xristus, ton filz, qui descendi
En terre et en la crois pendi,
Ot pour moy le costé fendu.
Sa grant rigour il destendi
Quant pour moy l'esperit rendi,
Son corps pendant et estendu ;
Pour moy son sanc fu espandu.
Se ceci j'ai bien entendu
A mon salut bien entendi,
Et pour ce, se l'ay offendu   250
Et il ne le m'a pas rendu,
Merci t'en rens, graces l'en di.

Ysaac le prefigura
Qui de sa mort rien ne cura
En obeïsant au pere.

Comme .j. aignel tout endura ;
En endurant tout espura
Par crueuse mort amere.
O très douce vierge mere,
Par ce fait fai que se pere   260
Par plour l'ame qui cuer dura ;
Fai que grace si m'apere ;
Et n'en soiez pas avere
Quar largement la mesura.

Zacharie de mon somme
Me exite, et si me somme
D'en toy ma merci atendre ;
Fontaine patent te nomme
Pour laver pecheür homme :
C'est leçon bonne a aprendre.   270

---

161. C. Xp̅c̅ (= Gk. χρς).   163. *All the MSS.* insert suffred *after* eek, *caught from the line above*; *see* note.   167. C. wole.   171. C. rouhte.   172. C. Riht soo thi. C. lust; *rest* list, liste.   173. C. ladi; merci; yow.   174. C. Sithe; merci.   177. C. yow; opene.   179. C. ouht.   180. C. thi.

I. AN A. B. C.

Now lady brighte, sith thou canst and wilt
Ben to the seed of Adam merciable,
So bring us to that palais that is bilt
To penitents that ben to mercy able. Amen. 184

Explicit carmen.

Se tu donc as le cuer tendre	Moy laver veillez entendre,
Et m'offense n'est pas mendre	Moy garder et moy deffendre,
De cil qui menga la pomme,	Que justice ne m'asomme.

---

181. C. ladi. Gg. bryȝt; *which the rest omit.* C. Gg. sithe; F. B. sith. Harl. 2251 *supplies* bothe *after* thou.   183. Sion MS. *alone supplies* So; Jo. *supplies* And. MS. Harl. 2251 *has* un-to; *rest* to.   184. Gl. penytentz; C. penitentes, Jo. Penitence (*for* penitents). C. merci.

II. THE COMPLEYNTE UNTO PITE.

PITE, that I have sought so yore ago,
With herte sore, and ful of besy peyne,
That in this world was never wight so wo
With-oute dethe; and, if I shal not feyne,
My purpos was, to Pite to compleyne 5
Upon the crueltee and tirannye
Of Love, that for my trouthe doth me dye.

And when that I, by lengthe of certeyn yeres,
Had ever in oon a tyme sought to speke,
To Pite ran I, al bespreynt with teres, 10
To preyen hir on Crueltee me awreke.
But, er I might with any worde out-breke,
Or tellen any of my peynes smerte,
I fond hir deed, and buried in an herte.

Adoun I fel, when that I saugh the herse, 15
Deed as a stoon, whyl that the swogh me laste;
But up I roos, with colour ful diverse,
And pitously on hir myn yën caste,
And ner the corps I gan to presen faste,
And for the soule I shoop me for to preye; 20
I nas but lorn; ther nas no more to seye.

The MSS. *are*: Tn. (Tanner 346); F. (Fairfax 16); B. (Bodley 638); Sh. (Shirley's MS., Harl. 78); Ff. (Ff. 1. 6, in Camb. Univ. Library); T., *here used for* Trin. (Trin. Coll. Camb. R. 3. 19); *also* Ha. (Harl. 7578). *I follow* F. *mainly, noting all variations of importance.*
 TITLE; *in* B. 1. F. agoo. 2. F. hert. 3. F. worlde; woo. 5. F. purpose. 8. F. be; B. Sh. T. by. F. certeyne. 9. Sh. Ha. a tyme sought; *rest* sought a tyme (*badly*). 10. F. bespreynte. 11. F. prayen. Sh. Ha. wreke; *rest* awreke. 14. F. fonde; dede. 15. F. Adovne. Ha. *alone supplies* that. 16. F. Dede; stone; while. T. (*and* Longleat) a; *rest om.* 17. F. roose; coloure. 18. F. petously; B. pitously. B. yen; F. eyen; *after which all but* Sh. *and* Ha. *insert* I. 19. Sh. Ha. to; *which the rest omit.* 20. Sh. shoope; *rest* shope. F. prey; Sh. preye. 21. *For* nas, *the* MSS. *wrongly have* was; *in both places.* F. lorne; sey.

II. THE COMPLEYNTE UNTO PITE. 273

Thus am I slayn, sith that Pite is deed;
Allas! that day! that ever hit shulde falle!
What maner man dar now holde up his heed?
To whom shal any sorwful herte calle? 25
Now Crueltee hath cast to sleen us alle,
In ydel hope, folk redelees of peyne—
Sith she is deed—to whom shul we compleyne?

But yet encreseth me this wonder newe,
That no wight woot that she is deed, but I; 30
So many men as in hir tyme hir knewe,
And yet she dyed not so sodeynly;
For I have sought hir ever ful besily
Sith first I hadde wit or mannes mynde;
But she was deed, er that I coude hir fynde. 35

Aboute hir herse ther stoden lustily,
Withouten any wo, as thoughte me,
Bountee parfit, wel armed and richely,
And fresshe Beautee, Lust, and Iolitee,
Assured Maner, Youthe, and Honestee, 40
Wisdom, Estaat, [and] Dreed, and Governaunce,
Confedred bothe by bonde and alliaunce.

A compleynt hadde I, writen, in myn hond,
For to have put to Pite as a bille,
But whan I al this companye ther fond, 45
That rather wolden al my cause spille
Than do me help, I held my pleynte stille;

---

22. F. slayne; dede.   23. Tn. shulde; F. shuld.   24. F. hold; hede.   25. *All but* Sh. *and* Ha. *ins.* now *bef.* any. F. eny.   26. F. caste. Sh. Ha. sleen; F. slee.   27. F. folke redelesse.   30. F. dede.   31. F. mony.   32. F. B. *omit* she; *the rest have it. Only* Sh. *and* T. *retain* so.   33. F. besely. *For ever,* Ten Brink *reads* ay.   34. *Only* Sh. *gives this line correctly; so* Ha. (*but with* any *for* mannes). F. Sith I hadde firste witte or mynde.   35. F. dede. Sh. Ha. that; *rest omit.*   36. F. there; lustely.   38. F. Bounte.   39. F. beaute; iolyte.   40. F. honeste.   41. F. Wisdome. F. B. estaat; *rest* estate; Ten Brink *rightly supplies* and *after* Estat (*sic*). F. drede.   43. Ha. hadde; Sh. hade; *rest* had. F. honde.   44. Sh. Ha. For; *rest omit.* F. pittee.   45. F. when. F. fonde.   46. Sh. wolden; F. wolde.   47. F. helpe; helde. Sh. Ha. compleynt; T. cause; *rest* pleynte *or* pleynt.

274   THE MINOR POEMS.

For to that folk, withouten any faile,
Withoute Pite may no bille availe.

Then leve I al thise virtues, sauf Pite,   50
Keping the corps, as ye have herd me seyn,
Confedred alle by bonde of Crueltee,
And been assented that I shal be sleyn.
And I have put my compleynt up ageyn;
For to my foos my bille I dar not shewe,   55
Theffect of which seith thus, in wordes fewe :—

The Bille.

¶ 'Humblest of herte, hyest of reverence,
Benigne flour, coroune of vertues alle,
Sheweth unto your rial excellence
Your servaunt, if I durste me so calle,   60
His mortal harm, in which he is y-falle,
And noght al only for his evel fare,
But for your renoun, as he shal declare.

'Hit stondeth thus: your contraire, Crueltee,
Allyed is ageynst your regalye   65
Under colour of womanly Beautee,
For men [ne] shuld not knowe hir tirannye,
With Bountee, Gentilesse, and Curtesye,
And hath depryved you now of your place
That hight "Beautee, apertenant to Grace."   70

---

48. F. folke. F. withoute; B. without; Ha. withouten.   49. F. pitee. Ha. may; Sh. ne may; *rest* ther may.   50. Sh. Ha. þanne leve I alle þees vertues sauf pitee; F. B. Then leve we al vertues saue oonly pite; Tn. Ff. T. Then leue all vertues saue onely pite.   51. F. Kepynge; herde.   52. F. Cofedered (*sic*). Sh. alle by bonde of (IIa. *om*. alle); F. Tn. B. Ff. by bonde and by; T. by bound and.   53. Sh. that; *rest* when.   54. F. complaynt.   55. F. Foes; Tn. foos.   57. F. highest.   59. F. youre rialle.   60. F. Youre; durst.   61. Sh. whiche he is Inne falle; *rest* in which he is falle : Thynne *has* yfal; *read* y-falle.   62. F. oonly.   64. *The* MSS. *insert* that *after* thus, *except* Sh. *and* Ha.   Sh. contraire; *rest* contrary.   65. Sh. ageynst; F. ayenst.   66. F. beaute.   67. *The* MSS. *omit* ne. F. shulde.   68. F. bounte.   69. Sh. nowe; *which the rest omit*.   70. Sh. heghte (*for* highte); Ha. hight; Tn. is hye; F. B. T. is hygh. F. beaute apertenent.   *The* MSS. (*except* Sh. *and* IIa.) *insert* your *after* to.

II. THE COMPLEYNTE UNTO PITE.

'For kyndly, by your heritage right,
Ye been annexed ever unto Bountee;
And verrayly ye oughte do your might
To helpe Trouthe in his adversitee.
Ye been also the coroune of Beautee;　　75
And certes, if ye wanten in thise tweyne,
The world is lore; ther nis no more to seyne.

¶ 'Eek what availeth Maner and Gentilesse
Withoute you, benigne creature?
Shal Crueltee be your governeresse?　　80
Allas! what herte may hit longe endure?
Wherfor, but ye the rather take cure
To breke that perilous alliaunce,
Ye sleen hem that ben in your obeisaunce.

'And further over, if ye suffre this,　　85
Your renoun is fordo than in a throwe;
Ther shal no man wite wel what Pite is.
Allas! that your renoun shuld be so lowe!
Ye be than fro your heritage y-throwe
By Crueltee, that occupieth your place;　　90
And we despeired, that seken to your grace.

'Have mercy on me, thou Herenus quene,
That you have sought so tenderly and yore;
Let som streem of your light on me be sene
That love and drede you, ay lenger the more.　　95
For, sothly for to seyne, I bere the sore,

---

71. F. kyndely; youre.　72. *Most* MSS. be; Ha. been; *read* been (*and in* l. 75).　73. F. verrely; youre.　75. F. beaute.　76. Tn. Ff. Ha. wante; *rest* want; *read* wanten. F. these tweyn.　77. F. worlde. *For* nis, *all have* is. F. seyn.　78. F. Eke.　79. F. yow.　82. F. Wherfore.　86. F. fordoo. Sh. than; *rest omit*.　87. F. wete well; *rest omit* well; Tn. wyte.　88. F. Tn. B. Ff. T. *insert* euer *after* that, *which* Sh. **rightly omits**. Sh. Ha. shoulde be; *rest* is falle.　89. Sh. thanne: *rest* also. F. youre.　90. F. youre.　91. Sh. sechen to; B. sekyn to; Tn. Ff. T. seken; F. speken to (*for* seken to).　92. Tn. F. B. Ff. herenus; T. herem*us*; Sh. vertuouse (!).　93. F. yow; tendirly.　94. B. som; F. som*m*e. F. streme. Sh. Ha. youre; *which the rest omit*.　95. Sh. ay; *rest* euer. Sh. Ha. *om.* the.　96. F. sothely. Sh. the hevy sore; Ha. the sore; *rest* so sore (*which gives no sense*).

And, though I be not cunning for to pleyne,
For goddes love, have mercy on my peyne!

¶ 'My peyne is this, that what so I desire
That have I not, ne no-thing lyk therto;   100
And ever set Desire myn herte on fire;
Eek on that other syde, wher-so I go,
What maner thing that may encrese wo
That have I redy, unsoght, everywhere;
Me [ne] lakketh but my deth, and than my bere.   105

'What nedeth to shewe parcel of my peyne?
Sith every wo that herte may bethinke
I suffre, and yet I dar not to you pleyne;
For wel I woot, al-though I wake or winke,
Ye rekke not whether I flete or sinke.   110
But natheles, my trouthe I shal sustene
Unto my deth, and that shal wel be sene.

'This is to seyne, I wol be youres ever;
Though ye me slee by Crueltee, your fo,
Algate my spirit shal never dissever   115
Fro your servyse, for any peyne or wo.
Sith ye be deed—allas! that hit is so!—
Thus for your deth I may wel wepe and pleyne
With herte sore and ful of besy peyne.'   119

Here endeth the exclamacion of the Deth of Pyte.

---

97. F. kunnynge.   98. F. goddis.   100. F. lyke.   101. F. Sh. setteth; Ha. set; *rest* settith; *see* note. F. hert.   102. F. Eke. F. sydes; *rest* side, syde. F. where so; goo.   103. Sh. Ha. wo; *rest insert* my *before* wo.   104. F. vnsoghte.   105. *All omit* ne; *see* note.   107. F. woo.   109. F. wote. Sh al-jaughe; *rest* though, thogh.   110. F. B. where; *rest* whether.   111. *All but* Sh. *and* Ha. *needlessly insert* yet *before* my.   114. F. soo; *rest* foo, fo.   115. F. spirite.   116. F. youre; eny.   117. B. yet (*sic*) be ded; F. Tn. Ff. T. ye be yet ded (*which will not scan*); Sh. Ha. *have a different line*—Now pitee þat I haue sought so yoore agoo.

III. THE BOOK OF THE DUCHESSE.

The Proem.

I HAVE gret wonder, by this lighte,
How that I live, for day ne nighte
I may nat slepe wel nigh noght;
I have so many an ydel thoght
Purely for defaute of slepe,   5
That, by my trouthe, I take kepe
Of no-thing, how hit cometh or goth,
Ne me nis no-thing leef nor loth.
Al is y-liche good to me—
Ioye or sorowe, wherso hit be—   10
For I have feling in no-thing,
But, as it were, a mased thing,
Alway in point to falle a-doun;
For [sory] imaginacioun
Is alway hoolly in my minde.   15
  And wel ye wite, agaynes kinde
Hit were to liven in this wyse;
For nature wolde nat suffyse
To noon erthely creature
Not longe tyme to endure   20
Withoute slepe, and been in sorwe;
And I ne may, ne night ne morwe,

The MSS. *are*: F. (Fairfax 16); Tn. (Tanner 346); B. (Bodley 638); *the fourth authority is* Th. (Thynne's edition of 1532). *I follow* F. *mainly, and note all but very trifling variations from it.* B. *usually agrees with* F.
  TITLE: *in* F. 1. Tn. gret; F. grete. Th. by; F. Tn. be.   5. Tn. Th. defaute; F. defaulte.   6. *All* take no kepe.   8. Tn. Th. lefe (*read* leef); F. leve.   9. Tn. Th. good; F. goode.   10. Tn. Ioye; F. Ioy.   11, 12. F. no thynge, thynge.   14. *All* sorwful (*badly*); *read* sory.   15. F. hooly. 16. F. woote; Th. B. wote; Tn. wotte; *read* wite.   19. *For* To *perhaps read* Unto. F. ertherly (*miswritten*).   21. *All* be.   22. Th. Tn. B. ne (*2nd time*); F. no.

Slepe; and thus melancolye,
And dreed I have for to dye,
Defaute of slepe, and hevinesse   25
Hath sleyn my spirit of quiknesse,
That I have lost al lustihede.
Suche fantasyes ben in myn hede
So I not what is best to do.
  But men mighte axe me, why so   30
I may not slepe, and what me is?
But natheles, who aske this
Leseth his asking trewely.
My-selven can not telle why
The sooth; but trewely, as I gesse,   35
I holdë hit be a siknesse
That I have suffred this eight yere,
And yet my bote is never the nere;
For ther is phisicien but oon,
That may me hele; but that is doon.   40
Passe we over until eft;
That wil not be, moot nede be left;
Our first matere is good to kepe.
  So whan I saw I might not slepe,
Til now late, this other night,   45
Upon my bedde I sat upright,
And bad oon reche me a book,
A romaunce, and he hit me took
To rede and dryve the night away;
For me thoghte it better play   50
Then playen either at chesse or tables.
  And in this boke were writen fables

---

23. *All* this. 24. *All* drede. 25. Th. Tn. Defaute; F. Defaulte. 26. Th. slayne; Tn. slain; F. *omits*. 27. F. loste. Tn. *omits* ll. 31-96; F. *has them in a later hand (the spelling of which I amend)*. 32. F. nathles whoe. 33. F. trewly. 34. F. tell. 35. Th. sothe; F. southe (!) F. trewly. 36. F. hold it; Th. holde it; *read* hold-ë hit. F. sicknes. 38. F. boote. 39. Th. F. For ther. (phisicien = fízishén). F. one. 40. F. heale; done. 41. F. vntill efte. 42. F. mote. Th. nede; F. nedes. F. lefte. 43. F. mater. 44. Th. So whan; F. Soe when. F. sawe. 45. Th. Tyl nowe late: F. Til now late; *but probably corrupt*. 46. F. sate. 47. F. bade one. F. booke. 48. F. it; Th. he it. F. toke. 50. F. thought; beter. 51. F. play; Ten Brink *reads* playen. 52. F. written.

III. THE BOOK OF THE DUCHESSE.

That clerkes hadde, in olde tyme,
And other poets, put in ryme
To rede, and for to be in minde 55
Whyl men loved the lawe of kinde.
This book ne spak but of such thinges,
Of quenes lyves, and of kinges,
And many othere thinges smale.
Amonge al this I fond a tale 60
That me thoughte a wonder thing.
 This was the tale: Ther was a king
That highte Seys, and hadde a wyf,
The beste that mighte bere lyf;
And this quene highte Alcyone. 65
So hit befel, therafter sone,
This king wolde wenden over see.
To tellen shortly, whan that he
Was in the see, thus in this wyse,
Soche a tempest gan to ryse 70
That brak hir mast, and made it falle,
And clefte hir ship, and dreinte hem alle,
That never was founden, as it telles,
Bord ne man, ne nothing elles.
Right thus this king Seys loste his lyf. 75
 Now for to speken of his wyf:—
This lady, that was left at home,
Hath wonder, that the king ne come
Hoom, for hit was a longe terme.
Anon her herte gan to erme; 80

---

53. F. had. 56. F. While. Th. of; F. in (*copied from line above*). 57. F. boke. Th. spake; F. speake (*read* spak). 58. F. kings. 59. Th. smale: F. smalle. 60. Th. al; F. all. F. fonde. 61. F. thought. 62. F. There. 63. F. hight. Th. Seys; F. Seyes. F. had. F. wife. 64. Th. beste; F. best. F. might beare lyfe. 65. F. hight. 66. F. Soe it befill thereafter. 67. F. woll; Th. wol. 70. *Perhaps read* gan aryse. 71. F. brake. (hir = *their*). F. maste; fal. 72. Th. her; F. ther (*see line above*). F. dreint; all. 73. Th. F. founde (*error for* founden). 74. F. Borde. 75. Th. Seys; F. Seyes. F. life. 76. Th. F. Now for to speke of Alcyone his wyfe; *read:* Now for to speken of his wyf. F. wife. 79. Th. F. Home; it. 80. Th. Anon; F. Anone. Th. F. began (*error for* gan). Th. F. yerne (*error for* erme); see note.

And for that hir thoughte evermo
Hit was not wel [he dwelte] so,
She longed so after the king
That certes, hit were a pitous thing
To telle hir hertely sorwful lyf   85
That hadde, alas! this noble wyf;
For him she loved alderbest.
Anon she sente bothe eest and west
To seke him, but they founde nought.
'Alas!' quoth she, 'that I was wrought!   90
And wher my lord, my love, be deed?
Certes, I nil never ete breed,
I make a-vowe to my god here,
But I mowe of my lorde here!'
Such sorwe this lady to her took   95
That trewely I, which made this book,
Had swich pite and swich rowthe
To rede hir sorwe, that, by my trowthe,
I ferde the worse al the morwe
After, to thenken on her sorwe.   100
So whan [she] coude here no word
That no man mighte fynde hir lord,
Ful oft she swouned, and seide 'alas!'
For sorwe ful nigh wood she was,
Ne she coude no reed but oon;   105
But doun on knees she sat anoon,
And weep, that pite was to here.
'A! mercy! swete lady dere!'
Quod she to Iuno, hir goddesse;
'Help me out of this distresse,   110

---

81. F. thought. 82. F. It; wele; thought soe. *Both* her thought so, *caught from l.* 81; *read* he dwelte (delayed). 83. F. soe. 84. F. it. 85. F. tell. Th. hertely; F. hartely. F. life. 86. Th. F. she had; *I omit* she, *and supply* alas *from l.* 87. 87. Th. *and* F. insert alas *after* him. 88. F. Anone; sent. 91. F. where. 92. Th. nyl; F. will. F. eate breede. 94. Th. lorde; F. Lord. 95. F. toke. 96. F. trewly; booke. 97. *The older hand recommences in* F. F. had; Tn. I Had. F. suche (*twice*). F. pittee. 100. F. And aftir; *but* Th. Tn. B. *omit* And. 101. *All* this lady (*for* she; *badly*). 102. F. myght; lorde. 103. F. ofte; sayed. 104. F. woode. 105. F. rede. 106. F. doune; sate. 107. *All* wepte (*read* weep). F. pittee. 109. Th. to; *which* F. Tn. *omit.* 110. F. Helpe; B. Help.

III. THE BOOK OF THE DUCHESSE.

And yeve me grace my lord to see
Sone, or wite wher-so he be,
Or how he fareth, or in what wyse,
And I shal make you sacrifyse,
And hoolly youres become I shal   115
With good wil, body, herte, and al;
And but thou wilt this, lady swete,
Send me grace to slepe, and mete
In my slepe som certeyn sweven,
Wher-through that I may knowen even   120
Whether my lord be quik or deed.'
With that word she heng doun the heed,
And fil a-swown as cold as ston;
Hir women caughte her up anon,
And broghten hir in bed al naked,   125
And she, forweped and forwaked,
Was wery, and thus the dede sleep
Fil on her, or she toke keep,
Through Iuno, that had herd hir bone,
That made hir [for] to slepe sone;   130
For as she prayde, so was don,
In dede; for Iuno, right anon,
Called thus her messagere
To do her erande, and he com nere.
Whan he was come, she bad him thus: 135
'Go bet,' quod Iuno, 'to Morpheus,
Thou knowest him wel, the god of sleep;
Now understond wel, and tak keep.
Sey thus on my halfe, that he
Go faste into the grete see,   140

---

112. F. Soone. Tn. B. wite; F. Th. wete.   114. F. yowe.   116. Th. Tn. B. good wyl; F. good wille (wil *is here a monosyllable*).   117. F. wilte.   118. Tn. Send; Th. F. Sende.   119. Th. som; F. som*m*e.   120. Th. through; F. thorgh. F. knowe.   121. F. lorde; quyke; ded.   122. F. worde; henge; hed.   123. Th. Tn. fel; F. felle (*see* l. 128). F. A swowne, Tn. a swowe (*for* a-swowen = a-swown); Th. in a swowne. F. colde; Tn. cold.   124. F. kaught; anoon.   127. Tn. dede; F. ded. *All* slepe.   128. F. tooke. *All* kepe.   129. Th. Through; F. Throgh. F. herde.   130. *I supply* for.   131. Th. Tn. prayde; F. prayede; *after which all insert* right (*but see next line*).   134. F. come.   137, 138. *All* slepe, kepe. F. vnderstonde; take.

And bid him that, on alle thing,
He take up Seys body the king,
That lyth ful pale and no-thing rody.
Bid him crepe into the body,
Aud do it goon to Alcyone   145
The quene, ther she lyth alone,
And shewe hir shortly, hit is no nay,
How hit was dreynt this other day;
And do the body speke so
Right as hit was wont to do,   150
The whyles that hit was on lyve.
Go now faste, and hy thee blyve!'
   This messager took leve and wente
Upon his wey, and never ne stente
Til he com to the derke valeye   155
That stant bytwene roches tweye,
Ther never yet grew corn ne gras,
Ne tree, ne nothing that ought was,
Beste, ne man, ne nothing elles,
Save ther were a fewe welles   160
Came renning fro the cliffes adoun,
That made a deedly sleping soun,
And ronnen doun right by a cave
That was under a rokke y-grave
Amid the valey, wonder depe.   165
Ther thise goddes laye and slepe,
Morpheus, and Eclympasteyre,
That was the god of slepes heyre,
That slepe and did non other werk.
   This cave was also as derk   170

---

141. Tn. B. all*e*; F. al.   142. Th. He; F. Tn. That he. F. kynge.   144. Tn. B. Bid; F. Bud.   145. Th. Alcyone; F. Tn. Alchione.   146. Th. alone; F. allone.   149. *After* speke *all insert* right (*see next line*).   150. *All* woned.   151. Tn. on; F. a.   152. F. hye the.   153. F. toke; went.   154. Th. he (*for* ne). F. stent.   155. Tn. com; F. come. F. valey.   156. Th. bytwene; F. betwex; Tn. betwix. F. twey.   157. F. corne.   158, 159. *All* noght (*for* nothing). F. oughte.   162. F. dedely; Th. deedly; Tn. dedli.   166. F. There these; lay.   167. Th. F. B. Eclympasteyre (*as in text*); Tn. Etlympasteyr*e* (*with* t *for* c).   168. Tn. heir*e*; F. eyre.   169, 170. F. werke, derke.

As helle pit over-al aboute;
They had good leyser for to route
To envye, who might slepe beste;
Some henge hir chin upon hir breste
And slepe upright, hir heed y-hed, 175
And some laye naked in hir bed,
And slepe whyles the dayes laste.
 This messager com flying faste,
And cryed, 'O ho! awak anon!'
Hit was for noght; ther herde him non. 180
'Awak!' quod he, 'who is, lyth there?'
And blew his horn right in hir ere,
And cryed 'awaketh!' wonder hyë.
This god of slepe, with his oon yë
Cast up, axed, 'who clepeth there?' 185
'Hit am I,' quod this messagere;
'Iuno bad thou shuldest goon '—
And tolde him what he shulde doon
As I have told yow here-tofore;
Hit is no need reherse hit more; 190
And wente his wey, whan he had sayd.
 Anon this god of slepe a-brayd
Out of his slepe, and gan to goon,
And did as he had bede him doon;
Took up the dreynte body sone, 195
And bar hit forth to Alcyone,
His wyf the quene, ther-as she lay,
Right even a quarter before day,
And stood right at hir beddes fete,
And called hir, right as she hete, 200

---

171. Tn. pit; F. pitte.   173. F. To envye; Tn. Th. vie.   175. Tn. slepte; F. slept; *see* 177.   Th. heed; F. hed.   B. Tn. I-hid; Th. yhed; F. yhedde. 176. *All* lay.   F. Tn. bedde.   177. F. slepe; Th. Tn. slepte.   178. F. com. Tn. flyyng; F. fleynge; Th. rennyng.   179. F. Tn. O how; Th. ho ho.   F. awake.   180. F. there.   181. F. Awake; lythe.   182. F. horne.   Tn. B. ere; F. heere.   184. Tn. oon; F. on.   F. ye; Th. eye; Tn. eiȝe.   185. Th. Tn. Cast; F. Caste.   *All ins.* and *after* up.   191. Th. wente; F. went. F. sayede; Tn. seide.   192. F. a-brayede; Tn. abraied.   195. F. Tooke; dreynt; *see* Cant. Ta. B. 69.   196. F. bare. Th. Alcione; F. Tn. Alchione. 197. F. wife.   199. Th. her; F. Tn. hys.   F. fete; *see* note.   200. *All* hete.

THE MINOR POEMS.

By name, and seyde, 'my swete wyf,
Awak! let be your sorwful lyf!
For in your sorwe ther lyth no reed;
For certes, swete, I nam but deed;
Ye shul me never on lyve y-see.   205
But good swete herte, [look] that ye
Bury my body, [at whiche] a tyde
Ye mowe hit finde the see besyde;
And far-wel, swete, my worldes blisse!
I praye god your sorwe lisse;   210
To litel whyl our blisse lasteth!'
   With that hir eyen up she casteth,
And saw noght; '[A]!' quod she, 'for sorwe!'
And deyed within the thridde morwe.
But what she sayde more in that swow   215
I may not telle yow as now,
Hit were to longe for to dwelle;
My first matere I wil yow telle,
Wherfor I have told this thing
Of Alcione and Seys the king.   220
   For thus moche dar I saye wel,
I had be dolven everydel,
And deed, right through defaute of slepe,
If I nad red and taken keep
Of this tale next before: 225
And I wol telle yow wherfore;
For I ne might, for bote ne bale,
Slepe, or I had red this tale
Of this dreynte Seys the king,
And of the goddes of sleping.   230

---

201. F. sayede; wyfe.   202. F. Awake; lyfe.   203. F. there; rede.
204. *I put* nam; *all have* am. F. dede.   206. *I supply* look, *for the sake of sense and metre; read*—But good swet' hert-ë, look that ye.   207. *All* for suche; *read* at whiche.   210. F. pray; youre.   211. F. while oure.   213. *All* allas (*for* A).   214. F. deyede; Tn. deid.   215. F. sayede. Tn. swow; Th. B. swowe; F. sorowe (!).   216. F. nowe.   219. Tn. told; F. tolde. F. thynge.   220. Th. Alcione; F. Tn. Alchione. F. kynge.   221. *All* say. Tn. wel; F. welle.   222. Tn. eueridel; F. euerydelle.   223. F. thorgh. Tn. defaute; F. defauite. *All* slepe.   224. Th. F. ne had (*read* nad); Tn. hade. Tn. red; F. redde. *All* take kepe.   226. F. *omits* I (*by mistake*).   228. F. redde.   229. F. kynge.   230. Th. goddes; F. Tn. goddis.

III. THE BOOK OF THE DUCHESSE.

Whan I had red this tale wel,
And over-loked hit everydel,
Me thoughte wonder if hit were so;
For I had never herd speke, or tho,
Of no goddes that coude make   235
Men [for] to slepe, ne for to wake;
For I ne knew never god but oon.
And in my game I sayde anoon—
And yet me list right evel to pleye—
'Rather then that I shulde deye   240
Through defaute of sleping thus,
I wolde yive thilke Morpheus,
Or his goddesse, dame Iuno,
Or som wight elles, I ne roghte who—
To make me slepe and have som reste—   245
I wil yive him the alder-beste
Yift that ever he abood his lyve,
And here on warde, right now, as blyve;
If he wol make me slepe a lyte,
Of downe of pure dowves whyte   250
I wil yive him a fether-bed,
Rayed with golde, and right wel cled
In fyn blak satin doutremere,
And many a pilow, and every bere
Of clothe of Reynes, to slepe softe;   255
Him thar not nede to turnen ofte.
And I wol yive him al that falles
To a chambre; and al his halles
I wol do peynte with pure golde,
And tapite hem ful many folde   260
Of oo sute; this shal he have,
If I wiste wher were his cave,

---

231. Tn. red; F. redde.   233. F. thoght.   234. Tn. herd; F. herde.
235. F. goddis.   236. *I supply the former* for.   237. I ne = I n'.   238.
F. sayede.   239. F. pley.   240. F. dey.   241. F. Thorgh defaulte.
Tn. sleping; F. slepynge.   244. Tn. sum; F. somme. F. ellis. F. roght;
Th. Tn. rought.   245. Tn. som; F. some.   247. F. Yifte. F. abode.
248. B. on warde; *rest* onwarde.   251. F. yif (*see* l. 246). Tn. fethirbed; F.
feder bedde.   252. Tn. cled; F. cledde.   253. Tn. fyn; F. fyne. Th.
doutremere; Tn. dou*tre*mere; F. de owter mere.   254. Tn. pilow; F. pelowe.
257, 8. F. fallys, hallys.

286 THE MINOR POEMS.

If he can make me slepe sone,
As did the goddesse Alcione.
And thus this ilke god, Morpheus,   265
May winne of me mo feës thus
Than ever he wan; and to Iuno,
That is his goddesse, I shal so do,
I trow that she shal holde her payd.'
  I hadde unneth that word y-sayd   270
Right thus as I have told hit yow,
That sodeynly, I niste how,
Swich a lust anoon me took
To slepe, that right upon my book
I fil aslepe, and therwith even   275
Me mette so inly swete a sweven,
So wonderful, that never yit
I trowe no man hadde the wit
To conne wel my sweven rede;
No, not Ioseph, withoute drede,   280
Of Egipte, he that redde so
The kinges meting Pharao,
No more than coude the leste of us;
Ne nat scarsly Macrobeus,
(He that wroot al thavisioun   285
That he mette, king Scipioun,
The noble man, the Affrican—
Swiche mervayles fortuned than)
I trowe, a rede my dremes even.
Lo, thus hit was, this was my sweven.   290

---

264. *All ins.* quene *after* goddesse. Th. Alcione; F. Tn. Alchione. 267. *All* wanne (!). 269. F. payede. 270. Tn. woord; F. worde. F. y-sayede. 271. Th. Tn. B. as; *which* F. *omits*. Tn. told; F. tolde. 273. Tn. lust; F. luste. F. tooke. 274. F. booke. 275. F. evene. 276. F. swevene. 277. Tn. ȝit; F. yitte. 278. Th. trowe; F. trow; Tn. trov. 281. Th. Tn. B. he; F. ho. F. red; Th. Tn. rad (*but read* redde *or* radde). 282. F. metynge. 283. B. leste; F. lest. 285. Tn. wrot; F. wrote. 286. F. kynge. 288. Th. Suche meruayles fortuned than; F. Tn. B. *omit this line*.

III. THE BOOK OF THE DUCHESSE.

The Dream.

> ME thoughte thus:—that hit was May,
> And in the dawning ther I lay,
> Me mette thus, in my bed al naked:—
> [I] loked forth, for I was waked
> With smale foules a gret hepe,   295
> That had affrayed me out of slepe
> Through noyse and swetnesse of hir song;
> And, as me mette, they sate among,
> Upon my chambre-roof withoute,
> Upon the tyles, al a-boute,   300
> And songen, everich in his wyse,
> The moste solempne servyse
> By note, that ever man, I trowe,
> Had herd; for som of hem song lowe,
> Som hye, and al of oon acorde.   305
> To telle shortly, at oo worde,
> Was never y-herd so swete a steven,
> But hit had be a thing of heven;—
> So mery a soun, so swete entunes,
> That certes, for the toune of Tewnes,   310
> I nolde but I had herd hem singe,
> For al my chambre gan to ringe
> Through singing of hir armonye.
> For instrument nor melodye
> Was nowher herd yet half so swete,   315
> Nor of acorde half so mete;
> For ther was noon of hem that feyned
> To singe, for ech of hem him peyned

---

291. F. thoght.   292. F. dawnynge. Th. there; *rest om.*   294. *All* And! (*for* I).   295. Tn. gret; F. grete.   296. *All insert* my *before* slepe; *it is not wanted.*   297. F. Thorgh; swettenesse; songe.   298. Th. as; F. Tn. B. al (*badly*). F. amonge.   299. F. roofe.   300. *All* ouer al; *but omit* ouer.   301. *All* songe, song.   304. F. herde. Tn. B. som; F. so*m*me. Tn. song; F. songe (*it can be singular*).   305. Tn. Som; F. Somme. F. high.   306. F. att.   307. F. harde; Tn. I-herd.   308. F. thynge.   309. F. soune. Th. Th. entunes; F. entewnes.   310. F. tewnes; Th. Tewnes; Tn. twnes.   311. F. herde.   313. F. Thorgh syngynge.   315. F. nowhere herde; halfe.   316. F. halfe.   318. Tn. ich; *rest* eche.

288   THE MINOR POEMS.

To finde out mery crafty notes;
They ne spared not hir throtes.   320
And, sooth to seyn, my chambre was
Ful wel depeynted, and with glas
Were al the windowes wel y-glased,
Ful clere, and nat an hole y-crased,
That to beholde hit was gret Ioye.   325
For hoolly al the storie of Troye
Was in the glasing y-wroght thus,
Of Ector and king Priamus,
Of Achilles and Lamedon,
Of Medea and of Iason,   330
Of Paris, Eleyne, and Lavyne.
And alle the walles with colours fyne
Were peynted, bothe text and glose,
[Of] al the Romaunce of the Rose.
My windowes weren shet echon,   335
And through the glas the sunne shon
Upon my bed with brighte bemes,
With many glade gilden stremes;
And eek the welken was so fair,
Blew, bright, clere was the air,   340
And ful atempre, for sothe, hit was;
For nother cold nor hoot hit nas,
Ne in al the welken was a cloude.
  And as I lay thus, wonder loude
Me thoughte I herde an hunte blowe   345
Tassaye his horn, and for to knowe

---

319. F. *wrongly inserts* of *after* out.   F. notys.   320. F. throtys.   321. F. soothe.   323. F. y-glasyd.   324. F. hoole y-crasyd.   326. Tn. hoolly; F. holy.   Tn. storie; F. story.   327. F. glasynge.   328. *All* and of king. 329. *All repeat* of king *before* Lamedon; *the words were caught from* l. 328. 330. *All insert* And eke *before* Of Medea.   331. *All* and of (*for* and). 332. Tn. colours; F. colouris.   334. *All* And; *read* Of.   335. Th. weren; F. were.   Tn. shet; F. shette.   336. F. throgh.   337. F. bryght. 338. F. gilde; Th. B. gyldy; Tn. gilti; *read* gilden.   339. F. eke.   F. welken; Th. Tn. welkyn.   *All* faire.   340. F. ayre.   341. Th. atempre; F. Tn. attempre.   342. *All ins.* to *bef.* cold.   F. colde; hoote.   Th. nas; F. Tn. was. 343. F. welkene; Th. welkyn; Tn. walkyn.   345. F. thoght.   346. F. Tassay; horne.

III. THE BOOK OF THE DUCHESSE.

Whether hit were clere or hors of soune.
I herde goinge, up and doune,
Men, hors, houndes, and other thing;
And al men speken of hunting, 350
How they wolde slee the hert with strengthe,
And how the hert had, upon lengthe,
So moche embosed, I not now what.
Anon-right, whan I herde that,
How that they wolde on hunting goon, 355
I was right glad, and up anoon;
[I] took my hors, and forth I wente
Out of my chambre; I never stente
Til I com to the feld withoute.
Ther overtook I a gret route 360
Of huntes and eek of foresteres,
With many relayes and lymeres,
And hyed hem to the forest faste,
And I with hem;—so at the laste
I asked oon, ladde a lymere:— 365
'Say, felow, who shal hunten here
Quod I; and he answerde ageyn,
'Sir, themperour Octovien,'
Quod he, 'and is heer faste by.'
'A goddes halfe, in good tyme,' quod I, 370
'Go we faste!' and gan to ryde.
Whan we came to the forest-syde,
Every man dide, right anoon,
As to hunting fil to doon.
The mayster-hunte anoon, fot-hoot, 375
With a gret horne blew three moot

---

347. Tn. B. hors; Th. F. horse. 348. *All insert* And *at the beginning of the line; but read* I herd-e. F. Th. goynge; Tn. goyng; *after which all insert* bothe (*which is not wanted*). 350. F. Th. speke; Tn. spake; *but read* speken. 355. F. huntynge. 357. *I supply* I. F. Tooke; forthe; went. 358. F. stent. 359. F. come; felde. 360. F. ouertoke; grete. 361. F. eke; foresterys. 362. F. lymerys. 364. Th. I; *which* F. Tn. *omit. For* at the *perhaps read* atte. 366. F. felowe whoo. *All* hunte (*read* hunten). 367. *All* answered (-id). 369. F. here fast. 370. *Read* goddes *as* god's. 373. F. didde. 374. F. huntynge fille. 375. F. fote hote. 376. F. blewe; mote.

At the uncoupling of his houndes.
Within a whyl the hert [y]-founde is,
Y-halowed, and rechased faste
Longe tyme; and at the laste, 380
This hert rused and stal away
Fro alle the houndes a prevy way.
The houndes had overshote hem alle,
And were on a defaute y-falle;
Therwith the hunte wonder faste 385
Blew a forloyn at the laste.

I was go walked fro my tree,
And as I wente, ther cam by me
A whelp, that fauned me as I stood,
That hadde y-folowed, and coude no good. 390
Hit com and creep to me as lowe,
Right as hit hadde me y-knowe,
Hild doun his heed and Ioyned his eres,
And leyde al smothe doun his heres.
I wolde han caught hit, and anoon 395
Hit fledde, and was fro me goon;
And I him folwed, and hit forth wente
Doun by a floury grene wente
Ful thikke of gras, ful softe and swete,
With floures fele, faire under fete, 400
And litel used, hit seemed thus;
For bothe Flora and Zephirus,
They two that make floures growe,
Had mad hir dwelling ther, I trowe;

---

377. F. vncoupylynge; Th. vncouplynge. 378. F. Withynne; while; herte. Th. F. founde; Tn. found; *read* y-founde. 380. *All* and so; *om.* so. 381. F. Tn. B. rused; Th. roused. F. staale. 383. Th. ouer-shot; F. ouershette; Tn. ouershet. Tn. hem; F. hym (*wrongly*). 384. Tn. on; F. vpon. Tn. defaute; F. defaulte. 386. F. Blewe. Th. Tn. forloyn; F. forleygne. *Perhaps read* atte *for* at the. 388. F. went; came. 389. F. whelpe. Th. fawned; F. Favned. F. stoode. 390. F. goode. 391. F. come. *All have* crepte (*wrongly*); *read* creep. 392. Tn. hade; F. had. 393. B. Hild; F. Hylde; Tn. Held. Th. heed; Tn. hed; F. hede. F. erys. 394. F. herys. 395. *All* haue; *read* han. 396. Tn. fledde; F. fled. 397. F. forthe went. 398. F. went. 399. *All* swete (*correctly*). 400. *All* fete; *see* 199. 402. Tn. bothe; F. both. 404. *All* made; *read* mad *or* maad. F dwellynge.

III. THE BOOK OF THE DUCHESSE.

For hit was, on to beholde, 405
As thogh the erthe envye wolde
To be gayer than the heven,
To have mo floures, swiche seven
As in the welken sterres be.
Hit had forgete the povertee 410
That winter, through his colde morwes,
Had mad hit suffren, and his sorwes;
Al was forgeten, and that was sene.
For al the wode was waxen grene,
Swetnesse of dewe had mad it waxe. 415
 Hit is no need eek for to axe
Wher ther were many grene greves,
Or thikke of trees, so ful of leves;
And every tree stood by him-selve
Fro other wel ten foot or twelve. 420
So grete trees, so huge of strengthe,
Of fourty or fifty fadme lengthe,
Clene withoute bough or stikke,
With croppes brode, and eek as thikke—
They were nat an inche a-sonder— 425
That hit was shadwe over-al under;
And many an hert and many an hinde
Was both before me and bihinde.
Of founes, soures, bukkes, does
Was ful the wode, and many roës, 430
And many squirelles, that sete
Ful hye upon the trees, and ete,
And in hir maner made festes.
Shortly, hit was so ful of bestes,

---

406. F. therthe; Th. the erthe. 408. F. moo; swche (*sic*). 409. Th. welken; F. walkene. F. sterris. 411. F. thorgh. 412. *All* suffre. 414. F. woode. 415. *All* made. 416. *All* nede eke. 417. F. Where there. 419. F. stoode. 420. Tn. ten; F. tene. Th. foote; F. fete; Tn. *om.* Th. or; F. Tn. fro other (*repeated*). 422. Th. Tn. B. Of; F. Or. Th. or; *rest om.* F. fedme; Th. fedome; Tn. fedim; *read* fadme. 424. Th. brode; F. Tn. bothe (*wrongly*). F. eke. 426. Tn. B. shadwe; F. shadewe. 427. Tn. hert; F. herte. 429. Th. fawnes; F. Tn. fovnes. F. Tn. sowres; Th. sowers. 430. Tn. wode; F. woode. 429, 430. B. doys, roys. 431. Th. squyrrels; F. sqwirels; Tn. squirels; B. squyrellys (*three syllables*). 432. F. high. 433. F. festys. 434. F. bestys.

292   THE MINOR POEMS.

    That thogh Argus, the noble countour,   435
Sete to rekene in his countour,
And rekened with his figures ten—
For by tho figures mowe al ken,
If they be crafty, rekene and noumbre,
And telle of every thing the noumbre—   440
Yet shulde he fayle to rekene even
The wondres, me mette in my sweven.
    But forth they romed wonder faste
Doun the wode; so at the laste
I was war of a man in blak,   445
That sat and had y-turned his bak
To an oke, an huge tree.
'Lord,' thoghte I, 'who may that be?
What ayleth him to sitten here?'
Anoon-right I wente nere;   450
Than fond I sitte even upright
A wonder wel-faringe knight—
By the maner me thoughte so—
Of good mochel, and yong therto,
Of the age of four and twenty yeer.   455
Upon his berde but litel heer,
And he was clothed al in blakke.
I stalked even unto his bakke,
And ther I stood as stille as ought,
That, sooth to saye, he saw me nought,   460
For-why he heng his heed adoune.
And with a deedly sorwful soune

---

435. Th. Tn. countour; F. counter (*and so in* l. 436). 437. F. Tn. rekene; Th. reken (*caught from above*); *read* rekened. F. figuris. 438. F. figuris. F. mowe; B. mow; Th. Tn. newe (*reading doubtful*). *All have* al ken; *see* note. 440. B. tell*e*; *rest* tel. F. thinge. 441. F. evene. 442. F. swevene. 443. *All ins.* right *bef.* wonder. 444. F. Doune; woode. 446. Th. sate; F. Tn. sete. Tn. Iturned; F. turned. 447. F. ooke. 448. Th. Tn. thought; F. thogh (!). 450. F. went. 451. Tn. fond; F. founde. 452. F. farynge. 454. *All but* B. insert ryght *before* yong. Tn. ȝung; F. Th. yonge. 455. *All* yere; *read* yeer. 456. *All* heere, here; *read* heer. 457. Th. blacke; F. blake. 458. Tn. bakke; F. bake. 459. F. stoode. 460. F. sawe. 461. Tn. heng; F. henge. Th. heed; Tn. hed; F. hede. 462. Tn. dedly; F. dedely.

III. THE BOOK OF THE DUCHESSE.

He made of ryme ten vers or twelve,
Of a compleynt to him-selve,
The moste pite, the moste rowthe, 465
That ever I herde; for, by my trowthe,
Hit was gret wonder that nature
Might suffren any creature
To have swich sorwe, and be not deed.
Ful pitous, pale, and nothing reed, 470
He sayde a lay, a maner song,
Withoute note, withoute song,
And hit was this; for wel I can
Reherse hit; right thus hit began.—
¶ 'I have of sorwe so gret woon, 475
That Ioye gete I never noon,
  Now that I see my lady bright,
  Which I have loved with al my might,
Is fro me deed, and is a-goon. 479
¶ Allas, [o] deeth! what ayleth thee, 481
That thou noldest have taken me,
  Whan that thou toke my lady swete?
That was so fayr, so fresh, so free,
So good, that men may wel [y]-see 485
  Of al goodnesse she had no mete!'—
Whan he had mad thus his complaynte,
His sorowful herte gan faste faynte,
And his spirites wexen dede;
The blood was fled, for pure drede, 490

---

463. Th. Tn. twelue; F. twelfe.   464. Th. Tn. selue; F. selfe.   465. Tn. pite; F. pitee.   468. *All* suffre; *read* suffren.   469. F. suche. Th. deed; F. Tn. ded.   470. Tn. pitous; B. pitouse; F. petuose. Tn. nothing; F. no thynge. Th. reed; F. Tn. red.   471. F. sayed; Tn. said.   471, 2. Tn. song; F. songe.   473. B. *alone supplies* it (=hit); *all insert* ful *before* wel.   475. F. grete; Tn. gret. *All* wone; *read* woon.   476. F. Ioy; none.   477, 8. *Read* brighte, mighte?   479. Th. deed; F. ded. *After* l. 479 Thynne *inserts* And thus in sorowe lefte me alone; *it is spurious; see note.* [Hence there is no l. 480.]   481. Koch *supplies* o. Tn. deth; F. dethe.   483. Tn. that; *which* F. Tn. *omit.*   484. F. faire. F. freshe; Tn. fressh.   485. *All* se; *but read* y-see.   486. F. goodenesse.   487. *All* made. Th. B complaynte; F. complaynt.   488. F. sorwful. Th. herte; F. hert. Th. B. faynte; F. faynt.   489. F. spiritis.   490. Tn. blood; F. bloode.

THE MINOR POEMS.

<blockquote>
Doun to his herte, to make him warm—
For wel hit feled the herte had harm—
To wite eek why hit was a-drad
By kinde, and for to make hit glad;
For hit is membre principal 495
Of the body; and that made al
His hewe chaunge and wexe grene
And pale, for no blood [was] sene
In no maner lime of his.

Anoon therwith whan I saw this, 500
He ferde thus evel ther he sete,
I wente and stood right at his fete,
And grette him, but he spak noght,
But argued with his owne thoght,
And in his witte disputed faste 505
Why and how his lyf might laste;
Him thoughte his sorwes were so smerte
And lay so colde upon his herte;
So, through his sorwe and hevy thoght,
Made him that he ne herde me noght; 510
For he had wel nigh lost his minde,
Thogh Pan, that men clepe god of kinde,
Were for his sorwes never so wrooth.

But at the laste, to sayn right sooth,
He was war of me, how I stood 515
Before him, and dide of myn hood,
And [grette] him, as I best coude.
Debonairly, and no-thing loude,
He sayde, 'I prey thee, be not wrooth,
I herde thee not, to sayn the sooth, 520
</blockquote>

---

491. Th. herte; F. hert. *All* warme. 492. Th. herte; F. hert. *All* harme. 493. B. wite; F. wete. *All* eke. 498. *All insert* ther *before* no. F. noo bloode. *All* is; *but read* was. 499. Th. lymme; B. Tn. lyme; F. hym (!). 500. B. saw; F. saugh. 501. F. Th. there; Tn. for. *All* sete (fete *is dat. pl.*). 502. F. went; stoode. 503. *All* spake (*wrongly*). 504. Th. Tn. owne; F. ovne. 506. F. Th. lyfe; Tn. life. 507. F. thought. 509. F. throgh. B. sorwe; Tn. sorov; F. sorwes. 511. Tn. lost; F. loste. 512. F. *inserts* the *before* god; Th. Tn. *omit*. 513. F. wrothe. 514. Th. laste; F. last. F. sothe. 515. F. stoode. 516. *All* did. F. hoode. 517. *All* had ygret; Lange *proposes* grette (*e* unelided). 519. F. wrothe. 520. F. sothe.

III. THE BOOK OF THE DUCHESSE.

Ne I saw thee not, sir, trewely.'
'A! goode sir, no fors,' quod I,
'I am right sory if I have ought
Destroubled yow out of your thought;
For-yive me if I have mis-take.' 525
'Yis, thamendes is light to make,'
Quod he, 'for ther lyth noon ther-to;
Ther is no-thing missayd nor do.'
Lo! how goodly spak this knight,
As it had been another wight; 530
He made it nouther tough ne queynte
And I saw that, and gan me aqueynte
With him, and fond him so tretable,
Right wonder skilful and resonable,
As me thoghte, for al his bale. 535
Anoon-right I gan finde a tale
To him, to loke wher I might ought
Have more knowing of his thought.
'Sir,' quod I, 'this game is doon;
I holde that this hert be goon; 540
Thise huntes conne him nowher see.'
'I do no fors therof,' quod he,
'My thought is ther-on never a del.'
'By our lord,' quod I, 'I trow yow wel,
Right so me thinketh by your chere. 545
But, sir, oo thing wol ye here?
Me thinketh, in gret sorwe I yow see;
But certes, [good] sir, yif that ye
Wolde ought discure me your wo,
I wolde, as wis god helpe me so, 550
Amende hit, yif I can or may;
Ye mowe preve hit by assay.

---

521. B. saw; F. sawgh. F. trewly. 522. Tn. goode; F. good. 523, 4. F. oughte, thoughte. 526. F. thamendys. 527. F. lyeth; Tn. lith. 528. F. There. *All* myssayde. 529. Th. goodly; F. goodely. *All* spake (!). Th. knyght; F. knyghte. 530. B. ben; *rest* be. 531. F. towgh. 532. F. sawe; aqueynt. 533. F. fonde. 535. F. thoght. 537. F. oughte. 538. F. knowynge; thoughte. 541. F. These huntys konne. 543. F. there on; dele (Tn. del). 544. Tn. Bi; Th. By; F. Be. F. oure lorde; wele (Tn. wel). 545. B. thinketh; F. thenketh. 547. F. grete. 548. *Ins.* good; see 714, 721. Th. Tn. if; F. yif. 550. F. wys; Th. wyse; Tn. wisse.

296   THE MINOR POEMS.

> For, by my trouthe, to make yow hool,
> I wol do al my power hool;
> And telleth me of your sorwes smerte,   555
> Paraventure hit may ese your herte,
> That semeth ful seke under your syde.'
>   With that he loked on me asyde,
> As who sayth, 'nay, that wol not be.'
> 'Graunt mercy, goode frend,' quod he,   560
> 'I thanke thee that thou woldest so,
> But hit may never the rather be do.
> No man may my sorwe glade,
> That maketh my hewe to falle and fade,
> And hath myn understanding lorn,   565
> That me is wo that I was born!
> May noght make my sorwes slyde,
> Nought the remedies of Ovyde;
> Ne Orpheus, god of melodye,
> Ne Dedalus, with playes slye;   570
> Ne hele me may phisicien,
> Noght Ypocras, ne Galien;
> Me is wo that I live houres twelve;
> But who so wol assaye him-selve
> Whether his herte can have pite   575
> Of any sorwe, lat him see me.
> I wrecche, that deeth hath mad al naked
> Of alle blisse that was ever maked,
> Y-worthe worste of alle wightes,
> That hate my dayes and my nightes;   580
> My lyf, my lustes be me lothe,
> For al welfare and I be wrothe.
> The pure deeth is so my fo,
> [Thogh] I wolde deye, hit wolde not so;

---

554. Th. al; F. alle; Tn. *om.*   556. B. ese; F. ease.   560. Tn. frend; F. frende.   564. *All* fal.   565. F. vnderstondynge lorne.   566. F. borne.   568. F. Th. *ins.* al (Tn. of) *before* the.   570. *All ins.* his *after* with.   571. *All ins.* no *after* may.   573. Th. Tn. houres; F. oures.   574. *All* assay.   575. B. Th. herte; F. Tn. hert.   577. F. wrechch; Tn. wrecch; Tn. wretche (*for* wrecche). *All* made.   578. F. al; Th. Tn. al the; B. alle (*read* al-le).   579. B. alle; *rest* al.   581. *All* lyfe. F. loothe.   582. F. wroothe (*it is plural*).   583. *All ins.* ful *after* so. F. foo.   584. *All* That; *read* Thogh. F. soo.

III. THE BOOK OF THE DUCHESSE.

For whan I folwe hit, hit wol flee; 585
I wolde have [hit], hit nil not me.
This is my peyne withoute reed,
Alway deying, and be not deed,
That Sesiphus, that lyth in helle,
May not of more sorwe telle. 590
And who so wiste al, by my trouthe,
My sorwe, but he hadde routhe
And pite of my sorwes smerte,
That man hath a feendly herte.
For who so seeth me first on morwe 595
May seyn, he hath [y]-met with sorwe;
For I am sorwe and sorwe is I.
'Allas! and I wol telle the why;
My [song] is turned to pleyning,
And al my laughter to weping, 600
My glade thoghtes to hevinesse,
In travaile is myn ydelnesse
And eek my reste; my wele is wo.
My good is harm, and ever-mo
In wrathe is turned my pleying, 605
And my delyt in-to sorwing.
Myn hele is turned into seeknesse,
In drede is al my sikernesse.
To derke is turned al my light,
My wit is foly, my day is night, 610

---

586. *For the former* hit, *all have* him; *but see line above.* 587. Th. reed; F. rede. 588. F. deynge. Th. deed; F. dede. 589. F. B. Thesiphus; Tn. Tesiphus; Th. Tesyphus. (*The two latter are miswritten for* Cesiphus = Sesiphus). Tn. lithe; F. Th. lyeth. 591. Th. Tn. al; F. alle. Th. by; F. Tn. be. 592. Tn. hade; F. had. 594. Tn. feenli (*sic*); Th. F. fendely. 596. Tn. met; Th. F. mette (!); *read* y-met. 598. B. telle; *rest* tel. 599. *For song,* F. Th. *have* sorowe, *and* Tn. *has* sorov, *which are absurd; the reading is obviously* song, *the* ng *being altered to* rowe *by influence of* l. 597, *which the scribes glanced at.* Tn. pleynyng; F. pleynynge. 600. Tn. laughter; F. lawghtre. Tn. weping; F. wepynge. 601. F. thoghtys. 603. *All* eke. 604. Th. Tn. good; F. goode. *All* harme. 605. Th. playeng; F. pleynge. 606. F. sorwynge. 607. Tn. sekenes; F. sekeenesse (*sic*). 609. Tn. liȝt; F. lyghte; Th. syght. 610. Tn. wit; F. wytte. Th. Tn. nyght; F. nyghte.

298   THE MINOR POEMS.

My love is hate, my sleep waking,
My mirthe and meles is fasting,
My countenaunce is nycete,
And al abaved wher-so I be,
My pees, in pleding and in werre;   615
Allas! how mighte I fare werre?
'My boldnesse is turned to shame,
For fals Fortune hath pleyd a game
Atte ches with me, allas! the whyle!
The trayteresse fals and ful of gyle,   620
That al behoteth and no-thing halt,
She goth upryght and yet she halt,
That baggeth foule and loketh faire,
The dispitousë debonaire,
That scorneth many a creature!   625
An ydole of fals portraiture
Is she, for she wil sone wryen;
She is the monstres heed y-wryen,
As filth over y-strawed with floures;
Hir moste worship and hir [flour is]   630
To lyen, for that is hir nature;
Withoute feyth, lawe, or mesure
She is fals; and ever laughinge
With oon eye, and that other wepinge.
That is broght up, she set al doun.   635
I lykne hir to the scorpioun,
That is a fals flatering beste;
For with his hede he maketh feste,
But al amid his flateringe
With his tayle he wol stinge,   640

---

611. *All* slepe. Tn. wakynge; F. wakynge.   612. Tn. fasting; F. fastynge.
614. Tn. abaved (*sic*); Th. F. abawed. *All* where so.   617. Tn. boldnes;
Th. F. boldenesse. (*Perhaps read* y-turned.)   618. F. pleyde; Th. played;
Tn. pleied.   619. F. Atte the (*wrongly*); Th. Tn. At the. Tn. ches; Th.
F. chesse.   621. Tn. halt; F. Th. halte (!).   622. Tn. goth; Th. gothe;
F. gethe (!). Th. halte; Tn. is halt; F. is halte.   627. Th. wrien; *rest*
varien (!).   628. Th. Tn. monstres; F. Mowstres. Th. heed; F. Tn. hed.
629. B. filth; *rest* fylthe. Th. Tn. ystrowed.   630. F. worshippe. Th. Tn.
floures; F. B. flourys; *read* flour is.   632. Tn. feith; F. feythe.   633.
F. lawghynge.   634. Tn. oon; Th. F. one. Th. eye; Tn. ei3; F. yghe; B.
ye. F. wepynge.   635. Th. set; F. sette.   637. F. flateyrynge; Tn. flateryng.
639. Th. Tn. amyd; F. amydde.   640. Th. he; F. hyt; Tn. it.

III. THE BOOK OF THE DUCHESSE.

And envenyme; and so wol she.
She is thenvyous charite
That is ay fals, and semeth wele,
So turneth she hir false whele
Aboute, for it is no-thing stable, 645
Now by the fyre, now at table;
Ful many oon hath she thus y-blent.
She is pley of enchauntement,
That semeth oon and is nat so,
The false theef! what hath she do, 650
Trowest thou? by our lord, I wol thee seye.
Atte ches with me she gan to pleye;
With hir false draughtes divers
She stal on me, and took my fers.
And whan I saw my fers aweye, 655
Alas! I couthe no lenger pleye,
But seyde, "farwel, swete, y-wis,
And farwel al that ever ther is!"
Therwith Fortune seyde "chek here!"
And "mate!" in mid pointe of the chekkere 660
With a poune erraunt, allas!
Ful craftier to pley she was
Than Athalus, that made the game
First of the ches: so was his name.
But god wolde I had ones or twyes 665
Y-koud and knowe the Ieupardyes
That coude the Grek Pithagores!
I shulde have pleyd the bet at ches,

---

642. F. thenvyouse; Tn. thenvious; Th. the enuyous. 644. Th. false; F. Tn. fals. 645. F. no thynge. 647. Th. Ful; *rest* For. F. thus she; Tn. Th. she thus. 649. Th. nat; F. Tn. not. 650. Th. false; F. Tn. fals. Th. F. thefe; Tn. knaue. 651. F. oure lorde; the sey. 652. *All* At the; Atte *is better.* Tn. ches; Th. F. chesse. F. pley. 653. Th. Tn. false; F. fals. 654. F. staale; toke. F. Tn. fers; Th. feers. 655. F. sawgh. B. a-waye; *rest* away. 656. B. pleye; Th. F. play; Tn. pley. 657. *All* farewel (farewell); *and in* l. 658. 660. *All insert* the *after* in (*badly*). 661. F. povne; Tn. pou*n*; Th. paune. Tn. erraunt; F. errante. 663. Tn. Athalaus. 664. Tn. ches; Th. F. chesse. 666. B. I-koude; Th. Tn. Iconde (!); F. y-konde (!); *see* l. 667. 667. Tn. Grek; F. Greke. Th. Pithagores; F. Tn. Pictagoras. 668. Tn. pleyd; F. pleyde.

And kept my fers the bet therby;
And thogh wherto? for trewely 670
I hold that wish nat worth a stree!
Hit had be never the bet for me.
For Fortune can so many a wyle,
Ther be but fewe can hir begyle,
And eek she is the las to blame; 675
My-self I wolde have do the same,
Before god, hadde I been as she;
She oghte the more excused be.
For this I say yet more therto,
Hadde I be god and mighte have do 680
My wille, whan my fers she caughte,
I wolde have drawe the same draughte.
For, also wis god yive me reste,
I dar wel swere she took the beste!
  'But through that draughte I have lorn 685
My blisse; allas! that I was born!
For evermore, I trowe trewly,
For al my wil, my lust hoolly
Is turned; but yet, what to done?
By our lord, hit is to deye sone; 690
For no-thing I [ne] leve it noght,
But live and deye right in this thoght.
Ther nis planete in firmament,
Ne in air, ne in erthe, noon element,
That they ne yive me a yift echoon 695
Of weping, whan I am aloon.
For whan that I avyse me wel,
And bethenke me every-del,

---

670. Tn. thogh; Th. thoughe; F. thoght (*sic*). F. trewly.   671. F. holde; wysshe.   675. *All* eke. B. las; F. lasse; Tn. lesse.   676. F. -selfe. 677. Th. had I ben; F. as I be (*wrongly*).   678. F. oght.   681. *All* she my fers; *read* my fers she (Koch). *All* kaught, *read* caughte; *and* draughte *in* ll. 682, 685.   683. Tn. wis; F. wys.   684. Th. she; F. Tn. B. he. F. tooke.   685. F. throgh; draught; lorne.   686. F. borne. 689. F. doone.   690. F. Be oure lorde; soone.   691. F. -thynge. *I supply* ne.   693. *All* For there (ther); *but omit* For.   694. F. ayre.   695. F. yifte.   696. F. wepynge.

III. THE BOOK OF THE DUCHESSE.

How that ther lyth in rekening,
In my sorwe, for no-thing;　　　　　　　　　700
And how ther leveth no gladnesse
May gladde me of my distresse,
And how I have lost suffisance,
And therto I have no plesance,
Than may I say, I have right noght.　　　　705
And whan al this falleth in my thoght,
Allas! than am I overcome!
For that is doon is not to come!
I have more sorowe than Tantale.'
　And whan I herde him telle this tale　　710
Thus pitously, as I yow telle,
Unnethe mighte I lenger dwelle,
Hit dide myn herte so moche wo.
'A! good sir!' quod I, 'say not so!
Have som pite on your nature　　　　　　715
That formed yow to creature,
Remembre yow of Socrates;
For he ne counted nat three strees
Of noght that Fortune coude do.'
'No,' quod he, 'I can not so.'　　　　　　720
'Why so? good sir! parde!' quod I;
'Ne say noght so, for trewely,
Thogh ye had lost the ferses twelve,
And ye for sorwe mordred your-selve,
Ye sholde be dampned in this cas　　　　725
By as good right as Medea was,
That slow hir children for Iason;
And Phyllis als for Demophon
Heng hir-self, so weylaway!
For he had broke his terme-day　　　　　730

---

699. Tn. lyth; F. lyeth. F. rekenynge.　　700. Th. Tn. In; F. Inne.　　701. F. levyth noe.　　702. B. Tn. glade; F. glad; *read* gladde.　　703. Th. lost; F. loste.　　710. Tn. telle; F. tel.　　711. Th. Tn. Thus; F. This.　　712. F. myght; duelle.　　713. Tn. dide, herte; F. dyd, hert.　　714. Th. good; F. goode.　　715. Tn. som; F. somme.　　721. *All insert* yis (*or* yes) *before* parde; *which spoils both sense and metre*.　　722. Th. say; *rest om*. F. trewly.　　723. Th. lost; F. loste.　　726. Th. good; F. goode.　　727. Tn. slowe; F. slowgh.　　728. *All* also; *read* als.　　729. F. Henge.

302   THE MINOR POEMS.

  To come to hir. Another rage
Had Dydo, quene eek of Cartage,
That slow hir-self, for Eneas
Was fals; [a!] whiche a fool she was!
And Ecquo dyed for Narcisus   735
Nolde nat love hir; and right thus
Hath many another foly don.
And for Dalida dyed Sampson,
That slow him-self with a pilere.
But ther is [noon] a-lyve here   740
Wolde for a fers make this wo!'
  'Why so?' quod he; 'hit is nat so;
Thou wost ful litel what thou menest;
I have lost more than thou wenest.'
  'Lo, [sir,] how may that be?' quod I;   745
'Good sir, tel me al hoolly
In what wyse, how, why, and wherfore
That ye have thus your blisse lore.'
  'Blythly,' quod he, 'com sit adoun;
I telle thee up condicioun   750
That thou hoolly, with al thy wit,
Do thyn entent to herkene hit.'
'Yis, sir.' 'Swere thy trouthe ther-to.'
'Gladly.' 'Do than holde her-to!'
'I shal right blythly, so god me save,   755
Hoolly, with al the witte I have,
Here yow, as wel as I can.'
  'A goddes half!' quod he, and began:—

---

732. *All* the quene; *omit* the. *All* eke. 733. Tn. slow; F. slough. F. selfe. 734. *I supply former* a. F. foole. 735. *All* Ecquo. 739 Tn. slow; F. slough. F. hym-selfe. 740. *All* no man; *but read* noon. 741. *Perhaps read* maken. 743. F. woste; menyst. 744. Th. lost; F. loste. F. thow wenyst. 745. F. Tn. Loo she that may be; Th. Howe that may be; *here* she *is an error for* sir, *and* Howe that may be *for* how may that be; (*ed*. 1550 *has* Howe may that be). 746. *All* sir. F. Tn. telle; Th. tel. F. hooly. 749. F. come. Tn. sit; F. sytte. 750. F. *inserts* hyt *after* telle; *which* Th. Tn. *omit*. Th. Tn. vpon a; F. vp a; *but* vp *is right*. 751. *All ins*. shalt *after* thou; *omit it* (Koch). F. hooly. Tn. wit; Th. wyt; F. wytte. 752. Tn. hit; F. hitte (!). 754. F. Tn. here lo; Th. here to. *Accent* thér- *and* hér-. 755. *Perhaps right should be omitted*. 756. F. Hooly. 758. B. half; F. halfe; (goddes = god's).

III. THE BOOK OF THE DUCHESSE. 303

'Sir,' quod he, 'sith first I couthe
Have any maner wit fro youthe, 760
Or kyndely understonding
To comprehende, in any thing,
What love was, in myn owne wit,
Dredeles, I have ever yit
Be tributary, and yiven rente 765
To love hoolly with goode entente,
And through plesaunce become his thral,
With good wil, body, herte, and al.
Al this I putte in his servage,
As to my lorde, and dide homage; 770
And ful devoutly prayde him to,
He shulde besette myn herte so,
That it plesaunce to him were,
And worship to my lady dere.
  'And this was longe, and many a yeer 775
Or that myn herte was set o-wher,
That I did thus, and niste why;
I trowe hit cam me kindely.
Paraunter I was therto most able
As a whyt wal or a table; 780
For hit is redy to cacche and take
Al that men wil therin make,
Wher-so men wol portreye or peynte,
Be the werkes never so queynte.
  'And thilke tyme I ferde so 785
I was able to have lerned tho,
And to have coud as wel or better,
Paraunter, other art or letter.

---

760. Tn. wit; F. wytte. 761. F. vnderstondynge. 763. Tn. wit; F. wytte. 764. Tn. yit; F. yitte. 765. Tn. youen; F. yive. 766. F. hooly. 767, 768. Th. thral, al; F. thralle, alle. Th. wyl; F. wille. 771. *All* deuoutely. *All insert* I *before* prayde. Th. prayde; F. prayed. 772. Th. Tn. herte; F. hert. 773. F. plesance; *see* l. 767. 774. F. worshippe. 775, 6. *All* yere, owhere. 778. Tn. cam; F. came. 779. F. Perauenture; *see* l. 788. *All insert* moste *before* able. 780. F. white walle. 781. F. cachche. 783. F. Tn. Whethir; Th. Whether; *read* Wher (*contracted form*). F. portrey or peynt; Tn. purtrey or paynte. 784. Tn. queynte; F. queynt. 785. *All insert* ryght *before* so. 787. Th. Tn. conde (*for* coude); F. kende (*for* kenned). 788. *All* arte.

But for love cam first in my thought,
Therfore I forgat it nought.   790
I chees love to my firste craft,
Therfor hit is with me [y]-laft.
Forwhy I took hit of so yong age,
That malice hadde my corage
Nat that tyme turned to no-thing   795
Through to mochel knowleching.
For that tyme youthe, my maistresse,
Governed me in ydelnesse ;
For hit was in my firste youthe,
And tho ful litel good I couthe ;   800
For al my werkes were flittinge,
And al my thoghtes varyinge ;
Al were to me y-liche good,
That I knew tho ; but thus hit stood.
'Hit happed that I cam on a day   805
Into a place, ther I say,
Trewly, the fayrest companyë
Of ladies, that ever man with yë
Had seen togedres in oo place.
Shal I clepe hit hap other grace   810
That broghte me ther? nay, but Fortune,
That is to lyen ful comune,
The false trayteresse, pervers,
God wolde I coude clepe hir wers !
For now she worcheth me ful wo,   815
And I wol telle sone why so.
'Among thise ladies thus echoon,
Soth to seyn, I saw [ther] oon

---

789. Tn. kam ; F. came.   790. *All* forgate.   791. Th. chees ; Tn. chese ; F. ches. Tn. fyrste ; F. first. *All* crafte (*but it will not rime*).   792. *All* lafte (*wrongly*) ; *read* y-laft.   793. *All* For-why ; *read* For ? *All* toke. *All* yonge.   795. F. no thynge.   796. F. Thorgh. Tn. knowlechynge ; F. knowlachynge.   799. Tn. firste ; F. first.   800. F. goode ; Th. good. 801. F. Tn. flyttynge.   802. *All ins.* That tyme (*see* l. 797) *bef.* And. Tn. thoughte*n* ; *rest* thoght. F. Tn. varyinge.   804. F. knewe ; stoode.   805. F. came. *Perhaps* on (*or* a) *should be omitted.*   806. *All* ther that I ; *om.* that.   808. F. euere. F. Tn. ye ; Th. eye.   810. Tn. hap ; F. happe. 811. F. broght ; Tn. broghte. *All* there.   813. Tn. false ; F. fals.   816. Tn. telle ; F. tel.   817. F. Amonge these.   818. *I supply* ther.

III. THE BOOK OF THE DUCHESSE.

That was lyk noon of [al] the route;
For I dar swere, withoute doute, 820
That as the someres sonne bright
Is fairer, clerer, and hath more light
Than any planete, [is] in heven,
The mone, or the sterres seven,
For al the worlde, so had she 825
Surmounted hem alle of beaute,
Of maner and of comlinesse,
Of stature and wel set gladnesse,
Of goodlihede so wel beseye—
Shortly, what shal I more seye? 830
By god, and by his halwes twelve,
It was my swete, right as hir-selve!
She had so stedfast countenaunce,
So noble port and meyntenaunce.
And Love, that had herd my bone, 835
Had espyed me thus sone,
That she ful sone, in my thoght,
As helpe me god, so was y-caught
So sodenly, that I ne took
No maner [reed] but at hir look 840
And at myn herte; for-why hir eyen
So gladly, I trow, myn herte seyen,
That purely tho myn owne thoght
Seyde hit were [bet] serve hir for noght
Than with another to be wel. 845
And hit was sooth, for, everydel,

---

819. *All* lyke (like). *I supply* al.   821. Tn. bryght; F. bryghte.   822. Th. lyght; F. lyghte.   823. *All* any other planete in; *see note*. F. hevene.   824. F. sevene.   826. Th. Tn. Surmounted; F. Surmountede. Tn. B. alle; F. al.   828. *All ins.* of *after* and. F. *ins.* so *before* wel; *which* Th. Tn. *omit*. Th. Tn. set; F. sette.   829. Th. goodlyhede; F. godelyhede. *All ins.* and *before* so, *probably caught from the line above*. B. beseye; *rest* besey.   830. Th. *supplies* more; F. Tn. *omit*. *All* sey.   831. Th. Tn. his; F. *omits*.   832. Tn. as; Th. F. al.   833. Th. stedfast; F. stedfaste.   835. F. Tn. had wel herd; *om.* wel.   838. F. y-kaught; Th. I cought; Tn. I caughte.   839. *All* toke.   840. *All* counseyl; *I propose* reed. *All* loke.   841. Th. And; F. Tn. But (*caught from* l. 840). Th. Tn. herte; F. hest (*wrongly*). *All* for why; *read* for?   842. F. hert; Th. Tn. herte.   843. F. ovne; *read* owne.   844. F. beter; Th. better; Tn. bettyr; *read* bet.   846. Tn. B. soth; F. Th. sothe.

I wil anoon-right telle thee why.
'I saw hir daunce so comlily,
Carole and singe so swetely,
Laughe and pleye so womanly,   850
And loke so debonairly,
So goodly speke and so frendly,
That certes, I trow, that evermore
Nas seyn so blisful a tresore.
For every heer [up]on hir hede,   855
Soth to seyn, hit was not rede,
Ne nouther yelw, ne broun hit nas;
Me thoghte, most lyk gold hit was.
And whiche eyen my lady hadde!
Debonair, goode, glade, and sadde,   860
Simple, of good mochel, noght to wyde;
Therto hir look nas not a-syde,
Ne overthwert, but beset so wel,
Hit drew and took up, everydel,
Alle that on hir gan beholde.   865
Hir eyen semed anoon she wolde
Have mercy; fooles wenden so;
But hit was never the rather do.
Hit nas no countrefeted thing,
It was hir owne pure loking,   870
That the goddesse, dame Nature,
Had made hem opene by mesure,
And close; for, were she never so glad,
Hir loking was not foly sprad,
Ne wildely, thogh that she pleyde;   875
But ever, me thoghte, hir eyen seyde,

---

848. Tn. saw; F. sawgh. F. comelely; Th. comely; Tn. comly. 850. F. Lawghe; pley. 852. Th. goodly; F. goodely. 854. Tn. seyn; F. seyne. 855. *All* on; *read* upon. 856. Tn. seyn; F. seyne. (*For* was *probably read* nas.) 857. F. yelowe; broune. 858. F. Tn. thoght. Th. F. lyke; Tn. likely. Th. golde; *which* F. Tn. *absurdly omit.* 861. F. goode. 862. F. looke. 863. F. ouertwert; Tn. ouyrthwerte; Th. ouertwhart (*sic*). Th. beset; Tn. biset; F. besette. 864. F. Tn. drewh. F. tooke. *All* euerydele. 865. Tn. B. All*e*; F. Th. Al. 867. F. foolys; B. folys. 869. F. thynge. 870. F. lokynge. 873. Th. close; Tn. clos; F. cloos. 874. F. lokynge. Th. folyche. 876. Tn. thoghte; F. thoght.

III. THE BOOK OF THE DUCHESSE.

"By god, my wrathe is al for-yive!"
'Therwith hir liste so wel to live,
That dulnesse was of hir a-drad.
She nas to sobre ne to glad; 880
In alle thinges more mesure
Had never, I trowe, creature.
But many oon with hir loke she herte,
And that sat hir ful lyte at herte,
For she knew no-thing of hir thoght; 885
But whether she knew, or knew hit noght,
Algate she ne roghte of hem a stree!
To gete hir love no ner nas he
That woned at home, than he in Inde;
The formest was alway behinde. 890
But goode folk, over al other,
She loved as man may do his brother;
Of whiche love she was wonder large,
In skilful places that bere charge.
'Which a visage had she ther-to! 895
Allas! myn herte is wonder wo
That I ne can discryven hit!
Me lakketh bothe English and wit
For to undo hit at the fulle;
And eek my spirits be so dulle 900
So greet a thing for to devyse.
I have no wit that can suffyse
To comprehenden hir beaute;
But thus moche dar I seyn, that she
Was rody, fresh, and lyvely hewed; 905
And every day hir beaute newed.

---

877. Th. By; F. Tn. Be. 882. Th. trowe; F. Tn. trow. 883. Th. herte; Tn. hyrte; F. hert. 884. *All* sate. B. lyte; Tn. lite; F. litel. Th. Tn. herte; F. hert. 885. Tn. knew; F. knowe (*sic*). F. no thynge. 886. *This line is in* Th. *only*; Th. *has* knewe (*twice*). 887. Tn. roghte; Th. F. rought. 888. Tn. ner; F. nerre. F. was; Th. Tn. nas. 889. Th. than; Tn. then; F. that. 891. Tn. gode; Th. F. good. *All* folke. 893. F. wounder. 894. F. placis. 895. *All* But which; *omit* But. 898. Th. bothe; F. both. 900. *All* eke. B. spyryts; F. spiritis. 901. *All* grete a thynge. 902. Th. wyt; Tn. F. witte. 903. Th. F. comprehende; Tn. comprehend; *read* comprehenden. 904. Tn. seyn; F. sayn. 905. *All insert* white *after* Was, *which spoils metre and story* (*see* l. 948). F. fressh.

THE MINOR POEMS.

And negh hir face was alder-best;
For certes, Nature had swich lest
To make that fair, that trewly she
Was hir cheef patron of beautee,　　　　910
And cheef ensample of al hir werke,
And moustre; for, be hit never so derke,
Me thinketh I see hir ever-mo.
And yet more-over, thogh alle tho
That ever lived were now a-lyve,　　　　915
[They] ne sholde have founde to discryve
In al hir face a wikked signe;
For hit was sad, simple, and benigne.
 'And which a goodly softe speche
Had that swete, my lyves leche!　　　　920
So frendly, and so wel y-grounded,
Up al resoun so wel y-founded,
And so tretable to alle gode,
That I dar swere by the rode,
Of eloquence was never founde　　　　925
So swete a sowninge facounde,
Ne trewer tonged, ne scorned lasse,
Ne bet coude hele; that, by the masse
I durste swere, thogh the pope hit songe,
That ther was never through hir tonge　　　　930
Man ne woman gretly harmed;
As for hir, [ther] was al harm hid;
Ne lasse flatering in hir worde,
That purely, hir simple recorde

---

908. Th. Tn. certes; F. certys.　　909. *All* faire *or* fayre.　　910, 911. B. chief; *rest* chefe. Th. Tn. patron; F. patrone.　　913. F. thynkyth. 914. Tn. B. all*e*; Th. F. al (*it is plural*).　　916. *I supply* They; Th. Ne wolde haue; Tn. Ne sholde haue; F. Ne sholde ha. *The right reading is* They ne sholde have (They ne *being read as* They n').　　919. Th. goodly; F. goodely.　　921. Th. frendly; F. frendely.　　922. F. B. Vp; Th. Tn. Vpon; *see* l. 750.　　923. Tn. B. all*e*; F. al. Tn. gode; F. goode.　　924. *After* swere *all insert* wel (*needlessly*). Tn. rode; F. roode.　　929. Th. Tn. pope; F. Pape.　　930. *All ins.* yet *after* never. Th. through; F. throgh.　　931. F. gretely.　　932. Th. Tn. her; F. hit (*sic*). *I supply* ther (*cf.* l. 930); *perhaps omitted, because* her *also ended in* her. *All* harme. 933. F. flaterynge; word.

III. THE BOOK OF THE DUCHESSE.

Was founde as trewe as any bonde, 935
Or trouthe of any mannes honde.
Ne chyde she coude never a del,
That knoweth al the world ful wel.
  'But swich a fairnesse of a nekke
Had that swete, that boon nor brekke 940
Nas ther non sene, that mis-sat.
Hit was whyt, smothe, streght, and flat,
Withouten hole; [and] canel-boon,
As by seming, had she noon.
Hir throte, as I have now memoire, 945
Semed a round tour of yvoire,
Of good gretnesse, and noght to grete.
  'And gode faire WHYTE she hete,
That was my lady name right.
She was bothe fair and bright, 950
She hadde not hir name wrong.
Right faire shuldres, and body long
She hadde, and armes, every lith
Fattish, flesshy, not greet therwith;
Right whyte handes, and nayles rede, 955
Rounde brestes; and of good brede
Hir hippes were, a streight flat bak.
I knew on hir non other lak
That al hir limmes nere sewing,
In as fer as I had knowing. 960
  'Therto she coude so wel pleye,
Whan that hir liste, that I dar seye,

---

937. *All* dele.   938. *All* worlde; wele.   939. *All* fairenesse (fayrenes). 941. Th. Tn. B. sene; F. seen. Th. F. myssatte; Tn. missate.   942. *All badly insert* pure (*dissyllabic*) *before* flat; *but* smothe *has two syllables.* Tn. flat; Th. F. flatte.   943. *All* or; *I read* and.   944. Th. by; *rest* be.   946. *All* rounde. Th. tour; F. Tn. toure.   947. Th. good; F. goode. F. gretenesse; grete.   948. B. het; *rest* hete.   949. Th. right; F. ryghte.   950. *All* faire. Th. bright; F. bryghte.   951. *All* had (*but it is emphatic*). *All* wronge.   952. *All* longe.   953. *All* had.   954. Th. great; F. Tn. grete.   957. Tn. bak; F. bakke.   958. B. knyw; *rest* knewe. *All* noon other; *perhaps read* no maner. Tn. lak; F. lakke.   959. *All insert* pure (*dissyllabic*) *after* nere; *but* limmes *is dissyllabic*.   960. Tn. fer; F. ferie. F. knowynge.   961. Th. playe; F. pley.   962. Tn. liste; F. list. Th. saye; F. sey.

310   THE MINOR POEMS.

  That she was lyk to torche bright,
  That every man may take of light
  Ynogh, and hit hath never the lesse.   965
   'Of maner and of comlinesse
  Right so ferde my lady dere;
  For every wight of hir manere
  Might cacche ynogh, if that he wolde,
  If he had eyen hir to beholde.   970
  For I dar sweren, if that she
  Had among ten thousand be,
  She wolde have be, at the leste,
  A cheef mirour of al the feste,
  Thogh they had stonden in a rowe,   975
  To mennes eyen that coude have knowe.
  For wher-so men had pleyd or waked,
  Me thoghte the felawship as naked
  Withouten hir, that saw I ones,
  As a coroune withoute stones.   980
  Trewely she was, to myn yë,
  The soleyn fenix of Arabye,
  For ther liveth never but oon;
  Ne swich as she ne knew I noon.
   'To speke of goodnesse; trewly she   985
  Had as moche debonairte
  As ever had Hester in the bible,
  And more, if more were possible.
  And, soth to seyne, therwith al
  She had a wit so general,   990
  So hool enclyned to alle gode,
  That al hir wit was set, by the rode,

---

963. *All* lyke. 965. F. hathe. 969. Tn. cacche; F. cachche. Th. Tn. if; F. yif (*and in* l. 970). 971. *All* swere wel; *read* sweren (*omitting the expletive* wel). 972. *All* thousande. 973. F. lest. 974. B. chieff; *rest* chefe. Th. Tn. myrrour; F. meroure. Th. Tn. feste; F. fest. 975. Th. F. stonde; *read* stonden. 976. Th. that; *rest* which Tn. F. *omit*. 977. Tn. B. pleyd; F. pleyed. 978. F. thoght. Th. felaushyp; Tn. feliship; F. felysshyppe. 979. Tn. saw; F. sawgh. 981. Th. F. Trewly; Tn. Truly. B. ye; Th. F. eye (*note the rime*). 982. Th. Tn. soleyn; F. soleyne. 983. Th. lyueth; F. levyth. 984. Tn. knew; *rest* knowe. 985. Th. goodnesse; F. godenesse. 988. Th. Tn. if; F. yif. 989. Tn. F. seyn; Th. sayne. F. alle. 990. Tn. wit; F. wytte. Th. general; F. generalle. 991. F. hoole. 992. *All* wytte.

III. THE BOOK OF THE DUCHESSE.

Withoute malice, upon gladnesse;
Therto I saw never yet a lesse
Harmful, than she was in doing. 995
I sey nat that she ne had knowing
What was harm; or elles she
Had coud no good, so thinketh me.
 'And trewly, for to speke of trouthe,
But she had had, hit had be routhe. 1000
Therof she had so moche hir del—
And I dar seyn and swere hit wel—
That Trouthe him-self, over al and al,
Had chose his maner principal
In hir, that was his resting-place. 1005
Ther-to she hadde the moste grace,
To have stedfast perseveraunce,
And esy, atempre governaunce,
That ever I knew or wiste yit;
So pure suffraunt was hir wit. 1010
And reson gladly she understood,
Hit folowed wel she coude good.
She used gladly to do wel;
These were hir maners every-del.
 'Therwith she loved so wel right, 1015
She wrong do wolde to no wight;
No wight might do hir no shame,
She loved so wel hir owne name.
Hir luste to holde no wight in honde;
Ne, be thou siker, she nolde fonde 1020
To holde no wight in balaunce,
By half word ne by countenaunce,

---

994. *All* And thereto; *but* And *is needless.* F. sawgh. 995. Th. Harmful; F. Harmeful. 996. *For* ne had *perhaps read* nad. 997. *I transpose; all have* What harme was (*but* harm *is monosyllabic, and the line is then bad*). 998. Tn. F. coude. Th. thynketh; F. thenketh. 1000. F. had hadde hyt hadde. 1001. *All* dele. 1002. *All* wele. 1003. F. al and alle. 1004. Th. principal; F. princ:palle. 1007. F. stedefaste. 1008. Th. Tn. B. attempre; F. atempry. 1009. Tn. knew; F. knewe. Tn. yit; F. yitte. 1010. Tn. wit; F. wytte. 1011. F. vnderstoode. 1012. F. goode. 1016. *All* wronge. 1019. Tn. luste; F. lust. 1020. *All* wolde not; *an error for* nolde (Koch). 1022. *All* halfe worde.

THE MINOR POEMS.

But-if men wolde upon hir lye,
Ne sende men in-to Walakye,
To Pruyse and in-to Tartarye,   1025
To Alisaundre, ne in-to Turkye,
And bidde him faste, anoon that he
Go hoodles to the drye see,
And come hoom by the Carrenare;
And seye, "Sir, be now right ware   1030
That I may of yow here seyn
Worship, or that ye come ageyn!"
She ne used no suche knakkes smale.
'But wherfor that I telle my tale?
Right on this same, as I have seyd,   1035
Was hoolly al my love leyd;
For certes, she was, that swete wyf,
My suffisaunce, my lust, my lyf,
Myn hap, myn hele, and al my blisse,
My worldes welfare and my [lisse],   1040
And I hirs hoolly, everydel.'
'By our lord,' quod I, 'I trowe yow wel!
Hardely, your love was wel beset,
I not how ye mighte have do bet.'
'Bet? ne no wight so wel!' quod he.   1045
'I trowe hit, sir,' quod I, 'parde!'
'Nay, leve hit wel!' 'Sir, so do I;
I leve yow wel, that trewely
Yow thoghte, that she was the beste,
And to beholde the alderfaireste,   1050
Who so had loked with your eyen.'
'With myn? nay, alle that hir seyen

1025. Th. F. pruyse; Tn. pruse; B. sprewse.   1027. Th. bydde; F. bid.
1028. Th. hoodlesse; F. hoodeles. *All* in-to; *read* to.   1029. B. hom; *rest*
home. Tn. Carrynare.   1030. F. Tn. sey; Th. *omits*.   1032. F. Worshyppe.   1034. F. wherfore. Tn. telle; F. tel.   1035. *All* seyde (sayde).
1036. F. hooly. *All* leyde (layde).   1037. *All* wyfe (wife).   1038. *All*
luste. *All* lyfe (life).   1039. Tn. F. happe; Th. hope.   1040. F. worldys.
I substitute lisse *for* goddesse; *see note*.   1041. F. hooly hires and; Th. Tn.
holy hers and; B. hooly hyres.   1042. F. oure.   1043. Th. beset; F.
besette; Tn. yset.   1044. F. myght haue doo bette.   1045. Th. Tn. Bet;
F. Bette. F. wele.   1046. F. hit wel sir; Th. Tn. *om*. hit wel.   1047.
F. sire.   1048. *All* trewly.   1049. Th. Tn. beste; F. best.   1050. Tn.
fayreste; F. fayrest.   1051. *All ins*. her *after* loked.   1052. Tn. B. alle; F. al.

III. THE BOOK OF THE DUCHESSE. 313

Seyde, and sworen hit was so.
And thogh they ne hadde, I wolde tho
Have loved best my lady fre,   1055
Thogh I had had al the beautee
That ever had Alcipyades,
And al the strengthe of Ercules,
And therto had the worthinesse
Of Alisaundre, and al the richesse   1060
That ever was in Babiloyne,
In Cartage, or in Macedoyne,
Or in Rome, or in Ninive;
And therto al-so hardy be
As was Ector, so have I Ioye,   1065
That Achilles slow at Troye—
And therfor was he slayn also
In a temple, for bothe two
Were slayn, he and Antilegius,
And so seyth Dares Frigius,   1070
For love of [hir] Polixena—
Or ben as wys as Minerva,
I wolde ever, withoute drede,
Have loved hir, for I moste nede!
"Nede!" nay, I gabbe now,   1075
Noght "nede," and I wol telle how,
For of good wille myn herte hit wolde,
And eek to love hir I was holde
As for the fairest and the beste.
'She was as good, so have I reste,   1080
As ever was Penelope of Grece,
Or as the noble wyf Lucrece,

1053. *All* swore; *read* sworen.   1054. *Perhaps read* nadde.   1056. F. had hadde (*better* hadde had).   1057. *All* Alcipyades.   1060. Th. Tn. Alisaundre; F. Alisaunder. *? omit* al *or* the.   1064. Th. therto; F. Tn. to (*see* 1059). Th. Tn. al so; F. also as.   1066. Tn. slow; F. slough.   1067. Tn. therfor; F. ther fore.   1069. Tn. slayn; F. slayne. Th. Tn. Antilegius; F. Antylegyus.   1071. *I supply* hir.   1074. Tn. moste; F. most.   1075. *All insert* trewly *after* nay; *we must omit it*.   1075, 6. F. nowe, howe. 1077. Th. good; F. goode. F. hert.   1078. *All* eke.   1081. *All ins*. was *after* ever. Th. Penelope; F. Penelopee; Tn. penelapie; *read* Pénelóp'). 1082. *All* wyfe (wife).

That was the beste—he telleth thus,
The Romain Tytus Livius—
She was as good, and no-thing lyke,　　　　1085
Thogh hir stories be autentyke;
Algate she was as trewe as she.
　'But wherfor that I telle thee
Whan I first my lady sey?
I was right yong, [the] sooth to sey,　　　　1090
And ful gret need I hadde to lerne;
Whan my herte wolde yerne
To love, it was a greet empryse.
But as my wit coude best suffyse,
After my yonge childly wit,　　　　1095
Withoute drede, I besette hit
To love hir in my beste wyse,
To do hir worship and servyse
That I tho coude, by my trouthe,
Withoute feyning outher slouthe;　　　　1100
For wonder fayn I wolde hir see.
So mochel hit amended me,
That, whan I saw hir first a-morwe,
I was warished of al my sorwe
Of al day after, til hit were eve;　　　　1105
Me thoghte no-thing mighte me greve,
Were my sorwes never so smerte.
And yit she sit so in myn herte,
That, by my trouthe, I nolde noght,
For al this worlde, out of my thoght　　　　1110
Leve my lady; no, trewly!'
　'Now, by my trouthe, sir,' quod I,

1083. Th. beste; F. best.　　1084. Tn. romayn; F. Romayne.　　1088. *All* wherfore.　　1089. F. firste. Th. sey; F. say.　　1090. *All* yonge. *I supply* the.　　1091. F. grete nede.　　1093. F. grete.　　1094. *All* wytte. Tn. best; F. beste.　　1095. *All* yonge. F. childely wytte.　　1097. B. beste; *rest* best.　　1098. F. worshippe. Th. F. *insert* the *before* servyse; *but* Tn. *omits*.　　1099. *All* coude tho; *read* tho coude. Tn. by; F. be.　　1100. F. Feynynge.　　1101. Tn. fayn; F. feyne.　　1103. Tn. saw; F. sawgh.　　1104. Th. warysshed; F. Tn. warshed.　　1106. F. thoght.　　1108. Tn. sit; Th. syt; F. sytte. Th. Tn. in; F. *om*.　　1110. Th. out; Tn. F. oute.　　1111. *All* trewly.

III. THE BOOK OF THE DUCHESSE.

'Me thinketh ye have such a chaunce
As shrift withoute repentaunce.'
    'Repentaunce! nay fy,' quod he;   1115
'Shulde I now repente me
To love? nay, certes, than were I wel
Wers than was Achitofel,
Or Anthenor, so have I Ioye,
The traytour that betraysed Troye,   1120
Or the false Genelon,
He that purchased the treson
Of Rowland and of Olivere.
Nay, whyl I am a-lyve here
I nil foryete hir never-mo.'   1125
    'Now, goode sir,' quod I [right] tho,
'Ye han wel told me her-before.
It is no need reherse hit more
How ye sawe hir first, and where;
But wolde ye telle me the manere,   1130
To hir which was your firste speche—
Therof I wolde yow be-seche—
And how she knewe first your thoght,
Whether ye loved hir or noght,
And telleth me eek what ye have lore;   1135
I herde yow telle her-before.'
    'Ye,' seyde he, 'thou nost what thou menest;
I have lost more than thou wenest.'
    'What los is that, [sir]?' quod I tho;
'Nil she not love yow? is hit so?   1140
Or have ye oght [y-]doon amis,
That she hath left yow? is hit this?'

1114. *All* shrifte (shryfte). 1117. Tn. certes; F. certis. 1118. Tn. Achitofell; F. Achetofel. 1120. Tn. traytour; F. traytor*e*. Tn. F. B. betraysed; Th. betrayed. 1121. Th. false; F. fals. *All* Genellon. 1123. Tn. rowland; F. Rowlande. 1124. *All* while (whyle). 1126. F. good; Tn. gode. *I supply* right. 1127. *All* tolde. B. her-; F. here-. 1128. *All* nede. F. Th. Tn. *insert* to *after* need; B. *omits it*. Tn. hit; Th. it; F. *om.* 1129. Tn. sawe; F. sawgh. Th. first; F. firste. 1130. Tn. telle; F. tel. 1131. Tn. her; F. hire. B. firste; *rest* first. 1133. *All* knewe (*subjunctive*). 1135. *All* eke. 1136. Tn. her-; F. here-. 1137. Tn. seyde he; F. he seyde. F. menyst. 1138. F. wenyst. 1139. Tn. los; F. losse. *I supply* sir. 1141. F. doon; Tn. Th. done (*read* y-doon). 1142. F. hathe lefte.

316   THE MINOR POEMS.

  For goddes love, tel me al.'
   'Before god,' quod he, 'and I shal.
I saye right as I have seyd,   1145
On hir was al my love leyd;
And yet she niste hit never a del
Noght longe tyme, leve hit wel.
For be right siker, I durste noght
For al this worlde telle hir my thoght,   1150
Ne I wolde have wratthed hir, trewly.
For wostow why? she was lady
Of the body; she had the herte,
And who hath that, may not asterte.
  'But, for to kepe me fro ydelnesse,   1155
Trewly I did my besinesse
To make songes, as I best coude,
And ofte tyme I song hem loude;
And made songes a gret del,
Al-thogh I coude not make so wel   1160
Songes, ne knowe the art al,
As coude Lamekes sone Tubal,
That fond out first the art of songe;
For, as his brothers hamers ronge
Upon his anvelt up and doun,   1165
Therof he took the firste soun;
But Grekes seyn, Pictagoras,
That he the firste finder was
Of the art; Aurora telleth so,
But therof no fors, of hem two.   1170

1143. Th. tel; F. telle. Th. al; F. alle.   1144. Th. shal; F. shalle.
1145. *All* say. Tn. seyd; F. seyde.   1146. Tn. leyd; F. leyde.   1147.
All needlessly insert not (*or* nat) *after* hit.   1150. F. tel.   1153. Tn.
herte; F. hert.   1154. Th. asterte; F. astert.   1155. *Omit* But for? F.
ins. so *before* fro; Tn. Th. *omit.*   1158. *All* songe.   1159. F. Th.
Tn. *ins.* this (B. thus) *before* a. F. grete dele.   1160. *All* wele.   1161.
Th. Tn. ne; B. to; F. the (!).   F. knowe (*infin.*); Tn. know; Th. knewe
(*wrongly*). *All* the arte; *perhaps read* that art.   1162. Th. Lamekes; F.
lamekys. Th. Tubal; F. Tuballe; Tn. B. Tuballe.   1163. B. fonde; *rest*
founde. Th. first; F. firste. *All* songe.   1164. Tn. brothers; F. brothres.
1165. Th. anvelt; Tn. anuelte; F. Anuelet. Tn. doun; F. doon.   1166. F.
tooke. B. fyrste; *rest* first. Tn. soune; F. soon.   1167. Th. of Pithagoras.
1168. Tn. fyrste; F. first.   1169. *All* arte.

III. THE BOOK OF THE DUCHESSE.

Algates songes thus I made
Of my feling, myn herte to glade;
And lo! this was [the] alther-firste,
I not wher [that] hit were the werste.—
¶ "Lord, hit maketh myn herte light, 1175
Whan I thenke on that swete wight
   That is so semely on to see;
   And wisshe to god hit might so be,
That she wolde holde me for hir knight,
My lady, that is so fair and bright!"— 1180
   'Now have I told thee, sooth to saye,
My firste song. Upon a daye
I bethoghte me what wo
And sorwe that I suffred tho
For hir, and yet she wiste hit noght, 1185
Ne telle hir durste I nat my thoght.
"Allas!" thoghte I, "I can no reed;
And, but I telle hir, I nam but deed;
And if I telle hir, to seye sooth,
I am a-dred she wol be wrooth; 1190
Allas! what shal I thanne do?"
   'In this debat I was so wo,
Me thoghte myn herte braste a-tweyn!
So atte laste, soth to seyn,
I me bethoghte that nature 1195
Ne formed never in creature
So moche beaute, trewely,
And bounte, withouten mercy.

1171. F. Algatis. 1172. F. felynge; hert. 1173. Th. this; F. Tn. thus. *I supply* the. Tn. firste; F. first. 1174. Th. werst; Tn. F. *repeat* first. *I supply* that. 1175. *All* Lorde. Tn. herte; F. hert. 1178. *All* myght (might). 1180. *All* faire (fayre). 1181. *All* tolde. Tn. soth; F. sothe. *All* say. 1182. Tn. firste; F. first. *All* songe; *all* day. 1183. Tn. bethoghte; F. bethoght. 1185. F. wyst. 1186. Tn. telle; F. tel. *All* durst. 1187. Tn. thoghte; F. thoght. F. rede. 1188. *All* am; *grammar requires* nam. F. dede. 1189. Tn. if; F. yif. *All* sey (say), *after which* ryght *is needlessly inserted; I omit it.* Tn. soth; F. sothe. 1190. Tn. wroth; F. wrothe. 1192. *All* debate. 1193. Tn. thoghte; F. thoght. F. brast; Th. Tn. braste (*subj.*). Tn. a tweyn; F. a tweyne. 1194. *All* at the; *read* atte. Tn. seyn; F. sayne. 1195. *All* bethoght (bethought) me 1197. *All* trewly *or* truly. 1198. F. wyth oute; *read* withouten.

318   THE MINOR POEMS.

'In hope of that, my tale I tolde
With sorwe, as that I never sholde,　　　　1200
For nedes; and, maugree my heed,
I moste have told hir or be deed.
I not wel how that I began,
Ful evel rehersen hit I can;
And eek, as helpe me god with-al,　　　　1205
I trowe hit was in the dismal,
That was the ten woundes of Egipte;
For many a word I over-skipte
In my tale, for pure fere
Lest my wordes mis-set were.　　　　1210
With sorweful herte, and woundes dede,
Softe and quaking for pure drede
And shame, and stinting in my tale
For ferde, and myn hewe al pale,
Ful ofte I wex bothe pale and reed;　　　　1215
Bowing to hir, I heng the heed;
I durste nat ones loke hir on,
For wit, manere, and al was gon.
I seyde "mercy!" and no more;
Hit nas no game, hit sat me sore.　　　　1220
 'So atte laste, sooth to seyn,
Whan that myn herte was come ageyn,
To telle shortly al my speche,
With hool herte I gan hir beseche
That she wolde be my lady swete;　　　　1225
And swor, and gan hir hertely hete
Ever to be stedfast and trewe,
And love hir alwey freshly newe,

1201. F. nedys; Mawgree. Th. heed; F. hede.　　1202. Tn. moste; F. most. All tolde. Th. deed; F. dede.　　1203. Th. began; F. beganne (!).　　1204. All reherse or reherce; but read rehersen.　　1205, 6. All eke. Th. -al, dismal; F. Tn. -alle, dismalle.　　1208. All worde.　　1210. F. wordys. Tn. mysset; F. mys sette.　　1212. F. quakynge.　　1213. F. styntynge.　　1215. Tn. wex; F. wexe. Th. reed; F. rede.　　1216. F. Bowynge. Th. heed; F. hede.　　1218. Tn. wit; F. witte. All maner.　　1220. All sate (!).　　1221. All at the; read atte. Tn. so'h; F. sothe. Tn. seyn; F. seyne.　　1222. Tn. herte; F. hert. Tn. agayn; F. ageyne.　　1223. Th. shortly; F. shortely. Th. al; Tn. B. alle; F. at (!).　　1226. All swore (!).　　1228. F. fresshly.

III. THE BOOK OF THE DUCHESSE.

And never other lady have,
And al hir worship for to save   1230
As I best coude; I swor hir this—
"For youres is al that ever ther is
For evermore, myn herte swete!
And never false yow, but I mete,
I nil, as wis god helpe me so!"   1235
  'And whan I had my tale y-do,
God wot, she acounted nat a stree
Of al my tale, so thoghte me.
To telle shortly as hit is,
Trewly hir answere, hit was this;   1240
I can not now wel counterfete
Hir wordes, but this was the grete
Of hir answere; she sayde, "nay"
Al-outerly. Allas! that day
The sorwe I suffred, and the wo!   1245
That trewly Cassandra, that so
Bewayled the destruccioun
Of Troye and of Ilioun,
Had never swich sorwe as I tho.
I durste no more say therto   1250
For pure fere, but stal away;
And thus I lived ful many a day:
That trewely, I hadde no need
Ferther than my beddes heed
Never a day to seche sorwe;   1255
I fond hit redy every morwe,
For-why I loved hir in no gere.
  'So hit befel, another yere,
I thoughte ones I wolde fonde
To do hir knowe and understonde   1260

1230. F. worshippe.   1231. *All* swore *or* swere (!).   1232. Th. al; F. alle.   1234. *All ins.* to *before* false.   1235. Tn. wisse; F. wysse; B. wys.   1237. *All* wote (!).   1238. Tn. thoghte; F. thoght.   1239. *All ins.* ryght *before* as.   1242. F. wordys.   1244. Th. Al; F. Alle.   1248. Th. Troye; F. Troy.   1250. Tn. durste; F. durst.   1251. F. stale.   1253. *All* trewly. *All* nede.   1254. *All* hede.   1256. *All* fonde *or* founde.

THE MINOR POEMS.

My wo; and she wel understood
That I ne wilned thing but good,
And worship, and to kepe hir name
Over al thing, and drede hir shame,
And was so besy hir to serve ;— 1265
And pite were I shulde sterve,
Sith that I wilned noon harm, y-wis.
So whan my lady knew al this,
My lady yaf me al hoolly
The noble yift of hir mercy, 1270
Saving hir worship, by al weyes ;
Dredles, I mene noon other weyes.
And therwith she yaf me a ring ;
I trowe hit was the firste thing ;
But if myn herte was y-waxe 1275
Glad, that is no need to axe !
As helpe me god, I was as blyve,
Reysed, as fro dethe to lyve,
Of alle happes the alder-beste,
The gladdest and the moste at reste. 1280
For trewely, that swete wight,
Whan I had wrong and she the right,
She wolde alwey so goodely
For-yeve me so debonairly.
In alle my youthe, in alle chaunce, 1285
She took me in hir governaunce.
'Therwith she was alway so trewe,
Our Ioye was ever y-liche newe ;
Our hertes wern so even a payre,
That never nas that oon contrayre 1290

1261. F. vnderstode.   1262. Th. thyng; F. Tn. B. no thynge; *but* no *is not required by idiom or metre.* All goode, gode.   1263. F. worshippe.   1264. All al (*or* alle) thynges ; *but* al thing *is the right idiom.* Th. drede ; Tn. to drede ; F. dred.   1266. *For* And *read* That (Lange).   1267. All harme.   1268. Tn. knew ; F. knewe.   1269. F. hooly.   1270. F. yifte.   1271. F. Savynge hir worshippe.   1273. All rynge (!).   1274. Tn. firste ; F. first. Th. thyng; F. thynge.   1275. Tn. if; F. yif. Tn. herte ; F. hert.   1276. Tn. Glad ; F. Gladde. All nede.   1279. Tn. alle ; F. al.   1281. All trewly (treuly).   1282. Th. Tn. B. the ; *which* F. *omits.*   1284. Th. debonairly ; F. debonairely.   1285. Tn. B. alle (*first time*) ; *the rest* al. B. alle (*second time*) ; *rest* al.   1286. F. tooke.   1289. F. Oure. Th. F. werne ; Tn. weren. Th. euen ; F. evene.   1290. Th. Tn. contrayre ; F. contrarye.

III. THE BOOK OF THE DUCHESSE.

To that other, for no wo.
For sothe, y-liche they suffred tho
Oo blisse and eek oo sorwe bothe;
Y-liche they were bothe gladde and wrothe;
Al was us oon, withoute were. 1295
And thus we lived ful many a yere
So wel, I can nat telle how.'
 'Sir,' quod I, 'wher is she now?'
'Now!' quod he, and stinte anoon.
 Therwith he wex as deed as stoon, 1300
And seyde, 'allas! that I was bore!
That was the los, that her-before
I tolde thee, that I had lorn.
Bethenk how I seyde her-beforn,
"Thou wost ful litel what thou menest; 1305
I have lost more than thou wenest"—
God wot, allas! right that was she!'
 'Allas! sir, how? what may that be?'
'She is deed!' 'Nay!' 'Yis, by my trouthe!'
'Is that your los? by god, hit is routhe!' 1310
 And with that worde, right anoon,
They gan to strake forth; al was doon,
For that tyme, the hert-hunting.
 With that, me thoghte, that this king
Gan [quikly] hoomward for to ryde 1315
Unto a place ther besyde,
Which was from us but a lyte,
A long castel with walles whyte,
By seynt Iohan! on a riche hil,
As me mette; but thus it fil. 1320

1293. *All* eke. 1294. *All* glad. 1300. Tn. B. wex; F. waxe; Th. woxe. Th. deed; F. dede. 1302. Tn. los; F. losse. 1303. F. hadde; *rest* had. *All* lorne (!). 1304. F. Bethenke. F. herebeforne. 1305. F. menyst. 1306. F. wenyst. 1307. F. wote. 1309. Th. deed; F. ded. Tn. bi; F. be. 1310. F. youre. Tn. los; F. losse. Th. by; F. be. 1312. *Read rather* They gonne forth straken (*or* striken). 1313. Th. hart; F. Tn. herte (!). 1314. F. thoght; kynge. 1315. *I supply* quikly; *the line is too short.* 1316. *All insert* was *after* place. 1318. *All* longe. F. wallys. 1319. Th. Tn. By; F. Be. Th. hyl; F. Tn. hille. 1320. Th. fyl; F. Tn. fille (!).

v

THE MINOR POEMS.

    Right thus me mette, as I yow telle,
That in the castel was a belle,
As hit had smiten houres twelve.—

    Therwith I awook my-selve,
And fond me lying in my bed;   1325
And the book that I had red,
Of Alcyone and Seys the king,
And of the goddes of sleping,
I fond it in myn honde ful even.
    Thoghte I, 'this is so queynt a sweven,   1330
That I wol, by processe of tyme,
Fonde to putte this sweven in ryme
As I can best'; and that anoon.—
This was my sweven; now hit is doon.   1334

Explicit the Boke of the Duchesse.

1322. F. castell. *All ins.* ther *before* was.   1323. Th. smytte; F. Tn. smyte; *read* smiten (*pp.*). Th. houres; F. oures.   1324. F. awooke.   1325. *All* fonde *or* founde. F. lyinge. Tn. bed; F. bedde.   1326. F. booke. Tn. had red; F. hadde redde.   1327. Th. Alcyone; F. Alchione. F. kynge. 1328. F. goddys of slepynge.   1329. Tn. euyn; F. evene.   1330. Tn. Thoghte; F. Thoght. Tn. sweuyn; F. sweuene.   1331. Th. by; F. be. 1332. *All* put. Tn. sweuyn; F. sweuene.   1334. Tn. sweuyn; F. sweuene. COLOPHON; *so in* F. B.

IV. THE COMPLEYNT OF MARS.

The Proem.

'GLADETH, ye foules, of the morow gray,
Lo! Venus risen among yon rowes rede!
And floures fresshe, honoureth ye this day;
For when the sonne uprist, then wol ye sprede.
But ye lovers, that lye in any drede,   5
Fleëth, lest wikked tonges yow espye;
Lo! yond the sonne, the candel of Ielosye!

With teres blewe, and with a wounded herte
Taketh your leve; and, with seynt Iohn to borow,
Apeseth somwhat of your sorowes smerte,   10
Tyme cometh eft, that cese shal your sorow;
The glade night is worth an hevy morow!'—
(Seynt Valentyne! a foul thus herde I singe
Upon thy day, er sonne gan up-springe).—

The authorities here used are: F. (Fairfax 16); Tn. (Tanner 346); Ju. (Julian Notary's edition); Harl. (Harleian 7333); T. (Trinity College, Cambridge, R. 3. 20); Ar. (Arch. Seld. B. 24, in the Bodleian Library). *Also* Th. (Thynne, ed. 1532). *I follow* F. *mainly; and note variations from it.*

    1. Ar. foules; Ju. fowles; T. fooles (!); Harl. floures (*see* l. 3); F. Tn. lovers (*wrongly*). F. Harl. on; Tn. in; *rest* of.   2. Ar. the; F. Harl. yow; Tn. Ju. you; T. your (*wrongly*; Thynne (1532) *has* yon, *which, after all, is clearly right*).   3. T. Ar. honoureth; F. Tn. honouren. F. the (!); *rest* ye. F. Tn. T. day; Ju. Harl. Ar. may (!)   4. F. Harl. sunne; *rest* sonne. Ar. vp risith. Ju. T. Ar. ye; F. they (!); Tn. the (!); Harl. he (!!).   5. Ar. any; F. eny.   7. F. Loo yonde; sunne; Ialosye.   8. F. blew; hert.   9. F. sent; Ar. seynt.   10. F. sum-; smert.   11. Ar. eft; Th. efte; T. efft; F. ofte.   12. Tn. Th. glade; F. glad.   13. F. foule; herd.   14. F. your; Ar. the; *rest* thy. F. sunne.

Yet sang this foul—'I rede yow al a-wake, 15
And ye, that han not chosen in humble wyse,
Without repenting cheseth yow your make.
And ye, that han ful chosen as I devyse,
Yet at the leste renoveleth your servyse;
Confermeth it perpetuely to dure, 20
And paciently taketh your aventure.

And for the worship of this hye feste,
Yet wol I, in my briddes wyse, singe
The sentence of the compleynt, at the leste,
That woful Mars made atte departinge 25
Fro fresshe Venus in a morweninge,
Whan Phebus, with his fyry torches rede,
Ransaked every lover in his drede.

The Story.

¶ Whylom the thridde hevenes lord above,
As wel by hevenish revolucioun 30
As by desert, hath wonne Venus his love,
And she hath take him in subieccioun,
And as a maistresse taught him his lessoun,
Comaunding him that never, in hir servyse,
He nere so bold no lover to despyse. 35

For she forbad him Ielosye at alle,
And cruelte, and bost, and tirannye;
She made him at hir lust so humble and talle,
That when hir deyned caste on him her yë,
He took in pacience to live or dye; 40
And thus she brydeleth him in hir manere,
With no-thing but with scourging of hir chere.

---

15. F. sange; foule.   17-19. *in wrong order in* F. Tn.   17. T. you; Ar. ʒow; Ju. ye; *rest om.*   19. F. this fest; *rest* the leste (lest, leest).   22. F. highe; Tn. high; *rest* hye. F. fest.   24. F. lest.   25. F. departyng; *see* l. 149.   26. F. morwnyng (*see* Kn. Tale, 204).   28. F. *ins.* hath *bef.* every; Tn. hat; Ju. had; *rest om.*   29. T. thridde; F. thrid.   35. Ju. Ar. nere; F. T. ner. F. bolde; dispise.   38. F. (*only*) *om.* him. F. calle (*for* talle); Harl. talle; Ju. Ar. tall; T. tal.   39. F. to cast; Ju. T. *rightly omit* to.   40. F. toke.   41. F. maner.   42. Ju. scourgyng; T. skowrginge; Ar. scurgeing; Tn. schouryng (*sic*); F. stering; Th. scornyng, *and ed.* 1561 scorning (*probably a substitution*). F. cher.

IV. THE COMPLEYNT OF MARS.

Who regneth now in blisse but Venus,
That hath this worthy knight in governaunce?
Who singeth now but Mars, that serveth thus   45
The faire Venus, causer of plesaunce?
He bynt him to perpetual obeisaunce,
And she bynt hir to loven him for ever,
But so be that his trespas hit dissever.

Thus be they knit, and regnen as in heven   50
By loking most; til hit fil, on a tyde,
That by hir bothe assent was set a steven,
That Mars shal entre, as faste as he may glyde,
Into hir nexte paleys, to abyde,
Walking his cours til she had him a-take,   55
And he preyde hir to haste hir for his sake.

Then seyde he thus—"myn hertes lady swete,
Ye knowe wel my mischef in that place;
For sikerly, til that I with yow mete,
My lyf stant ther in aventure and grace;   60
But when I see the beaute of your face,
Ther is no dreed of deth may do me smerte,
For al your lust is ese to myn herte."

She hath so gret compassion of hir knight,
That dwelleth in solitude til she come;   65
For hit stood so, that ilke tyme, no wight
Counseyled him, ne seyde to him welcome,
That nigh hir wit for wo was overcome;
Wherfore she spedde hir as faste in hir weye,
Almost in oon day, as he dide in tweye.   70

---

46. F. fair.   48. T. Ar. loven; *rest* loue.   49. Tn. trespas; F. trespace. T. Ar. disseuer; F. deseuer.   51. T. Ju. Tn. By; F. Be.   53. F. fast.   54. Tn. nexte; F. next.   55. Ar. our*e*-take.   56. T. preyde; F. preiede. F. faste (!); Harl. hasten; *rest* haste.   57. F. hertis; suete.   58. F. myschefe.   59. F. sikirly.   60. F. lyfe.   62. F. smert.   63. F. alle; hert.   64. F. grete. F. on; *rest* of.   66. F. stode.   67. Jn. Harl. T. Ar. *ins*. there *after* 1*st* him.   68. F. nyghe; witte. F. sorowe; Tn. sorow; *rest* wo, woo.   69. T. spedde; F. sped. T. Ar. als; *rest* as. F. fast; wey.   70. F. dyd; twey.

The grete Ioye that was betwix hem two,
Whan they be met, ther may no tunge telle,
Ther is no more, but unto bed they go,
And thus in Ioye and blisse I let hem dwelle;
This worthy Mars, that is of knighthod welle,   75
The flour of fairnes lappeth in his armes,
And Venus kisseth Mars, the god of armes.

Soiourned hath this Mars, of which I rede,
In chambre amid the paleys prively
A certeyn tyme, til him fel a drede,   80
Through Phebus, that was comen hastely
Within the paleys-yates sturdely,
With torche in honde, of which the stremes brighte
On Venus chambre knokkeden ful lighte.

The chambre, ther as lay this fresshe quene,   85
Depeynted was with whyte boles grete,
And by the light she knew, that shoon so shene,
That Phebus cam to brenne hem with his hete;
This sely Venus, dreynt in teres wete,
Enbraceth Mars, and seyde, "alas! I dye!   90
The torch is come, that al this world wol wrye."

Up sterte Mars, him liste not to slepe,
Whan he his lady herde so compleyne;
But, for his nature was not for to wepe,
In stede of teres, fro his eyen tweyne   95
The fyry sparkes brosten out for peyne;
And hente his hauberk, that lay him besyde;
Flee wolde he not, ne mighte him-selven hyde.

---

71. Ar. betuix; F. betwex; *rest* bytwene.   72. F. When; mette; tel.
74. F. duel.   75. F. knyghthode wel.   76. F. feyrenesse.   81. F.
Throgh.   82. F. (*alone*) *inserts* ful *before* sturdely.   83. F. bryght.   84. Ju.
Th. knockeden; Harl. knokkide; Tn. knokked; F. knokken (*wrongly*; *a copy in*
MS. Pepys 2006 *rightly has* knokkeden).   87. F. shone.   88. Tn. T. brenne;
F. bren.   89. F. cely (*for* sely); Tn. Ju. sely. MSS. nygh dreynt; *omit* nygh
92. Tn. sterte; F. stert.   Tn. liste; F. lust.   95. Tn. stede; F. stid. F. twyne
97. F. hent; hauberke; ley.   98. F. wold; myght.

IV. THE COMPLEYNT OF MARS.

He throweth on his helm of huge wighte,
And girt him with his swerde; and in his honde 100
His mighty spere, as he was wont to fighte,
He shaketh so that almost it to-wonde;
Ful hevy he was to walken over londe;
He may not holde with Venus companye,
But bad hir fleen, lest Phebus hir espye. 105

O woful Mars! alas! what mayst thou seyn,
That in the paleys of thy disturbaunce
Art left behinde, in peril to be sleyn?
And yet ther-to is double thy penaunce,
For she, that hath thyn herte in governaunce, 110
Is passed halfe the stremes of thyn yën;
That thou nere swift, wel mayst thou wepe and cryen.

Now fleeth Venus un-to Cylenius tour,
With voide cours, for fere of Phebus light.
Alas! and ther ne hath she no socour, 115
For she ne fond ne saw no maner wight;
And eek as ther she had but litil might;
Wher-for, hir-selven for to hyde and save,
Within the gate she fledde into a cave.

Derk was this cave, and smoking as the helle, 120
Not but two pas within the gate hit stood;
A naturel day in derk I lete hir dwelle.
Now wol I speke of Mars, furious and wood;
For sorow he wolde have seen his herte blood;
Sith that he mighte hir don no companye, 125
He ne roghte not a myte for to dye.

---

99. Tn. Ju. T. throweth; F. thrwe (*badly*). F. helme; wyght. 101. F. fyght. 102. Ar. to-wound; Harl. to-wond; *rest* to-wonde. 103. Ar. he was; *rest* was he. 108. F. (*alone*) *inserts* thou *after* Art. 110. F. hert. 112. Tn. Ju. Th. nere; F. ner. 113. F. Tn. in to; Harl. to; *rest* vn to. Ju. Cylenius; Harl. Cylenyus; Ar. Cilenius; T. Celenius; Tn. cilinius; F. cilinios. F. toure. 115. Harl. T. ne; Ar. so; *rest om.* 116. F. founde; saugh. 117. F. eke. 119. Harl. T. fledde; Tn. Ju. Ar. fled; F. fel. 120. F. Derke; hel. 121. F. pales; *rest* pas (pace). F. stode. 122. F. let; duel. 123. *So all.* F. wode. 124. F. wold; sene; hert blode. 125. F. myght. Harl. done hir; Ju. doo her; T. Ar. do hir; F. Tn. haue done her; *read* hir don. 126. Tn. roghte; Ju. Harl. Ar. rought; F. thoght (!).

THE MINOR POEMS.

So feble he wex, for hete and for his wo,
That nigh he swelt, he mighte unnethe endure;
He passeth but oo steyre in dayes two,
But ner the les, for al his hevy armure, 130
He foloweth hir that is his lyves cure;
For whos departing he took gretter yre
Thanne for al his brenning in the fyre.

After he walketh softely a pas,
Compleyning, that hit pite was to here. 135
He seyde, "O lady bright, Venus! alas!
That ever so wyde a compas is my spere!
Alas! whan shal I mete yow, herte dere,
This twelfte day of April I endure,
Through Ielous Phebus, this misaventure." 140

Now god helpe sely Venus allone!
But, as god wolde, hit happed for to be,
That, whyl that Venus weping made hir mone,
Cylenius, ryding in his chevauchè,
Fro Venus valance mighte his paleys see, 145
And Venus he salueth, and maketh chere,
And hir receyveth as his frend ful dere.

Mars dwelleth forth in his adversite,
Compleyning ever on hir departinge;
And what his compleynt was, remembreth me; 150
And therfore, in this lusty morweninge,
As I best can, I wol hit seyn and singe,
And after that I wol my leve take;
And God yeve every wight Ioye of his make!

---

128. F. myght.   129. Harl. o; T. oon; Ju. one; *rest* a. Tn. Ju. Harl. steyre; T. stayre; F. sterre (!).   130. F. lesse.   132. F. toke.   133. Harl. T. Thanne; F. Then.   134. F. paas.   135. F. heree.   137. F. speree.   138. F. hert.   139. T. twelfft (*but read* twelfte); Ju. twelfth; Harl. Ar. twelf (*wrongly*); F. Tn. xij. F. dayes; Tn. days; *rest* day (*rightly*). 140. F. Throgh Ielouse.   141. *Read* helpe god (Koch).   143. F. while. 144. Ju. Cylenius; F. Cilinius. Tn. Lt. cheuauche; F. cheuache.   145. F. Ju. Fro; Ar. From; Tn. Harl. T. For. Ar. valance; Tn. valauns; F. Valaunses; Th. (ed. 1532) Valanus (*for* Valauns?); Ju. balance; Harl. T. balaunce.   147. F. frende.   151. F. morwnynge.   154. Ju. Th. yeue; F. yif. F. Ioy.

The compleynt of Mars.

The Proem of the Compleynt.

¶ The ordre of compleynt requireth skilfully,   155
That if a wight shal pleyne pitously,
   There mot be cause wherfor that men pleyne;
Or men may deme he pleyneth folily
And causeles; alas! that am not I!
   Wherfor the ground and cause of al my peyne,   160
So as my troubled wit may hit ateyne,
I wol reherse; not for to have redresse,
But to declare my ground of hevinesse.

Devotion.

¶ The firste tyme, alas! that I was wroght,
And for certeyn effectes hider broght   165
   By him that lordeth ech intelligence,
I yaf my trewe servise and my thoght,
For evermore—how dere I have hit boght!—
   To hir, that is of so gret excellence,
That what wight that first sheweth his presence,   170
When she is wroth and taketh of him no cure,
He may not longe in Ioye of love endure.

This is no feyned mater that I telle;
My lady is the verrey sours and welle
   Of beaute, lust, fredom, and gentilnesse,   175
Of riche aray—how dere men hit selle!—
Of al disport in which men frendly dwelle,
   Of love and pley, and of benigne humblesse,
   Of soune of instruments of al swetnesse;
And therto so wel fortuned and thewed,   180
That through the world hir goodnesse is y-shewed.

TITLE. *In* F. Ar. Ju; T. Complaint of mars.   156. F. pleyn.   157. F. wherfore; pleyn.   158. F. Other; *rest* Or. Ju. Ar. folily; F. folely.   160. F. grounde; peyn.   161. F. witte; ateyn.   163. F. grounde.   164. F. first.   166. Tn. By; F. Be.   167. F. trwe; Tn. trewe.   169. F. That (*by mistake*); *rest* To. F. excelence.   171. F. wrothe.   175. F. fredam.   179. F. Instrumentes.   181. F. thorow; worlde.

330   THE MINOR POEMS.

What wonder is then, thogh that I besette
My servise on suche oon, that may me knette
  To wele or wo, sith hit lyth in hir might?
Therfor my herte for ever I to hir hette;   185
Ne trewly, for my dethe, I shal not lette
  To ben hir trewest servaunt and hir knight.
  I flater noght, that may wite every wight;
For this day in hir servise shal I dye;
But grace be, I see hir never with yë.   190

A Lady in fear and woe.

¶ To whom shal I than pleyne of my distresse?
Who may me helpe, who may my harm redresse?
  Shal I compleyne unto my lady free?
Nay, certes! for she hath such hevinesse,
For fere and eek for wo, that, as I gesse,   195
  In litil tyme hit wol hir bane be.
  But were she sauf, hit wer no fors of me.
Alas! that ever lovers mote endure,
For love, so many a perilous aventure!

For thogh so be that lovers be as trewe   200
As any metal that is forged newe,
  In many a cas hem tydeth ofte sorowe.
Somtyme hir ladies will not on hem rewe,
Somtyme, yif that Ielosye hit knewe,
  They mighten lightly leye hir heed to borowe; 205
  Somtyme envyous folke with tunges horowe
Depraven hem; alas! whom may they plese?
But he be fals, no lover hath his ese.

---

182. *All but* Tn. Th. *om.* that. T. besette; F. beset. 183. T. oone; Tn. Ar. one; F. on (*twice*). F. knet; Ar. knett; *rest* knette. 184. F. lythe. 185. F. Therfore. F. hert. Ju. Th. hette; Ar. het; F. T. hight; Tn. set; (Longleat MS. *has* hette). 186. F. truly. Tn. Ju. T. shal I. F. let. 187. F. truest; Tn. Ar. trewest. 188. Tn. wite; F. wete; T. wit; Ju. knowe. 191. T. thane (*for* than); *rest omit*. 192. F. harme. 193. F. compleyn. 195. F. eke. 197. Ju. Ar. sauf; T. sauff; F. Tn. safe. 200. Tn. thogh; F. tho. 201. Tn. any; F. eny. 202. Tn. many; F. mony. T. Ar. cas; F. case. 203. F. Somme; *rest* Somtyme. Ju. T. Ar. lady. 204. Ar. gif; *rest* if, yf; *read* yif. 205. F. ley; hede. 207. Ju. T. Th. Deprauen; Ar. Depeynen; F. Tn. Departen.

IV. THE COMPLEYNT OF MARS.

But what availeth suche a long sermoun
Of aventures of love, up and doun?
 I wol returne and speken of my peyne;
The point is this of my destruccioun,
My righte lady, my salvacioun,
 Is in affray, and not to whom to pleyne.
 O herte swete, O lady sovereyne!
For your disese, wel oghte I swoune and swelte,
Thogh I non other harm ne drede felte.

Instability of Happiness.

¶ To what fyn made the god that sit so hye,
Benethen him, love other companye,
 And streyneth folk to love, malgre hir hede?
And then hir Ioye, for oght I can espye,
Ne lasteth not the twinkeling of an yë,
 And somme han never Ioye til they be dede.
 What meneth this? what is this mistihede?
Wherto constreyneth he his folk so faste
Thing to desyre, but hit shulde laste?

And thogh he made a lover love a thing,
And maketh hit seme stedfast and during,
 Yet putteth he in hit such misaventure,
That reste nis ther noon in his yeving.
And that is wonder, that so Iust a king
 Doth such hardnesse to his creature.
 Thus, whether love breke or elles dure,
Algates he that hath with love to done
Hath ofter wo then changed is the mone.

---

209. F. longe. 210. *Read* lov-e (e *unelided*). F. dovne. 213. Tn. righte; F. right. F. sauacyoun; *rest* saluacioun. 214. F. pleyn. 215. F. hert suete. F. Tn. o; Ar. and; T. and my; Ju. *om.* 216. F. I oght wel; Tn. I oghte wel; Ju. T. Ar. wel ought I. Ju. swowne; Ar. suoun; T. swoone; Tn. swone; F. sowne. F. swelt. 217. F. none; harme; felt. 218. Ju. fyn; *rest* fyne. F. sitte; T. sit. 219. T. Tn. Ju. him; Ar. thame; F. *om.* F. other (= or); Tn. othyr (= or); Ju. T. or. 220. F. folke. 221. F. Ioy. 222. Tn. ye; *rest* eye. 223. F. Ioy. 225. F. folke; fast. 226. F. shuld last. 228. F. stidfast. 229. Ju. put; Ar. puttis. 230. Tn. T. reste; F. rest. T. noon; Ar. non; Ju. none; F. *om.* 231. F. Iuste.

Hit semeth he hath to lovers enmite,
And lyk a fissher, as men alday may see,
  Baiteth his angle-hook with som plesaunce,
Til mony a fish is wood til that he be
Sesed ther-with; and then at erst hath he   240
  Al his desyr, and ther-with al mischaunce;
  And thogh the lyne breke, he hath penaunce;
For with the hoke he wounded is so sore,
That he his wages hath for ever-more.

The Brooch of Thebes.

¶ The broche of Thebes was of suche a kinde,   245
So ful of rubies and of stones Inde,
  That every wight, that sette on hit an yë,
He wende anon to worthe out of his minde;
So sore the beaute wolde his herte binde,
  Til he hit hadde, him thoghte he moste dye;   250
  And whan that hit was his, than shulde he drye
Such wo for drede, ay whyl that he hit hadde,
That welnigh for the fere he shulde madde.

And whan hit was fro his possessioun,
Than had he double wo and passioun   255
  For he so fair a tresor had forgo;
But yet this broche, as in conclusioun,
Was not the cause of this confusioun;
  But he that wroghte hit enfortuned hit so,
  That every wight that had hit shuld have wo;   260
And therfor in the worcher was the vyce,
And in the covetour that was so nyce.

---

236. Tn. enmyte; F. enemyte.   237. F. lyke.   238. Tn. Ju. Bayteth; F. Bateth. Ju. hook; F. hoke. Tn. som; F. summe.   239. F. fissch; wode. F. to; *rest* til.   241. F. desire.   244. F. hathe.   245. F. such. 246. F. Tn. Ar. stones of; Ju. T. *om.* of; *see* Rom. Rose, 67.   247. T. Th. sette; Ar. sett; *rest* set.   248. Tn. wende; F. wend.   249. F. wold; hert. 250. T. hade; *rest* had. F. thoght. Tn. moste; F. must.   251. F. Ju. *om.* that. F. (*only*) *om.* his. F. shuld.   252. Ju. T. hadde; F. had.   253. Ju. sholde madde; F. shuld mad.   256. F. feir; tresore (Tn. Iuel).   259. F. wroght. Tn. Th. enfortuned; T. enfortund; F. enfortune (!).   261. F. therfore.

IV. THE COMPLEYNT OF MARS.

So fareth hit by lovers and by me;
For thogh my lady have so gret beaute,
  That I was mad til I had gete hir grace,   265
She was not cause of myn adversite,
But he that wroghte hir, also mot I thee,
  That putte suche a beaute in hir face,
That made me to covete and purchace
Myn owne deth; him wyte I that I dye,   270
And myn unwit, that ever I clomb so hye.

An Appeal for Sympathy.

¶But to yow, hardy knightes of renoun,
Sin that ye be of my divisioun,
  Al be I not worthy to so grete a name,
Yet, seyn these clerkes, I am your patroun;   275
Ther-for ye oghte have som compassioun
  Of my disese, and take it noght a-game.
The proudest of yow may be mad ful tame;
Wherfor I prey yow, of your gentilesse,
That ye compleyne for myn hevinesse.   280

And ye, my ladies, that ben trewe and stable,
By way of kinde, ye oghten to be able
  To have pite of folk that be in peyne:
Now have ye cause to clothe yow in sable;
Sith that your emperice, the honorable,   285
  Is desolat, wel oghte ye to pleyne;
Now shuld your holy teres falle and reyne.
Alas! your honour and your emperice,
Nigh deed for drede, ne can hir not chevise.

---

267. F. wroght. Ju. Ar. also; T. als; F. Tn. as.   268. F. Tn. Ju. Ar. put (*for* putte); T. list to putte. Tn. Ju. a; F. T. Ar. *om.*   269. T. Ar. to; *rest om.* F. coueten; Tn. Ju. coueyten; (*but* to covete *is better*).   270. F. ovne; Th. owne; Ju. T. Ar. owen. F. dethe.   271. F. ovne witte; Tn. *and rest* vnwi·. F. clombe.   273. F. deuisioun.   274. *Perhaps omit* to (*as* T.).   276. F. Therefore; oght; somme.   278. Tn. proudest; F. pruddest. Ar. maid; *rest* made (*for* mad, *pp.*).   279. F. Wherfore.   280. F. Tn. compleyn; Ju. Ar. compleyne; T. compleynen.   281. Ar. trewe; F. true.   282. Ar. By; F. Be.   283. F. folke; peyn.   285. Tn. emperice; F. emperise (*and in* l. 288).   286. Tn. oghte; F. oght; Ar. aughten.   289. F. Negh ded.

Compleyneth eek, ye lovers, al in-fere, 290
For hir that, with unfeyned humble chere,
  Was ever redy to do yow socour;
Compleyneth hir that ever hath had yow dere;
Compleyneth beaute, fredom, and manere;
  Compleyneth hir that endeth your labour; 295
  Compleyneth thilke ensample of al honour,
That never dide but al gentilesse;
Kytheth therfor on hir som kindenesse.' 298

---

290. F. eke.   293. Tn. Compleyneth; F. Comple*n* (*by mistake*); *see next line.*   297. Tn. dide; Ju. dyde; *rest* did. T. al; Ju. all; Ar. alway; F. Tn. *om.*   298. Ar. sum; F. summe.

V. THE PARLEMENT OF FOULES.

The Proem.

THE lyf so short, the craft so long to lerne,
Thassay so hard, so sharp the conquering,
The dredful Ioy, that alwey slit so yerne,
Al this mene I by love, that my feling
Astonyeth with his wonderful worching 5
So sore y-wis, that whan I on him thinke,
Nat wot I wel wher that I wake or winke.

For al be that I knowe not love in dede,
Ne wot how that he quyteth folk hir hyre,
Yet happeth me ful ofte in bokes rede 10
Of his miracles, and his cruel yre;
Ther rede I wel he wol be lord and syre,
I dar not seyn, his strokes been so sore,
But God save swich a lord! I can no more.

Of usage, what for luste what for lore, 15
On bokes rede I ofte, as I yow tolde.
But wherfor that I speke al this? not yore

The authorities are: F. (Fairfax 16); Gg. (Gg. 4. 27, Cambridge Univ. Library); Trin. (Trinity Coll. Camb. R. 3. 19); Cx. (Caxton's edition); Harl. (Harleian 7333); O. (St. John's Coll. Oxford); Ff. (Ff. 1. 6, Cambridge Univ. Library); *occasionally* Tn. (Tanner 346); D. (Digby 181); *and others. I follow F. mainly, corrected by* Gg. (*and others*); *and note all variations from F. of any consequence.*

TITLE; Gg. *has*—Here begynyth the parlement of Foulys; D. The parlement of Fowlis.   2. *So* F. Harl. Tn.; *some transpose* hard *and* sharp.   3. Gg. *and others* dredful; F. slyder. Gg. O. slit; Cx. flit (*for* slit); Ff. slydeth *(om.* so); F. slyd; Trin. fleeth.   5. Gg. (*and others*) with his wondyrful; F. soo with a dredeful.   7. F. Tn. wake or wynke; *rest* flete or synke; *see* 482.   9. Gg. Trin. Harl. that; *which the rest omit.*   10. Gg. Trin. Cx. Harl. Ff. ful ofte in bokis; F. in bookes ofte to.   11. F. *ins.* of *after* and; Gg. *om.*   13. F. Dar I; Gg. *and others* I dar.   14. F. suche; Gg. swich.   17. F. Tn. D. why; *rest* wherfore (wherfor).

Agon, hit happed me for to beholde
Upon a boke, was write with lettres olde;
And ther-upon, a certeyn thing to lerne,   20
The longe day ful faste I radde and yerne.

For out of olde feldes, as men seith,
Cometh al this newe corn fro yeer to yere;
And out of olde bokes, in good feith,
Cometh al this newe science that men lere.   25
But now to purpos as of this matere—
To rede forth hit gan me so delyte,
That al the day me thoughte but a lyte.

This book of which I make mencioun,
Entitled was al thus, as I shal telle,   30
'Tullius of the dreme of Scipioun';
Chapitres seven hit hadde, of hevene and helle,
And erthe, and soules that therinne dwelle,
Of whiche, as shortly as I can hit trete,
Of his sentence I wol you seyn the grete.   35

First telleth hit, whan Scipioun was come
In Afrik, how he mette Massinisse,
That him for Ioye in armes hath y nome.
Than telleth [hit] hir speche and al the blisse
That was betwix hem, til the day gan misse;   40
And how his auncestre, African so dere,
Gan in his slepe that night to him appere.

Than telleth hit that, fro a sterry place,
How African hath him Cartage shewed,

---

21. Gg. faste; F. fast. Harl. radde; F. rad; Gg. redde.   22. F. seyth; Gg. sey.   24. F. feythe; Gg. fey.   26. Gg. O. as of this; Trin. Cx. Harl. Ff. of this; F. of my firste.   28. Gg. Ff. me thou3te; Trin. Cx. Harl. me thought hit; F. thought me.   30. Gg. Cx. thus; F. Trin. Harl. there.   Gg. *and rest* as I schal; F. I shal yow.   31. F. *inserts* the *after* dreme of; *the rest omit.* Trin. Harl. O. Scipio*u*n; F. Cipio*u*n; Gg. sothion (!).   32. F. hyt had vij; Gg. *and the rest* seuene It hadde.   33. Ff. therInn*e*; F. *and the rest* theryn (*wrongly*).   34. Gg. it; O. of; *the rest omit.*   35. Gg. seyn; F. tel; *the rest* sey (say).   37. F. In-to; *rest* In. F. Aufryke; Gg. Affrik.   39. *For* hit *all wrongly have* he; see ll. 36, 43.   40. Harl. betwix; F. betwixt.   41. Gg. Affrican; F. Aufrikan.   42. F. on; *rest* in.   43. F. tolde he hym; Gg. Trin. Cx. Harl. tellith it; O. Ff. tellithe he.   44. Gg. Affrycan; F. Aufrikan. F. y-shewed; *rest* schewid, shewyd, &c.

V. THE PARLEMENT OF FOULES.

And warned him before of al his grace, 45
And seyde him, what man, lered other lewed,
That loveth comun profit, wel y-thewed,
He shal unto a blisful place wende,
Ther as Ioye is that last withouten ende.

Than asked he, if folk that heer be dede 50
Have lyf and dwelling in another place;
And African seyde, 'ye, withoute drede,'
And that our present worldes lyves space
Nis but a maner deth, what wey we trace,
And rightful folk shal go, after they dye, 55
To heven; and shewed him the galaxye.

Than shewed he him the litel erthe, that heer is,
At regard of the hevenes quantite;
And after shewed he him the nyne speres,
And after that the melodye herde he 60
That cometh of thilke speres thryes three,
That welle is of musyke and melodye
In this world heer, and cause of armonye.

Than bad he him, sin erthe was so lyte,
And ful of torment and of harde grace, 65
That he ne shulde him in the world delyte.
Than tolde he him, in certeyn yeres space,
That every sterre shulde come into his place
Ther hit was first; and al shulde out of minde
That in this worlde is don of al mankinde. 70

---

46. Gg. other; Th. eyther; *rest* or. 49. Gg. There as Ioye is that last with outy*n*; F. There Ioy is that lasteth with-out. 50. F. *inserts* the *after* if; *rest omit*. 52. Gg. Affrican; F. Aufrikan. 53. Gg. Ff. that; Trin. Cx. Harl. how; F. *om*. 54. Cx. Nis; Gg. Nys; F. Trin. Harl. Ff. Meneth. 55. Gg. *and rest* after; F. whan. Gg. Ff. gon; Harl. O. gone. 56. Cx. galaxye; F. Ff. galoxye; O. galoxie. i. watlynstrete; Harl. galorye; Trin. galry (!); Gg. galylye (!). 58. Gg. *and rest* the; Harl. tho; F. *om*. 62. T. Cx. Harl. O. That welles of musyk be (ben). 64. Gg. Ff. Tha*n* bad he hy*m* syn erthe was so lyte; F. Than bad he hym see the erthe that is so lite (*wrongly*). 65. Cx. Trin. Harl. O. ful of torment and; F. was somedel fulle; Gg. was su*m*del disseyuable and ful (!). 69. Gg. *and rest* schulde (schuld, shuld); F. shal. 70. F. was; *rest* is.

Than prayde him Scipioun to telle him al
The wey to come un-to that hevene blisse;
And he seyde, 'know thy-self first immortal,
And loke ay besily thou werke and wisse
To comun profit, and thou shalt nat misse   75
To comen swiftly to that place dere,
That ful of blisse is and of soules clere.

But brekers of the lawe, soth to seyne,
And lecherous folk, after that they be dede,
Shul alwey whirle aboute therthe in peyne,   80
Til many a world be passed, out of drede,
And than, for-yeven alle hir wikked dede,
Than shul they come unto that blisful place,
To which to comen god thee sende his grace!'—

The day gan failen, and the derke night,   85
That reveth bestes from hir besinesse,
Berafte me my book for lakke of light,
And to my bedde I gan me for to dresse,
Fulfild of thought and besy hevinesse;
For bothe I hadde thing which that I nolde,   90
Aud eek I ne hadde that thing that I wolde.

But fynally my spirit, at the laste,
For-wery of my labour al the day,
Took rest, that made me to slepe faste,
And in my slepe I mette, as I lay,   95
How African, right in that selfe aray

---

71. F. O. he; *rest* him. Gg. *and rest* to; F. *om.*   72. Gg. Trin. Harl. O. into that; Cx. unto that: F. to (*om.* that).   73. Gg. inmortal; O. Th. immortall*e*; F. *and rest* mortalle (!).   75. Gg. *and rest* not (nat, noght); F. never.   76. Gg. comyn: Cx. comen; F. come. Gg. O. to; *rest* into, vnto. 77. Trin. Cx. Harl. Ff. *retain of after* and; F. Gg. O. *omit.*   78. F. *ins.* for *before* to (*but* lawe *is dissyllabic*); *rest om.*   80. Gg. *wrongly puts* there *for* therthe; Harl. O. Ff. *place alwey before* in peyne; *the rest are bad.*   82. F. *ins.* hem *before* alle. Gg. And that for-ȝeuyn is his weked dede (*but* dede *is plural*). 84. Gg. comy*n*; *rest* come, com. Cx. Harl. the sende his; O. sende the his; Gg. synde us; Ff. send vs; F. sende ech lover (!).   85. Harl. faylen; Cx. fayllen; F. faile; Gg. folwy*n* (!).   87. F. Berefte; *rest* Berafte, Beraft.   90. F. had; Gg. hadde.   91. Harl. O. *give* 1*st* that; Trin. Cx. the; F. Ff. Gg. *om.* 95. *After* as, Gg. Trin. Harl. O. *insert* that; *it is hardly needed.*   96. Gg. Affrican; F. Aufrikan.

V. THE PARLEMENT OF FOULES.

That Scipioun him saw before that tyde,
Was comen, and stood right at my beddes syde.

The wery hunter, slepinge in his bed,
To wode ayein his minde goth anoon;   100
The Iuge dremeth how his plees ben sped;
The carter dremeth how his cartes goon;
The riche, of gold; the knight fight with his foon,
The seke met he drinketh of the tonne;
The lover met he hath his lady wonne.   105

Can I nat seyn if that the cause were
For I had red of African beforn,
That made me to mete that he stood there;
But thus seyde he, 'thou hast thee so wel born
In loking of myn olde book to-torn,   110
Of which Macrobie roghte nat a lyte,
That somdel of thy labour wolde I quyte!'—

Citherea! thou blisful lady swete,
That with thy fyr-brand dauntest whom thee lest,
And madest me this sweven for to mete,   115
Be thou my help in this, for thou mayst best;
As wisly as I saw thee north-north-west,
When I began my sweven for to wryte,
So yif me might to ryme hit and endyte!

The Story.

This forseid African me hente anoon,   120
And forth with him unto a gate broghte
Right of a parke, walled with grene stoon;
And over the gate, with lettres large y-wroghte,
Ther weren vers y-writen, as me thoghte,

---

102. Gg. Ff. carte is; O. cart is; *rest* cartes *or* cartis.   104, 5. Gg. Harl. O. met; F. Trin. Cx. meteth.   106. Gg. Cx. O. Ff. I nat; F. not I.   107. F. redde had; Gg. hadde red; *rest* had red (rad). Gg. affrican; F. Aufrican.   108. F. *omits* made; *the rest have it.*   110. to-torn] F. al to torne.   111. F. roght noght; Gg. roughte nat; Cx. roght not.   112. F. Cx. *ins.* the *after* I; *rest omit.*   114. Trin. Cx. fyrebronde; Gg. ferbrond; F. firy bronde.   119. Gg. ʒif; F. yeve. Trin. Cx. Harl. O. hit and; Ff. eke and; Gg. & ek; F. and to.   120. Gg. Affrican; F. Aufrikan.   122. F. *and rest* with; Gg. of.   124. *Read* weren; *all* were (weer). Gg. I-wrete; Th. ywritten; F. writen.

On eyther halfe, of ful gret difference, 125
Of which I shal yow sey the pleyn sentence.

'Thorgh me men goon in-to that blisful place
Of hertes hele and dedly woundes cure;
Thorgh me men goon unto the welle of Grace,
Ther grene and lusty May shal ever endure; 130
This is the wey to al good aventure;
Be glad, thou reder, and thy sorwe of-caste,
Al open am I; passe in, and hy the faste!'

'Thorgh me men goon,' than spak that other syde,
'Unto the mortal strokes of the spere, 135
Of which Disdayn and Daunger is the gyde,
Ther tree shal never fruyt ne leves bere.
This streem you ledeth to the sorwful were,
Ther as the fish in prison is al drye;
Theschewing is only the remedye.' 140

Thise vers of gold and blak y-writen were,
The whiche I gan a stounde to beholde,
For with that oon encresed ay my fere,
And with that other gan myn herte bolde;
That oon me hette, that other did me colde, 145
No wit had I, for errour, for to chese,
To entre or flee, or me to save or lese.

Right as, betwixen adamauntes two
Of even might, a pece of iren y-set,
That hath no might to meve to ne fro— 150
For what that on may hale, that other let—
Ferde I, that niste whether me was bet,

---

133. F. Ff. hye; *the rest* spede (sped). 135. F. stroke; *rest* strokes (strokis). 137. Cx. Harl. O. Ff. neuer tree shal. Cx. fruyt; Harl. O. fruyte; Trin. F. frute. 138. F. unto; *rest* to. 139. *All* is (ys). 140. O. Theschewing; Cx. Theschewyng; Harl. The eschuyng; F. Thescwynge (*sic*). 142. Trin. Cx. Harl. O. The; F. Gg. Of; Ff. On. F. Cx. a stounde (*which I think is correct*); Ff. astonde; (*alt. to*) Gg. a-stonyd; Trin. astonyed; Harl. O. astoned. 144. F. Cx. O. Ff. *insert* to *before* bolde (*wrongly*); Gg. Trin. Harl. *om*. 148. Gg. be-twixsyn; F. betwix. 149. F. y-sette; Gg. set. 150. F. That; Ff. *om.*; *rest* Ne (*which would be elided*). F. nor; *rest* ne (*better*). 152. Gg. *and rest* nyste; F. I ne wiste. Gg. *and rest* whether; F. wher that (*perhaps rightly*).

V. THE PARLEMENT OF FOULES. 341

To entre or leve, til African my gyde
Me hente, and shoof in at the gates wyde,

And seyde, 'hit stondeth writen in thy face, 155
Thyn errour, though thou telle it not to me;
But dred thee nat to come in-to this place,
For this wryting is no-thing ment by thee,
Ne by noon, but he Loves servant be;
For thou of love hast lost thy tast, I gesse, 160
As seek man hath of swete and bitternesse.

But natheles, al-though that thou be dulle,
Yit that thou canst not do, yit mayst thou see;
For many a man that may not stonde a pulle,
Yit lyketh him at the wrastling for to be, 165
And demeth yit wher he do bet or he;
And if thou haddest cunning for tendyte,
I shal thee shewen mater of to wryte.'

With that my hond in his he took anoon,
Of which I comfort caughte, and wente in faste; 170
But lord! so I was glad and wel begoon!
For over-al, wher that I myn eyen caste,
Were treës clad with leves that ay shal laste,
Eche in his kinde, of colour fresh and grene
As emeraude, that Ioye was to sene. 175

The bilder ook, and eek the hardy asshe;
The piler elm, the cofre unto careyne;
The boxtree piper; holm to whippes lasshe;

---

153. F. Affrikan. 156. Gg. Cx. O. to; *rest omit.* 158. Trin. Cx. by; Gg. bi; F. be. 159. Gg. Trin. Cx. by; F. be. 160. Gg. stat (!); *for* tast (taste). 162. F. Ff. *om.* that. 163. Gg. Harl. O. *supply* Yit; Cx. Yf; *rest om.* F. yet thou maist hyt; O. mayst thowe; *rest* yit mayst (may) thou. 165. F. Ff. *om.* for. 166. Gg. wher; *rest* whether. 167. Gg. Cx. tendite; F. Trin. to endite. 169. F. And with; *rest om.* And. 170. Gg. confort. Gg. that as; *rest* went in. 172. F. *om.* that (*but* over-al = ov'r-al). 173. F. Weren; *rest* Were. 174. Gg. O. Ff. of; F. Cx. with (*from line above*). 175. F. Emerawde. Gg. sothe (*for* Ioye, *wrongly*). 177. Cx. O. piler; Gg. pilere; Trin. pylor; F. Harl. peler. 178. F. box pipe tre; Gg. *and rest* box tre pipere (*or* piper). Trin. the holyn; Cx. holin; Ff. holye; Gg. O. holm; F. Harl. holme.

THE MINOR POEMS.

The sayling firr; the cipres, deth to pleyne;
The sheter ew, the asp for shaftes pleyne;   180
The olyve of pees, and eek the drunken vyne,
The victor palm, the laurer to devyne.

A garden saw I, ful of blosmy bowes,
Upon a river, in a grene mede,
Ther as that swetnesse evermore y-now is,   185
With floures whyte, blewe, yelowe, and rede;
And colde welle-stremes, no-thing dede,
That swommen ful of smale fisshes lighte,
With finnes rede and scales silver-brighte.

On every bough the briddes herde I singe,   190
With voys of aungel in hir armonye,
Som besyed hem hir briddes forth to bringe;
The litel conyes to hir pley gunne hye,
And further al aboute I gan espye
The dredful roo, the buk, the hert and hinde,   195
Squerels, and bestes smale of gentil kinde.

Of instruments of strenges in acord
Herde I so pleye a ravisshing swetnesse,
That god, that maker is of al and lord,
Ne herde never better, as I gesse;   200
Therwith a wind, unnethe hit might be lesse,
Made in the leves grene a noise softe
Acordant to the foules songe on-lofte.

The air of that place so attempre was
That never was grevaunce of hoot ne cold;   205
Ther wex eek every holsom spyce and gras,

---

180. Gg. Ew; *rest* ewe. 183. Harl. O. blosmy; Gg. blospemy (*for* blossemy); Cx. blossome; Trin. blossom; F. Ff. blossomed. 185. O. that; Gg. ther; *rest omit.* Gg. Ff. I-now; O. I-nowe; F. ynowh. 188. Ff. That swommen; Harl. That swommyn; Gg. That swemyn; Trin. That swymen; Cx. O. That swymmen; F. And swymmynge. 192. F. That; Gg. Ff. So (*error for* Som); *rest* Som, Some, Somme. 193. Gg. gunne; F. gunnen; *rest* gan, cane. 194. F. Trin. *om.* al. 196. Cx. Squerels; F. Squerel; *rest* Squyrelis (Squyrell*is*, Squerellis). 197. F. Cx. On; *rest* Of. Gg. Cx. O. strengis; Trin. stryngys; F. strynge. Gg. a-cord; *rest* accorde, acorde. 198. F. *om.* so. F. Gg. and (*for* a, *wrongly*); Ff. *om.*; *rest* a. 201. F. *om.* be; *rest* have it. 203. Gg. bryddis; *rest* foules. 205. F. ther of; *rest* of. 206. Gg. wex; Ff. waxed; F. growen; *rest* was (*error for* wex).

V. THE PARLEMENT OF FOULES. 343

Ne no man may ther wexe seek ne old;
Yet was ther Ioye more a thousand fold
Then man can telle; ne never wolde it nighte,
But ay cleer day to any mannes sighte.   210

Under a tree, besyde a welle, I say
Cupyde our lord his arwes forge and fyle;
And at his fete his bowe al redy lay,
And wel his doghter tempred al the whyle
The hedes in the welle, and with hir wyle   215
She couched hem after as they shulde serve,
Som for to slee, and som to wounde and kerve.

Tho was I war of Plesaunce anon-right,
And of Aray, and Lust, and Curtesye;
And of the Craft that can and hath the might   220
To doon by force a wight to do folye—
Disfigurat was she, I nil not lye;
And by him-self, under an oke, I gesse,
Sawe I Delyt, that stood with Gentilnesse.

I saw Beautee, withouten any atyr,   225
And Youthe, ful of game and Iolyte,
Fool-hardinesse, Flatery, and Desyr,
Messagerye, and Mede, and other three—
Hir names shul noght here be told for me—
And upon pilers grete of Iasper longe   230
I saw a temple of bras y-founded stronge.

---

207. Trin. Cx. Harl. Ne; *rest omit.*   208. F. more Ioye; *rest* Ioye more.   209. F. No; *rest* Then (*or* Than). F. *om.* ne; *rest* (*except* Ff.) *retain it.* Trin. was (*for* wolde).   214. Gg. Th. wel; F. O. wille; Cx. Trin. wylle; Harl. whille; *see* note.   215. Gg. *and rest* hire (hir, hyr); F. harde. F. fyle; Trin. vyle (*for* fyle); Harl. wyel; *rest* wile.   216. F. shul; *rest* shuld, shulde.   217. F. *om.* for.   221. O. doon by force; Trin. Cx. do by force; Harl. done be force; Gg. don be fore (*sic*); F. goo before.   222. F. Ff. Disfigured. Gg. Harl. nyl; Cx. Trin. Ff. wil; O. woll*e*; F. shal.   225. Gg. saw; F. sawgh. Gg. with outyn; Cx. Ff. with outen; F. with oute.   228. F. Ff. Trin. *omit* 1*st* and.   229. F. Ff. Trin. *omit* here.   230. F. pelers; *rest* pilers (pileris, pylors).   231. F. sawgh. F. glas; *rest* (*except* Ff.) bras *or* brasse. Gg. Harl. O. I-founded; Trin. enfoundyd; F. founded.

Aboute the temple daunceden alway
Wommen y-nowe, of whiche somme ther were
Faire of hem-self, and somme of hem were gay;
In kirtels, al disshevele, wente they there—   235
That was hir office alwey, yeer by yere—
And on the temple, of doves whyte and faire
Saw I sittinge many a hundred paire.

Before the temple-dore ful soberly
Dame Pees sat, with a curteyn in hir hond: 240
And hir besyde, wonder discretly,
Dame Pacience sitting ther I fond
With face pale, upon an hille of sond;
And alder-next, within and eek with-oute,
Behest and Art, and of hir folke a route.   245

Within the temple, of syghes hote as fyr
I herde a swogh that gan aboute renne;
Which syghes were engendred with desyr,
That maden every auter for to brenne
Of newe flaume; and wel aspyed I thenne   250
That al the cause of sorwes that they drye
Com of the bitter goddesse Ialousye.

The god Priapus saw I, as I wente,
Within the temple, in soverayn place stonde,
In swich aray as whan the asse him shente   255
With crye by night, and with his ceptre in honde;
Ful besily men gunne assaye and fonde
Upon his hede to sette, of sondry hewe,
Garlondes ful of fresshe floures newe.

---

232. Gg. daunsedyn; F. daunced.   233. F. O. om. ther.   234. F. om. were; rest retain.   236. Gg. ȝer be ȝeere; Trin. Cx. Harl. yere by yere; F. fro yere to yere.   237. Trin. O. of douys; Gg. of dowis; Cx. of duues; Harl. of dofes; Ff. of dowfs; F. saugh I (sic).   238. F. Of dowves white (sic); Ff. Saw I sitte; rest Saw I syttynge. Trin. Cx. Harl. O. thousand (for hundred).   240. F. om. with.   241. Gg. and rest by hire syde (for hir besyde).   244. F. om. eek; rest retain.   246. Gg. syḱys.   248. Gg. sikis.   250. Trin. Cx. flame. F. om. wel; rest retain it.   252. Gg. Cam; O. Com; F. Come; Cx. Comen; Trin. Harl. Ff. Cometh. Gg. Trin. Cx. goddesse; Harl. goddes (i. e. goddess); F. O. goddys.   253. F. sawgh.   255. Gg. swich; F. suche.   256. Trin. Cx. Ff. by; rest be.

V. THE PARLEMENT OF FOULES.

And in a privee corner, in disporte, 260
Fond I Venus and hir porter Richesse,
That was ful noble and hauteyn of hir porte;
Derk was that place, but afterward lightnesse
I saw a lyte, unnethe hit might be lesse,
And on a bed of golde she lay to reste, 265
Til that the hote sonne gan to weste.

Hir gilte heres with a golden threde
Y-bounden were, untressed as she lay,
And naked fro the breste unto the hede
Men might hir see; and, sothly for to say, 270
The remenant wel kevered to my pay
Right with a subtil kerchef of Valence,
Ther was no thikker cloth of no defence.

The place yaf a thousand savours swote,
And Bachus, god of wyn, sat hir besyde, 275
And Ceres next, that doth of hunger bote;
And, as I seide, amiddes lay Cipryde,
To whom on knees two yonge folkes cryde
To ben hir help; but thus I leet hir lye,
And ferther in the temple I gan espye 280

That, in dispyte of Diane the chaste,
Ful many a bowe y-broke heng on the wal
Of maydens, suche as gunne hir tymes waste
In hir servyse; and peynted over al
Of many a story, of which I touche shal 285
A fewe, as of Calixte and Athalaunte,
And many a mayde, of which the name I wante;

---

260. Gg. priue; F. prevy. 264. F. saugh. 267. Gg. goldene; Ff. golden; F. *and rest* golde *or* gold. 271. Cx. wel couerd; Harl. wel couered; Gg. was wel keuerede; Trin. was welle coueryd; F. keuered wel. 272. Harl. Trin. Ff. sotil. Trin. O. kerchyff; F. keuerchefe; Gg. couercheif; Cx. couerchef. 273. Gg. nas (*for* was). Gg. Harl. *alone insert* 2nd no (*but it is wanted*). 275. Trin. Cx. Bachus; *rest* Bacus. Gg. wyn; F. wyne. 277. F. Gg. Harl. Cipride (*rightly*); *the rest* Cupide (!); *see* l. 279. 278. Gg. Cx. O. two; Ff. to; F. the; Trin. Harl. *om.* Gg. O. Ff. folk ther (*for* folkes). 279. Gg. Trin. let; O. lat; Ff. lett; F. B. Cx. Harl. lete. 283. Gg. Harl. gunne; F. gonne; *rest* gan, can. 285. Gg. Cx. Ff. Ful (*for* Of).

Semyramus, Candace, and Ercules,
Biblis, Dido, Tisbe and Piramus,
Tristram, Isoude, Paris, and Achilles, 290
Eleyne, Cleopatre, and Troilus,
Silla, and eek the moder of Romulus—
Alle these were peynted on that other syde,
And al hir love, and in what plyte they dyde.

Whan I was come ayen into the place 295
That I of spak, that was so swote and grene,
Forth welk I tho, my-selven to solace.
Tho was I war wher that ther sat a quene
That, as of light the somer-sonne shene
Passeth the sterre, right so over mesure 300
She fairer was than any creature.

And in a launde, upon an hille of floures,
Was set this noble goddesse Nature;
Of braunches were hir halles and hir boures,
Y-wrought after hir craft and hir mesure; 305
Ne ther nas foul that cometh of engendrure,
That they ne were prest in hir presence,
To take hir doom and yeve hir audience.

For this was on seynt Valentynes day,
Whan every foul cometh ther to chese his make, 310
Of every kinde, that men thenke may;
And that so huge a noyse gan they make,
That erthe and see, and tree, and every lake
So ful was, that unnethe was ther space
For me to stonde, so ful was al the place. 315

---

288. Cx. O. Semiramis; Ff. Semiramis; *rest* Semiramus (*as in* Leg. Good Women, *Tisbe*, l. 2). Gg. Hercules.   289. Trin. Harl. Tysbe; F. Cx. Tesbe; Gg. Thisbe.   295. F. Cx. comen; *rest* come. F. Ff. that; *rest* the.   298. Gg. that; *which rest omit (though wanted)*.   303. F. O. *wrongly insert* of *before* Nature.   307. Gg. Trin. Cx. Ff. they; F. Harl. O. there. *After* were (*dissyllabic*) Gg. *inserts* al; *needlessly*.   308. Gg. dom; *rest* dome.   310. Gg. bryd (*for* foul); Cx. birde.   311. F. On; *rest* Of. Ff. thenke; *rest* thynke (*not so well*).   313. Gg. Ff. eyr (*for* see).

V. THE PARLEMENT OF FOULES.

And right as Aleyn, in the Pleynt of Kinde,
Devyseth Nature of aray and face,
In swich aray men mighten hir ther finde.
This noble emperesse, ful of grace,
Bad every foul to take his owne place,   320
As they were wont alwey fro yeer to yere,
Seynt Valentynes day, to stonden there.

That is to sey, the foules of ravyne
Were hyest set; and than the foules smale,
That eten as hem nature wolde enclyne,   325
As worm, or thing of whiche I telle no tale;
But water-foul sat lowest in the dale;
And foul that liveth by seed sat on the grene,
And that so fele, that wonder was to sene.

Ther mighte men the royal egle finde,   330
That with his sharpe look perceth the sonne;
And other egles of a lower kinde,
Of which that clerkes wel devysen conne.
Ther was the tyraunt with his fethres donne
And greye, I mene the goshauk, that doth pyne   335
To briddes for his outrageous ravyne.

The gentil faucon, that with his feet distreyneth
The kinges hond; the hardy sperhauk eke,
The quayles foo; the merlion that peyneth
Him-self ful ofte, the larke for to seke;   340
Ther was the douve, with hir eyen meke;
The Ialous swan, ayens his deth that singeth;
The oule eek, that of dethe the bode bringeth;

---

316. F. Alayne; Trin. Alen; *rest* Aleyn.   317. Gg. in (*for* of). *All but* Gg. Ff. *needlessly insert* suche *before* aray (*caught from line below*).   318. Gg. swich; F. suche. MSS. myghte, myght; *but read* mighten.   320. Gg. Ff. his; *rest* her, hir (*wrongly*). Cx. owen; Gg. owene; F. ovne; *rest* owne.   325. Gg. Cx. hem; Ff. them; O. *om.*; *rest* that.   327. Trin. vale (*for* dale).   330. Gg. ryal; Cx. Harl. O. rial.   338. F. *om.* hardy. *All* eke (*for* eek); *exceptionally.*   343. Trin. bood; Cx. bodword; *rest* bode (*dissyllabic*).

The crane the geaunt, with his trompes soune;
The theef, the chogh; and eek the Iangling pye;   345
The scorning Iay; the eles foo, the heroune;
The false lapwing, ful of trecherye;
The stare, that the counseyl can bewrye;
The tame ruddok; and the coward kyte;
The cok, that orloge is of thorpes lyte;   350

The sparow, Venus sone; the nightingale,
That clepeth forth the fresshe leves newe;
The swalow, mordrer of the flyës smale
That maken hony of floures fresshe of hewe;
The wedded turtel, with hir herte trewe;   355
The pecok, with his aungels fethres brighte;
The fesaunt, scorner of the cok by nighte;

The waker goos; the cukkow ever unkinde;
The popiniay, ful of delicasye;
The drake, stroyer of his owne kinde;   360
The stork, the wreker of avouterye;
The hote cormeraunt of glotonye;
The raven wys, the crow with vois of care;
The throstel olde; the frosty feldefare.

What shulde I seyn? of foules every kinde   365
That in this worlde han fethres and stature,
Men mighten in that place assembled finde
Before the noble goddesse Nature.
And everich of hem did his besy cure

---

344. Gg. Ff. *om.* the.   345. Trin. chowgh; F. choghe; Cx. choughe; Harl. chowhe; Gg. O. Ff. crow (*wrongly*).   346. Harl. Ff. eles; Gg. O. elis; Trin. elys; F. Cx. egles (!). Trin. Harl. O. *insert* the *before* heroun; *rest omit.*   347. Gg. false; F. fals. Trin. Cx. lapwynk; O. lappewynk.   348. Gg. starlyng; *rest* stare. Gg. bewreye (*but note the rime*).   349. Gg. rodok.   350. Gg. orloge; F. orlogge. Gg. thorpis; F. thropes.   352. Gg. Cx. Ff. grene (*for* fresshe). 353. Trin. Th. flyes; Ff. bryddis; Gg. O. foulis; *rest* foules (fowles). *But* flyes *is right*; see Cant. Ta. I. 468, Boeth. iii. met. 7.   355. F. his; O. *om.*; *rest* hire, hir, her.   356. Gg. clothis (*for* fethers).   357. F. be (*for* by). 359. F. papiay; Gg. popyniay.   361. F. Cx. Ff. *om.* the.   363. Gg. The rauen wys, the crowe wit voice of care; Ff. *same* (*omitting* wys); F. *and rest* The rauenes and the crowes with her voys of care (*badly*).   367. Gg. myghtyn; F. myghte.   368. F. that; Ff. this; Harl. *om.*; *rest* the.   *All but* Gg. Ff. *ins.* of *bef.* Nature.   369. Gg. eueriche; O. Ff. euery; F. eche (*badly*).

V. THE PARLEMENT OF FOULES.

Benignely to chese or for to take, 370
By hir acord, his formel or his make.

But to the poynt—Nature held on hir honde
A formel egle, of shap the gentileste
That ever she among hir werkes fonde,
The most benigne and the goodlieste; 375
In hir was every vertu at his reste,
So ferforth, that Nature hir-self had blisse
To loke on hir, and ofte hir bek to kisse.

Nature, the vicaire of thalmyghty lorde,
That hoot, cold, hevy, light, [and] moist and dreye 380
Hath knit by even noumbre of acorde,
In esy vois began to speke and seye,
'Foules, tak hede of my sentence, I preye,
And, for your ese, in furthering of your nede,
As faste as I may speke, I wol me spede. 385

Ye know wel how, seynt Valentynes day,
By my statut and through my governaunce,
Ye come for to chese—and flee your way—
Your makes, as I prik yow with plesaunce.
But natheles, my rightful ordenaunce 390
May I not lete, for al this world to winne,
That he that most is worthy shal beginne.

The tercel egle, as that ye knowen wel,
The foul royal above yow in degree,
The wyse and worthy, secree, trewe as stel, 395
The which I formed have, as ye may see,
In every part as hit best lyketh me,

---

370. Gg. Benygnely; F. Benyngly (*sic*). 374. fonde *is pt. t. subjunctive*. 375. Gg. Cx. the (*after* and); Ff. moste; *rest om.* 378. Gg. bek; F. beke. 379. Ff. Cx. vicaire; F. vyker. 380. *I insert* and *after* light. Gg. Cx. dreye; *rest* drye. 381. Trin. Cx. by; F. be; Gg. with. 383. Cx. Ff. kepe (*for* hede). 384. Gg. ese; F. ease. 385. Gg. Ff. ȝow; Cx. you (*for* me). 386. F. Cx. Harl. *insert* that *after* how. 387. Gg. By; F. Be. 389. F. Trin. Cx. Harl. O. *insert* With *before* Your; Gg. Ff. *rightly omit.* 390. Gg. Cx. Ff. ordenaunce; *rest* gouernaunce (*see* l. 387). 391. F. Trin. Harl. O. let (i.e. *let go*); Gg. breke; Ff. suffre; Cx. lette. 393. Gg. terslet (*for* tercel). Gg. ful wel; F. wele. 394. Gg. ryal. 395. Gg. stel; F. stele. 396. *All* have formed.

350   THE MINOR POEMS.

Hit nedeth noght his shap yow to devyse,
He shal first chese and speken in his gyse.

And after him, by order shul ye chese,   400
After your kinde, everich as yow lyketh,
And, as your hap is, shul ye winne or lese;
But which of yow that love most entryketh,
God sende him hir that sorest for him syketh.'
And therwith-al the tercel gan she calle,   405
And seyde, 'my sone, the choys is to thee falle.

But natheles, in this condicioun
Mot be the choys of everich that is here,
That she agree to his eleccioun,
Who-so he be that shulde been hir fere;   410
This is our usage alwey, fro yeer to yere;
And who so may at this time have his grace,
In blisful tyme he com in-to this place.'

With hed enclyned and with ful humble chere
This royal tercel spak and taried nought;   415
'Unto my sovereyn lady, and noght my fere,
I chese, and chese with wille and herte and thought,
The formel on your hond so wel y-wrought,
Whos I am al and ever wol hir serve,
Do what hir list, to do me live or sterve.   420

Beseching hir of mercy and of grace,
As she that is my lady sovereyne;
Or let me dye present in this place.
For certes, long may I not live in peyne;
For in myn herte is corven every veyne;   425
Having reward only to my trouthe,
My dere herte, have on my wo som routhe.

And if that I to hir be founde untrewe,
Disobeysaunt, or wilful negligent,
Avauntour, or in proces love a newe,   430

---

411. Cx. yere by yere (*for* fro yeer to yere).   413. Gg. cam.   414. Gg.
O. Ff. *om.* ful; *rest retain.*   415. Trin. Ff. Royalle; F. real; Gg. ryal.   424.
Gg. I may.   426. *Read* al only?   428. Gg. And if that I to hyre be founde;
F. And yf I be founde to hir.

V. THE PARLEMENT OF FOULES. 351

I pray to you this be my Iugement,
That with these foules I be al to-rent,
That ilke day that ever she me finde
To hir untrewe, or in my gilte unkinde.

And sin that noon loveth hir so wel as I, 435
Al be she never of love me behette,
Than oghte she be myn thourgh hir mercy,
For other bond can I noon on hir knette.
For never, for no wo, ne shal I lette
To serven hir, how fer so that she wende; 440
Sey what yow list, my tale is at an ende.'

Right as the fresshe, rede rose newe
Ayen the somer-sonne coloured is,
Right so for shame al wexen gan the hewe
Of this formel, whan she herde al this; 445
She neyther answerde 'wel,' ne seyde amis,
So sore abasshed was she, til that Nature
Seyde, 'doghter, drede yow noght, I yow assure.'

Another tercel egle spak anoon
Of lower kinde, and seyde, 'that shal not be; 450
I love hir bet than ye do, by seynt Iohn,
Or atte leste I love hir as wel as ye;
And lenger have served hir, in my degree,
And if she shulde have loved for long loving,
To me allone had been the guerdoning. 455

I dar eek seye, if she me finde fals,
Unkinde, Iangler, or rebel any wyse,
Or Ialous, do me hongen by the hals!
And but I bere me in hir servyse
As wel as that my wit can me suffyse, 460
Fro poynt to poynt, hir honour for to save,
Tak she my lyf, and al the good I have.'

---

436. F. As though; *rest* Al be.   438. F. knette; Gg. areete; *rest* knytte, knyt.   439. Gg. Cx. O. Ne (*for* For).   445. *So all. Read* whan that she?   446. Gg. She neythir; Cx. Harl. O. Ff. She neyther; F. Trin. Neyther she.   450. Gg. O. Ff. shal; *rest* shulde, shuld.   460. Gg. that; *rest omit*.   462. Gg the; Trin. Harl. ye; *rest* she.

352   THE MINOR POEMS.

The thridde tercel egle answerde tho,
'Now, sirs, ye seen the litel leyser here;
For every foul cryeth out to been a-go   465
Forth with his make, or with his lady dere;
And eek Nature hir-self ne wol nought here,
For tarying here, noght half that I wolde seye;
And but I speke, I mot for sorwe deye.

Of long servyse avaunte I me no-thing,   470
But as possible is me to dye to-day
For wo, as he that hath ben languisshing
Thise twenty winter, and wel happen may
A man may serven bet and more to pay
In half a yere, al-though hit were no more,   475
Than som man doth that hath served ful yore.

I ne say not this by me, for I ne can
Do no servyse that may my lady plese;
But I dar seyn, I am hir trewest man
As to my dome, and feynest wolde hir ese;   480
At shorte wordes, til that deth me sese,
I wol ben hires, whether I wake or winke,
And trewe in al that herte may bethinke.'

Of al my lyf, sin that day I was born,
So gentil plee in love or other thing   485
Ne herde never no man me beforn,
Who-[so] that hadde leyser and cunning
For to reherse hir chere and hir speking;
And from the morwe gan this speche laste
Til dounward drow the sonne wonder faste.   490

The noyse of foules for to ben delivered
So loude rong, 'have doon and let us wende!'
That wel wende I the wode had al to-shivered.
'Come of!' they cryde, 'allas! ye wil us shende!
Whan shal your cursed pleding have an ende?   495

---

463. Gg. thredde; Trin. Ff. thryd; F. thirdde.   467. F. *om.* Nature.   473. Gg. yeer and as (*for* winter and).   476. F. *om.* ful.   479. Gg. seyn; F. say.   480. Gg. Ff. ese; *rest* plese.   481. Gg. shorte; F. short.   482. Ff. hyres; F. hirse (!).   487. *I supply* so. Gg. hadde; F. had.   488. F. rehersen; *rest* reherse (reherce).   490. Gg. drow; Cx. wente; *rest* went (*badly*).   494. Cx. Harl. wil; F. wol.   495. Gg. pletynge; Trin. Cx. Harl. pletyng.

V. THE PARLEMENT OF FOULES. 353

How shulde a Iuge eyther party leve,
For yee or nay, with-outen any preve?'

The goos, the cokkow, and the doke also
So cryden 'kek, kek!' 'kukkow!' 'quek, quek!' hye,
That thorgh myn eres the noyse wente tho.   500
The goos seyde, 'al this nis not worth a flye!
But I can shape hereof a remedye,
And I wol sey my verdit faire and swythe
For water-foul, who-so be wrooth or blythe.'

'And I for worm-foul,' seyde the fool cukkow,   505
'For I wol, of myn owne auctorite,
For comune spede, take the charge now,
For to delivere us is gret charite.'
'Ye may abyde a whyle yet, parde!'
Seide the turtel, 'if hit be your wille   510
A wight may speke, him were as good be stille.

I am a seed-foul, oon the unworthieste,
That wot I wel, and litel of kunninge;
But bet is that a wightes tonge reste
Than entremeten him of such doinge   515
Of which he neyther rede can nor singe.
And who-so doth, ful foule himself acloyeth,
For office uncommitted ofte anoyeth.'

Nature, which that alway had an ere
To murmour of the lewednes behinde,   520
With facound voys seide, 'hold your tonges there!
And I shal sone, I hope, a counseyl finde
You to delivere, and fro this noyse unbinde;

---

498. *So* Gg.; *rest* The goos, the duk, and the cukkowe also (*wrongly; see next line*).   501. F. seyde tho; *rest omit* tho. Gg. Ff. nys not; Trin. O. ys nat; Cx. is not; F. Harl. *om.* not.   503. Gg. Cx. I; *rest om.*   507. Gg. O. profit; *rest* spede. Trin. For comon spede, take the chargë now. F. Cx. Harl. O. *ins.* on me *bef.* the; Ff. *ins.* vpon me. Gg. tak on no (!) *for* take the.   510. Trin. Seyde; Cx. Said; *rest* Quod.   511. F. good; Cx. better (*for* as good); *rest* fayr.   514. Gg. bet; *rest* better.   515. Gg. entirmety*n*; F. entremete. 517. *All but* Gg. Cx. *ins.* hyt (it, yt) *bef.* doth.   518. Ff. vncom*m*aundet; O. vnconveyid; Gg. onquit (!); *rest* vncommytted.   520. Gg. *om.* behynde; Trin. Harl. blynde; Cx. by kynde; *rest* behynde.   523. F. O. Ff. for to (*for* to). F. delyueren; *rest* delyuere (deliver). F. Gg. Harl. from; *rest* fro.

I Iuge, of every folk men shal oon calle
To seyn the verdit for you foules alle.'   525

Assented were to this conclusioun
The briddes alle; and foules of ravyne
Han chosen first, by pleyn eleccioun,
The tercelet of the faucon, to diffyne
Al hir sentence, and as him list, termyne;   530
And to Nature him gonnen to presente,
And she accepteth him with glad entente.

The tercelet seide than in this manere:
'Ful hard were hit to preve hit by resoun
Who loveth best this gentil formel here;   535
For everich hath swich replicacioun,
That noon by skilles may be broght a-doun;
I can not seen that arguments avayle;
Than semeth hit ther moste be batayle.'

'Al redy!' quod these egles tercels tho.   540
'Nay, sirs!' quod he, 'if that I dorste it seye,
Ye doon me wrong, my tale is not y-do!
For sirs, ne taketh noght a-gref, I preye,
It may noght gon, as ye wolde, in this weye;
Oure is the voys that han the charge in honde,   545
And to the Iuges dome ye moten stonde;

And therfor pees! I seye, as to my wit,
Me wolde thinke how that the worthieste
Of knighthode, and lengest hath used hit,
Moste of estat, of blode the gentileste,   550
Were sittingest for hir, if that hir leste;
And of these three she wot hir-self, I trowe,
Which that he be, for hit is light to knowe.'

---

524. Cx. charge (*for* Iuge).   527. *Most* MSS. *insert* the *before* foules; *which* Gg.Th. *and* Longleat MS. *omit.*   530. *All but* Cx. Ff. *ins.* to *after* list.   534. Trin.Th. preue; Gg. proue; F. preven.   536. Gg. swich; F. suche.   537. Gg. non by skillis; F. *and rest* by skilles may non (*badly*).   540. Cx. terselis egles.   543. Gg. ne; *rest omit.*   544. F. *om.* gon.   545. Gg. Cx. Oure; *rest* Oures, Ours.   549. Gg. O. hath; *rest* had.   551. Gg. sittyngest; *rest* sittynge.   553. Cx. Harl. ethe (*for* light).

V. THE PARLEMENT OF FOULES.

The water-foules han her hedes leyd
Togeder, and of short avysement,　　　　　555
Whan everich had his large golee seyd,
They seyden sothly, al by oon assent,
How that 'the goos, with hir facounde gent,
That so desyreth to pronounce our nede,
Shal telle our tale,' and preyde 'god hir spede.'　560

And for these water-foules tho began
The goos to speke, and in hir cakelinge
She seyde, 'pees! now tak kepe every man,
And herkeneth which a reson I shal bringe;
My wit is sharp, I love no taryinge;　　　　565
I seye, I rede him, though he were my brother,
But she wol love him, lat him love another!'

'Lo here! a parfit reson of a goos!'
Quod the sperhauk; 'never mot she thee!
Lo, swich hit is to have a tonge loos!　　　570
Now parde, fool, yet were hit bet for thee
Have holde thy pees, than shewed thy nycete!
Hit lyth not in his wit nor in his wille,
But sooth is seyd, "a fool can noght be stille."'

The laughter aroos of gentil foules alle,　　575
And right anoon the seed-foul chosen hadde
The turtel trewe, and gunne hir to hem calle,
And preyden hir to seye the sothe sadde
Of this matere, and asked what she radde;
And she answerde, that pleynly hir entente　580
She wolde shewe, and sothly what she mente.

'Nay, god forbede a lover shulde chaunge!'
The turtel seyde, and wex for shame al reed;
'Thogh that his lady ever-more be straunge,

---

556. Gg. O. gole; Ff. goler; Cx. golye; Ff. golee; Trin. Harl. wylle.　558. Gg. facounde so; Ff. facounde; Cx. faconde; F. faucond.　560. F. Cx. Ff. *needlessly insert* to *after* preyd-e.　564. *All but* Gg. *insert* forth *before* bringe. 569. *For* Quod *read* Seyde?　570. Gg. sich (*for* swich); F. suche.　575. F. laughtre.　576. F. Harl. Ff. foules; Trin. fowle; Cx. fowl; O. foule; Gg. ful (!).　577. Gg. gunne; Ff. gonne; *rest* gan.

A a 2

THE MINOR POEMS.

Yet let him serve hir ever, til he be deed; 585
For sothe, I preyse noght the gooses reed;
For thogh she deyed, I wolde non other make,
I wol ben hires, til that the deth me take.'

'Wel bourded!' quod the doke, 'by my hat!
That men shulde alwey loven, causeles, 590
Who can a reson finde or wit in that?
Daunceth he mury that is mirtheles?
Who shulde recche of that is reccheles?
Ye, quek!' yit quod the doke, ful wel and faire,
'There been mo sterres, god wot, than a paire!' 595

'Now fy, cherl!' quod the gentil tercelet,
'Out of the dunghil com that word ful right,
Thou canst noght see which thing is wel be-set:
Thou farest by love as oules doon by light,
The day hem blent, ful wel they see by night; 600
Thy kind is of so lowe a wrechednesse,
That what love is, thou canst nat see ne gesse.'

Tho gan the cukkow putte him forth in prees
For foul that eteth worm, and seide blyve,
'So I,' quod he, 'may have my make in pees, 605
I recche not how longe that ye stryve;
Lat ech of hem be soleyn al hir lyve,
This is my reed, sin they may not acorde;
This shorte lesson nedeth noght recorde.'

'Ye! have the glotoun fild ynogh his paunche, 610
Than are we wel!' seyde the merlioun;
'Thou mordrer of the heysugge on the braunche
That broghte thee forth, thou [rewthelees] glotoun!
Live thou soleyn, wormes corrupcioun!

---

588. Harl. hires; Gg. hire; Cx. hers; *rest* hirs. Trin. Harl. *om.* that (*perhaps rightly*).   589. Gg. Cx. Ff. doke; F. duk.   590. F. Ff. shulden.   592. F. Gg. murye; *rest* mery.   594. Gg. O. yit; Ff. yet; *rest om.*   599. Gg. by; F. be (*1st time*).   602. Gg. Th. nat; F. neyther.   603. F. put; Gg. putte.   606. Cx. Ff. recche; F. Gg. Harl. reche; Trin. O. rek.   611. Gg. Merlioun; Trin. O. Merlyon; Cx. merlion; F. Ff. Emerlyon.   612. F. *om. 1st* the. Harl. heysugge; O. heysugg; Cx. heysug; Ff. haysugge; F. haysogge; Gg. heysoge; Trin. heysoke.   613. Gg. reufulles (!); Pepys rowthfull; *rest* rewful (!).

V. THE PARLEMENT OF FOULES.

For no fors is of lakke of thy nature; 615
Go, lewed be thou, whyl the world may dure!'

'Now pees,' quod Nature, 'I comaunde here;
For I have herd al your opinioun,
And in effect yet be we never the nere;
But fynally, this is my conclusioun, 620
That she hir-self shal han the eleccioun
Of whom hir list, who-so be wrooth or blythe,
Him that she cheest, he shal hir have as swythe.

For sith hit may not here discussed be
Who loveth hir best, as seide the tercelet, 625
Than wol I doon hir this favour, that she
Shal have right him on whom hir herte is set,
And he hir that his herte hath on hir knet.
This Iuge I, Nature, for I may not lyë;
To noon estat I have non other yë. 630

But as for counseyl for to chese a make,
If hit were reson, certes, than wolde I
Counseyle yow the royal tercel take,
As seide the tercelet ful skilfully,
As for the gentilest and most worthy, 635
Which I have wroght so wel to my plesaunce;
That to yow oghte been a suffisaunce.'

With dredful vois the formel hir answerde,
'My rightful lady, goddesse of Nature,
Soth is that I am ever under your yerde, 640
Lyk as is everiche other creature,
And moot be youres whyl my lyf may dure;
And therfor graunteth me my firste bone,
And myn entente I wol yow sey right sone.'

---

621. Gg. han; *rest* haue. Gg. Cx. the; *rest* hir, hyr.   623. F. cheest; Gg. chesith; Trin. cheseth; Harl. chesithe. F. han hir; Gg. hire han; Trin. hyr hafe; Cx. Harl. Ff. her haue.   626. Gg. hire this fauour; Trin. Harl. to hyr thys fauour; F. *and rest* thys fauour to hir.   630. Ff. ye; Harl. yee; Trin. ey; *rest* eye.   632. F. Gg. I (*for* hit). Gg. certis; *rest omit.*   637. *All but* Gg. Cx. *insert* hit (*or* it) *after* That *or* yow. Th. ben; Cx. haue ben; *rest* to ben (be).   641. Gg. As is a-nothir lyuis creature. O. *alone ins.* Like *bef.* As.   642. Gg. mot; *rest* moste (muste).   643. Gg. grauntyth; *rest* graunte, graunt (*badly*).   644. Trin. Cx. Harl. I wyll yow; O. I woll ȝewe; F. Ff. yow wol I.

'I graunte it you,' quod she; and right anoon   645
This formel egle spak in this degree,
'Almighty quene, unto this yeer be doon
I aske respit for to avysen me.
And after that to have my choys al free;
This al and som, that I wolde speke and seye;   650
Ye gete no more, al-though ye do me deye.
I wol noght serven Venus ne Cupyde
For sothe as yet, by no manere wey.'
'Now sin it may non other wyse betyde,'
Quod tho Nature, 'here is no more to sey;   655
Than wolde I that these foules were a-wey
Ech with his make, for tarying lenger here'—
And seyde hem thus, as ye shul after here.

'To you speke I, ye tercelets,' quod Nature,
'Beth of good herte and serveth, alle three;   660
A yeer is not so longe to endure,
And ech of yow peyne him, in his degree,
For to do wel; for, god wot, quit is she
Fro yow this yeer; what after so befalle,
This entremes is dressed for you alle.'   665

And whan this werk al broght was to an ende,
To every foule Nature yaf his make
By even acorde, and on hir wey they wende.
A! lord! the blisse and Ioye that they make!
For ech of hem gan other in winges take,   670
And with hir nekkes ech gan other winde,
Thanking alwey the noble goddesse of kinde.

But first were chosen foules for to singe,
As yeer by yere was alwey hir usaunce
To singe a roundel at hir departinge,   675
To do Nature honour and plesaunce.
The note, I trowe, maked was in Fraunce;

---

652. F. Cipride; Harl. Cypride; Ff. Sypryde; *rest* Cupide (*cf.* ll. 212, 277).
654. F. other weyes; Cx. other wayes; O. othir wey (*perhaps best*); Gg. othirwise; Ff. other-wyse; Trin. Harl. other (*sic*).   655. Gg. Harl. tho; *rest om.*   659.
F. terceletys; Th. tercelets.   660. F. al; Gg. alle.   665. F. O. entremesse;
Ff. entremeese; Th. entremes; Gg. entyrmes; Harl. entermes.   666. F. wroght;
rest brought, broght.   669. F. A; Gg. But; *rest* And. Gg. Ioye; F. Ioy.
672. Gg. Thankynge; F. Thonkyng. Gg. queen; *rest* goddesse, goddes.

V. THE PARLEMENT OF FOULES.

The wordes wer swich as ye may heer finde,
The nexte vers, as I now have in minde.

Qui bien aime a tard oublie.

'Now welcom somer, with thy sonne softe,   680
That hast this wintres weders over-shake,
And driven awey the longe nightes blake!

Seynt Valentyn, that art ful hy on-lofte;—
Thus singen smale foules for thy sake—
  Now welcom somer, with thy sonne softe,   685
  That hast this wintres weders over-shake.

Wel han they cause for to gladen ofte,
Sith ech of hem recovered hath his make;
Ful blisful may they singen whan they wake;
  Now welcom somer, with thy sonne softe,   690
  That hast this wintres weders over-shake,
  And driven awey the longe nightes blake.'

And with the showting, whan hir song was do,
That foules maden at hir flight a-way,
I wook, and other bokes took me to   695
To rede upon, and yet I rede alway;
I hope, y-wis, to rede so som day
That I shal mete som thing for to fare
The bet; and thus to rede I nil not spare.   699

**Explicit tractatus de congregacione Volucrum
die sancti Valentini.**

---

678. Gg. sweche (*for* swiche); F. suche. Th. *Qui*; miswritten *Que* in F. Cx.; *Qe* in Trin.; rest omit. **aime**; F. ayme. **tard**; F. tarde. *Lines 680-692 only occur in* Gg. Th. *and* Digby 181; *lines* 683, 684, 687-9 *in* O. *I follow* Digby 181 *mainly.* 680. Digb. Nowe welcome. 681. Gg. wintres wedres; Digb. wynter wedirs. 682. Gg. And; Digb. Hast. Digb. drevyn; Gg. dreuyne. Digb. nyghtis; Gg. nyghtes. 684. Digb. syngen; Fowlis. 687. Gg. O. Wele. 688. Gg. O. hem; Digb. them. 689. Digb. Fulle blisfully they synge and endles ioy thei make (*wrongly*); Gg. Ful blisseful mowe they ben when they wake; O. Th. Ful blesfull may they synge when they wake (Th. awake). 693. F. showtynge. 694. Gg. mady*n*; Ff. maden; F. made. 698. Trin. fynde (*for* mete). 699. Ff. nyl; Gg. nele; F. O. wol; Trin. wyll*e*; Cx. wil. COLOPHON. *So in* F; Gg. *has*—Explicit parliamentum Auium in die sancti Valentini tentum, secundum Galfridum Chaucer; Ff. *has*—Explicit Parliamentum Auium; MS. Arch. Seld. B. 24 *has*—Here endis the parliament of foulis; Quod Galfride Chaucere; *the* Longleat MS. *has*—Here endith the Parlement of foules.

VI. A COMPLEINT TO HIS LADY.

I. (*In seven-line stanzas.*)

THE longe night, whan every creature
   Shulde have hir rest in somwhat, as by kinde,
Or elles ne may hir lyf nat long endure,
   Hit falleth most in-to my woful minde
   How I so fer have broght my-self behinde,   5
That, sauf the deeth, ther may no-thing me lisse,
So desespaired I am from alle blisse.

This same thoght me lasteth til the morwe,
   And from the morwe forth til hit be eve;
Ther nedeth me no care for to borwe,   10
   For bothe I have good leyser and good leve;
   Ther is no wight that wol me wo bereve
To wepe y-nogh, and wailen al my fille;
The sore spark of peyne doth me spille.

II. (*In Terza Rima; imperfect.*)

[The sore spark of peyne doth me spille;]   15
   This Love hath [eek] me set in swich a place
   That my desyr [he] never wol fulfille;
For neither pitee, mercy, neither grace

Of these fragments there are but two MS. copies, viz. in Shirley's MS. Harl. 78, *here called* 'Sh.' *and in* Ph. = MS. Phil. 9053, *in which (as in* Ed. = ed. 1561) *it is written in continuation of the* Complaint unto Pity. Ph. *is copied from* Sh. *The spelling is bad, and I alter it throughout.*

  1. Sh. nightes; *see* l. 8.   2, 3. hir] Sh. theyre.   7. Ed. (1561) dispaired.
12. Sh. me; Ed. my.   14. *All insert* now *before* doth.   15. *It seems necessary to repeat this line in order to start the series of rimes.*   16. Sh. This loue that hathe me set; *I omit* that, *and supply* eek.   17. *I supply* he (i. e. Love).

VI. A COMPLEINT TO HIS LADY. 361

Can I nat finde; and [fro] my sorwful herte,
For to be deed, I can hit nat arace. 20
The more I love, the more she doth me smerte;
Through which I see, with-oute remedye,
That from the deeth I may no wyse asterte;
[For this day in hir servise shal I dye].

III. (*In Terza Rima; imperfect.*)

[Thus am I slain, with sorwes ful dyverse; 25
Ful longe agoon I oghte have taken hede].
Now sothly, what she hight I wol reherse;
Hir name is Bountee, set in womanhede,
Sadnesse in youthe, and Beautee prydelees,
And Plesaunce, under governaunce and drede; 30
Hir surname eek is Faire Rewthelees,
The Wyse, y-knit un-to Good Aventure,
That, for I love hir, sleeth me giltelees.
Hir love I best, and shal, whyl I may dure,
Bet than my-self an hundred thousand deel, 35
Than al this worldes richesse or creature.
Now hath nat Lovë me bestowed weel
To lovë, ther I never shal have part?
Allas! right thus is turned me the wheel,
Thus am I slayn with loves fyry dart. 40
I can but love hir best, my swete fo;
Love hath me taught no more of his art
But serve alwey, and stinte for no wo.

IV. (*In ten-line stanzas.*)

[With]-in my trewe careful herte ther is
So moche wo, and [eek] so litel blis, 45
That wo is me that ever I was bore;
For al that thing which I desyre I mis,
And al that ever I wolde nat, I-wis,
That finde I redy to me evermore;

---

19. Sh. and yit my; *I omit* yit, *and supply* fro.   24. *Supplied to complete the rime from* Compl. Mars, 189.   25. *Supplied from* Compl. Pite, 22, 17.   26. *Supplied from* Anelida, 307.   31. Sh. is eek.   32. Sh. The wyse eknytte; Ph. The wise I-knyt (*corrupt?*)   33. Sh. hir she; *I omit* she.   36. *Corrupt? Perhaps read* richest creature.   40. Sh. fury.   42. *Read* of alle his?   44. Sh. In; *I read* With-in.   45. *I supply* eek.

362   THE MINOR POEMS.

And of al this I not to whom me pleyne.　　　　50
　For she that mighte me out of this bringe
　Ne reccheth nat whether I wepe or singe ;
So litel rewthe hath she upon my peyne.

Allas! whan sleping-time is, than I wake,
Whan I shulde daunce, for fere than I quake ;　　55
[Yow rekketh never wher I flete or sinke ;]
This hevy lyf I lede for your sake,
Thogh ye ther-of in no wyse hede take,
[For on my wo yow deyneth not to thinke.]
My hertes lady, and hool my lyves quene!　　60
　For trewly dorste I seye, as that I fele,
　Me semeth that your swete herte of stele
Is whetted now ageynes me to kene.

My dere herte, and best beloved fo,
Why lyketh yow to do me al this wo,　　65
　What have I doon that greveth yow, or sayd,
　But for I serve and love yow and no mo?
And whylst I live, I wol do ever so ;
And therfor, swete, ne beth nat evil apayd.
For so good and so fair as [that] ye be,　　70
　Hit were [a] right gret wonder but ye hadde
　Of alle servants, bothe goode and badde ;
And leest worthy of alle hem, I am he.

But never-the-les, my righte lady swete,
Thogh that I be unconning and unmete　　75
　To serve as I best coude ay your hynesse.
Yit is ther fayner noon, that wolde I hete,
Than I, to do yow ese, or elles bete
What-so I wiste were to [yow distresse].

---

50. *So in* Anelida, 237.　　54. Sh. *ins.* lo *after* is.　　55. Sh. *ins.* lo *after* fere.　　56, 59. *Both lines are missing; supplied from* Anelida, 181, 182.　　57. Sh. *ins.* lo *after* lede.　　68. Sh. euer do.　　70. *I supply* that.　　71. *I supply* a.　　72. Sh. *ins.* of *after* bothe.　　76. Sh. koude best; Ph. *om.* best.　　77. Sh. noon fayner.　　78. Sh. youre; *read* yow.　　79. Sh. wist that were; *om.* that. Sh. your hyenesse (*repeated from* l. 76 ; *wrongly*) ; *read* yow distresse.

VI. A COMPLEINT TO HIS LADY. 363

And hadde I might as good as I have wille,   80
  Than shulde ye fele wher it wer so or noon;
  For in this worlde living is ther noon
That fayner wolde your hertes wil fulfille.

For bothe I love, and eek dreed yow so sore,
And algates moot, and have doon yow, ful yore,   85
  That bet loved is noon, ne never shal;
  And yit I wolde beseche yow of no more
But leveth wel, and be nat wrooth ther-fore,
  And lat me serve yow forth; lo! this is al.
For I am nat so hardy ne so wood   90
  For to desire that ye shulde love me;
  For wel I wot, allas! that may nat be;
I am so litel worthy, and ye so good.

For ye be oon the worthiest on-lyve,
And I the most unlykly for to thryve;   95
  Yit, for al this, [now] witeth ye right wele,
That ye ne shul me from your service dryve
That I nil ay, with alle my wittes fyve,
  Serve yow trewly, what wo so that I fele.
For I am set on yow in swich manere   100
  That, thogh ye never wil upon me rewe,
  I moste yow love, and ever been as trewe
As any can or may on-lyve [here].

The more that I love yow, goodly free,
The lasse fynde I that ye loven me;   105
  Allas! whan shal that harde wit amende?
Wher is now al your wommanly pitee,
Your gentilesse and your debonairtee,
  Wil ye no thing ther-of upon me spende?
And so hool, swete, as I am youres al,   110
  And so gret wil as I have yow to serve,
  Now, certes, and ye lete me thus sterve,
Yit have ye wonne ther-on but a smal.

---

82. Sh. *ins.* þane *before* is.   83. Sh. wille; Ph. Ed. wil.   86. Sh. better.
88. Sh. leuethe; Ph. lovith.   96. *I supply* now.   98. Sh. ne wil (*for* nil).
100. Ed. (1561) *has* set so hy vpon your whele.   102. Sh. beon euer.   103.
Sh. man can; *I omit* man. *I supply* here; *the line is imperfect.*   104. Sh.
But the; *I omit* But.   113. Ed. *om.* a.

364 THE MINOR POEMS.

For, at my knowing, I do no-thing why,
And this I wol beseche yow hertely,　　　　　115
  That, ther ever ye finde, whyl ye live,
A trewer servant to yow than am I,
Leveth [me] thanne, and sleeth me hardely,
  And I my deeth to you wol al forgive.
And if ye finde no trewer [man than me],　　120
  [Why] will ye suffre than that I thus spille,
  And for no maner gilt but my good wille?
As good wer thanne untrewe as trewe to be.

But I, my lyf and deeth, to yow obeye,
And with right buxom herte hoolly I preye,　　125
  As [is] your moste plesure, so doth by me;
Wel lever is me lyken yow and deye
Than for to any thing or thinke or seye
  That mighte yow offende in any tyme.
And therfor, swete, rewe on my peynes smerte,　　130
  And of your grace granteth me som drope;
  For elles may me laste ne blis ne hope,
Ne dwellen in my trouble careful herte.

---

114. Sh. nought; *read* nothing.　　116. Sh. whyles.　　118. *I supply* me.
120. Sh. no trewer so verrayly; Ed. no trewer verely (*false rime*).　　121. *I supply*
Why.　　124-133. *Unique stanza, in* Ph. *only*.　　126. *I supply* is.　　127.
Ph. For wele; *omit* For.　　129. Ph. That yow myght offenden.　　132. Ph.
no blisse.　　133. Ph. dwelle withyn.　　*Colophon.* Ph. Explicit Pyte : dan
Chaucer Lauteire (?).

VII. ANELIDA AND ARCITE.

The compleynt of feire Anelida and fals Arcite.

Proem.

THOU ferse god of armes, Mars the rede,
That in the frosty country called Trace,
Within thy grisly temple ful of drede
Honoured art, as patroun of that place!
With thy Bellona, Pallas, ful of grace, 5
Be present, and my song continue and gye;
At my beginning thus to thee I crye.

For hit ful depe is sonken in my minde,
With pitous herte in English for tendyte
This olde storie, in Latin which I finde, 10
Of quene Anelida and fals Arcite,
That elde, which that al can frete and byte,
As hit hath freten mony a noble storie,
Hath nigh devoured out of our memorie.

Be favorable eek, thou Polymnia, 15
On Parnaso that, with thy sustres glade,
By Elicon, not fer from Cirrea,
Singest with vois memorial in the shade,
Under the laurer which that may not fade,

The chief authorities are: Harl. (Harl. 7333); F. (Fairfax 16); Tn. (Tanner 346); D. (Digby 181); Cx. (Caxton's edition); B. (Bodley 638); Lt. (Longleat MS.). Th. = Thynne's ed. 1532. *I follow* F. *mainly, correcting the spelling; and give selected* variations. *Title from* F. ; B. *has boke for* compleynt.

1. Tn. ferse; F. fers.   3. Harl. D. Cx. temple; *rest* temples.   6. F. songe. F. contynew; D. contynue. F. guye; Tn. gye.   7. F. I to the; Harl. Tn. D. to the I.   9. Cx. for tendyte; Harl. for to endite; *rest* to endyte.   11. F. Analida; Cx. Anelida; Tn. D. Annelida.   12. Harl. that; Cx. that (*for* which); *rest om.*   15. F. eke. Harl. Polymea; *rest* Polymya, Polymia; Th. Polymnia. 16. Harl. Cx. with; *rest* hath (!). Harl. Cx. sustren.   17. F. B. Cx. Cirrea; D. Cirea; Tn. Circa (*wrongly*).

366   THE MINOR POEMS.

  And do that I my ship to haven winne;   20
  First folow I Stace, and after him Corinne.

    The Story.
  Iamque domos patrias, &c.; Statii Thebais, xii. 519.

  Whan Theseus, with werres longe and grete,
  The aspre folk of Cithe had over-come,
  With laurer crouned, in his char gold-bete,
  Hoom to his contre-houses is y-come;—   25
  For which the peple blisful, al and somme,
  So cryden, that unto the sterres hit wente,
  And him to honouren dide al hir entente;—

  Beforn this duk, in signe of hy victorie,
  The trompes come, and in his baner large 30
  The image of Mars; and, in token of glorie,
  Men mighten seen of tresor many a charge,
  Many a bright helm, and many a spere and targe,
  Many a fresh knight, and many a blisful route,
  On hors, on fote, in al the felde aboute.   35

  Ipolita his wyf, the hardy quene
  Of Cithia, that he conquered hadde,
  With Emelye, hir yonge suster shene,
  Faire in a char of golde he with him ladde,
  That al the ground aboute hir char she spradde 40
  With brightnesse of the beautee in hir face,
  Fulfild of largesse and of alle grace.

---

20. Tn. ship; F. shippe. *After* l. 21, 3 Latin lines are quoted from Statius (see note). 23. F. folke. Cx. Cithye. 24. Harl. D. Cx. Lt. With; F. The (*caught from* l. 23). D. crowned; F. corovned. 25. *All* Home. Tn. ycome; F. he come. 27. Cx. cryden; *but rest* cryden, criden. Harl. unto; *rest* to. Tn. wente; F. went. 28. Tn. entente; F. entent. 29. F. Harl. Beforne; Cx. Biforn; Tn. D. B. Lt. Before. Harl. duk; F. duke. Harl. *inserts* hie (= hy); Addit. 16165 *has* his; *the rest wrongly omit; accent* o *in* victórie. 31. Cx. tokening. Harl. and tokenyng of his glorie. 32. F. sene; Harl. seen. 33. Tn. many; F. mony (5 *times*). 35. on] Harl. Cx. and. 36. Tn. Ypolita. F. wife. 37. Harl. D. Cithea. D. hadde; Lt. hade; *rest* had. 39. F. chare. D. ladde; Lt. lade; *rest* lad. 40. Harl. ground; F. grounde. D. spradde; *rest* sprad. 41. Harl. Cx. the; *rest omit.* 42. F. Fulfilled; al.

VII. ANELIDA AND ARCITE. 367

With his triumphe and laurer-crouned thus,
In al the floure of fortunes yevinge,
Lete I this noble prince Theseus   45
Toward Athenes in his wey rydinge,
And founde I wol in shortly for to bringe
The slye wey of that I gan to wryte,
Of quene Anelida and fals Arcite.

Mars, which that through his furious course of yre,   50
The olde wrath of Iuno to fulfille,
Hath set the peples hertes bothe on fyre
Of Thebes and Grece, everich other to kille
With blody speres, ne rested never stille,
But throng now her, now ther, among hem bothe,   55
That everich other slough, so wer they wrothe.

For whan Amphiorax and Tydeus,
Ipomedon, Parthonopee also
Were dede, and slayn [was] proud Campaneus,
And whan the wrecches Thebans, bretheren two,   60
Were slayn, and king Adrastus hoom a-go,
So desolat stood Thebes and so bare,
That no wight coude remedie of his care.

And whan the olde Creon gan espye
How that the blood roial was broght adoun,   65
He held the cite by his tirannye,
And did the gentils of that regioun
To been his frendes, and dwellen in the toun.
So what for love of him, and what for awe,
The noble folk wer to the toune y-drawe.   70

---

43. D. Cx. Lt. crowned; *rest* corouned.   44. F. yevyng; Tn. gifeynge.
45. F. B. Let; *rest* Lete.   46. F. ryding; Tn. ridinge.   47. F. bring; Tn. brynge.   48. D. slye (*rightly*); Tn. sly; F. sley.   50. F. thro. Harl. Tn. D. furious; F. furiouse.   51. Harl. Tn. wrath; F. wrethe.   52. F. hertis.
53. F. B. Tn. *insert* and *after* Grece; *which* D. Lt. Harl. Cx. *omit*.   Harl. yche othir for to kylle (*a good reading*). Cf. l. 56.   F. eueriche.   55. D. among; F. amonge.   D. bothe; F. both (*but* wrothe *in* l. 56).   56. F. eueriche.   58. Harl. Parthonopee; Cx. Parthonope; D. Partonope; Tn. Partinope; F. B. Prothonolope (!).   59. Harl. Tn. dede; F. ded.   *I supply* was, *which sense and metre require*; Cx. *supplies* and.   F. proude.   60. So F. Tn. B. Lt.; Harl. D. Cx. *put* wrechid (wrecchid) *for* wrecches.   61. Cx. hom; *rest* home.   62. F. stode.   66. F. helde.   70. F. folke.

THE MINOR POEMS.

Among al these, Anelida the quene
Of Ermony was in that toun dwellinge,
That fairer was then is the sonne shene;
Through-out the world so gan hir name springe,
That hir to seen had every wight lykinge;   75
For, as of trouthe, is ther noon hir liche,
Of al the women in this worlde riche.

Yong was this quene, of twenty yeer of elde,
Of midel stature, and of swich fairnesse,
That nature had a Ioye hir to behelde;   80
And for to speken of hir stedfastnesse,
She passed hath Penelope and Lucresse,
And shortly, if she shal be comprehended,
In hir ne mighte no-thing been amended.

This Theban knight [Arcite] eek, sooth to seyn,   85
Was yong, and ther-with-al a lusty knight,
But he was double in love and no-thing pleyn,
And subtil in that crafte over any wight,
And with his cunning wan this lady bright;
For so ferforth he gan hir trouthe assure,   90
That she him [trust] over any creature.

What shuld I seyn? she loved Arcite so,
That, whan that he was absent any throwe,
Anon hir thoghte hir herte brast a-two;
For in hir sight to hir he bar him lowe,   95
So that she wende have al his herte y-knowe;
But he was fals; it nas but feyned chere,
As nedeth not to men such craft to lere.

---

72. Tn. dwellynge; F. duellyng.   73. F. sunne; Harl. Tn. D. Cx. sonne.
74. D. Through; F. Thorogh. Tn. sprynge; F. spring.   75. Tn. likynge;
F. likyng.   77. Harl. Tn. D. Cx. the; F. thes.   78. twenty *is written*
xxti *in the* MSS. D. olde; Cx. olde; Lt. of olde; Harl. eld; *rest* of elde.
79. Tn. mydell*e*; F. mydil. F. suche.   80. F. Ioy.   81. D. stedfastnesse;
F. stidfastnesse.   82. F. B. both; *rest* hath. Harl. Th. penelope; F. *and
others* penolope.   84. Harl. ne; *rest om.* Tn. myghte; F. myght.   85.
I supply Arcite; *line too short.* F. seyne.   86. Harl. yong; F. yonge. Harl.
there with alle (*so* D. Cx. Lt.); *rest* therto with al.   87. F. pleyne.   88.
Harl. any; F. eny. 89. D. Lt. Cx. wan; F. whan (!). 90. F. ferforthe. F. can;
rest gan.   91. Th. Tn. Harl. trusteth; *rest* trusted; *read* trust. D. any; F. eny.
93. F. eny throw.   94. F. thoght; hert.   95. F. bare.   96. F. hert.

VII. ANELIDA AND ARCITE.

But never-the-les ful mikel besinesse
Had he, er that he mighte his lady winne,   100
And swoor he wolde dyen for distresse,
Or from his wit he seyde he wolde twinne.
Alas, the whyle! for hit was routhe and sinne,
That she upon his sorowes wolde rewe,
But no-thing thenketh the fals as doth the trewe.   105

Hir fredom fond Arcite in swich manere,
That al was his that she hath, moche or lyte,
Ne to no creature made she chere
Ferther than that hit lyked to Arcite;
Ther was no lak with which he mighte hir wyte,   110
She was so ferforth yeven him to plese,
That al that lyked him, hit did hir ese.

Ther nas to hir no maner lettre y-sent
That touched love, from any maner wight,
That she ne shewed hit him, er hit was brent;   115
So pleyn she was, and did hir fulle might,
That she nil hyden nothing from hir knight,
Lest he of any untrouthe hir upbreyde;
Withouten bode his heste she obeyde.

And eek he made him Ielous over here,   120
That, what that any man had to hir seyd,
Anoon he wolde preyen hir to swere
What was that word, or make him evel apayd;
Than wende she out of hir wit have brayd;
But al this nas but sleight and flaterye,   125
Withouten love he feyned Ielosye.

---

101. Harl. Tn. D. B. swore (*for* swoor); Cx. sware; F. sworne. 105. Tn. thenketh; F. thinketh. 106. F. fonde; suche. 107. F. B. *wrongly insert* both *before* moche; *rest omit.* F. B. and; *rest* or. 109. Harl. Cx. that; *rest omit.* 110. F. wiche; myght. 111. Tn. yeuen; F. yevin. 112. F. dyd her hert an ese; Harl. Cx. *omit* hert an; *others vary.* 114, 118. D. any; F. eny. 116. Tn. D. B. full*e*; *rest* ful. 119. (*See* 126.) Harl. Cx. heste; *rest* herte, hert. 120. F. eke. Tn. Ielous; F. Ielouse. D. Cx. here (*for the rime*); F. her. 121. Harl. any; F. eny. F. seyde. 123. F. worde. Harl. Tn. apayde; F. apaied; D. B. apaid. 124. F. wend. Cx. brayd; Tn. breyde; F. breyed. 125. Harl. Cx. this nas; *rest* was. D. sleight; Cx. sleyght; F. sleght. 126. Harl. Withouten; F. With out; (*and so in* 119).

And al this took she so debonerly,
That al his wille, hir thoghte hit skilful thing,
And ever the lenger loved him tenderly,
And did him honour as he were a king.   130
Hir herte was wedded to him with a ring;
So ferforth upon trouthe is hir entente,
That wher he goth, hir herte with him wente.

Whan she shal ete, on him is so hir thoght,
That wel unnethe of mete took she keep;   135
And whan that she was to hir reste broght,
On him she thoghte alwey til that she sleep;
Whan he was absent, prevely she weep;
Thus liveth fair Anelida the quene
For fals Arcite, that did hir al this tene.   140

This fals Arcite, of his new-fangelnesse,
For she to him so lowly was and trewe,
Took lesse deyntee for hir stedfastnesse,
And saw another lady, proud and newe,
And right anon he cladde him in hir hewe—   145
Wot I not whether in whyte, rede, or grene—
And falsed fair Anelida the quene.

But never-the-les, gret wonder was hit noon
Thogh he wer fals, for hit is kinde of man,
Sith Lamek was, that is so longe agoon,   150
To been in love as fals as ever he can;
He was the firste fader that began
To loven two, and was in bigamye;
And he found tentes first, but-if men lye.

---

127. F. toke. F. B. as; *rest* so.   128. Harl. Tn. wille; F. wil. F. thoght. Koch *proposes to omit* hit.   129. *All ins.* she *after* lenger; *it is not wanted.*
131. F. ringe.   132. Harl. Cx. So; *rest* For so. Harl. Tn. entente; F. entent.
133. Tn. herte; F. hert. Harl. Tn. wente; F. went.   135. F. toke; kepe.
136. Harl. Cx. that; *rest omit.* Harl. D. Cx. reste; F. rest.   137. Tn. thoghte; F. thoght. Harl. Tn. Cx. alwey; F. ay. F. slepe.   138. F. wepe.
139. Cx. fayr; F. feire.   141. D. newfangilnesse; Tn. newfangulnes; F. new fanglesse.   143. F. Toke. D. sted-; F. stid-.   144. F. proude.   145. Harl. D. cladde; F. clad.   146. F. whethir.   148. F. lesse grete.   149. Harl. Cx. *omit* the, *which* F. *and others insert after* is.   152. Harl. Tn. firste; F. first.   154. F. founde.

VII. ANELIDA AND ARCITE.

This fals Arcite sumwhat moste he feyne, 155
Whan he wex fals, to covere his traitorye,
Right as an hors, that can both byte and pleyne;
For he bar hir on honde of trecherye,
And swoor he coude hir doublenesse espye,
And al was falsnes that she to him mente; 160
Thus swoor this theef, and forth his way he wente.

Alas! what herte might enduren hit,
For routhe or wo, hir sorow for to telle?
Or what man hath the cunning or the wit?
Or what man might with-in the chambre dwelle, 165
If I to him rehersen shal the helle,
That suffreth fair Anelida the quene
For fals Arcite, that did hir al this tene?

She wepeth, waileth, swowneth pitously,
To grounde deed she falleth as a stoon; 170
Al crampissheth hir limes crokedly,
She speketh as hir wit were al agoon;
Other colour then asshen hath she noon,
Noon other word she speketh moche or lyte,
But 'mercy, cruel herte myn, Arcite!' 175

And thus endureth, til that she was so mate
That she ne hath foot on which she may sustene;
But forth languisshing ever in this estate,
Of which Arcite hath nother routhe ne tene;
His herte was elles-where, newe and grene, 180
That on hir wo ne deyneth him not to thinke,
Him rekketh never wher she flete or sinke.

---

156. Harl. Tn. D. couer; Cx. couere; F. coueren. 157. F. Tn. pleyn. 159, 161. *All* swore. 160. Harl. Tn. mente; F. ment. 161. D. Cx. theef; F. thefe. Harl. Tn. wente; F. went. 162. Tn. herte; F. hert. Cx. enduren; *rest* endure. 167. F. feir. 169. Cx. swowneth; D. sownyth; F. swoneth. 170. Harl. Tn. D. grounde; F. ground. F. dede; ston. 171. Harl. Al; *rest om.* Cx. Crampissheth; Lt. Crampuissheth; Tn. Crampicheth; F. cravmpysshe. 172. F. agon. 174. Harl. Noon; Cx. None; *the rest insert* Ne *before* Noon. *For* she speketh, *all the* MSS. *have* speketh she. 175. F. mercie; hert. 178. F. B. for; *rest* forth. 179. Tn. D. nothir; F. nouther. 180. F. wher; *rest* where. 182. Harl. nought; Cx. not (*for* never). Harl. D. Cx. whether; *but* wher *is short for* whether. Cf. Compt. unto Pite, 110; *see note.*

THE MINOR POEMS.

His newe lady holdeth him so narowe
Up by the brydel, at the staves ende,
That every word, he dradde hit as an arowe;   185
Hir daunger made him bothe bowe and bende,
And as hir liste, made him turne or wende;
For she ne graunted him in hir livinge
No grace, why that he hath lust to singe;

But drof him forth, unnethe liste hir knowe   190
That he was servaunt to hir ladyshippe,
But lest that he wer proude, she held him lowe;
Thus serveth he, withouten fee or shipe,
She sent him now to londe, now to shippe;
And for she yaf him daunger al his fille,   195
Therfor she had him at hir owne wille.

Ensample of this, ye thrifty wimmen alle,
Take here Anelida and fals Arcite,
That for hir liste him 'dere herte' calle,
And was so meek, therfor he loved hir lyte;   200
The kinde of mannes herte is to delyte
In thing that straunge is, also god me save!
For what he may not gete, that wolde he have.

Now turne we to Anelida ageyn,
That pyneth day by day in languisshing;   205
But whan she saw that hir ne gat no geyn,
Upon a day, ful sorowfully weping,
She caste hir for to make a compleyning,
And with hir owne honde she gan hit wryte;
And sente hit to hir Theban knight Arcite.   210

---

183. *All but* Harl. Cx. Th. *insert* up *before* so; *see next line*.   184. F. bridil.
185. F. worde. B. D. Lt. dredith; F. Tn. dred hit; Harl. Cx. drad; *read* dradde hit.   187. Tn. Cx. liste; Harl. lyste; F. lust.   190. Harl. Cx. vnnethe; F. vnneth. F. list.   191. *All* un-to; *read* to.   192. Cx. proud; F. proude. Harl. Cx. held; F. helde.   193. Harl. withouten; F. with out. Harl. Cx. mete; *rest* fee. F. B. Lt. shippe; D. shipe; Cx. sype; Harl. shepe (!); Tn. shep (!).   195. D. yaf; F. yafe.   196. Harl. owne; F. ovne.   197. Harl. Tn. D. thrifty; F. thrifte.   198. B. here; F. her (i. e. *here*); Tn. D. here of; Cx. Lt. hede of.   199. Tn. Cx. liste (*pt. t.*); F. list. Harl. Cx. dere herte; F. her der hert.   200. *All* meke.   201. *All* kynde (kinde). F. hert.   203. Harl. Cx. he (*twice*); F. *and others wrongly have* they *the 2nd time*.   205. F. Tn. be; *rest* by.   206. F. sawe.   208. Harl. Tn. caste; F. cast.   209. Harl. owne; F. ovne.   210. Th. sente; D. Cx. sende; *rest* sent. F. B. *omit* hit; *rest retain*.

VII. ANELIDA AND ARCITE.

The compleynt of Anelida the quene upon fals Arcite.

Proem.

So thirleth with the poynt of remembraunce,
The swerd of sorowe, y-whet with fals plesaunce,
  Myn herte, bare of blis and blak of hewe,
  That turned is in quaking al my daunce,
  My suretee in a-whaped countenaunce ;   215
Sith hit availeth not for to ben trewe ;
For who-so trewest is, hit shal hir rewe,
That serveth love and doth hir observaunce
Alwey to oon, and chaungeth for no newe.

(Strophe.)

1. I wot my-self as wel as any wight ;   220
For I loved oon with al my herte and might
  More then my-self, an hundred thousand sythe,
  And called him my hertes lyf, my knight,
  And was al his, as fer as hit was right ;
  And whan that he was glad, than was I blythe,   225
And his disese was my deeth as swythe ;
And he ayein his trouthe me had plight
For ever-more, his lady me to kythe.

2. Now is he fals, alas ! and causeles,
And of my wo he is so routheles,   230
  That with a worde him list not ones deyne
  To bring ayein my sorowful herte in pees,
  For he is caught up in a-nother lees.

TITLE. *So in* F. (*but misspelt* Analida) ; B. The compiaynt of feyre Anelida on fals Arcyte ; D. Litera Annelide Regine.   211. Harl. thirllethe ; Cx. thirleth ; F. B. thirled (!).   212. B. swerd ; F. suerde. F. y-whet ; B. I-whet ; *rest* whet ; 213. Tn. herte ; F. hert. Harl. Tn. D. blak ; F. blake.   214. Harl. Cx. in. *rest* to ; *see* 215.   215. Tn. B. Lt. surete ; F. suerte. F. B. in to ; *rest* in. D. Cx. a whaped ; Harl. a whaaped ; F. a waped.   216. Harl. for ; *rest om.* 217. Harl. trewest ; F. truest. Harl. hir ; Cx. her ; F. *and others* him (*but see* l. 218).   218. F. dothe.   220. Harl. any ; F. eny.   221. F. hert.   223. F. B. cleped ; *rest* called. F. hertis life.   227. Harl. D. Cx. B. plight ; F. I-plyght. 229. *So* Tn. Harl. Cx. D ; F. B. Alas now hath he left me causeles.   232. Tn herte, pees ; F. hert, pes.   233. B. caught ; F. caght. Tn. D. Cx. lees ; F. le-

THE MINOR POEMS.

  Right as him list, he laugheth at my peyne,
  And I ne can myn herte not restreyne,   235
   That I ne love him alwey, never-the-les;
   And of al this I not to whom me pleyne.

3. And shal I pleyne—alas! the harde stounde—
  Un-to my foo that yaf my herte a wounde,
   And yet desyreth that myn harm be more?   240
  Nay, certes! ferther wol I never founde
  Non other help, my sores for to sounde.
   My desteny hath shapen it ful yore;
   I wil non other medecyne ne lore;
  I wil ben ay ther I was ones bounde,   245
  That I have seid, be seid for ever-more!

4. Alas! wher is become your gentilesse!
  Your wordes ful of plesaunce and humblesse?
   Your obseruaunces in so low manere,
  And your awayting and your besinesse   250
  Upon me, that ye calden your maistresse,
   Your sovereyn lady in this worlde here?
   Alas! and is ther nother word ne chere
  Ye vouchesauf upon myn hevinesse?
  Alas! your love, I bye hit al to dere.   255

5.   Now certes, swete, thogh that ye
   Thus causeles the cause be
   Of my dedly adversitee,
  Your manly reson oghte it to respyte
   To slee your frend, and namely me,   260
   That never yet in no degree
   Offended yow, as wisly he,
  That al wot, out of wo my soule quyte!

---

234. F. B. me (!); *rest* him.   235. F. hert.   238. F. pleyn. Harl. Tn. harde; F. hard.   239. F. yafe; hert.   240. F. harme.   241. F. certis. *All* be founde; *but* be *is copied in from the line above*; *see* l. 47.   242. F. helpe.   243. Tn. desteny; F. destany. F. B. *om.* ful.   246. F. seide (*twice*).   252. F. souereigne.   253. *I supply* and *from* Cx.; Harl. *has* And is there nowe neyther.   254. Lt. vouchesauf; Cx. vouchen sauf; F. vouchesafe.   256. F. certis.   257. F. B. causer (*for* caus-e); *rest* cause.   258. F. dedely.   259. F. oght.   260. Harl. Lt. slee; Tn. D. Cx. sle; F. slene. F. frende.   263. Harl. wot; F. wote.

VII. ANELIDA AND ARCITE.

¶ But for I shewed yow, Arcite,
Al that men wolde to me wryte, 265
And was so besy, yow to delyte—
My honour save—meke, kinde, and free,
Therfor ye putte on me the wyte,
And of me recche not a myte,
Thogh that the swerd of sorow byte 270
My woful herte through your crueltee.

6. My swete foo, why do ye so, for shame?
And thenke ye that furthered be your name,
To love a newe, and been untrewe? nay!
And putte yow in sclaunder now and blame, 275
And do to me adversitee and grame,
That love yow most, god, wel thou wost!
alway?
Yet turn ayeyn, and be al pleyn som day,
And than shal this that now is mis be game,
And al for-yive, whyl that I live may. 280

(*Antistrophe.*)

1. Lo! herte myn, al this is for to seyne,
As whether shal I preye or elles pleyne?
Whiche is the wey to doon yow to be trewe?
For either mot I have yow in my cheyne,
Or with the dethe ye mot departe us tweyne; 285
Ther ben non other mene weyes newe;
For god so wisly on my soule rewe,
As verily ye sleen me with the peyne;
That may ye see unfeyned of myn hewe.

264, 265. Harl. Cx. But for I was so pleyne, Arcyte, In all*e* my werkes, much and lyte; *and omit* was *in* l. 266. 267. F. honor. Tn. saue; F. D. safe; Harl. Cx. sauf. 268. F. put. 269. Harl. Tn. recche; F. rek. 270. F. B. *om.* that. F. suerde. 271. Tn. herte; F. hert. F. thro. 272. F. suete. 274. Harl. Tn. vntrewe; F. vntrew. 275. Harl. putte; F. put. 278. Tn. D. Ff. Lt. turne; *rest* come. 279. Tn. Harl. Cx. D. Lt. And then shall this that now is mis ben (be); F. B. And turne al this that hath be mys to. 280. F. foryeve; Tn. foryife; Harl. 372, foryiue (*rightly*). 281. F. hert. Harl. seyne (*gerund*); F. seyn. 282. F. wheder; prey; pleyn. 284, 5, 8. F. cheyn, tweyn, peyn. 287. D. Cx. on; Harl. of; F. Tn. B. vpon. 288. D. verily; F. verrely.

THE MINOR POEMS.

2. For thus ferforth have I my deth [y]-soght, 290
    My-self I mordre with my prevy thoght;
    For sorow and routhe of your unkindenesse
    I wepe, I wake, I faste; al helpeth noght;
    I weyve Ioy that is to speke of oght,
        I voyde companye, I flee gladnesse; 295
    Who may avaunte hir bet of hevinesse
    Then I? and to this plyte have ye me broght,
        Withoute gilt; me nedeth no witnesse.

3. And sholde I preye, and weyve womanhede?
    Nay! rather deth then do so foul a dede, 300
    And axe mercy gilteles! what nede?
    And if I pleyne what lyf that I lede,
    Yow rekketh not; that know I, out of drede;
    And if I unto yow myn othes bede
        For myn excuse, a scorn shal be my mede; 305
    Your chere floureth, but hit wol not sede;
        Ful longe agoon I oghte have take hede.

4. For thogh I hadde yow to-morow ageyn,
    I might as wel holde Averill fro reyn,
        As holde yow, to make yow stedfast. 310
    Almighty god, of trouthe sovereyn,
    Wher is the trouthe of man? who hath hit sleyn?
    Who that hem loveth shal hem fynde as fast
        As in a tempest is a roten mast.
    Is that a tame best that is ay feyn 315
        To renne away, when he is leest agast?

---

290. Harl. Cx. *omit this stanza.* F. dethe (*wrongly*); *rest* deth. *All* soght, sought; *read* y-soght. 291. D. B. mordre; F. mou*r*dre. 292. F. vnkyndnesse. 293. Tn. D. faste; F. fast. 296. F. avaunt. Tn. B. Lt. bet; F. bet*er*. 298. Tn. Lt. With oute; F. With out. 299. *Some of the* final rimes *in this stanza are* forced *ones*. F. B. shal; *rest* sholde (shulde). F. prey. 300. F. dethe; Harl. Cx. dye. F. foule. 301. F. mercie. Tn. gilteles; F. giltles. 302. Harl. pleyne; F. pleyn. F. lyfe. Harl. Cx. *ins.* that; F. *and others omit.* 304. Tn. D. unto; F. to. 305. F. skorne. 306. F. B. *om.* hit. 307. F. *and others insert* to *before* have; Tn. D. Lt. Cx. *omit.* 308. D. hadde; F. had. 309. F. Apprile; Harl. Aueryll. 310. F. B. yow be; *rest om.* be. F. stidfast. 311. F. souereigne. 312. F. slayn. 313. Tn. D. Lt. She; Harl. Sheo; *rest* Who. F. B. *insert* she *before* shal. 314. F. *om.* 1st a. 315. Is] F. this (!) 316. Harl. fleen; Cx. fle (*for* renne). F. lest.

VII. ANELIDA AND ARCITE.

5. Now mercy, swete, if I misseye,
   Have I seyd oght amis, I preye?
   I not; my wit is al aweye.
   I fare as doth the song of *Chaunte-pleure*.   320
   For now I pleyne, and now I pleye,
   I am so mased that I deye,
   Arcite hath born awey the keye
   Of al my worlde, and my good aventure!

   ¶For in this worlde nis creature   325
   Wakinge, in more discomfiture
   Then I, ne more sorow endure;
   And if I slepe a furlong wey or tweye,
   Than thinketh me, that your figure
   Before me stant, clad in asure,   330
   To profren eft a newe assure
   For to be trewe, and mercy me to preye.

6. The longe night   this wonder sight   I drye,
   And on the day   for this afray   I dye,   334
      And of al this   right noght, y-wis, ye recche.
   Ne never mo   myn yën two   be drye,
   And to your routhe and to your trouthe I crye.
      But welawey!   to fer be they   to fecche;
   Thus holdeth me   my destinee   a wrecche.
   But me to rede   out of this drede   or gye   340
      Ne may my wit, so weyk is hit,   not strecche.

Conclusion.

Than ende I thus, sith I may do no more,
I yeve hit up for now and ever-more;

---

317. Harl. Cx. But; *rest* Now. F. mercie. F. myssey (*omitting* e *in* -eye *throughout, wrongly*); Harl. myssaye, &c.   318. *So* F. B.; *rest* Have I ought seyd out of the weye. F. seyde.   319. Harl. Cx. half (*for* al).   320. F. dothe; songe. F. chaunt plure; Harl. Chaunte pleure.   321. F. pleyn.   323. F. borne.   325. Harl. Cx. nys; F. B. D. ther is no; Tn. ther nis no (*too many syllables*). 328. F. furlonge. F. B. other (*for* or); *rest* or.   329. F. thenketh; Tn. thynketh.   330. Tn. stant; F. stont.   331. Harl. Cx. To profren efte; D. Tn. Lt. Efte to profre; F. B. To suere yet. Tn. D. Cx. Lt. assure; F. asure. 332. F. trew; mercie. Harl. and love me til I dye; Cx. and love me til he deye. 334. F. B. this; D. Tn. suche; Harl. Cx. thilke.   335. F. reche; Tn. D. recche; *and so with* feche, &c.   339. F. destany; Tn. destyne (*for the rime*). 341. F. weyke.   343. Harl. D. Cx. yeve; F. yf; Tn. gife.

378   THE MINOR POEMS.

   For I shal never eft putten in balaunce
   My sekernes, ne lerne of love the lore.   345
   But as the swan, I have herd seyd ful yore,
     Ayeins his deth shal singe in his penaunce,
     So singe I here my destiny or chaunce,
   How that Arcite Anelida so sore
     Hath thirled with the poynt of remembraunce! 350

The story continued.

   Whan that Anelida this woful quene
   Hath of hir hande writen in this wyse,
   With face deed, betwixe pale and grene,
   She fel a-swowe; and sith she gan to ryse,
   And unto Mars avoweth sacrifyse   355
   With-in the temple, with a sorowful chere,
   That shapen was as ye shal after here.   357

(*Unfinished.*)

---

344. F. efte. Tn. Cx. putten; F. put.   347. Tn. deth; F. dethe. Tn. D. Lt. Ff. *insert* in; *rest om.*   348. Harl. Tn. destenye; D. destynye; F. destany. 349. F. Analida. F. B. to; *rest* so.   351. *This stanza only occurs in* Tn. D. Lt. Ff. Th.; *I follow* Tn. *mainly.* Tn. Annelida; wofull.   352. Tn. Lt. Ff. of; D. with.   353. D. Th. deed; *rest* dede. D. betwixe; Th. betwyxe; Ff. bitwixte; Tn. Lt. betwix.   354. Tn. felle; Th. fel. Ff. a swowe; Tn. a swow. 355. Lt. Th. avoweth; D. avowith; Tn. avoyth.   356. Tn. With-Inne; *rest* With-in. Tn. sorofull*e*.   357. Tn. shapyn; aftyr. shal after] Lt. Th. may plainly.

VIII. CHAUCERS WORDES UNTO ADAM, HIS OWNE SCRIVEYN.

Adam scriveyn, if ever it thee bifalle
Boece or Troilus to wryten newe,
Under thy lokkes thou most have the scalle,
But after my making thou wryte trewe.
So ofte a daye I mot thy werk renewe, 5
Hit to correcte and eek to rubbe and scrape;
And al is through thy negligence and rape.

From T. (= MS. R. 3. 20 *in* Trin. Coll. Library, Cambridge). *It also occurs in* Stowe's edition (1561).

Title; T. *has*—Chauciers wordes .a. Geffrey vn-to Adame his owen scryveyne; Stowe *has*—Chaucers woordes vnto his owne Scriuener.

1. T. scryveyne; byfalle.   2. T. Troylus for to; nuwe.   3. T. thy long lokkes (*see* note); thowe.   4. T. affter; makyng thowe wryte more truwe (*see* note).   5. T. offt; renuwe.   6. T. It; corect; Stowe *has* correcte. T. eke. 7. T. thorugh; neclygence.

IX. THE FORMER AGE.

A BLISFUL lyf, a paisible and a swete
Ledden the peples in the former age;
They helde hem payed of fruites, that they ete,
Which that the feldes yave hem by usage;
They ne were nat forpampred with outrage; 5
Unknowen was the quern and eek the melle;
They eten mast, hawes, and swich pounage,
And dronken water of the colde welle.

Yit nas the ground nat wounded with the plough,
But corn up-sprong, unsowe of mannes hond, 10
The which they gniden, and eete nat half y-nough.
No man yit knew the forwes of his lond;
No man the fyr out of the flint yit fond;
Un-korven and un-grobbed lay the vyne;
No man yit in the morter spyces grond 15
To clarre, ne to sause of galantyne.

No mader, welde, or wood no litestere
Ne knew; the flees was of his former hewe;
No flesh ne wiste offence of egge or spere;
No coyn ne knew man which was fals or trewe; 20

From MS. I (= Ii. 3. 21, Camb. Univ. Library); *also in* Hh (= Hh. 4. 12, Camb. Univ. Library). *I note every variation from* I.
 1. I. Blysful; paysyble. 2. I. poeples; Hh. peplis. 3. I. paied of the; Hh. paied with the (*but omit* the). I. fructes; Hh. frutes. 4. I. Whiche. 5. I. weere; Hh. were. I. Hh. owtrage. 6. I. Onknowyn. I. quyerne; Hh. qwerne. I. ek. 7. I. swych pownage. 9. I. grownd; wownded; plowh. 11. I. gnodded; Hh. knoddyd; *read* gniden; *see* note. I. I-nowh. 12. I. knewe; Hh. knew. 13. I. owt; flynt; fonde. 15. I. spices. 16. I. sawse; Hh. sause. I. galentyne; Hh. galantine. 17. I. madyr; Hh. madder. Hh. wellyd (*wrongly*). I. wod; Hh. woode. 18. I. knewh. I. fles; Hh. flese (*for* flees). I. is (*for* his); Hh. hys. 19. I. flessh; wyste. 20. I. knewh. Hh. was; I. is.

IX. THE FORMER AGE.

No ship yit karf the wawes grene and blewe;
No marchaunt yit ne fette outlandish ware;
No trompes for the werres folk ne knewe,
No toures heye, and walles rounde or square.

What sholde it han avayled to werreye? 25
Ther lay no profit, ther was no richesse,
But cursed was the tyme, I dar wel seye,
That men first dide hir swety bysinesse
To grobbe up metal, lurkinge in darknesse,
And in the riveres first gemmes soghte. 30
Allas! than sprong up al the cursednesse
Of covetyse, that first our sorwe broghte!

Thise tyraunts putte hem gladly nat in pres,
No wildnesse, ne no busshes for to winne
Ther poverte is, as seith Diogenes, 35
Ther as vitaile is eek so skars and thinne
That noght but mast or apples is ther-inne.
But, ther as bagges been and fat vitaile,
Ther wol they gon, and spare for no sinne
With al hir ost the cite for tassaile. 40

Yit were no paleis-chaumbres, ne non halles;
In caves and [in] wodes softe and swete
Slepten this blissed folk with-oute walles,
On gras or leves in parfit quiete.
No doun of fetheres, ne no bleched shete 45
Was kid to hem, but in seurtee they slepte;
Hir hertes were al oon, with-oute galles,
Everich of hem his feith to other kepte.

---

22. I. owt-. 23. I. *inserts* batails (Hh. batayllys) *after* No. 24. I. towres; rownde. 26. I. profyt; rychesse. 27. I. corsed; Hh. cursyd. 28. I. fyrst; Hh. first. I. dede; bysynesse. 29. I. lurkynge. Hh. derknesse; I. dirkenesse. 30. I. Ryuerys fyrst gemmys sowhte. 31. I. cursydnesse. 32. Hh. couetyse; I. coueytyse. I. fyrst owr; browhte. 33. I. Thyse tyrauntz. *Both* put. 34. I. *inserts* places (Hh. place of) *after* No. I. wynne. 36. I. vitayle; ek. 37. I nat (*for* noght); Hh. nowt. 39. I. synne. 40. I. Cyte. I. forto asayle; Hh. for to asayle. 41. Hh. were; I. was. 42. I. kaues. I. Hh. *om*. 2nd in; *which I supply*. 43. I. Sleptin; blyssed; withowte. 44. Hh. On; I. Or. I. parfyt Ioye reste and quiete (!); Hh. parfite Ioy and quiete (!). 45. I. down. 46. I. kyd. I. surte; Hh. surt. 47. I. weere; on; -owte. 48. I. Euerych; oother.

Unforged was the hauberk and the plate;
The lambish peple, voyd of alle vyce, 50
Hadden no fantasye to debate,
But ech of hem wolde other wel cheryce;
No pryde, non envye, non avaryce,
No lord, no taylage by no tyrannye;
Humblesse and pees, good feith, the emperice, 55
[Fulfilled erthe of olde curtesye.]

Yit was not Iupiter the likerous,
That first was fader of delicacye,
Come in this world; ne Nembrot, desirous
To reynen, had nat maad his toures hye. 60
Allas, allas! now may men wepe and crye!
For in our dayes nis but covetyse
[And] doublenesse, and tresoun and envye,
Poysoun, manslauhtre, and mordre in sondry wyse. 64

Finit Etas prima. Chaucers.

---

49. I. hawberke.   50. I. lambyssh.   I. poeple; Hh. pepyl.   Hh. voyd; I. voyded.   Hh. vice; I. vyse.   51. I. fantesye.   52. I. eche; oother.   53. I. pride.   54. I. tyranye.   55. Hh. Humblesse; I. Vmblesse.   I. pes. 56. *Not in the* MSS.; *I supply it.* Koch *suggests*—Yit hadden in this worlde the maistrye.   57. I. Iuppiter; Hh. Iupiter. I. lykerous.   58. I. fyrst; fadyr; delicasie.   59. I. desyrous.   60. I. regne; towres.   61. Hh. men; *which* I. *omits*.   62. I. owre.   63. I. Hh. *omit first* And, *which I supply*. I. Hh. Dowblenesse.   64. I. Poyson and manslawtre; Hh. Poysonne manslawtyr. *Finit, &c.; in* Hh. *only*.

X. FORTUNE.

Balades de visage sanz peinture.

I. Le Pleintif countre Fortune.

This wrecched worldes transmutacioun,
As wele or wo, now povre and now honour,
With-outen ordre or wys discrecioun
Governed is by Fortunes errour;
But natheles, the lak of hir favour   5
Ne may nat don me singen, though I dye,
'*Iay tout perdu mon temps et mon labour:*'
For fynally, Fortune, I thee defye!

Yit is me left the light of my resoun,
To knowen frend fro fo in thy mirour.   10
So muche hath yit thy whirling up and doun
Y-taught me for to knowen in an hour.
But trewely, no force of thy reddour
To him that over him-self hath the maystrye!
My suffisaunce shal be my socour: 15
For fynally, Fortune, I thee defye!

O Socrates, thou stedfast champioun,
She never mighte be thy tormentour;
Thou never dreddest hir oppressioun,
Ne in hir chere founde thou no savour.   20

The spelling is conformed to that of the preceding poems; the alterations though numerous are slight; as *y* for *i*, *au* for *aw*, &c. The text mainly follows MS. I. (=Ii. 3. 21, Camb. Univ. Library). Other MSS. are A. (Ashmole 59); T. (Trin. Coll. Camb.); F. (Fairfax 16); B. (Bodley 638); H. (Harl. 2251).   2. F. pouerte; *rest* poure (poore, pore, poeere).   8, 16. I. fynaly; deffye.   11. I. mochel; *the rest* muche, moche.   13. I. fors; thi reddowr.   17. I. stidfast chaumpyoun.   18. I. myht; thi tormentowr.   20. I. fownde thow.

Thou knewe wel deceit of hir colour,
And that hir moste worshipe is to lye.
I knowe hir eek a fals dissimulour:
For fynally, Fortune, I thee defye!

II. La respounse de Fortune au Pleintif.

No man is wrecched, but him-self hit wene,   25
And he that hath him-self hath suffisaunce.
Why seystow thanne I am to thee so kene,
That hast thy-self out of my governaunce?
Sey thus: 'Graunt mercy of thyn haboundaunce
That thou hast lent or this.' Why wolt thou stryve? 30
What wostow yit, how I thee wol avaunce?
And eek thou hast thy beste frend alyve!

I have thee taught divisioun bi-twene
Frend of effect, and frend of countenaunce;
Thee nedeth nat the galle of noon hyene,   35
That cureth eyen derke fro hir penaunce;
Now seestow cleer, that were in ignoraunce.
Yit halt thyn ancre, and yit thou mayst arryve
Ther bountee berth the keye of my substaunce:
And eek thou hast thy beste frend alyve.   40

How many have I refused to sustene,
Sin I thee fostred have in thy plesaunce!
Woltow than make a statut on thy quene
That I shal been ay at thyn ordinaunce?
Thou born art in my regne of variaunce,   45
Aboute the wheel with other most thou dryve.
My lore is bet than wikke is thy grevaunce,
And eek thou hast thy beste frend alyve.

---

21. I. the deseyte; A. T. H. *om.* the.   22. I. most.   23. I. knew; *rest* knowe. I. ek.   24. I. fynaly; the deffye.   27. H. seystow; I. seysthow. I. (*only*) *om.* to.   30. So I.; *rest* Thou shalt not stryue.   31. I. woost thow; B. wostow; A. T. wostowe.   36. I. derkyd; *rest* derke (derk). T. from hir; H. from ther; A. frome theire; F. B. fro; I. for.   37. H. seestow; A. T. seestowe; I. *partly erased.*   43. I. Wolthow; B. Woltow.   46. I. most thow; H. thow must; *the rest* maystow, maisthow, maistow.

X. FORTUNE.

III. La respounse du Pleintif countre Fortune.

Thy lore I dampne, hit is adversitee.
My frend maystow nat reven, blind goddesse! 50
That I thy frendes knowe, I thanke hit thee.
Tak hem agayn, lat hem go lye on presse!
The negardye in keping hir richesse
Prenostik is thou wolt hir tour assayle;
Wikke appetyt comth ay before seknesse: 55
In general, this reule may nat fayle.

La respounse de Fortune countre le Pleintif.

Thou pinchest at my mutabilitee,
For I thee lente a drope of my richesse,
And now me lyketh to with-drawe me.
Why sholdestow my realtee oppresse? 60
The see may ebbe and flowen more or lesse;
The welkne hath might to shyne, reyne, or hayle;
Right so mot I kythen my brotelnesse.
In general, this reule may nat fayle.

Lo, thexecucion of the magestee 65
That al purveyeth of his rightwisnesse,
That same thing 'Fortune' clepen ye,
Ye blinde bestes, ful of lewednesse!
The hevene hath propretee of sikernesse,
This world hath ever resteles travayle; 70
Thy laste day is ende of myn intresse:
In general, this reule may nat fayle.

---

49. I. dempne; F. B. H. dampne. 50. I. maysthow; B. maistou; H. may-stow. 51. I. thanke to; F. thanke yt; B. thanke it; H. thank it nat : (Lansdowne *and* Pepys *also have* thank it). 60. I. apresse; *rest* oppresse. 61. I. A. or; *rest* and. 62. I. welkne; A. B. H. welkin; F. welkene; T. sky. 63. I. brutelnesse; T. brutilnesse; F. B. H. brotelnesse; A. brittelnesse. *After* l. 64, *a new rubric is wrongly inserted, thus*: I. Le pleintif; F. B. H. Le pleintif encontre Fortune; A. The Pleyntyff ageinst Fortune; T. Thaunswer of the Lover ayenst Fortune; *see* note. 65. A. F. þexecucion; B. thexecucyon; I. excussyoun. I. maieste; *rest* magestee (mageste). 71. I. intersse (*sic*); (Lansd. *and* Pepys intresse); T. F. B. interesse; A. H. encresse.

c c

Lenvoy de Fortune.

Princes, I prey you of your gentilesse,
Lat nat this man on me thus crye and pleyne,
And I shal quyte you your bisinesse 75
At my requeste, as three of you or tweyne;
And, but you list releve him of his peyne,
Preyeth his beste frend, of his noblesse,
That to som beter estat he may atteyne. 79

Explicit.

---

73. I. gentilesses; *the rest* gentilesse.   76. *In* I. *only*; *the rest omit this line.*
77. A. F. B. H. And; I. T. That.   I. lest; *rest* list (liste).   *At end*—B. Explicit.

XI. MERCILES BEAUTE: A TRIPLE ROUNDEL.

I. *Captivity.*

Your yën two wol slee me sodenly,
I may the beautè of hem not sustene,
So woundeth hit through-out my herte kene.

And but your word wol helen hastily
My hertes wounde, whyl that hit is grene,   5
  Your yën two wol slee me sodenly,
  I may the beautè of hem not sustene.

Upon my trouthe I sey yow feithfully,
That ye ben of my lyf and deeth the quene;
For with my deeth the trouthe shal be sene.   10
  Your yën two wol slee me sodenly,
  I may the beautè of hem not sustene,
  So woundeth hit through-out my herte kene.

II. *Rejection.*

So hath your beautè fro your herte chaced
Pitee, that me ne availeth not to pleyne;   15
For Daunger halt your mercy in his cheyne.

This excellent text is from P. (MS. Pepys 2006, p. 390). *I note all variations from the* MS.

  1. P. Yowre two yen; *but read* Your yen two; *for in* ll., 6, 11, *the* MS. *has* Your yen, &c. P. wolle sle.   2. them; *read* hem.   3. wondeth it thorowout (out *in the margin*).   4. wille.   5. Mi hertis wound while; it.   6, 7. Your yen, &c.   8. trouth.   9. liffe; deth.   10. deth; trouth.   11-13. Your yen, &c.   14. yowre.   15. nauailleth; pleyn.   16. danger.

388 THE MINOR POEMS.

Giltles my deeth thus han ye me purchaced;
I sey yow sooth, me nedeth not to feyne;
So hath your beautè fro your herte chaced
Pitee, that me ne availeth not to pleyne. 20

Allas! that nature hath in yow compassed
So greet beautè, that no man may atteyne
To mercy, though he sterve for the peyne.
So hath your beautè fro your herte chaced
Pitee, that me ne availeth not to pleyne; 25
For Daunger halt your mercy in his cheyne.

III. *Escape.*

Sin I fro Love escaped am so fat,
I never thenk to ben in his prison lene;
Sin I am free, I counte him not a bene.

He may answere, and seye this or that; 30
I do no fors, I speke right as I mene.
Sin I fro Love escaped am so fat,
I never thenk to ben in his prison lene.

Love hath my name y-strike out of his sclat,
And he is strike out of my bokes clene 35
For ever-mo; [ther] is non other mene.
Sin I fro Love escaped am so fat,
I never thenk to ben in his prison lene;
Sin I am free, I counte him not a bene. 39

Explicit.

---

17. deth.   18. soth; fayn.   19, 20. So hath yo*ur*, &c.   21. compased.
22. grete; atteyn.   23. peyn.   24-26. So hath yo*ur* beaute, &c.
28. neue*re*.   29. fre.   30. answe*re* & sey.   32, 33. Syn I fro loue, &c.
34. I strike.   36. this is (*read* ther is).   37-39. Syn I fro loue, &c.

XII. TO ROSEMOUNDE. A BALADE.

MADAME, ye ben of al beautè shryne
As fer as cercled is the mappemounde;
For as the cristal glorious ye shyne,
And lyke ruby ben your chekes rounde.
Therwith ye ben so mery and so iocounde, 5
That at a revel whan that I see you daunce,
It is an oynement unto my wounde,
Thogh ye to me ne do no daliaunce.

For thogh I wepe of teres ful a tyne,
Yet may that wo myn herte nat confounde; 10
Your seemly voys that ye so smal out-twyne
Maketh my thoght in Ioye and blis habounde.
So curteisly I go, with lovë bounde,
That to my-self I sey, in my penaunce,
Suffyseth me to love you, Rosemounde, 15
Thogh ye to me ne do no daliaunce.

Nas never pyk walwed in galauntyne
As I in love am walwed and y-wounde;
For which ful ofte I of my-self divyne
That I am trewe Tristam the secounde. 20
My love may not refreyd be nor afounde;
I brenne ay in an amorous plesaunce.
Do what you list, I wil your thral be founde,
Thogh ye to me ne do no daliaunce. 24

   Tregentil.   **Chaucer.**

From MS. Rawl. Poet. 163, leaf 114. *No title in the* MS. *Readings.* 2. mapamonde. 3. cristall. 4. chekys. 5. iocounde. 6. Reuell; se; dance. 8. Thoght (*see* 16); daliance. 11. semy (*sic*); *read* seemly; fynall, *for* final (*misreading of* fmal). 12. Makyth; ioy; blys. 13. curtaysly. 18. I wounde. 19. deuyne. 20. trew. 21. refreyde (*with* be *above the line, just before it*); affounde. 22. amorouse. 23. lyst; wyl. 24. daliance.

XIII. TRUTH.

Balade de bon conseyl.

FLEE fro the prees, and dwelle with sothfastnesse,
Suffyce unto thy good, though hit be smal;
For hord hath hate, and climbing tikelnesse,
Prees hath envye, and wele blent overal;
Savour no more than thee bihove shal; 5
Werk wel thy-self, that other folk canst rede;
And trouthe shal delivere, hit is no drede.

Tempest thee noght al croked to redresse,
In trust of hir that turneth as a bal:
Gret reste stant in litel besinesse; 10
And eek be war to sporne ageyn an al;
Stryve noght, as doth the crokke with the wal.
Daunte thy-self, that dauntest otheres dede;
And trouthe shal delivere, hit is no drede.

That thee is sent, receyve in buxumnesse, 15
The wrastling for this worlde axeth a fal.
Her nis non hoom, her nis but wildernesse:
Forth, pilgrim, forth! Forth, beste, out of thy stal!

TITLE. Gg. *has*—Balade de bone conseyl; F. *has*—Balade.
The MSS. *are* At. (Addit. 10340, Brit. Museum); Gg. (Camb. Univ. Library, Gg. 4. 27); E. (Ellesmere MS.); Ct. (Cotton. Cleop. D. 7); T. (Trin. Coll. Camb. R. 3. 20); F. (Fairfax 16); *and others. The text is founded on* E.
2. E. Suffise. E. good; T. goode; At. Ct. thing; Gg. þyng. 4. At. blent; T. blenteþe; Gg. blyndyþ; E. blyndeth; Ct. blindeth; *see* note. 5. E. the.
7. T. *inserts* thee *before* shal. 8. Tempest] Harl. F. T. Peyne. 9. E. trist; *the rest* trust. 10. Gg. Gret reste; T. Gret rest; E. For gret reste; Ct. I or greet rest; At. Mych wele. E. bisynesse; *rest* besynesse. 11. E. ek; agayn.
13. E. Ct. Daunt; *the rest* Daunte. 14. T. *inserts* thee *before* shal. 15. E. the; boxomnesse.

XIII. TRUTH.

Know thy contree, look up, thank God of al;
Hold the hye wey, and lat thy gost thee lede: 20
And trouthe shal delivere, hit is no drede.

Envoy.

Therfore, thou vache, leve thyn old wrecchednesse
Unto the worlde; leve now to be thral;
Crye him mercy, that of his hy goodnesse
Made thee of noght, and in especial 25
Draw unto him, and pray in general
For thee, and eek for other, hevenlich mede;
And trouthe shal delivere, hit is no drede. 28

Explicit Le bon counseill de G. Chaucer.

---

19. Know thy contree] Harl. F. T. Loke vp on hie. E. lok; *the rest* loke, looke. 20. *For* Hold the hye wey, Harl. F. *and others have* Weyve thy lust. E. the (*for* thee). 21. T. *inserts* thee *before* shal. 22-28. *This stanza is in* At. *only.* 22. At. þine olde wrechedenesse. 23. At. world. 24. At. Crie hym; hys hie. 25. At. þe; nouȝt. 26. At. Drawe; hym. 27. At. þe; eke; heuenelyche. 28. At. schal delyuere. COLOPHON: *so in* F.

XIV. GENTILESSE.

Moral Balade of Chaucer.

The firste stok, fader of gentilesse—
What man that claymeth gentil for to be,
Must folowe his trace, and alle his wittes dresse
Vertu to sewe, and vyces for to flee.
For unto vertu longeth dignitee,   5
And noght the revers, saufly dar I deme,
Al were he mytre, croune, or diademe.

This firste stok was ful of rightwisnesse,
Trewe of his word, sobre, pitous, and free,
Clene of his goste, and loved besinesse,   10
Ageinst the vyce of slouthe, in honestee ;
And, but his heir love vertu, as dide he,
He is noght gentil, thogh he riche seme,
Al were he mytre, croune, or diademe.

Vyce may wel be heir to old richesse ;   15
But ther may no man, as men may wel see,
Bequethe his heir his vertuous noblesse ;

TITLE ; *so in* Harl., *but spelt* Chaucier ; T. *has*—Balade by Chaucier.

The MSS. *are* A. (Ashmole 59) ; T. (Trin. Coll. R. 3. 20) ; Harl. (Harl. 7333) ; Ct. (Cotton, Cleopatra D. 7) ; Ha. (Harl. 7578) ; Add. (Additional 22139, Brit. Museum). *Also* Cx. (Caxton's printed edition). *I follow chiefly the last of these, and note variations.*

1. Cx. first ; Harl. ffirste ; Ct. firste. T. gentilesse ; *rest* gentilnesse.   3. Cx. *om.* alle.   4. A. T. suwe ; Harl. shew (*for* sewe) ; Cx. folowe (!).   5. Cx. vertue ; dignyte.   6. Cx. not ; *rest* nouȝt, nought, noȝte.   7. Cx. mytor ; A. T. Harl. Add. mytre. Cx. crowne ; dyademe.   8. Cx. rightwisnes.   9. A. Ct. Ha. pitous ; Cx. pyetous.   10. Cx. besynes.   11. A. Ageinst ; T. Ageynst ; Cx. Agayn. Cx. *om.* the. Cx. honeste.   12. Cx. eyer ; *rest* heire, heyre, eyre.   13. Cx. not ; Ct. Ha. nought. Cx. though ; Add. thogh. 14. Cx. mytor ; crowne.   15. Cx. *omits* heir. Cx. holde ; *rest* olde ; *but read* old.   16. Cx. al ; *rest* as.   17. Cx. eyer.

XIV. GENTILESSE.

That is appropred unto no degree,
But to the firste fader in magestee,
That maketh him his heir, that can him queme, 20
Al were he mytre, croune, or diademe.

---

18. Cx. degre.　　19. Cx. first; mageste.　　20. Ct. That maketh his heires hem that hym queme (*omitting* can); A. That maþe his heyre him that wol him qweme; T. That makeþe heos heyres hem þat wol him qweeme; Add. That maketh his eires hem that can him queme; Cx. That makes hem eyres that can hem queme; *with other variations. I follow* Cx., *supplying* his, *and putting* him *and* heir *in the singular*; *cf.* he *in* l. 21.　　21. Cx. crowne mytor.

XV. LAK OF STEDFASTNESSE.

Balade.

Som tyme this world was so stedfast and stable
That mannes word was obligacioun,
And now hit is so fals and deceivable,
That word and deed, as in conclusioun,
Ben no-thing lyk, for turned up so doun   5
Is al this world for mede and wilfulnesse,
That al is lost for lak of stedfastnesse.

What maketh this world to be so variable
But lust that folk have in dissensioun?
Among us now a man is holde unable,   10
But-if he can, by som collusioun,
Don his neighbour wrong or oppressioun.
What causeth this, but wilful wrecchednesse,
That al is lost, for lak of stedfastnesse?

Trouthe is put doun, resoun is holden fable;   15
Vertu hath now no dominacioun,
Pitee exyled, no man is merciable.
Through covetyse is blent discrecioun;
The world hath mad a permutacioun

The MSS *are*: Harl. (Harl. 7333); T. (Trin. Coll. R. 3. 20); Ct. (Cotton. Cleop. D. 7); F. (Fairfax 16); Add. (Addit. 22139); Bann. (Bannatyne); *and others*. Th. = Thynne (1532). *I follow* Ct. *chiefly*. *The title* Balade *is in* F.
1. Ct. Sumtyme. Ct. F. the; Harl. T. Add. this. Ct. worlde. 2. Ct. worde. 3. Ct. nowe it; false; desciuable.   4. Ct worde; dede.   5. Harl. T. Beon; Add. Ar; Ct. Is; F. Ys. Ct. lyke.   6. Ct. all; worlde.   8. Ct. worlde; veriable.   9. Ct. folke; discension.   10. *The* MSS. *have* For among vs now, *or* For nowe a dayes; *but* Bann. *omits* For, *which is not wanted*.   11. Bann. Harl. T. Th. collusion; Ct. F. Add. conclusioun (*but see* l. 4).   12. Ct. Do; neyghburgh.   15. Ct. putte.   17. Ct. Pite.   18. Ct. Thorugh.   19. Ct. worlde. T. F. Add. Th. a; Bann. ane; Ct. *om*.

XV. LAK OF STEDFASTNESSE.

Fro right to wrong, fro trouthe to fikelnesse, 20
That al is lost, for lak of stedfastnesse.

Lenvoy to King Richard.

O prince, desyre to be honourable,
Cherish thy folk and hate extorcioun!
Suffre no thing, that may be reprevable
To thyn estat, don in thy regioun. 25
Shew forth thy swerd of castigacioun,
Dred God, do law, love trouthe and worthinesse,
And wed thy folk agein to stedfastnesse. 28

Explicit.

---

20. Ct. trought; F. trouthe. TITLE. T. Lenvoye to Kyng Richard; F. Harl. Th. Lenvoy. 22. Ct. honurable. 23. Ct. Cherice thi. 25. Ct. thine estaat doen; thi. 26. Ct. Shewe; swerde. 27. Ct. Drede; truthe. 28. Ct. thi; ayen. Ct. Th. add *Explicit.*

XVI. LENVOY DE CHAUCER A SCOGAN.

To-broken been the statuts hye in hevene
That creat were eternally to dure,
Sith that I see the brighte goddes sevene
Mow wepe and wayle, and passioun endure,
As may in erthe a mortal creature.   5
Allas, fro whennes may this thing procede?
Of whiche errour I deye almost for drede.

By worde eterne whylom was hit shape
That fro the fifte cercle, in no manere,
Ne mighte a drope of teres doun escape.   10
But now so wepeth Venus in hir spere,
That with hir teres she wol drenche us here.
Allas, Scogan! this is for thyn offence!
Thou causest this deluge of pestilence.

Hast thou not seyd, in blaspheme of this goddes,   15
Through pryde, or through thy grete rakelnesse,
Swich thing as in the lawe of love forbode is?
That, for thy lady saw nat thy distresse,
Therfor thou yave hir up at Michelmesse!
Allas, Scogan! of olde folk ne yonge   20
Was never erst Scogan blamed for his tonge!

TITLE : *so in* F. *and* P.; Gg. *has*—Litera directa de Scogon per G. C.
The MSS. *are*: Gg. (Camb. Univ. Library, Gg. 4. 27); F. (Fairfax 16); P. (Pepys 2006). Th.=Thynne (1532). *I follow* F. *mainly.*
1. F. statutez.   2. F. weren eternaly.   3. F. bryght goddis.   4. F. Mowe.   5. F. Mortale.   6. F. thys thinge.   8. F. whilome. F. yshape; Gg. it schape; P. Th. it shape.   9. F. fyfte sercle; maner.   10. F. myght; teeres; eschape.   11. F. wepith.   12. F. teeres.   14. F. cawsest; diluge.   15. Gg. Hast þu; F. Hauesthow. F. this goddis; Gg. the goddis; P. Th. the goddes.   16. F. Thurgh; thrugh. F. they (*wrongly*); Gg. þyn; P. thi.   F. rekelnesse; P. Th. reklesnesse; Gg. rechelsnesse; *see* note.
17. F. P. forbede; Gg. forbodyn; Th. forbode.   18. Gg. saw; F. sawgh.
19. F. Therfore thow. Gg. Mychel-; F. Mighel-.   20. F. folke.

XVI. LENVOY A SCOGAN.

Thou drowe in scorn Cupyde eek to record
Of thilke rebel word that thou hast spoken,
For which he wol no lenger be thy lord.
And, Scogan, thogh his bowe be nat broken, 25
He wol nat with his arwes been y-wroken
On thee, ne me, ne noon of our figure;
We shul of him have neyther hurt ne cure.
Now certes, frend, I drede of thyn unhappe,
Lest for thy gilt the wreche of Love procede 30
On alle hem that ben hore and rounde of shape,
That ben so lykly folk in love to spede.
Than shul we for our labour han no mede;
But wel I wot, thou wilt answere and seye:
'Lo! olde Grisel list to ryme and pleye!' 35
Nay, Scogan, sey not so, for I mexcuse,
God help me so! in no rym, doutelees,
Ne thinke I never of slepe wak my muse,
That rusteth in my shethe stille in pees.
Whyl I was yong, I putte hir forth in prees, 40
But al shal passe that men prose or ryme;
Take every man his turn, as for his tyme.

Envoy.

Scogan, that knelest at the stremes heed
Of grace, of alle honour and worthinesse,
In thende of which streme I am dul as deed, 45
Forgete in solitarie wildernesse;
Yet, Scogan, thenke on Tullius kindenesse,
Minne thy frend, ther it may fructifye!
Far-wel, and lok thou never eft Love defye! 49

---

22. F. skorne; eke; recorde. 23. F. worde; thow. 24. F. lorde. 25. F. thow; P. Th. though. F. thy (*for* his, *wrongly*); Gg. P. his. 27. F. the. Th. our; Gg. oure; P. owre; F. youre. 28. F. hurte. Gg. P. Th. ne; F. nor. 29. F. dreed. 30. F. gilte. 31. Gg. P. hore; F. hoor. F. shappe; P. shape; Gg. schap. 32. F. folke. 33. P. shull; F. Gg. shal. Gg. P. han; F. haue. F. noo. 34. F. thow. F. wolt; Gg. wilt. 35. Gg. P. Lo olde; F. Loo tholde. F. lyste. 36. F. say; Gg. P. sey. F. soo. 37. P. help; Gg. F. helpe. F. soo. F. ryme dowteles. 38. F. Gg. to wake; P. Th. *om.* to. 40. F. While; yonge. Gg. putte; F. put. P. Th. her; F. hyt; Gg. it. 41. F. alle. 42. F. hys turne. 43. F. hede; Gg. hed. 45. F. dede; Gg. P. ded. 48. F. Mynne; there. 49. F. Fare; loke thow; dyffye.

N.B. *All have* —.i. a Windesore, *and* —.i. a Grenewich *opposite* ll. 43, 45.

XVII. LENVOY DE CHAUCER A BUKTON.

The counseil of Chaucer touching Mariage, which was sent to Bukton.

My maister Bukton, whan of Criste our kinge
Was axed, what is trouthe or sothfastnesse,
He nat a word answerde to that axinge,
As who saith: 'no man is al trewe,' I gesse.
And therfor, thogh I highte to expresse   5
The sorwe and wo that is in mariage,
I dar not wryte of hit no wikkednesse,
Lest I my-self falle eft in swich dotage.

I wol nat seyn, how that hit is the cheyne
Of Sathanas, on which he gnaweth ever,   10
But I dar seyn, were he out of his peyne,
As by his wille, he wolde be bounde never.
But thilke doted fool that eft hath lever
Y-cheyned be than out of prisoun crepe,
God lete him never fro his wo dissever,   15
Ne no man him bewayle, though he wepe.

But yit, lest thou do worse, tak a wyf;
Bet is to wedde, than brenne in worse wyse.
But thou shalt have sorwe on thy flesh, thy lyf,
And been thy wyves thral, as seyn these wyse,   20

TITLE: *so in* MS. Fairfax 16. Second Title *from* Ju.
The authorities are: F. (Fairfax 16); Th. (Thynne's edition, 1532); *and a printed copy by* Julian Notary (Ju.). *I follow* F. *mainly.*
2. F. ys; sothefastnesse.   3. F. worde.   4. F. noo. Ju. Th. trewe; F. trew.
5. F. therfore though; hight (Ju. hyghte).   6. F. woo.   7. F. writen; hyt noo.   8. Ju. Lest; F. Leste.   9. F. hyt.   10. F. euere.   11. F. oute.   12. F. neuere.   13. F. foole. Th. efte; F. ofte; Ju. oft. F. leuere.
15. F. woo disseuere.   16. F. noo   17. F. yet; thow doo; take; wyfe.
19. F. thow; flessh; lyfe.   20. F. ben. F. wifes; Ju. Th. wyues.

XVII. LENVOY A BUKTON. 399

And if that holy writ may nat suffyse,
Experience shal thee teche, so may happe,
That thee were lever to be take in Fryse
Than eft to falle of wedding in the trappe.

Envoy.

This litel writ, proverbes, or figure 25
I sende you, tak kepe of hit, I rede:
Unwys is he that can no wele endure.
If thou be siker, put thee nat in drede.
The Wyf of Bathe I pray you that ye rede
Of this matere that we have on honde. 30
God graunte you your lyf frely to lede
In fredom; for ful hard is to be bonde. 32

Explicit.

21. F. yſ; hooly writte. 22. F. the. 23. F. the. 24. F. Ju. *om.* to; *which* Th. *inserts.* 25. F. writte; Th. writ; Ju. wryt. 26. F. yow take; hyt. 27. F. Vnwise; kan noo. 28. F. thow; the. 29. F. wyfe; yow. 31. F. yow; lyfe. 32. F. fredam. F. harde it is; Ju. hard is; Th. foule is (*omitting* ful). *All add* Explicit.

XVIII. THE COMPLEYNT OF VENUS.

I. (*The Lover's worthiness.*)

THER nis so hy comfort to my plesaunce,
Whan that I am in any hevinesse,
As for to have leyser of remembraunce
Upon the manhod and the worthinesse,
Upon the trouthe, and on the stedfastnesse 5
Of him whos I am al, whyl I may dure;
Ther oghte blame me no creature,
For every wight preiseth his gentilesse.

In him is bountee, wisdom, governaunce
Wel more then any mannes wit can gesse; 10
For grace hath wold so ferforth him avaunce
That of knighthode he is parfit richesse.

I.

Il n'est confort que tant de biens me face,
Quant je ne puis a ma dame parler,
Comme d'avoir temps, loisir et espace
De longuement en sa valour penser,
Et [de] ses doulz fais femenins recorder 5
Dedens mon cuer. C'est ma vie, par m'ame,
Ne je ne truis nul homme qui me blasme,
Car chascun a joye de li loer.

Il a en li bonté, beauté et grace,
Plus que nulz homs ne saroit deviser. 10
C'est grant ëur quant en si pou de place
Dieux a voulu tous les biens assembler.

TITLE: *so in* F. Ff. Ar.; *see* Notes.
The MSS. *are*: T. (Trin. Coll. Cambridge, R. 3. 20); A. (Ashmole 59); Tn. (MS. Tanner 346); F. (Fairfax 16); Ff. (MS. Ff. 1. 6, Camb. Univ. Library); Ar. (Arch. Seld. P. 24); P. (Pepys 2006); etc. Th. = Thynne (1532). *I follow* F. *mainly*.
1. F. high; T. A. hye (hy *is better*).   2. F. When; eny.   4. F. manhod; *the rest have final* e.   5. F. stidfastnesse.   6. F. whiles; A. whilest; *rest* while.   7. F. oght; Tn. oghte to.   9. F. ys bounte. F. T A. Th. *insert* and *after* wisdom; *but the rest omit it.*   10. F. eny manes witte.   11. F. wolde (*wrongly*); Ff. wold. F. ferforthe.   12. F. parfite.

XVIII. THE COMPLEYNT OF VENUS.

Honour honoureth him for his noblesse;
Therto so wel hath formed him Nature,
That I am his for ever, I him assure,   15
For every wight preiseth his gentilesse.

And not-withstanding al his suffisaunce,
His gentil herte is of so greet humblesse
To me in worde, in werke, in contenaunce,
And me to serve is al his besinesse,   20
That I am set in verrey sikernesse.
Thus oghte I blesse wel myn aventure,
Sith that him list me serven and honoure;
For every wight preiseth his gentilesse.

II. (*Disquietude caused by Jealousy.*)

Now certes, Love, hit is right covenable   25
That men ful dere bye thy noble thing,
As wake a-bedde, and fasten at the table,
Weping to laughe, and singe in compleyning,

Honneur la vuelt sur toutes honnorer.
Oncques ne vi si [douce et] plaisant dame
De toutes gens avoir si noble femme;   15
Car chascun a joye de li loer.

Ou qu'elle soit, bien fait et mal efface.
Moult bien li siet le rire et le jouer.
Son cuer esbat et les autres soulace
Si liement qu'on ne l'en doit blasmer.   20
De li veoir ne se puet nulz lasser.

Son regart vault tous les biens d'un royaume.
Il semble bien qu'elle est tres noble femme,
Car chascun a joye de li loer.

II.

Certes, Amours, c'est chose convenable   25
Que voz grans biens [vous] faciez comparer :
Veillier ou lit et jeuner a la table,
Rire plourant et en plaignant chanter,

---

14. F. well. 16. F. preysith. 18. F. hert; grete. 19. F. werk. 21. F. sikirnesse. 22. F. oght. 25. F. certis. 26. T. A. Tn. Th. thy; F. Ff. the. 27. F. a-bed; T. A. a-bedde. 28. F. Wepinge; laugh; sing; compleynynge.

And doun to caste visage and loking,
Often to chaungen hewe and contenaunce, 30
Pleyne in sleping, and dremen at the daunce,
Al the revers of any glad feling.

Ialousye be hanged by a cable!
She wolde al knowe through hir espying;
Ther doth no wight no-thing so resonable, 35
That al nis harm in hir imagening.
Thus dere abought is love in yeving,
Which ofte he yiveth with-outen ordinaunce,
As sorow ynogh, and litel of plesaunce,
Al the revers of any glad feling. 40

A litel tyme his yift is agreable,
But ful encomberous is the using;
For sotel Ialousye, the deceyvable,
Ful often-tyme causeth destourbing.

Baissier les yeux quant on doit regarder,
Souvent changier couleur et contenance, 30
Plaindre en dormant et songier a la dance
Tout a rebours de ce qu'on vuelt trouver.

Jalousie, c'est l'amer du deable;
Elle vuelt tout veoir et escouter,
Ne nulz ne fait chose si raisonnable 35
Que tout a mal ne le vueille tourner.

Amours, ainsi fault voz dons acheter,
Et vous donnez souvent sanz ordonnance
Assez douleur et petit de plaisance,
Tout a rebours de ce qu'on vuelt trouver. 40

Pour un court temps le gieu est agreable;
Mais trop par est encombreux a user,
Et, ja soit il a dames honnorable,
A leurs amis est trop grief a porter.

---

29. F. cast; *the rest* caste. F. lokynge. 30. F. chaunge visage (*wrongly*); change hewe *in* MS. Arch. Selden, B. 24; T. A. chaunge huwe. 31. MSS. Pley, Pleye; *read* Pleyne (F. *Plaindre*). F. dreme; T. Tn. Ff. Th. dremen. 32. F. reuerse; eny. 33. Ff. T. Ialousye; F. Ielosie. Ff. P. be; F. Th. he (!). Ialousye be] T. þaughe Ialousye wer. T. Tn. Th. by; F. be; Ff. with. 34. F. wold; thro; espyinge. 35. F. dothe. 36. F. nys harme; ymagenynge. 37. F. yevynge. 38. F. yifeth. Ff. withouten; *rest* withoute. 40. F. reuerse; felynge. 42. T. Ff. encomberous; F. encombrouse. F. vsynge. 43. Tn. sotell; F. subtil. F. Ielosie. 44. T. destourbing; F. derturbynge (*sic*).

XVIII. THE COMPLEYNT OF VENUS.

Thus be we ever in drede and suffering, 45
In nouncerteyn we languisshe in penaunce,
And han ful often many an hard meschaunce,
Al the revers of any glad feling.

III. (*Satisfaction in Constancy*.)

But certes, Love, I sey nat in such wyse
That for tescape out of your lace I mente; 50
For I so longe have been in your servyse
That for to lete of wol I never assente;
No force thogh Ialousye me tormente;
Suffyceth me to see him whan I may,
And therfore certes, to myn ending-day 55
To love him best ne shal I never repente.

And certes, Love, whan I me wel avyse
On any estat that man may represente,
Than have ye maked me, through your franchyse,
Chese the best that ever on erthe wente. 60

Toudiz convient souffrir et en-
    durer, 45
Sans nul certain languir en esper-
    ance,
Et recevoir mainte male meschance,
Tout a rebours de ce qu'on vuelt
    trouver.

III.

Amours, sachiez que pas ne le vueil
    dire
Pour moy getter hors des amoureux
    las ; 50
Car j'ay porté si long temps mon
    martire

Que mon vivant ne le guerpiray pas.
Il me souffist d'avoir tant de soulas
Que veoir puisse la [belle et] gra-
    cieuse ;
Combien qu'el est [en]vers moy
    dangereuse, 55
De li servir ne serai jamaiz las.

Certes, Amours, quant bien droit
    [je] remire
Les haulx estas, les moyens et les
    bas,
Vous m'avez fait de tous les bons
    eslire,
A mon avis, le meilleur, en tous
    cas. 60

---

45. F. suffrynge; P. sufferyng; T. souffering. 46. F. Ff. noun-certeyn; T. noun-certaine; A. nouncerteine. F. langvisshen. 47. F. harde. F. *wrongly repeats* penaunce; T. A. meschaunce. 48. F. reuerse; ony; felynge. 49. F. certys; not. 50. F. youre; ment. 51. F. be; *the rest* ben *or* been. 52. F. wil; T. A. Ff. wol. F. assent. 53. F. fors; turment. 55. F. certys. 56. F. *om.* ne, *which* T. A. P. *insert*; Ar. *has* that. Tn. *inserts* me *before* never. 57. F. certis; when. 58. F. eny estate; represent. 59. F. Tn. Then; *rest* Than, Thanne, Thane. T. Ff. P. maked; *rest* made. F. thro. 60. F. went.

404   THE MINOR POEMS.

Now love wel, herte, and look thou never stente;
And let the Ielous putte hit in assay
That, for no peyne wol I nat sey nay;
To love him best ne shal I never repente.
Herte, to thee hit oghte y-nogh suffyse   65
That Love so hy a grace to thee sente,
To chese the worthiest in alle wyse
And most agreable unto myn entente.
Seche no ferther, neyther wey ne wente,
Sith I have suffisaunce unto my pay.   70
Thus wol I ende this compleynt or lay;
To love him best ne shal I never repente.

Lenvoy.

Princess, receyveth this compleynt in gree,
Unto your excellent benignitee
   Direct after my litel suffisaunce.   75
For eld, that in my spirit dulleth me,
Hath of endyting al the soteltee
   Wel ny bereft out of my remembraunce;
   And eek to me hit is a greet penaunce,
Sith rym in English hath swich scarsitee,   80
To folowe word by word the curiositee
   Of Graunson, flour of hem that make in Fraunce.

Or aime, cuer, ainsy que tu pourras;	Ne quiers [or] plus royaume ne empire,
Car ja n'aras paine si doulereuse,	Car si bonne jamaiz ne trouveras,
Pour ma dame, que ne me soit joieuse;	Ne si belle par mes yeux ne verras:
De li servir ne seray jamaiz las.	C'est jeunesce sachant et savoureuse. 70
Cuer, il te doit assez plus que souffire 65	Ja soit elle de m'amour desdaigneuse,
D'avoir choisy ce[lle] que choisi as.	De li servir ne seray jamaiz las.

61. F. hert; loke; stent. 62. P. Ielous; A. Ialous; T. Ialouse; F. Ielousie. A. putte; F. put. 63. F. peyn wille I not. 64. F. yow (*for* him); T. A. Tn. Ar. him (*see* l. 56). 65. F. Hert; the; ought ynogh. 66. F. highe; T. A. hye. T. A. Ff. Ar. thee; F. yow; Tn. you. F. sent. 67. F. al. 68. F. entent. 69. F. went. 70. F. Sithe. F. Tn. ye (*for* I); *rest* I. 71. *All but* Ju. (Julian Notary's edition) *repeat* this *before* lay. 72. *See* l. 56. 73. T. A. Pryncesse; *rest* Princes. F. resseyueth. 74. F. excelent benignite. 75. F. Directe aftir. 76. F. elde. 77. Tn. soteltee; F. subtilite. 78. F. nighe. 79. F. eke; grete. 80. F. ryme; englissh hat (*sic*) such skarsete. 81. F. worde by worde; curiosite. 82. F. floure; maken.

XIX. THE COMPLEINT OF CHAUCER TO HIS EMPTY PURSE.

To you, my purse, and to non other wight
Compleyne I, for ye be my lady dere!
I am so sory, now that ye be light;
For certes, but ye make me hevy chere,
Me were as leef be leyd up-on my bere;   5
For whiche un-to your mercy thus I crye:
Beth hevy ageyn, or elles mot I dye!

Now voucheth sauf this day, or hit be night,
That I of you the blisful soun may here,
Or see your colour lyk the sonne bright,   10
That of yelownesse hadde never pere.
Ye be my lyf, ye be myn hertes stere,
Quene of comfort and of good companye:
Beth hevy ageyn, or elles mot I dye!

Now purs, that be to me my lyves light,   15
And saveour, as doun in this worlde here,
Out of this toune help me through your might,
Sin that ye wole nat been my tresorere;
For I am shave as nye as any frere.

The MSS. *are*: F. (Fairfax 16); Harl (Harl. 7333); Ff. (Camb. Univ. Library, Ff. 1. 6) : P. (Pepys 2006) ; Add. (Addit. 22139); *also* Cx. (Caxton's edition); Th. (Thynne, 1532). I *follow* F. *mainly*.

TITLE. *So in* Cx. (*but with* Un-to *for* to); F. *om.* empty; P. La compleint de Chaucer a sa Bourse Voide.

1. F. yow.   2. F. Complayn; Harl. P. Compleyne.   3. Harl. be; F. been.   4. Add. That; P. But; *rest* For. P. Add. but ye; F. Harl. but yf ye; Ff. but yif ye; Cx. Th. ye now.   5. Add. leyd; F. layde.   7. F. Beeth; ageyne; mote.   8. F. hyt; nyght.   9. F. yow; sovne.   10. F. lyke; bryght.   11. *Read* That of yél-ownés-se.   12. F. lyfe; hertys.   14. F. ageyne; moote.   15. P. Cx. purs; F. Add. purse. F. ben.   17. F. Oute; helpe; thurgh.   18. F. bene.   19. Harl. P. Th. any; Add. eny; Cx. ony; F. is a.

But yit I pray un-to your curtesye : 20
Beth hevy ageyn, or elles mot I dye!

Lenvoy de Chaucer.

O conquerour of Brutes Albioun!
Which that by lyne and free eleccioun
Ben verray king, this song to you I sende;
And ye, that mowen al our harm amende, 25
Have minde up-on my supplicacioun!

---

21. F. Bethe; ayen; moote. F. Lenvoy de Chaucer; Harl. P. Lenvoye; Cx. Thenuoye of Chaucer vnto the kynge. 23. F. Whiche. F. lygne; Harl. Cx. Ff. P lyne. 24. F. Been; kynge; yow. 25. F. alle myn harme; Ff. alle oure harmes; Harl. all oure harmous; P. Cx. alle harmes.

XX. PROVERBS.

Proverbe of Chaucer.

I.

What shul thise clothes many-fold,
    Lo! this hote somers day?—
After greet heet cometh cold;
    No man caste his pilche away.   5

II.

Of al this world the wyde compas
    Hit wol not in myn armes tweyne.—
Who-so mochel wol embrace
    Litel therof he shal distreyne.

The MSS. *are*: F. (Fairfax 16); Ha. (Harl. 7578); Ad. (Addit. 16165). *I follow* F. *mainly.* Title; *in* F. Ha.; Ad. Prouerbe.
  1. Ad. þees; F. Ha. these. *All needlessly insert* thus *after* clothes. F. many-folde.   2. F. Loo; hoote.   3. F. grete hete; Ha. greet hete; Ad. heet. F. colde.   4. Ha. pilche; F. pilch.   5. F. all; worlde. Ad. wyde; F. Ha. large. Ad. Ha. compas; F. compace.   6. Ad. Hit; F. Yt. Ad. wol; F. Ha. wil. Ad. myn; F. Ha. my.   7. F. Whoo-so.

APPENDIX.

[The following Poems are also probably genuine; but are placed here for lack of external evidence.]

XXI. AGAINST WOMEN UNCONSTANT.

Balade.

MADAME, for your newe-fangelnesse,
Many a servaunt have ye put out of grace,
I take my leve of your unstedfastnesse,
For wel I wot, whyl ye have lyves space,
Ye can not love ful half yeer in a place ; 5
To newe thing your lust is ever kene ;
In stede of blew, thus may ye were al grene.

Right as a mirour nothing may enpresse,
But, lightly as it cometh, so mot it pace,
So fareth your love, your werkes bereth witnesse. 10
Ther is no feith that may your herte enbrace ;
But, as a wedercok, that turneth his face
With every wind, ye fare, and that is sene ;
In stede of blew, thus may ye were al grene.

TITLE. *None in* Ct.; Balade *in* F.; ed. 1561 *has*—A Balade which Chaucer made agaynst woman unconstaunt.
The text is from Ct. (Cotton, Cleopatra D. 7); *that in* ed. 1561 *is much the same, except in spelling. Another copy in* F. (Fairfax 16). *A third in* Ha. (Harl. 7578); *of less value.*
2. Ct. Manie; F. many. Ct. F. of youre; Ha. *om.* youre.   4. Ct. wote while. F. have lyves; Ct. to lyve haue.   5. Ct. kunnought; F. Ha. kan not.   6. F. thing; Ct. Ha. thinges. Ct. *inserts* so *before* kene; ed. (1561) *omits* so; F. *has* ay so.   7. Ct. sted; F. stede. Ct. Blue; F. blew.   8. Ct. Mirro*ur*; ed. mirour. Ct. Ha. ed. *ins.* that *bef.* nothing; F. *om.*   11. Ct. F. hert; Ha. ed. herte.   12. Ha. *om.* a. Ha. wethirkoc.   14. Ct. *om.* al; F. Ha. ed. *retain it.*

410   APPENDIX.

    Ye might be shryned, for your brotelnesse,   15
    Bet than Dalyda, Crescide or Candace;
    For ever in chaunging stant your sikernesse,
    That tache may no wight fro your herte arace;
    If ye lese oon, ye can wel tweyn purchace;
    Al light for somer, ye woot wel what I mene,   20
    In stede of blew, thus may ye were al grene.

Explicit.

---

15. Ct. *om.* your; F. Ha. ed. *retain it.*   16 Ct. Bettir; F. Ha. ed. Better; *read* Bet. F. Dalyda; Ct. Dalide. Ct. Cresside; F. Creseyde.   17. Ct. Changeng; F. chaungyng. *All* stondeth; *read* stant.   18. F. tache; Ct. tacche: ed. tatche. F. Ha. herte; Ct. ed. hert.   19. Ct. Ha. lese; F. ed. lose. Ct. kunne; F. kan; ed. can; Ha. kanne. Ct. ed. tweine; F. tweyn. 20. Ct. All; ed. Al. Ct. F. wote; Ha. woote; ed. wot; *cf.* Cant. Ta. A 740, 829. 21. Ct. *om.* al F ed *retain it.* Ct. *adds* Explicit.

XXII. AN AMOROUS COMPLEINT.
(COMPLEINT DAMOURS.)

An amorous Compleint, made at Windsor.

I, which that am the sorwefulleste man
That in this world was ever yit livinge,
And leest recoverer of him-selven can,
Beginne thus my deedly compleininge
On hir, that may to lyf and deeth me bringe, 5
Which hath on me no mercy ne no rewthe
That love hir best, but sleeth me for my trewthe.

Can I noght doon ne seye that may yow lyke,
[For] certes, now, allas! allas! the whyle!
Your plesaunce is to laughen whan I syke, 10
And thus ye me from al my blisse exyle.
Ye han me cast in thilke spitous yle
Ther never man on lyve mighte asterte;
This have I for I lovë you, swete herte!

In MS. Harl. 7333, fol. 133 b and 134. *Title*—And next folowyng begynnith an amerowse compleynte made at wyndesore in the laste May tofore Novembre (*sic*). *Also in* F. (Fairfax) *and* B. (Bodley 638); *entitled* Complaynt Damours. N. B. Unmarked *readings are from* Harl.

1. sorowfullest.   2. worlde; leving (F. lyvinge).   3. F. lest; Harl. B. leste. B. rekeuerer.   4. Begynne right thus; *so* F. B.; *I omit* right.   5. lyff; dethe.   6. Whiche hathe; rought (*for* rewthe).   7. beste; sleethe. 8. F. Kan I noght doon to seyn; B. Kan I nought don to seyn; Harl. Cane I nought ne saye.   9. *All* Ne; *read* For.   10. Youre.   11. frome.   12. Yee. F. B. han; Harl. haue. caste. F. B. thilke; Harl. that. *All* spitouse. 13. Harl. ne (*after* lyve); F. B. *om.*   14. beste (*after* you); F. B. *om.*

APPENDIX.

Sooth is, that wel I woot, by lyklinesse,   15
If that it were thing possible to do
Tacompte youre beutee and goodnesse,
I have no wonder thogh ye do me wo;
Sith I, thunworthiest that may ryde or go,
Durste ever thinken in so hy a place,   20
What wonder is, thogh ye do me no grace?

Allas! thus is my lyf brought to an ende,
My deeth, I see, is my conclusioun;
I may wel singe, 'in sory tyme I spende
My lyf;' that song may have confusioun!   25
For mercy, pitee, and deep affeccioun,
I sey for me, for al my deedly chere,
Alle thise diden, in that, me love yow dere.

And in this wyse and in dispayre I live
In lovë; nay, but in dispayre I dye!   30
But shal I thus [to] yow my deeth for-give,
That causeles doth me this sorow drye?
Ye, certes, I! For she of my folye
Hath nought to done, although she do me sterve;
Hit is nat with hir wil that I hir serve!   35

Than sith I am of my sorowe the cause
And sith that I have this, withoute hir reed,
Than may I seyn, right shortly in a clause,
It is no blame unto hir womanheed
Though swich a wrecche as I be for hir deed;   40

---

15. Soothe; weele.   16. F. B. that; Harl. *om.* F. B. a thing; Harl. *om.* a. thinge; doo.   17. F. B. Tacompte youre; Harl. For to acounte your.   18. noo wondre; yee; woo.   19. Sithe; goo.   20. F. neuer; B. euyr; Harl. euer. hie.   21. wondir; doo; noo.   22. Ellas; Eonde. F. myshefe; B. myschef (*for* my lyf).   23. dethe; conclucioun.   24. wele. F. sing; B. singe; Harl. say. Harl. sorye.   25. B. ys my (*for* may have). Confucioun. 26. B. my saluacioun (*for* deep affeccioun).   27, 28. B. I sey for me I haue noun [neuer?] felte Alle thes diden me in despeire to melte.   27. fo (?*for* for).   28. Alle this; yowe deere.   29. Harl. *om.* 2*nd* in.   30. F. B. nay; Harl. nay nay.   31. *I supply* to; yowe; dethe for-geve.   32. dothe. 33. certe (!); sheo.   34. Hathe; Al-thoughe sheo.   35. nought (*for* nat). 36. Thane sithe.   37. sitthe; rede.   38. seyne.   39. noo; womanhede.   40. Thaugh suche; dede.

XXII. AN AMOROUS COMPLEINT.

[And] yet alwey two thinges doon me dyë,
That is to seyn, hir beutee and myn yë.

So that, algates, she is the verray rote
Of my disese, and of my dethe also ;
For with oon word she mighte be my bote, 45
If that she vouched sauf for to do so.
But [why] than is hir gladnesse at my wo?
It is hir wone plesaunce for to take,
To seen hir servaunts dyen for hir sake!

But certes, than is al my wonderinge, 50
Sithen she is the fayrest creature
As to my dome, that ever was livinge,
The benignest and beste eek that nature
Hath wrought or shal, whyl that the world may dure,
Why that she lefte pite so behinde? 55
It was, y-wis, a greet defaute in kinde.

Yit is al this no lak to hir, pardee,
But god or nature sore wolde I blame;
For, though she shewe no pite unto me,
Sithen that she doth othere men the same, 60
I ne oughte to despyse my ladies game;
It is hir pley to laughen whan men syketh,
And I assente, al that hir list and lyketh!

Yit wolde I, as I dar, with sorweful herte
Biseche un-to your meke womanhede 65
That I now dorste my sharpe sorwes smerte
Shewe by worde, that ye wolde ones rede

---

41. Yette; *I supply* And; twoo; doone.   42. seyne; beaute; eye.   43. Harl. *om.* that. F. B. *om.* the. verraye Roote.   44. diseese; alsoo.   45. worde sheo myght; boote.   46. sheo wovched saufe; soo.   47. *I supply* why; woo.   48. wonne; *all ins.* to *after* wonne.   49. seon; sarvauntes; B. seruaunte.   50. thanne; all*e*; wondering.   51. sheo.   53. eke.   54. Hathe; shall*e*; Harl. *om.* that; worlde.   55. Whi; sheo lefe pitte; byhinde. Harl. so; F. alle; B. all.   56. ewisse; grete.   57. Yitte; noo. F. B. *om.* al.   58. Harl. *ins.* hem *before* soore (*sic*); F. B. hem (*but om.* sore).   59. thowe (*for* though); sheo; pette.   60. sheo doothe.   61. ought.   62. Harl. *om.* hir; pleye; lawhe when that men sikith.   63. liste; likethe.   64. B. Yit; F. Yet; Harl. Yeo (*sic*); *see* 57.   dare; sorowfull.   65. F. B. meke; Harl. mekly.   66. F. sorwes; B. sorwys; Harl. shoures.   67. Harl. and; F. B. that. yee; onys.

414   APPENDIX.

The pleynte of me, the which ful sore drede
That I have seid here, through myn unconninge,
In any worde to your displesinge.   70

Lothest of anything that ever was loth
Were me, as wisly god my soule save!
To seyn a thing through which ye might be wroth;
And, to that day that I be leyd in grave,
A trewer servaunt shulle ye never have;   75
And, though that I on yow have pleyned here,
Forgiveth it me, myn owne lady dere!

Ever have I been, and shal, how-so I wende,
Outher to live or dye, your humble trewe;
Ye been to me my ginning and myn ende,   80
Sonne of the sterre bright and clere of hewe,
Alwey in oon to love yow freshly newe,
By god and by my trouthe, is myn entente;
To live or dye, I wol it never repente!

This compleynt on seint Valentynes day,   85
Whan every foul [ther] chesen shal his make,
To hir, whos I am hool, and shal alwey,
This woful song and this compleynt I make,
That never yit wolde me to mercy take;
And yit wol I [for] evermore her serve   90
And love hir best, although she do me sterve.

                    Explicit.

68. compleynte (*for* pleynte); which I Fulle.   69. saide; thorowe. B. vnkonnynge; F. vnkunnynge; Harl. vnknowynge. F. B. *om.* here *and* myn.   70. yowre.   71. Loothest; loothe.   72. als; sowle safe.   73. seyne; thorughe; yee; wrothe.   74. leyde.   75. sarvaunt ne shulde yee. F. shul; B. shall; Harl. shulde.   76. thaughe. F. B. on yow haue pleyned; Harl. haue playned vnto yow.   77. For-gyvethe yt me, myne oune lady so dere.   78. howe.   79. youre.   80. Yee ben; gynnynge.   81. Harl. of; F. ouer; B. ovyr. F. B. *om.* and clere. Sterre so bright; huwe.   82. Harl. And I ay oon; F. B. Alwey in oon. fresshely.   84. wolle.   85. Conpleynte; valantines.   86. foughel cheesen shall; *I supply* ther *from* Parl. Foules, 310.   87. was (F. B. whos); hole; shall.   88. wofulle songe: conplaynte.   90. wolle; *I supply* for.   91. alle-thowhe sheo. F. B. Explicit; Harl. *om.*

XXIII. A BALADE OF COMPLEYNT.

COMPLEYNE ne coude, ne might myn herte never
My peynes halve, ne what torment I have,
Though that I sholde in your presence ben ever,
My hertes lady, as wisly he me save
That bountee made, and beutee list to grave   5
In your persone, and bad hem bothe in-fere
Ever tawayte, and ay be wher ye were.

As wisly he gye alle my Ioyes here
As I am youres, and to yow sad and trewe,
And ye, my lyf and cause of my good chere,   10
And deeth also, whan ye my peynes newe,
My worldes Ioye, whom I wol serve and sewe,
My heven hool, and al my suffisaunce,
Whom for to serve is set al my plesaunce.

Beseching yow in my most humble wyse   15
Taccepte in worth this litel povre dyte,
And for my trouthe my service nat despyse,
Myn observaunce eek have nat in despyte,
Ne yit to long to suffren in this plyte,
I yow beseche, myn hertes lady dere,   20
Sith I yow serve, and so wil yeer by yere.

In MS. Addit. 16165, fol. 256, back; *headed* Balade of compleynte.
1. koude; h*er*t.   2. turment.   3 Thaughe; shoulde; youre.   4. wissely.   5. beaute liste.   6. youre; bade; in-feere.   7. beo.   8. wissely.   9. yowe sadde; truwe.   10. lyff; gode.   11. dethe; whane; reewe, *altered by the scribe to* newe.   12. whome; suwe.   13. hole; souffisaunce.   14. sette.   15. yowe; moste.   16. Taccept; worthe; pore.   17. not despice.   18. eke; not.   19. longe; suffre.   20. here (*error for* dere; *see* XXII. 77).   21. yowe; yere by yere.

NOTES

TO

THE ROMAUNT OF THE ROSE.

THE French text, a portion of which is given in the lower part of pp. 93-164, is reprinted from Le Roman de la Rose, ed. Méon, Paris, 1814.

1. Scan :—Many | men seyn | that in | swev'níng-es‖. So, in the next line, read :—lesíng-es. In l. 3, read :—swev'nes. In l. 4, read 'hard-e-ly' as *three* syllables, and 'fals-e' as two; and, in general, throughout ll. 1-1705, apply the usual rules of Chaucerian pronunciation.

sweveninges, dreamings; see l. 3; cf. A. S. *swefen*, a dream, pl. *swefnu*; *swefnian*, v., to dream. The translation should be compared with the original F. text, as given below it.

On the subject of dreams, cf. Hous of Fame, ll. 1-52, and the notes to ll. 1, 7.

5. *apparaunte*, apparent, as coming true.

6. 'To warrant this, I may cite an author named Macrobius.' Macrobius, the commentator on Cicero's Somnium Scipionis (as here said) ; see notes to Parl. of Foules, 31 ; Book Duch. 284.

8-10. *halt*, holds, considers ; *lees*, deceptive. 'But explains to us the vision that king Scipio formerly dreamt.'

22. *taketh his corage*, assumes fresh confidence from the support of the young, is encouraged by the young, receives their tribute. The O. F. *paage* is the mod. F. *péage*, toll, lit. 'footing.'

24. Cf. 'Right ther as I was wont to done' ; Ho. Fame, 113.

27. Read—'That hit me lyked wonder wel.' *wonder wel*, wonderfully well. This use of *wonder* is common; see Cant. Ta., G 751, 1035. At a later time, *wonder*, when thus used adverbially, received the adverbial suffix -*s*; hence Th. has '*wonders* wel' here. So also '*wonders* dere' in the Test. of Love ; see *Wondrous* in my Etym. Dict.

38. *hote*, be called ; a less ambiguous spelling than *hatte*, as in Thynne ; cf. Cant. Ta. D 144. *rede you here*, advise you to hear.

44. *she*. These and similar allusions are merely translated, and have therefore no special significance.

49. 'Me thoghte thus; that hit was May'; Book Duch. 291.

56. *wreen*, cover; A. S. *wrēon*. Cf. *wrye*, I cover, Cant. Ta. D 1827.

59. Read:—And th'erth-e. Cf. Book Duch. 410-5; Good Wom. 125.

61. *Forget*, i. e. forgetteth; pres. tense. So in Ayenb. of Inwyt, p. 18, l. 9, we find the form *uoryet*. I supply *al*.

67. *inde*, azure; see Cursor Mundi, 9920. *pers*; see Prol. 439.

73. *grille*, keen, rough. '*Grym*, gryl, and horryble'; Prompt. Parv.

81. *chelaundre*, (cf. l. 663), a kind of lark; O. F. *calandre, caladre*, Lat. *caradrius*, Gk. χαραδριός. Cf. Land of Cockaigne, l. 97. *papingay*, parrot; Sir Topas, B 1957.

98. *aguiler*, needle-case. It occurs nowhere else. The rime *drow, y-now* occurs in Leg. Good Women, 1458.

118. *Seine*, the river of Paris. In the next line, *wel away straighter* means 'a good deal broader' or more expanded (F. text, *plus espandue*), though less in volume. *Wel away*, in this sense, occurs in P. Plowman, B. xii. 263, xvii. 42.

129. *Beet*, beat, struck, i. e. bordered closely; a translation of F. *batoit*.

131. So also 'And ful atempre'; Book Duch. 341.

147. The descriptions of allegorical personages in this poem are clearly imitated from similar descriptions in Latin poets. Compare the celebrated description of Envy in Ovid, Metam. ii. 775, and the like. MS. G. absurdly reads *a hate* for *Hate*.

149. The reading must, of course, be *moveresse*, as in the Fr. text; Speght corrected it in 1598; it means a mover or stirrer up of strife.

196. Read *miscounting* (Kaluza); F. text, *mesconter*.

197. *maketh*; pronounced *mak'th*. Note, once for all, that '*th* for final *-eth* is extremely common throughout all parts of this poem.

206. *thing*, pl. goods (A. S. *þing*, pl.). Cf. l. 387.

207. *Avarice*, i. e. Penuriousness, as distinct from *Coveitise*, i. e. Covetousness of the wealth of others. Compare the description of Avarice in Piers Plowman, B. v. 188.

220. *courtepy*, short coat, cape; see Prol. 290.

225. *perche*, a horizontal pole, on which clothes were sometimes hung.

226. *burnet*, a cloth of dyed wool, orig. of a dark brown colour. Gowns were nearly always trimmed with fur, but in this case only a common lambskin fur was used, instead of a costly fur such as *miniver*.

240. I supply *doun*, down. Cf. 'heng .. doun'; Cant. Ta. G 574.

247. *Envy*. Cf. Ovid, Met. ii. 775; P. Plowman, B. v. 76.

273. *maltalent*, ill-will; see 330. Cf. *talent*, Cant. Ta. C 540.

276. Read *melt'th. for pure wood*, as if entirely mad. The simple phrase *for wood*, as if mad, occurs in Ho. Fame, 1747; Leg. of Good Women, 2420 (unless *For-wood* is there a compound adjective).

292. *baggingly*, askant, sideways; cf. *baggeth*, looks askant, Book Duch. 623.

311. *fade*, withered. 'Thi faire hewe is al *fade*'; Will. of Palerne, 891. Compare the description of Sorrow in Sackville's 'Induction'; see my Specimens of Eng. Literature, iii. 286.

360. *dwyned*, dwindled, wasted; cf. *for-dwyned*, 366.

361. *forwelked*, much wrinkled; cf. *welked*, Cant. Ta. C 738.

368. *potente*, a crutch, staff; cf. Cant. Ta. D 1776.

369, 381. With these lines cf. Cant. Tales, B 20-24.

380. F. *trois tens*, three moments. It is here asserted that no one can think of the present moment; for while he tries to do so, three moments have fled.

387. *fret*, for *freteth*, devours. 'Tempus edax rerum'; Ovid, Met. xv. 234. *and shal*, and will ever do so. *thing* is pl., as in 206.

396. Bell and Morris here print *elde* with a capital letter, shewing that they did not make out the sense. But it is here a *verb*, as in 391, 392. The sense is:—' Time ... had made her grow so extremely old that, as far as I knew, she could in no wise help herself.'

401. *inwith*, for *within*, is common in Chaucer; the occurrence of *pith*, just before, probably caused the scribe to omit *with*.

413. *doon ther write*, caused to be written (or described) there.

415. *Pope-holy*; properly an adjective, meaning 'holy as a pope,' hence, hypocritical. Here used as a sb., as equivalent to 'hypocrite,' to translate F. *Papelardie*. Used as an adj. in P. Plowman, C. vii. 37; see my note, which gives references to Dyce's Skelton, i. 209, 216, 240, 386; Barclay, Ship of Fools, ed. Jamieson, i. 154; and Polit. Poems, ed. Wright, ii. 251.

429. 'Devoted to a religious life,' viz. by having joined one of the religious orders. See note to P. Plowman, C. xi. 88.

438. *haire*, hair-shirt; the F. text has *la haire*, borrowed from O. H. G. *hārrā*, with the same sense. The A. S. word is *hǣre*, a derivative from *hǣr*, hair. See *Haar* in Kluge. See Cant. Ta., G 133; P. Plowman, C. vii. 6, and the note.

442. The reading *ay* possibly stands for *aȝ*, i.e. *agh* or *ogh*. *Ogh* (A. S. *āh*) is the (obsolete) pres. t. of *ought*, which takes its place in mod. E. Cf. *ye owen*, in Melibeus, B 2691. See *ah* in Stratmann. ' From her the gate of Paradise ought to be kept.' But it is simpler to read *shal* (F. text, *ert*=Lat. *erit*).

445. Alluding to Matt. vi. 16. For *grace*, read *face* (l. 444).

454. Cf. 'like a worm'; Clerkes Ta. E 880.

464. *halke*, corner; Can. Yem. Ta. G 311.

482. *shepherd-e*, is trisyllabic; cf. *herd-e*, in Prol. 603.

490. *daungerous*, stingy; contrasted with *riche* (l. 492).

501. It is impossible to make sense without reading *nolde* for *wolde*. The Fr. text clearly shews that *nolde* is meant:—' Que *n*'en preisse pas ... Que ge *n*'entrasse.' The scribe stumbled over the double negative.

505. G. has:—' Thassemble, god kepe it fro care Of briddis, whiche therynne ware'; and Th. has the same reading. It cannot be right,

because *care* and *were* give a false rime. Even the scribe has seen this, and has altered *were* to *ware*, to give a rime to the eye. Perhaps such a rime may have passed in Northern English, but certainly not in Midland. I have no hesitation in restoring the reading, which must have been 'God *it kepe and were*,' or something very near it. It is obvious that *were* is the original word in this passage, because it is the precise etymological equivalent of *garisse* in the French text; and it is further obvious that the reason for expelling it from the text, was to avoid the apparent repetition of *were* in the rime; a repetition which the scribe too hastily assumed to be a defect, though examples of it are familiar to the student of Chaucer; cf. Prol. 17, 18. Chaucer has *were*, to defend, riming with *spere*, Cant. Ta. A 2550; and *were* (were) also riming with *spere*, Ho. Fame, 1047. He would therefore have had no hesitation in riming these words together; and we cannot doubt that he here did so. Cf. ll. 515, 516 below.

516. *where* would mean ' by which '; read *o-where*, i. e. anywhere.

520. The spelling *angwishis* is a false spelling of *anguissous*, i. e. full of anguish. For this form, see Pers. Tale, I 304.

535. Read *oft*; F. text, ' par maintes fois.'

562. *orfrays*, gold embroidered work, cloth-of-gold; cf. ll. 869, 1076. ' The golden bands fastened to, or embroidered on chasubles, copes, and vestments... Fringes or laces appended to the garments, as well as the embroidered work upon them, were so termed '; Fairholt, Costume in England. See Way's note on *Orfrey* in the Prompt. Parvulorum. Cotgrave has: ' *Orfrais*, m. Broad welts, or gards of gold or silver imbroidery laid on Copes, and other Church-vestments'; &c. There is a long note upon it, with quotations, in Thynne's Animadversions on Speght's Chaucer, ed. Furnivall, pp. 33-35; he says it is 'frised or perled cloothe of gold,' or 'a weued clothe of gold.' Here it seems to mean a gold-embroidered band, worn as a chaplet.

568. *tressour*; so spelt in Gawain and the Grene Knight, 1739, where a lady is described as having precious stones, in clusters of twenty, 'trased aboute hir *tressour*.' Roquefort also gives the O. F. forms *tressour*, *tressoir*, *tresson*, 'ornement de téte pour les femmes, ruban pour attacher les cheveux.' It differs from the heraldic term *tressure* (Lat. *tricatura*) in the form of the suffix. *Tressour* can rime with *mirrour*, whilst *tressure* (strictly) cannot do so. Her hair was entwined with gilt ribbons or threads.

574. *Gaunt*, Ghent; see Cant. Ta. A 448.

579, 580. *Iournee*, day's work. *wel bigoon*, might mean richly adorned; cf. 'With perle and gold so wel begoon'; Gower, C. A. ii. 45. But it is here equivalent to *mery*; see l. 693.

584. *graythe hir*, dress or adorn herself. *uncouthly*, strikingly, in an unusual way.

593. This is ' the porter Ydlenesse ' of the Knightes Tale; A 1940.

602. *Alexandryn*, of Alexandria; for *of* may well be omitted. It means that many trees have been imported from the east by way of

Alexandria. Many MSS. of the Fr. text read 'de la terre Alexandrins.' The damson, for example, came from Damascus.

603. I put *be hider* for *hider be*; but *be*, after all, is better omitted. *Made hider fet* is a correct idiom; see note to Cant. Ta. E 1098.

610. The images and pictures on the outside of the wall were made repellent, to keep strangers aloof.

624. *oon*, one; i.e. a place. *intil Inde*, as far as India.

656. The rime is only a single one, in *-ing*.

658. *Alpes*, bullfinches; also called *an awp*, or, corruptly, *a nope*. 'Alp, or *Nope*, a bulfinch. I first took notice of this word in *Suffolk*, but find since that it is used in other counties, almost generally all over England'; Ray's Collection of South and E. Country Words (1691).

wodewales, witwalls. In the Prompt. Parvulorum, the *wodewale* is identified with the *wodehake*, woodpecker; whilst Hexham explains Du. *Weduwael* as 'a kinde of a yellow bird.' There is often great confusion in such names. The true *witwall* is the Green Woodpecker (*Gecinus viridis*). We may omit *and*, and even *were* in l. 657.

662. *laverokkes*, larks. The A. S. *lāwerce*, *lāferce*, became *laverk*; then the final *k* was exchanged for the diminutive suffix *-ok*.

663. *Chalaundres*; see note to l. 81 above.

664. *wery*, weary (F. *lassees*); *nigh forsongen*, nearly tired out with singing.

665. *thrustles*, throstles, thrushes; see Parl. Foules, 364.

terins; F. *tarin*, which, Littré says, is the *Fringilla spinus*. Cotgrave has: '*Tarin*, a little singing bird, having a yellowish body, and an ash-coloured head'; by which (says Prof. Newton) he means the siskin, otherwise called the aberdevine.

mavys, mavises, song-thrushes. If we take the *mavis* to be the song-thrush, *Turdus musicus*, then the throstle may be distinguished as the missel-thrush, *Turdus viscivorus*. But the mavis is also called throstle. In Cambridge, the name is pronounced *mavish* (romic mei·vish).

672. 'As spiritual angels do.'

676. 'Of man liable to death'; by mortal man.

684. *sereyns*, i.e. Sirens. Cotgrave has: '*Sereine*, f. a Mermaid.' Chaucer takes no notice of G. de Lorris' notable etymology, by which he derives *Seraines* from the adj. *seri*. Cotgrave gives (marked as obsolete): '*Seri*, m. *ie*, f. Quiet, mild, calm, still; fair, clear.'

693. *wel bigo*, the opposite of 'woe begone'; as in l. 580. Cf. 'glad and wel begoon'; Parl. Foules, 171.

700. *leten*, pp. of *leten*, to let; 'and had let me in.'

705. Morris reads *Withoute*, which improves the line:—'Without·e fabl' I wol descryve.'

714. *sete*, sat; A. S. *sǣton*, pt. t. pl. (The correct form).

716. *Iargoning*, chattering; cf. E. *jargon*.

720. Read *reverdye* (see footnote). It means 'rejoicing'; from the renewal of green things in spring.

731. *mentes*, mints; Th. has *myntes*.

735. 'Where he abode, to amuse himself.'

744. *carole*, a dance; orig. a dance in a ring, accompanied with song. Hence, in l. 745, the verb *carolen*, to sing, in accompaniment to a dance of this character. In Rob. of Brunne's Handlyng Synne, 9138, there is a description of a company carolling 'hand in hand.' And see below, ll. 759-765, 781; Book Duch. 849.

746. I insert *the* (as Urry does) before *blisful*; cf. l. 797.

749. The line—'And couthe make in song swich refreininge' is obviously too long. The word *couthe* is needlessly repeated from l. 747, and must be omitted. The Fr. text shews that *refreininge* means the singing of a refrain at the end of each verse.

768. *in this contree*. This is an adaptation; the original Fr. says 'in *any* country.' Warton calmly observes: 'there is not a syllable of these songs and singers of Lorraine in the French.' But he consulted a defective copy.

769. *timbestere*, a female player on a timbrel. Tyrwhitt confuses the matter by quoting Lye, who mixed up this word with *tombestere*, a female tumbler; for which see Cant. Ta. C 477. They are quite unconnected, but are formed with the same fem. suffix, viz. that which appears also in the mod. E. *spin-ster*, and in the old words *webb-estere*, *bak-estere*, whence the surnames Webster, Baxter. In l. 772, *timbres* simply mean timbrels, and tambourine-players may still be performing the easy trick of throwing up a tambourine and catching it, spinning, on a finger-point. There is therefore no reason for explaining *timbre* as a basin. Nevertheless, such a mistake arose, and Junius quotes (s. v. *Timbestere*) some lines from an edition of Le Roman de la Rose, printed in 1529, in which the following lines here occur:—

> 'Apres y eut farces joyeuses,
> Et batelleurs et batelleuses,
> Qui de passe passe jouoyent,
> Et en l'air *ung bassin* ruoyent,
> Puis le scavoyent bien recueillir
> Sur ung doy, sans point y faillir.'

It is tolerably certain that this is a corrupt form of the passage, and only makes the matter darker. All it proves is, that *timbre* was, by some, supposed to mean a basin! No doubt it had that sense (see Cotgrave), but not here.

Timbestere is a mere English form of the O. F. *tymberesse*, a player on a *timbre*. Diez, in his Dictionary, cites a passage from a commentary on the Psalms, given in Roquefort, Poés. franç. p. 127, to this effect :—'li *tymbres* est uns estrumenz de musique qui est couverz d'un cuir sec de bestes'; i. e. it is the Lat. *tympanum*. So also, in Wright's Vocab. col. 616, l. 28, we have:—' *Timpanum*, a taber, or a tymbre.' In Allit. Poems, ed. Morris, ii. 1414, we read of the sound of '*tymbres* and *tabornes*,' and of '*symbales*,' i. e. cymbals. In King Alisaunder,

NOTES. LINES 731-892.

ed. Weber, 191, we again have *tymbres* meaning 'timbrels.' Wyclif, in his tr. of Isaiah, v. 12, has '*tymbre* and trumpe,' to translate 'tympanum et tibia'; and the word is well preserved in the mod. E. dimin. *timbr-el*.

770. *saylours*, dancers; from O. F. *saillir*, Lat. *salere*; cf. '*Salyyn*, salio'; Prompt. Parv. The M. E. *sailen*, to dance, occurs in P. Plowman, C xvi. 208 (see my note); and in Rob. of Glouc. l. 5633 (or p. 278, ed. Hearne).

791. *Ne bede I*. The Fr. text means—'I would never seek to go away.' As *e* and *o* are constantly confused, I change *bode* (which gives no sense) into *bede*; i. e. 'I would never pray.' *Bede* is the pt. t. subj. of *bidden*, to pray. Gower uses *ne bede* in the same sense; 'That I ne bede never awake'; Conf. Am. ii. 99.

826. *girdilstede*, the *stead* or place of the girdle, i. e. the waist.

836. *samyt*, samite, a very rich silk; see Halliwell and my Etym. Dict.

840. *to-slitered*, very much 'slashed' with small cuts. It is well known that slashed or snipped sleeves, shewing the colour of the lining beneath them, were common in the Tudor period; and it here appears that they were in vogue much earlier. *Slideren* is the frequentative form of *sliten*, to slit.

843. *decoped*, cut, slashed. The shoes were slashed like the dress; the Fr. text has here *decopes*, which, only just above, is translated by *to-slitered*. Cf. the expression 'galoches *y-couped*' in P. Plowman, C. xxi. 12, and see my note on that passage. Halliwell is quite wrong in confusing *decoped* with *coppid*, i. e. peaked. See note to Mill. Ta. A 3318.

860. The readings *pleye*, *ply* are evidently false; the scribe has omitted the stroke for *n* above the vowel. The right reading is obviously *playn*, i. e. plain, smooth; it translates F. *poli*, just as *frounceles* translates *sans fronce*, without a wrinkle.

865. If the reader prefers to keep *eleven* (or *twelve*) syllables in this line, I am sorry for him.

869. *orfrays*, gold embroidery; see note to l. 562. In this case, the gold seems to have been embroidered on silk; see l. 872.

886. *quistroun*, a kitchen-boy, scullion. Godefroy gives the forms *coistron, coitron, coisteron, quistron, coestron*, with the sense 'marmiton.' His examples include the expressions '*coitron* de la cuisine,' and 'un *quistroun* de sa quisyne.' The addition of *de la (sa) cuisine* shew that the word meant no more than 'boy' or 'lad'; such a lad as was often employed in the kitchen.

> 'Ther nas knave, ne *quystron*,
> That he ne hadde god waryson';
>   King Alisaunder, ed. Weber, 2511.

892. *amorettes*, (probably) love-knots. Such seems also to be the meaning in the passage in the Kingis Quair, st. 47, which was probably

imitated from the present one. But both passages are sufficiently obscure. The word occurs again, below, in l. 4755, where the meaning is different, viz. young girls, sweethearts; but we must remember that it is there employed by a different translator. In the present passage, the Fr. text is obscure, and it is possible that *par fines amoretes* means 'by beautiful girls.' The note in Bell's Chaucer says accordingly:— 'these flowers were painted by amorous young ladies;' and adds that '*with* here means *by*.' But this will hardly serve. We have no proof that Chaucer so understood the French; and if '*with* means *by*' here, it must have the same sense in l. 894, which would mean that birds, leopards, and lions all lent a hand in painting. On the whole, the sense 'love-knots' seems the safest.

893. *losenges and scochouns*, lozenges (or diamond-shaped figures) and escutcheons.

911. *felden*, caused to fall, knocked off.

914. *chalaundre*; see note to l. 81. *wodewale*; see note to l. 658.

915. *archaungel*, supposed to mean 'a titmouse,' answering to F. *mesange*. But no other example of this use is known.

923. This line is too long; I omit *ful wel devysed*, which is not in the original.

933. *thwiten*, cut, shaped; pp. of *thwyten*, to cut (see Hous of Fame, 1938); cf. *thwitel* in the Reves Ta. A 3933, and E. *whittle*.

938. *gadeling*, vagabond; see Gamelyn, 102, 106.

971. The idea of the two sets of arrows is taken from Ovid, Met. i. 468-471.

998. William de Lorris did not live to fulfil this promise.

1008. I. e. Beauty was also the name of an arrow; see l. 952. The allegory is rather of a mixed kind.

1014. *byrde*, i. e. bride (though the words are different); Fr. *espousee*. *bour*, bower; the usual name for a lady's chamber.

1018. I alter the *wintred* of the old copies to *windred*, to make the form agree with that in l. 1020. To *windre* is evidently a form suggested by the Fr. *guignier*. There are two verbs of this form; the more common is *guigner*, to wink (see Cotgrave); the other is given by Godefroy as *guignier, guigner, guingnier, guinier, gignier*, with the senses 'parer, farder,' i.e. to trick out. Note the original line: 'Ne fu fardee ne guignie'; and again in l. 2180: 'Mais ne te farde ne guigne.' The sense, in the present passage, is evidently 'to trim,' with reference to the eyebrows. 'Her eyebrows were not artificially embellished.'

Poppen, in l. 1019, has much the same sense, and is evidently allied to F. *popin*, 'spruce, neat, briske, trimme, fine,' in Cotgrave.

1031. I read *Wys* for want of a better word; it answers to one sense of Lat. *sapidus*, whence the F. *sade* is derived. However, Cotgrave explains *sade* by 'pretty, neat, spruce, fine, compt, minion, quaint.' Perhap *Queint* or *Fine* would do better.

1049. *in hir daungere*, under her control ; see Prol. A 663, and the note. And see l. 1470.

1050. *losengere*, deceiver, flatterer ; see Non. Pr. Ta. B 4516 ; Legend of Good Women, 352. Cf. ll. 1056, 1064 below.

1057. ' And thus anoint the world with (oily) words.'

1058. I cannot find that there is any such word as *prill* (as in Th.) or *prile* (as in G.) in any suitable sense ; the word required is clearly *prikke*. As it was usual to write *kk* like *lk*, the word probably looked, to the eye, like *prilke*, out of which *prille* may have been evolved. Numerous mistakes have thus arisen, such as *rolke* for *rokke* (a rock) in Gawain Douglas, and many more of the same kind. M. Michel here quotes an O. F. proverb—' Poignez vilain, il vous oindra : Oignez vilain, il vous poindra.'

1068. Read *aryved*, for the Fr. text has *arives* ; cf. Ho. Fame, 1047.

1079. *bend*, band, strip ; as used in heraldry.

1080. Read *améled*, as in Speght ; of which *enameled* is a lengthened form, with the prefix *en-*. It signifies ' enamelled.' Palsgrave gives a good example. ' I *ammell*, as a goldesmyth dothe his worke, *Iesmaille*. Your broche is very well amelled : *vostre deuise est fort bien esmaillee*.' See *Ameled* in the New Eng. Dict. See also the long note in Warton (sect. xiii, where this passage is quoted) on enamelling in the middle ages. He cites the Latin forms *amelitam* and *amelita* in the sense ' enamelled,' and shews that the art flourished, in particular, at Limoges in France.

1081. *of gentil entaile*, of a fine shape, referring to her neck, apparently ; or it may refer to the collar. Halliwell quotes from MS. Douce 291 ' the hors of gode *entaile*,' i. e. of a good shape. Cf. *entaile*, to shape, in l. 609 above ; and see l. 3711.

1082. *shet*, shut, i. e. clasped, fastened. *Chevesaile*, a collar; properly, the neckband of the robe, as explained in the New E. Dict. Though it does not here occur in the Fr. text, it occurs below in a passage which Chaucer does not exactly translate, though it answers to the ' colere ' of l. 1190, q. v. There seems to be no sufficient reason for explaining it by ' necklace ' or ' gorget,' as if it were a separable article of attire. It answers to a Lat. type *capitiale*, from *capitium*, the opening in a tunic through which the head passed; which explains how the word arose.

1089. The right word is *thurte*, which the scribe, not understanding, has turned into *durst* ; both here, and in l. 1324 below. *Thurte him* means ' he needed,' the exact sense required. The use of the dative *him* is a clear trace of the use of this phrase.

The idea that a gem would repel venom was common ; see P. Plowman, B. ii. 14, and my note.

1093. *and Fryse*, and Friesland. Not in the original, and merely added for the rime.

1094. *mourdaunt*, mordant, chape, tag. Halliwell explains it ' the tongue of a buckle,' which is probably a guess ; it is often mentioned as if it were quite distinct from it. It was probably ' the metal chape or tag fixed to the end of a girdle or strap,' viz. to the end *remote* from the buckle; see Fairholt's 'Costume.' Godefroy explains it in the same way; it terminated the dependent end of the girdle; and this explains how it could be made of a stone. Warton, in a note on this passage (sect. xiii.), quotes from a wardrobe roll, in which there is mention of one hundred garters 'cum boucles, barris, et pendentibus de argento.'

1103. *barres*, bars; fixed transversely to the satin tissue of the girdle, and perforated to receive the tongue of the buckle. See note to Prol. A 329.

1106. 'In each bar was a bezant-weight of gold.' A *bezant* was a gold coin, originally struck at Byzantium, whence the name. It 'varied in weight between the English sovereign and half-sovereign, or less'; New E. Dict.

1117. The false reading *ragounces* is easily corrected by the original. In Lydgate's Chorle and Bird, st. 34, we find:—'There is a stone which called is *iagounce*.' Warton rather hastily identifies it with the jacinth. Godefroy says that some make it to be a jacinth, but others, a garnet. Warnke explains *iagunce* (in Marie de France, Le Fraisne, 130) by 'ruby.'

1120. *carboucle*, carbuncle; see notes to Ho. Fame, 1352, 1363.

1137. That is, he would have expected to be accused of a crime equal to theft or murder, if he had kept in his stable such a horse as a hackney. The F. text has *roucin*, whence Chaucer's *rouncy*, in Prol. A 390.

1148. I. e. as if his wealth had been poured into a garner, like so much wheat. *daungere* here means 'parsimony.'

1152. I. e. Alexander was noted for his liberality.

1163. *to hir baundon*, (so as to be) at her disposal.

1182. *adamaunt*, lodestone; *leyd therby*, laid beside it.

1188. The form *sarlynysh* (in G.) evidently arose from the common mistake of reading a long *s* (f) as an *l*. The right reading is, of course, *Sarsinesshe*, i.e., Saracenic, or coloured by an Eastern dye. Compare the mod. E. *sarsnet*, a derivative from the same source.

1190. Her neck-band was thrown open, because she had given away the brooch, with which she used to fasten it.

1199. The knight is said to be *sib*, i.e., akin, to king Arthur, because of the great celebrity of that flower of chivalry.

1201. The reading *gousfaucoun* is a queer mistake; the scribe seems to have thought that it meant a goshawk! But the sense is 'war-banner.' See *Gonfanon* in my Etym. Dict.

1215. *at poynt devys*, with great exactness, with great regularity; cf. l. 830. The same expression occurs in the Ho. of Fame, 917.

1216. *tretys*, long and well-shaped; hence this epithet, as applied to the nose of the Prioress; see Prol. A 152. See ll. 932, 1016.

1227. *bistad*, bestead; i.e. hard beset.

1232. *sukkenye*, an E. adaptation of the O. F. *sorquanie*. Cotgrave has: '*Souquenie*, f. a canvas Jacket, frock, or Gaberdine; such a one as our Porters wear.' Mod. F. *souquenille*, a smock-frock. It was therefore a loose frock, probably made, in this case, of fine linen. For a note in the glossary to Méon's edition says that linen was sometimes the material used for it; and we are expressly told, in the text, that it was *not* made of hempen hards. Cf. Russ. *sukno*, cloth.

1235. *rideled*, 'gathered,' or pleated; F. *coillie*. Not 'pierced like a riddle,' as suggested in Bell's Chaucer, but gathered in folds like a curtain or a modern surplice; from O. F. *ridel* (F. *rideau*), a curtain. Cf. 'filettis, and wymplis, and *rydelid* gownes and rokettis, colers, lacis,' &c.; Reliquiæ Antiquæ, i. 41. Hence, in ll. 1236, 7, the statement that every point was in its right place; because it was so evenly gathered.

1240. 'A *roket*, or *rochet*, is a loose linen frock synonymous with *sukkenye*. The name is now appropriated to the short surplice worn by bishops over their cassocks.'—Bell.

1249, 50. *Al hadde he be*, even if he had been. As the French copy consulted by Warton here omitted two lines of the original, Warton made the singular mistake of supposing that, in l. 1250, Chaucer intended 'a compliment to some of his patrons.' But William de Lorris died in 1260, so that the *seignor de Gundesores* was 'Henry of Windsor,' as he was sometimes termed[1], i.e. no other than Henry III; and the reference was probably suggested by the birth of prince Edward in 1239, unless these two lines were added somewhat later.

1263. *avenant*, comely, graceful; see the New E. Dict.

1282. The absolutely necessary correction in this line was suggested by Ten Brink, in his Chaucer Studien, p. 30.

1284. *volage*, flighty, giddy; see Manc. Ta. H 239.

1294. I should like to read—'They ne made force of privetee'; pronounced *They n' mad-e*, &c. But *no fors* is usual.

1321. *his thankes*, willingly; see Kn. Ta. A 1626, 2107.

1324. *durst* is an error for *thurte*; see note to l. 1089.

1334. For *hadde* (which gives no sense), read *bad*; confusion of *b* and *h* is not uncommon. And for *bent*, read *bende it*; see l. 1336.

1341. Some mending of the text is absolutely necessary, because *shette* is altogether a false form; the pp. of *sheten*, to shoot, is *shoten*. The suggested emendation satisfies the conditions, and makes better sense. So, in l. 1343, read *wol me greven*.

1348. In ll. 1461, 1582, the F. *vergier* is translated by *yerde*. So here, and in l. 1447 (as Dr. Kaluza suggests) we must read *yerde in*, to make sense. The scribe easily turned *yerde in* into *gardin*, but ruined the sense by it. So in l. 1366, *yerde* would be better than *gardin*.

1359. *greet foisoun*, a great abundance (of them).

1361. *notemygge* is the form given in the Prompt. Parv. In Sir

---

[1] As, e.g. in the curious satirical ballad 'Against the King of Almaigne,' printed in Percy's Ballads, Series II. Book I, and in Wright's 'Political Songs,' p. 69. Henry was also called Henry of Winchester, from the place of his birth.

Topas, 1953, *notemuge* occurs in all the seven MSS. See note to the same, B 1950, which explains *clow-gelofre*, i.e. clove, and *setewale*, i.e., zedoary.

1363. The form *alemandres* is justified by the Fr. text, which has *Alemandiers*. The O.F. for 'almond' was at first *alemande*, before it was shortened to *almande*; see *Almond* in the New E. Dict. The sense is 'almond-trees.'

1369. *parys* or *paris* is a stupid blunder for *paradys*, as the Fr. text shews. It was a well-known term. Cotgrave has '*Graine de paradis*, the spice called Grains.' Philips explains *Paradisi grana* as 'cardamum-seed.' Compare the quotation from Langham in the New E. Dict., s. v. *Cardamom*. *Canelle* (in l. 1370) is 'cinnamon.'

1374. *coyn* is the word which has been twisted into *quin*; and the pl. *quins* has become the sing. *quince*.

1377. *aleys*. 'Aley [adapted from O. Fr. *alie*, *alye* (also *alis*), mod. Fr. *alise*, *alize*, from O. H. G. *eliza*, mod. G. *else(beere)*; the suppression of the *s* in the O. Fr. is anomalous.] The fruit of the Wild-Service tree'; New E. Dict. No other example of the word is known in English. *bolas*, bullace; the rime is only a *single* one.

1379. *lorer*, laurel; miswritten *lorey* in G.; cf. l. 1313 above, where *loreres* is miswritten *loreyes*.

1384. Compare the tree-lists in Parl. Foules, 176, and in the Kn. Ta. A 2921.

1385. I should read *Pyn, ew*, instead of *Fyn ew*; only we have had *pyn* already, in l. 1379.

1391. Imitated in the Book Duch. 419; again, l. 1401 is imitated in the same, 429.

1397, 8. The rimed words must needs be *knet, set*, as in the Parl. Foules, 627, 628.

1405. *claperes*, burrows. '*Clapier*, m. A clapper of conies, a heap of stones, &c., whereinto they retire themselves'; Cotgrave. See *Clapper* in the New E. Dict.

1414. *condys*, conduits; Fr. text, *conduis*. Godefroy gives numerous examples of *conduis* as the pl. of O. F. *conduit*, in the sense of safe-conduct, &c. So, in the Ayenbite of Inwyt, p. 91, we find :—'Thise uif wytes byeth ase uif *condwys*,' i.e. these five wits (senses) are as five channels. *by devys*, by contrivances (l. 1413).

1420. *vel-u-et* is here a trisyllabic word; and the *u* is a vowel, as in A. F. *veluet*. The mod. E. *velvet* arose from misreading the *u* as a *v*. The Prompt. Parv. has also the form *velwet*. So in Lydgate, Compl. of the Black Knight, l. 80 : ' And soft as vel-u-et,' &c.

1426. *as mister was*, as was need, as was necessary.

1447. As *garden* makes no sense here, Kaluza reads *yerde in*; see note to l. 1348.

1448. *estres* (F. text, *l'estre*), inner parts; see Rev. Ta. A 4295, and the note.

1453. *at good mes*, to advantage, from a favourable position; Fr. *en* *bel leu.* In l. 3462, the phrase translates F. *en bon point.* *Mes* (*Lat. missum*) is an old Anglo-French hunting-term, answering (nearly) to mod. E. *shot.* Thus, in Marie de France, Guigemar, 87 :—'Traire voleit, si *mes* ëust,' he wished to shoot, if he could get a good shot. See Ducange, ed. 1887, ix. 270, for two more examples.

1458. *Pepyn*; the F. text says 'Charles, the son of Pepin.' Charles the Great, who died in 814, was the son of Pepin Le Bref, king of the Franks, who died in 768.

1469. This story of Narcissus is from Ovid, Met. iii. 346.

1470. *in his daungere,* within his control; in l. 1492, *daungerous* means 'disdainful.' See note to l. 1049.

1498. The right spelling is *vilaynsly*; it occurs in the Pers. Tale, I 279; and the adj. *vilayns* in the same, I 627, 715, 854.

1517, 18. The right spellings are *sene*, adj., visible, and *shene*, adj., showy, bright.

1525. *bere,* bore; but it is in the subjunctive mood; A. S. *bǣre.*

1537. *warisoun,* reward; F. *guerredon.* But this is not the usual sense; it commonly means healing, cure, or remedy; see *Guarison* in Cotgrave. However, it also means provision, store, assistance; whence it is no great step to the sense of 'reward.' To 'winne a warisun' is to obtain a reward; Will. of Palerne, 2253, 2259. Cf. note to l. 886.

1550. *scatheles,* without harm. There is actually a touch of humour here; the poet ran no risk of falling in love with such a face as his own.

1561. *welmeth up,* boils up, bubbles up; from A. S. *wylm,* a spring.

1564. *For moiste,* because it was moist, because of its moisture. The adj. has almost the force of a sb. Cf. note to l. 276.

1591. *entrees* is, of course, a blunder for *estres*, as the F. text shews. See l. 1448 above, where *estres* rightly occurs, to represent F. *l'estre. accuseth,* reveals, shews; see the New Eng. Dict.

1604. 'That made him afterwards lie on his back,' i. e. lie dead (F. *mors*). The alteration of *lye* to *ligge* in MS. G. is a clear example of the substitution of a Northern form.

1608. Here *laughyng* is a very queer travesty of *loving,* owing to a similarity in the sound. But the F. text has *d'amer,* which settles it.

1621. *panteres,* nets; see Leg. of Good Women, 131, and the note.

1624. *lacche,* trap. The usual sense is 'the latch of a door'; but the sense here given is clearly caught from the related verb *lacchen,* which sometimes meant to catch birds. Thus in P. Plowman, B. v. 355, we find 'forto lacche foules,' i.e. to catch birds. We must not confuse *lacche,* as here used, with *lace,* a snare.

1641. We must read *syked,* not *sighede,* in order to rime with *entryked.* Observe that *syketh* rimes with *entryketh* in the Parl. of Foules, 404. Further, as the rime is a double one, the word *have* must be inserted, to fill up the line. It is in the Fr. text, 'tant en *ai* puis souspire.'

1652. *enclos,* enclosed; a French form, used for the rime. Cf. *clos,* in the same sense; The Pearl, l. 2.

1663. Speght made the obvious correction of *be*, for *me*.

1666. *My thankes*, with my goodwill; cf. *his thankes*, l. 1321.

1673. *gret woon*, a great quantity.

1674. *roon* (in place of *Rone*); F. text, *sous ciaus*, 'under the skies.' Bell suggests that there is a reference to the river Rhone, and to the roses of Provence. But the prep. *in* must mean 'in' or 'upon'; and as roses do not grow on a river, but upon bushes, perhaps *roon* answers to Lowland Scotch *rone*, a bush; see Jamieson. Thus Henrysoun, Prol. to Moral Fables, l. 15, has:—' The roisis reid arrayit on *rone* and ryce'; and G. Douglas has *ronnis*, bushes. *In Roon* might mean ' in Rouen'; spelt *Roan* in Shakespeare.

1677. *moysoun*, size; Cotgrave has : ' *Moyson*, size, bignesse, quantity'; from Lat. *mensionem*, a measuring. See P. Plowman, C. xii. 120, and my note. Not connected with *moisson*, harvest, as suggested in Bell.

1701. ' The stalk was as upright as a rush.'

1705. Here ends Chaucer's portion of the translation, in the middle of an incomplete sentence, without any verb. It may have been continued thus (where *dide fulfild* = caused to be filled) :—

> The swote smelle sprong so wyde,
> That it dide al the place aboute
> *Fulfild of baume, withouten doute.*

We can easily understand that the original MS. ended here suddenly, the rest being torn away or lost. An attempt was made to join on another version, without observing the incompleteness of the sentence. Moreover, the rime is a false one, since *swote* and *aboute* have different vowel-sounds. Hence the point of junction becomes visible enough.

Dr. Max Kaluza was the first to observe the change of authorship at this point, though he made Chaucer's portion end at l. 1704. He remarked, very acutely, that Chaucer translates the F. *bouton* by the word *knoppe*; see ll. 1675, 1683, 1685, 1691, 1702, whereas the other translator merely keeps the word *botoun*; see ll. 1721, 1761, 1770.

It is easily seen that ll. 1706-5810 are by a second and less skilful hand. This portion abounds with non-Chaucerian rimes, as explained in the Introduction, and is not by any means remarkable for accuracy. Some of the false rimes are noted below.

As the remaining portion is of less interest and value, I only draw attention, in the notes, to the most important points. I here denote the second portion (ll. 1706-5810) by the name of Section B.

1713. *muche*, in Sect. B, is usually dissyllabic; perhaps the original had *mikel*.

1721. In sect. B, the word *botoun* is invariably misspelt *bothum* or *bothom*. That this ridiculous form is wrong, is proved by the occurrence of places where the pl. *botouns* rimes with *sesouns* (4011) and with *glotouns* (4308). I therefore restore the form *botoun* throughout.

1776. Sect. B is strongly marked by the frequent use of *withouten wene, withouten were, withouten drede,* and the like tags.

1820. A common proverb, in many languages. 'Chien eschaudé craint l'eau froide, the scaulded dog fears even cold water;' Cotgrave. 'Brend child fur dredeth' is one of the Proverbs of Hending, l. 184. The Fr. text has : 'Qu'eschaudés doit iaue douter.' See Cant. Ta. G 1407. At this point, the translation somewhat varies from the Fr. text, as usually printed. The *third* arrow is here called Curtesye (1802, cf. 957) instead of Fraunchise (955).

1853, 4. Both *thore, more,* evidently for *thar, mar*; see ll. 1857, 8.

1871. *allegeaunce,* alleviation ; F. text, *aleiance.* Cf. *aleggement,* 1890; F. text, *alegement*; and see l. 1923.

1906. Both texts have *Rokyng.* A better spelling is either *rouking* or *rukking.* It means—'crouching down very closely on account of the pain.' See Kn. Ta. A 1308. (Not in the French text.)

1909. The other four arrows are Beauty (1750), Simplesse (1774), Curtesye (1802, and note to l. 1820), and Companye (1862). But the names, even in the F. text, are not exactly the same as in a former passage ; see ll. 952-963 above.

2002. 'For I do not vouchsafe to churls, that they shall ever come near it.' For *of* (suggested by *sauf*) we should read *to.*

2017. *Lord* seems to be dissyllabic; read (perhaps) *laverd.*

2037. As in l. 4681, there is here an allusion to the mode of doing homage, wherein the kneeling vassal places his joined hands between those of his lord. This is still the attitude of one who receives a degree at Cambridge from the Vice-chancellor.

2044. For *taken* read *tan,* the Northern form. So again in l. 2068.

2046. *Disteyned* is, of course, a blunder for *Disceyued.*

2051. 'If I get them into my power.'

2063. *For-why,* i. e. why ; F. 'por quoi.'

2076. *disseise,* oust you from possessing it. *Disseisin* is the opposite of *seisin,* a putting in possession of a thing ;

2087. *aumener,* purse, lit. bag for alms ; F. *aumoniere.*

2092. I take *iowell* (with a bar through the *ll*) to be the usual (Northern) contraction for *Iowellis,* jewels ; F. text, *joiau,* pl. I can find no authority for making it a collective noun, as Bell suggests.

2099. *spered,* for *sperred,* fastened ; F. *ferma.* See l. 3320.

2141. I supply *sinne*; perhaps the exact word is *erre,* as suggested by Urry ; F. 'Tost porroie *issir de la voie.*'

2154. Read *ginn'th*; only one syllable is wanted here. Cf. l. 2168.

2161. *poyntith ille,* punctuates badly. This is a remarkable statement. As the old MSS. had no punctuation at all, the responsibility in this respect fell entirely on the reader. Ll. 2157-62 are not in the French.

2170. *Romaunce,* the Romance language, Old French.

2190. This important passage is parallel to one in the Wife of

Bath's Tale, D 1109. Ll. 2185-2202 are not in the French; so they may have been suggested by Chaucer's Tale.

2203. 'Gravis est culpa, tacenda loqui'; Ovid, Ars Amat. ii. 604.

2206. *Keye*, Sir Kay, one of the knights of the Round Table, who was noted for his discourtesy. For his rough treatment of Sir Beaumains, see Sir T. Malory's Morte d'Arthur, bk. vii. c. 1. On the other hand, Sir Gawain was famed for his courtesy; see Squi. Ta. F 95.

2271. The word *aumenere* is here used, as in l. 2087 above, to translate the F. *aumosniere* or *aumoniere*. In Th., it is miswritten *aumere*, and in G. it appears as *awmere*. Hence *awmere* has gained a place in the New E. Dict., to which it is certainly not entitled. It is not a 'contraction for *awmenere*,' as is there said, but a mere blunder.

2278. *Of Whitsonday*, suitable for Whitsunday, a time of great festivity; F. text—'a Penthecouste.'

2279. Both texts have *costneth*, which makes the line halt. *Cost* (short for *costeth*) has the same sense, and suits much better; the F. text has simply *couste*.

2280-4. Copied from Ovid, Ars Amat. i. 515-9.

2285. It is clear that *Fard*, not *Farce*, is the right reading. *Farce* would mean 'stuff' or 'cram'; see Prol. A 233. The F. text has— 'Mais ne te *farde* ne ne guigne.' Among the additions by Halliwell and Wright to Nares' Glossary will be found : '*Fard*, to paint the face'; with three examples. Cotgrave also has : '*Fardé*, Farded, coloured, painted.'

2294. *knowith* is a strange error for *lowhith*, or *lauhwith*, forms of *laugheth*; F. text, *rit*.

2296. *meynd*, mingled; see Kn. Ta. A 2170.

2301-4. Not in the F. text. I alter *pleyneth* in l. 2302 to *pleyeth*, to suit the context more closely.

2309. *sitting*, becoming; cf. *sit*, Clk. Ta. E 460.

2318. 'Make no great excuse'; F. *essoine*. From Ovid, Ars Am. i. 595.

2327. For *meuen* I read *meve hem*, move them. Ll. 2325-8 are not in the French text.

2336. Read *Loves*. 'Whoever would live in Love's teaching must be always ready to give.' F. text, 'Se nus se vuelt *d'amors* pener.'

2341. Cf. F. text :—'Doit bien, apres si riche don.' See ll. 2381.

2354. *alosed*, praised (for liberality); see *Alose* in the New E. Dict.

2365. 'Against treachery, in all security.' *For* is here used for 'against.' F. text, ' Tous entiers sans tricherie.'

2386. *maugre his*, in spite of himself; against the giver's will.

2463. 'That thou wouldst never willingly leave off.'

2471. *fere*, fire; spelt *fyr* in l. 2467. But *desyr* rimes with *nere*, l. 2441.

2473. Obscure. The French text helps but little; it means—'whenever thou comest nearer *her*.' Hence *Thought* should be *That swete*, or some such phrase.

2522. 'To conceal (it) closely'; F. de soi celer.

2561. 'Now groveling on your face, and now on your back.'

2564. 'Like a man that should be defeated in war.' To get a rime to *abrede* or *abreed*, abroad, read *forwerreyd*; see l. 3251.

2573. 'Thou shalt imagine delightful visions.' The 'castles in Spain' are romantic fictions. Cf. Gower, Conf. Am. ii. 99.

2617, 2624. In both lines, *wher* is short for 'whether.'

2628. *To liggen*, to lie, is a Northern form; I alter *liggen* to *ly*, which occurs in the next line.

2641. *contene,* contain (thyself). But the F. text has *te contendras*, which perhaps means 'shalt struggle.'

2650. *What whider* gives no sense; read *What weder*, i. e. whatever weather it be; see next line.

2660. *score*, (perhaps) cut, i. e. crack; F. text, fendéure.

2669. I supply *a,* i. e. by; or we may supply *al.*

2676. There is something wrong here; the F. text has:—

'Si te dirai que tu dois faire
Por l'amour de la debonnaire [*or*, du haut seintueire]
De qui tu ne pues avoir aise;
Au departir la porte baise.'

The lover is here directed to kiss the door!

2684-6. From Ovid, Ars Amat. i. 729, 733.

2695. All from Ovid, Ars Amat. ii. 251-260.

2710. Read *fare*, short for *faren*, gone; cf. Ovid, Ars Am. ii. 357-8. A note in Bell says—'*fore* means absent, from the Lat. *foris*, abroad.' This is a cool invention.

2775. *Hope,* do thou hope; imperative mood.

2824. The reading *not ben* ruins sense and metre.

'Et se tu l'autre refusoies,
Qui n est mie mains doucereus,
Tu seroies moult dangereus.'

2883. Such was the duty of sworn brethren; See Kn. Ta. A 1132.

2888. The trilled *r* in *darst* perhaps constitutes a syllable.

2951. 'When the God of Love had all day taught me.'

2971. *hay(e)*, hedge; F. *haie*. Perhaps not *hay-e*; see l. 2987.

2984. *Bial-Acoil*, another spelling of *Bel-Acueil*, i. e. 'a graceful address'; which would be useful in propitiating the lady.

3105. *doth me drye*, makes me suffer; Scotch 'gars me dree.'

3132. *chere,* face; *kid,* manifested, displayed.

3137. *kirked,* probably 'crooked,' as Morris suggests. It may be a mere dialectal form of 'crooked,' or it may be miswritten for *kroked,* the usual old spelling. Halliwell gives, '*kirked,* turning upwards,' on the authority of Skinner; but a reference to Skinner shows that his reason for giving the word this sense was solely owing to a notion of deriving it from A. S. *cerran,* to turn, which is out of the question. On the strength of this Wright, in his Provincial Dictionary, makes up the verb: '*Kirk*, to turn upwards.' This is how glossaries are frequently written. The F. text merely has: 'Le nes froncié.'

3144. *maugree*, disfavour, ill will.

3185. *with the anger*, against the pain.

3231. *trasshed*, betrayed; F. traï. *Trasshen* is from the stem *traiss-*.

3234. *verger*, orchard; F. vergier; Lat. *uiridiarium*; so in ll. 3618, 3831.

3249. *to garisoun*, to protection, to safety; here, to your cure.

'Je ne voi mie ta santé,
Ne ta garison autrement.'

3251. *thee to werrey*, to war against thee; F. guerroier.

3256. *musarde*, sluggard; one who delays; F. musarde; see l. 4034.

3264. G. has *seyne*; Th. *sayne*. I prefer *feyne*. Not in the F. text.

3277. *passioun*, suffering, trouble; F. *poine* pain.

3284. *but in happe*, only in chance, i. e. a matter of chance.

3292. *a rage*, as in Th.; G. *arrage*. Cf. l. 3400.

3303. *leve*, believe; for the F. text has *croit*.

3326. *in the peine*, under torture; see Kn. Ta. A 1133.

3337. *chevisaunce*, resource, remedy. Both G. and Th., and all old editions, have *cherisaunce*, explained by Speght to mean 'comfort,' though the word is fictitious. Hence Kersey, by a misprint, gives '*cherisaunei*, comfort'; which Chatterton adopted.

3346. The F. text has 'Amis ot non'; so that 'Freend' is here a proper name.

3356. *meygned*, maimed. This word takes numerous forms both in M. E. and in Anglo-French.

3462. *at good mes*, at a favourable time (en bon point); see note to l. 1453.

3501. 'And Pity, (coming) with her, filled the Rosebud with gracious favour.' *of* = with.

3508. Supply *word*; F. La parole a premiere prise.

3539. Cf. 'Regia, crede mihi, res est succurrere lapsis'; Ovid, Ex Ponto, Ep. lib. ii. ix. 11.

3548. *This*, put for *This is*; as in Parl. Foules, 411.

3579. *moneste*, short for *amoneste*, i. e. admonish.

3604. 'You need be no more afraid.' Here Thynne has turned *thar* into *dare*; see l. 3761, and note to l. 1089.

3633. *to spanisshing*, to its (full) expansion. F. text, *espanie*, expanded, pp. fem. of *espanir*, which Cotgrave explains by 'To grow or spread, as a blooming rose.'

3645, 6. *vermayle*, ruddy, lit. vermilion. *abawed*, dismayed; variant of *abaved*, Book Duch. 614; cf. l. 4041 below.

3699. *werreyeth*, makes war upon; cf. Knight Ta. A 2235, 6. The corrections here made in the text are necessary to the sense.

3715. I. e. she did not belong to a religious order.

3718. *attour*; better *atour*; F. text *ator*; array, dress.
3740. *chasteleyne*, mistress of a castle; F. chastelaine.
3751. The reading is easily put right, by help of the French :—

> ' Car tant cum vous plus atendrez,
> Tant plus, sachies, de tens perdrez.'

3774. Read *it nil*, it will not; F. Qu'el ne soit troble (l. 3505).

3811. The F. text has *une vielle irese*, and M. Méon explains *irese* by angry, or full of ire. Hence, a note in Bell suggests that *irish* here means 'full of ire.' But I think M. Méon is wrong; for the O. F. for 'full of ire' is *irous*, whence M. E. *irous*; and M. Michel prints *Irese* with a capital letter, and explains it by 'Irlandaise.' Besides, there is no point in speaking of 'an old angry woman'; whereas G. de Lorris clearly meant something disrespectful in speaking of 'an old Irishwoman.' M. Michel explains, in a note, that the Irish character was formerly much detested in France. I therefore believe that *Irish* has here its usual sense.

3826. Where *Amyas* is, is of no consequence; for the name is wrongly given. The F. text has 'a Estampes ou a Miaus,' i.e. at Étampes or at Meaux. Neither place is very far from Paris. *Reynes* means Rennes in Brittany; see note to Book Duch. 255.

3827. *foot-hoot*, foot-hot, immediately; see note to Cant. Ta. B 438.

3832. *reward*, regard; as in Parl. Foules, 426.

3845. Insert *not*, because the F. text has 'Si *ne* s'est *mie*.'

3855. We should probably insert *him* after *hid*.

3856. *took*, i.e. caught; see l. 3858.

3880. Read *leye*, lay; both for rime and sense.

3882. *loigne*, leash for a hawk. Cotgrave gives: '*Longe*,... a hawks lune or leash.' This is the mod. F. *longe*, a tether, quite a different word from *longe*, the loin. *Longe*, a tether, was sometimes spelt *loigne* in O. F. (see Godefroy), which accounts for the form here used. It answers to Low Lat. *longia*, a tether, a derivative of *longus*, long. Perhaps *lune* is only a variant of the same word. The expression ' to have a long loigne ' means ' to have too much liberty.'

3895. Read *trecherous*, i.e. treacherous people, for the sake of the metre and the rime. *Trechours* means 'traitors.'

3907. Read *loude*; for *loude and stille* is an old phrase; see Barbour's Bruce, iii. 745. It means, 'whether loudly or silently,' i.e. under all circumstances.

3912. *blered is myn ye*, I am made a fool of; see Cant. Ta. G 730.

3917. Read *werreyed*, warred against; see note to l. 3699.

3928. I.e. 'I must (have) fresh counsel.'

3938. 'And come to watch how to cause me shame.'

3940-3. The F. text has :—

> ' Il ne me sera ja peresce
> Que ne face une forteresce
> Qui les Roses clorra entor.'

3954. 'And to blind him with their imposture.'

3962. Perhaps read *he durste*.

3987. *purpryse*, enclosure ; F. porprise, fem. Cotgrave has *pourpris*, m., in the same sense. See l. 4171.

4021. Read *in hy*, in haste, a common phrase ; see l. 3591.

4032. ' No man, by taming it, can make a sparrow-hawk of a buzzard.' A buzzard was useless for falconry, but a sparrow-hawk was excellent. The F. text gives this as a proverb. Two similar proverbs are given in Cotgrave, s. v. *Esparvier*.

4034. *musarde*, a sluggish, and hence a useless person ; see l. 3256.

4038. *recreaundyse*, recreant conduct ; F. *recreantise*.

4073. *goth afere*, goes on fire, is inflamed.

4096. *me* sometimes occurs in M. E. as a shorter form of *men*, in the sense of ' one ' ; but it is better to read *men* at once, as it receives the accent. If written ' mē,' it might easily be copied as ' me.'

4126. ' Unless Love consent, at another time.'

4149. *querrour*, a quarrier, stone-cutter ; see *quarrieur* in Cotgrave.

4176. *ginne*, war-engine. *skaffaut*, scaffold ; a wooden shed on wheels, to protect besiegers. See the description of one, called 'a sow,' employed at the siege of Berwick in 1319, in Barbour's Bruce, xvii. 597-600 ; together with other sundry 'scaffatis' in the same, l. 601.

4191. *Springoldes* (F. *perrieres*, from Lat. *petrariae*), engines for casting-stones ; spelt *spryngaldis* in Barbour's Bruce, xvii. 247. From O. F. *espringale*, a catapult ; from G. *springen*, to spring.

4195. *kernels*, battlements ; F. text, *creniaus*. Cf. P. Plowm. C. viii. 235 ; B. v. 597.

4196. *arblasters* (answering to Lat. *arcuballistra*), a variant form of *arblasts* or *arbalests* (answering to Lat. *arcuballista*), huge cross-bows, for discharging missiles. See *Arbalest* in the New E. Dict.

4229. *for stelinge*, i. e. to prevent stealing.

4248. *distoned*, made different in tone, out of tune. Cotgrave gives : '*Destonner*, to change or alter a tune, to take it higher or lower.'

4249. *Controve*, compose or invent tunes. *foule fayle*, fail miserably.

4250. *horn-pypes*, pipes made of horn ; but the F. text has *estives*, pipes made of straw. *Cornewayle* is doubtful ; some take it to mean Cornwall ; but it was more probably the name of a place in Brittany. A note in Méon's edition of Le Roman de la Rose, iii. 300, suggests ' la ville de *Cornouaille*, aujourd'hui *Quimper-Corentin*, qui est en basse Bretagne.' The F. text has *Cornoaille*.

4286. *vekke*, an old woman ; as in l. 4495. Cf. Ital. *vecchia*, the same ; but it is difficult to see how we came by the Ital. form.

4291. Some late editions read *expert*, which is clearly right ; *except* gives no sense. *Expt*, with a stroke through the *p*, may have been misread as *except*.

4300. F. ' Qu'el scet toute la vielle dance ' ; see Prol. A 476.

4322. The old reading gives no sense ; the corrected reading is due

NOTES. LINES 3954-4705. 437

to Dr. Kaluza. It means 'I weened to have bought it very knowingly';
F. Ges cuidoie avoir achetés, I weened to have bought them. *Ges =
Ge les*, i.e. *les biens*, the property. See note to l. 4352.

4333. For *also* perhaps read *als*, or *so*.

4352. *wend*, for *wende*, weened, supposed; F. cuidoie.

4372. For *wol* read *wal*; F. 'Qui est entre les *murs* enclose.'

4389. M. Méon here quotes a Latin proverb :—'Qui plus castigat, plus amore ligat.'

4432. G. de Lorris here ended his portion of the poem (containing 4070 lines), which he did not live to complete. His last line is :—

'A poi que ne m'en desespoir.'

When Jean de Meun, more than forty years later, began his continuation, he caught up the last word, commencing thus :—

'Desespoir, las! ge non ferai,
Jà ne m'en desespererai.'

4464. *a-slope*, on the slope, i.e. insecure, slippery.

4472. Perhaps *stounde* should be *wounde*. F. 'S'ele ne me fait desdoloir.' *Stounde* arose from repeating the *st* in *staunche*.

4499. *enforced*, made stronger, i.e. increased.

4510. Read *simpilly*; this trisyllabic form is Northern, occurring in Barbour's Bruce, i. 331, xvii. 134. Cf. l. 3861.

4525. 'Who was to blame?' Cf. l. 4529.

4532. *for to lowe*, to appraise; hence, to be valued at. F. 'De la value d'une pome.' See *Allow* in the New E. Dict.

4549. *The develles engins*, the contrivances of the devil.

4556. *yolden*, requited; cf. Somp. Ta. D 2177.

4559. 'Ought I to shew him ill-will for it?'

4568. 'And lie awake when I ought to sleep.'

4574. *taken atte gree*, receive with favour.

4617, 8. *not*, know not; *nist* (knew not) would suit better; see l. 4626. *eche*, eke out, assist.

4634. I insert *pyned*, punished; F. 'N'as tu mie éu mal assés?'

4646. 'Thou didst act not at all like a wise man.'

4668. 'See, there's a fine knowledge.' *Noble* is ironical, as in 4639.

4681. *with myn honde*; see note to l. 2037 above.

4689, 90. 'Si sauras tantost, sans science,
Et congnoistras, sans congnoissance.'

4697-4700. To him who flees love, its nature is explicable; to you, who are still under its influence, it remains a riddle.

4705. In Tyrwhitt's Gloss., s. v. *Fret*, he well remarks :—'In Rom. Rose, l. 4705, *And through the* fret full, read *A trouthe* fret full.' In fact, the F. text has: 'C'est loiautes la desloiaus.' *Fret full* is adorned or furnished, so as to be full; from A. S. *frætwian*, to adorn; cf. *fretted full*, Leg. of Good Women, 1117; and see Mätzner. Cf. l. 7259. On the whole, I do not think it is an error for *bret-ful*, i.e. brimful.

4712. This line is not in the F. text; it seems to mean—'a wave, harmful in wearing away the shore.'

4713. *Caribdis*, Charybdis, the whirlpool; cf. Horace, Carm. i. 27. 19.

4720. *Havoir*, property; usually spelt *avoir*.

4722. 'A thirst drowned in drunkenness'; F. 'C'est la soif qui tous jors est ivre.'

4728. *drerihed*, sadness; F. 'tristor'; cf. G. *Traurigkeit*.

4732. F. 'De pechies pardon entechies.' *without*, on the outside.

4747. *Pryme temps*, spring-time; F. 'Printems.'

4751. *a slowe*, a moth; F. taigne (Lat. tinea). But I know of no other example. Hence *were*, in the next line, must mean to wear away, to fret; cf. note to 4712.

4755. 'And sweethearts are as good in black mourning as when adorned in shining robes.' Cotgrave, s. v. *Amourette*, quotes a proverb: 'Aussi bien sont amourettes Soubs bureau, que soubs brunettes; Love bides in cottages, as well as in courts.' A *burnet* was a cloth of a superior quality; see note to l. 226.

4764. For *That* read *But*, answering to the F. *Qui...ne*.

4768. *Genius* is one of the characters in a later part of the F. text, l. 16497 (ed. Méon).

4790. *avaunt*, forward; F. 'Ge n'en sai pas plus que devant.'

4793. For *ever* read *er*, i. e. ere, before; for the rime.

4796. *can*, know. *parcuere*, by heart; F. 'par cuer.'

4831. 'For paramours only feign.' But the original has: 'Mes *par Amors* amer ne daignent,' i. e. 'But they do not deign to love like true lovers'; unless it is a mere exclamation, 'I swear by Love.'

4859. 'To save the progeny (or strain) of our species'; cf. Cl. Ta. E 157.

4875, 6. Not in the original. It seems to mean—'who very often seek after destroyed increase (abortion) and the play of love.' Cf. *tenen*, to harm. But no other instance of *for-tened* is known, nor yet of *crece* as short for *increes* (increase). However, the verb *cresen*, to increase, is used by Wyclif; see *cresce* in Stratmann, ed. Bradley.

4882-4. Alluding to Cicero's treatise De Senectute.

4901. 'And considers himself satisfied with no situation.'

4904. *Yalt him*, yields himself, goes; F. 'se rent.'

4910. I. e. to remain till he professes himself, his year of probation being over. So, in l. 4914, *leve his abit*, to give up his friar's dress.

4923. *Conteyne*, contain or keep himself; F. 'le tiegne.'

4943. *And mo* seems a mistake for *Demand*, i. e. 'he may go and ask them.' F. 'Ou le demant as anciens.'

5014. This sentence is incomplete; the translator has missed the line—'Et qu'ele a sa vie perdue.' And he missed it thus. He began: 'That, but [i. e. unless] aforn hir,' &c., and was going to introduce, further on, 'She findeth she hath lost hir lyf,' or something of that kind. But by the time he came to 'wade' at the end of l. 5022, where

NOTES. LINES 4712-5443.

this line should have come in, he had lost the thread of the sentence, and so left it out!

5028. *Who list have Ioye*; F. 'Qui .. veut joir.'

5047. *arn*, with the trilled *r*, is dissyllabic; see l. 5484.

5051. *so*, clearly an error for *sho*, Northern form of *she*.

5064. *druery*, courtship; but here, apparently, improperly used in the sense of 'mistress,' answering to 'amie' in the F. text.

5080. *ado*, short for *at do*, i. e. to do; *at* = to, is Northern.

5085. Read *they*; F. 'Més de la fole Amor se gardent.'

5107. Read *herberedest*; see Lounsbury, Studies in Chaucer, ii. 14. Pronounce it as *herb'redest*. F. 'hostelas,' from the verb *hosteler*.

5123, 4. As these lines are not in the original, the writer may have taken them from Chaucer's Hous of Fame, ll. 1257, 8. The converse seems to me unlikely; however, they are not remarkable for originality. Cf. note to l. 5486.

5124. *recured*, recovered; see examples in Halliwell.

5137. *That* refers to *love*, not to the *sermon*; and *hir* refers to Reason.

5162. The sense is doubtful; perhaps—'Then must I needs, if I leave it (i. e. Love), boldly essay to live always in hatred, and put away love from me, and be a sinful wretch, hated by all who love that fault.' Ll. 5165, 6 are both deficient, and require filling up.

5176. 'He who would not believe you would be a fool.' The omission of the relative is common; it appears (as *qui*) in the F. text. The line is ironical. Cf. ll. 5185-7.

5186. 'When that thou wilt approve of nothing.'

5191. 'But I know not whether it will profit.'

5223. I supply *Ne lak* (defect) *in hem*, to make some sense; the F. text does not help here. Half the line is lost; the rest means—'whom they, that ought to be true and perfect in love, would wish to prove.'

5266. A proverbial phrase; not in the F. text.

5274. *him* is here reflexive, and means 'himself.'

5278, 9, *fered*, fired, inflamed. *depart*, part, share.

5285. Read *amitee*; F. 'amitié.'

5286. Alluding to Cicero, De Amicitia: capp. xiii, xvii.

5292. The sense is; one friend must help another in every reasonable request; if the request seem unjust, he need not do so, except in two cases, viz. when his friend's life is in danger, or his honour is attacked: 'in quibus eorum aut caput agatur aut fama.' Read *in cases two*; F. 'en deux cas.'

5330. *bit not*, abides not, at any time; *bit* = *bideth*.

5341. For *hir* read *the*.

5353. The original reading would be *It hit*, i. e. it hideth; then *It* was dropped, and *hit* became *hidith*.

5384. *gote*, goat; but the F. text has *cers*, i. e. stag. *ramage*, wild.

5443. Obscure. The F. text has: 'Et que por seignors ne les

tiengnent' Perhaps it means: 'They perform it (their will) wholly; see l. 5447.

5452. Here *chere of* is for *there of*, with the common mistake of *c* for *t*.

5470. *Of*, i. e. off, off from.

5484. *arn*, with trilled *r*, is dissyllabic; as in l. 5047.

5486. 'Friend from affection (*affect*), and friend in appearance.' Chaucer, in his Balade on Fortune, l. 34, has 'Frend of *effect* [i. e. in reality], and frend of countenance.' And as the passage is not in the French, but is probably borrowed from Chaucer, we see that *effect* (not *affect*) is the right reading here; see l. 5549.

5491. The reading of Th. and G. is clearly wrong. The F. text helps but little. I read *al she*, i. e. all that she.

5507. *flaterye* is very inappropriate; we should expect *iaperye*, i. e. mockery. F. text, 'a vois jolie.'

5510. I. e. 'Begone, and let us be rid of you.' See Troilus, iii. 861, and note. (Probably borrowed from Chaucer.)

5513. From Prov. xvii. 17.

5523-9. 'This appears to be taken from Ecclus. xxii. 26.'—Bell. This reference is to the Vulgate; in the A. V., it is Ecclus. xxii. 22. Compare ll. 5521-2 with the preceding verse. With l. 5534 cf. Eccles. vii. 28.

5538. *valoure*, value; F. text, 'valor.' See 5556.

5541. So in Shakespeare; 2 Hen. IV. v. i. 34. Michel cites: 'Verus amicus omni praestantior auro.'

5569. F. text; 'Que vosist-il acheter lores'; &c.

5585, 6. I fill up the lines so as to make sense. *miches*, F. 'miches.' A *miche* is a loaf of fine manchet bread, of good quality; see Cotgrave. *chiche* (l. 5588) is 'niggardly.'

5590. *mauis*, (as in G. and Th.) is clearly an error for *muwis*, or, *muis*, bushels. The F. text has *muis*, i. e. bushels (from Lat. *modius*). For the M. E. form *muwe* or *mue*, cf. M. E. *puwe* or *pue* (Lat. *podium*). The A. F. form *muy* occurs in the Liber Custumarum, ed. Riley, i. 62.

5598. *that*, perhaps 'that gold'; see l. 5592. 'And though that (gold) lie beside him in heaps.' It is better to read *it*.

5600. *Asseth*, a sufficiency, enough; see note to P. Plowman, C. xx. 203; and the note to Catholicon Anglicum, p. 13, n. 6.

5619. *maysondewe*, hospital, lit. 'house of God.' See Halliwell.

5649. *Pictagoras*, Pythagoras; the usual form, as in Book Duch. 1167. He died about B.C. 510. He was a Greek philosopher, who taught the doctrine of the transmigration of souls, and he is here said to have taught the principle of the absorption of the soul into the supreme divinity. None of his works are extant. Hierocles of Alexandria, in the fifth century, wrote a commentary on the Golden Verses, which professed to give a summary of the views of Pythagoras.

5661. From Boethius, de Consolatione Philosophiæ, lib. i. pr. 5; lib. v. pr. 1. See notes to the Balade of Truth, ll. 17, 19.

5668. 'According as his income may afford him means.'

5673. *ribaud*, here used in the sense of 'a labouring man.' In the F. text he is spoken of as carrying 'sas de charbon,' i.e. sacks of coal.

5683. It is quite possible that Shakespeare caught up the phrase 'who would fardels bear,' &c., from this line in a black-letter edition of Chaucer. His next line—'To grunt and sweat under a weary life'—resembles ll. 5675-6; and 'The undiscovered country' may be from ll. 5658-5664. And see note to l. 5541. (But it is proper to add that Shakespearian scholars in general do not accept this as a possibility.)

5699. Read 'in sich a were'; F. 'en tel guerre.'

5700. Insert 'more'; F. ' Qu'il art tous jors de *plus* acquerre.'

5702. *yeten*, poured; a false form; correctly, *yoten*, pp. of *yeten*, to pour (A. S. *gēotan*, pp. *goten*).

5710. *Seyne*; F. 'Saine'; the river Seine (at Paris).

5739-5744. Not in the F. text, but inserted as a translation of some lines by Guiot de Provins, beginning: 'Fisicien sont apelé Sanz *fi* ne sont-il pas nommé.' See La Bible Guiot de Provins, v. 2582, in Fabliaux et Contes, édit. de Méon, tom. ii. p. 390. We must spell the words *fysyk* and *fysycien* as here written. A mild joke is intended. These words begin with *fy*, which (like E. *fie !*) means 'out upon it'; and go on with *sy* (=*si*), which means 'if,' and expresses the precariousness of trusting to doctors. Cf. Lounsbury, Studies in Chaucer, ii. 222.

5749. 'Because people do not live in a holy manner.' This is ironical. The word 'Her' refers to 'tho that prechen,' i.e. the clergy; F. 'devins.' But the F. text has—'*Cil* [i.e. the preachers] ne vivent pas loiaument.' See ll. 5750-1.

5759. Proverbial. F. 'Deceus est tex decevierres.' See Reves Ta. A 4321; P. Plowman, C. xxi. 166, and the note.

5799. *yeve*, gave, i.e. were to give; past pl. subjunctive.

5810. This answers to l. 5170 of the original; after which there is a gap of some 6000 lines, which are entirely lost in the translation. L. 5811 answers to l. 10717 of the F. text. The last portion, or part C, of the E. text (ll. 5811-7698) may be by a *third* hand. Part C is considerably better than Part B, and approaches very much nearer to Chaucer's style; indeed, Dr. Kaluza accepts it as genuine, but I am not myself (as yet) fully convinced upon this point. See further in the Introduction.

5811. At l. 10715 of the original, we have the lines :—

> 'Ainsinc Amors a eus parole,
> Qui bien reçurent sa parole.
> *Quant il ot sa raison fenie,*
> *Conseilla soi la baronnie.*'

Ll. 5811-2 of the E. text answer to the two last of these.

5824. *lyf* answers to F. *âme*; but the F. text has *arme*, a weapon.

5837. *To-moche-yeving*; F. 'Trop-Donner.'

5855, 6. *To,* i.e. against; F. 'Contre.' *Fair-Welcoming*; F. 'Bel-Acueil'; called *Bialacoil* in Fragment B of the translation.

5857. *Wel-Helinge,* good concealment; F. 'Bien-Celer.'

5894. *tan,* taken; common in the Northern dialect. So, perhaps, in l. 5900.

5931. *letting,* hindrance; F. 'puisse empéeschier.' He cannot prevent another from having what he has himself paid for.

5953. According to one account, Aphrodite was the daughter of Cronos and Euonyme; and the Romans identified Aphrodite with Venus, and Cronos with Saturnus. The wife of Cronos was Rhea.

5962. Two of the fathers were Mars and Anchises; and there are several other legends about the loves of Venus.

5966. *pole,* pool; F. 'la palu d'enfer.'

5978. Here *sparth,* with trilled *r,* appears to be dissyllabic; cf. ll. 3962, 5047, 5484, 6025. Or supply *with* before *gisarme.*

5984. *pulle,* pluck; as in Prol. A 652, &c.

5988. 'Unless they continue to increase (F. sourdent) in his garner.'

6002. *chinchy,* niggardly. For *grede* read *gnede,* i. e. stingy (person); A. S. *gnēð.*

6006. *beautee;* F. 'volonte'; read *leautee;* see l. 5959.

6009. For *wol* read *wolde;* F. 'Tous les méisse.'

6017. *they;* i. e. a number of barons; see l. 5812.

6024. 'They act like fools who are outrageous,' i. e. they act foolishly. F. 'Il ne feront mie que sage'; which seems to mean just the contrary.

6025. *forsworn,* with trilled *r,* seems to be trisyllabic; see note to l. 5978. But it is better to read *forsworen.*

6026. *Ne lette,* nor cease. Cf. l. 5967. But read *let,* pp. prevented.

6027. *piment* is much the same as *clarree;* in fact, in l. 5967, where the E. has *clarree,* the F. text has *piment.* Tyrwhitt says, s. v. *clarre;* 'wine mixed with honey and spices, and afterwards strained till it is clear. It is otherwise called *Piment,* as appears from the title of the following reccipt, in the *Medulla Cirurgiae Rolandi,* MS. Bodl. 761, fol. 86: Claretum bonum, sive Pigmentum,' &c., shewing that *piment* is spiced wine, with a third part of honey; see *Piment* in Halliwell.

6033. *vicaire,* deputy. In Méon's edition, the F. text has: 'Ja n'i querés autres victaires'; but Kaluza quotes five MSS. that read *vicaires.*

6037. *Lat ladies worche,* let ladies deal.

6044. 'Shall there never remain to them' (F. demorra).

6057. *This,* a common contraction for *This is;* cf. E. *'tis;* see 3548.

6068. *King of harlots;* F. 'rois des ribaus.' The sense is 'king of rascals.' There is a note on the subject in Méon's edition. It quotes Fauchet, Origine des Dignités, who says that the *roi des ribauds* was an officer of the king's palace, whose duty it was to clear out of it the men of bad character who had no business to be there. M. Méon quotes an extract from an order of the household of king Philippe, A.D. 1290:—'Le Roy des Ribaus, vi. d. de gages, une provende de xl. s. pour robbe pour tout l'an, et mengera à court et n'aura point de livraison.'

NOTES. LINES 5855-6264.

It further appears that the title of *Roi des ribaus* was often jocularly conferred on any conspicuous vagabond; as e. g. on the chief of a gang of strolling minstrels. See the note at p. 369 of Political Songs, ed. T. Wright, where it is shewn that the *ribaldi* were usually 'the lowest class of retainers, who had no other mode of living than following the courts of the Barons, and who were employed on all kinds of disgraceful and wicked actions.' The word *harlot* had, in Middle English, a similar sense.

6078. *mister*, need, use; F. 'mestier.'

6083. 'Which I do not care should be mentioned'; cf. l. 6093, which means—'They do not care to hear such tales.'

6103. 'If I say anything to impair (or lessen) their fame.'

6111. *Let*, short for *ledeth* : 'that he leads his life secretly.'

6120. 'Whilst every one here hears.'

6146. *to hulstred be*, to be concealed; cf. A.S. *heolstor*, a hiding-place.

6149. Remember that the speaker is Fals-Semblant, who often speaks ironically; he explains that he has nothing to do with *truly* religious people, but he dotes upon hypocrites. See l. 6171.

6169. *lete*, let alone, abandon; *lette* gives no sense.

6186. 'They offer the world an argument.'

6192. 'Cucullus non facit monachum'; a proverb.

'Non tonsura facit monachum, nec horrida uestis,
  Sed uirtus animi, perpetuusque rigor'; &c.
                    Alex. de Neckam (Michel).

6198. *cut*, for *cutteth*, cuts; F. trenche. 'Whom Guile cuts into thirteen branches.' I. e. Guile makes thirteen tonsured men at once; because the usual number in a convent was thirteen, viz. a prior and twelve friars.

6204. *Gibbe*, Gib (Gilbert); a common name for a tom-cat. Shak. has *gib-cat*, 1 Hen. IV. i. 2. 83. The F. text has *Tibers*, whence E. *Tibert, Tybalt*.

6205. A blank line in G.; Th. has—'That awayteth mice and rattes to killen,' which will not rime, and is spurious. I supply a line which, at any rate, rimes; *went his wyle* means 'turns aside his wiliness.' F. text—'Ne tent qu'a soris et a ras.'

6220. *aresoneth*, addresses him, talks to him.

6223. *what, devel*; i. e. what the devil.

6247. The legend of St. Ursula and the eleven thousand virgins, who were martyred by the Huns at Cologne in the middle of the fifth century, is mentioned by Alban Butler under the date of Oct. 21, and is told in the Legenda Aurea. The *ciergis* (in l. 6248) are wax-candles.

6256. Read *mak'th*, and (in 6255) *the god-e*.

6260. *wolf*; F. Sire Isangrin; such is the name given to the wolf in the Roman de Renard.

6264. *wery*, worry. Thynne has *wirry*. In P. Plowman, C. x. 226, we find the pl. *wyryeth*, with the various readings *wirieth*, *werien*, *werrieth*, *wery*. See *wurʒen* in Stratmann.

6267. *treget*, trickery; cf. Frank. Ta. F 1141, 1143.

6279. *trepeget*, a machine for casting stones; see *trepeget* in Halliwell, and my note to P. Plowman, A. xii. 91. A *mangonel* is a similar machine.

6280. *pensel*, banner; cf. P. Plowm. C. xix. 189. Short for *penoncel*.

6290. *stuffen*, furnish the wall with defenders.

6305. *my lemman*, my sweetheart (Abstinence), see l. 6341.

6317-8. Kaluza supplies the words within square brackets; G. has only 'But so sligh is the aperceyuyng,' followed by a blank line, in place of which Th. has the spurious line—'That al to late cometh knowyng.' F. text; 'Mès tant est fort la decevance Que trop est grief l'apercevance.'

6332. 'I am a man of every trade.'

6337. Sir Robert was a knight's name; Robin, that of a common man, as Robin Hood.

6338. *Menour*. The Friars Minors were the Franciscan, or Grey Friars; the Jacobins were the Dominicans, or Black Friars.

6339. *loteby*, wench; see P. Plowman, B. iii. 150, and note.

6341. Elsewhere called 'Streyned-Abstinence,' as in ll. 7325, 7366; F. 'Astenance-Contrainte,' i. e. Compulsory-Abstinence.

6345. I. e. 'Sometimes I wear women's clothes.'

6352. 'Trying all the religious orders.'

6354. All the copies wrongly have *bete* or *beate* for *lete*, i. e. leave. Some fancy the text is wrong, because Méon's edition has 'G'en pren le grain et laiz la paille.' But (says Kaluza) three MSS. have—'Je les le grain et pren la paille'; which better suits the context.

6355. *To blynde*, to hoodwink; F. 'avugler.' For *blynde*, G. and Th. actually have *Ioly*! I supply *ther*, i. e. where; for sense and metre.

6359. *bere me*, behave; *were me*, defend myself. The F. text varies.

6365. *lette*, hinder. The friars had power of absolution, independently of the bishop; and it was a bitter grievance.

6374. *tregetry*, a piece of trickery; see l. 6267.

6379. 'Through their folly, whether man or woman.'

6385. I. e. at Easter; see Pers. Tale, I 1027. See l. 6435.

6390. Note that the penitent is here supposed to address his **own** parish-priest. Thus *he* in l. 6391 means the friar.

6398. This is like the argument in the Somn. Ta. D 2095.

6418. *I*, for *me*, would be better grammar. As it stands, *me* is governed by *pleyne*, and *I* is understood. The F. text has: 'Si que ge m'en aille complaindre.'

6423. That is, the penitent will again apply to the friar.

6424. 'Whose name is not.' This means; such is his right name, but he does not answer to it; see l. 6428.

6425. 'He will occupy himself for me,' i. e. will take my part; **see** *Chevise* in the New E. Dict., sect. 4 b.

6434. 'Unless you admit me to communion.'

6449. *may never have might*, will never be able. If the priest is not confessed to, he will not understand the sins of his flock.

6452. *this*, i.e. this is; see notes to ll. 3548, 6057.

6454. See Prov. xxvii. 23; and cf. John, x. 14.

6464. 'I care not a bean for the harm they can do me.'

6469. 'Shall lose, by the force of the blow.' The rime is a bad one.

6491. Read *the acqueyntance*, as in Th.; F. 'l'acointance.'

6500. *yeve me dyne*, give me something to dine off.

6532. Read *thrittethe*, i.e. thirtieth. See Prov. xxx. 8, 9.

6541, 2. *Unnethe that he nis*, it is hard if he is not; i.e. he probably is. *micher*, a petty thief, a purloiner; F. 'lierres.' See the examples of *mich* in Halliwell. For *goddis*, read *god is*; F. 'ou Diex est mentieres.' See Prov. xxx. 9.

6556. 'The simple text, and neglect the commentary.'

6571. *bilden* is here used as a pt. tense; 'built.' In the next line, read *leye*, lay, lodged. There is an allusion to the splendid houses built by the friars.

6584. Not in the F. text.

6585. *writ*, writeth. Alluding to St. Augustine's work De Opere Monachorum, shewing how monks ought to exercise manual labour. His arguments are here made to suit the friars.

6615. '*De Mendicantibus validis;* Codex Justin. xi. 25. Justinian, whose celebrated code (called the Pandects) forms the basis of the Civil and Canon Law, was emperor of the Eastern Empire in 527.'—Bell.

6636. 'The allusion seems to be to Matt. xxiii. 14.'—Bell.

6645-52. Not in the F. text, ed. Méon; but found in some MSS.

6653. See Matt. xix. 21.

6665. Alluding, probably, to Eph. iv. 28.

6682. Alluding to Acts xx. 33-35.

6691. Alluding to St. Augustine's treatise De Opere Monachorum ad Aurelium episc. Carthaginensem. Of course he does not mention the Templars, &c.; these are only noticed by way of example.

6693. *templers*; 'the Knights Templars were founded in 1119 by Hugh de Paganis. Their habit was a white garment with a red cross on the breast. See Fuller, Holy Warre, ii. 16, v. 2.'—Bell. The Knights Hospitallers are described in the same work, ii. 4. The Knights of Malta belonged to this order.

6694. *chanouns regulers*, Canons living under a certain rule; see the Chan. Yemannes Tale.

6695. 'The White Monks were Cistercians, a reformed order of Benedictines; the Black, the unreformed.'—Bell.

6713. *I may abey*, 'I may suffer for it'; see Cant. Ta. C 100. The F. text varies.

6749. 'In the rescue of our law (of faith)'; i.e. of Christianity.

6763. William of Saint-Amour, a doctor of the Sorbonne, and a canon of Beauvais, about A.D. 1260, wrote a book against the friars, entitled De Periculis nouissimorum Temporum. He was answered by St. Bonaventure and St. Thomas Aquinas, his book was condemned by Pope Alexander IV, and he was banished from France (see l. 6777). See the note in Méon's edition of Le Roman.

6782. *This noble*, this brave man; F. 'Le vaillant homme.'

6787. *ich reneyed*, that I should renounce.

6796. *papelardye*, hypocrisy; see note to l. 415.

6810. *garners*; i. e. their garners contain things of value.

6811. *Taylagiers* (not in F. text), tax-gatherers. Cf. *taillage*, tax, tribute; P. Plowm. C. xxii. 37.

6814. 'The poor people must bow down to them.'

6819. *wryen himself*, cover himself, clothe himself.

6820. *pulle*, strip them, skin them. A butcher scalds a hog to make the hair come off more easily (Bell).

6824. 'And beguile both deceived men and deceivers.'

6831. *entremees*. Cotgrave has: '*Entremets*, certain choice dishes served in between the courses at a feast.'

6834. 'For, when the great bag (of treasure) is empty, it comes right again (i. e. is filled again) by my tricks.'

6838. Quoted in the Freres Tale, D 1451.

6861. *Bigyns*, Beguines; these were members of certain lay sisterhoods in the Low Countries, from the twelfth century onwards.

6862. *palasyns* (F. dames palasines), ladies connected with the court. Allied to F. *palais*, palace; cf. E. *palatine*.

6875. *Ayens me*, in comparison with me.

6887-6922. See Matt. xxiii. 1-8.

6911. *burdens*, repeated from ll. 6902, 6907, is clearly wrong. Perhaps read *borders*; F. 'philateres.'

6912. *hemmes*, borders of their garments, on which were phylacteries.

6948. *our alder dede*, the action of us all.

6952. *parceners*, partners; see *Partner* in my Etym. Dict.

6964. See 2 Cor. vi. 10.

6971. 'I intermeddle with match-makings.' See my note to P. Plowman, C. iii. 92 (B. ii. 87); and cf. Ch. Prol. A 212.

6976. I. e. 'yet it is no real business of mine.'

7000. The friars did not seek retirement, like the monks.

7016. *ravisable* (F. ravissables), ravenous, ravening; Matt. vii. 15.

7017. Imitated from Matt. xxiii. 15.

7018. *werreyen*, war; F. 'avons pris guerre.'

7022. *bougerons*, sodomites; see Godefroy; F. 'bogres.' This long sentence goes on to l. 7058; *if* (7021) is answered by *He shal* (7050).

7029. In G. and Th., *thefe* has become *these*, by confusion of *f* with long *s*; hence also *or* has become *that*. But the F. text has—'Ou lerres ou simoniaus.'

7038. *But*, unless; unless the sinners bribe the friars.

7043. *caleweys*, sweet pears of Cailloux in Burgundy. See my note to P. Plowman, B. xvi. 69. *pullaille*, poultry.

7044. *coninges*, conies, rabbits; F. 'connis.'

7049. *groine*, murmur; see note to Kn. Ta. A 2460.

7050. *loigne*, a length, long piece; see l. 3882.

7057. *smerten*, smart for; F. 'sera pugni.'

7063. *vounde* (so in G. and Th.), if a genuine word, can only be another form of *founde*, pp. of the strong verb *finden*, to find. I suppose 'found stone' to mean good building-stone, *found* in sufficient quantities in the neighbourhood of a site for a castle. The context shews that it here means stone of the first quality, such as could be wrought with the *squire* (mason's square) and to any required *scantilone* (scantling, pattern). The general sense clearly is, that the friars oppress the weak, but not the strong. If a man is master of a castle, they let him off easily, even if the castle be not built of freestone of the first quality, wrought by first-rate workmen. (Or read *founded*.)

7071. *sleightes*, missiles. The translator could think of no better word, because the context is jocular. If the lord of the castle pelted the friars, not exactly with stones, but with barrels of wine and other acceptable things, then the friars took his part.

7076. *equipolences*, equivocations. The next line suggests that he should refrain from coarse and downright lies *(lete* = let alone).

7089. 'And if it had not been for the good keeping (or watchfulness) of the University of Paris.' Alluding to William de St. Amour and his friends; see ll. 6554, 6766.

7092. See the footnote. We must either read *They had been turmented* (as I give it) or else *We had turmented* (as in Bell). I prefer *They*, because it is a closer translation, and suits better with *Such* in the next line.

7093. I insert *fals*, for the metre; it is countenanced by *traitours* in l. 7087. The reference is to the supporters of the book mentioned below.

7102. The book here spoken of really emanated from the friars, but was too audacious to succeed, and hence Fals-Semblant, for decency's sake, is made to denounce it. We may note how the keen satire of Jean de Meun contrives to bring in a mention of this work, under the guise of a violent yet half-hearted condemnation of it by a representative of the friars.

The book appeared in 1255 (as stated in the text), and was called Euangelium Eternum, siue Euangelium Spiritus Sancti. It was compiled by some Dominican and Franciscan friars, from notes made by an abbot named Joachim, and from the visions of one Cyril, a Carmelite. It is thus explained in Southey's Book of the Church, chap. xi. 'The opinion which they started was ... that there should be *three* Dispensations, one from each Person. That of the Father had terminated when the Law was abolished by the Gospel; ... the uses of the Gospel were obsolete; and in its place, they produced a book, in the name of the Holy Ghost, under the title of the Eternal Gospel. ... In this, however, they went too far: the minds of men were not yet subdued to this. The Eternal Gospel was condemned by the church; and the Mendicants were fain to content themselves with disfiguring the religion which they were not allowed to set aside.'

7108. 'In the porch before the cathedral of Notre Dame, at Paris.' A school was for some time held in this porch; and books could be bought there, or near it. Any one could there buy this book, 'to copy it, if the desire took him.'

7113. This is a quotation from the Eternal Gospel. L. 7118 means: 'I am not mocking you in saying this; the quotation is a true one.'

7116. *troubler*, dimmer; F. 'plus troble.'

7152. This shews that Fals-Semblaunt does not *really* condemn the book; he only says it is best to suppress it *for the present*, till Antichrist comes to strengthen the friars' cause. The satire is of the keenest. Note that, in l. 7164, Fals-Semblaunt shamelessly calls the Eternal Gospel '*our* book.' See also ll. 7211-2.

7173. I am obliged to supply two lines by guess here, to make out the sense. The F. text has:—

'Par Pierre voil le Pape entendre,
Et les clers seculiers comprendre
Qui la loi Iesu-Crist tendront,' &c.

I. e. By Peter I wish you to understand the pope, and to include also the secular clerks, &c. John represents the friars (l. 7185).

7178. I. e. 'against those friars who maintain all (this book), and falsely teach the people; and John betokens those (the friars) who preach, to the effect that there is no law so suitable as that Eternal Gospel, sent by the Holy Ghost to convert such as have gone astray.' The notion is, that the teaching of John (the type of the law of love, as expounded by the friars) is to supersede the teaching of Peter (the type of the pope and other obsolete secular teachers). Such was the 'Eternal Gospel'; no wonder that the Pope condemned it as being too advanced.

7197-7204. Obscure; and not fully in the F. text.

7217. The mother of Faux-Semblaunt was Hypocrisy (l. 6779).

7227. 'But he who dreads my brethren more than Christ subjects himself to Christ's wrath.'

7243. *patren*, to repeat Pater-nosters; see Plowm. Crede, 6.

7256. *Beggers* is here used as a proper name, answering to F. *Beguins*. The *Beguins*, members of certain lay brotherhoods which arose in the Low Countries in the beginning of the thirteenth century, were also called *Beguards* or *Begards*, which in E. became *Beggars*. There can be now no doubt that the mod. E. *beggar* is the same word, and the verb *to beg* was merely evolved from it. See the articles on *Beg, Beggar, Beghard,* and *Beguine* in the New E. Dict. All these names were derived from a certain Lambert Bègue. The Béguins were condemned at the council of Cologne in 1261, and at the general council of Vienne, in 1311. It seems probable that the term *Beggars* (*Beguins*) is here used derisively; the people really described seem to be the Franciscan friars, also called Gray friars; see l. 7258.

7259. *fretted*, ornamented, decked; from A. S. *frætwian*, to adorn; cf. l. 4705, and Leg. of Good Women, 1117; here ironical.

tatarwagges, ragged shreds, i. e. patches coarsely sewn on. See *tatter* in my Etym. Dict. The ending *-wagges* is allied to *wag*.

The F. text has: 'Toutes fretelées de crotes,' which means all bedaubed with dirt; see *frestelé* in Godefroy. The translation freely varies from the original, in a score of places. See next line.

7260. *knopped*, knobbed. *dagges*, clouts, patches. A more usual sense of *dagge* is a strip of cloth; see *dagge* in Stratmann.

7261. *frouncen*, shew wrinkles; cf. ll. 155, 3137. The comparison to a quail-pipe seems like a guess; in the F. text, we have *Hosiaus froncis*, wrinkled hose, and 'large boots like a *borce à caillier*,' said (in Méon) to mean a net for quails. Any way, the translation is sufficiently inaccurate.

7262. *riveling*, shewing wrinkles; *gype*, a frock or cassock; cf. *gipoun* in Prol. A 75.

7265. *Take*, betake, offer.

7282. Here again, *Beggar* answers to F. *Beguin*; see l. 7256.

7283. *papelard*, hypocrite; see l. 6796 and note to l. 415.

7288. *casting*, vomit; see 2 Pet. ii. 22.

7302. See note to l. 6068.

7316. 'Read *flayn* for *slayn*; F. Tant qu'il soit escorchiés.'—Kaluza.

7325. *Stryned*, constrained; F. 'Contrainte-Astenance.'

7348. *batels*, battalions, squadrons; see Gloss. to Barbour's Bruce.

7363. *in tapinage*, in secret. Cotgrave has: '*Tapinois, en tapinois*, Crooching, lurking ... also, covertly, secretly.' Also: '*Tapineux*, lurking, secret'; '*Tapi*, hidden'; '*Tapir*, to hide; *se tapir*, to lurk.'

7367. *camelyne*, a stuff made of camel's hair, or resembling it.

7372. *peire of bedis*, set of beads, rosary; see Prol. A 159.

7374. *bede*, might bid; pt. s. subjunctive.

7388. I. e. they often kissed each other.

7392. *that salowe horse*, that pale horse; Rev. vi. 8.

7403. *burdoun*, staff; F. 'bordon'; see ll. 3401, 4092.

7406. *elengeness*, cheerlessness; F. 'soussi,' i. e. *souci*, care, anxiety. See Wyf of B. Ta. D 1199.

7408. *saynt*, probably 'girt,' i. e. with a girdle on him like that of a Cordelier (Franciscan). The F. has 'qui bien se ratorne,' who attires himself well. (The epithet 'saint' is weak.) A better spelling would be *ceint*, but no other example of the word occurs. We find, however, the sb. *ceint*, a girdle, in the Prol. A 329, spelt *seint* in MS. Ln., and *seynt* in MSS. Cm. and Hl. *ie vous dy*, I tell you, occurs in the Somn. Ta. D 1832.

7422. *Coupe-Gorge*, Cut-throat; F. 'Cope-gorge.'

7455. *Joly Robin*, Jolly Robin, a character in a rustic dance; see Troil. v. 1174, and note.

7456. *Jacobin*, a Jacobin or Dominican friar. They were also called Black Friars and Friars Preachers (as in l. 7458). Their black robes gave them a melancholy appearance.

7459. 'They would but wickedly sustain (the fame of) their order, if they became jolly minstrels.'

7461. *Augustins*, Austin Friars; *Cordileres*, Cordeliers, Franciscan Friars; *Carmes*, Carmelites, or White Friars; *Sakked Friars*, Friars of the Sack. The orders of friars were generally counted as *four*; see note to Prol. A 210. These were the Dominican, Austin, Franciscan, and Carmelite Friars, all of whom had numerous houses in England. There were also Croutched Friars and Friars de Penitentia or de Sacco. The last had houses at Cambridge, Leicester, Lincoln, London, Lynne, Newcastle, Norwich, Oxford, and Worcester; see Godwin, Archæologist's Handbook, p. 178.

7467. 'But you will never, in any argument, see that a good result can be concluded from the mere outward appearance, when the inward substance has wholly failed.' Cf. Hous of Fame, 265-6.

7492. *fisshen*, fish for; see Somn. Ta. D 1820. Cf. Matt. iv. 19.

7520. We are here referred back to ll. 3815-3818, where Wicked-Tongue reports evil about the author (here called the 'young man') and Bialacoil (here called Fair-Welcoming).

7534. 'You have also caused the man to be chased.'

7538. The repetition of *thought* (in the rime) is correct; the F. text repeats *pensee*.

7562. 'Meditate there, you sluggard, all day.'

7573. 'Take it not amiss; it were a good deed.'

7578. F. text—'Vous en irez où puis [pit] d'enfer.' And, for *puis*, some MSS. have *cul*; a fact which at once sets aside the argument in Lounsbury's Studies in Chaucer, ii. 119.

7581. 'What? you are anything but welcome.'

7588. *tregetours*, deceivers; cf. *treget* above, l. 6267.

7605. *bemes*, trumpets; see Ho. Fame, 1240.

7628. *come*, coming; see *cume* in Stratmann.

7633. 'You would necessarily see him so often.'

7645. 'The blame (lit. the ill will) would be yours.' For the use of *maugre* as a sb., compare l. 4399.

7664. *Iolyly*, especially; a curious use; F. 'bien.'

7680, 1. 'To shrive folk that are of the highest dignity, as long as the world lasts.' So in the F. text.

7682. I. e. the Mendicant friars had license to shrive in any parish whatever.

7693. 'To read (i. e. give lectures) in divinity'; a privilege reserved for doctors of divinity.

7694. Here G. merely has a wrong half-line:—'And longe haue

red'; with which it abruptly ends, the rest of the page being blank, except that *explicit* is written, lower down, on the same page.

The last four lines in the F. text are :—

> 'Se vous volés ci confessier,
> Et ce pechié sans plus lessier
> Sans faire en jamés mencion,
> Vous auréz m'asolucion.'

The last of these lines is l. 12564 in Méon's edition. The last line in the whole poem is l. 22052; leaving 9488 lines untranslated, in addition to the gap of 5546 lines of the F. text at the end of Fragment B. Thus the three fragments of the translation make up less than a third of the original.

The fact that Thynne gives the last six lines correctly shews that his print was *not* made from the Glasgow MS. Indeed, it frequently preserves words which that MS. omits.

NOTES
TO
THE MINOR POEMS.

I. AN A B C.

THIS poem is a rather free translation of a similar poem by Guillaume de Deguileville, as pointed out in the Preface, p. 60. The original is quoted beneath the English text.

Explanations of the harder words should, in general, be sought for in the Glossarial Index, though a few are discussed in the Notes.

The language of this translation is, for the most part, so simple, that but few passages call for remark. I notice, however, a few points.

Chaucer has not adhered to the complex metre of the original, but uses a stanza of eight lines of five accents in place of de Deguileville's stanza of twelve lines of four accents.

3. Dr. Koch calls attention to the insertion of a second *of*, in most of the MSS., before *sorwe*. Many little words are often thus wrongly inserted into the texts of nearly all the Minor Poems, simply because, when the final *e* ceased to be sounded, the scribes regarded some lines as imperfect. Here, for example, if *sinne* be regarded as monosyllabic, a word seems required after it; but when we know that Chaucer regarded it as a dissyllabic word, we at once see that MSS. Gg. and Jo. (which omit this second *of*) are quite correct. We know that *sinne* is properly a dissyllabic word in Chaucer, because he rimes it with the infinitives *biginne* (Cant. Ta. C 941) and *winne* (same, D 1421), and never with such monosyllables as *kin* or *tin*. This is easily tested by consulting Mr. Cromie's very useful Rime-index to the Canterbury Tales. The above remark is important, on account of its wide application. The needless insertions of little words in many of the 15th-century MSS. are easily detected.

4. Scan the line by reading – Gloríous virgín', of all-e flóur-es flóur. Cf. l. 49.

6. *Debonaire*, gracious lady; used as a sb. Compare the original, l. 11.

8. Answers to l. 6 of the original—'Vaincu m'a mon aversaire.' Perhaps *Venquisht* is here the right form; similarly, in the Squieres Tale, F 342, the word *vanisshed* is to be read as *vanish'd*, with the accent on

I. AN A B C. LINES 3-29. 453

the second syllable, and elision of *e*. See Ten Brink, Chaucers Sprache, § 257. Otherwise, read *Venquis-shed m'hath*; cf. *mexcuse*, XVI. 37 (p. 397).

11. *Warne*, reject, refuse to hear. So in P. Plowman, C. xxiii. 12, 'whanne men hym *werneth*' means ' when men refuse to give him what he asks for.'

12. *Free*, liberal, bounteous. So in Shak. Troilus, iv. 5. 100—' His heart and hand both open and both *free*.' It may be remarked, once for all, that readers frequently entirely misunderstand passages in our older authors, merely because they forget what great changes may take place in the sense of words in the course of centuries.

13. *Largesse*, i.e. the personification of liberality; 'thou bestowest perfect happiness.'

14. Cf. original, l. 15—' Quer [*for*] tu es de salu porte.' Scan by reading—Háv'n of refút. But in l. 33, we have *réfut*.

15. *Theves seven*, seven robbers, viz. the seven deadly sins. We could easily guess that this is the meaning, but it is needless; for the original has—' Par sept larrons, pechies mortez,' l. 17; and a note in the Sion Coll. MS. has—' i. seven dedly synnes.' The theme of the Seven Deadly Sins is one of the commonest in our old authors; it is treated of at great length in Chaucer's Persones Tale, and in Piers Plowman.

16. 'Ere my ship go to pieces'; this graphic touch is not in the original.

17. *Yow*, you. In addressing a superior, it was customary to use the words *ye* and *you*, as a mark of respect; but, in prayer, the words *thou* and *thee* were usual. Hence, Chaucer has mixed the two usages in a very remarkable way, and alternates them suddenly. Thus, we have *thee* in l. 5, *thou* in l. 6, &c., but *yow* in l. 17, *thy* in l. 19, *you* in l. 24; and so on. We even find the plural verbs *helpen*, l. 104; *Beth*, l. 134; and *ben*, l. 176.

20. *Accioun*, action, is here used in the legal sense; 'my sin and confusion have brought an action (i.e. plead) against me.' It is too close a copy of the original, l. 25—' Contre moy font une accion.'

21. I.e. 'founded upon rigid justice and a sense of the desperate nature of my condition.' Cf. ' Rayson et desperacion Contre moy veulent maintenir'; orig. l. 29. *Maintenir*, to maintain an action, is a legal term. So, in l. 22, *sustene* means ' sustain the plea.'

24. ' If it were not for the mercy (to be obtained) from you.'

25. Literally—' There is no doubt that thou art not the cause'; meaning, ' Without doubt, thou art the cause.' *Misericorde* is adopted from the original. According to the usual rule, viz. that the syllable *er* is usually slurred over in Chaucer when a vowel follows, the word is to be read as *mis'ricord-e*. So also *sov'reyn*, l. 69.

27. *Vouched sauf*, vouchsafed. *Tacorde*, to accord; cf. *talyghte*, *tamende*, &c. in the Cant. Tales.

29. Cf. 'S'encore fust l'arc encordé'; orig. l. 47; and 'l'arc de

justice,' l. 42. The French expression is probably borrowed (as suggested in Bell's Chaucer) from Ps. vii. 13—' arcum suum tetendit.' Hence the phrase *of Iustice and of yre* refers to *the bowe*.

30. *First*, at first, before the Incarnation.

36. For examples of the use of *great assize*, or *last assize*, to signify the Last Judgment, see the New E. Dict., s. v. *Assize*.

39. Most MSS. read here—'That but thou er [*or* or] that day correcte me'; this cannot be right, because it destroys the rime. However, the Bedford MS., instead of *correcte me*, has *Me chastice*; and in MS. C *me chastyse* is written over an erasure (doubtless of the words *correcte me*). Even thus, the line is imperfect, but is completed by help of the Sion MS., which reads *me weel chastyce*.

40. *Of verrey right*, in strict justice; not quite as in l. 21.

41. Rather close to the original—' Fuiant m'en viens a ta tente Moy mucier pour la tormente Qui ou monde me tempeste,' &c. *Mucier* means ' to hide,' and *ou* means ' in the,' F. *au*.

45. *Al have I*, although I have. So in l. 157.

49. MS. Gg. has *Gracyouse*; but the French has *Glorieuse*.

50. *Bitter*; Fr. text ' amere.' The allusion is to the name *Maria*, Gk. Μαρία, Μαριάμ, the same as *Miriam*, which is explained to mean ' bitterness,' as being connected with *Marah*, i. e. bitterness; see Exod. xv. 23 (Gesenius). Scan the line by reading: *neith'r in érth-ë nór*.

55. *But-if*, except, unless (common).

56. *Stink* is oddly altered to *sinke* in some editions.

57, 58. Closely copied from the French, ll. 85-87. But the rest of the stanza is nearly all Chaucer's own. Cf. Col. ii. 14.

67. The French means, literally—' For, when any one goes out of his way, thou, out of pity, becomest his guide, in order that he may soon regain his way.'

70. The French means—' And thou bringest him back into the right road.' This Chaucer turns into—' bringest him out of the wrong road '; which is all that is meant by *the crooked strete*.

71. In the ending *-eth* of the third pers. sing. present, the *e* is commonly suppressed. Read *lov'th*. So also *com'th* in l. 99.

73. The French means—' Calendars are illumined, and other books are confirmed (or authenticated), when thy name illumines them.' Chaucer has 'illuminated calendars, in this world, are those that are brightened by thy name.' ' An allusion to the custom of writing the high festivals of the Church in the Calendar with red, or illuminated, letters'; note in Bell's Chaucer. The name of Mary appears several times in old calendars; thus the Purification of Mary is on Feb. 2; the Annunciation, on Mar. 25; the Visitation, on July 2; the Assumption, on Aug. 15; the Nativity, on Sept. 8; the Presentation, on Nov. 21; the Conception, on Dec. 8. Our books of Common Prayer retain all of these except the Assumption and the Presentation. *Kalenderes* probably has four syllables; and so has *enlumined*. Otherwise, read Kálendér's (Koch).

76. *Him thar*, i.e. it needs not for him to dread, he need not dread. It occurs again in the Cant. Tales, A 4320, D 329, 336, 1365, &c.

80. *Resigne* goes back to l. 112 of the original, where *resiné* (=*resigne*) occurs.

81. Here the French (l. 121) has *douceur*; Koch says it is clear that Chaucer's copy had *douleur*; which refers to the *Mater dolorosa*.

86. This line runs badly in the MSS., but is the same in nearly all. Read *both' hav-e*. I should prefer *hav' both-e*, where *bothe* is dissyllabic; see ll. 63, 122. This runs more evenly. The sense of ll. 84-6 seems to be—'Let not the foe of us all boast that he has, by his wiles (*listes*), unluckily convicted (of guilt) that (soul) which ye both,' &c.

88. Slur over the last syllable of *Continue*, and accent *us*.

89. The French text refers to Exod. iii. 2. Cf. The Prioresses Tale, C. T. Group B, l. 1658.

97. Koch points out that *per-e* is here dissyllabic; as in the Compleint to His Purse, l. 11. The French has *per*, l. 146. Read— Nóble princésse, &c.

100. *Melodye or glee*; here Koch remarks that Chaucer 'evidently mistook *tirelire* for *turelure*.' The Fr. *tirelire* means a money-box, and the sense of l. 150 of the original is—'We have no other place in which to secure what we possess.' See l. 107 of Chaucer's translation below. But Chaucer's mistake was easily made; he was thinking, not of the mod. Fr. *turelure* (which, after all, does not mean a 'melody,' but the refrain of a song, like the Eng. *tooral looral*) but of the O. F. *tirelire*. This word (as Cotgrave explains) not only meant 'a box having a cleft on the lid for mony to enter it,' but 'also the warble, or song of a lark.' Hence Shakespeare speaks of 'the lark, that *tirra-lyra* chants,' Wint. Tale, iv. 3. 9.

102. Read *N'ad'vócat noón*. That the M. E. *advocat* was sometimes accented on the *o*, is proved by the fact that it was sometimes cut down to *vócat*; see P. Plowman, B. ii. 60; C. iii. 61.

109. Cf. Luke, i. 38—'Ecce *ancilla* Domini.'

110. *Oure bille*, &c., i.e. 'to bring forward (or offer) a petition on our behalf.' For the old expression 'to put up (or forth) a bill,' see my note to P. Plowman, C. v. 45. Compare also Compleynte unto Pite, l. 44 (p. 273).

113. Read *tym-e*. *Tenquere*, for *to enquere*; cf. note to l. 27. Cf. the French *d'enquerre*, l. 169.

116. *To werre*; F. 'pour guerre,' l. 173; i.e. 'by way of attack.' *Us* may be taken with *wroughte*, i.e. 'wrought for us such a wonder.' *Werre* is not a verb; the verb is *werreyen*, as in Squi. Ta. l. 10.

119. *Ther*, where, inasmuch as. 'We had no salvation, inasmuch as we did not repent; if we repent, we shall receive it.' But the sentence is awkward. Cf. Mark i. 4; Matt. vii. 7.

122. Pause after *both-e*; the *e* is not elided.

125. *Mene*, mediator; lit. mean (intermediate) person. So in P. Plowman, B. vii. 196—'And Marie his moder be owre *mene* bitwene.'

132. Koch thinks that the false reading *it* in some MSS. arose from a reading *hit* (=hitteth) as a translation of F. *fiert*, l. 196. Anyway, the reading *is* seems best. Surely, 'his reckoning hitɛ so hideous' would be a most clumsy expression.

136. *Of pitee*, for pity; the usual idiom. Cf. *of al*, XIII. 19 (p. 301).

140. *Vicaire*, deputed ruler; not in the original. See note to Parliament of Foules, l. 379.

141. *Governeresse*; copied from the French text, l. 214. This rare word occurs, as the last word, in a poem beginning 'Mother of norture, printed in the Aldine Edition of Chaucer's Poems, vi. 275. Chaucer himself uses it again in the Complaint to Pity, l. 80 (p. 275).

144. Compare the expressions *Regina Celi*, *Veni coronaberis*, 'Heil crowned queene,' and the like; Polit., Religious, and Love Poems, ed. Furnivall, p. 147; Hymns to the Virgin, ed. Furnivall, pp. 1, 4. Suggested by Rev. xii. 1.

146. Koch notes that the reading *deprived* arose from its substitution for the less familiar form *prived*.

150. The reference is, obviously, to Gen. iii. 18; but thorns here mean sins. Cf. 'Des espines d'iniquite'; F. text, l. 224.

158. Copied from the French, l. 239—'Ou tu a la court m'ajournes.' It means 'fix a day for me to appear at thy court,' cite me to thy court.

159. Not in the original. Chaucer was thinking of the courts of the Common Bench and King's Bench, as mentioned, for example, in Wyclif's Works, ed. Arnold, iii. 215.

161. The word *Xristus*, i.e. *Christus*, is written Xpc (with a mark of contraction) in MSS. C., Gl., Gg., and Xpūs in F. Xpc is copied from the French; but it is very common, being the usual contracted form of the Gk. Χριστός, or, in capital letters, ΧΡΙCΤΟC, obtained by taking the two first and the last letters. The old Greek *sigma* was written C; as above. De Deguileville could think of no French word beginning with X; so he substituted for it the Greek *chi*, which resembled it in form.

163, 164. These lines answer to ll. 243, 247 of the French; 'For me He had His side pierced; for me His blood was shed.' Observe that the word *Christus* has no verb following it; it is practically an objective case, governed by *thanke* in l. 168. 'I thank thee because of Christ and for what He has done for me.' In l. 163, the word *suffre* is understood from the line above, and need not be repeated. Unfortunately, all the scribes *have* repeated it, to the ruin of the metre; for the line then contains two syllables too many. However, it is better omitted. *Longius* is trisyllabic, and *herte* (as in the next line) is dissyllabic. The sense is—'to suffer His passion on the cross, and also (to suffer) that Longius should pierce His heart, and make,' &c. *Pighte*, *made*, are in the subjunctive. The difficulty really resides in the word *that* in l. 161. If Chaucer had written *eek* instead of it, the whole could be parsed.

Koch reads 'Dreygh eek' for 'And eek,' in l. 163, where 'Dreygh' means 'endured.' But I do not think *Dreygh* could be used in this connection, with the word *that* following it.

I. AN A B C. LINES 132-184.

The story of Longius is very common; hence Chaucer readily introduced an allusion to it, though his original has no hint of it. The name is spelt *Longeus* in Piers Plowman, C. xxi. 82 (and is also spelt *Longinus*). My note on that passage says—'This story is from the Legenda Aurea, cap. xlvii. Longinus was a blind centurion, who pierced the side of Christ; when drops of the Sacred Blood cured his infirmity. The day of St. Longinus is Mar. 15; see Chambers, Book of Days. The name *Longinus* is most likely derived from λόγχη, a lance, the word used in John xix. 34; and the legend was easily developed from St. John's narrative. The name Longinus first appears in the Apocryphal Gospel of Nicodemus.' See also the Chester Plays, ed. Wright; Cursor Mundi, p. 962; Coventry Mysteries, ed. Halliwell, p. 334; York Mystery Plays, p. 368; Lamentation of Mary Magdalen, st. 26; &c.

164. *Herte* is the true M. E. genitive, from the A. S. gen. *heortan*. *Herte blood* occurs again in the Pardoneres Tale, C 902.

169-171. Close to the French, ll. 253-5; and l. 174 is close to l. 264 of the same. Cf. Heb. xi. 19; Jo. i. 29; Isaiah, liii. 7.

176. This line can best be scanned by taking *That* as standing *alone*, in the first foot. See note to Compl. to Pite, l. 16. Koch suggests that *our-e* is dissyllabic; but this would make an unpleasing line; 'That yé | ben fróm | veng'áunce | ay oú | re targe||.' I hope this was not intended; 'fróm | veng'áun | cë áy | our' would be better.

177. The words of Zechariah (xiii. 1) are usually applied to the blood of Christ, as in Rev. i. 5. Chaucer omits ll. 266-7 of the French.

180. 'That were it not (for) thy tender heart, we should be destroyed.'

181. Koch, following Gg, reads—'Now lady bright, siththe thou canst and wilt.' I prefer 'bright-e, sith'; *brighte* is a vocative.

184. *To mercy able*, fit to obtain mercy; cf. Cant. Ta. Prol. 167.

II. THE COMPLEYNTE UNTO PITE.

TITLE. In MS. B., the poem is entitled, 'The Complaynte vnto Pyte,' which is right. In MS. Trin., there is a colophon—'Here endeth the exclamacioun of the Deth of Pyte'; see p. 276. In MS. Sh. (in Shirley's handwriting) the poem is introduced with the following words—'And nowe here filowing [*following*] begynnethe a complaint of Pitee, made by Geffray Chaucier the aureat Poete that euer was fonde in oure vulgare to-fore hees [*for* thees?] dayes.' The first stanza may be considered as forming a Proem; stanzas 2-8, the Story; and the rest, the Bill of Complaint. The title 'A complaint of Pitee' is not necessarily incorrect; for *of* may be taken in the sense of 'concerning,' precisely as in the case of 'The Vision of Piers the Plowman.' As to the connection of this poem with the Thebaid of Statius, see notes to ll. 57 and 92.

1. I do not follow Ten Brink in putting a comma after *so*. He says: 'That *so* refers to the verb [*sought*] and not to *yore ago*, is evident from l. 3. Compare the somewhat different l. 93.' I hope it shews no disrespect to a great critic if I say that I am not at all confident that the above criticism is correct; l. 93 rather tells against it. Observe the reading of l. 117 in MS. Sh. (in the footnotes, p. 276).

4. *With-oute dethe*, i.e. without actually dying.

Shal not, am not to.

7. *Doth me dye*, makes me die.

9. *Ever in oon*, continually, constantly, always in the same way; cf. Cant. Tales, E 602, 677, F 417.

11. *Me awreke*. 'The *e* of *me* is elided'; Ten Brink. He compares also Cant. Ta. Prol. 148; (the correct reading of which is, probably—

'But sorë weep sche if oon of hem were deed';

the *e* of *sche* being slurred over before *i* in *if*). He also refers to the Prioresses Tale (B 1660), where *thalighte = thee alighte*; and to the Second Nonnes Tale (G 32), where *do me endyte* is to be read as *do mendyte*. Cf. note to A B C, l. 8.

14. The notion of Pity being '*buried in* a heart' is awkward, and introduces an element of confusion. If Pity could have been buried *out of* the heart, and thus *separated* from it, the whole would have been a great deal clearer. This caution is worth paying heed to; for it will really be found, further on, that the language becomes confused in consequence of this very thing. In the very next line, for example, the hearse of Pity appears, and in l. 19 the corpse of Pity; in fact, Pity is never fairly buried out of sight throughout the poem.

15. *Herse*, hearse; cf. l. 36 below. It should be remembered that the old *herse* was a very different thing from the modern *hearse*. What Chaucer refers to is what we should now call 'a lying in state'; with especial reference to the array of lighted torches which illuminated the bier. See the whole of Way's note in Prompt. Parvulorum, pp. 236, 237, part of which is quoted in my Etym. Dict., s. v. *hearse*. The word *hearse* (F. *herce*) originally denoted a harrow; next, a frame with spikes for holding lights in a church service; thirdly, a frame for lights at a funeral pageant or 'lying in state'; fourthly, the funeral pageant itself; fifthly, a frame on which a body was laid, and so on. 'Chaucer,' says Way, 'appears to use the term *herse* to denote the decorated bier, or funeral pageant, and not exclusively the illumination, which was a part thereof; and, towards the sixteenth century, it had such a general signification alone.' In ll. 36-42, Chaucer describes a company of persons who stood round about the hearse. Cf. Brand's Popular Antiquities, ed. Ellis, ii. 236-7; Eng. Gilds, ed. Toulmin Smith, p. 176.

'The *hearse* was usually a four-square frame of timber, which was hung with black cloth, and garnished with flags and scutcheons and lights'; Strutt, Manners and Customs of the English, iii. 159. See the whole passage, which describes the funeral of Henry VII.

II. COMPLEYNTE UNTO PITE. LINES 1-64.

16. In most MSS., *Deed* stands alone in the first foot. In which case, scan—Deed | as stoon | whyl that | the swogh | me laste. Cf. A B C, l. 176, and the note. However, two MSS. insert *a*, as in the text.

27. Cf. *Deth of Blaunche*, l. 587—'This is my peyne withoute reed'; Ten Brink. See p. 297.

33. Ten Brink reads *ay* for *ever*, on the ground that *ever* and *never*, when followed by a consonant, are dissyllabic in Chaucer. But see Book of the Duchesse, l. 73 (p. 279).

34. *Hadde*, dissyllabic; it occasionally is so; mostly when it is used by itself, as here. Cf. Book of the Duch. l. 951 (p. 309).

37. 'Without displaying any sorrow.' He now practically identifies Pity with the fair one in whose heart it was said (in l. 14) to be buried. This fair one was attended by Bounty, Beauty, and all the rest; they are called a *folk* in l. 48.

41. Insert *and* after *Estaat* or *Estat*, for this word has no final -*e* in Chaucer; see Prol. A 522; Squi. Tale, F 26; &c.

44. 'To have offered to Pity, as a petition'; see note to A B C, 110.

47. 'I kept my complaint quiet,' i. e. withheld it; see l. 54.

50. MS. Sh. is right. The scribe of the original of MSS. Tn. Ff. T. left out *I* and *these*, and then put in *only*; then another scribe, seeing that a pronoun was wanted, put in *we*, as shewn by MSS. F. B. (Ten Brink). Here, and in l. 52, the *e* of *alle* is either very lightly sounded after the cæsural pause, or (more likely) is dropped altogether, as elsewhere.

53. *And been assented*, and (who) are all agreed.

54. *Put up*, put by. Cf. 'to *put up* that letter'; K. Lear, i. 2. 28: &c.

57. He here addresses his fair one's Pity, whom he personifies, and addresses as a mistress.

By comparison of this passage with l. 92, it becomes clear that Chaucer took his notion of personifying *Pity* from Statius, who personifies *Pietas* in his Thebaid, xi. 457-496. I explained this at length in a letter to The Academy, Jan. 7, 1888, p. 9. In the present line, we find a hint of the original; for Statius describes *Pietas* in the words 'pudibundaque longe Ora reducentem' (l. 493), which expresses her *humility*; whilst the *reverence* due to her is expressed by *reuerentia* (l. 467).

59. *Sheweth ... Your servaunt*, Your servant sheweth. *Sheweth* is the word used in petitions, and *servant* commonly means 'lover.'

63. Accented *rénoun*, as in the Ho. of Fame, 1406. Cf. l. 86.

64. *Crueltee*, Cruelty, here corresponds to the Fury Tisiphone, who is introduced by Statius (*Theb.* xi. 483) to suppress the peaceful feelings excited by Pietas, who had been created by Jupiter to control the passions even of the gods (l. 465). At the siege of Thebes, Pietas was for once overruled by Tisiphone; and Chaucer complains here that she is again being controlled; see ll. 80, 89-91. Very similar is the character of *Daungere* or Danger (F. *Dangier*) in the Romaunt of

the Rose; in l. 3549 of the English Version (l. 3301 of the original), we find Pity saying—

> 'Wherefore I pray you, Sir Daungere,
> For to mayntene no lenger here
> Such cruel werre agayn your man.'

We may also compare Machault's poem entitled Le Dit du Vergier, where we find such lines as—

> 'Einssi encontre Cruauté
> Deffent l'amant douce Pité.'

66. *Under colour*, beneath the outward appearance.

67. 'In order that people should not observe her tyranny.'

70. *Hight*, is (rightly) named. The final -*e*, though required by grammar, is suppressed; the word being conformed to other examples of the third person singular of the *present* tense, whilst *hight-e* is commonly used as the *past* tense. Pity's right name is here said to be 'Beauty, such as belongs to Favour.' The poet is really thinking of his mistress rather than his personified Pity. It is very difficult to keep up the allegory.

71. '*Heritage*, of course, stands in the gen. case'; Ten Brink.

76. *Wanten*, are lacking, are missing, are not found in, fall short. 'If you, Pity, are missing from Bounty and Beauty.' There are several similar examples of this use of *want* in Shakespeare; e.g. 'there *wants* no junkets at the feast'; Tam. Shrew, iii. 2. 250.

78. This *Bille*, or Petition, may be divided into three sets of 'terns,' or groups of three stanzas. I mark this by inserting a paragraph-mark (¶) at the beginning of each tern. They are marked off by the rimes; the first tern ends with *seyne*, l. 77; the next with the riming word *peyne*, l. 98; and again with *peyne*, l. 119.

83. *Perilous* is here accented on the *i*.

87. Ten Brink omits *wel*, with most of the MSS.; but the *e* in *wite* seems to be suppressed, as in Book of the Duch. 112. It will hardly bear a strong accent. Mr. Sweet retains *wel*, as I do.

91. Pronounce the third word as *despeir'd*. 'Compare 1 Kings x. 24: And all the earth *sought to* Solomon'; Ten Brink.

92. *Herenus* has not hitherto been explained. It occurs in four MSS., Tn. F. B. Ff.; a fifth (T.) has 'herem*us*'; the Longleat MS. has 'heremus' or 'herenius'; Sh. substitutes 'vertuouse,' and MS. Harl. 7578 has 'Vertoues'; but it is highly improbable that *vertuouse* is original, for no one would ever have altered it so unintelligibly. Ten Brink and Mr. Sweet adopt this reading *vertuousë*, which they make four syllables, as being a vocative case; and of course this is an easy way of *evading* the difficulty. Dr. Furnivall once suggested *hevenus*, which I presume is meant for 'heaven's'; but this word could not possibly be accented as *hevénus*. The strange forms which proper names assume in Chaucer are notorious; and the fact is, that *Herenus* is a mere error for *Herines* or *Herynes*. *Herynes* (accented on *y*),

occurs in St. 4 of Bk. iv of Troilus and Criseide, and is used as the plural of *Erinnys*, being applied to the three Furies:—'O ye *Herynes*, nightes doughtren thre.' Pity may be said to be the *queen* of the Furies, in the sense that pity (or mercy) can alone control the vindictiveness of vengeance. Shakespeare tells us that mercy 'is mightiest in the mightiest,' and is 'above this sceptred sway'; Merch. Ven. iv. 1. 188.

Chaucer probably found this name precisely where he found his personification of Pity, viz. in Statius, who has the sing. *Erinnys* (Theb. xi. 383), and the pl. *Erinnyas* (345). Cf. Æneid, ii. 337, 573.

In a poem called The Remedy of Love, in Chaucer's Works, ed. 1561, fol. 322, back, the twelfth stanza begins with—'Come hither, thou Hermes, and ye furies all,' &c., where it is plain that 'thou Hermes' is a substitution for 'Herines.'

95. The sense is—'the longer I love and dread you, the more I do so.' If we read *ever* instead of *ay*, then the *e* in *the* must be suppressed. 'In *ever lenger the moore, never the moore, never the lesse*, Chaucer not unfrequently drops the *e* in *the*, pronouncing *lengerth, neverth*'; cf. Clerkes Tale, E 687; Man of Lawes Tale, B 982; Ten Brink.

96. Most MSS. read *so sore*, giving no sense. Ten Brink has— 'For sooth to seyne, I bere the hevy soore'; following MS. Sh. It is simpler to correct *so* to *the*, as suggested by Harl. 7578, which has— 'For soith [*error for* sothly] for to saye I bere the sore.'

101. *Set*, short for *setteth*, like *bit* for *biddeth*, Cant. Tales, Prol. 187, &c. Ten Brink quotes from the Sompnoures Tale (D 1982)—'With which the devel *set* your herte a-fyre,' where *set* = sets, present tense.

105. Ten Brink inserts *ne*, though it is not in the MSS. His note is: '*Ne* is a necessary complement to *but* = "only," as *but* properly means "except"; and a collation of the best MSS. of the Cant. Tales shows that Chaucer never omitted the negative in this case. (The same observation was made already by Prof. Child in his excellent paper on the language of Chaucer and Gower; see Ellis, *Early Eng. Pronunciation*, p. 374.) *Me ne* forms but one syllable, pronounced *meen* [i.e. as mod. E. *main*]. In the same manner *I ne = iin* [pron. as mod. E. *een*] occurs, Cant. Tales, Prol. 764 (from MS. Harl. 7334)—

"I *ne* saugh this yeer so mery a companye";

and in the Man of Lawes Tale (Group B, 1139)—

"*I ne* seye but for this ende this sentence."

Compare Middle High German *in* (= *ich ne*), e.g. *in kan dir nicht*, Walter v. d. Vogelweide, ed. Lachmann, 101. 33. In early French and Provençal *me, te, se,* &c., when preceded by a vowel, often became *m, t, s,* &c.; in Italian we have *cen* for *ce ne*, &c.' Cf. *They n' wer-e* in The Former Age, l. 5; and Book of the Duch. 244 (note).

110. See Anelida, 182; and the note.

119. Observe that this last line is a repetition of l. 2.

III. THE BOOK OF THE DUCHESSE.

I MAY remark here that the metre is sometimes difficult to follow; chiefly owing to the fact that the line sometimes begins with an accented syllable, just as, in Milton's L'Allegro, we meet with lines like 'Zéphyr, with Aurora playing.' The accented syllables are sometimes indistinctly marked, and hence arises a difficulty in immediately detecting the right flow of a line. A clear instance of a line beginning with an accented syllable is seen in l. 23—' Slép', and thús meláncolÿë.'

1. The opening lines of this poem were subsequently copied (in 1384) by Froissart, in his Paradis d'Amour—

> 'Je sui de moi en grant merveille
> Comment je vifs, quant tant je veille,
> Et on ne porrait en veillant
> Trouver de moi plus travaillant:
> Car bien sacies que pour veiller
> Me viennent souvent travailler
> Pensees et melancolies,' etc.
>   Furnivall; Trial Forewords, p. 51.

Chaucer frequently makes words like *have* (l. 1), *live* (l. 2), especially in the present indicative, mere monosyllables. As examples of the fully sounded final *e*, we may notice the dative *light-e* (l. 1), the dative (or adverbial) *night-e* (l. 2), the infinitive *slep-e* (3), the adverb *ylich-e* (9), the dative *mind-e* (15), &c. On the other hand, *hav-e* is dissyllabic in l. 24. The *e* is elided before a following vowel in *defaute* (5), *trouthe* (6), *falle* (13), *wite* (16), &c. We may also notice that *com'th* is a monosyllable (7), whereas *trewely* (33) has three syllables, though in l. 35 it makes but two. It is clear that Chaucer chose to make *some* words of variable length; and he does this to a much greater extent in the present poem and in the House of Fame than in more finished productions, such as the Canterbury Tales. But it must be observed, on the other hand, that the number of these variable words is *limited*; in a far larger number of words, the number of syllables never varies at all, except by regular elision before a vowel.

14. The reading *For sorwful ymaginacioun* (in F., Tn., Th.) cannot be right. Lange proposes to omit *For*, which hardly helps us. It is clearly *sorwful* that is wrong. I propose to replace it by *sory*. Koch remarks that *sorwful* has only two syllables (l. 85); but the line only admits of one, or of one and a very light syllable.

15. Observe how frequently, in this poem and in the House of Fame, Chaucer concludes a sentence with the *former* of two lines of a couplet. Other examples occur at ll. 29, 43, 51, 59, 67, 75, 79, 87, 89; i.e. at least ten times in the course of the first hundred lines. The same arrangement occasionally occurs in the existing translation of the Romaunt of the Rose, but with such less frequency as, in itself, to form a presumption against Chaucer's having written the whole of it.

III. BOOK OF THE DUCHESSE. LINES 1-56.

Similar examples in Milton, though he was an admirer of Chaucer, are remarkably rare; compare, however, Comus, 97, 101, 127, 133, 137. The metrical effect of this pause is very good.

23. The texts read *this*. Ten Brink suggests *thus* (Ch. Sprache, § 320); which I adopt.

31. *What me is*, what is the matter with me. *Me* is here in the dative case. This throws some light on the common use of *me* in Shakespeare in such cases as 'Heat *me* these irons hot,' K. John, iv. 1. 1; &c.

31-96. These lines are omitted in the Tanner MS. 346; also in MS. Bodley 638 (which even omits ll. 24-30). In the Fairfax MS. they are added in a much later hand. Consequently, Thynne's edition is here our only satisfactory authority; though the late copy in the Fairfax MS. is worth consulting.

32. *Aske*, may ask; subjunctive mood.

33. *Trewely* is here three syllables, which is the normal form; cf. Prologue, 761; Kn. Ta. A 1267. In l. 35, the second *e* is hardly sounded.

36. We must here read 'hold-e,' *without* elision of final *e*, which is preserved by the cæsura.

37. 'The most obvious interpretation of these lines seems to be that they contain the confession of a hopeless passion, which has lasted for eight years—a confession which certainly seems to come more appropriately and more naturally from an unmarried than a married man. 'For eight years,'—he says—'I have loved, and loved in vain—and yet my cure is never the nearer. There is but one physician that can heal me—but all that is ended and done with. Let us pass on into fresh fields; what cannot be obtained must needs be left'; Ward, Life of Chaucer, p. 53. Dr. Furnivall supposes that the relentless fair one was the one to whom his Complaint unto Pite was addressed; and chronology would require that Chaucer fell in love with her in 1361. There is no proof that Chaucer was married before 1374, though he may have been married not long after his first passion was 'done.'

43. 'It is good to regard our first subject'; and therefore to return to it. This first subject was his sleeplessness.

45. *Til now late* follows *I sat upryght*, as regards construction. The reading *Now of late*, in some printed editions, is no better.

48. This 'Romaunce' turns out to have been a copy of Ovid's Metamorphoses, a book of which Chaucer was so fond that he calls it his 'own book'; Ho. of Fame, 712. Probably he really had a copy of his own, as he constantly quotes it. Private libraries were very small indeed.

49. *Dryve away*, pass away; the usual phrase. Cf. 'And dryuen forth the longe day'; P. Plowman, B. prol. 224.

56. 'As long as men should love the law of nature,' i.e. should continue to be swayed by the natural promptings of passion; in other words, for ever. Certainly, Ovid's book has lasted well. In l. 57, *such thinges* means 'such love-stories.'

62. 'Alcyone, or Halcyone: A daughter of Æolus and Enarete or Ægiale. She was married to Ceyx, and lived so happy with him, that they were presumptuous enough to call each other Zeus and Hera, for which Zeus metamorphosed them into birds, *alkuōn* (a king-fisher) and *kēuks* (a greedy sea-bird, Liddell and Scott; a kind of sea-gull; Apollod. i. 7. § 3, &c.; Hygin. Fab. 65). Hyginus relates that Ceyx perished in a shipwreck, that Alcyone for grief threw herself into the sea, and that the gods, out of compassion, changed the two into birds. It was fabled that, during the seven days before, and as many after the shortest day of the year, while the bird *alkuōn* was breeding, there always prevailed calms at sea. An embellished form of the story is given by Ovid, Met. xi. 410, &c.; compare Virgil, Georg. i. 399.'—Smith's Dictionary. Hence the expression 'halcyon days'; see Holland's Pliny, b. x. c. 32, quoted in my Etym. Dict. s. v. *Halcyon*.

M. Sandras asserts that the history of Ceyx and Alcyone is borrowed from the Dit de la Fontaine Amoureuse, by Machault, whereas it is evident that Chaucer took care to consult his favourite Ovid, though he *also* copied several expressions from Machault's poem. Consult Max Lange, as well as Furnivall's Trial Forewords to Chaucer's Minor Poems, p. 43. Surely, Chaucer himself may be permitted to know; his description of the book, viz. in ll. 57-59, applies to Ovid, rather than to Machault's Poems. But the fact is that we have further evidence; Chaucer himself, elsewhere, plainly *names* Ovid as his authority. See Cant. Tales, Group B, l. 53 (as printed in vol. v.), where he says—

'For he [Chaucer] hath told of loveres up and doun
Mo than *Ovyde* made of mencioun
In his Epistelles, that been ful olde.
What sholde I tellen hem, sin they ben tolde?
In youthe he made of *Ceys and Alcion*;' &c.

It is true that Chaucer here mentions Ovid's Heroides rather than the Metamorphoses; but that is only because he goes on to speak of *other* stories, which he took from the Heroides; see the whole context. It is plain that he wishes us to know that he took the present story chiefly from Ovid; yet there are some expressions which he owes to Machault, as will be shown below. It is worth notice, that the whole story is also in Gower's Confessio Amantis, bk. iv. (ed. Pauli, ii. 100); where it is plainly copied from Ovid throughout.

Ten Brink (Studien, p. 10) points out one very clear indication of Chaucer's having consulted Ovid. In l. 68, he uses the expression *to tellen shortly*, and then proceeds to allude to the shipwreck of Ceyx, which is told in Ovid at great length (Met. xi. 472-572). Of this shipwreck Machault says never a word; he merely says that Ceyx died in the sea.

There is a chapter *De Alcione* in Vincent of Beauvais, Speculum Naturale, bk. xvi. c. 26; made up from Ambrosius, Aristotle, Pliny (bk. 10), and the Liber de Natura Rerum.

III. BOOK OF THE DUCHESSE. LINES 62-80.

66. Instead of quoting Ovid, I shall quote from Golding's translation of his Metamorphoses, as being more interesting to the English reader. (The whole story is also told by Dryden, whose version is easily accessible.) As the tale is told at great length, I quote only a few of the lines that most closely correspond to Chaucer. Compare—

'But fully bent
He [*Ceyx*] seemed neither for to leaue the iourney which he ment
To take by sea, nor yet to giue Alcyone leaue as tho
Companion of his perlous course by water for to go . . . .
When toward night the wallowing waues began to waxen white,
And eke the heady eastern wind did blow with greater might . . .
And all the heauen with clouds as blacke as pitch was ouercast,
That neuer night was halfe so darke. There came a flaw [*gust*] at last,
That with his violence brake the Maste, and strake the Sterne away . . . .
Behold, euen full vpon the waue a flake of water blacke
Did breake, and vnderneathe the sea the head of Ceyx stracke.'
fol. 137-9.

See further in the note to l. 136.

67. Koch would read *wolde* for *wol*; I adopt his suggestion.

76. Alcyone (in the MSS.) was introduced as a gloss.

78. *Come* (dissyllabic) is meant to be in the pt. t. subjunctive.

80. Of the restoration of this line, I should have had some reason to be proud; but I find that Ten Brink (who seems to miss nothing) has anticipated me; see his Chaucers Sprache, §§ 48, 329. We have here, as our guides, only the edition of Thynne (1532), and the late insertion in MS. Fairfax 16. Both of these read—'Anon her herte began to yerne'; whereas it of course ought to be—'Anon her herte gan to erme.' The substitution of *began* for *gan* arose from forgetting that *herte* (A.S. *heorte*) is dissyllabic in Chaucer, in countless places. The substitution of *yerne* for *erme* arose from the fact that the old word *ermen*, to grieve, was supplanted by *earn*, to desire, to grieve, in the sixteenth century, and afterwards by the form *yearn*. This I have already shewn at such length in my note to the Pardoner's Prologue (Cant. Ta. C. 312), in my edition of the Man of Lawes Tale, pp. 39, 142, and yet again in my Etym. Dict., s. v. *Yearn* (2), that it is needless to repeat it all over again. Chaucer was quite incapable of such a mere assonance as that of *terme* with *yerne*; in fact, it is precisely the word *terme* that is rimed with *erme* in his Pardoner's Prologue. Mr. Cromie's index shews that, in the Cant. Tales, the rime *erme*, *terme*, occurs only once, and there is no third word riming with either. There is, however, a rime of *conferme* with *ferme*, Troil. ii. 1525, and with *afferme* in the same, 1588. There is, in Chaucer, no *sixth* riming word in *-erme* at all, and none in either *-irme* or *-yrme*.

Both in the present passage and in the Pardoner's Prologue the verb to *erme* is used with the same sb., viz. *herte*; which clinches the matter. By way of example, compare 'The bysschop weop for *ermyng*'; King Alisaunder, ed. Weber, l. 1525.

86, 87. L. 86 is too short. In l. 87 I delete *alas* after *him*, which makes the line a whole foot too long, and is not required. Koch ingeniously suggests, for l. 86: 'That hadde, alas! this noble wyf.' This transference of *alas* mends both lines at once.

91. *Wher*, short for *whether* (very common).

93. *Avowe* is all one word, though its component parts were often written apart. Thus, in P. Plowman, B. v. 457, we find *And made avowe*, where the other texts have *a-vou, a-vowe*; see *Avow* in the New E. Dict. See my note to Cant. Tales, Group C, 695.

97. Here the gap in the MSS. ceases, and we again have their authority for the text. For *Had* we should, perhaps, read *Hadde*.

105. Doubtless, we ought to read:—'Ne coude she.'

106. This phrase is not uncommon. 'And on knes she sat adoun'; Lay le Freine, l. 159; in Weber's Met. Romances, i. 363. Cf. 'This Troilus ful sone on knees him sette'; Troilus, iii. 953.

107. *Weep* (not *wepte*) is Chaucer's word; see Cant. Tales, B 606, 1052, 3852, E 545, F 496, G 371.

120. For *knowe* (as in F. Tn. Th.) read *knowen*, to avoid hiatus.

126. 'And she, exhausted with weeping and watching.' Gower (Confes. Amantis, ed. Pauli, i. 160) speaks of a ship that is *for-stormed and forblowe*, i. e. excessively driven about by storm and wind.

130. Or read: 'That madë her to slepe sone'; without elision of *e* in *made* (Koch).

136. *Go bet*, go quickly, hasten, lit. go better, i. e. faster. See note to Group C, 667. Cf. *Go now faste*, l. 152.

Morpheus is dissyllabic, i. e. *Morph'us*; cf. *Mórph'us* in l. 167.

I here add another illustration from Golding's Ovid, fol. 139:—

'Alcyone of so great mischaunce not knowing ought as yit,
Did keepe a reckoning of the nights that in the while did flit,
And hasted garments both for him and for her selfe likewise
To weare at his homecomming which she vainely did surmize.
To all the Gods deuoutly she did offer frankincense:
But most aboue them all the Church of Iuno she did sence.
And for her husband (who as then was none) she kneeld before
The Altar, wishing health and soone arriuall at the shore.
And that none other woman might before her be preferd,
Of all her prayers this one peece effectually was herd.
For Iuno could not finde in heart entreated for to bee
For him that was already dead. But to th'intent that shee
From Dame Alcyons deadly hands might keepe her Altars free
She sayd: most faithfull messenger of my commandements, O
Thou Rainebow to the sluggish house of slumber swiftly go,

III. BOOK OF THE DUCHESSE. LINES 86-155.

And bid him send a dreame in shape of Ceyx to his wife
Alcyone, for to shew her plaine the loosing of his life.
Dame Iris takes her pall wherein a thousand colours were,
And bowing like a stringed bow vpon the cloudie sphere,
Immediately descended to the drowzye house of Sleepe,
Whose court the cloudes continually do closely ouerdreepe.
  Among the darke Cimmerians is a holow mountaine found
And in the hill a Caue that farre doth run within the ground,
The C[h]amber and the dwelling place where slouthfull sleepe
    doth couch.
The light of Phœbus golden beames this place can never
    touch . . .
No boughs are stird with blasts of winde, no noise of tatling
    toong
Of man or woman euer yet within that bower roong.
Dumbe quiet dwelleth there. Yet from the rockes foote doth
    go
The riuer of forgetfulnesse, which runneth trickling so
Upon the litle peeble stones which in the channell ly,
That vnto sleepe a great deale more it doth prouoke thereby . . .
Amid the Caue of Ebonye a bedsted standeth hie,
And on the same a bed of downe with couering blacke doth lie:
In which the drowzie God of sleepe his lither limbes doth rest.
About him forging sundry shapes as many dreams lie prest
As eares of corne do stand in fields in haruest time, or leaues
Doe grow on trees, or sea to shoore of sandie cinder heaues.
Assoone as Iris came within this house, and with her hand
Had put aside the dazeling dreames that in her way did stand,
The brightnesse of her robe through all the sacret house did
    shine.
The God of sleepe scarce able for to raise his heauie eine,
A three or foure times at the least did fall againe to rest,
And with his nodding head did knock his chinne against his
    brest.
At length he waking of himselfe, vpon his elbowe leande.
And though he knew for what she came: he askt her what she
    meand': &c.

139. The first accent falls on *Sey*; the *e* in *halfe* seems to be suppressed.

154. *His wey.* Chaucer substitutes a male messenger for Iris; see ll. 134, 155, 180-2.

155. Imitated from Machault's Dit de la Fontaine:—

> '*Que venue est en une grant valee,*
> *De deus grans mons entour environnee,*
> *Et d'un russel qui par my la contree,*' &c.

See Ten Brink, Studien, p. 200; Furnivall, Trial Forewords, p. 44.

It is worth notice that the visit of Iris to Somnus is also fully described by Statius, Theb. x. 81-136; but Chaucer does not seem to have copied him.

158, 159. Two bad lines in the MSS. Both can be mended by changing *nought* into *nothing*, as suggested by Ten Brink, Chaucers Sprache, § 299.

160. See a very similar passage in Spenser, F. Q. i. 1. 39, 40, 41, 42, 43. And cf. Ho. of Fame, 70.

167. *Eclympasteyre.* 'I hold this to be a name of Chaucer's own invention. In Ovid occurs a son of Morpheus who has two different names : " Hunc *Icelon* superi, mortale *Phobetora* vulgus Nominat ; " *Met.* xi. 640. *Phobetora* may have altered into *Pastora*: *Icelonpastora* (the two names linked together) would give *Eclympasteyre*.'— Ten Brink, Studien, p. 11, as quoted in Furnivall's Trial Forewords, p. 116. At any rate, we may feel sure that *Eclym-* is precisely Ovid's *Icelon*. And perhaps *Phobetora* comes nearer to *-pasteyre* than does *Phantasos*, the name of another son of Morpheus, whom Ovid mentions immediately below. Gower (ed. Pauli, ii. 103) calls them *Ithecus* and *Panthasas*; and the fact that he here actually turns *Icelon* into *Ithecus* is a striking example of the strange corruption of proper names in medieval times. Prof. Hales suggests that *Eclympasteyre* represents *Icelon plastora*, where *plastora* is the acc. of Gk. πλαστώρ, i. e. moulder or modeller, a suitable epithet for a god of dreams ; compare the expressions used by Ovid in ll. 626 and 634 of this passage. *Icelon* is the acc. of Gk. ἴκελος, or εἴκελος, like, resembling. For my own part, I would rather take the form *plastera*, acc. of πλαστήρ, a form actually given by Liddell and Scott, and also nearer to the form in Chaucer. Perhaps Chaucer had seen a MS. of Ovid in which *Icelon* was explained by *plastora* or *plastera*, written beside or over it as a gloss, or by way of explanation. This would explain the whole matter. Mr. Fleay thinks the original reading was *Morpheus, Ecelon, Phantastere*; but this is impossible, because Morpheus had but *one* heir (l. 168).

Froissart has the word *Enclimpostair* as the name of a son of the god of sleep, in his poem called Paradis d'Amour. But *as he is merely copying this precise passage*, it does not at all help us.

For the remarks by Prof. Hales, see the Athenæum, 1882, i. 444; for those by Mr. Fleay, see the same, p. 568. Other suggestions have been made, but are not worth recording.

173. *To envye*; to be read as *T'envý-e.* The phrase is merely an adaptation of the F. *à l'envi*, or of the vb. *envier*. Cotgrave gives : '*à l'envy l'vn de l'autre*, one to despight the other, or in emulation one of the other'; also '*envier* (au ieu), to vie.' Hence E. *vie*; see *Vie* in my Etym. Dict. It is etymologically connected with Lat. *inuitare*, not with Lat. *inuidia.* See l. 406, below.

175. Read *slepe*, as in ll. 169, 177; A.S. *slépon*, pt. t. pl.

Upright, i. e. on their backs ; see The Babees Book, p. 245.

181. *Who is*, i. e. who is it that.

III. BOOK OF THE DUCHESSE. LINES 158-255.

183. *Awaketh* is here repeated in the plural form.

184. *Oon ye*, one eye. This is from Machault, who has: 'ouvri l'un de ses yeux.' Ovid has the pl. *oculos*.

185. *Cast* is the pp., as pointed out by Ten Brink, who corrects the line; Chaucers Sprache, § 320.

192. *Abrayd*, and not *abrayde*, is the right form; for it is a strong verb (A. S. *ábregdan*, pt. t. *ábrægd*). So also in the Ho. of Fame, 110 However, *brayde* (as if weak) also occurs; Ho. of Fame, 1678.

195. *Dreynt-e* is here used as an adj., with the weak declension in *-e*. So also in Cant. Tales, B 69. Cf. also Ho. of Fame, 1783.

199. *Fet-e* is dat. pl.; see l. 400, and Cant. Ta., B 1104.

206. The word *look* must be supplied. MS. B. even omits *herte*; which would give—' But good-e swet-e, [look] that ye'; where *good-e* and *swet-e* are vocatives.

213. I adopt Ten Brink's suggestion (Chaucers Sprache, § 300), viz. to change *allas* into *A*. Lange omits *quod she*; but see l. 215.

218. *My first matere*, my first subject; i. e. sleeplessness, as in l. 43.

219. *Whérfor* seems to be accented on the former syllable. MS. B. inserts *you* after *told*; perhaps it is not wanted. If it is, it had better come before *told* rather than after it.

222. *I had be*, I should have been. *Deed and dolven*, dead and buried; as in Cursor Mundi, 5494. Chaucer's *dolven and deed* is odd.

244. *I ne roghte who*, to be read *In' roght-e who*; i. e. I should not care who; see note to Compl. to Pite, 105. *Roghte* is subjunctive.

247. *His lyve*, during his life.

248. The readings are *here onwarde*, Th. F.; *here onward*, Tn.; *here on warde*, B. I do not think *here onward* can be meant, nor yet *hereon-ward*; I know of no examples of such meaningless expressions. I read *here on warde*, and explain it: ' I will give him the very best gift that he ever expected (to get) in his life; and (I will give it) here, in his custody, even now, as soon as possible,' &c. *Ward*=custody, occurs in the dat. *warde* in William of Palerne, 376 —' How that child from here *warde* was went for evermore.'

250. Here Chaucer again takes a hint from Machault's Dit de la Fontaine, where we find the poet promising the god a hat and a soft bed of gerfalcon's feathers. See Ten Brink, Studien, p. 204.

> 'Et por ce au dieu qui moult sout (?) et moult vault
> Por mielx dormir un chapeau de pavaut
> Et un mol lit de plume de gerfaut
>   Promes et doing.'

See also Our English Home, p. 106.

255. *Reynes*, i. e. Rennes, in Brittany; spelt *Raynes* in the Paston Letters, ed. Gairdner, iii. 358. Linen is still made there; and by 'clothe of Reynes' some kind of linen, rather than of woollen cloth, is meant. It is here to be used for pillow-cases. It was also used for sheets. ' Your shetes shall be of clothe of *Rayne*'; Squyr of Lowe

Degre, l. 842 (in Ritson, Met. Rom. iii. 180). 'A peyre schetes of *Reynes*, with the heued shete [head-sheet] of the same'; Earliest Eng. Wills, ed. Furnivall, p. 4, l. 16. 'A towaile of Raynes'; Babees Book, p. 130, l. 213; and see note on p. 208 of the same. 'It [the head-sheet] was more frequently made of the fine white linen of Reynes'; Our Eng. Home, p. 109. 'Hede-shetes of Rennes' are noticed among the effects of Hen. V; see Rot. Parl. iv. p. 228; footnote on the same page. Skelton mentions rochets 'of fyne Raynes'; Colin Clout, 316. The mention of this feather-bed may have been suggested to Machault by Ovid's line about the couch of Morpheus (Metam. **xi.** 611)—
'Plumeus, unicolor, pullo velamine tectus.'

264. We must delete *quene*; it is only an explanatory gloss.

279. 'To be well able to interpret my dream.'

282. The modern construction is—'The dream of King Pharaoh.' See this idiom explained in my note to the Prioresses Tale, Group F, l. 209. Cf. Gen. xli. 25.

284. As to Macrobius, see note to the Parl. of Foules, 31. And cf. Ho. of Fame, 513-7. We must never forget how frequent are Chaucer's imitations of Le Roman de la Rose. Here, for example, he is thinking of ll. 7-10 of that poem:—

'Ung acteur qui ot non Macrobes . . . .
Ancois escrist la vision
Qui avint au roi Cipion.'

After *Macrobeus* understand *coude* (from l. 283), which governs the infin. *arede* in l. 289.

286. *Mett-e* occupies the second foot in the line. Koch proposes *him* for *he*; but it is needless; see Cant. Tales, B 3930. In l. 288, read *fortuned*.

288. This line, found in Thynne only, is perhaps not genuine, but interpolated. Perhaps *Whiche* is better than *Swiche*.

292. Cf. Rom. de la Rose, 45-47 :—

'Avis m'iere qu'il estoit mains . . . .
En Mai estoie, ce songoie.'

And again, cf. ll. 295, &c. with the same, ll. 67-74. See pp. 95, 96.

301. Read *songen*, not *songe*, to avoid the hiatus.

304. Chaucer uses *som* as a singular in such cases as the present. A clear case occurs in '*Som* in *his* bed'; Kn. Tale, 2173. (C. T A 3031.) Hence *song* is the sing. verb.

309. *Entunes*, tunes. Cf. *entuned*, pp.; C. T. Prol. 123.

310. *Tewnes*, Tunis; vaguely put for some distant and wealthy town; see ll. 1061-4, below. Its name was probably suggested by the preceding word *entunes*, which required a rime. Gower mentions *Kaire* (Cairo) just as vaguely :—

'That me were lever her love winne
Than Kaire and al that is therinne'; Conf. Amant, ed. Pauli, ii. 57.

III. BOOK OF THE DUCHESSE. LINES 264-334.

The sense is—'that certainly, even to gain Tunis, I would not have (done other) than heard them sing.' Lange thinks these lines corrupt; but I believe the idiom is correct.

323. As stained glass windows were then rare and expensive, it is worth while observing that these gorgeous windows were not real ones, but only seen in a dream. This passage is imitated in the late poem called the Court of Love, st. 33, where we are told that 'The temple shone with windows al of glasse,' and that in the glass were portrayed the stories of Dido and Annelida. These windows, it may be observed, were equally imaginary.

328. The caesural pause comes after *Ector*, which might allow the intrusion of the word *of* before *king*. But Mr. Sweet omits *of*, and I follow him. The words *of king* are again inserted before *Lamedon* in l. 329, being caught from l. 328 above.

Lamedon is Laomedon, father of King Priam of Troy. *Ector* is Chaucer's spelling of Hector; Man of Lawes Tale, B 198. He here cites the usual examples of love-stories, such as those of Medea and Jason, and Paris and Helen. *Lavyne* is Lavinia, the second wife of Æneas; Vergil, Æn. bk. vii; Rom. Rose, 21087; cf. Ho. of Fame, 458. Observe his pronunciation of *Médea*, as in Ho. of Fame, 401; Cant. Ta., B 72.

332. 'There is reason to believe that Chaucer copied these imageries from the romance of *Guigemar*, one of the Lays of Marie de France; in which the walls of a chamber are painted with Venus and the *Art of Love* from Ovid. Perhaps Chaucer might not look further than the temples of Boccaccio's *Theseid* for these ornaments'; Warton, Hist. E. Poetry, 1871, iii. 63. Cf. Rom. of the Rose, ll. 139-146; see p. 99.

333. *Bothe text and glose*, i.e. both in the principal panels and in the margin. He likens the walls to the page of a book, in which the *glose*, or commentary, was often written in the margin. Mr. Sweet inserts *with* before *text*, and changes *And* into *Of* in the next line; I do not think the former change is necessary, but I adopt the latter.

334. It had all sorts of scenes from the Romance of the Rose on it. Chaucer again mentions this Romance by name in his Merchant's Tale; C. T., E 2032; and he tells us that he himself translated it; Prol. to Legend, 329. The celebrated Roman de la Rose was begun by Guillaume de Lorris, who wrote ll. 1-4070, and completed about forty years afterwards (in a very different and much more satirical style) by Jean de Meung (or Meun), surnamed (like his father) Clopinel, i.e. the Cripple, who wrote ll. 4071-22074; it was finished about the year 1305. The story is that of a young man who succeeded in plucking a rose in a walled garden, after overcoming extraordinary difficulties; allegorically, it means that he succeeded in obtaining the object of his love. See further above, pp. 16-19.

The E. version is invariably called the Romaunt of the Rose, and we find the title Rommant de la Rose in the original, l. 20082; cf. our *romant-ic*. But Burguy explains that *romant* is a false form, due to confusion with words rightly ending in -*ant*. The right O. F. form is *romans*, originally an adverb; from the phrase *parler romans*, i.e. loqui Romanice. In the Six-text edition of the Cant. Tales, E 2032, four MSS. have *romance*, one has *romans*, and one *romauns*.

For examples of walls or ceilings being painted with various subjects, see Warton's Hist. of E. Poetry, ed. Hazlitt, ii. 131, 275; iii. 63.

340. The first accent is on *Blew*, not on *bright*. Cf. Rom. de la Rose, **124, 125** (see p. 98, above):—

> 'Clere et serie et bele estoit
> La matinee, et atrempee.'

343. *Ne in* is to be read as *Nin*; we find it written *nin* in the Squieres Tale, F 35. See l. 694.

347. *Whether* is to be read as *Wher*; it is often so spelt.

348. The line, as it stands in the authorities, viz. 'And I herde goyng, bothe vp and doune'—cannot be right. Mr. Sweet omits *bothe*, which throws the accent upon *I*, and reduces *herde* to *herd* (unaccented!). To remedy this, I also omit *And*. Perhaps *speke* (better *speken*) is an infinitive in l. 350, but it may also be the pt. t. plural (A. S. *spræcon*); and it is more convenient to take it so.

352. *Upon lengthe*, after a great length of course, after a long run.

M. Sandras points out some *very* slight resemblances between this passage and some lines in a French poem in the Collection Mouchet, vol. ii. fol. 106; see the passage cited in Furnivall's Trial Forewords to the Minor Poems, p. 51. Most likely Chaucer wrote independently of this French poem, as even M. Sandras seems inclined to admit.

353. *Embosed*, embossed. This is a technical term, used in various senses, for which see the New Eng. Dict. Here it means 'so far plunged into the thicket'; from O. F. *bos* (F. *bois*), a wood. In later authors, it came to mean 'driven to extremity, like a hunted animal'; then 'exhausted by running,' and lastly, 'foaming at the mouth,' as a result of exhaustion.

362. A *relay* was a fresh set of dogs; see *Relay* in my Etym. Dict.

> 'When the howndys are set an hert for to mete,
> And other hym chasen and folowyn to take,
> Then all the *Relais* thow may vppon hem make.'
>   Book of St. Alban's, fol. e 8, back.

A *lymere* was a dog held in a *liam*, *lime*, or leash, to be let loose when required; from O. F. *liem* (F. *lien*, Lat. *ligamen*), a leash. In the Book of St. Alban's, fol. e 4, we are told that the beasts which should be 'reride with the *lymer*,' i. e. roused and pursued by the dog so called, are 'the hert and the bucke and the boore.'

365. *Oon, ladde*, i. e. one who led. This omission of the relative is common.

368. 'The emperor Octovien' is the emperor seen by Chaucer in his dream. In l. 1314, he is called *this king*, by whom Edward III. is plainly intended. He was 'a favourite character of Carolingian legend,

III. BOOK OF THE DUCHESSE. LINES 340-386. 473

and pleasantly revived under this aspect by the modern romanticist Ludwig Tieck—probably [here] a flattering allegory for the King'; Ward's Life of Chaucer, p. 69. The English romance of Octouian Imperator is to be found in Weber's Metrical Romances, iii. 157; it extends to 1962 lines. He was an emperor of Rome, and married Floraunce, daughter of Dagabers [Dagobert], king of France. The adventures of Floraunce somewhat resemble those of Constance in the Man of Lawes Tale. 'The Romance of the Emperor Octavian' was also edited by Halliwell for the Percy Society, in 1844. The name originally referred to the emperor Augustus.

370. The exclamation 'A goddes halfe' was pronounced like 'A god's half'; see l. 758. See note to l. 544.

374. *Fil to doon*, fell to do, i. e. was fitting to do.

375. *Fot-hoot*, foot-hot, immediately; see my note to Man of Lawes Tale, B 438.

376. *Moot*, notes upon a horn, here used as a plural. See Glossary. 'How shall we blowe whan ye han sen the hert? I shal blowe after one *mote*, ij *motes* [i. e. 3 motes in all]; and if myn howndes come not hastily to me as I wolde, I shall blowe iiij. *motes*'; Venery de Twety, in Reliquiæ Antiquæ, i. 152.

Cf. a passage in the Chace du Cerf, quoted from the Collection Mouchet, i. 166, in Furnivall's Trial Forewords, p. 51 (though Chaucer probably wrote his account quite independently of it):—

'Et puis si corneras apel
.iij. lons *mots*, pour les chiens avoir.'

379. *Rechased*, headed back. Men were posted at certain places, to keep the hart within certain bounds. See next note.

386. *A forloyn*, a recall (as I suppose; for it was blown when the hounds were all a long way off their object of pursuit). It is thus explained in the Book of St. Alban's, fol. f 1 :—

'Yit mayster, wolde I fayn thus at yow leere,
What is a *forloyng*, for that is goode to here.
That shall I say the, quod he, the soth at lest.
When thy houndes in the wode sechyn any beest,
And the beest is stoll away owt of the fryth,
Or the houndes that thou hast meten therwith,
And any other houndes before than may with hem mete,
Thees oder houndes are then *forloyned*, I the hete.
For the beste and the houndes arn so fer before,
And the houndes behynde be weer[i]e and soore,
So that they may not at the best cum at ther will,
The houndes before *forloyne* [distance] hem, and that is the
  skyll.
They be ay so fere before, to me iff thou will trust;
And thys is the *forloyne*; lere hit, iff thou lust.'

The 'chace of the forloyne' is explained (very obscurely) in the

Venery de Twety; see Reliquiæ Antiquæ, i. 152. But the following passage from the same gives some light upon *rechased* : 'Another chace ther is whan a man hath set up archerys and greyhoundes, and the best be founde, and passe out the boundys, and myne houndes after; then shall y blowe on this maner a mote, and aftirward the *rechace* upon my houndys that be past the boundys.'

387. *Go*, gone. The sense is—'I had gone (away having) walked from my tree.' The idiom is curious. *My tree*, the tree at which I had been posted. Chaucer dreamt that he was one of the men posted to watch which way the hart went, and to keep the bounds.

396. The final *e* in *fled-de* is not elided, owing to the pause after it. See note to l. 685.

398. *Wente*, path. Chaucer often rimes words that are pronounced alike, if their meanings be different. See ll. 439, 440; and cf. ll. 627-630. The very same pair of rimes occurs again in the Ho. of Fame, 181, 182; and in Troil. ii. 62, 813; iii. 785, v. 603, 1192.

402. Read—*For both-e Flor-a*, &c. The *-a* in *Flora* comes at the cæsural pause; cf. ll. 413, 414. Once more, this is from Le Roman de la Rose, ll. 8449-51 :—

> 'Zephirus et Flora, sa fame,
> Qui des flors est déesse et dame,
> Cil dui font les floretes nestre.'

Cf. also ll. 5962-5 :—

> 'Les floretes i fait parair,
> E *cum estoiles* flamboier,
> Et les herbetes verdoier
> *Zephirus*, quant sur mer chevauche.'

405. The first accent is on *For*; not happily.

408. 'To have more flowers than the heaven (has stars, so as even to rival) seven such planets as there are in the sky.' Rather involved, and probably all suggested by the necessity for a rime to *heven*. See l. 824. Moreover, it is copied from Le Roman de la Rose, 8465-8 :—

> 'Qu'il vous fust avis que la terre
> Vosist emprendre estrif et guerre
> Au ciel d'estre miex estelée,
> Tant iert par ses flors revelée.'

410-412. From Le Roman de la Rose, 55-58 (see p. 95, above) :—

> 'La terre . . . .
> Et oblie la poverte
> Ou ele a tot l'yver este.'

419. Imitated from Le Roman de la Rose, 1373-1391; in particular :—

> 'Li ung [arbre] fu loing de l'autre assis
> Plus de cinq toises, ou de sis,' &c.

III. BOOK OF THE DUCHESSE. LINES 387-438.

Chaucer has treated a *toise* as if it were equal to two feet; it was really about six. In his own translation of the Romaunt, l. 1393, he translates *toise* by *fadome*. See p. 151 (above).

429. According to the Book of St. Albans, fol. e 4, the buck was called *a fawne* in his first year, a *preket* in the second, *a sowrell* in the third, *a sowre* in the fourth, *a bucke of the fyrst hede* in the fifth, and *a bucke* (simply) in the sixth year. Also *a roo* is the female of the *roobucke*.

435. *Argus* is put for *Algus*, the old French name for the inventor of the Arabic numerals; it occurs in l. 16373 of the Roman de la Rose, which mentions him in company with Euclid and Ptolemy—

'*Algus*, Euclides, Tholomees.'

This name was obviously confused with that of the hundred-eyed Argus.

This name *Algus* was evolved out of the O. F. *algorisme*, which, as Dr. Murray says, is a French adaptation 'from the Arab. *al-Khowār-azmī*, the *native of Khwārazm (Khiva)*, surname of the Arab mathematician Abu Ja'far Mohammed Ben Musa, who flourished early in the 9th century, and through the translation of whose work on Algebra, the Arabic numerals became generally known in Europe. Cf. *Euclid* = plane geometry.' He was truly 'a noble countour,' to whom we all owe a debt of gratitude. That *Algus* was sometimes called *Argus*, also appears from the Roman de la Rose, ll. 12994, &c., which is clearly the very passage which Chaucer here copies:—

'Se mestre *Argus* li bien contens
I vosist bien metre ses cures,
E venist *o ses dix figures*,
Par quoi tout certefie et nombre,
Si ne péust-il pas le nombre
Des grans contens certefier,
Tant seust bien monteplier.'

Here *o* means 'with'; so that Chaucer has copied the very phrase 'with his figures ten.' But still more curiously, Jean de Meun here rimes *nombre*, pres. sing. indic., with *nombre*, sb.; and Chaucer rimes *noumbre*, infin., with *noumbre*, sb. likewise. *Countour* in l. 435 means 'arithmetician'; in the next line it means an abacus or counting-board, for assisting arithmetical operations.

437. *His figures ten*; the ten Arabic numerals, i.e. from 1 to 9, and the cipher o.

438. *Al ken*, all kin, i.e. mankind, all men. This substitution of *ken* for *kin* (A. S. *cyn*) seems to have been due to the exigencies of rime, as Chaucer uses *kin* elsewhere. However, Gower has the same form— 'And of what *ken* that she was come'; Conf. Am. b. viii; ed. Pauli, iii. 332. So also in Will. of Palerne, 722—'Miself knowe ich nouȝt mi *ken*'; and five times at least in the Ayenbite of Inwyt, as it is a Kentish form. It was, doubtless, a permissible variant.

442. The strong accent on *me* is very forced.

445. *A man in blak*; John of Gaunt, in mourning for the loss of his wife Blaunche. Imitated by Lydgate, in his Complaint of the Black Knight, l. 130, and by Spenser, in his Daphnaida:—

> 'I did espie
> Where towards me a sory wight did cost
> Clad all in black, that mourning did bewray.'

452. *Wel-faring-e*; four syllables.

455. John of Gaunt, born in June, 1340, was 29 years old in 1369. I do not know why a poet is *never to make a mistake*; nor why critics should lay down such a singular law. But if we are to lay the error on the scribes, Mr. Brock's suggestion is excellent. He remarks that *nine and twenty* was usually written xxviiij.; and if the *v* were omitted, it would appear as .xxiiij., i. e. *four and twenty*. The existing MSS. write 'foure and twenty' at length; but such is not the usual practice of earlier scribes. It may also be added that .xxiiij. was at that time always read as *four and twenty*, never as *twenty-four*; so that no ambiguity could arise as to the mode of reading it. See Richard the Redeless, iii. 260.

There is a precisely similiar confusion in Cant. Ta. Group B, l. 5, where *eightetethe* is denoted by ' xviijthe ' in the Hengwrt MS., whilst the Harl. MS. omits the *v*, and reads *threttenthe*, and again the Ellesmere MS. inserts an *x*, and gives us *eighte and twentithe*. The presumption is, that Chaucer knew his patron's age, and that we ought to read *nine* for *four*; but even if he inadvertently wrote *four*, there is no crime in it.

475. The knight's lay falls into two stanzas, one of five, and one of six lines, as marked. In order to make them more alike, Thynne inserted an additional line—And thus in sorowe lefte me alone—after l. 479. This additional line is numbered 480 in the editions; so I omit l. 480 in the numbering. The line is probably spurious. It is not grammatical; grammar would require that *has* (not *is*, as in l. 479) should be understood before the pp. *left*; or if we take *left-e* as a past tense, then the line will not scan. But it is also unmetrical, as the arrangement of lines should be the same as in ll. 481-6, if the two stanzas are to be made alike. Chaucer says the lay consisted of 'ten verses or twelve' in l. 463, which is a sufficiently close description of a lay of eleven lines. Had he said *twelve* without any mention of *ten*, the case would have been different.

479. Lange proposes: 'Is deed, and is fro me agoon.' F. Tn. Th. agree as to the reading given; I see nothing against it.

481. If we must needs complete the line, we must read 'Allas! o deth!' inserting *o*; or 'Allas! the deth,' inserting *the*. The latter is proposed by Ten Brink, Sprache, &c. § 346.

490. *Pure*, very; cf. ' pure fettres,' Kn. Tale, A 1279. And see l. 583, below.

III. BOOK OF THE DUCHESSE. LINES 442-589.

491. Cf. 'Why does my blood thus muster to my heart?' Meas. for Meas. ii. 4. 20.

501. The MSS. have *seet*, sat, a false form for *sat* (A. S. *sæt*) ; due to the plural form *seet-e* or *sēt-e* (A. S. *sǣt-on*). We certainly find *seet* for *sat* in the Kn. Tale, A 2075. Read *sete*, as the pt. t. subj. (A. S. *sǣte*) ; and *fete* as dative pl. form, as in Cant. Ta. B 1104.

510. *Made*, i. e. they made ; idiomatic.

521. *Ne I*, nor I ; to be read *N'I* ; cf. note to l. 343.

526. 'Yes ; the amends is (are) easily made.'

532. *Me acqueynte* = *m'acqueynt-e*, acquaint myself.

544. *By our Lord*, to be read as *by'r Lord*. Cf. *by'r lakin*, Temp. iii. 3. 1. So again, in ll. 651, 690, 1042.

547. *Me thinketh* (= *me think'th*), it seems to me.

550. *Wis*, certainly : 'As certainly (as I hope that) God may help me.' So in Nonne Prestes Tale, 587 (B 4598); and cf. Kn. Tale, 1928 (B 2786) ; Squ. Ta. F 469, &c. And see l. 683, below.

556. *Paraventure*, pronounced as *Paraunter* ; Thynne so has it.

Compare this passage with the long dialogue between Troilus and Pandarus, in the latter part of the first book of Troilus.

568. Alluding to Ovid's Remedia Amoris. Accent *remédies* on the second syllable.

569. The story of Orpheus is in Ovid's Metamorphoses, bk. x. The allusion is to the harp of Orpheus, at the sound of which the tortured had rest. Cf. Ho. of Fame, 1202 :—

'To tyre on Titius growing hart the gredy Grype forbeares:
The shunning water Tantalus endeuereth not to drink ;
And Danaus daughters ceast to fil their tubs that haue no brink.
Ixions wheel stood still : and downe sate Sisyphus vpon
His rolling stone.'— GOLDING'S Ovid, fol. 120.

570. Cf. Ho. of Fame, 919 ; Rom. Rose, 21633. Dædalus represents the mechanician. No mechanical contrivances can help the mourner.

572. Cf.
'Par Hipocras, ne Galien,
Tant fussent bon phisicien.'
Roman de la Rose, 16161.

Hippocrates and Galen are meant; see note to Cant. Tales, C 306.

579. *Y-worthe*, (who am) become ; pp. of *worthen*.

582. 'For all good fortune and I are foes,' lit. angry (with each other). Hence *wroth-e* is a plural form.

589. *S* and *C* were so constantly interchanged before *e* that *Sesiphus* could be written *Cesiphus* ; and *C* and *T* were so often mistaken that *Cesiphus* easily became *Tesiphus*, the form in the Tanner MS. Further, initial *T* was sometimes replaced by *Th* ; and this would give the *Thesiphus* of MS. F.

Sesiphus, i. e. Sisyphus, is of course intended ; it was in the author's mind in connection with the story of Orpheus just above ; see note to l. 569. In the Roman de la Rose, we have the usual allusions to *Yxion*

(l. 19479), *Tentalus*, i.e. Tantalus (l. 19482), *Ticius*, i.e. Tityus (l. 19506), and *Sisifus* (l 19499).

But whilst I thus hold that Chaucer probably wrote *Sesiphus*, I have no doubt that he really meant *Tityus*, as is shewn by the expression *lyth*, i.e. lies extended. See Troil. i. 786, where Bell's edition has *Siciphus*, but the Campsall MS. has *Ticyus*; whilst in ed. 1532 we find *Tesiphus*.

599. With this string of contrarieties compare the Eng. version of the Roman de la Rose, 4706-4753. See p. 212, above.

614. *Abaved*, confounded, disconcerted. See Glossary.

618. Imitated from the Roman de la Rose, from l. 6644 onwards—

> 'Vez cum fortune le servi . . . .
> N'est ce donc chose bien provable
> Que sa roë n'est pas tenable?' . . . .

Jean de Meun goes on to say that Charles of Anjou killed Manfred, king of Sicily, in the first battle with him [A.D. 1266]—

> 'En la premeraine bataille
> L'assailli por li desconfire,
> *Eschec* et *mat* li ala dire
> Desus son destrier auferrant,
> Du trait d'un paonnet errant
> Ou milieu de son eschiquier.'

He next speaks of Conradin, whose death was likewise caused by Charles in 1268, so that these two (Manfred and Conradin) lost all their pieces at chess—

> 'Cil dui, comme folz garçonnés,
> Roz et fierges et paonnés,
> Et chevaliers as gieus perdirent,
> Et hors de l'eschiquier saillirent.'

And further, of the inventor of chess (l. 6715)—

> 'Car ainsinc le dist Athalus
> Qui des eschez controva l'us,
> Quant il traitoit d'arismetique.'

He talks of the queen being taken (at chess), l. 6735—

> 'Car la fierche avoit este prise
> Au gieu de la premiere assise.'

He cannot recount all Fortune's tricks (l. 6879)—

> 'De fortune la semilleuse
> Et de sa roë perilleuse
> Tous les tors conter ne porroie.'

629. Cf. 'whited sepulchres'; Matt. xxiii. 27; Rom. de la Rose, 8946.

630. The MSS. and Thynne have *floures, flourys*. This gives no sense; we must therefore read *flour is*. For a similar rime see that of

nones, noon is, in the Prologue, 523, 524. Strictly, grammar requires *ben* rather than *is*; but when two nominatives express much the same sense, the singular verb may be used, as in Lenvoy to Bukton, 6. The sense is—'her chief glory and her prime vigour is (i.e. consists in) lying.'

634. The parallel passage is one in the Remède de Fortune, by G. de Machault:—

> '*D'un œil rit, de l'autre lerme*;
>   C'est l'orgueilleuse humilité,
>   *C'est l'envieuse charité* [l. 642]. . .
>   La peinture d'une vipère
>   Qu'est mortable;
>   En riens à li ne se compère.'

See Furnivall's Trial Forewords, p. 47; and compare the remarkable and elaborate description of Fortune in the Anticlaudian of Alanus de Insulis (Distinctio 8, cap. 1), in Wright's Anglo-Latin Satirists, vol. ii. pp. 399, 400.

636. Chaucer seems to have rewritten the whole passage at a later period:—

> 'O sodeyn hap, o thou fortune instable,
> Lyk to the scorpioun so deceivable,
> That flaterest with thyn heed when thou wolt stinge;
> Thy tayl is deeth, thurgh thyn enveniminge.
> O brotil Ioye, o swete venim queynte,
> O monstre, that so subtilly canst peynte
> Thy giftes under hewe of stedfastnesse,
> That thou deceyvest bothe more and lesse,' &c.
>   Cant. Tales, 9931 (E 2057).

Compare also Man of Lawes Tale, B 361, 404. 'The scorpiun is ones cunnes wurm thet haueth neb, ase me seith, sumdel iliche ase wummon, and is neddre bihinden; maketh feir semblaunt and fiketh mit te heaued, and stingeth mid te teile'; Ancren Riwle, p. 206. Vincent of Beauvais, in his Speculum Naturale, bk. xx. c. 160, quotes from the Liber de Naturis Rerum—'Scorpio blandum et quasi virgineum dicitur vultum habere, sed habet in cauda nodosa venenatum aculeum, quo pungit et inficit proximantem.'

642. A translated line; see note to l. 634.

651. Read—*Trow'st thou? by'r lord*; see note to l. 544.

653. *Draught* is a move at chess; see ll. 682, 685. Thus in Caxton's Game of the Chesse—'the alphyn [bishop] goeth in vj. *draughtes* al the tablier [board] rounde about.' So in The Tale of Beryn, 1779, 1812. It translates the F. *trait*; see note to l. 618 (second quotation).

654. '*Fers*, the piece at chess next to the king, which we and other European nations call the *queen*; though very improperly, as Hyde has observed. *Pherz*, or *Pherzan*, which is the Persian name for the same piece, signifies the King's *Chief Counsellor*, or *General*—Hist.

Shahilud. [*shahi-ludii*, chess-play], pp. 88, 89.'—Tyrwhitt's Glossary. Chaucer follows Rom. Rose, where the word appears as *fierge*, l. 6688, and *fierche*, l. 6735; see note to l. 618 above. (For another use of *fers*, see note to l. 723 below.) Godefroy gives the O. F. spellings *fierce*, *fierche*, *fierge*, *firge*, and quotes two lines, which give the O. F. names of all the pieces at chess :—

'Roy, roc, chevalier, et alphin,
Fierge, et peon.'—

Caxton calls them *kyng, quene, alphyn, knyght, rook, pawn*. Richardson's Pers. Dict. p. 1080, gives the Pers. name of the queen as *farzī* or *farzīn*, and explains *farzīn* by 'the queen at chess, a learned man'; compare Tyrwhitt's remark above. In fact, the orig. Skt. name for this piece was *mantrī*, i.e. the adviser or counsellor. He also gives the Pers. *farz*, learned; *farz* or *firz*, the queen at chess. I suppose it is a mere chance that the somewhat similar Arab. *faras* means 'a horse, and the knight at chess'; Richardson (as above). Oddly enough, the *latter* word has also some connection with Chaucer, as it is the Arabic name of the 'wedge' of an astrolabe; see Chaucer's Astrolabe, Part i. § 14 (footnote), in vol. iii.

655. When a chess-player, by an oversight, loses his queen for nothing, he may, in general, as well as give up the game. Beryn was 'in hevy plyghte,' when he only lost a rook for nothing; Tale of Beryn, 1812.

660. The word *the* before *mid* must of course be omitted. The lines are to be scanned thus :—

'Therwith | fortun | e seid | e chek | here
And mate | in mid | pointe of | the chek | kere.'

The rime is a feminine one. Lines 660 and 661 are copied from the Rom. Rose; see note to l. 618, above. To be checkmated by an 'errant' pawn in the very middle of the board is a most ignominious way of losing the game. Cf. *check-mate* in Troil. ii. 754.

663. *Athalus*; see note to l. 618, above. Jean de Meun follows John of Salisbury (bishop of Chartres, died 1180) in attributing the invention of chess to Attalus. 'Attalus Asiaticus, si Gentilium creditur historiis, hanc ludendi lasciuiam dicitur inuenisse ab exercitio numerorum, paululum deflexa materia;' Joan. Saresburiensis Policraticus, lib. i. c. 5. Warton (Hist. E. Poet. 1871, iii. 91) says the person meant is Attalus Philometor, king of Pergamus; who is mentioned by Pliny, Nat. Hist. xviii. 3, xxviii. 2. It is needless to explain here how chess was developed out of the old Indian game for four persons called *chaturaṅga*, i.e. consisting of four members or parts (Benfey's Skt. Dict. p. 6). I must refer the reader to Forbes's History of Chess, or the article on *Chess* in the English Cyclopædia. See also the E. version of the Gesta Romanorum, ed. Herrtage, p. 70; A. Neckam, De Naturis Rerum, ed. Wright, p. 324; and Sir F. Madden's article in the Archæologia, xxiv. 203.

666. *Ieupardyes*, hazards, critical positions, problems; see note on Cant. Tales, Group G, 743.

667. *Pithagores*, put for Pythagoras; for the rime. Pythagoras of Samos, born about B.C. 570, considered that all things were founded upon numerical relations; various discoveries in mathematics, music, and astronomy, were attributed to him.

682. 'I would have made the same move'; i.e. had I had the power, I would have taken her *fers* from her, just as she took mine.

684. *She*, i.e. Fortune; so in Thynne. The MSS. have *He*, i.e. God, which can hardly be meant.

685. The cæsural pause preserves *e* in *draughte* from elision. It rimes with *caughte* (l. 682). Similar examples of 'hiatus' are not common: Ten Brink (Sprache, § 270) instances Cant. Tales, Group C, 599, 772 (Pard. Tale).

694. *Ne in* is to be read as *nin* (twice); see note to l. 343.

700. 'There lies in reckoning (i.e. is debited to me in the account), as regards sorrow, for no amount at all.' In his account with Sorrow he is owed nothing, having received payment in full. There is no real difficulty here.

705. 'I have nothing'; for (1) Sorrow has paid in full, and so owes me nothing; (2) I have no gladness left; (3) I have lost my true wealth; (4) and I have no pleasure.

708. 'What is past is not yet to come.'

709. *Tantale*, Tantalus. He has already referred to *Sisyphus*; see note to l. 589. In the Roman de la Rose, we find *Yxion*, l. 19479; *Tentalus*, l. 19482; and *Sisifus*, l. 19499; as I have already remarked.

717. Again from the Rom. de la Rose, l. 5869—

'Et ne priseras une prune
Toute la roë de fortune.
A *Socrates* seras semblables,
Qui tant fu fers et tant estables,
Qu'il n'ert liés en prospérités,
Ne tristes en aversités.'

Chaucer's *three strees* (i.e. straws) is Jean de Meun's *prune*.

723. By *the ferses twelve* I understand all the pieces except the king, which could not be taken. The guess in Bell's Chaucer says 'all the pieces except the pawns'; but as a player only has *seven* pieces beside the pawns and king, we must then say that the knight exaggerates. My own reckoning is thus: pawns, *eight*; queen, bishop, rook, knight, *four*; total, *twelve*. The fact that each player has *two* of three of these, viz. of the *bishop, rook*, and *knight*, arose from the conversion of *chaturanga*, in which each of four persons had a king, bishop, knight, rook [to keep to modern names] and four pawns, into chess, in which each of two persons had two kings (afterwards king and queen), two bishops, knights, and rooks, and eight pawns. The bishop, knight, and rook, were thus duplicated, and so count but one apiece, which

makes *three* (sorts of) pieces; and the queen is a *fourth*, for the king cannot be taken. The case of the pawns was different, for each pawn had an individuality of its own, no two being made alike (except in inferior sets). Caxton's Game of the Chesse shews this clearly; he describes each of the eight pawns separately, and gives a different figure to each. According to him, the pawns were (beginning from the King's Rook's Pawn) the Labourer, Smyth, Clerke (or Notary), Marchaunt, Physicien, Tauerner, Garde, and Ribauld. They denoted 'all sorts and conditions of men'; and this is why our common saying of 'tinker, tailor, soldier, sailor, gentleman, apothecary, ploughboy, thief' enumerates *eight* conditions [1].

As the word *fers* originally meant counsellor or monitor of the king, it could be applied to any of the pieces. There was a special reason for its application to each of the pawns; for a pawn, on arriving at its last square, could not be exchanged (as now) for any piece at pleasure, but only for a queen, i.e. the fers *par excellence*. For, as Caxton says again, 'he [the pawn] may not goo on neyther side till he hath been in the fardest ligne of theschequer, & that he hath taken the nature of the draughtes of the quene, & than he is a *fiers*, and than may he goo on al sides cornerwyse fro poynt to poynt onely as the quene'; &c.

726. These stock examples all come together in the Rom. de la Rose; viz. *Jason* and *Medee*, at l. 13433; *Philis* and *Demophon*, at l. 13415; '*Dido*, roine de Cartage,' at l. 13379. The story of Echo and Narcissus is told fully, in an earlier passage (see ll. 1469-1545 of the English version, at p. 154); also that of 'Dalida' and 'Sanson' in a later passage, at l. 16879. See also the Legends of Dido, Medea, and Phillis in the Legend of Good Women; and the story of Sampson in the Monkes Tale, B 3205:—

'Ne Narcissus, the faire,' &c.; Kn. Tale, 1083 (A 1941).

'And dye he moste, he seyde, as dide Ekko
 For Narcius'; C. T. 11263 (Frank. Tale, F 951).

779. M. Sandras points out the resemblance to a passage in G. de Machault's Remède de Fortune:—

'Car le droit estat d'innocence
Ressemblent (?) proprement la table
Blanche, polie, *qui est able*
A recevoir, sans nul contraire,
Ce qu'on y veut peindre ou portraire.'

The rime of *table* and *able* settles the point. Mr. Brock points out a parallel passage in Boethius, which Chaucer thus translates:—'the soule hadde ben naked of it-self, as a mirour or a clene parchemin ... Right as we ben wont som tyme by a swifte pointel to ficchen lettres emprented in the smothenesse or in the pleinnesse of the table of wex,

---

[1] The thief is the Ribauld; the ploughboy, the Labourer; the apothecary, the Physicien; the soldier, the Garde; the tailor, the Marchaunt; the tinker, the Smyth. Only two are changed.

III. BOOK OF THE DUCHESSE. LINES 726-837.

or in parchemin that ne hath no figure ne note in it'; bk. v. met. 4. But I doubt if Chaucer knew much of Boethius in 1369; and in the present passage he clearly refers to a prepared white surface, not to a tablet of wax. 'Youth and white paper take any impression'; Ray's Proverbs.

791. An allusion to the old proverb which is given in Hending in the form—'Whose yong lerneth, olt [old] he ne leseth'; Hending's Prov. l. 45. Kemble gives the medieval Latin—'Quod puer adsuescit, leviter dimittere nescit'; Gartner, Dicteria, p. 24 b. Cf. Horace, Epist. i. 2. 69; also Rom. de la Rose, 13094.

799. John of Gaunt married Blaunche at the age of nineteen.

805. Imitated from Machault's Dit du Vergier and Fontaine Amoureuse.

'Car il m'est vis que je veoie,
Au joli prael ou j'estoie,
La plus tres belle compaignie
Qu'oncques fust veue ne oïe:'
    Dit du Vergier, ed. Tarbé, p. 14.

'Tant qu'il avint, qu'en une compagnie
Où il avait mainte dame jolie
Juene, gentil, joïeuse et envoisie
 Vis, par Fortune,
(Qui de mentir à tous est trop commune),
 Entre les autres l'une
Qui, tout aussi *com li solaus la lune*
 Veint de clarté,
Avait-elle les autres sormonté
De pris, d'onneur, de grace, de biauté;' &c.
    Fontaine Amoureuse (in Trial Forewords, p. 47).

These are, no doubt, the lines to which Tyrwhitt refers in his remarks on the present passage in a note to the last paragraph of the Persones Tale. Observe also how closely the fifth line of the latter passage answers to l. 812.

823. *Is*, which is; as usual. I propose this reading. That of the MSS. is very bad, viz. 'Than any other planete in heven.'

824. 'The seven stars' generally mean the planets; but, as the sun and moon and planets have just been mentioned, the reference may be to the well-known seven stars in Ursa Major commonly called Charles's Wain. In later English, the *seven stars* sometimes mean the Pleiades; see *Pleiade* in Cotgrave's French Dictionary, and G. Douglas, ed. Small, i. 69. 23, iii. 147. 15. The phrase is, in fact, ambiguous; see note to P. Plowman, C. xviii. 98.

831. Referring to Christ and His twelve apostles.

835-7. Resembles Le Roman de la Rose, 1689-91 (see p. 164)—

'Li Diex d'Amors, qui, l'arc tendu,
Avoit toute jor atendu
A moi porsivre et espier.'

840. Koch proposes to omit *maner*, and read—' No counseyl, but at hir loke.' It is more likely that *counseyl* has slipped in, as a gloss upon *reed*, and was afterwards substituted for it.

849. *Carole*, dance round, accompanying the dance with a song. The word occurs in the Rom. de la Rose several times; thus at l. 747, we have:—

'Lors veissies *carole* aler,
Et gens mignotement baler.' (See p. 125, above.)

Cf. Chaucer's version, ll. 759, 810; also 744. Dante uses the pl. *carole* (Parad. xxiv. 16) to express swift circular movements; and Cary quotes a comment upon it to the effect that '*carolæ* dicuntur tripudium quoddam quod fit saliendo, ut Napolitani faciunt et dicunt.' He also quotes the expression 'grans danses et grans *karolles*' from Froissart, ed. 1559, vol. i. cap. 219. That it meant singing as well as dancing appears from the Rom. de la Rose, l. 731.

858. Chaucer gives Virginia golden hair; Doct. Tale, C 38. Compare the whole description of the maiden in the E. version of the Rom. of the Rose, ll. 539-561 (p. 116, above).

861. *Of good mochel*, of an excellent size; *mochel* = size, occurs in P. Plowman, B. xvi. 182. Scan the line—

'Simpl' of | good moch | el noght | to wyde.'

894. ' In reasonable cases, that involve responsibility.'

908. Somewhat similar are ll. 9-18 of the Doctoures Tale.

916. Scan by reading—They n' shóld' hav' foúnd-e, &c.

917. *A wikked signe*, a sign, or mark, of wickedness.

919. Imitated from Machault's Remède de Fortune (see Trial Forewords, p. 48):—

'*Et sa gracieuse parole*,
Qui n'estoit diverse ne folle,
Etrange, *ne mal ordenée*,
Hautaine, mès bien affrenèe,
Cueillie à point et de saison,
Fondée sur toute raison,
Tant plaisant et *douce à oïr*,
Que chascun faisoit resjoir'; &c.

Line 922 is taken from this word for word.

927-8. ' Nor that scorned less, nor that could better heal,' &c.

943. *Canel-boon*, collar-bone; lit. channel-bone, i. e. bone with a channel behind it. See Three Metrical Romances (Camden Soc.), p. 19; Gloss. to Babees Book, ed. Furnivall; and the Percy Folio MS., i. 387. I put *and* for *or*; the sense requires a conjunction.

948. Here *Whyte*, representing the lady's name, is plainly a translation of *Blaunche*. The insertion of *whyte* in l. 905, in the existing authorities, is surely a blunder, and I therefore have omitted it. It anticipates the climax of the description, besides ruining the scansion of the line.

III. BOOK OF THE DUCHESSE. LINES 840-1024.   485

950. There is here some resemblance to some lines in G. Machault's Remède de Fortune (see Trial Forewords, p. 49):—

—'ma Dame, qui est clamée
De tous, sur toutes belle et bonne,
Chascun por droit ce nom li donne.'

957. For *hippes*, Bell prints *lippes*; a comic reading.

958. This reading means—'I knew in her no other defect'; which, as *no* defect has been mentioned, seems inconsistent. Perhaps we should read *no maner lak*, i. e. no 'sort of defect in her (to cause) that all her limbs should not be proportionate.'

964. A common illustration. See Rom. de la Rose, 7448; Alexander and Dindimus, ll. 233-5. Duke Francesco Maria had, for one of his badges, a lighted candle by which others are lighted; with the motto *Non degener addam*, i. e. I will give without loss; see Mrs. Palliser's Historic Devices, p. 263. And cf. Cant. Ta. D 333-5.

973. The accents seem to fall on *She* and *have*, the *e* in *wold-e* being elided. Otherwise, read: She wóld-e háv' be.

982. Liddell and Scott explain Gk. φοῖνιξ as 'the fabulous Egyptian bird phœnix, first in Hesiod, Fragment 50. 4; then in Herodotus, ii. 73.' Vincent of Beauvais, Speculum Naturale, bk. 16. c. 74, refers us to Isidore, Ambrosius (lib. 5), Solinus, Pliny (lib. 10), and Liber de Naturis Rerum; see Solinus, Polyhistor. c. 33. 11; A. Neckam, De Naturis Rerum, c. 34. Philip de Thaun describes it in his Bestiaire, l. 1089; see Popular Treatises on Science, ed. Wright, p. 113. 'The Phœnix of Arabia passes all others. Howbeit, I cannot tell what to make of him; and first of all, whether it be a tale or no, that there is neuer but one of them in all the world, and the same not commonly seen'; Holland, tr. of Pliny, bk. 10. c. 2.

'Tous jors est-il ung seul *Fenis*'; &c.
Rom. de la Rose, 16179.

'Una est, quæ reparet, seque ipsa reseminet, ales;
Assyrii phœnica uocant.'—Ovid, Met. xv. 392.

Scan: Th' soléyn | feníx | of A | rabye ‖. Cf. 'Com la fenix souleine est au sejour En Arabie': Gower, Balade 35.

987. Chaucer refers to Esther again; e. g. in his Merchant's Tale (E 1371, 1744); Leg. of G. Women, prol. 250; and in the Tale of Melibee (B 2291).

997. Cf. Vergil, Æn. i. 630: 'Haud ignara mali.'

1021. *In balaunce*, i. e. in a state of suspense. F. *en balance*; Rom. de la Rose, 13871, 16770.

1024. This sending of lovers on expeditions, by way of proving them, was in accordance with the manners of the time. Gower explains the whole matter, in his Conf. Amant, lib. 4 (ed. Pauli, ii. 56):—

'Forthy who secheth loves grace,
Where that these worthy women are,
He may nought than him-selve spare

> Upon his travail for to serve,
> Wherof that he may thank deserve, . . .
> So that by londe and ek by ship
> He mot travaile for worship
> And make many hastif rodes,
> Somtime in *Pruse*, somtime in Rodes,
> And somtime into *Tartarie*,
> So that these heralds on him crie
> "Vailant! vailant! lo, where he goth!"' &c.

Chaucer's Knight (in the Prologue) sought for renown in *Pruce, Alisaundre*, and *Turkye*.

There is a similar passage in Le Rom. de la Rose, 18499-18526. The first part of Machault's Dit du Lion (doubtless the Book of the Lion of which Chaucer's translation is now lost) is likewise taken up with the account of lovers who undertook feats, in order that the news of their deeds might reach their ladies. Among the places to which they used to go are mentioned *Alexandres*, Alemaigne, Osteriche, Behaigne, Hongnerie, Danemarche, *Prusse*, Poulaine, Cracoe, *Tartarie*, &c. Some even went 'jusqu'à l'Arbre sec, Ou li oisel pendent au bec.' This alludes to the famous *Arbre sec* or Dry Tree, to reach which was a feat indeed; see Yule's edition of Marco Polo, i. 119; Maundeville, ed. Halliwell, p. 68; Mätzner, Sprachproben, ii. 185.

As a specimen of the modes of expression then prevalent, Warton draws attention to a passage in Froissart, c. 81, where Sir Walter Manny prefaces a gallant charge upon the enemy with the words— 'May I never be embraced by my mistress and dear friend, if I enter castle or fortress before I have unhorsed one of these gallopers.'

1028. *Go hoodles*, travel without even the protection of a hood; by way of bravado. Warton, Hist. Eng. Poet. § 18 (ed. Hazlitt, iii. 4), says of a society called the Fraternity of the Penitents of Love— 'Their object was to prove the excess of their love, by shewing with an invincible fortitude and consistency of conduct ... that they could bear extremes of heat and cold. ... It was a crime to wear fur on a day of the most piercing cold; or to appear *with a hood*, cloak, gloves or muff.' See the long account of this in the Knight de la Tour Landry, ed. Wright, p. 169; and cf. The Squyer of Low Degree, 171-200.

What is meant by *the drye se* (dry sea) is disputed; but it matters little, for the general idea is clear. Mr. Brae, in the Appendix to his edition of Chaucer's Astrolabe (p. 101), has a long note on the present passage. Relying on the above quotation from Warton, he supposes *hoodless* to have reference to a practice of going unprotected in winter, and says that 'dry sea' may refer to any *frozen* sea. But it may equally refer to going unprotected in summer, in which case he offers us an alternative suggestion, that 'any arid sandy desert might be metaphorically called a dry sea.' The latter is almost a sufficient explanation; but if we must be particular, Mr. Brae has yet more to

III. BOOK OF THE DUCHESSE. LINES 1028, 1029.

tell us. He says that, at p. 1044 (Basle edition) of Sebastian Munster's Cosmographie, there is a description of a large lake which was dry in summer. 'It is said that there is a lake near the city of Labac, adjoining the plain of Zircknitz [Czirknitz], which in winter-time becomes of great extent.... But in summer the water drains away, the fish expire, the bed of the lake is ploughed up, corn grows to maturity, and, after the harvest is over, the waters return, &c. The Augspourg merchants have assured me of this, and it has been since confirmed to me by Vergier, the bishop of Cappodistria' [Capo d'Istria]. The lake still exists, and is no fable. It is the variable lake of *Czirknitz*, which sometimes covers sixty-three square miles, and is sometimes dry. It is situate in the province of Krain, or Carniola; *Labac* is the modern Laybach or Laibach, N.E. of Trieste. See the articles *Krain*, *Czirknitz* in the Engl. Cyclopædia, and the account of the lake in The Student, Sept. 1869.

That Chaucer really referred to this very lake becomes almost certain, if we are to accept Mr. Brae's explanation of the next line. See the next note.

1029. *Carrenare.* Mr. Brae suggests that the reference is to the 'gulf of the *Carnaro* or *Quarnaro* in the Adriatic,' to which Dante alludes in the Inferno, ix. 113, as being noted for its perils. Cary's translation runs thus :—

'As where Rhone stagnates on the plains of Arles,
Or as at Pola, near *Quarnaro's* gulf,
That closes Italy and laves her bounds,
The place is all *thick spread with sepulchres.*'

It is called in Black's Atlas the Channel of Quarnerolo, and is the gulf which separates Istria from Croatia. The head of the gulf runs up towards the province of Carniola, and approaches within forty miles (at the outside) of the lake of Czirknitz (see note above). I suppose that *Quarnaro* may be connected with *Carn-iola* and the *Carn-ic* Alps, but popular etymology interpreted it to mean 'charnel-house,' from its evil reputation. This appears from the quotations cited by Mr. Brae; he says that the Abbé Fortis quotes a Paduan writer, Palladio Negro, as saying—'E regione Istriæ, sinu Palatico, quem nautæ *carnarium* vocitant'; and again, Sebastian Munster, in his Cosmographie, p. 1044 (Basle edition) quotes a description by Vergier, Bishop of Capo d'Istria—'par deça le gouffre enragé lequel on appelle vulgairement *Carnarie*, d'autantque le plus souvent on le voit agité de tempestes horribles; et là s'engloutissent beaucoup de navires et se perdent plusieurs hommes.' In other words, the true name *Quarnaro* or *Carnaro* was turned by the sailors into *Carnario*, which means in Italian 'the shambles'; see Florio's Dict., ed. 1598. This *Carnario* might become *Careynaire* or *Carenare* in Chaucer's English, by association with the M. E. *careyne* or *caroigne*, carrion. This word is used by Chaucer in the Kn. Tale, 1155 (Six-text, A 2013), where the

Ellesmere MS. has *careyne*, and the Cambridge and Petworth MSS. have *careyn*.

For myself, I am well satisfied with the above explanation. It is probable, and it suffices; and stories about this *dry sea* may easily have been spread by Venetian sailors. I may add that Maundeville mentions 'a gravely see' in the land of Prestre John, 'that is alle gravele and sonde, with-outen any drope of watre; and it ebbethe and flowethe in grete wawes, as other sees don': ed. Halliwell, p. 272. This curious passage was pointed out by Prof. Hales, in a letter in the Academy, Jan. 28, 1882, p. 65.

We certainly ought to reject the explanation given with great assurance in the Saturday Review, July, 1870, p. 143, col. 1, that the allusion is to the chain of mountains called the *Carena* or *Charenal*, a continuation of the Atlas Mountains in Africa. The writer says— 'Leonardo Dati (A. D. 1470), speaking of Africa, mentions a chain of mountains in continuation of the Atlas, 300 miles long, "commonly called Charenal." In the fine chart of Africa by Juan de la Coxa (1500), this chain is made to stretch as far as Egypt, and bears the name of Carena. La Salle, who was born in 1398, lays down the same chain, which corresponds, says Santarem (Histoire de la Cosmographie, iii. 456), to the Καρήνη of Ptolemy. These allusions place it beyond doubt [?] that the *drie see* of Chaucer was the Great Sahara, the return from whence [*sic*] homewards would be by the chain of the Atlas or [*sic*] Carena.' On the writer's own shewing, the Carena was *not* the Atlas, but a chain stretching thence towards Egypt; not an obvious way of returning home! Whereas, if the 'dry sea' were the lake of Czirknitz, the obvious way of getting away from it would be to take ship in the neighbouring gulf of Quarnaro. And how could Chaucer come to hear of this remote chain of mountains?

1034. 'But why do I tell you my story?' I. e. let me go on with it, and tell you the result.

1037. Again imitated from Machault's Remède de Fortune:—

> 'Car c'est mes cuers, c'est ma creance,
> C'est *mes desirs*, c'est *m'esperaunce*,
> C'est *ma santé* ....
> C'est *toute ma bonne éürté*,
> C'est ce qui me soustient en vie,' &c.

Line 1039 is closely translated. See Furnivall's Trial Forewords, p. 48.

1040. I here substitute *lisse* for *goddesse*, as in the authorities. The blunder is obvious; *goddesse* clogs the line with an extra syllable, and gives a false rime such as Chaucer never makes[1]. He rimes *blisse* with *kisse, lisse, misse,* and *wisse*. Thus in the Frankelein's Tale, F 1237—

---

[1] Koch instances *góddes* in the Envoy to Scogan, 15, which he assumes was *góddis*. Not at all; it is like Chaucer's rime of *clérkes, derk is*; the *-es* being unaccented. This could never produce *goddís*, and still less *goddísse*.

III. BOOK OF THE DUCHESSE. LINES 1034-1070.

'What for his labour and his hope of blisse,
His woful herte of penaunce hadde a lisse.'

Lisse is alleviation, solace, comfort; and l. 1040 as emended, fairly corresponds to Machault's ' C'est ce qui me soustient en vie,' i. e. it is she who sustains my life. The word *goddesse* was probably substituted for *lisse*, because the latter was obsolescent.

1041. I change *hoolly hirs* into *hirs hoolly*, and omit the following *and*. In the next line we have—By'r lord; as before (ll. 544, 651, 690).

1047. *Leve* (i.e. believe) is here much stronger than *trowe*, which merely expresses general assent.

1050. Read—' And to | behold | e th'alder | fayrest | e.' After *beholde* comes the cæsural pause, so that the final *e* in *beholde* does not count. Koch proposes to omit *alder-*. But how came it there?

1057. The spelling *Alcipiades* occurs in the Roman de la Rose, 8981, where he is mentioned as a type of beauty—' qui de biauté avoit adès '—on the authority of ' Boece.' The ultimate reference is to Boethius, Cons. Phil. b. iii. pr. 8. l. 32—' the body of Alcibiades that was ful fayr.'

1058. Hercules is also mentioned in Le Rom. de la Rose, 9223, 9240. See also Ho. Fame, 1413.

1060. Koch proposes to omit *al*; I would rather omit *the*. But we may read *al th*.'

1061. See note to l. 310.

1067. *He*, i. e. Achilles himself; see next note.

1069. *Antilegius*, a corruption of *Antilochus*; and again, *Antilochus* is a mistake for *Archilochus*, owing to the usual medieval confusion in the forms of proper names. For the story, see next note.

1070. *Dares Frigius*, i. e. Dares Phrygius, or Dares of Phrygia. Chaucer again refers to him near the end of Troilus, and in Ho. Fame, 1467 (on which see the note). The works of Dares and Dictys are probably spurious. The reference is really to the very singular, yet popular, medieval version of the story of the Trojan war which was written by Guido of Colonna, and is entitled ' Historia destructionis Troie, per iudicem Guidonem de Columpna Messaniensem.' Guido's work was derived from the Roman de Troie, written by Benoit de Sainte-Maure ; of which romance there is a late edition by M. Joly. In Mr. Panton's introduction to his edition of the Gest Historiale of the Destruction of Troy (Early Eng. Text Society), p. ix., we read—' From the exhaustive reasonings and proofs of Mons. Joly as to the person and age and country of his author, it is sufficiently manifest that the *Roman du Troie* appeared between the years 1175 and 1185. The translation, or version, of the *Roman* by Guido de Colonna was finished, as he tells us at the end of his *Historia Trioana*, in 1287. From one or other, or both, of these works, the various Histories, Chronicles, Romances, Gestes, and Plays of *The Destruction of Troy*, *The*

Prowess and Death of Hector, *The Treason of the Greeks*, &c., were translated, adapted, or amplified, in almost every language of Europe.'

The fact is, that the western nations of Europe claimed connexion, through Æneas and his followers, with the Trojans, and repudiated Homer as favouring the Greeks. They therefore rewrote the story of the Trojan war after a manner of their own; and, in order to give it authority, pretended that it was derived from two authors named Dares Phrygius (or Dares of Phrygia) and Dictys Cretensis (or Dictys of Crete). Dares and Dictys were real names, as they were cited in the time of Ælian (A.D. 230); and it was said that Dares was a Trojan who was killed by Ulysses. See further in Mr. Panton's introduction, as above; Morley's English Writers, vi. 118; and Warton, Hist. Eng. Poetry, ed. Hazlitt, ii. 127 (sect. 3). But Warton does not seem to have known that Guido mainly followed Benoit de Sainte-Maure.

The story about the death of Achilles is taken, accordingly, not from Homer but from Guido de Colonna and his predecessor Benoit. It may be found in the alliterative Geste Hystoriale, above referred to (ed. Panton and Donaldson, p. 342); or in Lydgate's Siege of Troye, bk. iv. c. 32. Hecuba invites Achilles and Archilochus to meet her in the temple of Apollo. When they arrive, they are attacked by Paris and a band of men and soon killed, though Achilles first slays seven of his foes with his own hand.

'There kyld was the *kyng*, and the *knight* bothe,
And by treason *in the temple* tirnyt to dethe.'

Here 'the kyng' is Achilles, and 'the knyght' is Archilochus. It may be added that Achilles was lured to the temple by the expectation that he would there meet Polyxena, and be wedded to her; as Chaucer says in the next line. Polyxena was a daughter of Priam and Hecuba; she is alluded to in Shakespeare's Troilus, iii. 3. 208. According to Ovid, Metam. xiii. 448, she was sacrificed on the tomb of Achilles.

Lydgate employs the forms *Archylogus* and *Anthylogus*.

1071. I supply *hir*; Koch would supply *queen*. I do not find that she *was* a queen.

1075. *Trewely* is properly (though not always) trisyllabic. It was inserted after *nay*, because *nede* and *gabbe* were thought to be monosyllables. Even so, the 'amended' line is bad. It is all right if *trewly* be omitted; and I omit it accordingly.

1081. *Penelope* is accented on the first *e* and on *o*, as in French. Chaucer copies this form from the Roman de la Rose, l. 8694, as appears from his coupling it with *Lucrece*, whilst at the same time he borrows a pair of rimes. The French has:—

'Si n'est-il mès nule *Lucrece*,
Ne *Penelope* nule *en Grece*.'

In the same passage, the story of Lucretia is told in full, on the authority of Livy, as here. The French has: 'ce dit Titus Livius'; l. 8654. In the prologue to the Legend of Good Women, Chaucer alludes again

III. BOOK OF THE DUCHESSE. LINES 1071-1123.

to Penelope (l. 252), Lucrece of Rome (l. 257), and Polixene (l. 258); and he gives the Legend of Lucrece in full. He again alludes to Lucrece and Penelope in the lines preceding the Man of Lawes Prologue (B 63, 75); and in the Frankelein's Tale (F 1405, 1443).

1085. This seems to mean—'she (Blaunche) was as good (as they), and (there was) nothing like (her), though their stories are authentic (enough).' But the expression 'nothing lyke' is extremely awkward, and seems wrong. *Nothing* also means 'not at all'; but this does not help us. In l. 1086, *stories* should perhaps be *storie*; then *her storie* would be the story of Lucrece; cf. l. 1087.

1087. 'Any way, she (Blaunche) was as true as she (Lucrece).'

1089, 1090. Read *seyë*, subjunctive, and *seyë*, gerund. Cf. *knewë*, subj., 1133.

Yong is properly monosyllabic. Read—'I was right yong, the sooth to sey.' In. l. 1095, *yong-e* is the *definite* form.

1096. Accent *besette* (= besett') on the prefix. Else, we must read *Without'* and *besettë*. We should expect *Without-e*, as in 1100. *Without* is rare; but see IV. 17.

1108. *Yit*, still. *Sit*, sittteth; pres. tense.

1113. I. e. you are like one who confesses, but does not repent.

1118. *Achitofel*, Ahitophel; see 2 Sam. xvii.

1119. According to the Historia Troiana of Guido (see note to l. 1070) it was Antenor (also written Anthenor) who took away the Palladium and sent it to Ulysses, thus betraying Troy. See the Geste Hystoriale, p. 379; or see the extract from Caxton in my Specimens of English from 1394 to 1579, p. 89. Or see Chaucer's Troilus, bk. iv. l. 204.

1121. *Genelon*; also *Genilon*, as in the Monkes Tale, B 3579. He is mentioned again in the Nonne Preestes Tale, B 4417 (C. T. 15233), and in the Shipmannes Tale, B 1384 (C. T. 13124), where he is called 'Geniloun of France.' Tyrwhitt's note on *Genelon* in his Glossary is as follows: 'One of Charlemaigne's officers, who, by his treachery, was the cause of the defeat at Roncevaux, the death of Roland, &c., for which he was torn to pieces by horses. This at least is the account of the author who calls himself Archbishop Turpin, and of the Romancers who followed him; upon whose credit the name of *Genelon* or *Ganelon* was for several centuries a synonymous expression for *the worst of traitors.*' See the Chanson de Roland, ed. Gautier; Dante, Inf. xxxii. 122, where he is called *Ganellone*; and Wheeler's Noted Names of Fiction. Cf. also the Roman de la Rose, l. 7902-4:—

'Qu'onques Karles n'ot por Rolant,
Quant en Ronceval mort reçut
Par *Guenelon* qui les deçut.'

1123. *Rowland and Olivere*, the two most celebrated of Charlemagne's Twelve Peers of France; see *Roland* in Wheeler's Noted Names of Fiction, and Ellis's Specimens of Early Eng. Metrical Romances, especially the account of the Romance of Sir Otuel.

NOTES TO THE MINOR POEMS.

1126. I supply *right*. We find *right tho* in C. T. 6398, 8420 (D 816, E 544).

1133. *Knew-e*, might know; subjunctive mood. See note to l. 1089.

1137. Accent *thou*. This and the next line are repeated, nearly, from ll. 743, 744. See also ll. 1305-6.

1139. I here insert the word *sir*, as in most of the other places where the poet addresses the stranger.

1152-3. Cf. Rom. de la Rose, 2006-7 :—

'Il est asses *sires du cors*
Qui a le *cuer* en sa commande.'

1159. For *this*, B. has *thus*. Neither *this* nor *thus* seems wanted; I therefore pay no regard to them.

The squire Dorigen, in the Frankelein's Tale, consoled himself in the same way (F 947) :—

'Of swich matere made he manye layes,
Songes, compleintes, roundels, virelayes.'

1162. *Tubal*; an error for *Jubal*; see Gen. iv. 21. But the error is Chaucer's own, and is common. See Higden's Polychronicon, lib. iii. c. 11, ed. Lumby, iii. 202 ; Higden cites the following from Isidorus, lib. ii. c. 24 :—'Quamvis *Tubal* de stirpe Cayn ante diluvium legatur fuisse musicæ inventor, . . tamen apud Græcos *Pythagoras* legitur ex malleorum sonitu et chordarum extensione musicam reperisse.' In Genesis, it is Jubal who 'was the father of all such as handle the harp and organ'; and Tubal-cain who was 'an instructor of every artificer in brass and iron.' The notion of the discovery of music by the former from the observation of the sounds struck upon the anvil of the latter is borrowed from the usual fable about Pythagoras. This fable is also given by Higden, who copies it from Macrobius. It will be found in the Commentary by Macrobius on the Somnium Scipionis, lib. ii. c. 1; and is to the effect that Pythagoras, observing some smiths at work, found that the tones struck upon their anvils varied according to the weights of the hammers used by them ; and, by weighing these hammers, he discovered the relations to each other of the various notes in the gamut. The story is open to the objection that the facts are not so ; the sound varies according to variations in the anvil or the thing struck, not according to the variation in the striking implement. However, Pythagoras is further said to have made experiments with stretched strings of varying length ; which would have given him right results. See Mrs. Somerville's Connection of the Physical Sciences, sect. 16 and 17.

1169. *Aurora*. The note in Tyrwhitt's Glossary, s. v. *Aurora*, runs thus :—'The title of a Latin metrical version of several parts of the Bible by *Petrus de Riga*, Canon of Rheims, in the twelfth century. Leyser, in his *Hist. Poet. Med. Ævi*, pp. 692-736, has given large extracts from this work, and among others the passage which Chaucer seems to have had in his eye (p. 728) :—

III. BOOK OF THE DUCHESSE. LINES 1126-1206.

> 'Aure Jubal varios ferramenti notat ictus.
> Pondera librat in his. Consona quæque facit.
> Hoc inventa modo prius est ars musica, quamvis
> Pythagoram dicant hanc docuisse prius.'

Warton speaks of 'Petrus de Riga, canon of Rheims, whose *Aurora*, or the *History of the Bible allegorised*, in Latin verses .. was never printed entire.'—Hist. E. Poet. 1871, iii. 136.

1175. A song in six lines; compare the eleven-line song above, at l. 475. Lines 1175-6 rime with lines 1179-80.

1198. Koch scans: Ánd | bounté | withoút' | mercý‖. This is no better than the reading in the text.

1200. 'With (tones of) sorrow and by compulsion, yet as though I never ought to have done so.' Perhaps read *wolde*, wished (to do).

1206. *Dismal.* In this particular passage the phrase *in the dismal* means 'on an unlucky day,' with reference to an etymology which connected *dismal* with the Latin *dies malus*. Though we cannot derive *dismal* immediately from the Lat. *dies malus*, it is now known that there was an Anglo-French phrase *dis mal* (=Lat. *dies mali*, plural); whence the M.E. phrase *in the dismal*, 'in the evil days,' or (more loosely), 'on an evil day.' When the exact sense was lost, the suffix *-al* seemed to be adjectival, and the word *dismal* became at last an adjective. The A.F. form *dismal*, explained as *les mal jours* (evil days), was discovered by M. Paul Meyer in a Glasgow MS. (marked Q. 9. 13, fol. 100, back), in a poem dated 1256; which settles the question. Dr. Chance notes that Chaucer probably took *dis-mal* to be derived from O.F. *dis mal*, i.e. 'ten evils'; see l. 1207.

We can now see the connexion with the next line. The whole sentence means: 'I think it must have been in the evil days (i.e. on an unlucky day), such as were the days of the ten plagues of Egypt'; and the allusion is clearly to the so-called *dies Ægyptiaci*, or unlucky days; and *woundes* is merely a rather too literal translation of Lat. *plaga*, which we generally translate by *plague*. In Vincent of Beauvais, Speculum Naturale, lib. xv. c. 83, we find:—'In quolibet mense sunt duo dies, qui dicuntur *Ægyptiaci*, quorum unus est a principio mensis, alter a fine.' He goes on to shew how they are calculated, and says that, in January, the Egyptian days are the 1st, and the 7th from the end, i.e. the 25th; and he expressly refers the name *Ægyptiaci* to the plagues of Egypt, which (as some said) took place on Egyptian days; for it was asserted that there were minor plagues besides the ten. See also Brand's Pop. Antiquities, ed. Ellis, from which I extract the following. Barnabe Googe thus translates the remarks of Naogeorgus on this subject [of days]:—

> 'But some of them Egyptian are, and full of jeopardee,
> And some again, beside the rest, both good and luckie bee.'
> Brand (as above), ii. 45.

'The Christian faith is violated when, so like a pagan and apostate, any man doth observe those days which are called *Ægyptiaci*,' &c.— Melton's Astrologaster, p. 56; in Brand, ii. 47. 'If his Journey began unawares *on the dismal day*, he feares a mischiefe'; Bp. Hall, Characters of Virtues and Vices; in Brand, ii. 48. 'Alle that take hede to *dysmal dayes*, or use nyce observaunces in the newe moone,' &c.; Dialogue of Dives and Pauper (1493); in Brand, i. 9. 'A *dismol* day'; Tale of Beryn, 650. Compare also the following:—

> 'Her *disemale daies*, and her fatal houres';
> Lydgate, Storie of Thebes, pt. iii. (ed. 1561, fol. 370).

In the Pistil of Swete Susan (Laing's Anc. Pop. Poetry of Scotland), l. 305, Daniel reproves one of the elders in these terms:—

> 'Thou hast i-be presedent, the people to steere,
> Thou dotest now on thin olde tos, *in the dismale*.'

In Langtoft's Chronicle, l. 477 (in Wright's Polit. Songs, p. 303), John Baliol is attacked in some derisive verses, which conclude with:— 'Rede him at ride *in the dismale*'; i.e. advise him to ride on an unlucky day. Cf. The Academy, Nov. 28, 1891, p. 482; &c.

The consequence of 'proposing' on an unlucky day was a refusal; see l. 1243.

1208. A priest who missed words in chanting a service was called an *overskipper*; see my note to P. Plowman, C. xiv. 123.

1219. Similarly, Troilus was reduced to saying—

> 'Mercy, mercy, swete herte!'—Troil. iii. 98.

1234. 'Unless I am dreaming,' i.e. unintentionally.

1246. *Cassandra*. The prophetic lamentation of Cassandra over the impending fate of Troy is given in the alliterative Geste Hystoriale (E. E. T. S.), p. 88, and in Lydgate's Siege of Troye, bk. ii. c. 12, from Guido de Colonna; cf. Vergil, Æn. ii. 246.

1248. Chaucer treats *Ilion* as if it were different from *Troye*; cf. Nonne Prestes Tale, B 4546 (C. T. 15362). He merely follows Guido de Colonna and others, who made *Ilion* the name of the *citadel* of Troy; see further in note to Ho. of Fame, l. 158.

1288. M. Sandras (Étude sur Chaucer, p. 95) says this is from Machault's Jugement du Bon Roi de Behaigne—

> 'De nos deux cuers estoit si juste paire
> Qu'onques ne fu l'un à l'autre contraire.
> Tuit d'un accord, une pensee avoient.
> De volenté, de desir se sambloient.
> Un bien, un mal, une joie sentoient
>   Conjointement.
> N'onques ne fu entre eux deux autrement.'

1305-6. Repeated from ll. 743, 744. Cf. ll. 1137-8.

1309. Imitated in Spenser's Daphnaida, 184. The Duchess Blaunche

IV. THE COMPLAINT OF MARS. LINES 1, 2.

died Sept. 12, 1369. The third great pestilence lasted from July to September in that year.

1314. *King*, i.e. Edward III; see note to l. 368.

1318. Possibly the *long castel* here meant is Windsor Castle; this seems likely when we remember that it was in Windsor Castle that Edward III. instituted the order of the Garter, April 23, 1349; and that he often resided there. *A riche hil* in the next line appears to have no special significance. The suggestion, in Bell's Chaucer, that it refers to Richmond (which, after all, is not Windsor) is quite out of the question, because that town was then called Sheen, and did not receive the name of Richmond till the reign of Henry VII., who renamed it after Richmond in Yorkshire, whence his own title of Earl of Richmond had been derived.

1322. *Belle*, i. e. bell of a clock, which rang out the hour. This bell, half heard in the dream, seems to be meant to be real. If so, it struck midnight; and Chaucer's chamber must have been within reach of its sound.

IV. THE COMPLAINT OF MARS.

FOR general remarks on this poem, see p. 64, above.

By consulting ll. 13 and 14, we see that the whole of this poem is supposed to be uttered by a bird on the 14th of February, before sunrise. Lines 1-28 form the proem; the rest give the story of Mars and Venus, followed by the Complaint of Mars at l. 155. The first 22 stanzas are in the ordinary 7-line stanza. The Complaint is very artificial, consisting of an Introductory Stanza, and five Terns, or sets of three stanzas, making sixteen stanzas of nine lines each, or 144 lines Thus the whole poem has 298 lines.

Each tern is occupied with a distinct subject, which I indicate by headings, viz. Devotion to his Love; Description of a Lady in an anxiety of fear and woe; the Instability of Happiness; the story of the Brooch of Thebes; and An Appeal for Sympathy. A correct appreciation of these various 'movements' of the Complaint makes the poem much more intelligible.

1. *Foules*. The false reading *lovers* was caught from l. 5 below. But the poem opens with a call from a bird to all other birds, bidding them rejoice at the return of Saint Valentine's day. There is an obvious allusion in this line to the common proverb —' As fain as fowl of a fair morrow,' which is quoted in the Kn. Tale, 1579 (A 2437), in P. Plowman, B. x. 153, and is again alluded to in the Can. Yeom. Tale, G 1342. In l. 3, the bird addresses the *flowers*, and finally, in l. 5, the *lovers*.

2. Venus, the planet, supposed to appear as a morning-star, as it sometimes does. See note to Boethius, bk. i. met. 5. l. 9.

Rowes, streaks or rays of light, lit. rows. In the Complaint of the Black Knight, l. 596, Lydgate uses the word of the streaks of light at eventide—'And while the twilight and the *rowes* rede Of Phebus light,' &c. Also in Lydgate's Troy-Book, bk. i. c. 6, ed. 1555, fol. E I, quoted by Warton, Hist. E. Poetry, 1871, iii. 84 :—'Whan that the *rowes* and the rayes rede Estward to us full early gonnen sprede.' Hence the verb *rowen*, to dawn; P. Plowm. C. ii. 114, xxi. 28; see my Notes to P. Plowman. Tyrwhitt's Glossary ignores the word.

3. For *day*, Bell's edition has *May*! The month is February.

4. *Uprist*, upriseth. But in Kn. Tale, 193 (A 1051), *uprist-e* (with final *e*) is the dat. case of a sb.

7. The final *e* in *sonn-e* occurs at the cæsural pause; *candle* is pronounced nearly as *candl'*. The sun is here called the *candle of Ielosye*, i. e. torch or light that discloses cause for jealousy, in allusion to the famous tale which is the foundation of the whole poem, viz. how Phœbus (the Sun) discovered the amour between Mars and Venus, and informed Vulcan of it, rousing him to jealousy; which Chaucer doubtless obtained from his favourite author Ovid (Metam. bk. iv). See the description of ' Phebus,' with his 'torche in honde,' in ll. 27, 81 84 below. Gower also, who quotes Ovid expressly, has the whole story; Conf. Amant. ed. Pauli, ii. 149. The story first occurs in Homer, Odys. viii. 266-358. And cf. Statius, Theb. iii. 263-316; Chaucer's Kn. Tale, 1525 (A 2383), &c. Cf. also Troil s, iii. 1457.

8. *Blewe*; 'there seems no propriety in this epithet; it is probably a corruption'; Bell. But it is quite right; in M. E., the word is often applied to the colour of a wale or stripe caused by a blow, as in the phrase 'beat black and *blue*'; also to the gray colour of burnt-out ashes, as in P. Plowman, B. iii. 97; also to the colour of lead; 'as blo as led,' Miracle-Plays, ed. Marriott, p. 148. 'Ashen-gray' or 'lead-coloured' is not a very bad epithet for tears :—

'And round about her tear-distained eye
Blue circles streamed.' Shak. Lucrece, 1586.

9. *Taketh*, take ye. *With seynt Iohn*, with St. John for a surety; *borwe* being in the dat. case; see note to Squi. Tale, F 596. It occurs also in the Kingis Quair, st. 23; Blind Harry's Wallace, bk. ix. l. 46; &c.

13. *Seynt Valentyne*; Feb. 14. See note to Sect. V. l. 309.

21. Cf. 'And everich of us take his aventure'; Kn. Tale, 328 (A 1186).

25. See note to line 7 above; and cf. Troilus, iii. 1450-70 :—'O cruel day,' &c.

29. In the Proem to Troilus, bk. iii. st. 1, Chaucer places *Venus* in the third heaven; that is, he begins to reckon from the earth outwards, the spheres being, successively, those of the Moon, Mercury, Venus, Sun, Mars, Jupiter, and Saturn; see the description of the planets in Gower's Confessio Amantis, bk. vii. So also, in Troilus, v. 1809, by the *seventh* sphere he means the outermost sphere of Saturn. But in

IV. COMPLAINT OF MARS. LINES 3-55. 497

other poems he adopts the more common ancient mode, of reckoning the spheres in the reverse order, taking Saturn *first*; in which case Mars comes third. In this he follows Macrobius, who, in his Commentary on the Somnium Scipionis, lib. i. c. 19, has :—' A sphaera Saturni, quae est *prima* de septem,' &c. ; see further on this borrowing from Macrobius in the note to l. 69. The same mode of reckoning places Venus in the *fifth* sphere, as in Lenvoy to Scogan, l. 9. In the curious manual of astronomy called The Shepheards Kalendar (pr. in 1604) we find, in the account of Mars, the following : ' The planet of Mars is called the God of battel and of war, and he is the *third* planet, for he raigneth next vnder the gentle planet of Jupiter . . . And Mars goeth about the twelue signes *in two yeare*.' The account of Venus has :—' Next after the Sun raigneth the gentle planet *Venus*, . . . and she is lady ouer all louers : . . . and her two signes is *Taurus* and Libra . . . This planet Venus runneth *in twelue months* ouer the xii. signes.' Also :—' Next under Venus is the faire planet Mercury . . and his principall signes be these : *Gemini* is the first . . and the other signe is *Virgo*,' &c. See Furnivall's Trial Forewords, p. 121.

Hence the ' third heaven's lord ' is *Mars* ; and Chaucer tells us, that by virtue of his motion in his orbit (as well as by desert) he had won Venus. That is, Venus and Mars were seen in the sky very near each other. We may explain *wonne* by ' approached.'

36. *At alle*, in any and every case. There is a parallel passage to this stanza in Troilus, bk. iii. st. 4 of the Proem.

38. *Talle*, obedient, docile, obsequious. See the account of this difficult word in my Etym. Dictionary, s. v. *tall*.

42. *Scourging*, correction. Compare the phr. *under your yerde*; Parl. Foules, 640, and the note. I see no reason for suspecting the reading.

49. ' Unless it should be that his fault should sever their love.'

51. *Loking*, aspect ; a translation of the Latin astrological term *aspectus*. They regard each other with a favourable aspect.

54. *Hir nexte paleys*, the next palace (or mansion), which belonged to Venus. In astrology, each planet was said to have two *mansions*, except the sun and moon, which had but one apiece. A *mansion*, or *house*, or *palace*, is that Zodiacal sign in which, for some imaginary reason, a planet was supposed to be peculiarly at home. (The whole system is fanciful and arbitrary.) The mansions of Venus were said to be Taurus and Libra ; those of Mars, Aries and Scorpio ; and those of Mercury, Gemini and Virgo. See the whole scheme in the introduction to Chaucer's Astrolabe. The sign here meant is *Taurus* (cf. l. 86) ; and the arrangement was that Mars should ' glide ' or pass out of the sign of Aries into that of Taurus, which came next, and belonged specially to Venus.

55. *A-take*, overtaken ; because the apparent motion of Venus is swifter than that of Mars. This shews that Mars was, at first, further advanced than Venus along the Zodiac.

* K k

61. Actually repeated in the Nonne Prestes Tale, l. 340 (B 4350) :—'For whan I see the beautee of your face.' Compare also l. 62 with the same, l. 342 ; and l. 63 with the same, l. 350.

65. *come*, may come ; pres. subj. (Lounsbury says 'preterite').

69. That is, the apparent motion of Venus was twice as great as that of Mars. Chaucer here follows Macrobius, Comment. in Somnium Scipionis, lib. i. ch. 19, who says :—' Rursus tantum a Iove sphæra Martis recedit, ut eundum cursum *biennio* peragat. Venus autem tanto est regione Martis inferior, ut ei annus satis sit ad zodiacum peragrandum'; that is, Mars performs his orbit in *two* years, but Venus in *one*; accordingly, she moves as much in *one day* as Mars does in *two days*. Mars really performs his orbit in rather less than two years (about 687 days), and Venus in less than one (about 225 days), but Chaucer's statement is sufficiently near to facts, the apparent motion of the planets being variable.

71. This line resembles one in the Man of Lawes Tale, B 1075 :—'And swich a blisse is ther bitwix hem two'; and ll. 71, 72 also resemble the same, ll. 1114, 1115 :—

'Who can the pitous Ioye tellen al
Betwix hem three, sin they ben thus y-mette?'

81. Phebus here passes the palace-gates ; in other words, the sun enters the sign of Taurus, and so comes into Venus' chamber, within her palace. Cf. note to l. 54.

In Chaucer's time, the sun entered Taurus on the twelfth of April. This is actually mentioned below, in l. 139.

84. *Knokkeden*, knocked at the door, i. e. demanded admission.

86. That is, both Mars and Venus are now in Taurus. The entry of Venus is noticed in l. 72.

89. The latter syllable of *Venus* comes at the cæsural pause ; but the scansion is best mended by omitting *nygh* ; see footnote.

96. In the Shepheards Kalendar, Mars is said to be 'hot and dry'; and Venus to be 'moist and colde.' Thus Mars was supposed to cause heat, and Venus to bring rain. The power of Venus in causing rain is fully alluded to in Lenvoy to Scogan, st. 2.

100. *Girt*, short for *girdeth* ; not *gerte*, pt. t.

104. Nearly repeated in Kn. Tale, 1091 (A 1949) :—'Ne may with Venus holde champartye.'

105. *Bad her fleen*, bade her flee ; because her motion in her orbit was faster than his. Cf. l. 112.

107. 'In the palace (Taurus) in which thou wast disturbed.'

111. *Stremes*, beams, rays ; for the eyes of Mars emitted streams of fire (l. 95). Venus is already half past the distance to which Mars's beams extend. Obscure and fanciful.

113. *Cylenius*, Cyllenius, i. e. Mercury, who was born on Mount Cyllene in Arcadia ; Vergil, Æn. viii. 139. *Tour*, tower ; another word for *mansion*. The tower of Cyllenius, or mansion of Mercury, is

the sign Gemini; see note to l. 29. Venus passes out of Taurus into the next sign Gemini. 'The sign *Gemini* is also *domus Murcurii*, so that when Venus fled into "the tour" of Cyllenius, she simply slipped into the next door to her own house of *Taurus*, leaving poor Mars behind to halt after her as he best might'; A. E. Brae, in Notes and Queries, 1st Series, iii. 235.

114. *Voide*, solitary; Mars is left behind in Taurus. Besides (according to l. 116) there was no other planet in Germini at that time.

117. *But litil myght*. A planet was supposed to exercise its greatest influence in the sign which was called its *exaltation*; and its least influence in that which was called its *depression*. The *exaltation* of Venus was in Pisces; her *depression*, in Virgo. She was now in Gemini, and therefore halfway from her exaltation to her depression. So her influence was slight, and waning.

119. *A cave*. In l. 122 we are told that it stood only two paces within the gate, viz. of Gemini. The gate or entrance into Gemini is the point where the sign begins. By *paces* we must understand *degrees*; for the F. word *pas* evidently represents the Lat. *gradus*. Venus had therefore advanced to a point which stood only two degrees within (or from the beginning of) the sign. In plain words, she was now in the second degree of Gemini, and there fell into *a cave*, in which she remained for *a natural day*, that is (taking her year to be of nearly the same length as the earth's year) for the term during which she remained within that second degree. Venus remained in the cave as long as she was in that second degree of the sign; from the moment of entering it to the moment of leaving it.

A *natural day* means a period of twenty-four hours, as distinguished from the *artificial day*, which was the old technical name for the time from sunrise to sunset. This Chaucer says plainly, in his Treatise on the Astrolabe, pt. ii. § 7, l. 12—'the *day natural*, that is to seyn 24 houris.'

We thus see that the *cave* here mentioned is a name for the *second degree* of the sign Gemini.

This being so, I have no doubt at all, that *cave* is here merely a translation of the Latin technical astrological term *puteus*. In Vincent of Beauvais, Speculum Naturale, lib. xv. c. 42, I find:—'Et *in signis* sunt quidam *gradus*, qui dicuntur *putei*; cum fuerit planeta in aliquo istorum, dicitur esse *in puteo*, vt 6 gradus Arietis, et 11, etc.' There are certain degrees in the signs called *putei*; and when a planet is in one of these, it is said to be *in puteo*; such degrees, in Aries, are the 6th, 11th, &c. Here, unfortunately, Vincent's information ceases; he refers us, however, to Alcabitius.

Alcabitius (usually Alchabitius), who should rather be called Abd-el-Aziz, was an Arabian astrologer who lived towards the middle of the tenth century. His treatise on judicial astrology was translated into Latin by Johannes Hispalensis in the thirteenth century. This translation was printed at Venice, in quarto, in 1481, 1482, and 1502; see Didot, Nouv. Biograph. Universelle.

I found a copy of the edition of 1482 in the Cambridge University Library, entitled Libellus ysagogic*us* abdilazi .i. serui gloriosi dei. q*ui* d*i*c*i*tu*r* alchabit*ius* ad *m*agisteriu*m* iudicior*um* astror*um* ; i*n*terpretat*us* a ioa*n*ne hispale*n*si. At sign. a 7, back, I found the passage quoted above from Vincent, and a *full list* of the *putei*. The *putei* in the sign of Gemini are the degrees numbered 2, 12, 17, 26, 30. After this striking confirmation of my conjecture, I think no more need be said.

But I may add, that Chaucer expressly mentions 'Alkabucius' by name, and refers to him; Treat. on Astrolabe, i. 8. 9. The passage which he there quotes occurs in the same treatise, sign. a 1, back.

120. *Derk*, dark. I think it is sufficient to suppose that this word is used, in a purely astrological sense, to mean inauspicious; and the same is true of l. 122, where Venus remains under this sinister influence as long as she remained in the ill-omened second degree of Gemini. There is no need to suppose that the planet's light was really obscured.

129. The Fairfax MS. and some editions have the false reading *sterre*. As Mars was supposed to complete his orbit (360 degrees) in *two years* (see note to l. 69), he would pass over one degree of it in about *two days*. Hence Mr. Brae's note upon this line, as printed in Furnivall's Trial Forewords, p. 121:—'The mention of *dayes two* is so specific that it cannot but have a special meaning. Wherefore, either *sterre* is a metonym for *degree*; or which is more probable, Chaucer's word was originally *steppe* (*gradus*), and was miscopied *sterre* by early scribes.' Here Mr. Brae was exceedingly near the right solution; we now see that *sterre* was miswritten (not for *steppe*, but) for *steyre*, by the mere alteration of one letter. If the scribe was writing from dictation, the mistake was still more easily made, since *steyre* and *sterre* would sound very nearly alike, with the old pronunciation. As to *steyre*, it is the exact literal translation of Lat. *gradus*, which meant a degree or stair. Thus Minsheu's Dict. has:— 'a *Staire*, Lat. *gradus*.' This difficulty, in fact, is entirely cleared up by accepting the reading of the majority of the MSS.

131. *He foloweth her*, i.e. the motions of Mars and Venus were in the same direction; neither of them had a 'retrograde' motion, but advanced along the signs in the direction of the sun's apparent motion.

133. *Brenning*, burning in the fire of the sun's heat.

137. 'Alas; that my orbit has so wide a compass'; because the orbit of Mars is so very much larger than that of Venus. Still larger was the orbit of Saturn; Kn. Tale, 1596 (A 2454). *Spere* is sphere, orbit.

139. *Twelfte*, twelfth. The false reading *twelve* arose from misreading the symbol '.xij.,' which was used as an abbreviation both for

IV. COMPLAINT OF MARS. LINES 120-145.

twelfte and for *twelve*. See Furnivall, Trial Forewords, p. 88. As a fact, it was on the 12*th day of April* that the sun entered Taurus; see note to l. 81.

144. *Cylenius*, Mercury; as in l. 113. *Chevauche*, equestrian journey, ride. Used ludicrously to mean a feat of horsemanship in l. 50 of the Manciple's Prologue. The closely related word *chivachye*, in Prologue to C. T. 85, means a military (equestrian) expedition. In the present case it simply means 'swift course,' with reference to the rapid movement of Mercury, which completes its orbit in about 88 days. Thus the line means—'Mercury, advancing in his swift course.'

145. *Fro Venus valance.* This is the most difficult expression in the poem, but I explain it by reading *fallance*, which of course is only a *guess*. I must now give my reasons, as every preceding commentator has given up the passage as hopeless.

The readings of the MSS. all point back to a form *valance* (as in Ar.) or *valauns* (as in Tn.); whence the other readings, such as *Valaunses*, *valanus* (for *valauns*), *balance*, *balaunce*, are all deduced, by easy corruptions. But, as no assignable sense has been found for *valance*, I can only suppose that it is an error for *falance* or *fallance*. I know of no instance of its use in English, but Godefroy gives examples of *fallance* and *falence* in O. French, though the usual spelling is *faillance*. The change from *faillance* or *fallance* to *vallance* or *valance* would easily be made by scribes, from the alliterative influence of the initial letter of the preceding word *Venus*. Moreover, we have *v* for *f* in E. *vixen* (for *fixen*), and in Southern English generally. Even in a Chaucer MS., the curious spelling *vigour* or *vigur* for *figure* occurs over and over again; viz. in the Cambridge MS. (Dd. 3. 53) of Chaucer's 'Astrolabe.'

The sense of *fallance* or *faillance* is failure, defection. Cotgrave gives us: 'Faillance, f. a defection, failing, decaying.' The numerous examples in Godefroy shew that it was once a common word. It represents a Lat. fem. **fallentia*.

I hold it to be the exact literal translation into French of the Lat. technical (astrological) term *detrimentum*. In my edition of Chaucer's Astrolabe (E. E. T. S.), p. lxvii., I explained that every planet had either one or two *mansions*, and one or two *detrimenta*. The *detrimentum* is the sign of the Zodiac opposite to the planet's mansion. The mansions of Venus were Taurus and Libra (see note to l. 54); and her *detrimenta* were Scorpio and Aries. The latter is here intended; so that, after all, this apparently mysterious term 'Venus valance' is nothing but another name for *the sign Aries*, which, *from other considerations*, must necessarily be here intended.

If the correction of *valance* to *fallance* be disallowed, I should plead that *valance* might be short for *avalance* (mod. E. *avalanche*, literally *descent*), just as every reader of our old literature knows that *vale* is a common form instead of *avale*, to descend or lower, being the verb from which *avalance* is derived. This *valance* (= *avalance*) is a fair translation of the Lat. *occasus*, which was an alternative name for the sign called *detrimentum*; see my edition of the Astrolabe, as above. The result would then be just the same as before, and would bring us back to *the sign of Aries* again.

But we know that Aries is meant, from purely astronomical considerations. For the planet Mercury is always so near the sun that it can never have a greater elongation, or angular distance, from it than 29°, which is just a little less than the length of a sign, which was 30°. But, the sun being (as said) in the 1st degree of Taurus on the 12th of April, it is quite certain that Mercury was either in Taurus or in Aries. Again, as there was no mention of Mercury being in Taurus when Mars and Venus were there and were undisturbed (see note to l. 114), we can only infer that Mercury was then *in Aries*.

Moreover, he continued his swift course, always approaching and tending to overtake the slower bodies that preceded him, viz. the Sun, Mars, and Venus. At last, he got so near that he was able to 'see' or get a glimpse of his mansion Gemini, which was not so very far ahead of him. This I take to mean that he was swiftly approaching the end of Aries.

We can now tell the exact position of all the bodies on the 14th of April, two days after the sun had burst into Taurus, where he had found Mars and Venus at no great distance apart. By that time, Venus was in the second degree of Gemini, Mars was left behind in Taurus, the sun was in the third degree of Taurus, and Mercury near the end of Aries, sufficiently near to Venus to salute and cheer her with a kindly and favourable aspect.

I will add that whilst the whole of the sign of Aries was called the *occasus* or *detrimentum* of Venus, it is somewhat curious that the last ten degrees of Aries (degrees 20 to 30) were called *the face of Venus*. Chaucer uses this astrological term *face* elsewhere with reference to the *first* ten degrees of Aries, which was 'the face of Mars' (see my note to Squieres Tale, F 47). Hence another possible reading is *Fro Venus facë mighte*, &c.

In any case, I think we are quite sufficiently near to Chaucer's meaning; especially as he is, after all, only speaking in allegory, and there is no need to strain his words to suit rigid astronomical calculations.

I only give this as a guess, for what it is worth; I should not care to defend it.

150. *Remembreth me*, comes to my memory; the nom. case being the preceding part of the sentence. *Me*, by the way, refers to the extraordinary bird who is made responsible for the whole poem, with the sole exception of lines 13 and 14, and half of l. 15. The bird tells us he will say and sing the Complaint of Mars, and afterwards take his leave.

155. We now come to the part of the poem which exhibits great

IV. COMPLAINT OF MARS. LINES 150-206.

metrical skill. In order to shew the riming more clearly, I have 'set back' the 3rd, 6th, and 7th lines of each stanza. Each stanza exhibits the order of rimes *a a b a a b b c c*; i.e. the first rime belongs to lines 1, 2, 4, 5; the second rime to lines 3, 6, 7; and the last rime to lines 8 and 9. The first stanza forms an Introduction or Proem. The rest form five Terns, or sets of three stanzas, as has been already said. Each Tern has its own subject, quite separate from the rest.

The first line can only be scanned by reading *The ordre* as *Th'ordr'* (monosyllable).

164. The first Tern expresses his Devotion to his love's service. I gave my love, he says, to her for ever; She is the very source of all beauty; and now I will never leave her, but will die in her service.

170. That is—who ever approaches her, but obtains from her no favour, loses all joy in love, and only feels its bitterness.

176. *Men*, people; *men hit selle* = it is sold. This parenthetical ejaculation is an echo to that in l. 168.

185. *Hette*, promised (incorrectly). The M. E. *haten*, to promise, is a complicated verb; see the excellent examples in Mätzner's Dictionary, and in Grein's A. S. Dict., s. v. *hátan*. It had two past tenses; the first *heet*, a strong form, meaning 'promised, commanded,' answering to A.S. *héht* and Goth. *haihait*; and the second *hette*, *hatte*, a weak form, meaning 'I was named,' answering to A. S. *hátte* (used both as a present and a past tense without change of form) and to the Goth. present passive *haitada*. Chaucer has here used the intransitive weak past tense with the sense of the transitive strong one; just as he uses *lernen* with the sense of 'teach.' The confusion was easy and common.

190. *But grace be*, unless favour be shewn me. *See*, shall see; present as future.

191. Tern 2. Shall I complain to my lady? Not so; for she is in distress herself. Lovers may be as true as new metal, and yet suffer. To return: my lady is in distress, and I ought to mourn for her, even though I knew no other sorrow.

197. 'But if *she* were safe, it would not matter about *me*.'

205. 'They might readily leave their head as a pledge,' i.e. might devote themselves to death.

206. *Horowe*, foul, unclean, filthy, scandalous; pl. of *horow*, an adj. formed from the A.S. sb. *horu* (gen. *horwes*). filth; cf. A. S. *horweht*, filthy, from the same stem *horw-*. The M. E. adj. also takes the form *hori*, *hory*, from A. S. *horig*, an adj. formed from the closely related A. S. sb. *horh*, *horg*, filth. As the M. E. adj. is not common, I give some examples (from Mätzner). 'Hit nis bote a *hori* felle,' it is only a dirty skin; Early Eng. Poems, ed. Furnivall, p. 19, l. 13. 'Thy saule .. thorugh fulthe of synne Sone is mad wel *hory* wythinne,' thy soul, by filth of sin, is soon made very foul within; Reliquiæ Antiquæ, ii. 243. 'Eny uncleene, whos touchynge is *hoory*,' any unclean person, whose touch is defiling; Wyclif, Levit. xxii. 5. 'Still used in Devon, pronounced *horry*'; Halliwell.

218. Tern 3. Why did the Creator institute love? The bliss of lovers is so unstable, that in every case lovers have more woes than the moon has changes. Many a fish is mad after the bait; but when he is hooked, he finds his penance, even though the line should break.

219. *Love other companye*, love or companionship.

229. Read *putt'th*; as a monosyllable.

245. Tern 4. The brooch of Thebes had this property, that every one who saw it desired to possess it; when he possessed it, he was haunted with constant dread; and when he lost it, he had a double sorrow in thinking that it was gone. This was due, however, not to the brooch itself, but to the cunning of the maker, who had contrived that all who possessed it should suffer. In the same way, my lady was as the brooch; yet it was not she who caused me wo, but it was He who endowed her with beauty.

The story referred to occurs in the account of the war between Eteocles and Polynices for the possession of Thebes, as related in the Thebaïd of Statius.

In the second book of that poem, the story relates the marriage of Polynices and Tydeus to the two daughters of Adrastus, king of Argos. The marriage ceremony was marred by inauspicious omens, which was attributed to the fact that Argia, who was wedded to Polynices, wore at the wedding a magic bracelet (here called a brooch) which had belonged to Harmonia, *a daughter of Mars and Venus*, and wife of Cadmus. This ornament had been made by Vulcan, in order to bring an evil fate upon Harmonia, to whom it was first given, and upon all women who coveted it or wore it. See the whole story in Statius, Thebais, ii. 265; or in Lewis's translation of Statius, ii. 313.

246. It must be remembered that great and magical virtues were attributed to precious stones and gems. See further in the note to Ho. of Fame, l. 1352.

259. *Enfortuned hit so*, endued it with such virtues. 'He that wrought it' was Vulcan; see note to l. 245.

262. *Covetour*, the one who coveted it. *Nyce*, foolish.

270. 'For my death I blame Him, and my own folly for being so ambitious.'

272. Tern 5. I appeal for sympathy, first to the knights who say that I, Mars, am their patron; secondly, to the ladies who should compassionate Venus their empress; lastly, to all lovers who should sympathise with Venus, who was always so ready to aid them.

273. *Of my divisioun*, born under my influence. The same word is used in the same way in Kn. Tale, 1166 (A 2024). Of course Mars was the special patron of martial knights.

280. 'That ye lament for my sorrow.'

293. *Compleyneth hir*, lament for her.

298. 'Therefore display, on her behalf, some kindly feeling.'

The Complaint of Venus, which formerly used to be printed as a part of this poem, is really a distinct piece. See Sect. XVIII.

V. THE PARLEMENT OF FOULES.

TITLE. Gg. *has* Here begynyth the parlement of Foulys; Harl. *has* The Parlament of Foules; Tn. *has* The Parlement of Briddis; Trin. *has* Here foloweth the parlement of Byrdes reducyd to loue, &c. We also find, at the end of the poem, such notes as these: Gg. Explicit parliamentum Auium in die sancti Valentini tentum secundum Galfridum Chaucer; Ff. Explicit parliamentum Auium; Tn. Explicit tractatus de Congregacione volucrum die Sancti Valentini; and in MS. Arch. Seld. B. 24—Here endis the parliament of foulis Quod Galfride Chaucere.

1. Part of the first aphorism of Hippocrates is—'O βίος βραχύς, ἡ δὲ τέχνη μακρή. This is often quoted in the Latin form—Ars longa, uita breuis. Longfellow, in his Psalm of Life, well renders it by—'Art is long, but life is fleeting.'

2. Several MSS. transpose *hard* and *sharp*; it is of small consequence.

3. *Slit*, the contracted form of *slideth*, i.e. passes away; cf. 'it *slit* awey so faste,' Can. Yeom. Tale; C. T., Group G, l. 682. The false reading *flit* arose from mistaking a long *s* for *f*.

4. *By*, with respect to. In l. 7, *wher* = whether.

8. Evidently this disclaimer is a pretended one; the preceding stanza and ll. 13, 14 contradict it. So does l. 160. In this stanza we have an early example of Chaucer's humour, of which there are several instances below, as e.g. in ll. 567-570, 589, 599, 610, &c. Cf. Troilus, i. 15, where Chaucer again says he is no lover himself, but only serves Love's servants.

15. Cf. Prol. to Legend of Good Women, 29-39.

22. *Men* is here a weakened form of *man*, and is used as a singular sb., with the same force as the F. *on* or the G. *man*. Hence the vb. *seith* is in the singular. This construction is extremely common in Middle English. In ll. 23 and 25 *com'th* is monosyllabic.

31. *Tullius*, i.e. M. Tullius Cicero, who wrote a piece entitled Somnium Scipionis, which originally formed part of the sixth book of the De Republica. Warton (Hist. Eng. Poetry, ed. Hazlitt. iii. 65) remarks:—'Had this composition descended to posterity among Tully's six books *De Republica*, to the last of which it originally belonged, perhaps it would have been overlooked and neglected. But being preserved and illustrated with a prolix commentary by Macrobius, it quickly attracted the attention of readers who were fond of the marvellous, and with whom Macrobius was a more admired classic than Tully. It was printed [at Venice] subjoined to Tully's *Offices*, in [1470]. It was translated into Greek by Maximus Planudes, and is frequently [i.e. four times] quoted by Chaucer ... Nor is it improbable that not only the form, but the first idea, of Dante's *Inferno* was suggested by this apologue.' The other allusions to it in Chaucer are in the Nonnes Prestes Tale, B 4314; Book of the Duchesse, 284; Ho. of Fame, 514.

See also l. 111 below, where *Macrobie* is expressly mentioned. In the E. version of the Romance of the Rose, l. 7, he is called *Macrobes*.

Aurelius Theodosius Macrobius, about A. D. 400, not only preserved for us Cicero's Somnium Scipionis, but wrote a long commentary on it in two books, and a work called Saturnalia in seven books. The commentary is not very helpful, and discusses collateral questions rather than the dream itself.

32. Chaucer's MS. copy was, it appears, divided into seven chapters. A printed copy now before me is divided into nine chapters. As given in an edition of Macrobius printed in 1670, it is undivided. The treatise speaks, as Chaucer says, of heaven, hell, and earth, and men's souls. It recalls the tale of Er, in Plato's Republic, bk. x.

35. *The grete*, the substance. Accordingly, in the next seven stanzas, we have a fair summary of the general contents of the Somnium Scipionis. I quote below such passages as approach most closely to Chaucer's text.

36. *Scipioun*, i. e. P. Cornelius Scipio Æmilianus Africanus Minor, the hero of the third Punic War. He went to Africa in B.C. 150 to meet Masinissa, King of Numidia, who had received many favours from Scipio Africanus Major in return for his fidelity to the Romans. Hence Masinissa received the younger Africanus joyfully, and so much was said about the elder Africanus that the younger one dreamt about him after the protracted conversation was over, and all had retired to rest. The younger Africanus was the grandson, by adoption, of the elder.

'Cum in Africam venissem, ... nihil mihi potius fuit, quam ut Masinissam convenirem .. Ad quem ut veni, complexus me senex collacrymavit. ... multisque verbis .. habitis, ille nobis consumptus est dies ... me .. somnus complexus est .. mihi .. Africanus se ostendit'; &c.

43. 'Ostendebat autem Carthaginem de excelso, et pleno stellarum .. loco ... tu eris unus, in quo nitatur civitatis salus, &c. ... Omnibus qui patriam conservârint, adiuverint, auxerint, certum esse in cælo definitum locum, ubi beati ævo sempiterno fruantur.'

50. 'Quæsivi tamen, viveretne ipse et Paullus pater et alii, quos nos exstinctos arbitraremur. Immo vero, inquit, ii vivunt ... vestra vero. quæ dicitur vita, mors est ..... corpore laxati illum incolunt locum, quem vides. Erat autem is splendissimo candore inter flammas circus elucens, quem vos, ut a Graiis accepistis, *orbem lacteum* nuncupatis.'

56. *Galaxye*, milky way; see note to Ho. Fame, 936.

57. 'Stellarum autem globi terræ magnitudinem facile vincebant. Iam ipsa terra ita mihi parva visa est, &c. ... Novem tibi orbibus, vel potius globis, connexa sunt omnia ... Hic, inquam, quis est, qui complet aures meas, tantus et tam dulcis sonus? ... impulsu et motu ipsorum orbium conficitur.'

59. The 'nine spheres' are the spheres of the seven planets (Moon, Mercury, Venus, Sun, Mars, Jupiter, Saturn), that of the fixed stars, and the *primum mobile*; see notes to the Treatise on the Astrolabe, part i, § 17, in vol. iii.

61. This is an allusion to the so-called 'harmony of the spheres.' Chaucer makes a mistake in attributing this harmony to *all* of the nine spheres. Cicero plainly excludes the *primum mobile*, and says that, of the remaining eight spheres, two sound alike, so that there are but *seven* tones made by their revolution. 'Ille autem *octo* cursus, in quibus *eadem vis est duorum, septem* efficiunt distinctos intervallis sonos.' He proceeds to notice the peculiar excellence of the number *seven*. By the two that sounded alike, the spheres of Saturn and the fixed stars must be meant; in fact, it is usual to ignore the sphere of fixed stars, and consider only those of the seven planets. Macrobius, in his Commentary, lib. ii. c. 4, quite misses this point, and clumsily gives the same note to Venus and Mercury. Each planetary sphere, in its revolution, gives out a different note of the gamut, so that all the notes of the gamut are sounded; and the result is, that the 'music of the spheres' cannot be heard at all, just as the dwellers by the cataract on the Nile fail to hear the sound of its fall. 'Hoc sonitu oppletæ aures hominum obsurduerunt; nec est ullus hebetior sonus in vobis; sicut ubi Nilus ad illa, quæ Catadupa [καταδουποι] nominantur, præcipitat ex altissimis montibus, ea gens, quæ illum locum accolit, *propter magnitudinem sonitus*, sensu audiendi caret.' Macrobius tries to explain it all in his Commentary, lib. ii. c. 1-4. The fable arose from a supposed necessary connection between the number of the planets and the number of musical notes in the scale. It breaks down when we know that the number of the planets is *more* than seven. Moreover, modern astronomy has exploded the singular notion of revolving hollow concentric spheres, to the surface of which each planet was immoveably nailed. These 'spheres' have disappeared, and their music with them, except in poetry.

Shakespeare so extends the old fable as to give a voice to every star. See Merch. of Venice, v. 60 :—

> 'There's not the smallest orb which thou behold'st,
> But in his motion like an angel sings,' &c.

The notion of the music of the spheres was attributed to Pythagoras. It is denied by Vincent of Beauvais, Speculum Naturale, lib. xv. c. 32— Falsa opinio de concentu cæli. Vincent puts the old idea clearly— 'Feruntur septem planetæ, et hi septem orbes (vt dicitur) cum dulcissima harmonia mouentur, ac suauissimi concentus eorum circumitione efficiuntur. Qui sonus ad aures nostras ideo non peruenit, quia vltra ærem fit':—a sufficient reason. He attributes the notion to the Pythagoreans and the Jews, and notes the use of the phrase 'concentum cæli' in Job xxxviii. 37, where our version has 'the bottles of heaven,' which the Revised Version retains. Cf. also—'Cum me laudarent simul astra matutina'; Job xxxviii. 7.

Near the end of Chaucer's Troilus, v. 1811, we have the singular passage :—

'And ther he saugh with ful avysement
The erratik sterres, herkening armonye
With sounes fulle of hevenish melodye'; &c.

This passage, by the way, is a translation from Boccaccio, Teseide, xi. 1. Cf. Rom. de la Rose, 17151-5.

See also Longfellow's poem on the Occultation of Orion, where the poet (heretically but sensibly) gives the *lowest* note to Saturn, and the *highest* to the Moon; whereas Macrobius says the contrary; lib. ii. c. 4.

A. Neckam (De Naturis Rerum, lib. i. c. 15) seems to say that the sound of an eighth sphere is required to make up the octave.

64. 'Sentio, inquit, te sedem etiam nunc hominum ac domum contemplari: quæ si tibi parva, ut est, ita videtur, hæc cælestia semper spectato; illa humana contemnito ... Cum autem ad idem, unde semel profecta sunt, cuncta astra redierint, eandemque totius anni descriptionem longis intervallis retulerint, tum ille vere vertens *annus* appellari potest ... Sermo autem omnis ille .. obruitur hominum interitu, et oblivione posteritatis exstinguitur.'

The great or mundane year, according to Macrobius, Comment. lib. 2. c. 11, contained 15,000 common years. In the Roman de la Rose, l. 17,018, Jean de Meun makes it 36,000 years long; and in the Complaint of Scotland, ed. Murray, p. 33, it is said, on the authority of Socrates, to extend to 37,000 years. It is not worth discussion.

71. 'Ego vero, inquam, o Africane, siquidem bene meritis de patria quasi limes ad cæli aditum patet,' &c. 'Et ille, Tu vero enitere, et sic habeto, non esse te mortalem, sed corpus hoc ... Hanc [naturam] tu exerce in optimis rebus; sunt autem optimæ curæ de salute patriæ: quibus agitatus et exercitatus animus velocius in hanc sedem et domum suam pervolabit.'

78. 'Nam eorum animi, qui se corporis voluptatibus dediderunt, ... corporibus elapsi circum terram ipsam volutantur; nec hunc in locum, nisi multis exagitati sæculis, revertuntur.' We have here the idea of purgatory; compare Vergil, Æn. vi.

80. *Whirle aboute*, copied from *volutantur* in Cicero; see last note. It is remarkable that Dante has copied the same passage, and has the word *voltando*; Inf. v. 31-8. Cf. 'blown with restless violence round about The pendent world'; Meas. for Meas. iii. 1. 125; and 'The sport of winds'; Milton, P. L. iii. 493.

85. Imitated from Dante, Inf. ii. 1-3 (with which cf. Æneid, ix. 224). Cary's translation has—

'Now was the day departing, and the air,
Imbrowned with shadows, from their toils released
All animals on earth.'

90. 'I had what I did not want,' i. e. care and heaviness. 'And I had not what I wanted,' i. e. my desires. Not a personal reference, but borrowed from Boethius, bk. iii. pr. 3; see vol. ii. p. 57, l. 24.

V. PARLEMENT OF FOULES. LINES 64-117.

Moreover, the same idea is repeated, but in clearer language, in the Complaint to his Lady, ll. 47-49 (p. 361); and again, in the Complaint to Pity, ll. 99-104 (p. 276).

99. Chaucer discusses dreams elsewhere; see Ho. of Fame, 1-52; Nonne Prestes Tale, 76-336; Troil. v. 358. Macrobius, Comment. in Somn. Scipionis, lib. i. c. 3, distinguishes five kinds of dreams, giving the name ἐνύπνιον to the kind of which Chaucer here speaks. 'Est enim ἐνύπνιον quotiens oppressi animi corporisve sive fortunæ, qualis vigilantem fatigaverat, talem se ingerit dormienti: animi, *si amator deliciis suis aut fruentem se videat* aut carentem: . . corporis, si . . esuriens cibum aut *potum sitiens* desiderare, quærere, vel etiam *invenisse videatur*,' &c. But the real original of this stanza (as shewn by Prof. Lounsbury) is to be found in Claudian, In Sextum Consulatum Honorii Augusti Præfatio, ll. 3-10.

'Venator defessa toro cum membra reponit,
 Mens tamen ad silvas et sua lustra redit.
Iudicibus lites, aurigæ somnia currus,
 Vanaque nocturnis meta cavetur equis.
Furto gaudet amans; permutat navita merces;
 Et vigil elapsas quærit avarus opes.
Blandaque largitur frustra sitientibus ægris
 Irriguus gelido pocula fonte sopor.'

Cf. Vincent of Beauvais, lib. xxvi. c. 62 and c. 63; Batman upon Bartholome, lib. vi. c. 27, ed. 1582, fol. 84. And see the famous passage in Romeo and Juliet, i. 4. 53; especially ll. 70-88. The Roman de la Rose begins with remarks concerning dreams; and again, at l. 18564, there is a second passage on the same subject, with a reference to Scipio, and a remark about dreaming of things that occupy the mind (l. 18601).

109. Compare Dante, Inf. i. 83; which Cary translates—

'May it avail me, that I long with zeal
 Have sought thy volume, and with love immense
 Have conn'd it o'er. My master thou, and guide!'

111. 'Of which Macrobius recked (thought) not a little.' In fact, Macrobius concludes his commentary with the words—'Vere igitur pronunciandum est nihil hoc opere perfectius, quo universa philosophiæ continetur integritas.'

113. *Cithérea*, Cytherea, i. e. Venus; see Kn. Tale, 1357 (A 2215).

114. In the Roman de la Rose, 15980, Venus speaks of her bow (F. *arc*) and her firebrand or torch (*brandon*). Cf. Merch. Tale, E 1777.

117. 'As surely as I saw thee in the north-north-west.' He here refers to the planet Venus. As this planet is never more than 47° from the sun, the sun must have been visible to the north of the west point at sunset; i. e. the poem must have been written in the summer-time. The same seems to be indicated by l. 21 (*the longe day*), and still more clearly by ll. 85-88; Chaucer would hardly have gone to bed at

sunset in the winter-time. It is true that he dreams about Saint Valentine's day, but that is quite another matter. Curiously enough, the landscape seen in his dream is quite a summer landscape; see ll. 172, 184-210.

120. *African*, Africanus; as above.

122. *Grene stone*, mossy or moss-covered stone; an expression copied by Lydgate, Complaint of the Black Knight, l. 42.

Prof. Hales, in the Gent. Magazine, April, 1882, has an interesting article on 'Chaucer at Woodstock.' He shews that there was a park there, surrounded by a stone wall; and that Edward III. often resided at Woodstock, where the Black Prince was born. It is possible that Chaucer was thinking of Woodstock when writing the present passage. See the account of Woodstock Palace in Abbeys, Castles, &c. by J. Timbs; vol. ii. But Dr. Köppel has shewn (Anglia, xiv. 234) that Chaucer here partly follows Boccaccio's poem, Amorosa Visione, ii. 1-35, where we find 'un muro antico.' So also the Roman de la Rose has an allusion to Scipio's dream, and the following lines (129-131, p. 99, above):—

'Quant j'oi ung poi avant alé
Si vi ung *vergier* grant et lé,
Tot clos d'ung *haut mur* bataillié;' &c.

123. *Y-wroght-e*; the final *-e* here denotes the plural form.

125. *On eyther halfe*, on either side; to right and left.

127. Imitated from Dante, Inf. iii. 1; Cary's translation has—

'Through me you pass into the city of woe: . . .
Such characters in colour dim, I mark'd
Over a portal's lofty arch inscribed.'

See also l. 134. The gate is the entrance into Love, which is to some a blessing, and to some a curse; see ll. 158, 159. Thus *men gon* is, practically, equivalent to 'some men go'; and so in l. 134. The idea is utterly different from that of the *two* gates in Vergil, Æn. vi. 893. The successful lover finds 'the well of Favour,' l. 129. The unsuccessful one encounters the deadly wounds caused by the spear (or dart) guided to his heart by Disdain and Power-to-harm (Daunger); for him, the opened garden bears no fruit, and the alluring stream leads him only to a fatal weir, wherein imprisoned fish are left lying dry.

Cf. 'As why this fish, and nought that, comth to were';

Troil. iii. 35.

140. 'Avoiding it is the only remedy.' This is only another form of a proverb which also occurs as 'Well fights he who well flies.' See Proverbs of Hending (in Spec. of English), l. 77; Owl and Nightingale, l. 176. Sir T. Wiat has—'The first eschue is remedy alone'; Spec. of Eng. Part III. p. 235. Probably from the Roman de la Rose, l. 16818—'Sol foïr en est medicine.' (O. F. *foir* = Lat. *fugere*.)

141. The alluring message (ll. 127-133) was written in gold; the forbidding one (ll. 134-140) in black; see Anglia, xiv. 235.

142. *A stounde*, for a while (rightly); the reading *astonied* is to be rejected. The attitude is one of deliberation.

143. *That oon*, the one, the latter. In l. 145, it means the former.

148. An adamant was, originally, a diamond; then the name was transferred to the loadstone; lastly, the diamond was credited with the properties of the loadstone. Hence we find, at the end of ch. 14 of Mandeville's Travels, this remarkable experiment:—'Men taken the Ademand, that is the Schipmannes Ston, that drawethe the Nedle to him, and men leyn the Dyamand upon the Ademand, and leyn the Nedle before the Ademand; and yif the Dyamand be good and vertuous, the Ademand drawethe not the Nedle to him, whils the Dyamand is there present.' Cf. A. Neckam, De Naturis Rerum, lib. ii. c. 98, where the story is told of an iron statue of Mahomet, which, being surrounded by adamants (*lapides adamantini*), hangs suspended in the air. The modern simile is that of a donkey between two bundles of hay. For *adamaunt*, see Rom. of the Rose, 1182 (p. 142).

156. *Errour*, doubt; see l. 146 above.

158. 'This writing is not at all meant to apply to thee.'

159. *Servant* was, so to speak, the old technical term for a lover; cf. *serveth*, Kn. Tale, 2220, 2228 (A 3078, 3086); and *servant* in the same, 956 (A 1814); and in Two Gent. of Verona, ii. 1. 106, 114, 140, &c.

163. I. e. 'at any rate you can come and look on.'

169. Imitated from Dante, Inf. iii. 19. Cary has—

'And when his hand he had stretch'd forth
To mine, with pleasant looks, whence I was cheer'd,
Into that secret place he led me on.'

171. Cf. 'So Iolyf, nor so wel bigo'; Rom. Rose, 693.

176. Imitated by Spenser, F. Q. i. 1. 8, 9. Chaucer's list of trees was suggested by a passage in the Teseide, xi. 22-24; but he extended his list by help of one in the Roman de la Rose, 1338-1368; especially ll. 1363-8, as follows (see p. 151, above)—

'Et d'*oliviers* et de *cipres*,
Dont il n'a gaires ici pres;
Ormes y ot branchus et gros,
Et avec ce charmes et fos,
Codres droites, *trembles* et *chesnes*,
Erables haus, *sapins* et *fresnes*.'

Here *ormes* are elms; *charmes*, horn-beams; *fos*, beeches; *codres*, hasels; *trembles*, aspens; *chesnes*, oaks; *erables*, maples; *sapins*, firs; *fresnes*, ashes. Hence this list contains seven kinds of trees out of Chaucer's thirteen. See also the list of 21 trees in Kn. Tale, A 2921. Spenser has—

'The builder oake, sole king of forrests all.'

This tree-list is, in fact, a great curiosity. It was started by Ovid, Metam. x. 90; after whom, it appears in Seneca, Œdipus, 532; in

Lucan, Phars. iii. 440; in Statius, Thebaid, vi. 98; and in Claudian, De Raptu Proserpinae, ii. 107. Statius was followed by Boccaccio, Tes. xi. 22-24; Rom. de la Rose, 1361; Chaucer (twice); Tasso, Gier. Lib. iii. 73; and Spenser. Cf. Vergil, Æn. vi. 179.

I here quote several notes from Bell's Chaucer, marked 'Bell.'

'The reader will observe the life and spirit which the personification of the several trees gives to this catalogue. It is common in French, even in prose; as, for instance, the weeping willow is *le saule pleureur*, the weeper willow. The oak is called *builder*, because no other wood was used in building in this country in the middle ages, as may be seen in our old churches and farm-houses, in which the stairs are often made of solid blocks of the finest oak.'—Bell.

177. 'The elm is called *piler*, perhaps because it is planted as a pillar of support to the vine [cf. Spenser's 'vine-prop elme']; and *cofre unto careyne* because coffins for carrion or corpses were [and are] usually made of elm.'—Bell. In fact, Ovid has 'amictae uitibus ulmi,' Met. x. 100; Claudian has 'pampinus induit ulmos'; and Boccaccio —'E l'olmo, che di viti s'innamora'; Tes. xi. 24.

178. *Piper*, suitable for pipes or horns. 'The box, being a hard, fine-grained wood, was used for making pipes or horns, as in the Nonne Prestes Tale, B 4588—"Of bras they broghten bemes [trumpets] and of box."'—Bell. Boxwood is still used for flutes and flageolets.

Holm to whippes lasshe; 'the holm used for making handles for whip-lashes.'—Bell. Spenser calls it 'The carver holm,' i. e. the holm suitable for carving. It is the holly (A. S. *holegn*), not the holm-oak.

179. *The sayling firr;* this 'alludes to the ship's masts and spars being made of fir.'—Bell. 'Apta fretis abies'; Claudian, De Raptu Proserpinae, ii. 107. Spenser substitutes for it 'The sailing pine.' *The cipres;* 'tumulos tectura cupressus,' in Claudian.

180. *The sheter ew.* 'The material of our [ancient] national weapon, the bow, was yew. It is said that the old yews which are found in country churchyards were planted in order to supply the yeomanry with bows.'—Bell. Spenser has—'The eugh, obedient to the benders will.'

'*The asp* is the aspen, or black poplar, of which shafts or arrows were made.'—Bell. Spenser has—'The aspine good for staves'; and 'The birch for shaftes.' See Ascham's Toxophilus, ed. Arber, p. 126.

181. The olive is the emblem of peace; and the palm, of victory. Boccaccio has—"e d' ogni vincitore Premio la palma'; Tes. xi. 24; from Ovid—'uictoris praemia palmae'; Met. x. 102.

182. 'The laurel (used) for divination,' or 'to divine with.' 'Venturi praescia laurus'; Claudian, de Raptu Proserpinae, ii. 109. It was 'sacred to Apollo; and its branches were the decoration of poets, and of the flamens. The leaves, when eaten, were said to impart the power of prophesying; Tibull. 2. 5. 63; Juvenal, 7. 19.'—Lewis and Short's Lat. Dict., s. v. *laurus*.

V. PARLEMENT OF FOULES. LINES 177-255.

183. In a note to Cant. Tales, l. 1920, Tyrwhitt says—'Chaucer has [here] taken very little from Boccace, as he had already inserted a very close imitation of this part of the Teseide in his Assemblee of Foules, from verse 183 to verse 287.' In fact, eleven stanzas (183-259) correspond to Boccaccio's Teseide, Canto vii. st. 51-60; the next three stanzas (260-280) to the same, st. 63-66; and the next two (281-294) to the same, st. 61, 62. See the whole extract from Boccaccio, given and translated in the Introduction; see p. 68, above.

On the other hand, this passage in Chaucer is imitated in the Kingis Quair, st. 31-33, 152, 153; and ll. 680-9 are imitated in the same, st. 34.

The phrase 'blosmy bowes' occurs again in Troilus, ii. 821.

185. 'There where is always sufficient sweetness.'

214. According to Boccaccio, the name of Cupid's daughter was Voluttade (Pleasure). In the Roman de la Rose, ll. 913, 927 (Eng. version, 923, 939), Cupid has two bows and ten arrows.

216. Read : 'aft'r ás they shúld-e.' So Koch. Or read 'couch'd.'

217. See Ovid, Metam. i. 468-471.

218. This company answer to Boccaccio's Grace, Adornment, Affability, Courtesy, Arts (plural), Vain Delight, and Gentleness. Instead of Craft, Boccaccio speaks of 'the Arts that have power to make others perforce do folly, in their aspect much disfigured.' Hypocritical Cajolery seems to be intended. Cf. 'Charmes and Force'; Kn. Tale, 1069 (A 1927).

225. Ed. 1561 has *with a nice atire*, but wrongly; for compare Boccaccio. Cf. Kn. Tale, 1067-9 (A 1925-7).

226. Cf. 'Jest and youthful Jollity'; L'Allegro, 26.

228. *Messagerye* and *Mede* represents the sending of messages and giving of bribes. For this sense of *Mede*, see P. Plowman, C. iv. (or B. iii.). The *other three* are Audacity (too forward Boldness), Glozings (Flatteries), and Pimps; all of bad reputation, and therefore not named. Boccaccio's words are—'il folle Ardire Con Lusinghe e Ruffiani.'

231. *Bras*, brass. Boccaccio has *rame*, i. e. copper, the metal which symbolised Venus; see Can. Yeom. Tale, G 829. In fact, this temple is the very temple of Venus which Chaucer again describes in the Knightes Tale, ll. 1060-1108 (A 1918); which see.

234. *Faire*, beautiful by nature; *gay*, adorned by art.

236. *Office*, duty; viz. to dance round.

237. These are the *dowves flikeringe* in Kn. Tale, 1104 (A 1962).

243. *Sonde*, sand. 'Her [Patience's] chief virtue is quiet endurance in the most insecure and unhopeful circumstances'; Bell.

245. Answering to Boccaccio's 'Promesse ad arte,' i.e. 'artful Promises.'

246. Cf. Kn. Tale, 1062-1066, 1070 (A 1920-4, 1928).

255. 'The allusion is to the adventure of Priapus, related by Ovid in the Fasti, lib. i. 415'; Bell. The ass, by braying, put Priapus to confusion.

261. But in Kn. Tale, 1082 (A 1940), the porter of Venus is Idleness, as in the Rom. de la Rose, 636 (E. version, 643, at p. 120, above).

267. *Gilte*; cf. Leg. of Good Women, 230, 249, 1315.

272. *Valence*, explained by Urry as Valentia in Spain. But perhaps it may refer to Valence, near Lyons, in France; as Lyons is especially famous for the manufacture of silks, and there is a considerable trade in silks at Valence also. Probably 'thin silk' is here meant. Boccaccio merely speaks of 'texture so thin,' or, in the original 'Testa, tanto *sottil*,' which accounts for Chaucer's 'subtil.' Coles's Dict. (1684) gives: '*Valence,-tia*, a town in Spain, France, and Milan.' In the Unton Inventories, for the years 1596 and 1620, ed. J. G. Nichols, I find: 'one covering for a fielde bedde of green and *valens*,' p. 4; 'one standinge bedsteed with black velvett testern, black *vallance* fringed and laced,' p. 21; 'one standinge bed with yellow damaske testern and *vallence*,' p. 21; '*vallance* frindged and laced,' p. 22; 'one bedsteed and testern, and *valance* of black velvett,' p. 22; 'one bedsteed .. with *vallance* imbroydered with ash couler,' p. 23; 'one bedsteed, with .. *vallance* of silke,' p. 29. It is the mod. E. *valance*, and became a general term for part of the hangings of a bed; Shakespeare has 'Valance of Venice gold,' spelt *Vallens* in old editions, Tam. Shrew, ii. 1. 356. Spenser imitates this passage, F. Q. ii. 12. 77.

275. Compare the well-known proverb—'sine Cerere et Libero friget Venus'; Terence, Eun. 2. 3. 4.

277. Read *Cipryde*, not *Cupide*; for in l. 279 we have *hir* twice, once in the sense of 'their,' but secondly in the sense of 'her.' Boccaccio also here speaks of Venus, and refers to the apple which she won from Paris. *Cipride* is regularly formed from the accus. of *Cypris* (gen. *Cypridis*), an epithet of Venus due to her worship in Cyprus. Chaucer found the genitive *Cypridis* in Alanus de Planctu Naturæ (ed. Wright, p. 438); see note to l. 298. Cf. 'He curseth Ceres, Bacus, and *Cipryde*'; Troilus, v. 208.

281. The best way of scansion is perhaps to read *despyt-e* with final *e*, preserved by cæsura, and to pronounce *Diane* as *Dián*'. So in Kn. Tale, 1193 (A 2051), which runs parallel with it.

282. 'Trophies of the conquest of Venus'; Bell.

283. *Maydens*; of these Callisto was one (so says Boccaccio); and this is Chaucer's *Calixte* (l. 286), and his *Calistopee* in the Kn. Tale, l. 1198 (A 2056). She was the daughter of the Arcadian king Lycaon, and mother of Arcas by Jupiter; changed by Juno, on account of jealousy, into a she-bear, and then raised to the heavens by Jupiter in the form of the constellation Helice or Ursa Major; see Ovid, Fasti, ii. 156; Metamorph. ii. 401; &c. (Lewis and Short).

286. *Athalaunte*, Atalanta. There were two of this name; the one here meant (see Boccaccio) was the one who was conquered in a foot-race by the lover who married her; see Ovid, Metam. x. 565. The other, who was beloved by Meleager, and hunted the Calydonian boar, is the one mentioned in the Kn. Tale, A 2070; see Ovid, Metam.

V. PARLEMENT OF FOULES. LINES 261-292.

viii. 318. It is clear that Chaucer thought, at the time, that they were one and the same.

287. *I wante*, I lack; i.e. I do not know. Boccaccio here mentions the mother of Parthenopæus, whose name Chaucer did not know. She was *the other* Atalanta, the wife of Meleager; and Boccaccio did not name her, because he says 'that other proud one,' meaning the other proud one of the same name. See the story in Dryden; tr. of Ovid's Metamorphoses, bk. viii. Cf. Troilus, v. 1473.

288. Boccaccio only mentions 'the spouse of Ninus,' i.e. Semiramis, the great queen of Assyria, Thisbe and Pyramus, 'Hercules in the lap of Iole,' and Byblis. The rest Chaucer has added. Compare his lists in Prol. to Leg. of Good Women, 250, and in Cant. Tales, Group B, 63; see the note. See the Legend for the stories of Dido, Thisbe and Pyramus, and Cleopatra. Paris, Achilles, Troilus, and Helen are all mentioned in his Troilus; and Hercules in Cant. Ta., B 3285.

Candace is mentioned again at p. 410, above, l. 16. There was a Candace, queen of Meroë, mentioned by Pliny, vi. 29; and there is the Candace in the Acts of the Apostles, viii. 27. But the Candace of fiction was an Indian queen, who contrived to get into her power no less a person than the world's conqueror, Alexander the Great. See King Alisaunder, ed. Weber, l. 7646, and the Wars of Alexander, ed. Skeat, l. 5314. It is probable that Candace was sometimes confused with the Canace of Ovid's Heroides, Epist. xi. (wholly translated by Dryden). In fact, we have sufficient proof of this confusion; for one MS. reads *Candace* in the Legend of Good Women, 265, where five other MSS. have *Canace* or *Canacee*. *Biblis* is Byblis, who fell in love with Caunus, and, being repulsed, was changed into a fountain; Ovid, Metam. ix. 452.

Tristram and *Isoude* are the Tristran (or Tristan) and Ysolde (or Ysolt) of French medieval romance; cf. Ho. Fame, 1796, and Balade to Rosemounde, l. 20. Gower, in his Conf. Amantis, bk. 8 (ed. Pauli, iii. 359) includes Tristram and Bele Isolde in his long list of lovers, and gives an outline of the story in the same, bk. 6 (iii. 17). Ysolde was the wife of King Mark of Cornwall, and the mistress of her nephew Sir Tristram, of whom she became passionately enamoured from having drunk a philter by mistake; see Wheeler, Noted Names of Fiction, s.v. *Isolde*. The Romance of Sir Tristram was edited by Sir W. Scott, and has been re-edited by Kölbing, and by G. P. McNeill (for the Scottish Text Society). The name *Ysoude* is constantly misprinted *Ysonde*, even by the editors. Chaucer mentions her again; see Leg. G. Women, 254; Ho. of Fame, 1796.

292. *Silla*, Scylla; daughter of Nisus, of Megara, who, for love of Minos, cut off her father's hair, upon which his life depended, and was transformed in consequence into the bird Ciris; see Ovid, Metam. viii. 8. Another Scylla was changed by Circe into a sea-monster; Ovid, Metam. xiv. 52. Their stories shew that the former is meant; see Leg. of Good Women, 1910, and the note.

Moder of Romulus, Ilia (also called Rhæa Silvia), daughter of Numitor, dedicated to Vesta, and buried alive for breaking her vows; see Livy, bk. 1; Verg. Æn. i. 274.

The quotation from Boccaccio ends here.

296. *Of spak,* spake of; see l. 174.

298. This *quene* is the goddess Nature (l. 303). We now come to a part of the poem where Chaucer makes considerable use of the work which he mentions in l. 316, viz. the Planctus Naturæ (Complaint of Nature) by Alanus de Insulis, or Alein Delille, a poet and divine of the 12th century. This work is printed in vol. ii. of T. Wright's edition of the Anglo-Latin Satirical Poets (Record Series), which also contains the poem called Anticlaudianus, by the same author. The description of the goddess is given at great length (pp. 431-456), and at last she declares her name to be *Natura* (p. 456). This long description of Nature and of her vesture is a very singular one; indeed, all the fowls of the air are supposed to be depicted upon her wonderful garments (p. 437). Chaucer substitutes a brief description of his own, and represents the birds as real live ones, gathering around her; which is much more sensible. For the extracts from Alanus, see the Introduction, p. 74. As Prof. Morley says (Eng. Writers, v. 162)—'Alain describes Nature's changing robe as being in one of its forms so ethereal that it is like air, and the pictures on it seem to the eye a Council of Animals (*Animalium Concilium*). Upon which, beginning, as Chaucer does, with the Eagle and the Falcon, Alain proceeds with a long list of the birds painted on her transparent robe, that surround Nature as in a council, and attaches to each bird the most remarkable point in its character.' Professor Hales, in The Academy, Nov. 19, 1881, quoted the passages from Alanus which are here more or less imitated, and drew attention to the remarkable passage in Spenser's F. Q. bk. vii. c. 7. st. 5-10, where that poet quotes and copies Chaucer. Dunbar imitates Chaucer in his Thrissill and Rois, and describes Dame Nature as surrounded by beasts, birds, and flowers; see stanzas 10, 11, 18, 26, 27 of that poem.

The phrase 'Nature la déesse' occurs in Le Roman de la Rose, l. 16480.

309. Birds were supposed to choose their mates on St. Valentine's day (Feb. 14); and lovers thought they must follow their example, and then 'choose their loves.' Mr. Douce thinks the custom of choosing valentines was a survival from the Roman feast of the Lupercalia. See the articles in Brand, Pop. Antiq. i. 53; Chambers, Book of Days, i. 255; Alban Butler, Lives of Saints, Feb. 14; &c. The custom is alluded to by Lydgate, Shakespeare, Herrick, Pepys, and Gay; and in the Paston Letters, ed. Gairdner, iii. 169, is a letter written in Feb. 1477, where we find: 'And, cosyn, uppon Fryday is Sent Volentynes Day, and every brydde chesyth hym a make.' See also the Cuckoo and Nyghtingale, l. 80.

316. *Aleyn,* Alanus de Insulis; *Pleynt of Kynde,* Complaint of

V. PARLEMENT OF FOULES. LINES 296-343.

Nature, Lat. Planctus Naturæ; see note to l. 298. Chaucer refers us to Aleyn's description on account of its unmerciful length; it was hopeless to attempt even an epitome of it. Lydgate copies this passage; see Political, Religious and Love Poems, ed. Furnivall, p. 45, l. 17; or his Minor Poems, ed. Halliwell, p. 47.

323. *Foules of ravyne*, birds of prey. Chaucer's division of birds into birds of prey, birds that eat worms and insects, water-fowl, and birds that eat seeds, can hardly be his own. In Vincent of Beauvais, lib. xvi. c. 14, Aristotle is cited as to the food of birds :—'quædam comedunt *carnem*, quædam *grana*, quædam utrumque; ... quædam vero comedunt *vermes*, vt passer. ... Vivunt et *ex fructu* quædam aues, vt palumbi, et turtures. Quædam viuunt in ripis *aquarum lacuum*, et cibantur ex eis.'

330. *Royal*; because he is often called the king of birds, as in Dunbar's Thrissill and Rois, st. 18. Vincent of Beauvais, Spec. Nat., lib. xvi. c. 32, quotes from Iorath (*sic*) :—'Aquila est auis magna *regalis*.' And Philip de Thaun, Bestiary, 991 (in Wright's Pop. Treatises, p. 109) says :—'Egle est rei de oisel. . En Latine raisun *clerveant* le apellum, Ke le solail verat quant il plus cler serat.'

331. See the last note, where we learn that the eagle is called in Latin 'clear-seeing,' because 'he will look at the sun when it will be brightest.' This is explained at once by the remarkable etymology given by Isidore (cited by Vincent, as above), viz. :—'*Aqu*-ila ab *acumine oculorum vocata est*.'

332. Pliny, Nat. Hist. bk. x. c. 3, enumerates six kinds of eagles, which Chaucer leaves us to find out ; viz. Melænaetos, Pygargus, Morphnos, which Homer (Il. xxiv. 316) calls *perknos*, Percnopterus, Gnesios (the true or royal eagle), and Haliæetos (osprey). This explains the allusion in l. 333.

334. *Tyraunt*. This epithet was probably suggested by the original text in Alanus, viz.—'Illic ancipiter [accipiter], civitatis præfectus aeriæ, violenta *tyrannide* a subditis redditus exposcebat.' Sir Thopas had a 'grey goshauk'; C. T., Group B, 1928.

337. See note on the *faucon peregrin*, Squi. Tale, 420 (F 428). 'Beautifully described as "distreining" the king's hand with its foot, because carried by persons of the highest rank'; Bell. Read, 'with 's feet.'

339. *Merlion*, merlin. 'The merlin is the smallest of the long-winged hawks, and was generally carried by ladies'; Bell.

342. From Alanus (see p. 74) :—' Illic olor, sui funeris præco, mellitæ citherizationis organo vitæ prophetabat apocopam.' The same idea is mentioned by Vincent of Beauvais, Spec. Nat. lib. xvi. c. 50; Pliny says he believes the story to be false, Nat. Hist. lib. x. c. 23. See Compl. of Anelida, l. 346. 'The wild swan's death-hymn'; Tennyson, The Dying Swan. Cf. Ovid, Heroid. vii. 2.

343. From Alanus :—' Illic bubo, propheta miseriæ, psalmodias funereæ lamentationis præcinebat.' So in the Rom. de la Rose, 5999 :—

'Li chahuan . . .
Prophetes de male aventure,
Hideus messagier de dolor.'

Cf. Vergil, Æn. iv. 462; Ovid, Metam. v. 550, whence Chaucer's allusion in Troilus, v. 319; Shakespeare, Mid. Nt. D. v. 385.

344. *Geaunt*, giant. Alanus has :—' grus ... in *giganteæ* quantitatis evadebat excessum.' Vincent (lib. xvi. c. 91) quotes from Isidore :— ' Grues nomen de propria voce sumpserunt, tali enim sono susurrant.'

345. 'The chough, who is a thief.' From Alanus, who has :— ' Illic monedula, *latrocinio* laudabili reculas thesaurizans, innatæ avaritiæ argumenta monstrabat.' ' It was an old belief in Cornwall, according to Camden (Britannia, tr. by Holland, 1610, p. 189) that the chough was an incendiary, "and thievish besides; for oftentimes it secretly conveieth fire-sticks, setting their houses a-fire, and as closely filcheth and hideth little pieces of money."'—Prov. Names of Brit. Birds, by C. Swainson, p. 75. So also in Pliny, lib. x. c. 29, choughs are called thieves. Vincent of Beauvais quotes one of Isidore's delicious etymologies :—' Monedula dicitur quasi *mone-tula*, quæ cum aurum inuenit aufert et occultat'; i. e. from *monetam tollere*. ' The Jackdaw tribe is notoriously given to pilfering'; Stanley, Hist. of Birds, ed. 1880, p. 203.

Iangling, talkative; so Alanus :—' Illic pica .. curam *logices* perennabat insomnem.' So in Vincent—' pica loquax'—' pica garrula,' &c.; and in Pliny, lib. x. c. 42.

346. *Scorning*, ' applied to the jay, probably, because it follows and seems to mock at the owl, whenever the latter is so unfortunate as to be caught abroad in the daylight; for this reason, a trap for jays is always baited with a live owl'; Bell.

' The *heron* will stand for hours in the shallow water watching for eels'; Bell. Vincent quotes from Isidore :—' Ciconeæ ... serpentium hostes.' So also A. Neckam, De Naturis Rerum, lib. i. c. 64 :— ' Ranarum et locustarum et serpentum hostis est.'

347. *Trecherye*, trickery, deceit. ' During the season of incubation, the cock-bird tries to draw pursuers from the nest by wheeling round them, crying and screaming, to divert their attention ... while the female sits close on the nest till disturbed, when she runs off, feigning lameness, or flaps about near the ground, as if she had a broken wing; cf. Com. Errors, iv. 2. 27; Much Ado, iii. 1. 24; ' Prov. Names of Brit. Birds, by C. Swainson, p. 185. And cf. ' to seem the *lapwing* and to jest, Tongue far from heart'; Meas. for Meas. i. 4. 32.

348. *Stare*, starling. As the starling can speak, there is probably ' an allusion to some popular story like the Manciple's Tale, in which a talking starling betrays a secret'; Bell. The same story is in Ovid, Metam. bk. ii. 535; and in Gower, Conf. Amant. bk. iii. ' Germanicus and Drusus had one *stare*, and sundry nightingales, taught to parle Greeke and Latine'; Holland's Pliny, bk. x. c. 42. In the Seven Sages, ed. Weber, p. 86, the bird who ' bewrays counsel' is a magpie.

349. *Coward kyte.* See Squi. Tale, F 624; and note. 'Miluus .. fugatur a niso, quamuis in triplo sit maior illo'; Vincent of Beauvais, lib. xvi. c. 108. 'A kite is .... a coward, and fearefull among great birds'; Batman on Bartholomè, lib. xii. c. 26.

350. Alanus has :—' Illic gallus, tanquam vulgaris astrologus, suæ vocis *horologio* horarum loquebatur discrimina.' Cf. Nonne Prestes Tale, B 4044. We also see whence Chaucer derived his epithet of the cock—'common astrologer'—in Troilus, iii. 1415. Tusser, in his Husbandry, ed. Payne, § 74, says the cock crows—'At midnight, at three, and an hower ere day.' Hence the expressions 'first cock' in K. Lear, iii. 4. 121, and 'second cock' in Macbeth, ii. 3. 27.

351. The sparrow was sacred to Venus, from its amatory disposition (Meas. for Meas. iii. 2. 185). In the well-known song from Lyly's Alexander and Campaspe, Cupid 'stakes his quiver, bow, and arrows, His Mother's *doves*, and team of *sparrows*;' Songs from the Dramatists, ed. R. Bell, p. 50.

352. Cf. Holland's Pliny, bk. x. c. 29—' The nightingale ... chaunteth continually, namely, at that time as the trees begin to put out their leaues thicke.'

353. 'Nocet autem apibus sola inter animalia carnem habentia et carnem comedentia'; Vincent of Beauvais, De hyrundine; Spec. Nat. lib. xvi. c. 17. 'Culicum et muscarum et apecularum infestatrix'; A. Neckam, De Naturis Rerum (De Hirundine), lib. i. c. 52. 'Swallowes make foule worke among them,' &c.; Holland's Pliny, bk. xi. c. 18. Cf. Vergil, Georg. iv. 15; and Tennyson, The Poet's Song, l. 9.

Flyes, i. e. bees. This, the right reading (see footnote), occurs in two MSS. only; the scribes altered it to *foules* or *briddes*!

355. Alanus has :—' Illic turtur, suo viduata consorte, amorem epilogare dedignans, in altero bigamiæ refutabat solatia.' 'Etiam vulgo est notum turturem et amoris veri prærogatiua nobilitari et castitatis titulis donari'; A. Neckam, i. 59. Cf. An Old Eng. Miscellany, ed. Morris, p. 22.

356. 'In many medieval paintings, the feathers of angels' wings are represented as those of peacocks'; Bell. Cf. Dunbar, ed. Small, 174. 14 : 'Qhois angell fedderis as the pacok schone.'

357. Perhaps Chaucer mixed up the description of the pheasant in Alanus with that of the 'gallus silvestris, privatioris galli *deridens* desidiam,' which occurs almost immediately below. Vincent (lib. xvi. c. 72) says :—' Fasianus est gallus syluaticus.' Or he may allude to the fact, vouched for in Stanley's Hist. of Birds, ed. 1880, p. 279, that the Pheasant will breed with the common Hen.

358. 'The Goose likewise is very vigilant and watchfull : witnesse the Capitoll of Rome, which by the means of Geese was defended and saued'; Holland's Pliny, bk. x. c. 22.

> ' There is no noise at all
> Of waking dog, nor gaggling goose more *waker* then the hound.'
> Golding, tr. of Ovid's Metam. bk. xi. fol. 139, back.

Unkinde, unnatural; because of its behaviour to the hedge-sparrow; K. Lear, i. 4. 235.

359. *Delicasye*, wantonness. 'Auis est luxuriosa nimium, bibitque vinum'; Vincent (quoting from Liber de Naturis Rerum), lib. xvi. c. 135, De Psittaco; and again (quoting from Physiologus)—'cum vino inebriatur.' So in Holland's Pliny, bk. x. c. 42—' She loueth wine well, and when shee hath drunk freely, is very pleasant, plaifull, and wanton.'

360. 'The farmers' wives find the drake or mallard the greatest enemy of their young ducks, whole broods of which he will destroy unless removed.'—Bell. Chaucer perhaps follows the Liber de Naturis Rerum, as quoted in Vincent, lib. xvi. c. 27 (De Anate) :—' Mares aliquando cum plures fuerint simul, tanta libidinis insania feruntur, vt fœminam solam . . occidant.'

361. From A. Neckam, Liber de Naturis Rerum (ed. Wright, lib. i. c. 64); cited in Vincent, lib. xvi. c. 48. The story is, that a male stork, having discovered that the female was unfaithful to him, went away; and presently returning with a great many other storks, the avengers tore the criminal to pieces. Another very different story may also be cited. 'The stork is the Embleme of a gratefull Man. In which respect Ælian writeth of a storke, which bred on the house of one who had a very beautiful wife, which in her husband's absence used to commit adultry with one of her base servants : which the storke observing, in gratitude to him who freely gave him house-roome, flying in the villaines face, strucke out both his eyes.'—Guillim, Display of Heraldry, sect. iii. c. 19.

In Thynne's Animadversions on Speght's Chaucer, ed. Furnivall, p. 68 (Chau. Soc.), we find :—'for Aristotle sayethe, and Bartholomeus de proprietatibus rerum, li. 12. c. 8, with manye other auctors, that yf the storke by any meanes perceve that his female hath brooked spousehedde, he will no moore dwell with her, but strykethe and so cruelly beateth her, that he will not surcease vntill he hathe killed her yf he maye, to wreake and reuenge that adulterye.' Cf. Batman vppon Bartholome, ed. 1582, leaf 181, col. 2; Stanley, Hist. of Birds, 6th ed. p. 322; and story no. 82 in Swan's translation of the Gesta Romanorum. Many other references are given in Oesterley's notes to the Gesta; and see the Exempla of Jacques de Vitry, ed. Crane (Folklore Soc.), 1890, p. 230. Cf. Skelton's Phyllyp Sparowe, 469-477.

362. 'The voracity of the cormorant has become so proverbial, that a greedy and voracious eater is often compared to this bird'; Swainson, Prov. Names of British Birds, p. 143. See Rich. II, ii. 1. 38.

363. *Wys*; because it could predict; it was therefore consecrated to Apollo; see Lewis and Short, s. v. *corvus*. *Care*, anxiety; hence, ill luck. 'In folk-lore the crow always appears as a bird of the worst and most sinister character, representing either death, or night, or winter'; Prov. Names of British Birds, by C. Swainson, p. 84; which see.

Chaucer here mistranslates Vergil precisely as Batman does (l. xii. c. 9).

V. PARLEMENT OF FOULES. LINES 359-380.

'Nunc plena cornix pluuiam uocat improba uoce'; Georg. i. 388.
'That is to vnderstande, Nowe the Crowe calleth rayne *with an eleinge voyce*'; Batman vppon Bartholome, as above.

364. *Olde.* I do not understand this epithet; it is usually the crow who is credited with a long life. *Frosty*; i. e. that is seen in England in the winter-time; called in Shropshire the *snow-bird*; Swainson's Prov. Names of Brit. Birds, p. 6. The explanation of the phrase 'farewell feldefare,' occurring in Troil. iii. 861 and in Rom. Rose, 5510, and marked by Tyrwhitt as not understood, is easy enough. It simply means—'good bye, and we are well rid of you'; when the fieldfare goes, the warm weather comes.

371. *Formel*, perhaps 'regular' or 'suitable' companion; as F. *formel* answers to Lat. *formalis*. Tyrwhitt's Gloss. says: '*formel* is put for the *female* of any fowl, more especially for a female eagle (ll. 445, 535 below).' It has, however, no connection with *female* (as he seems to suppose), but answers rather, in sense, to *make*, i. e. match, fit companion. Godefroy cites the expression 'faucon *formel*' from L'Aviculaire des Oiseaux de proie (MS. Lyon 697, fol. 221 *a*). He explains it by 'qui a d'amples formes,' meaning (as I suppose) simply 'large'; which does not seem to be right; though the *tercel* or male hawk was so called because he was a third less than the female. Ducange gives *formelus*, and thinks it means 'well trained.'

379. *Vicaire*, deputy. This term is taken from Alanus, De Planctu Naturæ, as above, where it occurs at least *thrice*. Thus, at p. 469 of Wright's edition, Nature says:—'Me igitur tanquam sui [Dei] *vicariam*'; at p. 511—'Natura, Dei gratia mundanæ civitatis *vicaria procuratrix*'; and at p. 516, Nature is addressed as—'O supracælestis Principis fidelis *vicaria*!' M. Sandras supposes that Chaucer took the term from the Rom. de la Rose, but it is more likely that Chaucer and Jean de Meun alike took it from Alanus.

> 'Cis Diex meismes, par sa grace, . . .
> Tant m'ennora, tant me tint chiere,
> Qu'il m'establi sa chamberiere . . .
> Por chamberiere! certes vaire,
> Por connestable, et por *vicaire*,' &c.
> Rom. de la Rose, 16970, &c.

Here Nature is supposed to be the speaker. Chaucer again uses *vicaire* of Nature, Phis. Tale, D 20, which see; and he applies it to the Virgin Mary in his A B C, l. 140. See also Lydgate, Compl. of Black Knight, l. 491.

380. That l. 379 is copied from Alanus is clear from the fact that ll. 380-1 are from the same source. At p. 451 of Wright's edition, we find Nature speaking of the concordant discord of the four elements— 'quatuor elementorum concors discordia'—which unites the buildings of the palace of this world—'mundialis regiæ structuras conciliat.' Similarly, she says, the four humours are united in the human body:

'quæ qualitates inter elementa mediatrices conveniunt, hæ eædem inter quatuor humores pacis sanciunt firmitatem'; &c.

Compare also Boethius, bk. iii. met. 9. 13, in Chaucer's translation. 'Thou bindest the elements by noumbres proporcionables, that the colde thinges mowen acorden with the hote thinges, and the drye thinges with the moiste thinges; that the fyr, that is purest, ne flee nat over hye, ne that the hevinesse ne drawe nat adoun over-lowe the erthes that ben plounged in the wateres. Thou knittest togider the mene sowle of treble kinde, moeving alle thinges'; &c.

'Et froit, et chaut, et sec, et moiste';
Rom. Rose, 17163.
'For hot, cold, moist, and dry, four champions fierce,
Strive here for mastery.' Milton, P. L. ii. 898.

386. *Seynt*, &c.; i.e. *on* St. Valentine's day; as in l. 322.

388. 'Ye come to choose your mates, and (then) to flee (on) your way.'

411. It appears that Chaucer and others frequently crush the two words *this is* into the time of one word only (something like the modern *it's* for *it is*). Hence I scan the line thus:—

This 's oúr | uság' | alwéy, | &c.

So again, in the Knight's Tale, 233 (A 1091):—

We mót | endúr' | it thís 's | the shórt | and pleýn.

And again, in the same, 885 (A 1743):—

And seíd | e thís 's | a shórt | conclú | sioun.

And frequently elsewhere. In the present case, both *this* and *is* are unaccented, which is much harsher than when *this* bears an accent.

I find that Ten Brink has also noted this peculiarity, in his Chaucers Sprache, § 271. He observes that, in C. T. Group E, 56, the Ellesmere and Hengwrt MSS. actually substitute *this* for *this is;* see footnote; and hence note that the correct reading is—'But this his tale, which,' &c. See *This* in Schmidt, Shak. Lexicon. Cf. l. 620.

413. *Com*, came. The *o* is long; A. S. *cóm*, Goth. *kwam*.

417. 'I choose the formel to be my sovereign lady, not my mate.'

421. 'Beseeching her *for* mercy,' &c.

435. Read *lov'th*; monosyllabic, as frequently.

464. 'Ye see what little leisure we have here.'

471. Read *possibl'*, just as in French.

476. *Som*; quite indefinite. 'Than *another* man.'

482. *Hir-ës*, hers; dissyllabic. *Whether*=*whe'r*. Cf. l. 7.

485. 'The dispute is here called a *plee*, or plea, or pleading; and in the next stanza the terms of law, adopted into the Courts of Love, are still more pointedly applied'; Bell.

499. *Hye*, loudly. *Kek kek* represents the goose's cackle; and *quek* is mod. E. *quack*.

504. *For*, on behalf of; see next line.

V. PARLEMENT OF FOULES. LINES 386-610.

507. *For comune spede*, for the common benefit.

508. 'For it is a great charity to set us free.'

510. 'If it be *your* wish for any one to speak, it would be as good for him to be silent; it were better to be silent than to talk as you do.' That is, the cuckoo only wants to listen to those who will talk nonsense. A mild rebuke. The turtle explains (l. 514) that it is better to be silent than to meddle with things which one does not understand.

518. Lit. 'A duty assumed without direction often gives offence.' A proverb which appears in other forms. In the Canon's Yeoman's Tale, G 1066, it takes the form—'Profred servyse stinketh'; see note on the line. *Uncommitted* is not delegated, not entrusted to one. Cotgrave has: '*Commis*, assigned, appointed, delegated.'

524. *I Iuge*, I decide. *Folk*, kind of birds; see note to l. 323.

545. *Oure*, ours; it is the business of us who are the chosen spokesmen. The *Iuge* is Nature.

556. *Goler* in the Fairfax MS. is doubtless merely miswritten for *golee*, as in Ff.; Caxton turns it into *golye*, to keep it dissyllabic; the reading *gole* (in O. and Gg.) also=*golee*. Godefroy has: '*Golee, goulee, goullee, gulee, gculee*, s. f. cri, parole'; and gives several examples. Cotgrave has: '*Goulée*, f. a throatfull, or mouthful of, &c.' One of Godefroy's examples gives the phrase—'Et si dirai ge ma *goulee*,' and so I shall say my say. Chaucer uses the word sarcastically: *his large golee*=his tedious gabble. Allied to E. *gullett, gully*.

564. *Which a reson*, what sort of a reason.

568. Cf. Cant. Tales, 5851, 5852 (D 269, 270). Lydgate copies this line in his Hors, Shepe, and Goos, l. 155.

572. 'To have held thy peace, than (to have) shewed.'

574. A common proverb. In the Rom. de la Rose, l. 4750 (E. version, l. 5265), it appears as: 'Nus fox ne scet sa langue taire,' i. e. No fool knows how to hold his tongue. In the Proverbs of Hendyng, it is: 'Sottes bolt is sone shote,' l. 85. In later English, 'A fool's bolt is soon shot'; cf. Henry V, iii. 7. 132, and As You Like It, v. 4. 67. Kemble quotes from MS. Harl. fol. 4—'Ut dicunt multi, cito transit lancea stulti.'

578. *The sothe sadde*, the sober truth.

595. Another proverb. We now say—'There's as good fish in the sea as ever came out of it'; or, 'as ever was caught.'

599. See Chaucer's tr. of Boethius, bk. iv. pr. 4. l. 132.

603. 'Pushed himself forward in the crowd.'

610. Said sarcastically—'Yes! when the glutton has filled his paunch sufficiently, the rest of us are sure to be satisfied!'

Compare the following. 'Certain persones... saiyng that Demades had now given over to bee suche an haine [niggardly wretch] as he had been in tymes past—"Yea, marie, quoth Demosthenes, for now ye see him full paunched, as lyons are." For Demades was covetous and gredie of money, and indeed the lyons are more gentle when their bealyes are well filled.'—Udall, tr. of Apothegmes of Erasmus;

Anecdotes of Demosthenes. The merlin then addresses the cuckoo directly.

612. *Heysugge*, hedge-sparrow; see note to l. 358.

613. Read *rewtheles* (*reufulles* in Gg); cf. Cant. Ta., B 863; and see p. 361, l. 31. *Rewtheles* became *reufulles*, and then *rewful*.

614. 'Live thou unmated, thou destruction (destroyer) of worms.'

615. 'For it is no matter as to the lack of thy kind,' i.e. it would not matter, even if the result was the loss of your entire race.

616. 'Go! and remain ignorant for ever.'

620, 1. Cf. note to l. 411. Read *th'eleccioun*; i.e. the choice.

623. *Cheest*, chooseth; spelt *chyest*, Ayenbite of Inwyt, p. 126; spelt *chest* (with long *e*) in Shoreham's Poems, ed. Wright, p. 109, where it rimes with *lest* = *leseth*, i.e. loseth; A. S. *císt*, Deut. xxviii. 9.

626. Accent *favour* on the second syllable; as in C. T., Group B, 3881 (Monkes Tale). So (perhaps) *colóur-ed* in l. 443.

630. 'I have no other (i.e. no wrongful) regard to any rank,' I am no respecter of persons.

633. 'I would counsel you to take'; two infinitives.

640. 'Under your rod,' subject to your correction. So in the Schipmannes Tale, C. T. 13027 (B 1287).

641. The first accent is on *As*.

653. *Manér-e* is trisyllabic; and *of* is understood after it.

657. *For tarying*, to prevent tarrying; see note to C. T. Group B, 2052.

664, 5. 'Whatever may happen afterwards, this intervening course is ready prepared for all of you.'

670. They embraced each other with their wings and by intertwining their necks.

675. Gower, Conf. Amant. bk. i. (ed. Pauli, i. 134) speaks of 'Roundel, balade, and virelay.' Johnson, following the Dict. de Trevoux, gives a fair definition of the roundel; but I prefer to translate that given by Littré, s. v. *rondeau*. '1. A short poem, also called *triolet*, in which the first line or lines recur in the middle and at the end of the piece. Such poems, by Froissart and Charles d'Orleans, are still extant. 2. Another short poem peculiar to French poetry, composed of thirteen lines broken by a pause after the fifth and eighth lines, eight having one rime and five another. The first word or words are repeated after the eighth line and after the last, without forming part of the verse; it will readily be seen that this *rondeau* is a modification of the foregoing; instead of repeating the whole line, only the first words are repeated, often with a different sense.' The word is here used in the *former* sense; and the remark in Morley's Eng. Writers (v. 271), that the Roundel consists of thirteen lines, eight having one rime, and five another, is not to the point here, as it relates to the later French *rondeau* only. An examination of Old French roundels shews us that Littré's definition of the *triolet* is quite correct, and is purposely left somewhat indefinite; but we can apply a somewhat more exact

description to the form of the roundel as used by Machault, Deschamps, and Chaucer.

The form adopted by these authors is the following. First come three lines, rimed *abb*; next two more, rimed *ab*, and then the first refrain; then three more lines, rimed *abb*, followed by the second refrain. Now the first refrain consists of either one, or two, or three lines, being the first line of the poem, or the first two, or the first three; and the second refrain likewise consists of either one, or two, or three lines, being the same lines as before, but not necessarily the same number of them. Thus the whole poem consists of eight unlike lines, three on one rime, and five on another, with refrains of from two to six lines. Sometimes one of the refrains is actually omitted, but this may be the scribe's fault. However, the least possible number of lines is thus reduced to nine; and the greatest number is fourteen. For example, Deschamps (ed. Tarbé) has roundels of nine lines—second refrain omitted—(p. 125); of ten lines (p. 36); of eleven lines (p. 38); of twelve lines (p. 3); and of fourteen lines (pp. 39, 43). But the prettiest example is that by Machault (ed. Tarbé, p. 52), which has thirteen lines, the first refrain being of *two*, and the second of *three* lines. And, as thirteen lines came to be considered as the normal length, I here follow this as a model, both here and in 'Merciless Beaute'; merely warning the reader that he may make either of his refrains of a different length, if he pleases.

There is a slight art in writing a roundel, viz. in distributing the pauses. There *must* be a full stop at the end of the third and fifth lines; but the skilful poet takes care that complete sense can be made by the first line taken alone, and also by the first *two* lines taken alone. Chaucer has done this.

Todd, in his Illustrations of Chaucer, p. 372, gives a capital example of a roundel by Occleve; this is of *full* length, both refrains being of three lines, so that the whole poem is of fourteen lines. This is quite sufficient to shew that the definition of a roundel in Johnson's Dictionary (which is copied from the Dict. de Trevoux, and relates to the latter *rondeau* of *thirteen* lines) is quite useless as applied to roundels written in Middle English.

677. *The note*, i.e. the tune. Chaucer adapts his words to a known French tune. The words *Qui bien aime, a tard*[1] *oublie* (he who loves well is slow to forget) probably refer to this tune; though it is not quite clear to me how lines of five accents (normally) go to a tune beginning with a line of four accents. In Furnivall's Trial Forewords, p. 55, we find:—'Of the *rondeau* of which the first line is cited in the Fairfax MS., &c., M. Sandras found the music and the words in a MS. of Machault in the National Library, no. 7612, leaf 187. The verses form the opening lines of one of two pieces entitled *Le Lay de plour*:—

---

[1] In old French, *a tard* means 'slowly, late'; later French drops *a*, and uses *tard* only.

'Qui bieu aime, a tart oublie,
Et cuers, qui oublie a tart,
Ressemble le feu qui art,' &c.

M. Sandras also says (Étude, p. 72) that Eustache Deschamps composed, on this burden slightly modified, a pretty ballad, inedited till M. Sandras printed it at p. 287 of his Étude; and that, a long time before Machault, Moniot de Paris began, by this same line, a hymn to the Virgin that one can read in the Arsenal Library at Paris, in the copy of a Vatican MS., B. L. no. 63, fol. 283 :—

'Ki bien aime a tart oublie;
Mais ne le puis oublier
La douce vierge Marie.'

In MS. Gg. 4. 27 (Cambridge), there is a poem in 15 8-line stanzas. The latter half of st. 14 ends with :—' Qui bien ayme, tard oublye.'

In fact, the phrase seems to have been a common proverb; see Le Roux de Lincy, ii. 383, 496. It occurs again in Tristan, ed. Michel, ii. 123, l. 700; in Gower, Balade 25 (ed. Stengel, p. 10); in MS. Digby 53, fol. 15, back; MS. Corp. Chr. Camb. 450, p. 258, &c.

683. See note above, to l. 309.

693. This last stanza is imitated at the end of the Court of Love, and of Dunbar's Thrissill and Rois.

VI. A COMPLEINT TO HIS LADY.

In the two MSS., this poem is written as if it were a continuation of the Compleint unto Pity. The printed edition of 1651 has this heading—' These verses next folowing were compiled by Geffray Chauser, and in the writen copies foloweth at the ende of the complainte of petee.' This implies that Stowe had seen more than one MS. containing these lines.

However, the poem has nothing to do with the Complaint of Pity; for which reason the lines are here numbered separately, and the title 'A Compleint to his Lady' is supplied, for want of a better.

The poem is so badly spelt in Shirley's MS. (Harl. 78) as quite to obscure its diction, which is that of the fourteenth century. I have therefore re-spelt it throughout, so as to shew the right pronunciation. The Phillipps MS. is merely a copy of the other, but preserves the last stanza.

The printed copy resembles Shirley's MS. so closely, that both seem to have been derived from a common source. But there is a strange and unaccountable variation in l. 100. The MS. here has—' For I am sette on yowe in suche manere'; whilst ed. 1561 has—' For I am set so hy vpon your whele.' The latter reading does not suit the right order of the rimes; but it points to a lost MS.

VI. COMPLEINT TO HIS LADY. LINES 1-39.

The poem evidently consists of several fragments, all upon the same subject, of hopeless, but true love.

It should be compared with the Complaint of Pity, the first forty lines of the Book of the Duchess, the Parliament of Foules (ll. 416-441), and the Complaint of Anelida. Indeed, the last of these is more or less founded upon it, and some of the expressions (including one complete line) occur there again.

1. MSS. *nightes*. This will not scan, nor does it make good sense. Read *night*; cf. l. 8, and Book of the Duchess, l. 22.

3. Cf. Compl. Pite, 81—'Allas! what herte may hit longe endure?'

7. *Desespaired*, full of despair. This, and not *dispaired* (as in ed. 1561), is the right form. Cf. *desespeir*, in Troil. i. 605.

8, 9. Cf. Anelida, 333, 334.

14, 15. I repeat this line, because we require a rime to *fulfille*, l. 17; whilst at the same time l. 14 evidently ends a stanza.

16. I omit *that*, and insert *eek*, in order to make sense.

17. I supply *he*, meaning *Love*. Love is masculine in l. 42, precisely as in the Parl. of Foules, l. 5.

19. I alter *and yit* to *and fro*, to make sense; the verb to *arace* absolutely requires *from* or *fro*; see Clerkes Tale, E 1103, and particularly l. 18 of sect. XXI, where we find the very phrase 'fro your herte arace.' Cf. Troilus, v. 954.

24. I supply this line from Compl. Mars, 189, to rime with l. 22.

If Fragments II and III were ever joined together, we must suppose that at least *five* lines have been lost, as I have already shewn in the note to Dr. Furnivall's Trial Forewords, p. 96.

Thus, after l. 23, ending in *asterte*, we should require lines ending in *-ye*, *-erse*, *-ye*, *-erse*, and *-ede* respectively, to fill the gap. However, I have kept fragments II and III apart, and it is then sufficient to supply *three* lines. Lines 25 and 26 are from the Compl. of Pite, 22, 17, and from Anelida, 307.

32. I suspect some corruption; MS. Sh. has *The wyse eknytte*, Ph. has *The wise I-knyt*, and ed. 1561 has *The Wise, eknit*. As it stands, it means—'Her surname moreover is the Fair Ruthless one, (or) the Wise one, united with Good Fortune.' Fair Ruthless is a translation of the French phrase *La Belle Dame sans Merci*, which occurs as the title of a poem once attributed to Chaucer. The Wise one, &c., means that she is wise and fortunate, and will not impair her good fortune by bestowing any thought upon her lover. Shirley often writes *e* for initial *y-*.

35. Almost identical with Anelida, 222—'More then myself, an hundred thousand sythe.'

36. Obviously corrupt; neither sound nor sense is good. Read:—
'Than al this worldes richest (*or* riche) creature.' *Creature* may mean 'created thing.' Or scan by reading *world's richéss*'.

39. Cf. Kn. Tale, l. 380 (A 1238)—'Wel hath Fortune y-turned thee the dys.'

41. *My swete fo.* So in Anelida, l. 272; and cf. l. 64 below.

42, 43. Cf. Parl. of Foules, ll. 439, 440.

44. Ed. 1561 also reads *In.* Perhaps the original reading was *Inwith.* Moreover, the copies omit *eek* in l. 45, which I supply.

47-49. This remarkable statement re-appears twice elsewhere; see Parl. Foules, 90, 91, and note; and Compl. of Pite, ll. 99-104.

50. Repeated in Anelida, 237.

51, 52. Cf. Anelida, 181, 182; Compl. Pite, 110; Parl. Foules, 7.

55. Cf. Anelida, 214—'That turned is to quaking al my daunce.'

56. Here a line is missing, as again at l. 59. This appears from the form of the stanza, in which the rimes are arranged in the order *a a b a a b c d d c.* I supply the lines from Anelida, 181, 182.

63. Cf. the use of *y-whet* in Anelida, 212.

64, 65. Cf. Anelida, 272—'My swete fo, why do ye so for shame?'

73. For *leest*, ed. 1561 has *best*!

79. The MSS. have—'What so I wist that were to youre hyenesse'; where *youre hyenesse* is absurdly repeated from l. 76. Ed. 1561 has the same error. It is obvious that the right final word is *distresse*, to be preceded by *yow* or *your*; of which I prefer *yow*.

83. Ch. uses both *wille* and *wil*; the latter is, e. g., in Cant. Ta. A 1104. We must here read *wil*.

86. *shal*, i. e. shall be. See also XXII. ll. 78, 87.

88. *leveth wel*, believe me wholly. MS. Ph. and ed. 1561 wrongly have *loveth*.

98. I read *nil*, as being simpler. The MSS. have *ne wil*, which would be read—'That I n'wil ay'; which comes to much the same thing.

100. *set*, fixed, bound. Ed. 1561 has—'For I am set so hy vpon your whele,' which disturbs the rimes.

102. MS. Sh. *beon euer als trewe*; ed. 1561 has—*bene euer as trewe.*

103. MS. Sh. 'As any man can er may on lyue'; ed. 1561 and MS. Ph. have—'As any man can or maye on liue.' It is clear that a final word has been dropped, because the scribe thought the line ought to rime with *fyve* (l. 98). The dropped word is clearly *here*, which rimes with *manere* in the Miller's Prologue, and elsewhere. After *here* was dropped, *man* was awkwardly inserted, to fill up the line. Ch. employs *here* at the end of a line more than thirty times; cf. Kn. Tale, A 1260, 1670, 1711, 1819, &c.

107, 108. Cf. Anelida, 247, 248.

123. Cf. Anelida, 216. MS. Ph. alone preserves ll. 124-133.

124. *My lyf and deeth* seems to be in the vocative case. Otherwise, *my* is an error for *in*.

125. For *hoolly I* perhaps we should read *I hoolly*.

126. The rime *by me, tyme*, is Chaucerian; see Cant. Ta. G 1204.

130. This resembles Cant. Tales, F 974 and A 2392.

133. *trouble*, troubled. A like use occurs in Boethius, bk. i. met. 7, l. 2. *Drope, hope*, rime in Troil. i. 939, and Gower, C. A., ii. 286.

VII. ANELIDA AND ARCITE.

THIS Poem consists of several distinct portions. It begins with a Proem, of three stanzas, followed by a part of the story, in twenty-seven stanzas, all in seven-line stanzas. Next follows the Complaint of Anelida, skilfully and artificially constructed; it consists of a Proem in a single stanza of nine lines; next, what may be called a Strophe, in six stanzas, of which the first four consist of nine lines, the fifth consists of sixteen lines (with only two rimes), and the sixth, of nine lines (with internal rimes). Next follows what may be called an Antistrophe, in six stanzas arranged precisely as before; wound up by a single concluding stanza corresponding to the Proem at the beginning of the Complaint. After this, the story begins again; but the poet had only written *one* stanza when he suddenly broke off, and left the poem unfinished; see note to l. 357.

The name of Arcite naturally reminds us of the Knightes Tale; but the 'false Arcite' of the present poem has nothing beyond the name in common with the 'true Arcite' of the Tale. However, there are other connecting links, to be pointed out in their due places, which tend to shew that this poem was written *before* the Knightes Tale, and was never finished; it is also probable that Chaucer actually wrote an earlier draught of the Knightes Tale, with the title of Palamon and Arcite, which he afterwards partially rejected; for he mentions 'The Love of Palamon and Arcite' in the prologue to the Legend of Good Women as if it were an independent work. However this may be, it is clear that, in constructing or rewriting the Knightes Tale, he did not lose sight of 'Anelida,' for he has used some of the lines over again; moreover, it is not a little remarkable that the very lines from Statius which are quoted at the beginning of the fourth stanza of Anelida are also quoted, in some of the MSS., at the beginning of the Knightes Tale.

But this is not all. For Dr. Koch has pointed out the close agreement between the opening stanzas of this poem, and those of Boccaccio's Teseide, which is the very work from which Palamon and Arcite was, of course, derived, as it is the chief source of the Knightes Tale also. Besides this, there are several stanzas from the Teseide in the Parliament of Foules; and even three near the end of Troilus, viz. the seventh, eighth, and ninth from the end of the last book. Hence we should be inclined to suppose that Chaucer originally translated the Teseide rather closely, substituting a seven-line stanza for the *ottava rima* of the original; this formed the original Palamon and Arcite, a poem which he probably never finished (as his manner was). Not wishing, however, to abandon it altogether, he probably used some of the lines in this present poem, and introduced others into his Parliament of Foules. At a later period, he rewrote, in a complete form, the whole story in his own fashion, which has come down to us as The Knightes Tale. Whatever the right explanation may be, we are at

NOTES TO THE MINOR POEMS.

any rate certain that the Teseide is the source of (1) sixteen stanzas in the Parliament of Foules; (2) of part of the first ten stanzas in the present poem; (3) of the original Palamon and Arcite; (4) of the Knightes Tale; and (5) of three stanzas near the end of Troilus, bk. v. 1807-27 (Tes. xi. 1-3).

1. In comparing the first three stanzas with the Teseide, we must reverse the order of the stanzas in the latter poem. Stanza 1 of Anelida answers to st. 3 of the Italian; stanza 2, to st. 2; and stanza 3 to st. 1. The first two lines of lib. i. st. 3 (of the Italian) are :—

'*Siate presenti*, O *Marte rubicondo*,
Nelle tue *arme* rigido e *feroce*.'

I. e. *Be present*, O *Mars the red*, strong and *fierce* in thy *arms* (battle-array). For the words *Be present*, see l. 6.

2. *Trace*, Thrace. Cf. Kn. Tale, 1114-6 (A 1972-4). Chaucer was here thinking of Statius, Theb. lib. vii. 40, who describes the temple of Mars on Mount Hæmus, in Thrace, which had a frosty climate. In bk. ii, l. 719, Pallas is invoked as being superior to Bellona. Chaucer seems to confuse them; so does Boccaccio, in his De Genealogia Deorum.

6, 7. Partly imitated from Tes. i. 3 :—

' E sostenete la mano e la voce
Di me, che intendo i vostri effecti dire.'

8-10. Imitated from Tes. i. 2 :—

'Chè m' è venuta voglia con *pietosa*
Rima di scriver *una storia antica*,
Tanto negli anni riposta e nascosa,
Che *latino* autor non par ne dica,
Per quel ch' io senta, in libro alcuna cosa.'

Thus it appears that, when speaking of his finding an old story in Latin, he is actually translating from an Italian poem which treats of a story not found in Latin! That is, his words give no indication whatever of the source of his poem; but are merely used in a purely conventional manner. His 'old story' is really that of the siege of Thebes; and his *Latin* is the Thebais of Statius. And neither of them speaks of Anelida!

15. Read *favourabl'*. Imitated from Tes. i. 1 :—

' O *sorelle* Castalie, che nel monte
Elicona contente dimorate
D' intorno al sacro gorgoneo fonte,
Sottesso l' ombra delle frondi amate
Da Febo, delle quali ancor la fronte
I' spero ornarmi sol che 'l concediate
Gli santi orecchi a' miei prieghi porgete,
E quegli udite come voi volete.'

Polymnia, Polyhymnia, also spelt Polymnia, Gk. Πολυμνία; one of the

VII. ANELIDA AND ARCITE. LINES 1-23.

nine Muses. Chaucer invokes the muse Clio in Troil. bk. ii, and Calliope in bk. iii. Cf. Ho. of Fame, 520-2. *Parnaso*, Parnassus, a mountain in Phocis sacred to Apollo and the Muses, at whose foot was Delphi and the Castalian spring. *Elicon*, mount Helicon in Bœotia; Chaucer seems to have been thinking rather of the Castalian spring, as he uses the prep. *by*, and supposes *Elicon* to be near *Parnaso*. See the Italian, as quoted above; and note that, in the Ho. of Fame, 522, he says that Helicon is a *well*.

A similar confusion occurs in Troilus, iii. 1809:—

'Ye sustren nyne eek, that by Elicone
In hil Parnaso listen for tabyde.'

17. *Cirrea*, Cirra. Chaucer was thinking of the adj. *Cirræus*. Cirra was an ancient town near Delphi, under Parnassus. Dante mentions *Cirra*, Parad. i. 36; and *Parnaso* just above, l. 16. Perhaps Chaucer took it from him.

20. A common simile. So Spenser, F. Q. i. 12. 1, 42; and at the end of the Thebaid and the Teseide both.

21. *Stace*, Statius; i.e. the Thebaid; whence some of the next stanzas are more or less borrowed. Chaucer epitomises the general contents of the Thebaid in his Troilus; v. 1484, &c.

Corinne, not Corinna (as some have thought, for she has nothing to do with the matter), but Corinnus. Corinnus was a disciple of Palamedes, and is said to have written an account of the Trojan War, and of the war of the Trojan king Dardanus against the Paphlagonians, in the Dorian dialect. Suidas asserts that Homer made some use of his writings. See Zedler, Universal Lexicon; and Biog. Universelle. How Chaucer met with this name, is not known. Possibly, however, Chaucer was thinking of *Colonna*, i.e. Guido di Colonna, author of the medieval Bellum Trojanum. But this does not help us, and it is at least as likely that the name *Corinne* was merely introduced by way of flourish; for no source has been discovered for the latter part of the poem, which may have been entirely of his own invention. For Palamedes, see Lydgate's Troy-book, bk. v. c. 36.

22. The verses from Statius, preserved in the MSS., are the three lines following; from Thebais, xii. 519:—

'Jamque domos patrias Scythicæ post aspera gentis
Prælia laurigero subeuntem Thesea curru,
Lætifici plausus missusque ad sidera vulgi,' &c.

The first line and half the second appear also in the MSS. of the Canterbury Tales, at the head of the Knightes Tale, which commences, so to speak, at the same point (l. 765 in Lewis's translation of the Thebaid). Comparing these lines of Statius with the lines in Chaucer, we at once see how he came by the word *aspre* and the expression *With laurer crouned*. The whole of this stanza (ll. 22-28) is expanded from the three lines here quoted.

23. *Cithe*, Scythia; see last note. See Kn. Tale, 9 (A 867).

532   NOTES TO THE MINOR POEMS.

24. Cf. Kn. Tale, 169, 121 (A 1027, 979).

25. *Contre-houses*, houses of his country, homes (used of Theseus and his army). It exactly reproduces the Lat. *domos patrias*. See Kn. Tale, 11 (A 869).

29-35. Chaucer merely takes the general idea from Statius, and expands it in his own way. Lewis's translation of Statius has :—

'To swell the pomp, before the chief are borne
The spoils and trophies from the vanquish'd torn;'

but the Lat. text has—

'Ante ducem spolia et *duri Mauortis imago*,
Uirginei currus, cumulataque fercula cristis.'

And, just below, is a brief mention of Hippolyta, who had been wedded to Theseus.

30, 1. Cf. Kn. Tale, 117, 118 (A 975). See note above.

36, 7. Cf. Kn. Tale, 23, 24 (A 881, 2); observe the order of words.

38. Repeated in Kn. Tale, 114 (A 972); changing *With* to *And*.

Emelye is not mentioned in Statius. She is the *Emilia* of the Teseide; see lib. ii. st. 22 of that poem.

43-6. Cf. Kn. Tale, 14, 15, 169 (A 872-3, 1027).

47. Here we are told that the story is really to begin. Chaucer now returns from Statius (whom he has nearly done with) to the Teseide, and the next three stanzas, ll. 50-70, are more or less imitated from that poem, lib. ii. st. 10-12.

50-6. Boccaccio is giving a sort of summary of the result of the war described in the Thebaid. His words are :—

'Fra tanto Marte i popoli lernei
Con furioso corso avie commossi
Sopro i Tebani, e miseri trofei
Donati avea de' Principi percossi
Più volte già, e de' greci plebei
Ritenuti tal volta, e tal riscossi
Con asta sanguinosa fieramente,
Trista avea fatta l' una e l' altra gente.'

57-63. Imitated from Tes. ii. 11 :—

'Perciò che dopo Anfiarao, Tideo
Stato era ucciso, e 'l buon Ippomedone,
E similmente il bel Partenopeo,
E più Teban, de' qua' non fo menzione,
Dinanzi e dopo al fiero Capaneo,
E dietro a tutti in doloroso agone,
Eteocle e Polinice, ed ispedito
Il solo Adrastro ad Argo era fuggito.'

See also Troilus, v. 1499-1510.

57. *Amphiorax*; so in Troilus, ii. 105, v. 1500; Cant. Tales, 6323 (D 741); and in Lydgate's Siege of Thebes. Amphiaraus is meant;

he accompanied Polynices, and was swallowed up by the earth during the siege of Thebes; Statius, Thebais, lib. vii. (at the end); Dante, Inf. xx. 34. Tydeus and Polynices married the two daughters of Adrastus. The heroic acts of Tydeus are recorded in the Thebaid. See Lydgate, Siege of Thebes; or the extract from it in my Specimens of English.

58. *Ipomedon*, Hippomedon; one of the seven chiefs who engaged in the war against Thebes. *Parthonopee*, Parthenopæus, son of Meleager and Atalanta; another of the seven chiefs. For the account of their deaths, see the Thebaid, lib. ix.

59. *Campaneus*; spelt *Cappaneus, Capaneus* in Kn. Tale, 74 (A 932); Troil. v. 1504. Thynne, in his Animadversions on Speght's Chaucer (ed. Furnivall, p. 43), defends the spelling *Campaneus* on the ground that it was the usual medieval spelling; and refers us to Gower and Lydgate. In Pauli's edition of Gower, i. 108, it is *Capaneus*. Lydgate has *Campaneus*; Siege of Thebes, pt. iii. near the beginning. Capaneus is the right Latin form; he was one of the seven chiefs, and was struck with lightning by Jupiter whilst scaling the walls of Thebes; Statius, Theb. lib. x (at the end). Cf. Dante, Inf. xiv. 63. As to the form *Campaneus*, cf. Ital. *Campidoglio* with Lat. *Capitolium*.

60. 'The Theban wretches, the two brothers;' i.e. Eteocles and Polynices, who caused the war. Cf. Troil. v. 1507.

61. *Adrastus*, king of Argos, who assisted his son-in-law Polynices, and survived the war; Theb. lib. xi. 441.

63. 'That no man knew of any remedy for his (own) misery.' *Care*, anxiety, misery. At this line Chaucer begins upon st. 12 of the second book of the Teseide, which runs thus:—

> 'Onde il misero gente era rimaso
> Vôto[1] di gente, e pien d' ogni dolore;
> Ma a picciol tempo da Creonte invaso
> Fu, che di quello si fe' re e signore,
> Con tristo augurio, in doloroso caso
> Recò insieme il regno suo e l' onore,
> Per fiera crudeltà da lui usata,
> Mai da null' altro davanti pensata.

Cf. Knightes Tale, 80-4 (A 938).

71. From this point onward, Chaucer's work is, as far as we know at present, original. He seems to be intending to draw a portrait of a queen of Armenia who is neglected by her lover, in distinct contrast to Emilia, sister of the queen of Scythia, who had a pair of lovers devoted to her service.

72. *Ermony*, Armenia; the usual M. E. form.

78. *Of twenty yeer of elde*, of twenty years of age; so in MSS. F., Tn., and Harl. 372. See note to l. 80.

80. *Behelde*; so in MSS. Harl., F.; and Harl. 372 has *beheelde*.

---

[1] *Voto*, 'hollow, voide, empty'; Florio.

I should hesitate to accept this form instead of the usual *beholde*, but for its occurrence in Gower, Conf. Amant., ed. Pauli, iii. 147 :—

> 'The wine can make a creple sterte
> And a deliver man unwelde;
> It maketh a blind man to *behelde*.

So also in the Moral Ode, l. 288, the Trinity MS. has the infin. *behealde*, and the Lambeth MS. has *bihelde*. It appears to be a Southern form, adopted here for the rime, like *ken* for *kin* in Book of the Duch. 438.

There is further authority; for we actually find *helde* for *holde* in five MSS. out of seven, riming with *welde* (*wolde*); C. T., Group D, l. 272.

82. Penelope and Lucretia are favourite examples of constancy; see C. T., Group B, 63, 75; Book Duch. 1081-2; Leg. Good Women, 252, 257. Read Penélop', not Pénelóp', as in B. D. 1081.

84. *Amended.* Compare what is said of Zenobia; C. T., B 3444.

85. I have supplied *Arcite*, which the MSS. strangely omit. It is necessary to *name* him here, to introduce him; and the line is else too short. Chaucer frequently shifts the accent upon this name, so that there is nothing wrong about either *Arcíte* here, or *Árcite* in l. 92. See Kn. Tale, 173, 344, 361, &c. on the one hand; and lines 1297, 1885 on the other. And see l. 140 below.

91. Read *trust*, the contracted form of *trusteth*.

98. 'As, indeed, it is needless for men to learn such craftiness.'

105. A proverbial expression; see Squi. Tale, F 537. The character of Arcite is precisely that of the false tercelet in Part II. of the Squieres Tale; and Anelida is like the falcon in the same. Both here and in the Squieres Tale we find the allusions to Lamech, and to blue as the colour of constancy; see notes to ll. 146, 150, 161-9 below.

119. Cf. Squi. Tale, F 569.

128. 'That all his will, it seemed to her,' &c. A common idiom. Koch would omit *hit*, for the sake of the metre; but it makes no difference at all, the *e* in *thoghte* being elided.

141. *New-fangelnesse*; see p. 409, l. 1, and Squi. Tale, F 610.

145. *In her hewe*, in her colours : he wore the colours which she affected. This was a common method of shewing devotion to a lady.

146. Observe the satire in this line. Arcite is supposed to have worn *white*, *red*, or *green*; but he did not wear *blue*, for that was the colour of *constancy*. Cf. Squi. Tale, F 644, and the note; and see l. 330 below; also p. 409, l. 7.

150. Cf. Squi. Tale, F 550. I have elsewhere drawn attention to the resemblance between this poem and the Squieres Tale, in my note to l. 548 of that Tale. Cf. also Cant. Tales, 5636 (D 54). The reference is to Gen. iv. 19—'And Lamech took unto him two wives.' In l. 154, Chaucer curiously confounds him with Jabal, Lamech's *son*, who was 'the father of such as dwell in tents'; Gen. iv. 20.

155. *Arcit-e*; trisyllabic, as frequently in Kn. Tale.

157. 'Like a wicked horse, which generally shrieks when it bites'; Bell. This explanation is clearly wrong. The line is repeated, with the slight change of *pleyne* to *whyne*, in C. T. 5968 (D 386). To *pleyne* or to *whyne* means to utter a plaintive cry, or to whinny; and the sense is—'Like a horse, (of doubtful temper), which can either bite or whinny (as if wanting a caress).'

161. *Theef*, false wretch; cf. Squi. Tale, F 537.

162. Cf. Squi. Tale, F 462, 632.

166. Cf. Squi. Tale, F 448.

169. Cf. Squi. Tale, F 412, 417, 430, 631.

171. *Al crampissheth*, she draws all together, contracts convulsively; formed from *cramp*. I know of but four other examples of the use of this word.

In Lydgate's Flour of Curtesie, st. 7, printed in Chaucer's Works, ed. 1561, fol. 248, we have the lines:—

'I gan complayne min inwarde deedly smert
That aye so sore *crampeshe at* min herte.'

As this gives no sense, it is clear that *crampeshe at* is an error for *crampisheth* or *crampished*, which Lydgate probably adopted from the present passage.

Again, in Lydgate's Life of St. Edmund, in MS. Harl. 2278, fol. 101 (ed. Horstmann, p. 430, l. 930), are the lines:—

'By pouert spoiled, which made hem sore smerte,
Which, as they thouhte, *craumpysshed* at here herte.'

Skelton has *encraumpysshed*, Garland of Laurell, 16; and Dyce's note gives an example of *craumpishing* from Lydgate's Wars of Troy, bk. iv. c. 33, sig. Xv. col. 4, ed. 1555.

Once more, Lydgate, in his Fall of Princes, bk. i. c. 9 (pr. by Wayland, leaf 18, col. 2), has the line—

'Deth *crampishing* into their hert gan crepe.'

175. In Kn. Tale, 1950 (A 2808), it is Arcite who says '*mercy!*'

176. Read *endur'th*. *Mate*, exhausted.

177. Read *n'hath*. *Sustene*, support herself; cf. C. T. 11173 (F 861).

178. *Forth* is here equivalent to 'continues'; *is* or *dwelleth* is understood. Read *languisshing*.

180. *Grene*, fresh; probably with a reference to *green* as being the colour of inconstancy.

182. Nearly repeated in Kn. Tale, 1539 (A 2397); cf. Comp. unto Pity, 110. Cf. Compl. to his Lady, 52.

183. If *up* is to be retained before *so*, change *holdeth* into *halt*. 'His new lady reins him in by the bridle so tightly (harnessed as he is) at the end of the shaft (of her car), that he fears every word like an arrow.' The image is that of a horse, tightly fastened to the ends of the shafts of a car, and then so hardly reined in that he fears every word of the driver; he expects a cut with the whip, and he cannot get away.

193. *Fee or shipe*, fee or reward. The scarce word *shipe* being misunderstood, many MSS. give corrupt readings. But it occurs in the Persones Tale, Group I, 568, where Chaucer explains it by 'hyre'; and in the Ayenbite of Inwit, p. 33. It is the A. S. *scipe*. '*Stipendium*, scipe'; Wright's Vocabularies, 114. 34.

194. *Sent*, short for *sendeth*; cf. *serveth* above. Cf. Book of Duch. 1024.

202. *Also*, as; 'as may God save me.'

206. *Hir ne gat no geyn*, she obtained for herself no advantage.

211. The metre now becomes extremely artificial. The first stanza is introductory. Its nine lines are rimed *a a b a a b b a b*, with only two rimes. I set back lines 3, 6, 7, 9, to show the arrangement more clearly. The next four stanzas are in the same metre. The construction is obscure, but is cleared up by l. 350, which is its echo, and again by ll. 270-1. *Swerd* is the nom. case, and *thirleth* is its verb; 'the sword of sorrow, whetted with false complaisance, so pierces my heart, (now) bare of bliss and black in hue, with the (keen) point of (tender) recollection.' Chaucer's 'with . . . remembrance' is precisely Dante's 'Per la puntura della rimembranza'; Purg. xii. 20.

214. Cf. The Compleint to his Lady, l. 55.

215. *Awhaped*, amazed, stupified. To the examples in the New E. Dict. add—'Sole by himself, *awhaped* and amate'; Compl. of the Black Knight, 168.

216. Cf. the Compleint to his Lady, l. 123.

218. *That*, who: relative to *hir* above.

220. Observe how the stanza, which I here number as 1, is echoed by the stanza below, ll. 281-289; and so of the rest.

222. Nearly repeated in the Compl. to his Lady, l. 35.

237. Repeated from the Compl. to his Lady, l. 50.

241. *Founde*, seek after; A. S. *fundian*. For *founde*, all the MSS. have *be founde*, but the *be* is merely copied in from *be more* in l. 240. If we retain *be*, then *befounde* must be a compound verb, with the same sense as before; but there is no known example of this verb, though the related strong verb *befinden* is not uncommon. But see l. 47 above. With l. 242 cf. Rom. Rose, 966 (p. 134).

247. Cf. Compl. to his Lady, ll. 107, 108.

256-71. This stanza is in the same metre as that marked 5 below, ll. 317-332. It is very complex, consisting of 16 lines of varying length. The lines which I have set back have but *four* accents; the rest have *five*. The rimes in the first eight lines are arranged in the order *a a a b a a a b*; in the last eight lines this order is precisely reversed, giving *b b b a b b b a*; so that the whole forms a *virelay*.

260. *Namely*, especially, in particular.

262. 'Offended you, as surely as (I hope that) He who knows everything may free my soul from woe.'

265. This refers to ll. 113-5 above.
267. Read *sav-e, mek-e*; or the line will be too short.
270. Refers to ll. 211-3 above.
272. This stanza answers to that marked 6 below, ll. 333-341. It is the most complex of all, as the lines contain internal rimes. The lines are of the normal length, and arranged with the end-rimes *a a b a a b b a b*, as in the stanzas marked 1 to 4 above. Every line has an internal rime, viz. at the second and fourth accents. In ll. 274, 280, this internal rime is a feminine one, which leaves but *one* syllable (viz. *nay, may*) to complete these lines.

The expression 'swete fo' occurs again in the Compleint to his Lady, l. 41 (cf. ll. 64, 65); also in Troil. v. 228.

279. 'And then shall this, which is now wrong, (turn) into a jest; and all (shall be) forgiven, whilst I may live.'

281. The stanza here marked 1 answers to the stanza so marked above; and so of the rest. The metre has already been explained.

286. 'There are no other fresh intermediate ways.'

299. 'And must I pray (to you), and so cast aside womanhood?' It is not for the woman to sue to the man. Compare l. 332.

301. *Nēd-e*, with long close *e*, rimes with *bēde, mēde, hēde*.

302. 'And if I lament as to what life I lead.'

306. 'Your demeanour may be said to flower, but it bears no seed.' There is much promise, but no performance.

309. *Holde*, keep back. The spelling *Averyll* (or *Auerill*) occurs in MS. Harl. 7333, MS. Addit. 16165, and MSS. T. and P. It is much better than the *Aprill* or *Aprille* in the rest. I would also read *Averill* or *Aperil* in Troil. i. 156.

313. *Who that*, whosoever. *Fast*, trustworthy.

315. *Tame*, properly tamed. From Rom. Rose, 9945:—

'N'est donc bien privée tel beste
Qui de foir est toute preste.'

320. *Chaunte-pleure*. Godefroy says that there was a celebrated poem of the 13th century named *Chantepleure* or *Pleurechante*; and that it was addressed to those who sing in this world and will weep in the next. Hence also the word was particularly used to signify any complaint or lament, or a chant at the burial-service. One of his quotations is:—'Heu brevis honor qui vix duravit per diem, sed longus dolor qui usque ad mortem, gallicè *la chantepleure*'; J. de Aluet, *Serm.*, Richel. l. 14961, fol. 195, verso. And again:—

'Car le juge de vérité
Pugnira nostre iniquité
Par la balance d'équité
Qui où val de la *chantepleure*
Nous boute en grant adversité
Sanz fin à perpétuité,
Et y parsevere et demeure.'

J. de Meung, Le Tresor, l. 1350; ed. Méon.

Tyrwhitt says:—'A sort of proverbial expression for *singing and weeping* successively [rather, little singing followed by much weeping]. See Lydgate, Trag. [i. e. Fall of Princes] st. the last; where he says that his book is 'Lyke *Chantepleure*, now singing now weping.' In MS. Harl. 4333 is a Ballad which turns upon this expression. It begins: 'Moult vaut mieux *pleure-chante* que ne fait *chante-pleure.*' Clearly the last expression means, that short grief followed by long joy is better than brief joy followed by long grief. The fitness of the application in the present instance is obvious.

Another example occurs in Lydgate's Fall of Princes, bk. i. c. 7, *lenvoy*:—

'It is like to the *chaunte-pleure*,
Beginning with ioy, ending in wretchednes.'

So also in Lydgate's Siege of Troye, bk. ii. c. 11; ed. 1555, Fol. F 6, back, col. 2.

328. *A furlong-wey* meant the time during which one can walk a furlong, at three miles an hour. A *mile-way* is twenty minutes; a *furlong-wey* is two minutes and a half; and the double of it is five minutes. But the strict sense need not be insisted on here.

330. *Asure*, true blue; the colour of *constancy*; see l. 332.

'Her habyte was of manyfolde colours,
Watchet-*blewe* of fayned *stedfastnesse*,
Her golde allayed like son in watry showres,
Meynt with *grene*, for *chaunge and doublenesse*.'
Lydgate's Fall of Princes, bk. vi. c. 1. st. 7.

So in Troil. iii. 885—'bereth him this *blewe* ring.' And see Sect. XXI. l. 7 (p. 409), and the note.

332. 'And to pray to me for mercy.' Cf. ll. 299, 300.

338. *They*, i. e. your ruth and your truth.

341. 'My wit cannot reach, it is so weak.'

342. Here follows the concluding stanza of the Complaint.

344. Read—*For I shal ne'er* (or *nev'r*) *eft putten*.

346. See note to Parl. of Foules, 342.

350. This line re-echoes l. 211.

357. The reason why the Poem ends here is sufficiently obvious. Here must have followed the description of the temple of Mars, *written in seven-line stanzas*. But it was all *rewritten* in a new metre, and is preserved to us, for all time, in the famous passage in the Knightes Tale; ll. 1109-1192 (A 1967).

VIII. CHAUCERS WORDES UNTO ADAM.

ONLY extant in MS. T., written by Shirley, and in Stowe's edition of 1561. Dr. Koch says—'It seems that Stowe has taken his text from Shirley, with a few modifications in spelling, and altered Shirley's

IX. THE FORMER AGE. LINES 1-7.

Scriveyn into *scrivener*, apparently because that word was out of use in his time. *Scriveyn* is O. Fr. *escrivain*, F. *écrivain*. Lines 3 and 4 are too long [in MS. T. and Stowe], but *long* and *more* are unnecessary for the sense, wherfore I have omitted them.' Dr. Sweet omits *long*, but retains *more*, though it sadly clogs the line. Again, in l. 2, we find *for to*, where *for* is superfluous.

2. *Boece*, Chaucer's translation of Boethius. *Troilus*, Chaucer's poem of Troilus and Creseyde; in 5 books, all in seven-line stanzas. See vol. II.

3. 'Thou oughtest to have an attack of the scab under thy locks, unless thou write exactly in accordance with my composition.'

IX. THE FORMER AGE.

'THE former Age' is a title taken from l. 2 of the poem. In MS. Hh., at the end, are the words—'Finit Etas prima: Chaucers.'

Both MSS. are poor, and omit a whole line (l. 56), which has to be supplied by conjecture; as we have no other authority. The spelling requires more emendation than usual.

The poem is partly a verse translation of Boethius, De Consolatione Philosophiæ, lib. ii. met. 5. We possess a prose translation by Chaucer of the entire work (see vol. II. p. 40). This therefore contains the same passage in prose; and the prose translation is, of course, a much closer rendering of the original. Indeed there is nothing in the original which corresponds to the last four stanzas of the present poem, excepting a hint for l. 62.

The work of Boethius, in Latin, consists of five books. Each book contains several sections, written in prose and verse alternately. Hence it is usual to refer to bk. ii. prose 5 (liber ii. prosa 5); bk. ii. metre 5 (liber ii. metrum 5); and the like. These divisions are very useful in finding one's place.

Chaucer was also indebted to Ovid, Metam. i. 89-112, for part of this description of the Golden Age; of which see Dryden's fine translation. See also Le Roman de la Rose, ll. 8395-8492: and compare the Complaint of Scotland, ed. Murray, p. 144; and Dante, Purg. xxii. 148. For further remarks, see the Introduction.

1. 'Decaearchus... refert sub Saturno, id est, in aureo saeculo, cum omnia humus funderet, nullum comedisse carnes: sed uniuersos uixisse frugibus et pomis, quae sponte terra gignebat'; Hieron. c. Iouin. lib. ii.

2. *The former age*; Lat. prior etas.

3. *Payed of*, satisfied with; Lat. contenta.

4. *By usage*, ordinarily; i.e. without being tilled.

5. *Forpampred*, exceedingly pampered; Lat. perdita. *With outrage*, beyond all measure.

6. *Quern*, a hand-mill for grinding corn. *Melle*, mill.

7. Dr. Sweet reads *hawes, mast* instead of *mast, hawes*. This sounds better, but is not necessary. *Haw-es* is dissyllabic. *Pounage*, mod. E. *pannage*, mast, or food given to swine in the woods; see the Glossary. Better spelt *pannage* or *paunage* (Manwood has *pawnage*), as cited in Blount's Nomolexicon. Koch wrongly refers us to O. F. *poün*, *poön*, a sickle (Burguy), but mast and haws were never reaped. Cf. Dante, Purg. xxii. 149.

11. 'Which they rubbed in their hands, and ate of sparingly.' *Gnodded* is the pt. t. of *gnodden* or *gnudden*, to rub, examples of which are scarce. See Ancren Riwle, pp. 238, 260 (footnotes), and *gnide* in Halliwell's Dictionary. But the right reading is obviously *gniden* or *gnide* (with short *i*), the pt. t. pl. of the strong verb *gniden*, to rub. This restores the melody of the line. In the Ancren Riwle, p. 260, there is a reference to Luke vi. 1, saying that Jesus' disciples '*gniden* the cornes ut bitweonen hore honden'; where another MS. has *gnuddeden*. The Northern form *gnade* (2 p. sing.) occurs in the O. E. Psalter, Ps. lxxxviii. 45. Dr. Sweet reads *gnodde*, but the pt. t. of *gnodden* was *gnodded*. *Nat half*, not half of the crop; some was wasted.

16. 'No one as yet ground spices in a mortar, to put into *clarrè* or galantine-sauce.' As to *clarre*, see Knightes Tale, 613 (A 1471); R. Rose, 6027; and the Babees Book, ed. Furnivall, p. 204, and Index.

In the Liber Cure Cocorum, ed. Morris, p. 30, is the following recipe for *Galentyne*:—

'Take crust of brede and grynde hit smalle,
Take powder of galingale, and temper with-alle;
Powder of gyngere and salt also;
Tempre hit with venegur er þou more do;
Drawȝe hit þurughe a streynour þenne,
And messe hit forth before good menne.'

'*Galendyne* is a sauce for any kind of roast Fowl, made of Grated Bread, beaten Cinnamon and Ginger, Sugar, Claret-wine, and Vinegar, made as thick as Grewell'; Randell Holme, bk. iii. ch. iii. p. 82, col. 2 (quoted in Babees Book, ed. Furnivall, p. 216). Roquefort gives O. F. *galatine*, *galantine*, *galentine*, explained by 'gelée, daube, sauce, ragoût fort épicé; en bas Latin, *galatina*.' Beyond doubt, Chaucer found the word in the Roman de la Rose, l. 21823—'En friture et en *galentine*.' See *Galantine* in Littré, and see note to Sect. XII. l. 17. Cf. Rom. de la Rose, 8418:—

'Et de l'iaue simple bevoient
Sans querre piment ne clare,' &c.

17. 'No dyer knew anything about madder, weld, or woad.' All three are plants used in dyeing. Madder is *Rubia tinctoria*, the roots of which yield a dye. I once fancied *weld* was an error for *welled* (i.e. flowed out); and Dr. Sweet explains *welde* by 'strong.' Both of these fancies are erroneous. *Weld* is the *Reseda Luteola* of Linnæus, and grows wild in waste places; I have seen it growing near Beachey Head. It is better known as Dyer's Rocket. In Johns' Flowers of the Field, we duly find—'*Reseda Luteola*, Dyer's Rocket, Yellow-

IX. THE FORMER AGE. LINES 11-47.

weed, or Weld.' Also called Ash of Jerusalem, Dyer's Weed, &c.; see Eng. Plant-names, by Britten and Holland. It appears in mod. G. as *Wau* (Du. *wouw*), older spelling *Waude*. Its antiquity as a Teut. word is vouched for by the derivatives in the Romance languages, such as Span. *gualda*, Port. *gualde*, F. *gaude*; see *Gualda* in Diez. *Weld* is a totally distinct word from *woad*, but most dictionaries confound them. Florio, most impartially, coins a new form by mixing the two words together (after the fashion adopted in Alice through the Looking-glass). He gives us Ital. *gualdo*, 'a weede to die yellow with, called *woald*.' The true *woad* is the *Isatis tinctoria*, used for dyeing blue before indigo was known; the name is sometimes given to *Genista tinctoria*, but the dye from this is of a yellow colour. Pliny mentions the dye from madder (Nat. Hist. xix. 3); and says the British women used *glastum*, i.e. woad (xxii. 1).

18. *Flees*, fleece; Lat. ' uellera.'

20. ' No one had yet learnt how to distinguish false coins from true ones.'

27-9. Cf. Ovid, Metam. i. 138-140.

30. *Ri-ver-es;* three syllables. Dr. Sweet suggests putting *after* in place of *first*.

33. 'These tyrants did not gladly venture into battle to win a wilderness or a few bushes where poverty (alone) dwells—as Diogenes says —or where victuals are so scarce and poor that only mast or apples are found there; but, wherever there are money-bags,' &c. This is taken either from Jerome, in his Epistle against Jovinian, lib. ii. (Epist. Basil. 1524, ii. 73), or from John of Salisbury's Policraticus, lib. viii. c. 6. Jerome has: 'Diogenes *tyrannos* et subuersiones urbium, bellaque uel hostilia, uel ciuilia, non pro simplici uictu holerum pomorumque, sed pro carnibus et epularum deliciis asserit excitari.' John of Salisbury copies this, with *subuersores* for *subuersiones*, which seems better. Gower relates how Diogenes reproved Alexander for his lust of conquest; Conf. Amantis, ed. Pauli, i. 322.

41. This stanza seems more or less imitated from Le Rom. de la Rose, 8437 :—

> ' Et quant par nuit dormir voloient,
> En leu de coites [*quilts*] aportoient
> En lor casiaus monceaus de gerbes,
> De foilles, ou de mousse, ou d'erbes; . . .
> Sor tex couches cum ge devise,
> Sans rapine et sans convoitise,
> S'entr'acoloient et baisoient . . .
> Les simples gens asséurées,
> De toutes cures escurées.'

47. 'Their hearts were all united, without the gall (of envy).' Curiously enough, Chaucer has here made an oversight. He ends the line with *galles*, riming with *halles* and *walles*; whereas the line should

542   NOTES TO THE MINOR POEMS.

end with a word riming to *shete*, as, e.g. 'Hir hertes knewen nat to counterfete.'

49. Here again cf. Rom. de la Rose, 8483:—

'N'encor n'avoit fet roi ne prince
Meffais qui l'autrui tolt et pince.
Trestuit pareil estre soloient,
Ne riens propre avoir ne voloient.

55, 6. 'Humility and peace, (and) good faith (who is) the empress (of all), filled the earth full of ancient courtesy.' Line 56 I have supplied; Dr. Koch supplies the line—'Yit hadden in this worlde the maistrie.' Either of these suggestions fills up the sense intended.

57. Jupiter is mentioned in Ovid's Metamorphoses immediately after the description of the golden, silver, brazen, and iron ages. At l. 568 of the same book begins the story of the love of Jupiter for Io.

59. *Nembrot*, Nimrod; so that *his toures hye* refers to the tower of Babel. In Gen. x, xi, the sole connection of Nimrod with Babel is in ch. x. 10—'And the beginning of his kingdom was Babel.' But the usual medieval account is that he built the tower. Thus, in the Cursor Mundi, l. 2223:—

'Nembrot than said on this wise, . . .
"I rede we bigin a laboure,
And do we wel and make a toure,"' &c.

So also in Sir D. Lyndsay, Buke of the Monarché, bk. ii. l. 1625.

62-4. These last lines are partly imitated from Boethius; lines 33-61 are independent of him.

X. FORTUNE.

THIS poem consists of *three* Ballads and an Envoy. Each Ballad contains three stanzas of eight lines, with the rimes *a b a b b c b c*, and the rimes of the second and third stanzas are precisely the same as those of the first. Thus the rime *a* recurs six times, the rime *b* twelve times, and the rime *c* likewise six times. Moreover, each stanza ends with the same line, recurring as a refrain. Hence the metrical difficulties are very great, and afford a convincing proof of Chaucer's skill. The Envoy is of seven lines, rimed *a b a b b a b*.

The three ballads are called, collectively, Balades de visage sanz peinture, a title which is correctly given in MS. I., with the unlucky exception that *visage* has been turned into *vilage*. This curious blunder occurs in all the MSS. and old editions, and evidently arose from mistaking a long *s* (f) for an *l*. *Vilage*, of course, makes no sense; and we are enabled to correct it by help of Chaucer's translation of Boethius, bk. ii. pr. 1; l. 39. 'Right swich was she [Fortune] whan she flatered thee, and deceived thee with unleveful lykinges of fals welefulnesse. Thou hast now knowen and ataynt the doutous or double *visage* of thilke blinde goddesse *Fortune*. She, that yit *covereth* hir and

X. FORTUNE. LINE 1.

wimpleth hir to other folk, hath shewed hir everydel to thee.' Or the Ballads may refer to the unmasking of false friends : '*Fortune* hath departed and uncovered to thee bothe the *certein visages* and eek the doutous *visages* of thy felawes'; id. bk. ii. pr. 8 ; l. 25. The whole poem is more or less founded on the descriptions of Fortune in Boethius ; and we thus see that the visage meant is the *face of Fortune*, or else the *face of a supposed friend*, which is clearly revealed to the man of experience, in the day of adversity, without any covering or wimpling, and even without any painting or false colouring.

In MS. T. we are told that 'here filoweþe [*followeth*] a balade made by Chaucier of þe louer and of Dame Fortune.' In MS. A. we are told that 'here foloweþe nowe a compleynte of þe Pleintyff agenst fortune translated oute of Frenshe into Englisshe by þat famous Rethorissyen Geffrey Chaucier.' This hint, that it is translated out of French, can scarcely be right, unless Shirley (whose note this is) means that it partially resembles passages in Le Roman de la Rose ; for Chaucer's work seems to contain some reminiscences of that poem as well as of the treatise of Boethius, though of course Le Roman is indebted to Boethius also.

Le Pleintif is the complainant, the man who brings a charge against Fortune, or rather, who exclaims against her as false, and defies her power. The first Ballad, then, consists of this complaint and defiance.

The close connection between this poem and Boethius is shewn by the fact that (like the preceding poem called The Former Age) it occurs in an excellent MS. of Chaucer's translation of Boethius, viz. MS. I. (Ii. 3. 21, in the Cambridge University Library). I may also remark here, that there is a somewhat similar dialogue between Nobilitas and Fortuna in the Anticlaudianus of Alanus de Insulis, lib. viii. c. 2 ; see Anglo-Latin Satirists, ed. T. Wright, ii. 401.

In Morley's English Writers, ii. 283, is the following description. 'The argument of the *first* part [or Ballad] is : I have learnt by adversity to know who are my true friends ; and he can defy Fortune who is master of himself. The argument of the *next* part [second Ballad], that Fortune speaks, is : Man makes his own wretchedness. What may come you know not ; you were born under my rule of change ; your anchor holds. Of the *third* part of the poem [third Ballad], in which the Poet and Fortune each speak, the sum of the argument is, that what blind men call fortune is the righteous will of God. Heaven is firm, this world is mutable. The piece closes with Fortune's call upon the Princes to relieve this man of his pain, or pray his best friend " of his noblesse " that he may attain to some better estate.'

The real foundation of these three Ballads is (1) Boethius, bk. ii. proses 1, 2, 3, 4, 5, 8, and met. 1 ; and (2) a long passage in Le Roman de la Rose, ll. 4853-4994 (Eng. version, 5403-5584). More particular references are given below.

1. The beginning somewhat resembles Boethius, bk. ii. met. 1, l. 5 :—'She, cruel Fortune, casteth adoun kinges that whylom weren

y-drad; and she, deceivable, enhaunseth up the humble chere of him that is discomfited.' Cf. Rom. Rose (E. version), ll. 5479-83.

2. The latter part of this line is badly given in the MSS. The readings are: F. now pouerte and now riche honour (*much too long*); I. now poe*er*e and now honour; A. T. nowe poure and nowe honour; H. now poore and now honour. But the reading *poure, poer, pore*, i.e. poor, hardly serves, as a sb. is required. *Pouerte* seems to be the right word, but this requires us to omit the former *now*. *Pouerte* can be pronounced *povért'*; accented on the second syllable, and with the final *e* elided. For this pronunciation, see Prol. to Man of Lawes Tale, Group B, l. 99. Precisely because this pronunciation was not understood, the scribes did not know what to do. They inserted *now* before *pouerte* (which they thought was *póverte*); and then, as the line was too long, cut it down to *poure, poore*, to the detriment of the sense. I would therefore rather read—'As wele or wo, poverte and now honour,' with the pronunciation noted above.

7. In the Introduction to the Persones Tale (Group I, 248), we find: 'wel may that man, that no good werke ne dooth, singe thilke newe Frenshe song, *Iay tout perdu mon temps et mon labour*.' In like manner, in the present case, this line of 'a new French song' is governed by the verb *singen* in l. 6; cf. Sect. XXII. l. 24. The sense is —'the lack of Fortune's favour shall never (though I die) make me sing—"I have wholly lost my time and my labour."' In other words, 'I will not own myself defeated.'

9. With this stanza cf. Rom. de la Rose (E. version), 5551-2, 5671-78, 5579-81:—

> 'For Infortune makith anoon
> To knowe thy freendis fro thy foon . . .
> A wys man seide, as we may seen,
> Is no man wrecched, but he it wene, . .
> For he suffrith in pacience . . .
> Richesse riche ne makith nought
> Him that on tresour set his thought;
> For richesse stont in *suffisaunce*;' &c.

13. *No force of*, it does not matter for; i.e. 'thy rigour is of no consequence to him who has the mastery over himself.' From Boethius, bk. ii. pr. 4, l. 98, which Chaucer translates: 'Thanne, yif it so be that thou art mighty over thy-self, that is to seyn, by tranquillitee of thy sowle, than hast thou thing in thy power that thou noldest never lesen, ne Fortune ne may nat beneme it thee.'

17. Socrates is mentioned in Boeth. bk. i. pr. 3, l. 39, but ll. 17-20 are from Le Rom. de la Rose, ll. 5871-4:—

> 'A Socrates seras semblables,
> Qui tant fu fers et tant estables,
> Qu'il n'ert liés en prospérités,
> Ne tristes en aversités.'

20. **Chere**, look. *Savour*, pleasantness, attraction; cf. Squi. Tale, F 404. All the MSS. have this reading; Caxton alters it to *favour*.

25. This Second Ballad gives us Fortune's response to the defiance of the complainant. In Arch. Seld. B. 10, it is headed—'Fortuna ad paupertatem.' See Boethius, bk. ii. prose 2, where Philosophy says —'Certes, I wolde *pleten* with thee a fewe thinges, *usinge the wordes of Fortune*.' Cf. 'nothing is wrecched but whan thou wenest it'; Boeth. ii. pr. 4, l. 79; and see Rom. Rose (E. version, 5467-5564).

28. 'Who possessest thy (true) self (as being quite) beyond my control.' A fine sentiment. *Out of*, beyond, independent of.

29. Cf. 'thou hast had grace as he that hath used of foreine goodes; thou hast no right to pleyne thee'; Boethius, bk. ii. pr. 2, l. 17.

31. Cf. 'what eek yif my mutabilitee yiveth thee rightful cause of hope to han yit beter thinges?' id. l. 58.

32. *Thy beste frend*; possibly John of Gaunt, who died in 1399; but see note to l. 73 below. There is a curious resemblance here to Le Rom. de la Rose, 8056-60:—

> 'Et sachies, compains, que sitost
> Comme *Fortune* m'ot ça mis,
> *Je perdi trestous mes amis*,
> *Fors ung*, ce croi ge vraiement,
> Qui m'est remès tant solement.'

34. Cf. 'For-why this ilke Fortune hath departed and uncovered to thee bothe the certein visages and eek the doutous visages of thy felawes ... thow hast founden the moste precious kinde of richesses, that is to seyn, thy verray freendes'; Boeth. bk. ii. pr. 8, l. 25.

Cf. Rom. Rose (E. version), l. 5486, and ll. 5547-50. The French version has (ll. 4967, &c.):—

> 'Si lor fait par son mescheoir
> Tretout si clerement veoir,
> Que lor fait lor amis trover,
> Et par experiment prover
> Qu'il valent miex que nul avoir
> Qu'il poïssent où monde avoir.'

35. Vincent de Beauvais, Speculum Naturale, bk. 19, c. 62, headed De medicinis ex hyæna, cites the following from Hieronymus, Contra Iouinianum [lib. ii. Epist. Basileæ, 1524, ii. 74]:—'Hyænæ fel oculorum claritatem restituit,' the gall of a hyena restores the clearness of one's eyes. So also Pliny, Nat. Hist. bk. xxviii. c. 8. This exactly explains the allusion. Compare the extract from Boethius already quoted above, at the top of p. 543.

38. 'Still thine anchor holds.' From Boethius, bk. ii. pr. 4, l. 40:—whan that thyn ancres cleven faste, that neither wolen suffren

the counfort of this tyme present, ne the hope of tyme cominge, to passen ne to faylen.'

39. 'Where Liberality carries the key of my riches.'

43. *On*, referring to, or, that is binding on.

46. Fortune says :—'I torne the whirlinge wheel with the torning cercle'; Boethius, bk. ii. pr. 2, l. 37.

47. 'My teaching is better, in a higher degree, than your affliction is, in its degree, evil'; i. e. my teaching betters you more than your affliction makes you suffer.

49. In this third Ballad, the stanzas are distributed between the Complainant and Fortune, one being assigned to the former, and two to the latter. The former says :—'I condemn thy teaching; it is (mere) adversity.' M. S. Arch. Seld. B. 10 has the heading 'Paupertas ad Fortunam.'

50. *My frend*, i. e. my true friend. In l. 51, *thy frendes* means 'the friends I owed to thee,' my false friends. From Boethius, bk. ii. pr. 8, l. 23 :—'this aspre and horrible Fortune hath discovered to thee the thoughtes of thy trewe freendes ; . . . Whan she departed awey fro thee, she took awey *hir* freendes and lafte thee *thyne* freendes.'

51. *I thanke hit thee*, I owe thanks to thee for it. But very likely *hit* has been inserted to fill up, and the right reading is, probably, *I thank-e thee*; as Koch suggests.

52. *On presse*, in a throng, in company, all together.

53. 'Their niggardliness, in keeping their riches to themselves, foreshews that thou wilt attack their stronghold ; just as an unnatural appetite precedes illness.'

56. Cf. Rom. de la Rose, 19179 :—

'Ceste ruile est si généraus,
Qu'el ne puet defaillir vers aus.'

57. Here Fortune replies. This stanza is nearly made up of extracts from Boethius, bk. ii. pr. 2, transposed and rearranged. For the sake of comparison, I give the nearest equivalents, transposing them to suit the order here adopted.

'That maketh thee now inpacient ayeins me. . . I norisshede thee with my richesses. . . Now it lyketh me to with-drawen my hand . . . shal I than only ben defended to usen my right ? . . . The see hath eek his right to ben somtyme calme . . . and somtyme to ben horrible with wawes. . . Certes, it is leveful to the hevene to make clere dayes. . . The yeer hath eek leve . . . to confounden hem [*the flowers*] somtyme with reynes . . . shal it [*men's covetousness*] binde me to ben stedefast ?'

Compare also the defence of Fortune by Pandarus, in Troilus, bk. i. 841-854.

65. Above this stanza (ll. 65-72) all the MSS. insert a new heading, such as 'Le pleintif,' or 'Le pleintif encountre Fortune,' or 'The

pleyntyff ageinst Fortune,' or ' Paupertas ad Fortunam.' But they are all wrong, for it is quite certain that this stanza belongs to Fortune. Otherwise, it makes no sense. Secondly, we know this by the original (in Boethius). And thirdly, Fortune cannot well have the 'envoy' unless she has the stanza preceding it. Dr. Morris, in his edition, rightly omits the heading; and so in Bell's edition.

66. Compare :—' For purviaunce is thilke divyne reson that is establisshed in the soverein prince of thinges ; the whiche purviaunce disponeth alle thinges'; Boeth. bk. iv. pr. 6, l. 42.

68. *Ye blinde bestes*, addressed to men; evidently by *Fortune*, not by the *Pleintif.* Compare the words *forth, beste*, in the Balade on Truth, Sect. XIII. l. 18.

71. Here we have formal proof that the speaker is Fortune ; for this is copied from Boethius, bk. ii. pr. 3, l. 60—' natheles the laste day of a mannes lyf is a manere deeth to Fortune.' Hence *thy* refers to *man*, and *myn* refers to *Fortune* ; and the sense is—' Thy last day (O man) is the end of my interest (in thee)'; or 'dealings (with thee).' The word *interesse*, though scarce, is right. It occurs in Lydgate's Minor Poems, ed. Halliwell, p. 210; and in Spenser, F. Q. vii. 6. 33 :—

'That not the worth of any living wight
May challenge ought in Heaven's *interesse*.'

And in Todd's Johnson :—' I thought, says his Majesty [K. Charles I.] I might happily have satisfied all *interesses*'; Lord Halifax's Miscell. p. 144. The sb. also occurs as Ital. *interesse* ; thus Florio's Ital. Dict. (1598) has :—' *Interesse, Interesso*, the interest or profite of money for lone. Also, what toucheth or concerneth a mans state or reputation.' And Minsheu's Spanish Dict. (1623) has :—' *Interes*, or *Interesse*, interest, profite, auaile.' The E. vb. to *interess* was once common, and occurs in K. Lear, i. 1. 87 (unless Dr. Schmidt is right in condemning the reading of that line).

73. *Princes.* Who these princes were, it is hard to say; according to l. 76 (found in MS. I. only), there were *three* of them. If the reference is to the Dukes of Lancaster, York, and Gloucester, then the 'beste frend' must be the king himself. Cf. l. 33.

75, 76. 'And I (Fortune) will requite you for your trouble (undertaken) at my request, whether there be three of you, or two of you (that heed my words).' Line 76 occurs in MS. I. *only*, yet it is difficult to reject it, as it is not a likely sort of line to be thrust in, unless this were done, in revision, by the author himself. Moreover, we should expect the Envoy to form a stanza with the usual seven lines, so common in Chaucer, though the rime-arrangement differs.

77. ' And, unless it pleases you to relieve him of his pain (yourselves), pray his best friend, for the honour of his nobility, that he may attain to some better estate.'

The assigning of this petition to *Fortune* is a happy expedient. The poet thus escapes making a direct appeal in his own person.

XI. MERCILESS BEAUTY.

THE title 'Mercilesse Beaute' is given in the Index to the Pepys MS. As it is a fitting title, and no other has been suggested, it is best to use it.

I think this Roundel was suggested by one written in French, in the thirteenth century, by Willamme d'Amiens, and printed in Bartsch, Chrestomathie de l'ancien Français. It begins—

> 'Jamais ne serai saous
> D'esguarder les vairs ieus dous
> Qui m'ont ocis';—

i.e. I shall never be sated with gazing on the gray soft eyes which have slain me.

1. The MS. has *Yowre two yen*; but the scribe lets us see that this ill-sounding arrangement of the words is not the author's own; for in writing the refrain he writes 'Your yen, &c.' But we have further evidence: for the whole line is quoted in Lydgate's Ballade of our Ladie, printed in Chaucer's Works, ed. 1550, fol. 347 b, in the form—'Your eyen two wol slee me sodainly.' The same Ballad contains other imitations of Chaucer's language. Cf. also Kn. Tale, 260 and 709 (A 1118, 1567).

3. *So woundeth hit . . . kene*, so keenly it (your beauty) wounds (me). The MS. has *wondeth*, which is another M. E. spelling of *woundeth*. Percy miscopied it *wendeth*, which gives but poor sense; besides, Chaucer would probably have used the contracted form *went*, as his manner is. In l. 5, the scribe writes *wound* (better *wounde*).

4. *And but*, and unless. For *word* Percy printed *words*, quite forgetting that the M. E. plural is dissyllabic (*word-es*). The final *d* has a sort of curl to it, but a comparison with other words shews that it means nothing; it occurs, for instance, at the end of *wound* (l. 5), and *escaped* (l. 27).

Wounde (MS. *wound*) is dissyllabic in Mid. English, like mod. G. *Wunde*. See *wunde* in Stratmann.

6. I give *two* lines to the first refrain, and *three* to the second. The reader may give *three* lines to both, if he pleases; see note to sect. V, l. 675. We cannot confine the first refrain to *one* line only, as there is no stop at the end of l. 14.

8. *Trouth-e* is dissyllabic; see *treouthe* in Stratmann.

15. *Ne availeth*; with elided *e*. MS. nauailleth; Percy prints *n'availeth*.

16. *Halt*, i. e. holdeth; see Book of Duch. 621.

17. MS. *han ye me*, correctly; Percy omits *me*, and so spoils both sense and metre.

27. Lovers should be *lean*; see Romaunt of the Rose (E. version), 2684. The F. version has (l. 2561):—

> 'Car bien saches qu' Amors ne lesse
> Sor fins amans color ne gresse.'

XII. TO ROSEMOUNDE. LINES 2-17.   549

28. MS. neue*re*; Percy prints *nere*; but the syllables *in his* occupy the time of *one* syllable. I suspect that the correct reading is *thenke ben*; *to* is not wanted, and *thenke* is better with a final *e*, though it is sometimes dropped in the pres. indicative. Percy prints *thinke*, but the MS. has *thenk*; cf. AS. *þencan*. With l. 29 cf. Troil. v. 363.

31. *I do no fors*, I don't care; as in Cant. Ta. 6816 (D 1234).

XII. TO ROSEMOUNDE.

THIS graceful Balade is a happy specimen of Chaucer's skill in riming. The metre is precisely that of 'Fortune,' resembling that of the Monkes Tale with the addition of a refrain; only the same rimes are used throughout. The formula is *a b a b b c b c*.

2. 'As far as the map of the world extends.' *Mappemounde* is the F. *mappemonde*, Lat. *mappa mundi*; it is used also by Gower, Conf. Amant. iii. 102.

9. *tyne*, a large tub; O. F. *tine*. The whole phrase occurs in the Chevalier au Cigne, as given in Bartsch, Chrest. Française, 350. 23:—
'Le jour i ot plore de larmes plaine tine.' Cotgrave has:—'*Tine*, a Stand, open Tub, or Soe, most in use during the time of vintage, and holding *about four or five pailfuls*, and commonly borne, by a Stang, between two.' We picture to ourselves the brawny porters, staggering beneath the '*stang*,' on which is slung the 'tine' containing the 'four or five pailfuls' of the poet's tears.

10. The poet, in all his despair, is sustained and refreshed by regarding the lady's beauty.

11. *seemly*, excellent, pleasing; this is evidently meant by the *semy* of the MS.

smal, fine in tone, delicate; perhaps treble. A good example occurs in the Flower and the Leaf, 180:—

> 'With voices sweet entuned, and so *smalle*,
> That it me thoughte the swetest melodye,' &c.

Cf. 'his vois gentil and *smal*'; Cant. Tales, A 3360. The reading *fynall* (put for *finall*) is due to mistaking the long f (*s*) for *f*, and *m* for *in*.

out-twyne, twist out, force out; an unusual word.

17. 'Never was pike so involved in galantine-sauce as I am completely involved in love.' This is a humorous allusion to a manner of serving up pikes which is well illustrated in the Fifteenth-Century Cookery-books, ed. Austin, p. 101, where a recipe for 'pike in Galentyne' directs that the cook should 'cast the sauce *under him and aboue him, that he be al y-hidde in the sauce*.' At p. 108 of the same we are told that the way to make 'sauce galentyne' is to steep crusts of brown bread in vinegar, adding powdered cinnamon till it is brown; after which the vinegar is to be strained twice or thrice through a strainer, and some pepper and salt is to be added. Thus

'sauce galentine' was a seasoned pickle. See further in the note to l. 16 of Sect. IX.

20. 'True Tristram the second.' For *Tristram*, see note to Sect. V. l. 290. Tristram was a famous example of 'truth' or constancy, as his love was inspired by having drunk a magical love-potion, from the effects of which he never recovered. The MS. has *Tristam*.

21. *refreyd*, cooled down; lit. 'refrigerated.' This rare word occurs twice in Troilus; see bk. ii. 1343, v. 507; cf. Pers. Ta. I 341. Dr. Murray tells me that no writer but Chaucer is known to have used this form of the word, though Caxton has *refroid*, from continental French, whereas *refreid* is from Anglo-French.

afounde, sink, be submerged. See O. F. *afonder*, to plunge under water, also, to sink, in Godefroy; and *affonder* in Cotgrave. Chaucer found this rare word in Le Roman de la Rose, 19914. (I once thought it was the pp. of *afinden*, and meant 'nor be explored'; but it is better to take it as infin. after *may not*). See *Afounder* in the New E. Dict.

XIII. TRUTH.

THE Titles are: Gg. Balade de bone conseyl; Lansd. 699, La bon Counseil de le Auttour; Caxton, The good counceyl of Chawcer; Harl. Moral balade of Chaucyre. Shirley calls it—Balade that Chaucier made on his deeth-bedde; a note that has been frequently repeated, and is probably no better than a bad guess.

1. Koch considers that the source of the poem is a passage in Boethius, lib. iii. met. 11, at the beginning, but the resemblance is very slight. It contains no more than a mere hint for it. However, part of st. 3 is certainly from the same, bk. i. pr. 5, as will appear; see note to l. 17.

The former passage in Boethius is thus translated by Chaucer: 'Who-so that seketh sooth by a deep thoght, and coveiteth nat to ben deceived by no mis-weyes, lat him rollen and trenden [*revolve*] with-inne himself the light of his inward sighte; and lat him gadere ayein, enclyninge in-to a compas, the longe moevinges of his thoughtes; and lat him techen his corage that he hath enclosed and hid in his tresors, al that he compaseth or seketh fro with-oute.' See also bk. ii. pr. 5 of the same, which seems to me more like the present poem than is the above passage.

2. Koch reads *thing* for *good*, as in some MSS. He explains the line:—'Devote thyself entirely to one thing, even if it is not very important in itself (instead of hunting after a phantom).' This I cannot accept; it certainly means nothing of the kind. Dr. Sweet has the reading: *Suffise thin owene thing*, &c., which is the reading of *one* MS. only, but it gives the right idea. The line would then mean: 'let your own property, though small, suffice for your wants.' I think we are bound to follow the MSS. generally; of these, *two* have

XIII. TRUTH. LINES 1-8.

Suffice unto thi thing; seven have *Suffice unto thy good*; one has *Suffice unto thi lyuynge* (where *lyuynge* is a gloss upon *good*); and F. has the capital reading *Suffice the* (=*thee*) *thy good*. It seems best to follow the majority, especially as they allow *suffice* to be followed by a vowel, thus eliding the final *e*. The sense is simply: 'Be content with thy property, though it be small'; and the next line gives the reason why—'for hoarding only causes hatred, and ambition creates insecurity; the crowd is full of envy, and wealth blinds one in every respect.' *Suffice unto thy good* is much the same as the proverb— 'cut your coat according to your cloth.' Chaucer elsewhere has *worldly suffisaunce* for 'wealth'; Cler. Tale, E 759. Of course this use of *suffice unto* (be content with) is peculiar; but I do not see why it is not legitimate. The use of *Savour* in l. 5 below is at least as extraordinary.

Cf. Chaucer's tr. of Boethius, bk. ii. pr. 5, l. 54:—'And if thou wolt fulfille thy nede after that it suffiseth to nature, than is it no nede that thou seke after the superfluitee of fortune.'

3. Cf. 'for avarice maketh alwey mokereres [*hoarders*] to ben hated'; Boeth. ii. pr. 5, l. 11.

5. *Savour*, taste with relish, have an appetite for. 'Have a relish for no more than it may behove you (to taste).'

6. Most MSS. read *Werk* or *Do*; only two have *Reule*, which Dr. Sweet adopts. Any one of these three readings makes sense. 'Thou who canst advise others, work well thyself,' or 'act well thyself,' or 'rule thyself.' To quote from Hamlet, i. 3. 47 :—

'Do not, as some ungracious pastors do,
Show me the steep and thorny way to heaven;
Whiles, like a puff'd and reckless libertine,
Himself the primrose path of dalliance treads,
And recks not his own rede.'

It is like the Jewish proverb—' Physician, heal thyself.'

7. *Trouthe shal delivere*, truth shall give deliverance. 'The truth shall make you free,' Lat. 'ueritas liberabit uos'; John viii. 32. This is a general truth, and there is no need for the insertion of *thee* after *shal*, as in the inferior MSS., in consequence of the gradual loss of the final *e* in *trouthe*, which in Chaucer is properly dissyllabic. The scribes who turned *trouthe* into *trouthe thee* forgot that this makes up *trou-thè thee*.

8. *Tempest thee neght*, do not violently trouble or harass thyself, do not be in a state of agitation. Agitation will not redress everything that is crooked. So also :—' *Tempest* thee nat thus with al thy fortune'; Boeth. bk. ii. pr. 4, l. 50. Chaucer (as Koch says) obtained this curious verb from the third line of section F (l. 63 of the whole poem) of the French poem from which he translated his A B C. This section begins (see p. 263 above) :—

'Fuiant m'en viens a ta tente
Moy mucier pour la tormente
Qui ou monde me *tempeste*';

i.e. I come fleeing to thy tent, to hide myself from the storm which harasses me in the world. Goldsmith speaks of a mind being 'tempested up'; Cit. of the World, let. 47.

9. 'Trusting to the vicissitudes of fortune.' There are several references to the wheel of Fortune in Boethius. Thus in bk. ii. pr. 2 of Chaucer's translation :—' I torne the whirlinge wheel with the torning cercle,' quoted above, in the note to X. 46.

10. 'Much repose consists in abstinence from fussiness.'

11. 'To spurn against an awl,' i.e. against a prick, is the English equivalent of the Gk. phrase which our bibles render by 'to kick against the pricks,' Acts ix. 5. Wyclif has 'to kike ayens the pricke.' In MS. Cotton, Otho A. xviii, we find the reading *a nall*, the *n* being transferred from *an* to the sb. Tusser has *nall* for 'awl' in his Husbandry, § 17, st. 4, l. 3. This MS., by the way, has been burnt, but a copy of it (too much corrected) is given in Todd's Illustrations of Chaucer, p. 131.

12. An allusion to the fable in Æsop about the earthern and brazen pots being dashed together. An earthen pot would have still less chance of escape if dashed against a wall. In MS. T., the word *crocke* is glossed by 'water-potte.'

13. 'Thou that subduest the deeds of another, subdue thyself.'

15. Cf. 'it behoveth thee to suffren with evene wille in pacience al that is don .. in this world'; Boeth. bk. ii. pr. 1, l. 66.

16. *Axeth*, requires ; i.e. will surely cause.

17. When Boethius complains of being exiled, Philosophy directs him to a heavenly home. 'Yif thou remembre of what contree thou art born, it nis nat governed by emperours ... but oo lord and oo king, and that is god'; bk. i. pr. 5, l. 11. This is copied (as being taken from 'Boece') in Le Roman de la Rose, l. 5049 (Eng. version, l. 5659).

18. The word *beste* probably refers to the passage in Boethius where wicked men are likened to various animals, as when the extortioner is a wolf, a noisy abusive man is a hound, a treacherous man is a fox, &c.; bk. iv. pr. 3. The story of Ulysses and Circe follows; bk. iv. met. 3.

19. 'Recognise heaven as thy true country.' *Lok up*, gaze upwards to heaven. Cf. the expression 'thy contree' at the end of bk. iv. pr. 1 of his translation of Boethius. There is also a special reference here to Boeth. bk. v. met. 5, where it is said that quadrupeds look *down*, but man is upright ; 'this figure amonesteth thee, that axest the hevene with thy righte visage'; l. 14. See Ovid, Met. i. 85.

> But, man, as thou wittlees were,
> Thou lokist euere dounwarde as a beest.'
> Polit. and Love Poems, ed. Furnivall, p. 185, l. 273.

Thank god of al, thank God for all things. In like manner, in the Lamentation of Mary Magdalen, st. 53, we find : 'I thanke God *of* al, if I nowe dye.' Mätzner (Gram. ii. 2. 307) quotes from the Towneley

Mysteries, p. 128:—'Mekyll thanke *of* youre good wille'; and again (Gram. ii. 1. 238) from King Alisaunder, l. 7576:—'And thankid him *of* his socour.' Henrysoun, in his Abbay Walk, l. 8, has:—'Obey, and thank thy God of al'; but he is probably copying this very passage. Cf. also—'of help I him praye'; Lydgate, London Lyckpeny, st. 6; 'beseech you of your pardon'; Oth. iii. 3. 212. In Lydgate's Minor Poems, ed. Halliwell, p. 225, is a poem in which every stanza ends with 'thonk God of alle.' Cf. Cant. Tales, B 1113.

'Lyft wp thyne Ene [*not* orne], and thank thi god of al.'
Ratis Raving, ed. Lumby, p. 10.

20. *Hold the hye wey*, keep to the high road. Instead of *Hold the hye wey*, some MSS. have *Weyve thy lust*, i.e. put aside thy desire, give up thine own will.

22. This last stanza forms an Envoy. It exists in *one* copy only (MS. Addit. 10340); but there is no reason at all for considering it spurious. *Vache*, cow; with reference to the 'beast in the stall' in l. 18. This animal was probably chosen as being less offensive than those mentioned by Boethius, viz. the wolf, hound, fox, lion, hart, ass, and sow. Possibly, also, there is a reference to the story of Nebuchadnezzar, as related by Chaucer in the Monkes Tale; Group B, 3361.

XIV. GENTILESSE.

FOR remarks upon Scogan's quotation of this Ballad in full, see the Introduction.

The titles are: Harl. Moral balade of Chaucier; T. Balade by Chaucier.

Caxton's text is unusually good, and is often superior to that in the existing MSS.

The general idea of the poem is that Christ was the true pattern of 'gentleness' or gentility, i.e. of noble behaviour. Cf. Dekker's noble line, in which he speaks of Christ as 'The first true gentleman that ever breathed.'

But the finest poetical essay upon this subject is that by Chaucer himself, in the Wife of Bath's Tale; C. T. 6691-6758 (D 1109); which see. And cf. Tale of Melibeus, B 2831-2.

Another passage on this subject occurs in the Eng. version of the Romance of the Rose, ll. 2188-2202, which, curiously enough, is in neither Michel's nor Méon's edition of the French Poem (in which l. 2184 of the E. version is immediately succeeded by l. 2203 of the same). Again, in Le Roman de la Rose, ll. 6603-6616, there is a definition of *Gentillesce*; but this passage is not in the Eng. version.

The original passage, to which both Chaucer and Jean de Meun were indebted, is one in Boethius, bk. iii. pr. 6; which Chaucer thus translates:—'For yif the name of gentilesse be referred to renoun and cleernesse of linage, than is gentil name but a foreine thing, that is to seyn, to hem that glorifyen hem of hir linage. For it semeth that gentilesse be a maner preysinge that comth of deserte of ancestres .. yif thou ne have no gentilesse of thy-self—that is to seyn, preyse that comth of thy deserte—foreine gentilesse ne maketh thee nat gentil.' And again, just below, in metre 6 :—'On allone is fader of thinges .. Thanne comen alle mortal folk of noble sede ; why noisen ye or bosten of youre eldres ?' But we must not overlook a long passage near the end of Le Roman de la Rose, ll. 18807-19096, which Chaucer certainly also consulted. I quote some of these lines below.

1. With this first stanza compare R. Rose, 18881 :—

> 'Quiconques tent à gentillece
> D'orguel se gart et de parece ;
> Aille as armes, ou à l'estuide,
> Et de vilenie se vuide ;
> Humble cuer ait, cortois et gent
> En tretous leus, vers toute gent.'

Two MSS., both written out by Shirley, and MS. Harl. 7333, all read :—'The first fader, and foundour (*or* fynder) of gentylesse.' This is wrong, and probably due to the dropping of the final *e* in the definite adjective *firste*. We must keep the phrase *firste stok*, because it is expressly repeated in l. 8.

The first line means—'With regard to, *or* As to the first stock (or source), who was the father of *gentilesse*.' The substantives *stok* and *fader* have *no verb* to them, but are mentioned as being the *subject* of the sentence.

3. The former *his* refers to *fader*, but the latter to *man*.

4. *Sewe*, follow. In a Ballad by King James the First of Scotland, printed at p. 54 of my edition of the Kingis Quair, the first five lines are a fairly close imitation of the opening lines of the present poem, and prove that King James followed a MS. which had the reading *sewe*.

> 'Sen throu vertew encressis dignite,
> And vertew flour and rut [*root*] is of noblay,
> Of ony weill or quhat estat thou be,
> His steppis *sew*, and dreid thee non effray :
> Exil al vice, and folow trewth alway.'

Observe how his first, third, and fourth lines answer to Chaucer's fifth, second, and fourth lines respectively.

5. 'Dignitees apertienen ... to vertu '; Boeth. iii. pr. 4, l. 25.

7. *Al were he*, albeit he may wear ; i. e. although he may be a bishop, king, or emperor.

8. *This firste stok*, i.e. Christ. In l. 12, *his heir* means mankind in general.

Compare Le Rom. de la Rose, 18819 :—

> 'Noblece vient de bon corage,
> Car gentillece de lignage

XV. LAK OF STEDFASTNESSE.

> N'est pas gentillece qui vaille,
> Por quoi bonté de cuer i faille,
> Por quoi doit estre en li parans [*apparent*]
> La proece de ses parens
> Qui la gentillece conquistrent
> Par les travaux que grans i mistrent.
> Et quant du siecle trespasserent,
> Toutes lor vertus emporterent,
> Et lessierent as hoirs l'avoir ;
> Que plus ne porent d'aus avoir.
> L'avoir ont, plus riens n'i a lor,
> Ne gentillece, ne valor,
> Se tant ne font que gentil soient
> Par sens ou par vertu qu'il aient.'

And cf. Dante, Purg. vii. 121-3, to which Ch. refers in his Wife of Bath's Tale (D 1128).

15. *Vyc-e* is dissyllabic ; hence two MSS. turn it into *Vices*, and one even has *Vicesse* !

With this stanza compare part of the French quotation above, and compare Rom. Rose, 19064, &c. :—

> 'Mes il sunt mauvais, vilain nastre,
> Et d'autrui noblece se vantent ;
> Il ne dient pas voir, ains mentent,
> Et le non [*name*] de gentillece emblent,
> Quant lor bons parens ne resemblent ;' &c.

16. In MS. A. is this side-note, in a later hand :—

> ' Nam genus et proauos et quæ non fecimus ipsi
> Vix ea nostra voco.'

20. This is a difficult line to obtain from the MSS. It is necessary to keep *heir* in the singular, because of *he* in l. 21. In MS. A., *maþe* clearly stands for *makeþe*, i. e. *maketh*, as in nearly all the MSS. This gives us—That maketh his heir him that wol [*or* can] him queme. The change from *his heir him* to the more natural order *him his heir* is such a gain to the metre that it is worth while to make it.

XV. LAK OF STEDFASTNESSE.

IN MS. Harl. 7333 is the following note, probably correct :—' This balade made Geffrey Chauuciers the Laureall Poete of Albion, and sent it to his souerain lorde kynge Rycharde the secounde, thane being in his Castell of Windesore.' In MS. T. is the heading :—' Balade Royal made by oure laureal poete of Albyon in hees laste yeeres '; and above l. 22 is :—' Lenvoye to Kyng Richard.' In MS. F. it is simply headed ' Balade.' For another allusion to King Richard at Windsor, see note to Lenvoy to Scogan, l. 43.

The general idea is taken from Boethius, bk. ii. met. 8, which Chaucer thus translates:—' That the world with stable feith varieth acordable chaunginges, that the contrarious qualitee of elements holden among hem-self aliaunce perdurable, . . . al this acordaunce of thinges is bounden with love, that governeth erthe and see, and hath also commaundements to the hevenes. And yif this love slakede the brydeles, alle thinges that now loven hem to-gederes wolden maken a bataile continuely, and stryven to fordoon the fasoun of this worlde, the whiche they now leden in acordable feith by faire moevinges . . . O weleful were mankinde, yif thilke love that governeth hevene governed youre corages!'

4. *Word and deed*; or read *Word and werk*, as in Harl. 7333 and T.

5. *Lyk*, alike; or read *oon*, one, as in Harl. and T. *Up so doun* is the old phrase, and common. Modern English has 'improved' it into *upside down*, where *side* has to mean 'top.'

10. *Unable*, not able, wanting in ability or strength.

21. Here the Bannatyne MS. inserts a spurious *fourth* stanza. It runs thus:—

> 'Falsheid, that sowld bene abhominable,
> Now is regeing, but reformatioun,
> Quha now gifis lergly ar maist dissavable,
> For vycis are the grund of sustentatioun;
> All wit is turnit to cavillatioun,
> Lawtie expellit, and al gentilnes,
> That all is loist for laik of steidfastnes.'

This is very poor stuff.

24, 25. *Suffre . . don*, suffer (to be) done; correct as being an old idiom. See my note to the Clerkes Tale, E 1098.

28. For *wed*, two MSS. have *drive*; a reading which one is glad to reject. It would be difficult to think of a more unfitting word.

XVI. Lenvoy a Scogan.

THERE are but three MSS., all much alike. As to Scogan, see the Introduction. MSS. F. and P. have the heading—' Lenvoy de Chaucer a Scogan'; Gg. has—' Litera directa de Scogon per G. C.'

1, 2. These two lines are quite Dantesque. Cf. Purg. i. 47, 76; Inf. iii. 8:—' Son le leggi . . . cosi rotte'; 'gli editti eterni . . . guasti'; 'io eterno duro.'

3. The 'seven bright gods' are the seven planets. The allusion is to some great floods of rain that had fallen. Chaucer says it is because the heavenly influences are no longer controlled; the seven planets are allowed to weep upon the earth. The year was probably 1393, with respect to which we find in Stowe's Annales, ed. 1605, p. 495:—
' In September, lightnings and thunders, in many places of England

did much hurt, but esp[e]cially in Cambridge-shire the same brent houses and corne near to Tolleworke, and in the Towne it brent terribly. Such abundance of water fell in October, that at Bury in Suffolke the church was full of water, and at Newmarket it bare downe walles of houses, so that men and women hardly escaped drowning.' Note the mention of Michaelmas in l. 19, shewing that the poem was written towards the close of the year.

7. *Errour*; among the senses given by Cotgrave for F. *erreur* we find 'ignorance, false opinion.' Owing to his ignorance, Chaucer is almost dead for fear; i.e. he wants to know the reason for it all.

9. *Fifte cercle*, fifth circle or sphere of the planets, reckoning from without; see note to Mars, l. 29. This fifth sphere is that of *Venus*.

14. *This deluge of pestilence*, this late pestilential flood. There were several great pestilences in the fourteenth century, notably in 1348-9, 1361-2, 1369, and 1375-6; cf. note to IV. 96. Chaucer seems to imply that the bad weather may cause another plague.

15. *Goddes*, goddess, Venus; here spoken of as the goddess of *love*.

16. *Rakelnesse*, rashness. The MSS. have *rekelnesse, reklesnesse, rechelesnesse*; the first is nearly right. *Rakelnesse* is Chaucer's word, Cant. Tales, 17232 (H 283); five lines above, Phœbus blames his *rakel hond*, because he had slain his wife.

17. *Forbode is*; rather a forced rime to *goddes*; see p. 488 (note).

21. *Erst*, before. I accept Chaucer's clear evidence that his friend Scogan (probably Henry Scogan) was not the same person as the John (or Thomas) Scogan to whom various silly jests were afterwards attributed.

22. *To record*, by way of witness. *Record*, as Koch remarks, is here a sb., riming with *lord*; not the gerund *record-e*.

27. *Of our figure*, of our (portly) shape; see l. 31.

28. *Him*, i.e. Cupid. The Pepys MS. has *hem*, them, i.e. the arrows. Koch reads *hem*, and remarks that it makes the best sense. But it comes to much the same thing. Cf. Parl. of Foules, 217, where some of Cupid's arrows are said to slay, and some to wound. It was the spear of Achilles that could both wound and cure; see Squi. Tale, F 240, and the note. Perhaps, in some cases, the arrow of Cupid may be supposed to cure likewise; but it is simpler to ascribe the cure to Cupid himself. Observe the use of *he* in ll. 24 and 26, and of *his* in ll. 25 and 26. Thynne has *hym*.

29. *I drede of*, I fear for thy misfortune.

30. *Wreche*, vengeance; distinct from *wrecche*.

31. 'Gray-headed and round of shape'; i.e. like ourselves. Cf. what Chaucer says of his own shape; C. T. Group B, 1890.

35. 'See, the old gray-haired man is pleased to rime and amuse himself.' For *ryme* (as in the three MSS.), the old editions have *renne*. This would mean, 'See, the old gray horse is pleased to run about and play.' And possibly this is right; for the O. F. *grisel* properly means a gray horse, as shewn in Godefroy's O. F. Dict.

36. *Mexcuse*, for *me excuse*, excuse myself. Cf. *mawreke*, Compleint to Pite, 11.

43. For *stremes*, Gg. has *wellis*; but the whole expression *stremes heed* is equivalent to *well*, and we have *which streme* in l. 45 (Koch).

In the MSS., the words *stremes heed* are explained by *Windesore* (Windsor), and *ende of whiche streme* in l. 45 by *Grenewich* (Greenwich); explanations which are probably correct. Thus the *stream* is the Thames; Chaucer was living, in a solitary way, at Greenwich, whilst Scogan was with the court at Windsor, much nearer to the source of favour.

47. *Tullius.* Perhaps, says Koch, there is an allusion to Cicero's Epist. vi. ad Cæcinam. For myself, I think he alludes to his De Amicitia; see note to Rom. Rose, 5286.

XVII. LENVOY A BUKTON.

1. *Bukton.* Most old editions have the queer reading :—' My mayster. &c. whan of Christ our kyng.' Tyrwhitt was the first to correct this, and added :—' It has always been printed at the end of the *Book of the Duchesse*, with an &c. in the first line instead of the name of *Bukton*; and in Mr. Urry's edition the following most unaccountable note is prefixed to it—"This seems an Envoy to the Duke of *Lancaster* after his loss of *Blanch*." From the reference to the *Wife of Bathe*, l. 29, I should suppose this to have been one of our author's later compositions, and I find that there was a *Peter de Buketon*, the King's Escheator for the County of York, in 1397 (Pat. 20 R. II. p. 2, m. 3, ap. Rymer) to whom this poem, from the familiar style of it, is much more likely to have been addressed than to the Duke of Lancaster.' Julian Notary's edition is the only one that retains Bukton's name.

My maister Bukton is in the vocative case.

2. 'What is truth?' See John xviii. 38.

5. *Highte*, promised; by confusion with *heet* (A.S. *hēht*).

8. *Eft*, again, a second time. This seems to assert that Chaucer was at this time a widower. Cf. C. T. 9103 (E 1227).

9. 'Mariage est maus liens,' marriage is an evil tie; Rom. de la Rose, 8871. And again, with respect to marriage—'Quel forsenerie [*witlessness*] te maine A cest torment, a ceste paine?' R. Rose, 8783; with much more to the same effect. Cf. Cant. Tales, Marchauntes Prologue (throughout); and Barbour's Bruce, i. 267.

18. Cf. 1 Cor. vii. 9, 28. And see Wife of Bath's Prol. D 154-160.

23. 'That it would be more pleasant for you to be taken prisoner in Friesland.' This seems to point to a period when such a mishap was not uncommon. In fact, some Englishmen were present in an expedition against Friesland which took place in the autumn of 1396. See the whole account in Froissart, Chron. bk. iv. cc. 77, 78. He tells us that the Frieslanders would not ransom the prisoners taken by their enemies; consequently, they could not exchange prisoners, and at last

they put their prisoners to death. Thus the peculiar peril of being taken prisoner in Friesland is fully explained.

25. *Proverbes*, set of proverbs. Koch remarks—'*Proverbes* is rather curious, referring to a singular, but seems to be right, as *proverbe* would lose its last syllable, standing before a vowel.' Perhaps we should read *or proverbe*.

27. This answers to the modern proverb—'Let well alone.'

28. I. e. learn to know when you are well off. 'Half a loaf is better than no bread.' 'Better sit still than rise and fall' (Heywood). 'Better some of a pudding than none of pie' (Ray). In the Fairfax MS., the following rimed proverb is quoted at the end of the poem :—

'Better is to suffre, and fortune abyde,
Than[1] hastely to clymbe, and sodeynly to slyde.'

The same occurs (says Hazlitt) at the end of Caxton's edition of Lydgate's Stans Puer ad Mensam ; but does not belong to that poem.

29. The reference is to the Wife of Bathes Prologue, which curiously enough, is again referred to by Chaucer in the Marchauntes Tale, C.T. 9559 (E 1685). This reference shews that the present poem was written quite late in life, as the whole tone of it shews ; and the same remark applies to the Marchauntes Tale also. We may suspect that Chaucer was rather proud of his Prologue to the Wife of Bathes Tale. Unquestionably, he took a great deal of pains about it.

XVIII. COMPLEYNT OF VENUS.

THIS poem has frequently been printed as if it formed a part of The Compleynt of Mars ; but it is a separate poem, and belongs to a later period.

The Compleynt of Mars is an original poem ; but the present poem is a translation, being partly adapted, and partly translated from three Balades by Sir Otes de Graunson (l. 82). The original Balades have been lately recovered by Dr. Piaget, and are printed below the text. See the Introduction.

It consists of three Ballads and an Envoy, and bears a strong resemblance, in metrical form, to the poem on Fortune, each Ballad having three stanzas of eight lines each, with a refrain. It differs from 'Fortune' only in the arrangement of the rimes, which occur in the order *a b a b b c c b*, instead of (as in Fortune) in the order *a b a b b c b c*. One rime (in *-aunce*) occurs in the second Ballad as well as in the first ; but this is quite an accidental detail, of no importance. It must be remembered that the metre was not chosen by Chaucer, but by Graunson. The Envoy, which alone is original, consists of ten lines, rimed *a a b a a b b a a b*. This arrangement is very unusual. See further in the note to l. 82.

In the MSS. T. and A. we have notes of some importance, written

---

[1] The MS. has *And* for *Than* (wrongly).

by Shirley. T. has :—'The Compleynt of Venus. And filowing be-gynnethe a balade translated out of frenshe in-to englisshe by Chaucier, Geffrey; the frenshe made sir Otes de Grauntsome, knight Savosyen.' A. has :—' Here begynnethe a balade made by that worthy Knight of Savoye in frenshe, calde sir Otes Graunson; translated by Chauciers.' At the end of the copy in T. is :—' Hit is sayde that Graunsome made this last balade for Venus, resembled to my lady of york ; aunswering the complaynt of Mars.' We certainly find that Chaucer has materially altered the first of the three Balades ; so perhaps he wished to please his patron. But the title (probably *not* Chaucer's) is a bad one. See the Introduction. Cf. note to l. 73.

1. We must suppose Venus, i. e. the lady, to be the speaker. Hence the subject of the first Ballad is the worthiness of the lover of Venus, in another word, of *Mars*; indeed, in Julian Notary's edition, the poem is headed 'The Compleint of Venus for Mars.' But Mars is merely to be taken as a general type of true knighthood.

I have written the general subject of each Ballad at the head of each, merely for convenience. The subjects are :—(1) The Lover's worthiness ; (2) Disquietude caused by Jealousy ; (3) Satisfaction in Constancy. We thus have three movements, expressive of Admiration, Passing Doubt, and Reassurance.

The lady here expresses, when in a pensive mood, the comfort she finds in the feeling that her lover is worthy ; for every one praises his excellence.

9. This portrait of a worthy knight should be placed side by side with that of a worthy lady, viz. Constance. See Man of Law's Tale, B 162-8.

11. *Wold*, willed. The later E. *would* is dead, as a past participle, and only survives as a past tense. It is scarce even in Middle English, but occurs in P. Plowman, B. xv. 258—'if God hadde *wolde* [better *wold*] hym-selue.' See also Leg. Good Women, 1209, and note.

22. *Aventure*, luck ; in this case, good luck.

23. Here is certainly a false rime ; Chaucer nowhere else rimes *-oure* with *-ure*. But the conditions under which the poem was written were quite exceptional (see note to l. 79); so that this is no proof that the poem is spurious. There is a false rime in Sir Topas, Group B, l. 2092 (see my note).

25. In this second Ballad or Movement, an element of disturbance is introduced ; jealous suspicions arise, but are put aside. Like the third Ballad, it is addressed to Love, which occurs, in the vocative case, in ll. 25, 49, and 57.

The lady says it is but suitable that lovers should have to pay dearly for ' the noble thing,' i. e. for the valuable treasure of having a worthy lover. They pay for it by various feelings and expressions of disquietude.

26. *Men*, one ; the impersonal pronoun ; quite as applicable to a woman as to a man. Cf. F. *on*.

31. The French text shews that we must read *Pleyne*, not *Pleye*; besides, it makes better sense. This correction is due to Mr. Paget Toynbee; see his Specimens of Old French, p. 492.

33. 'May Jealousy be hanged, for she is so inquisitive that she would like to know everything. She suspects everything, however innocent.' Such is the general sense.

37. The final *e* in *lov-e* is sounded, being preserved from elision by the cæsura. The sense is—'so dearly is love purchased in (return for) what he gives; he often gives inordinately, but bestows more sorrow than pleasure.'

46. *Nouncerteyn*, uncertainty; as in Troilus, i. 337. A parallel formation to *nounpower*, impotence, which occurs in Chaucer's tr. of Boethius, bk. iii. pr. 5, l. 14.

49. In this third Ballad, Venus says she is glad to continue in her love, and contemns jealousy. She is thankful for her good fortune, and will never repent her choice.

50. *Lace*, snare, entanglement. Chaucer speaks of the *lace of love*, and the *lace of Venus*; Kn. Tale, 959, 1093 (A 1817, 1951).

52. *To lete of*, to leave off, desist.

56. All the MSS. read *never*; yet I believe it should be *nat* (not).

62. 'Let the jealous (i.e. Jealousy) put it to the test, (and so prove) that I will never, for any woe, change my mind.'

69. *Wey*, highroad. *Wente*, footpath.

70. The reading *ye*, for *I*, is out of the question; for *herte* is addressed as *thou*. So in l. 66, we must needs read *thee*, not *you*.

73. *Princess*. As the MSS. vary between *Princesse* and *Princes*, it is difficult to know whether the Envoy is addressed to a *princess* or to *princes*. It is true that Fortune seems to be addressed to three princes collectively, but this is unusual, and due to the peculiar form of that Envoy, which is supposed to be spoken by *Fortune*, not by the author. Moreover, the MSS. of Fortune have only the readings *Princes* and *Princis*; not one of them has *Princesse*.

The present case seems different. Chaucer would naturally address his Envoy, in the usual manner, to a single person. The use of *your* and *ye* is merely the complimentary way of addressing a person of rank. The singular number seems implied by the use of the word *benignitee*; 'receive this complaint, addressed to your benignity in accordance with my small skill.' *Your benignity* seems to be used here much as we say *your grace, your highness, your majesty*. The plural would (if this be so) be *your benignitees*; cf. Troil. v. 1859. There is no hint at all of the plural number.

But if the right reading be *princess*, we see that Shirley's statement (see p. 560, l. 6) should rather have referred to Chaucer, who may have produced this adaptation at the request of 'my lady of York.' Princesses are usually scarce, but 'my lady of York' had the best of claims to the title, as she was daughter to no less a person than Pedro, king of Spain. She died in 1394 (Dugdale's Baronage, ii. 154;

Stowe's Annales, 1605, p. 496) ; and this Envoy may have been written in 1393.

76. *Eld*, old age. See a similar allusion in Lenvoy to Scogan, 35, 38.

79. *Penaunce*, great trouble. The great trouble was caused, not by Chaucer's having any difficulty in finding rimes (witness his other Ballads), but in having to find rimes, to translate somewhat closely, and yet to adapt the poem in a way acceptable to the 'princess,' all at once. See further in the Introduction.

Chaucer's translation of the A B C should be compared ; for there, in every stanza, he begins by translating rather closely, but ends by deviating widely from the original in many instances, merely because he wanted to find rimes to words which he had already selected.

Moreover, the difficulty was much increased by the great number of lines ending with the same rime. There are but 8 different endings in the 72 lines of the poem, viz. 6 lines ending in *-ure, -able, -yse*, and *-ay*, and 12 in *-aunce, -esse, -ing*, and *-ente*. In the Envoy, Chaucer purposely limits himself to 2 endings, viz. *-ee* and *-aunce*, as a proof of his skill.

81. *Curiositee*, i. e. intricacy of metre. The line is too long. I would read *To folwe in word the curiositee* ; and thus get rid of the puzzling phrase *word by word*, which looks like a gloss.

82. *Graunson.* He is here called the flower of the poets of France. He was, accordingly, not an Englishman. According to Shirley, he was a knight of Savoy, which is correct. Sir Oto de Graunson received an annuity of £126 13s. 4d. from Richard II., in November, 1393, for services rendered ; see the mention of him in the Patent Rolls, 17 Rich. II., p. 1, no. 339, sixth skin ; printed in Furnivall's Trial Forewords, p. 123. It is there expressly said that his sovereign *seigneur* was the Count of Savoy, but he had taken an oath of allegiance to the king of England. The same Graunson received a payment from Richard in 1372, and at other times. See the article by Dr. Piaget referred to in the Introduction.

XIX. THE COMPLEINT TO HIS EMPTY PURSE.

THE date of the Envoy to this Poem can be determined almost to a day. Henry IV. was received as king by the parliament, Sept. 30, 1399. Chaucer received his answer, in the shape of an additional grant of forty marks yearly, on Oct. 3 of the same year. Consequently, the date of the Envoy is Sept. 30 or Oct. 1 or 2 in that year. It is obvious that the poem itself had been written (perhaps some time) beforehand ; see note to l. 17. As far as we know, the Envoy is Chaucer's last work.

A somewhat similar complaint was addressed to the French king John II. by G. de Machault in 1351-6 ; but it is in short rimed lines ; see his works, ed. Tarbé, p. 78. But the real model which Chaucer

XIX. COMPLEINT TO HIS PURSE. LINES 4-12.

had in view was, in my opinion, the Ballade by Eustache Deschamps, written in 1381, and printed in Tarbé's edition, at p. 55.

This Ballade is of a similar character, having three stanzas of eight lines each, with a somewhat similar refrain, viz. 'Mais de paier n'y sçay voie ne tour,' i.e. but how to pay I know therein no way nor method. It was written on a similar occasion, viz. after the death of Charles V. of France, and the accession of Charles VI., who had promised Deschamps a pension, but had not paid it. Hence the opening lines:—

> 'Dieux absoille le bon Roy trespassé!
> Et Dieux consault cellui qui est en vie!
> Il me donna rente le temps passé
> A mon vivant; laquelle je n'ay mie.'

The Envoy has but six lines, though the stanzas have eight; similarly, Chaucer's Envoy has but five lines (rimed $a\,a\,b\,b\,a$), though the stanzas have seven. Chaucer's Envoy is in a *very* unusual metre, which was copied by the author of the Cuckoo and the Nightingale.

The Title, in MS. F. is—'The Complaynt of Chaucer to his Purse.' In Caxton's print, it is—'The compleint of Chaucer vnto his empty purse.' In MS. P.—'La Compleint de Chaucer a sa Bourse voide.' MS. Harl. has—'A supplicacion to Kyng Richard by chaucier.' The last of these, written by Shirley, is curious. If not a mere mistake, it seems to imply that the Complaint was first prepared before king Richard was deposed, though, by means of the Envoy, it was addressed to his successor. However, this copy of Shirley's gives the Envoy; so it may have been a mere mistake. Line 23 is decisive; see note below.

I remark here, for completeness' sake, that this poem has sometimes been ascribed to Hoccleve; but, apparently, without any reason.

4. Koch remarks, that the Additional MS. 22139, which alone has *That*, is here superior to the rest; and he may be right. Still, the reading *For* is quite intelligible.

8. *This day.* This hints at impatience; the poet did not contemplate having long to wait. But we must take it in connexion with l. 17; see note to that line.

10. *Colour*; with reference to golden coins. So also in the Phisiciens Tale (C. T. 11971, or C 37), the golden colour of Virginia's hair is expressed by—

> 'And Phebus dyed hath hir tresses grete
> Lyk to the stremes of his burned hete.'

11. Four MSS., as well as the printed copies, read *That of yelow-nesse*, &c.; and this may very well be right. If so, the scansion is:— That of yél|ownés|se hád|de név|er pere. MS. Harl. 2251 has *That of yowre Ielownesse*, but the *yowre* is merely copied in from l. 10.

12. *Stere*, rudder; see Man of Lawes Tale, B 448, 833.

17. *Out of this toune.* This seems to mean—'help me to retire from London to some cheaper place.' At any rate, *toune* seems to refer to some large town, where prices were high. From the tone of this line, and that of l. 8, I should conclude that the poem was written on some occasion of special temporary difficulty, irrespectively of general poverty; and that the *Envoy* was hastily added afterwards, without revision of the poem itself. (I find that Ten Brink says the same.) Compare Thackeray's Carmen Lilliense.

19. 'That is, I am as bare of money as the tonsure of a friar is of hair'; Bell.

22. *Brutes Albioun*, the Albion of Brutus. *Albion* is the old name for England or Britain in the histories which follow Geoffrey of Monmouth and profess to give the ancient history of Britain before the coming of the Romans. See Layamon's Brut, l. 1243; Higden's Polychronicon, bk. i. c. 39; Fabyan's Chronicle, ed. Ellis, pp. 1, 2, 7. According to the same accounts, Albion was first reigned over by Brutus, in English spelling *Brute*, a descendant of Æneas of Troy, who arrived in Albion (says Fabyan) in the eighteenth year of Eli, judge of Israel. Layamon's poem is a translation from a poem by Wace, entitled Brut; and Wace borrowed from Geoffrey of Monmouth. See *Brute* (2) in the New E. Dict.

23. This line makes it certain that the king meant is Henry IV.; and indeed, the title *conquerour* in l. 21 proves the same thing sufficiently. 'In Henry IV's proclamation to the people of England he founds his title on *conquest, hereditary right*, and *election*; and from this inconsistent and absurd document Chaucer no doubt took his cue'; Bell.

XX. PROVERBS.

THE titles in the MSS. are: Ad. Prouerbe; F. Proverbe of Chaucer; Ha. Prouerbe of Chaucers.

Each proverb takes the form of a question or objection, in two lines, followed by an answer in two lines more.

There is a fair copy of them (but not well spelt) in the black-letter edition of 1561, fol. cccxl. They there appear without the addition of fourteen unconnected lines (not by Chaucer) which have been recklessly appended to them in modern editions. The title in ed. 1561 is— 'A Prouerbe agaynst couitise and negligence.'

For the metre, compare the Envoy to a Ballad by Deschamps, ed. Tarbé, pp. 23, 24.

7. At the head of a Ballad by Deschamps, ed. Tarbé, i. 132, is the French proverb—'Qui trop embrasse, mal étreint.' Cotgrave, s. v. *embrasser*, has: '*Trop embrasser, et peu estraigner*, to meddle with more business then he can wield; to have too many irons in the fire; to lose all by coveting all.'

But the most interesting point is the use of this proverb by Chaucer elsewhere, viz. in the Tale of Melibeus, Group B, 2405—'For the proverbe seith, he that to muche embraceth, distreyneth litel.' It is also quoted by Lydgate, in his description of the Merchant in the Dance of Machabre.

7. *Embrace* must be read as *embrac'*, for the rime. Similarly, Chaucer puts *gras* for *grac-e* in Sir Thopas (Group B, l. 2021).

XXI. BALADE AGAINST WOMEN UNCONSTANT.

5. *In a place*, in one place. In the New E. Dictionary, the following is quoted from Caxton's print of *Geoffroi de la Tour*, leaf 4, back:—
'They satte att dyner in *a* hall and the quene in another.'

7. From Machault, ed. Tarbé, p. 56 (see p. 88 above):—'Qu'en lieu de bleu, Damë, vous vestez vert'; on which M. Tarbé has the following note:—'*Bleu*. Couleur exprimant la sincérité, la pureté, la constance; le *vert*, au contraire, exprimait les nouvelles amours, le changement, l'infidélité; au lieu de bleu se vêtir de vert, c'était avouer que l'on changeait d'ami.' Blue was the colour of constancy, and green of inconstancy; see Notes to Anelida, l. 330; and my note to the Squire's Tale, F 644.

In a poem called Le Remède de Fortune, Machault explains that *pers*, i.e. *blue*, means loyalty; *red*, ardent love; *black*, grief; *white*, joy; *green*, fickleness; *yellow*, falsehood.

8. Cf. James i. 23, 24; and see The Marchantes Tale (Group E, ll. 1582-5).

9. *It*, i.e. the transient image; relative to the word *thing*, which is implied in *no-thing* in l. 8.

10. Read *far'th*, *ber'th*; as usual in Chaucer. So *turn'th* in l. 12.

12. Cf. 'chaunging as a vane'; Clerkes Tale, E 996.

13. *Sene*, evident; A.S. *ge-séne*, *ge-sýne*, adj., evident, quite distinct from the pp. of the verb, which appears in Chaucer as *seen* or *yseen*. Other examples of the use of this adjective occur in *ysene*, C.T. Prol. 592; C.T. 11308 (Frank. Tale, F 996); *sene*, Compl. of Pite, 112; Merciless Beauty, 10.

15. *Brotelnesse*, fickleness. Cf. 'On *brotel* ground they bilde, and *brotelnesse* They finde, whan they wene *sikernesse*,' with precisely the same rime, Merch. Tale, 35 (E 1279).

16. *Dalýda*, Delilah. It is *Dálida* in the Monkes Tale, Group B, 3253; but see Book of the Duchesse, 738.

Creseide, the heroine of Chaucer's Troilus.

Candáce, hardly for *Canace*; see note to Parl. of Foules, 288. Rather, it is the queen Candace who tricked Alexander; see Wars of Alexander, ed. Skeat, p. 264; Gower, Conf. Amant. ii. 180.

18. *Tache*, defect; cf. P. Plowman, B. ix. 146. This is the word which best expresses the sense of *touch* (which Schmidt explains by *trait*) in the famous passage—'One *touch* of nature makes the whole world kin'; Shak. Troil. iii. 3. 175. I do not assert that *touch* is an error for *tache*, though even that is likely; but I say that the context

shews that it is used in just the sense of *tache*. The same context also entirely condemns the forced sense of the passage, as commonly misapplied. It is somewhat curious that *touchwood* is corrupted from a different *tache*, which had the sense of dried fuel or tinder.

Arace, eradicate; precisely as in VI. 20, q. v.

19. Compare the modern proverb—'She has two strings to her bow.'

20. *Al light for somer;* this phrase begins l. 15 of the Canon's Yeoman's Prologue, Group G, 568; and the phrase *wot what I mene* occurs again in C. T., Group B, 93. This allusion to the wearing of light summer garments seems here to imply wantonness or fickleness. Canacee in the Squi. Tale was arrayed lightly (F 389, 390); but she was taking a walk in her own park, attended by her ladies. Skelton has, 'he wente so all for somer lyghte'; Bowge of Courte, 355; and again, in Philip Sparowe, 719, he tells us that Pandarus won nothing by his help of Troilus but 'lyght-for-somer grene.' It would seem that green was a favourite colour for summer garments.

XXII. AN AMOROUS COMPLEINT (COMPLEINT DAMOURS).

THERE are three MS. copies of this poem, viz. in MSS. F., B., and Harl. 7333. See remarks upon these in the Introduction, p. 89.

1. In Troil. iv. 516, the parallel line is—'Of me, that am the wofulleste wight'; where *wofullest-e* has four syllables. Chaucer constantly employs *sorwe* or *sorw* so as to occupy the time of a monosyllable; hence the right reading in this case is *sorw'fullest-e*, with final *-e*. See also Troil. ii. 450—'So as she was the ferfulleste wight.' And 'Bicomen is the sorwefulleste man'; Cant. Tales. E 2098.

3. *Recoverer*, recovery, cure; answering to O. F. *recovrier*, sb. succour, aid, cure, recovery; see examples in La Langue et la Littérature Française, by Bartsch and Horning, 1887. Gower uses *recoverir* in a like sense; ed. Pauli, i. 265. In Specimens of English, ed. Morris and Skeat, pt. ii. p. 156, l. 394, *recouerer* may likewise mean 'succour': and the whole line may mean, 'they each of them cried for succour (to be obtained) from the Creator.'

6. Cf. Sect. VI. l. 53:—'So litel rewthe hath she upon my peyne.'

7. Cf. Sect. VI. l. 33:—'That, for I love hir, sleeth me giltelees.' So also Frank. Ta. F 1322:—'Er ye me sleen bycause that I yow love.'

12. *Spitous*, hateful. The word in Chaucer is usually *despitous*; see Prol. 516, Cant. Ta. A 1596, D 761, Troil. ii. 435, v. 199; but *spitously* occurs in the Cant. Tales. D 223. Trevisa translates *ignominiosa seruitute* by 'in a *dispitous* bondage'; Higden's Polychron. v. 87. The sense is—'You have banished me to that hateful island whence no man may escape alive.' The allusion is to the isle of Naxos, here used as a synonym for a state of hopeless despair. It was the island in which Ariadne was left, when deserted by Theseus; and Chaucer alludes to it at least thrice in a similar way: see C. T. Group B, 68, Ho. of Fame, 416, Legend of Good Women, 2163.

XXII. AN AMOROUS COMPLEINT. LINES 1-85.

14. *This have I*, such is my reward. *For*, because.

16. Another reading is—'If that it were a thing possible to do.' In that case, we must read *possibl'*, with the accent on *i*.

17. Cf. Sect. VI. l. 94 :—'For ye be oon the worthiest on-lyve.'

19. Cf. Sect. VI. l. 93 :—'I am so litel worthy.'

24, 25. Cf. X. 7, and the note (p. 544).

28. Perhaps corrupt; it seems to mean—'All these things caused me, in that (very state of despair), to love you dearly.'

31. The insertion of *to* is justified by the parallel line—'And I my deeth to yow wol al forgive'; VI. 119.

36, 37. Perhaps read—'And sithen I am of my sorwe the cause, And sithen I have this,' &c.; as in MSS. F. and B.

43. Perhaps read—'So that, algates, she is verray rote'; as in F. B.

45. Cf. C. T. 11287 (F 975) :—'For with a word ye may me sleen or save.'

52. *As to my dome*, in my judgment, as in V. 480; and see Troil. iv. 386, 387.

54. Cf. 'whyl the world may dure'; V. 616.

55. *Bihynde*, in the rear, far away; cf. VI. 5.

57. The idea is the same as in the Compl. of Mars, ll. 264-270.

62. See l. 10 above.

70, 71. Cf. C. T. 11625 (F 1313)—'And lothest wer of al this world displese.'

72. Compare the description of Dorigen, C. T. 11255-66 (F 943-54). We have similar expressions in Troil. iii. 1501 :—'As wisly verray God my soule save'; and in Legend of Good Women, 1806 :—'As wisly Iupiter my soule save.' And see XXIII. 4.

76. Chaucer has both *pleyne unto* and *pleyne on*; see C. T., Cler. Tale, Group E, 97; and Pard. Tale, Group C, 512.

77. Cf. Troil. iii. 1183, and v. 1344 :—'Foryeve it me, myn owne swete herte.'

79. Cf. Troil. iii. 141—'And I to ben your verray humble trewe.'

81. 'Sun of the bright and clear star'; i. e. source of light to the planet Venus. The 'star' can hardly be other than this bright planet, which was supposed to be auspicious to lovers. Cf. Troil. v. 638 :— 'O sterre, of which I lost have al the light.' Observe that MSS. F. and B. read *over* for *of*; this will not scan, but it suggests the sense intended.

82. *In oon*, in one state, ever constant; C. T., E 602. Cf. also Troil. iii. 143 :—'And ever-mo desire *freshly newe* To serven.'

83. So in Troil. iii. 1512 :—'For I am thyn, by god and by my trouthe'; cf. Troil. iii. 120.

85. See Parl. of Foules, 309, 310, whence I supply the word *ther*. These lines in the Parl. of Foules may have been borrowed from the present passage, i. e. if the 'Amorous Compleint' is the older poem of the two, as is probable. In any case, the connexion is obvious. Cf. also Parl. Foules, 386.

87. Cf. Parl. Foules, 419 :—'Whos I am al, and ever wol her serve.' *Shal*, shall be; as in l. 78 above, and in Troil. iii. 103; cf. Kn. Tale, 286 (A 1144), and note to VI. 86.

90, 91. Cf. Kn. Tale, 285, 286 (A 1143, 1144); Parl. Foules, 419, 420. All three passages are much alike.

XXIII. A Balade of Compleynt.

1. Cf. Troil. iii. 104 :—'And thogh I dar ne can unto yow pleyne.'

4. See note to XXII. 72, and l. 8 below.

13, 14. Cf. VI. 110, 111.

16. *Dyt-e*, ditty (dissyllabic); see Ho. of Fame, 622. It here rimes with *despyte* and *plyte*. In the Cant. Tales the usual forms are *despyt* and *plyt-e* respectively, but *despyt-e* may here be taken as a dative case.

20. *Hertes lady*; see VI. 60. *Dere* is the best reading, being thus commonly used by Chaucer as a vocative. If we retain the MS. reading *here*, we must insert a comma after *lady*, and explain *I yow beseche . . here* by 'I beseech you to hear.'

*** For Errata and Addenda, see p. lxiv.

COSIMO

COSIMO is a specialty publisher of books and publications that inspire, inform, and engage readers. Our mission is to offer unique books to niche audiences around the world.

COSIMO BOOKS publishes books and publications for innovative authors, nonprofit organizations, and businesses. **COSIMO BOOKS** specializes in bringing books back into print, publishing new books quickly and effectively, and making these publications available to readers around the world.

COSIMO CLASSICS offers a collection of distinctive titles by the great authors and thinkers throughout the ages. At **COSIMO CLASSICS** timeless works find new life as affordable books, covering a variety of subjects including: Business, Economics, History, Personal Development, Philosophy, Religion & Spirituality, and much more!

COSIMO REPORTS publishes public reports that affect your world, from global trends to the economy, and from health to geopolitics.

FOR MORE INFORMATION CONTACT US AT
INFO@COSIMOBOOKS.COM

* if you are a book lover interested in our current catalog of books

* if you represent a bookstore, book club, or anyone else interested in special discounts for bulk purchases

* if you are an author who wants to get published

* if you represent an organization or business seeking to publish books and other publications for your members, donors, or customers.

COSIMO BOOKS ARE ALWAYS
AVAILABLE AT ONLINE BOOKSTORES

VISIT COSIMOBOOKS.COM
BE INSPIRED, BE INFORMED